DATE DUE

GAYLORD			PRINTED IN U S A.

The Mental
Health Interview
(PGPS-47)

Pergamon Titles of Related Interest

Catalano—*Health, Behavior and the Community:
An Ecological Perspective*

Gatchel & Price—*Clinical Applications of Biofeedback:
Appraisal and Status*

Goldstein—*Prescriptions for Child Mental Health and
Education*

Gurman & Razin—*Effective Psychotherapy: A
Handbook of Research*

Keat, II—*Multimodal Therapy with Children*

Moses & Byham—*Applying the Assessment Center
Method*

Sherman—*Personality: Inquiry and Application*

The Mental Health Interview/Research and Application

Benjamin Pope

Pergamon Press

NEW YORK • OXFORD • TORONTO • SYDNEY • FRANKFURT • PARIS

Pergamon Press Offices:

U.S.A.   Pergamon Press Inc., Maxwell House, Fairview Park, Elmsford, New York 10523, U.S.A.

U.K.   Pergamon Press Ltd., Headington Hill Hall, Oxford OX3 0BW, England

CANADA   Pergamon of Canada Ltd., 150 Consumers Road, Willowdale, Ontario M2J 1P9, Canada

AUSTRALIA   Pergamon Press (Aust) Pty. Ltd., P O Box 544, Potts Point, NSW 2011, Australia

FRANCE   Pergamon Press SARL, 24 rue des Ecoles, 75240 Paris, Cedex 05, France

FEDERAL REPUBLIC OF GERMANY   Pergamon Press GmbH, 6242 Kronberg/Taunus, Pferdstrasse 1, Federal Republic of Germany

Library of Congress Cataloging in Publication Data

Pope, Benjamin.
    The mental health interview.

    (Pergamon general psychology series ; 47)
    Bibliography: p.
    Includes index.
    1. Interviewing in mental health. 2. Interpersonal communication. 3. Interpersonal relations.
I. Title. (DNLM: 1. Interview, Psychological.
2. Psychotherapy. WM141 P825m)
RC480.7.P66   1979   362.2   78-17809
ISBN 0-08-019583-0

Printed in the United States of America

To Allan and Irvin - two good friends,

at different times and different places

Contents

PREFACE ix

ACKNOWLEDGEMENTS xiii

PART I. INTRODUCTION 1

CHAPTER 1. INTRODUCTION TO INTERVIEWING 3

PART II. COMMUNICATION IN THE INTERVIEW 35

2. THE COMMUNICATION OF VERBAL CONTENT 37

3. CONTROL AND DIRECTION OF VERBAL CONTENT IN THE INTERVIEW 97

4. STUDIES ON STYLE IN INTERVIEW COMMUNICATION 129

5. EXPRESSIVE COMMUNICATION IN THE INTERVIEW 184

PART III. RELATIONSHIP IN THE INTERVIEW 231

6. RELATIONSHIP WITHIN THE INTERVIEW 233

7.   EXPECTATION AND INTERPERSONAL
     PERCEPTION IN RELATIONSHIP   288

8.   INTERVIEWER ATTRIBUTES IN RELATIONSHIP   332

9.   INTERVIEWEE ATTRIBUTES IN RELATIONSHIP   393

PART IV.   DEMOGRAPHIC VARIABLES FOR
           INTERVIEWERS AND INTERVIEWEES   439

10. SEX, RACE AND SOCIAL CLASS IN THE
     INTERVIEW   441

PART V.   THE INTERVIEW –
           A TEMPORAL PERSPECTIVE   511

11. SEQUENCE EFFECTS IN THE INTERVIEW   513

NAME INDEX   527

SUBJECT INDEX   536

ABOUT THE AUTHOR   541

Preface

Practitioners of the mental health interview are aware of diversity in their styles of interviewing, associated with the schools to which they adhere, their background experiences, the models they have emulated, and their personal attributes and dynamics. Thus, a client-centered interview is readily distinguishable from a psychoanalytic one; and the former two from a behavioral assessment interview. Just as varied are the modes of communication and relationship of interviewees, and the interactions that occur between the two participants in a dyadic encounter.

What is not as evident, on first glance, is the operation of certain correlations and contingencies which traverse the range and diversity of interview types and idiosyncracies. These represent the system aspects of an interview interaction. In a generic sense the interview is a dyadic communication system, in which certain variables are primarily related to the communication of information, and others, more directly to relationship. Both communication and relationship are overlapping aspects of an interview interaction, distinguishable but not independent of each other.

The studies reviewed in the present book deal with the interview at both the individual dynamic and dyadic communication system levels. But the author must confess a fascination with the survival of a dyadic exchange model through the vicissitudes of idiosyncratic interviewer and interviewee behavior and the clinically varied interactions that result. This is particularly evident in the research reviewed in the last chapter. There, certain sequence effects occurred over the duration of the intial interview, whether conducted by a total novice or a skilled professional. In these sequence effects it was possible to trace the contours of a communication system that develops when two people relate and speak to each other, one assuming the role of an elicitor of information of a personally revealing kind, and the other, of a provider of this information.

This fascination with the dyadic system aspects of the interview has not served to negate the more clinically visible ones. Both are equally represented. Moreover there is no intention to diminish the importance of the differences that are introduced into an interview by the personalities of the participants, their demographic attributes, their training and experience, and their individual dynamics. Clearly, the clinician who uses the initial interview as the major assessment instrument must be equally sensitive to the play of individual dynamics within the interview and to the attributes of the communication system. But the frequent failure to emphasize system sensitivity in clinical training is likely to lead the interviewer to confound indiviual with system components, thus attenuating the accuracy of the clinical assessments made.

The data on which the present work is based are derived from both clinical and experimental investigations that cannot be contained in any single specialty of psychology. The reader will recognize much that is psycholinguistic in the studies included. Many bear the mark of the social psychologist's interest in the variables and conditions that govern relationship and interaction between the members of a dyad, and others are directly clinical. The central concourse that all studies traverse is the mental health interview.

There are many roads that lead to this central concourse. Consider, for example, the following sampling of topics that occur in the book and how they might be classified: selected topics in verbal and nonverbal communication, stylistic aspects of verbal and nonverbal communication, the verbal and nonverbal expression of affect, dimensions in dyadic relationship, the matching of two communicants, demographic variables in relationship and communication, expectation and interpersonal perception in relationship, clinical theory and practice in communication and relationship, and communication system theory and research. The author explored the realm of psychology without regard to specialty boundaries. In this search he was prompted by problems posed by clinical practice and by the dyadic communication system model of the interview.

The book will therefore speak to those students and professionals who are engaged in training to conduct interviews or, if already in professional practice, in examining their interview behavior and attitudes. But they must be prepared to consider both the practice of interviewing and the roots of this practice in clinical and general psychological theory and research. This volume may also appeal to nonpractitioners who are interested in tracing the transposing of general psychological theory and research findings into a clinical area of application. For them, it will be a case illustration of the practical application of research investigations, many of them not directed toward the interview by those who have designed and implemented them.

In brief, this book has been written primarily for the clinical novice, both in the late undergraduate pre-clinical training years or in the early graduate training years. But it should also be useful as an illustration of the many channels that connect psychological theory and research with clinical application. It could therefore serve in an introductory clinical psychology course in which there is an emphasis on the articulation between the scientific and the applied. An additional area of instruction that may draw from this volume is that of psycholinguistics and communication. Although not suitable as the primary text in this domain, it could offer supplementary resource material illustrating the application of findings in psycholinguistic and communication research. There has been a deliberate attempt, not always successful, to write the book· in nontechnical English, and thus render it readable at undergraduate as well as graduate levels.

As might have been expected, it has not been possible in most instances to develop specific prescriptions for interviewer behavior from the research findings reviewed. Nevertheless, these findings do provide interviewers with an informational context for their work, and possibly with an outline of the options available to them, and the contingencies that operate, as each picks his/her way through an emerging interaction with another person. There may be some who will decry the lack of prescriptive specificity for the trainee. At a time when capsule or micro-approaches to the development of clinical skills are so prevalent, a book that appears to reintroduce an element of uncertainty into the practice of clinicians may be regarded as regressive. To such a possible criticism there are two replies. (1) The present volume is not primarily one that is technique oriented. However, it may be paired with texts that focus on technique, for it can function as a bridge between the practice of interviewing and its scientific foundations. (2) It may provide the clinical trainee with an attitudinal counterweight for the impression that one may become an accomplished interviewer by mastering a narrow range of skills. An interview is a complex interaction between two people, encompassing a wide range of communication and relationship behaviors. Both clinical experience and the findings of interview-relevant research should serve to sensitize the student to the various interactional possibilities that operate in an emerging exchange between two people who have only recently been total strangers to each other.

Finally, a word is in order about a current stylistic dilemma. It is not always easy to steer an easy course between the Scylla of male "chauvinism" and the Charybdis of a sort of linguistic diplopia, exemplified by such expressions as "him/her" and "s(he)." Here I ask for the reader's indulgence. The reefs of "chauvinism" have, I think, been safely avoided. But the occasional encounter with the type of bipolar construction referred to above was inevitable. If the experience is not always an elegant one, the reader and author may both derive comfort from the purpose that it serves.

Acknowledgements

I am grateful to the Bruner Foundation of New York City for generously supporting a training program for mental health paraprofessionals out of which the idea for the present volume, and indeed the intention to write it, grew. I am appreciative of the time and effort spent by Ms. Joyce Jenkins in the typing of the manuscript, and I am indebted to the following individuals and publishers for permission to quote from their work.

Bordin, E.S. Psychological counseling. New York: Appleton-Century-Crofts, 1955, p. 49. © by Edward S. Bordin.

Carson, R.C. Interaction concepts of personality. Chicago: Aldine, p. 11. © 1969 by Robert C. Carson.

Cautela, J.P. Behavior therapy. In L. Hersher (Ed.), Four psychotherapies. pp. 85-124. New York: Appleton-Century-Crofts, pp. 102-104. © 1970 by Appleton-Century-Crofts.

Curry, A. The Negro worker and the white client: A commentary on the treatment relationship. Social Casework, 1964, pp. 131-136 (p. 132). Published by Family Service Association of America.

Danzier, K. Interpersonal communication. New York: Pergamon Press, 1976, pp. 15, 16. © by Pergamon Press Publishers, Inc.

Fenlason, A.F. Essentials in interviewing. New York: Harper & Row, 1952, pp. 204, 285, 286. © 1952 by Harper & Row Publishers, Inc.

Frank, J.D. Persuasion and healing. Baltimore: The Johns Hopkins Press, Inc., 1961, pp. 67, 129. © 1961 by The Johns Hopkins Press, Baltimore, Maryland.

Frank, J.D. The role of influence in psychotherapy. In M.I. Stein (Ed.), Contemporary psychotherapies. New York: The Free Press of Glencoe, 1961, p. 51. © 1961 by the Free Press of Glencoe, Inc.

Goldstein, A.P. Structured learning therapy. New York: Academic Press, 1973, p. 51. © 1973 by Academic Press, Inc.

Grier, W.H., & Cobbs, P.M. Black rage. New York: Basic Books, 1968, p. 155. © 1968 by William H. Grier and Price M. Cobbs, Basic Books, Inc., Publishers, New York. © 1968 for British Rights by Jonathan Cape Ltd.

Heider, F. Consciousness, the perceptual world and communications with others. In R. Tagiuri and L. Petrullo (Eds.) Person perception and interpersonal behavior. Stanford, California: Stanford University Press, 1958, p. 30. © 1958 by the Board of Trustees of Leland Stanford Junior University.

Hollingshead, A. & Redlich, F.C. Social class and mental illness. New York: John Wiley & Sons, 1958, p. 176. © 1958 by John Wiley & Sons.

Isaacs, K.S. & Haggard, E.A. Some methods used in the study of affect in psychotherapy. In L.A. Gottschalk & A.A. Auerbach (Eds.) Methods of research in psychotherapy. New York: Appleton-Century-Crofts, 1966, p. 227. © by Plenum Publishing Corporation.

Jourard, S.M. The transparent self. Revised Edition. New York: D. Van Nostrand, 1971, p. 138. © 1971 by D. Van Nostrand. By permission of D. Van Nostrand.

Lewis, N.D.C. Outlines for psychiatric examinations. Albany, New York: The New York State Department of Mental Hygiene, 1934, p. 34. By permission of the New York State Department of Mental Hygiene.

Maccoby, E.E. The interview: A tool of social science. In G. Lindzey (Ed.) Handbook of social psychology, Reading, Mass.: Addison Wesley Publishing Co., 1954, p. 462. © 1954 by Addison Wesley Publishing Co., Inc.

MacKinnon, R.A. & Michels, R. The psychiatric interview in clinical practice. Philadelphia, Pa.: W. B. Saunders Co., 1971, p. 158. © 1971 by W. B. Saunders Co.

Matarazzo, R.G. Research on the teaching and learning of psychotherapeutic skills. In A.E. Bergin & S.L. Garfield (Eds.) Handbook of psychotherapy and behavior change. New York: John Wiley & Sons, Inc., 1971, p. 901. © 1971 by John Wiley & Sons, Inc.

Mehrabian, A. Encoding of attitude by seated communication via posture and posture cues. Journal of consulting and clinical psychology, 1969, p. 330. © 1969 by the American Psychology Association, Inc.

Nemiah, J.C. Foundations of psychopathology. New York: Oxford University Press, 1961. pp. 101-111. Reprinted from the Journal of medical education, 1960, 35, 1983-186. Permission granted by the Journal of medical education.

Nemiah, J.C. Foundations of psychopathology. New York: Oxford University Press, 1961, pp. 28-30. © 1961 by Oxford University Press, Inc.

Polansky, N.A. Ego psychology and communication. New York: Aldine Publishing Co., 1971, pp. 159, 160. © 1971 by Aldine Publishing Co.

Pope, B. & Scott, W. Psychological diagnosis in clinical practice. New York: Oxford University Press, 1967, p. 133. © 1967 by Oxford University Press.

Rogers, C. The characteristics of a helping relationship. In M.I. Stein (Ed.) Contemporary psychotherapies. New York: The Free Press of Glencoe, 1961, p. 98. © 1961 by the Free Press of Glencoe, Inc.

Sattler, J. Racial "experimenter effects" in experimentation, testing, interviewing and psychotherapy. Psychological bulletin, 1970. p. 148. © 1970 by the American Psychological Association, Inc.

Seeman, J. The case of Jim. Nashville, Tennessee: Counselor Recordings and Tests, 1957, pp. 7-9, 10-15. By permission of Counselor Recordings and Tests.

Seeman, J. Perspectives in client-centered therapy. In B.B. Wolman (Ed.) Handbook of clinical psychology. New York: McGraw-Hill, Inc., 1965, p. 1221. © 1965 by McGraw-Hill, Inc.

Simmel, G. Sociology of the senses; Visual interaction. In R.E. Park & E.W. Burgess, Introduction of the science of sociology, 1921. Chicago, Illinois: The University of Chicago Press, 1921. © 1921 by the University of Chicago Press.

Snyder, W.U. The psychotherapy relationship. New York: The Macmillan Co., 1961, p. 53. © 1961 by W.U. Snyder.

Tagiuri, R. Social preference and its perception. In R. Tagiuri & L. Petrullo (Eds.) Person perception and interpersonal behavior. Stanford, California: Stanford University Press, 1958, p. 322. © 1958 by the Board of Trustees of the Leland Stanford Junior University.

Truax, C.B. & Carkhuff, R.R. Toward effective counseling and psychotherapy. Chicago: Aldine Publishing Co., pp. 34, 47-48, 66-67, © 1967 by Charles B. Truax and Robert R. Carkhuff.

Watzlawick, P. An anthology of human communication; Text & tape, Palo Alto, California: Science and Behavior Books, 1964, p. 77. © 1964 by Science and Behavior Books.

Watzlawick, P., Beavin, J.H. & Jackson, D.D. Pragmatics of human communication. New York: W.W. Norton & Co., Inc., 1967, p. 77. © 1967 by W.W. Norton & Co., Inc.

Wiener, M.S. Language within language: Immediacy, a channel of communication. New York: Irvington Publishers, Inc., 1968, p. 16. © by Irvington Publishers, Inc.

Will, O.H. & Cohen, R.A. A report of a recorded interview in the course of psychotherapy. Psychiatry, 1953, 16, 263-282. Pp. 266-270 & 272-273. Reprinted by special permission of the William Alanson White Psychiatric Foundation, Inc. © by the William Alanson White Psychiatric Foundation, Inc.

                                                                                        Benjamin Pope

Baltimore, Maryland
January 1978

I

Introduction

1 Introduction to Interviewing

An interview is a conversational encounter between two individuals encompassing both verbal and nonverbal interactions. It is not an encounter between equals for it is based on a differentiation of roles between the two participants. The one to whom the major responsibility for the conduct of the interview is assigned is designated the <u>interviewer</u>; the other, the <u>interviewee</u>. Although the interviewee may request the interview as a consequence of his/her own motivations or needs and thus introduce his/her personal objectives into the exchange, the goals of the interview as a dyadic system are generally determined by the interviewer. The following are frequently occurring goals: The interviewer elicits information from the interviewee (e.g., a physician obtains a medical history from a patient); s(he) imparts information to the interviewee (e.g., a school counselor conveys college entrance information to a student), s(he) assesses or evaluates the interviewee as in the diagnostic interview; s(he) influences, changes, or modifies the behavior of the interviewee as in the psychotherapeutic interview. An interview may, in fact, be characterized by one or more of the above goals depending on the context within which it occurs and the purposes of the interviewer.

Riesman and Benney (1956) remark that over the last half century the interview has become a major white-collar industry, used as an important instrument in social research, market research, industry, social work, and psychotherapy. It is used by such diverse professionals

...as psychologists, psychiatrists, economists, social workers, sociologists, anthropologists, professional nurses, business executives, salesmen, newspaper reporters, television interviewers, pollsters, motivation researchers, and public opinion takers, college and other educational guidance specialists, vocational rehabilitation and othe types of counselors, bank personnel who specialize in loans, finance company interviewers, welfare caseworkers, employment agency specialists, detectives, and... thought reform interrogators....

(Matarazzo, 1965, p. 403)

The chapters that follow will be concerned primarily with clinical and research information pertaining to the initial or diagnostic interview within the field of mental health. In the initial interview the interviewer's purpose is to obtain the information required to make a diagnostic formulation, to plan treatment, or to determine some other course for dealing with the problem presented. All other objectives such as the establishment of rapport, the motivation of the patient, the promotion of a positive relationship, and possibly the provision of an initial therapeutic experience are secondary.

The initial or intake interview is the first encounter between the clinician and the client or patient. In this sense it is, of course, readily distinguishable from the interviews that follow in a counseling or psychotherapy sequence. However, this distinction does not negate the undoubted overlap between the diagnostic and the psychotherapy interview. To begin with, the diagnostic interview may be the first in a psychotherapy sequence. The point is often made that the two types of interviews are closely related in an historical sense. "The history of the interview as a clinical diagnostic method used by psychology and psychiatry cannot be separated from the use of interviewing techniques in psychotherapy. Since the medium for carrying out most forms of psychotherapy is a two-person interaction...the history of interviewing is inextricably wed to the history of psychotherapy as a form of interpersonal influence" (Matarazzo, 1965, p. 404). Moreover, both the diagnostic and the psychotherapeutic interviews are interactional encounters between two individuals; they are certain, therefore, to have many points of similarity both in objectives and in process. It should, therefore, be anticipated that a primary focus on the diagnostic interview will not exclude the use of examples from the psychotherapy interview whenever they appear to be relevant to the topic under discussion.

It should also be noted that the designation of the initial interview as an instrument for obtaining diagnostically relevant information is by no means completely definitive in itself. For example, in a traditional medical history the physician may conduct the interview on the basis of a schedule of precise questions, formulated in advance, with the object of obtaining specific bits of information regarding the patient's medical history. The focus is on information that is specific, and objective (e.g., "Have you ever had whooping cough?"). By contrast, the psychiatrist, psychologist, or social worker may be interested primarily in the interviewee's mode of relating within the interview and his/her style of communication as sources of information about his/her interpersonal behavior.

This contrast is the point that Gill, Newman, and Redlich (1954) have in mind when they speak about a trend "to reorient the initial interview from its old setting of diagnostic fact gathering to its new setting of diagnostic evaluation of an interpersonal relationship" (p.18). Clearly, the kind of information that one wishes to obtain in the initial interview will determine to a large extent the course that it follows.

It is not the purpose of the present book to lay down specific instructions regarding the practice of interviewing. Instead, the concern is with clinical and research information regarding the consequences within the interview of different interview practices. Stated otherwise, the findings summarized here are regarded as contributing toward an informational context within which the interviewer may pick his/her clinical or pragmatic way. It is hoped that they provide him/her with some awareness of options that are open. But it is unlikely that they can supply a priori generalized prescriptions for each step that s(he) takes.

EXCERPTS FROM VARIED INTERVIEWS

The interview excerpts that follow represent a number of divergent approaches to the art of interviewing. All but one are assessment interviews. The exception is the fourth interview, by Dr. Otto Will (Will & Cohen, 1953), selected because it exemplifies an approach to interviewing for which an example in published assessment interviews could not be found. In addition, it should be noted that the first excerpt is not a transcription of an actual interview. Instead, it is a recommended outline for the guidance of the interviewer.

The Traditional Information-gathering Diagnostic Interview in Psychiatry

In a book on procedures for psychiatric examination that has been widely used (Lewis, 1934), the following questions are recommended for the diagnostic evaluation of a patient. The items cited are a sampling of those that occur in the examination guide.

I. General intelligence, knowledge and judgment

Learning at school easy or difficult.

Did he keep up with his classes; if not, what was the apparent reason?

Especially smart in certain subjects but deficient in others.

What did the teacher say about it?

Attention and concentration (at school and later).

Memory capacity and characteristics.

Education commensurate with opportunities ...

II. Output of energy-activity levels

As a child lively and active at play or work, or sluggish and lazy.

Was imagination lively or not noticeable in play?

Naturally talkative or inclined to be quiet or silent.

Awkward or graceful in speech.

Hard worker, energetic, hustler, or slow, sluggish, deliberate or intermediate.

Temperamental worker.

Work easily blocked by scruples or doubts. (Lewis, 1934, p.34)

Although the preceding excerpt is part of an outline or guide for conducting an interview and is not an actual transcript, it does strongly suggest a particular approach to conducting an interview. Concerned with a systematic sampling of a number of topical areas considered to be essential for making a personality assessment, the interviewer is urged to follow the guide in all its explicit detail. One would therefore expect him/her to "interrogate" the patient with specific questions in a preset order. The indicated information and not the interaction with the interviewee is assigned a position of primary importance. If the patient is not able to provide the desired information, other members of the family or otherwise related individuals might. If such others are interviewed, they too would be asked for specific information as required by the examination guide. Moreover, there is no doubt about where the initiative in this particular interview lies. The author himself summarizes his goals for the psychiatrist in the following terms:

Owing to the variety and complexity of the situation dealt with in the investigation of life histories and the difficulties encountered in the examination of many types of mental disorder, the student or physician who approaches the case without a definite plan in mind is certain to overlook important facts or permit the patient to lead too much in the examination, often with the result that the time is not spent to the best advantage or that he is misled into drawing false conclusions. (Lewis, 1934, p. 11)

Clearly, then, the emphasis in the traditional psychiatric diagnostic interview is on specific, a priori selected topical areas and on the active direction of the interview by the physician. Any initiative on the part of the interviewee is regarded as potentially distracting.

A Behavior Therapist's Inquiry

The interview segment that follows was taken from an assessment interview conducted by a behavior therapist. The objective of the interview was the eliciting of information from a male patient about his headaches. The therapist wished this information to be specific enough to permit him to formulate a treatment program that would zero in on the troublesome symptom.

ER: Yesterday you told me about some of the things that were bothering you. Today, I'd like to go into more detail about some of the things that bothered you alright, alright? Now you talked about headaches remember that you mentioned that you had

EE: Yes

ER: Now how frequent do you have the headaches in any one day?

EE: I - I have 'em everyday now.

ER: How many times a day would you say you have the

EE: Well

ER: headaches?

EE: It's usually one headache I have starts about 10:00 or 11:00 in the morning and then it gets worse and ah during the day and I take something Darvon for it usually it helps about 2:00 and ah it gets better then and ah then I get home I still have the headache, then sometimes during the evening if I got any work to do especially if I'm under any pressure I

ER: Pressure, pressure, ah, seems to bring on the headache, does it?

EE: Yea, yes, I, if I got a report to write or I, I gotta hurry up and grade some tests

ER: Other words, in other words are you telling me that there are certain times when the headache is more apt to occur than other times and some of them seem to be tense or pressure situations?

EE: Especially then, sometimes though I, I can get em when I'm not. I, I don't seem to have anything bothering me but, but mostly when I'm, when I feel I'm under some kind of pressure I got to perform in something.

ER: Ah, you, ah, quite a tense person you think?

EE: Yeh my wife tells me that I, I'm too tense that I should loosen up but I, I guess I am pretty tense.

ER: I noticed the way you said it you're quite tense. Why don't you sit back and relax? Sit back relax a little okay. Come on. Lean back in the chair a little. Alright relax take a deep breath, take a deep breath and relax, okay? I think we'll teach you how to do that later. That's kind of important. Now, ah, is anybody else in the family that, ah, gets headaches or got headaches?

EE: You me- you me- not my wife or my kids ah they-.

ER: Ah, well I was thinking about your mother or father. Your father's a pharmacist, was he?

EE: Yeh I, I don't think he got headaches. He was, he was tense though. He was, ah, he was always worried about his work you know.

ER: Look, do you know if he got headaches?

EE: I don't think he got headaches.

ER: Since he was a pharmacist and you got headaches did he, ah, ever give you the, ah, aspirin or the medication for the headaches?

EE: Well it didn't, the headaches never really, I, I never did anything about 'em and they never really bothered me that much until I started college and I felt a lot of pressure in college to get my work done and and..

ER: Your pressure again; it's always pressure.

EE: Yeh, yeh, when I was in school earlier than that, when I was, ah, a sophomore in high school I didn't. I gave up. I, I didn't care anymore.. I went around with this, this group of guys that, ah I, I kind of gave up studying or worrying about it.

ER: Well what situations now, ah, during the day, if I asked you to make a list of the situations during the day that put you under pressure what will be some of the things you would say?

EE: Well first thing that gets me i- and I may get a headache is if if I have my homeroom group and they're particularly boisterous that day.. if if I got, you know, I got some of these behavior problems and sometimes they, they feel they don't have to obey the rules that they can they they can mouth off if they want to and immediately I have to tell them to sit down and to to control them.   (Cautela, 1970, pp. 102-104)

The behavior therapist's inquiry is similar to the preceding diagnostic interrogation in one respect only - its specificity. There was no general invitation to speak, no unplanned, emergent interaction. The interviewer was quite specific and behavioral (i.e., objective) in the questions he asked. Indeed, the rapid-fire tempo of the questioning had some of the quality of an interrogation. But in one crucial respect the interview differed from one that would conform with the traditional type of psychiatric inquiry. It was not based on an a priori set of questions in preset sequence. Each question followed from the cumulative information provided by the interviewee at any given moment in time. Thus, the interviewer could not have known what his second question would be without the information elicited by his first; and similarly with each succeeding question.

In this limited sense the interview was interactional. But there was no doubt about who was in command. The interviewer was active, leading, and not greatly concerned with the interviewee's style of communicating, personal expressiveness, or the associative patterns of his verbalizations.

A Psychoanalytically Oriented Initial Interview

The next excerpt is taken from an initial interview conducted on the psychiatric ward of a general hospital (Nemiah, 1961). The interview bears the mark of a psychoanalytic orientation both in its associative flow and in its topical focus. The patient, a male aged 41, was admitted to the psychiatric ward of a general hospital because of a variety of anxieties and disturbing thoughts. Talking to the doctor on the way to his office, the patient complained that he had a phobia of elevators. Then, during the interview, the following transpired:

Dr.   Tell me about the elevator - how that bothered you.

Pt.   Well, I was an elevator operator, and I've never had no accident.
        But still, lately, the last six months or so, it's been bothering
        me. Where I live...there's a self-service passenger elevator, and
        I don't use it; I walk upstairs; when I go by it, I make sure the
        door is closed. It is funny - I walk by to go out and I have to pass
        it to go outside, so I make sure the door is closed. I dream I'm
        driving an elevator and falling down in it. That sorta got me
        scared,   but I've never had any accident in an elevator...(p. 101)

Later the patient went on to say:

        The last time I was here - I was here for five days, and this girl
        said she had cancer. So it upset me so much I had to leave the
        hospital...and as soon as she mentioned that, I didn't want her
        touching me. I had this shirt on; she touched my back when I
        was sitting down playing cards...I know if she had cancer, she
        wouldn't be on that ward. If only I could tell my mind that. I
        mean, it keeps going around.

Dr.   How does it go around?

Pt.   Well, I mean, I knock it off for awhile. I'll say to myself, try to
        convince myself that if she had cancer, she wouldn't be in this
        ward. So I'd be alright for a few seconds. Then it would come
        back to me again, and I'd say 'oh, oh! - maybe she has'; and then
        I'd say, 'No' and try to convince myself again, and that's all I
        would be doing all day long, until I couldn't stick it out any
        longer...I wouldn't stay in the hospital near her. (p. 103)

The patient described his fear of touching things. For example, he tries to enter doors without touching the doorknob because of a fear that he might contract a disease by doing so. In the same vein he is compelled to wash his hands very frequently. And recently he felt that he had to discontinue the sport of wrestling because of possible contamination by the sweat of his competitor's body.

The interview continued:

Dr.   Are there any other things you are afraid of?

Pt.   I'm afraid of sewers in the street...I know that the sewer - if I walked over the sewer, I couldn't fall in. But still, when I walk over the sewer - I know it would take two or three men to lift the sewer, but still, when I walk and see a sewer, I try to walk around it; I'm afraid of it...I wouldn't want to fall down a sewer...that's what comes to my mind: sewer is liable to tip; I'm liable to fall down a sewer. (p. 104)

Later the patient returned to his obsession with the girl in the hospital who said that she had cancer. This girl had touched one of his shirts, and the patient felt compelled to keep his mother from taking the shirt to the cleaners out of a fear that she would contract cancer by picking up the garment.

Dr.   Are you worried about other people the way you are worried about yourself?

Pt.   Yes. I'm worried about other people very much. I make sure my hands are washed very thoroughly before I handle the food on the table, because if I take something and dirt or something from my hands should fall on the milk or something - whatever I'm handling - upsets me.

Dr.   How does it upset you?

Pt.   Well, I wouldn't want any dirt to fall in the milk. It upsets me. I try to tell myself, 'My hands are washed, my hands are washed.' I shouldn't worry about it...I have to convince myself. I have to keep fighting with myself. I have to say, 'No - your hands. You washed your hands, Chet. There's nothing on your hands.' And I have to keep doing that most of the day - telling myself that I washed my hands and nothing would go into the milk to harm anybody. (p. 107)

As the doctor continued to explore the patient's fear of harming others, the interview proceeded:

Dr.   In what other ways do you feel you hurt people?

Pt.   Well, going on street cars. If I'm going on a street car and there is a crowd - especially if there is a crowd - I'm afraid that somebody might fall beneath the street car. Like last year, my sister took me to her house, so I went on the street car with her. And it was kinda crowded, so I thought I accidentally pushed somebody...under the street car wheels. So it took me about two or three weeks to convince myself I didn't do it. I was even going to call up the street car company and find out if any accidents had happened there. My sister was right along there aside of me... .

Dr. How do you think you have pushed them?

Pt. I don't know. It just comes into my mind - it just comes into my mind, 'Did you harm anybody, Chet? Did you push anybody?', and I said, 'No - I didn't push anybody. I had my hands in my pockets to make sure I don't push anybody. I hold myself like this (The patient demonstrates how he held his arms tight against his body), and I stand alongside my sister. It makes it awfully hard for me. I can't even go by street cars. If I want to go in town or something, I can't even go by myself. It's an awful feeling... .

Dr. You are terribly scared you are going to hurt people.

Pt. Accidentally I might. I figure maybe accidentally you get in crowds going on the street car. You <u>accidentally</u> might bump into somebody and push them underneath the car tracks, but that's an accident. I mean, not that I want to do it. I mean - but gosh, you can't take somebody and throw them under the street car unless you really took him. He's not going to stand there to let you throw him under the streetcar. He's going to put up a fight. And I'm sure with so many people around me - I'm sure they're not going to stop me...I'd rather not go on the street car so it wouldn't happen to me - I mean, it wouldn't occur in my mind, I've never harmed nobody in my life, doctor.

(Nemiah, 1961, pp. 110-111)

The above interview differs from the two that preceded it both in the content elicited and in the process that characterizes it. In the place of a focus on tangible historical events and observable traits and behaviors, it is concerned with the patient's fantasies, feelings, and thoughts. It would not provide the interviewer with the data needed to write a detailed medical and psychiatric history about his patient, an accomplishment possible if the psychiatric examination guide were followed. Although both the behavioral interview and the psychoanalytic one deal with patient symptomatology, they do this in different ways. The behavioral interview seeks only the objective attributes of the patient's symptoms (e.g., time and frequency of occurrence and triggering stimuli). The psychoanalytic interview, by contrast, delves into the subjective experience of the symptom, associated fantasies, drives, and other aspects that permit a dynamic formulation of the meaning of the symptom.

The patient's symptoms covered a wide spectrum. The fear of elevators has already been designated as a <u>phobia</u>. Irrational anxieties that invade the patient's thoughts as though they were unwelcome intrusions from the outside - such as his fear of dirt, his fear of disease, his fear of cancer, and his preoccupation with possibly hurting others - are designated as <u>obsessions</u>. In part, the patient's fears have a passive referent (i.e., he visualizes himself as the object of harm inflicted). In part, the referent is active (i.e., he fears that he may harm others). His need to repeatedly wash his hands as a means of allaying his anxiety about dirt and disease is further designated as a <u>compulsive act</u>. In discussing the patient's obsession about pushing a stranger under the wheels of a streetcar, the author has the following to say: "Judged by the fantasy alone, this act has a violently aggressive and destructive quality, and we wonder at this point whether it is related in some way to the patient's own aggressive impulses" (Nemiah, 1961, p. 109).

The information elicited by the interview and the inferences made on the basis of this information will not be developed any further at this point. Suffice it to say that the author, operating within a psychoanalytic framework, obtained certain classes of information that are relevant to the kinds of inferences that he makes. To obtain the type of information required within this context, it was necessary for the interview to proceed much differently from one that would be based on the examination guide presented above in outline in the section on "The Traditional Information-Gathering Diagnostic Interview in Psychiatry." Thus, it was important to let the patient tell his own story, and to pursue his associations as they occurred to him. Accordingly, the interviewer's questions lacked the specificity that characterized the first two interviews. Moreover, the interviewer maintains a low level of activity and an attitude of permissiveness because he regarded the patient's initiative not as a distraction but as an important source of information.

For example, he justifies his low activity level and his frequent ambiguity as a means of circumventing the usual reluctance of a patient to speak about daydreams, fantasies, and unverbalized thoughts.

There are...ways of gaining knowledge of a person's inner mental life without directly challenging him to reveal it; and by the same methods of interviewing one obtains insight into the patient's manner of concealing and disguising his thoughts. The picture of the psychiatrist as a sphinx-like creature who stares, occasionally grunts, and mostly listens is a caricature, but like any caricature it has a likeness, though exaggerated, to the original. The psychiatrist is often silent, he does listen because he wants his patient to talk freely and spontaneously. When the doctor asks a direct question (e.g., "Were you angry at your husband when he forgot your birthday?"), he asks it because he has a notion in his own mind as to what the patient is experiencing. He may be right, but it is also possible that his questions may slant and distort the patient's account of his own thought processes. With such a question, he abandons the position of a neutral observer who is watching and listening to discover what comes from the patient spontaneously. This should not be construed to mean that the doctor does not guide or control the interview. On the contrary, by his questions he focuses the patient's attention on the area he is interested in hearing about. But about that area he allows the patient to talk freely in his own way. For as the patient talks, he gives clues in his tone of voice, his phrasings, his pauses, his imagery, to important attitudes, feelings, and fantasies that he cannot directly talk about, and of which in fact he may not really be aware himself." (Nemiah, 1961, p. 28)

The interviewer's purpose is therefore to focus and to direct the course of the interview in such a manner as to leave the interviewee considerable latitude for generating the information that he communicates in his own way, and with his own expressive style. One reason for according this latitude to the interviewee is found in the information that may be transmitted by his train of thought.

The importance of a train of thought derives from the principle of the association of ideas: thoughts, even during the most chaotic and fragmented daydreaming, do not come into conscious awareness simply by chance; their appearance, content and sequence are causally determined. Seemingly disparate ideas are related to one another by their connection with a central underlying theme, motive, feeling, or impulse, which may not in itself be immediately apparent but which determines the nature of the conscious associations. If, therefore, one allows a person to associate freely, that is, to observe and to communicate all the ideas that flow through his consciousness, one can arrive eventually at an understanding of the central factor determining the ideas. If an interviewer interrupts a patient frequently, or interjects too many of his own ideas into the flow of associations, that flow will be contaminated and distorted, and may not reveal the underlying motivating factor... Moreover, the observation of where a patient seems to be holding back ideas, to be breaking the smooth train of associations, or to be resisting the unfettered flow of thoughts, provides important information about his whole personality structure. (Nemiah, 1961, p. 30)

Excerpts from a Sullivanian Interview

Will and Cohen (1953) published the verbatim transcript of an interview conducted by the former author, along Sullivanian lines. This particular interview does not happen to be an initial encounter between the therapist and the patient. In fact, it is the eighteenth in a series of some 50 recorded interviews, made after the patient had been in treatment for a number of months. However, it exemplifies some of the salient features of a Sullivanian interview so well that it was included in the present series. The patient is a single woman in her middle twenties, a college graduate, socially active, and employed in clerical work in a large office. Her complaints include a lack of interest in her work and an inability to form lasting close attachments with others. In the therapy interviews that had preceded the present one, the therapist had learned that the patient

was a cautious, guarded person who rarely dreamed, who felt anxious if she had no logical, prepared story to present in the hours, was threatened by the idea of free association, had little awareness of her emotions, and little freedom to express them. Beneath her controlled exterior there lay considerable loneliness and isolation, with strong feelings of rage, which were usually covered by a multitude of obsessional substitutions. (Will & Cohen, 1953, p. 264)

During the therapy hour, she was careful about what she said and how she said it, experiencing particular difficulty in expressing her feelings to the physician. She presented hereself as a "passive," "subdued" person who could never be guilty of assertive behavior. Nevertheless, she was able to let her therapist know, however indirectly, that she had some doubt about his commitment to her. She treated him in a distant and formal manner, only occasionally approaching him shyly and hesitantly. Apparently there was a period during which the physician was seen as an angry, domineering, deprecating person who made the patient feel afraid, very careful, and occasionally angry.

In the hour before the interview excerpted below, the patient and the therapist had listened together to a portion of a recording of an earlier hour. The patient reported feeling anxious as she listened, with the distinct impression that the therapist lacked understanding and consideration. After a few opening exchanges regarding the scheduling of the next session, the following ensued:

Dr.   That suits me fine. Do you want to listen to some of that record?

Pt.   No, I want to tell you what I think about it.

Dr.   Yeah - okay.

Pt.   You know, I was just astonished. First I wanted to hear it to see what there was in it that had sort of made me dislike you real much that day.

Dr.   Yeah!

Pt.   But I don't think that we got to that yet, but that - I was real surprised! You know, I really didn't have the slightest idea that I was talking like that - the first 15 minutes, you know. One statement and then two minutes' silence, and this and that, and 'isn't it,' and 'it's sort of,' and 'it was kind of,' and so uncertain, and so - you know.

Dr.   Ummm (assent).

Pt.   - so difficult... I was completely unaware that I was talking like that. You know, it seems very easy to understand why I could feel you were not responding, or you weren't understanding what I was saying, when I didn't know what I was saying, doesn't it? 'Cause I didn't feel like that; I mean I didn't feel timid, frightened, or anxious at that time at all. I thought I had a message, and I thought I was stating it.

Dr.   Yeah.

Pt.   And it seems to me - you know, I mean, it seems to me clear why I don't sort of feel like I'm making any progress; you know, because I feel like I've said something I really haven't said.

Dr.   Yeah. Um-hum. So a lot of the forcefulness of what you have to say, and the clarity, and so on, is sort of internal, and it doesn't -

Pt.   There wasn't even much content to that first 10 or 15 minutes,
       was there? It took a long time to say it and I didn't really say
       much - was there? - Did I? (pp. 266-267)

Later on in the interview the patient complained about a party that she
attended at which there were several discussions about international conflict
situations. Thus, there was some reference to anti-Semitism in Germany and
some reference to anti-German feeling in Israel. The patient then expressed
a wish to get away from such conflict, to find a place where people were not
fighting with each other. The physician at this point made a rather long
response in which he attempted to discuss the relevance to the therapy
situation of the patient's avoidance of hostility at the party. His remark
follows:

Dr.   Well, that stops me there for a minute - I think you are pretty
       used to it in a way that has chilled you off a lot. This sounds
       like a pretty routine sort of shooting back and forth. You know,
       you have spoken to me at times - and I, sometimes, you know,
       have been not too clear when you said that you didn't like to
       fight with me - or that I jumped on you, or something; and on
       some occasions I literally wasn't aware of too much fighting or
       jumping on you, or being jumped on by you. And I think that -
       that doesn't mean that you're wrong. I don't think so, but I think
       that we're not getting right down to what you feel in that
       situation. But we're talking - probably I'm talking a little more
       about content - that is, what's said and the way it's said, and
       you're talking a little more about feeling, based on your past
       experience. So, sometimes when you say something rather
       mildly and I may say something which sounds to me rather
       mildly because I can distort some of my words in a tone of voice
       in the same way you can yours, why I guess to you it comes out
       as fighting, and to me it comes out as some kind of exchange,
       huh? And what we have to do, I think, is to get real clear so we
       have some kind of consensus about it - not that one of us is
       right or wrong, but that we at least know how the other person
       feels about this thing. So, that I know when it is like fighting to
       you and you know when it is not to me. And - so we are not
       talking on two different levels about the same thing. (Pause). I
       want to pause now for just one moment. What you started at a
       little bit was that you felt that some of this mode of speech and
       all that you had noted related to your Dad, and here we see it as
       being repeated with me - and to a fair extent with me.

Pt.   I think it is more with everybody than you realize, because I
       think that you don't go around with me every day and hear me,
       but I think that if you'd ask the people I talk to, most of them
       would agree that I talk like that - and I think that I'm just as
       completely unaware of that with other people as with you.

Dr.   That, I think, is possible - or - the place I think it hit me as being - you have a good example of it on a couple of occasions when you referred to talking to your professor - and we did talk a little bit about that.   I had the feeling, there, that you presented yourself as a much more insecure and sort of feeble person than you needed to.   That isn't a very good way to put it, but, anyhow, you didn't put yourself out anywhere near, as I thought, as the person that you were.   By that, I mean with the intelligence and with the background, etc., which you have. That's one place that I picked some of that up.

Pt.   I went home and talked to my roommate, Edith, about it, and she said I did - that I talked in a low tone of voice, and slowly always, and she said that people who talk slowly usually are mild and gentle, you know - and that I just always do, and I am willing to accept that, I think I always do, insofar that I don't know I am doing it.   And then I called up Mr. Howard (a friend), you know, and said this was me and that Jane had told me that he had invited me to his party, but she didn't know that I was going with John and could I bring John to the party, and he said 'yes' and when I hung up and Edith said, 'Now, the minute you started talking to him your voice got very slow and low.' So, I think it happens all of the time except that I think that sometime I start talking about things like Archeology which is an -

Dr.   Ah!

Pt.   - intellectual problem which I let myself move around in it because there is no place that I am going to step on anybody's toes in Archeology.

Dr.   Now, by Jove, that does remind me - let me just add 'Yes' to that, because I do know now that on some occasions when you talk about your Archeology and you have done it about Astronomy on a few occasions - you do it with quite a bit of enthusiasm, with a fairly firm tone of voice, although there frequently has been here a little note of apology in it because it's as if you were talking about this instead of something else - which I think makes you a little bit hesitant.

Pt.   Yes - but I notice that difference.   True enough!
                                              (Will & Cohen, 1953, pp. 272-273)

The content of this interview deals largely with the interaction between the two participants.   Thus, the patient speaks at length about her disappointment in her own style of speaking, her apparent constriction and timidity. She then, however defensively, complains that the therapist lacks in empathy and in his capacity to understand her. The therapist confirms some of the patient's impressions of her own behavior and then gives his own observations of his behavior and his inferences of how it must be perceived by the patient.   The focus is therefore almost completely on the interaction between the two members of the dyad, and additionally on the patient's interpersonal behavior outside of the therapy situation.

If the above interview stands out from the two preceding ones in its particular topical focus, it is even more divergent in the style of the therapist. Clearly he is considerably more active and productive than the preceding interviewers. This does not, however, imply that he is more directive. The patient is given the lead, and the therapist responds with his eye and his ear on the interaction between them. This interview is unusual in its approach to an egalitarian exchange between the two participants. The therapist is quite willing to speak at length about his own feelings, his own reactions, and to admit his misperceptions. He is spontaneous, highly productive, and personally expressive. While it may be assumed that the particular content emphasis and the style of the therapist are in part consequences of the status of the interview as one in a psychotherapy sequence, rather than an initial encounter between the therapist and patient, it is still fair to note that in general one would expect a Sullivanian interview, even an initial one, to emphasize relationship and the therapist's active participation in the exchange to a greater extent than interviews conducted by adherents of other schools.

A Rogerian Type of Interview

Finally, there follows the first interview in a counseling sequence that extended over a two-year period (Seeman, 1957). The patient was described as a young man in his early 20s, with a speech handicap of many years standing, which had apparently affected his personality and behavior. A number of attempts at speech therapy had failed. When he sought counseling it was not with his speech impediment as the primary point of reference but rather his general unhappiness and feelings of inadequacy. The following is the first interview:

C1: Well, I'm having q-q-quite a bit of trouble in class talking and it s-seems like I- will, I want to talk in class but I'm unable to. I, oh I just get sc-scared and tied up and oh-everything else.

T1: Is it that you want to so much and yet the very thought of it is frightening? Is that the way it works?

C2: Yes, I, I, oh I just get scared and I begin to sweat and I, I have- and my stomach bothers me and everything else and w-well when I t-try to get the word out somethin' gets st- stuck in my m-m-mouth or something. I, I, just, I just feel like quitting school.

T2: It's a terribly discouraging thing to you when it happens this way?

C3: Yeah, I t- try so hard and-well it seems like the harder I try the more trouble I have.

T3:   It must seem unfair to you that, here you try, you do the best you can, and still you can't get anywhere - I mean there's something pretty awful about that thought.

C4:   And, oh, when I have trouble I feel like I am sorta dumb, sorta worthless, and I think everybody else thinks I am stupid or something. (pause). It's talking, and I guess it's just about, I guess it's about everything I do, I just feel like that I'm no good, I just sorta crack up when I try hard. I don't know, I guess there isn't any use in trying hard anymore.

T4:   You get to feeling worthless yourself, and you're sure that everybody else just thinks the same way about you, is that the way you feel?

C5:   Everybody else thinks that I'm, 'oh well, he's crazy, or there's something wrong with him, he can't talk right, he can't do anything right. So, well, we'll just simply let him go. Oh, well, I guess we'll be nice to him but he's no good, he's just sorta worthless.' That's the way I feel other people think about me; they think I'm crazy or something; I don't, I guess I am.

T5:   Is it that you come to feel those things yourself, about yourself, too?

C6:   Well, whenever I'm alone I feel so depressed, oh it seems like nobody loves me, nobody cares for me anymore. Well when I'm out with, when I'm out in a crowd I feel so lo- lo- lonely, and all by myself, and oh, it seems like I want to talk, and I don't want to make a fool of myself either.

T6:   No matter what you do you feel very deeply alone when you are with people.

C7:   I don't know, I get tight and I sweat, I'm sweating now; and my voice is jerky and shaky, and I feel tight and stuff and everything in my heart seems to be beating faster and everything else.

T7:   It seems like everything comes together at that very point where you have to speak, where it seems like a big crisis for you, doesn't it?

C8:   Yeah. It seems like every time I talk it seems to be quite an ordeal, I guess. It seems like s- something, something very important to my life. Might as well get a job in some factory or something. Just quit the whole thing.

T8:   I'm sure there are times when you just feel like giving up the whole business of trying to get anywhere.

C9:   Yeah, okay, I think -

T9:   Okay, yeah, I think it's about time - (Seeman, 1957, pp. 7-9)

The content in this rather brief intake interview focuses almost entirely on the client's perceptions and feelings about himself. Thus, he makes the following remarks: "I'm sort of dumb, sorta worthless," "everybody else thinks I'm stupid or something," "they think I'm crazy or something," and others in a similar vein. This is not surprising since the therapist consistently reinforces the patient or the client whenever he makes a remark of this kind, by reflecting back to him feelings and perceptions of himself that he has expressed. In order to do this the therapist remains moderately productive, expressing an empathic attitude of acceptance toward the client.

***

The five interviews exemplify approaches that differ in the content that is emphasized in the interviewer's style of expression and in the nature of the relationship between the two participants.

INTERVIEW STUDIES

In the preceding section certain concepts have been used repeatedly to describe the dyadic interactions and to suggest distinctions between them. Thus, there has been reference to such interviewer variables as the specificity (ambiguity) of his questions or remarks, the content he has emphasized (personal history, fantasies, feelings, symptoms, defensive patterns of behavior, motivational dynamics), the initiative or lead he has assumed in the conduct of the interview, and his activity level and degree of personal expressiveness. In addition, there has been some mention of particular interviewer techniques such as reflection of affect. One interviewee variable mentioned was his train of thought; his associational flow. The relationship or interaction between the two members of the dyad was given a central focus in the discussion of the Sullivanian interview (e.g., its egalitarian character) as were certain interviewer attributes that color and modulate relationship such as his personal expressiveness.

As indicated earlier in this chapter, the intention in the present book is not that of offering an authoritative sanction in clinical and research findings for specifically prescribed interview practices. Rather, it is to provide the reader with a knowledge of interview dimensions that have been widely investigated and that may be used to describe and evaluate both communication and other aspects of interaction within the interview.

Although research findings will be referred to frequently, there will be no attempt to present a searching critical analysis of each study cited. Instead, the approach will be that of examining the implications of the results for the practice of interviewing. The objective is not the review of an encyclopedically exhaustive list of studies but rather a sampling that is relevant to the work of the clinician who uses the interview in both patient assessment and treatment. Nevertheless, the intention is to favor research investigations that have already run a considerable critical gauntlet in the review literature and that are regarded as meeting standard criteria of acceptability in research design and statistical analysis.

THE ORGANIZATION OF THE BOOK

For present purposes, the conceptualization of the interview as a communication system is particularly apt (Lennard & Bernstein, 1960). Within this communication system, it is possible to focus on variables that are primarily related to the communication of information and on others that are concerned more directly with relationship. It is not assumed that these two aspects of the interview are independent of each other. In fact, much of the work pertaining to variables included under informational exchange is concerned with the correlation between these and others subsumed under relationship.

The chapters that follow immediately deal with interviewer and interviewee variables associated with the communication of information and the expression of affect. These are followed by others that consider the relationship aspects of the dyadic interaction. One of these presents a psychological analysis of relationship in such terms as initial expectations and the interpersonal perceptions that follow; one discusses interviewer attributes in relationship; and another, interviewee attributes in relationship. These are followed by a chapter dealing with demographic variables for both interviewer and interviewee (i.e., sex, race, and social class) that affect the course of the interview. A final integrative chapter brings the preceding ones to a focus by treating the interview as a communication system that is governed by certain principles of interaction between the two members of the dyad.

If the clinically based topics outlined above form the warp of the material contained in the book, others pertaining to the various channels of communication, grouped under linguistics, paralinguistics, and nonverbal communication, form its woof. This book is not a work in psycholinguistics. But an acquaintance with the major channels of verbal and nonverbal communication will provide the reader with some of the language and concepts used in interview research. With this as justification, much of the remainder of this chapter will include a concise outline of some of the major channels of communication.

CHANNELS OF COMMUNICATION

While language is central to human communication, it is not the sole channel through which people send messages to each other. "People interact not only through words but also through spatial relations, as when a boy sidles up to a girl. They interact through temporal relations, as when the girl keeps the boy waiting. And people interact through gesture and touch and many other media" (Smith, 1966, p. 3). The interview as a dyadic interaction draws on a wide range of channels of communication.

Linguistic Channels

Much of what is communicated in an interview is linguistic in nature. Therefore, it need surprise no one that a considerable portion of interview research is concerned with verbal content. Because the boundary between the linguistic and other communication channels is not always as clear as it might be, some definition of language is in order.

One author defines it as "the articulated sound patterns which form words, phrases, and sentences...presenting semantically meaningful material" (Vetter, 1970, p. 17). The domain of language may be further specified by designating three ways in which it may be studied. The first is known as "syntactics" and refers to its structural aspect which focuses on "the relation of signs to signs within a system of signs" (Lounsbury, 1966, p. 408). Words, phrases, and clauses are classified, and a complex of rules is developed which governs the relationships of words and groups of words to each other. In general, syntactics is not of primary interest in the study of the interview.

The second approach is known as "semantics," or the study of verbal meaning. Semantics does intrude appreciably into the investigation of the interview, when the research deals with what is said - i.e., with content. Does the interviewee talk about emotional experiences, personal relationships, or about objective events that are external to himself/herself? How much anxiety is associated with the topics s(he) is asked to talk about? Indeed, what topics are appropriate for inclusion in an initial mental health interview? Matters such as these, pertaining to verbal content, touch on semantics.

A third approach is referred to as "pragmatics." The term "pragmatics" is not a precise one in the present context. It refers to the correlation between language on the one hand and any other variables that influence verbal communication on the other. These "other" variables could include the communication situation (e.g., interviewer-interviewee, parent-child, teacher-pupil), the personality traits of the communicators, their styles of communicating, and others. Much interview research would qualify as studies in the pragmatics of language.

Clinicians have shown a considerable interest in the relative emphasis a speaker might give to the use of linguistic and other channels of communication. When an interviewee is prepared to be direct and explicit about a topic, s(he) will usually communicate it in the verbal channel. But there is much that an interviewee is not able to speak about explicitly. While the interviewee may, in fact, deliberately avoid the verbal expression of such material, s(he) may simultaneously "leak" it from the unconscious through nonlinguistic channels. For example, a middle-aged schoolteacher, weary of the strain of her profession but unable to accept or directly express this weariness, begins an interview by telling her therapist of the joy she experienced in a recent class discussion. The therapist hears her, but also notes that she speaks of the classroom incident through a strained smile, a tense face, and hands that grip each other with great intensity.

Psychotherapists are well acquainted with the message that appears to express one emotion in one channel and a contradictory emotion in another. "If a communication is about an experience which is taboo or socially unacceptable for the speaker or the addressee, then it is likely that these contents of experience will be communicated primarily by a less explicit channel" (Wiener & Mehrabian, 1968, p. 61).

The various paralinguistic and nonverbal channels discussed below are particularly apt for nonexplicit communications.

Paralinguistic Channels

Included in the paralinguistic aspects of speech are those forms that are vocal but not, strictly speaking, verbal. They have been referred to as "qualities and noises separable from language itself" (Pittenger & Smith, 1966, p. 176). Another author has defined paralinguistics as the study of "how something is said, not...what is said" (Weitz, 1974, p. 94). The four paralinguistic channels that are dealt with below should not be regarded as a complete list.

Vocal signals through tone of voice

Included in this channel are all forms of vocal coloration and emphasis that communicate some special meaning to the listener. Some of these vocal signals are closely associated with verbal messages and shape the meaning of that which is verbally expressed. Miller (1973) cites the example of a person who might say: "Oh, isn't that wonderful!," sounding genuinely enthusiastic, in contrast to another who might say, "Oh, isn't that wonderful!" with heavy sarcasm, in fact implying that it isn't at all wonderful.

In general, linquists would tend to agree that "variations in 'manner of delivery'...indicate the speaker's attitude toward what he is saying, or towards something in the context in which he is speaking" (Pittenger, Hockett, & Danehy, 1960, p. 254).

Vocal tone may provide clues about the emotion being felt by a speaker. "Rapid and highly inflected speech usually communicates excitement; extremely distinct speech usually communicates anger; very loud speech usually communicates pomposity; and a slow monotone usually communicates boredom" (Miller, 1973, p. 239). In addition, rapid speech has been found to be associated with anxiety, and slow speech with depression (Pope, Blass, Siegman, & Raher, 1970).

Interviewers are well aware that the meaning of the words spoken by the interviewee can be accurately heard only within the context of the vocal tone with which they are uttered. "A psychiatrist asked a woman patient how she felt. With a tremulous voice and an anguished expression, she replied that she felt fine" (Vetter, 1970, p. 18). The verbal denial notwithstanding, what the interviewer understood was that the patient was depressed. The emotion communicated in vocal tone and facial expression was assumed to be more authentic than that expressed linguistically. Indeed, paralinguistic cues are generally given precedence over verbal ones as modalities for the expression of affect.

The ungrammatical pause

The pause that is of particular interest to the mental health interviewer is the ungrammatical rather than the grammatical one. The latter serves as a vocal punctuation mark. It separates grammatical units from each other, functioning as an audible comma, semicolon, or period. It is part of the structure of spoken language. The former usually occurs within a grammatical unit, disrupting the flow of speech. It is readily recognized by the listener as a nonfluency. To be sure, it is an integral part of unrehearsed, spontaneous speech. Its occurrence marks the difference between a "canned" speech (e.g., one that may be read from a script) and one that unfolds spontaneously. However, its naturalistic character does not strip it of meaning or interest to the interviewer. When an interviewee pauses, s(he) signals a need to hesitate because s(he) is thinking about what to say next.

The interviewer notes such attributes of a person's speech as frequency of hesitation. During an interview, s(he) becomes attuned to an interviewee's "normal" frequency of pausing. Having once developed a feel for this "norm," s(he) attends with particular care to passages that are delivered more smoothly than the "norm" or, conversely, to others that are more hesitant. The former will alert the interviewer to the likelihood that the interviewee has resorted to the use of well-rehearsed, overlearned phrases. S(he) may wonder what personally uncomfortable thoughts have prompted the interviewee to move in an avoidant direction. The latter is a clear signal of the interviewee's uncertainty, whatever its cause. Is s(he) simply undecided about what to say next? Is s(he) hesitant for emotional reasons to utter a thought that has occurred? Or is s(he) blocking because of the threatening nature of an association that has not quite reached a level of conscious awareness?

Rate of speech

Rate of speech is widely recognized as a characteristic of personal and cultural style in verbal communication. That there are marked differences between cultures on this variable was suggested to this author by a Brazilian audience with whom he discussed some of his interview studies. To this audience, the speech of the American Ss in the studies reported seemed unusually hesitant and slow. The author was assured that, were he to repeat his studies in Brazil, hesitation would decrease markedly while rate of speech would increase.

Equally evident as the differences between cultures are individual differences in rate of speech within a given culture. "Some of our friends or acquaintances seem to talk and act very speedily compared to ourselves; others are slow and deliberate. These characteristics of individuals are something we intuitively recognize, and we often are at variance with the rates at which others act" (Chapple & Arensberg, 1940, p. 31).

Several studies (Chapple & Arensberg, 1940; Saslow & Matarazzo, 1959) have demonstrated that individuals tend to have characteristic patterns of silent hesitation and rate of speech. Coincidentally, other studies have shown that two participants in a dyadic exchange tend to influence each other on the above two attributes. Thus, one investigation found "that the depressed patient responds best to active stimulation, and the one who talks easily gets the best chance with the passive interview technique" (Goldman-Eisler, 1952, p. 670). Two individuals may indeed have different patterns of silence and rate of speech, but once they enter into a conversation, each tends to move toward the position occupied by the other.

Speech disturbances

In his book entitled The Psychiatric Interview, Sullivan (1954) remarked: "Much attention may profitably be paid to the telltale aspects of intonation, rate of speech, difficulty in enunciation" (p. 5). Sullivan made this comment in a discussion of the various "signs or indicators of meaning" to which the interviewer might well attend. The present section on paralinguistic channels has already dealt with "intonation" and "rate of speech." The final paralinguistic channel to be considered here, that of speech disturbances, is pointed to by Sullivan when he speaks of "difficulty in enunciation."

In clinical literature disturbances in the interviewee's speech have been generally accepted as cues of the occurrence of anxiety or some other disruptive emotion. But the systematic investigation of speech disturbances is a relatively new development, stemming in part from the work of George F. Mahl, a psychologist at Yale University (Mahl, 1961). Mahl observed that the interviewer usually perceives flustered or garbled speech as occurring in separate episodes intruding into communication that is otherwise free-flowing. He contends that this perception by the interviewer is wrong. Actually, recordings of interviews demonstrate that speech disturbances occur fairly constantly, but at frequency levels below the interviewer's perceptual threshold. Only when anxiety or some other disruptive experience increases the frequency of speech disturbance above the interviewer's threshold does s(he) take note of them and possibly respond to them as signals of distress.

Mahl (1961) noted also that speech disturbances do not fall into a chaotic mass but are susceptible to systematic distribution into the following classes: sentence changes, repetitions of words or phrases, stutters, omissions of parts of words, sentence incompletions, tongue slips, and intruding incoherent sounds. In his earlier studies Mahl had included "Ah" and other expressions of hesitation in his list of speech disturbances. Because he later found that hesitations did not have the same psychological meaning as the remaining speech disturbances, he removed "Ah" from the speech disturbance ratio that he came to use, designating the remaining categories as "Non-Ah."

An examination of the various Non-Ah categories suggests their division into two groupings, each representing a different response to the experience of anxiety. One grouping appears to represent the direct, disorganizing impact of the discharge of strong feeling. If sufficiently intense, anxiety has been observed to disrupt complex, coordinated behavior patterns. Tongue slips and intruding incoherent sounds may exemplify the disorganizing effect on speech of the direct discharge of anxiety. The speech disturbances in the second grouping appear to function as defenses against the expression of anxiety-arousing thoughts. For example, sentence incompletions, omissions, and sentence corrections seem to be attempts to revise, censor, or block a communication in process or one that is about to begin.

Although there is some disagreement about the various implications of the different speech disturbances, both clinicians and investigators regard them all as significant aspects of interviewee speech.

Nonverbal Communication

In an article that appeared in the October 1974 issue of Psychology Today, Ernest G. Beier reported briefly on a study he had conducted with 50 married couples. This study is a striking demonstration of the eloquence of nonverbal communication. His purpose was to investigate the use of body language in the communication of marital harmony and conflict. First, the degree of conflict in each marriage was determined by a questionnaire administered to each couple. Then each couple was interviewed. Husband and wife, in each instance, were asked to take turns in talking about what each had expected from the marriage and how each felt about it. These interviews were videotaped and later played back without sound to judges trained in rating nonverbal behavior. The judges had no information about how each couple had rated its marriage. Using the judges' ratings, the investigator found that the "happy couples would sit closer together, look more frequently into each other's eyes, would touch each other more often than themselves, and would talk more to their spouses. The couples who were experiencing the most conflict...tended to cross their arms and legs, had less eye contact, and touched themselves more frequently than they touched each other" (Beier, 1974, p. 55). It was evident that nonverbal cues expressed the feelings that members of couples had toward each other with sufficient clarity to enable the judges to distinguish between the relatively happy and unhappy ones.

The study conducted by Beier investigated a number of channels of nonverbal communication. Some of these and others will be examined briefly in the section that follows with a particular emphasis on their role in the interview.

Communication through choice of clothing and ornamentation

In reporting the appearance of a 17-year-old girl during a psychological examination, the psychologist made the following observations: "She is a particularly cute, blonde-haired teenager, who gives a rather sensuous appearance, although dressed very much like a tomboy. She was clothed in a grey, pink, and black striped T-shirt and sat barefooted during the testing. Her hair was in a mod shag cut and she wore no make up."

Apparently the psychologist felt that the patient's appearance and garb emitted conflicting signals, suggesting some ambivalence about appearing heterosexually attractive. To be sure, the psychologist could have misinterpreted the nonverbal message he received. Rather than telling him something about her inner dynamics, the patient may simply have been displaying her acceptance of the dress code of a peer group. At any rate, the patient's dress and appearance did communicate something about her concept of herself, whether it pertained only to peer group norms or to clinically significant attitudes about self. If the psychologist were indeed wrong, his error would simply exemplify one of the attributes of nonverbal communication. Its significance is more ambiguous than that of verbal communication, because a nonverbal message has less autonomy of meaning than one that is verbally expressed. It can be "read" only within the context of the situation in which it occurs and the other channels through which communication may be flowing at the moment.

Gaze and eye contact

"The use of clothing as an avenue of communication is relatively obvious, of course. A somewhat subtle kind of communication occurs in the way people use their eyes" (Miller, 1973, p. 234).

Direct eye contact between two people is a signal that each has the other's attention and that something is about to happen. And what happens very frequently is an interaction of some kind, such as a conversation. In the event that a conversation ensues there is a characteristic pattern of eye contact which functions as a regulator of the exchange between the two participants. It is usual for the listener in a conversation to look fairly steadily at the talker's mouth and eyes. During his/her speech, the talker may briefly check the listener with his/her eyes from time to time, and avert his/her gaze the rest of the time. "As the moment arrives for the talker to become a listener, and for his partner to begin talking, there will often be a preliminary eye signal. The talker will often look toward the listener, and the listener will signal that he is ready to talk by glancing away" (Miller, 1973, p. 235).

In the preceding description gaze and eye contact play an active role in regulating the conversation. But a person's gaze may also be passively and silently expressive. Miller (1973) speaks of the interest and excitement that may be communicated by the size of the pupils in a person's eyes. He summarizes an experiment in which a psychologist showed each of his male Ss two pictures of the face of a pretty girl, completely identical with the exception that in one the girl's pupils were constricted, and in the other, dilated. When asked to express their preferences, the Ss voted for the pictures with the dilated pupils. Findings such as those in this experiment have prompted another investigator to conclude that eye contact conveys emotionality and intimacy in a conversation (Mehrabian, 1972). In brief, gaze and eye contact between two communicators perform both expressive and regulatory functions.

Physical and psychological distance as modalities of communication

The eyes of people are not the only avenues of silent communication. Much is transmitted and, indeed, much interaction between people is controlled by the distances that they assume from one another. Edward T. Hall, an anthropologist, has developed the discipline of proxemics, his name for the study of spatial relations appropriate for different levels of communication.

It is generally known that there are cultural differences for the distances that two conversationalists take from each other. South Americans, for example, are comfortable at closer conversational quarters than those preferred by North Americans. In the North American culture a distance of four feet is considered to be suitable for an impersonal exchange between two strangers. Two South Americans, though strangers, would consider four feet too great a distance, even for an impersonal exchange. In fact, strangers in South America would not consider two to three feet as improperly close.

Within a single culture there are spatial zones that accord with widely accepted conventions of propriety for conversation.

If two North Americans are talking at a distance of one foot or less, you know that what they are saying is highly confidential. At a distance of two or three feet it will be some personal subject matter. At four or five feet it is impersonal, and if they are conversing at a distance of seven or eight feet, we know that they expect others to be listening to what they are saying." (Miller, 1973, p. 236)

What consequences might one expect if one member of a dyad disregards the spatial norm that applies to a given conversation? Sommer (1974) reviewed a number of studies in which the investigators systematically violated usual personal distances, with the result that the Ss experienced "avoidance, bewilderment, and embarrassment" (Sommer, 1974, p. 247). In one investigation to which he refers, systematic invasions of conventional personal distances were carried out under natural conditions (e.g., people seated on benches and at library tables). The unsuspecting Ss simply took to their heels; they fled. In general, the studies demonstrated that the violation of normative personal distances for specified levels of communication resulted in discomfort extreme enough to impel the person subjected to this type of intrusion to move away.

It need only be added that proxemics is concerned with both physical distance and something that might be called psychological distance. For example, there is less psychological distance between a speaker and a listener if the body of the former is turned toward the latter rather than away from him/her and if there is eye contact between them rather than an avoidance of such contact.

There is no reason to expect that the interview situation would be immune from the silent communication of physical and psychological distance. When the chairs in an interview room are easily movable, the interviewee may signal his/her wish to communicate at a designated level of intimacy by the distance that s(he) chooses to sit from the interviewer. If the chairs are too heavy to move, the interviewer's arrangement of his/her furniture might signal his/her expectation regarding the level at which s(he) wishes the interviewee to communicate. A reserved interviewee who is distrustful of the interviewer would be discomfitted by excessive proximity, whether it be expressed through physical closeness, the directness of orientation of the interviewer to the interviewee, or a frequency of eye contact in excess of that which the interviewee finds comfortable.

Gesture

Possibly the most interesting channel of nonverbal communication is that of gesture. "A gesture is an expressive motion or action, usually made with the hands and arms, but also with the head or even the whole body. Gestures can occur with or without speech" (Miller, 1973, p. 237).

Although the scientific study of gesture is a recent and as yet rudimentary development, it would be inconceivable to omit gesture from a review of interview research. The reason is that "we respond to gesture with an extreme alertness and, one might almost say, in accordance with an elaborate and secret code that is written nowhere, known by none, and understood by all" (Sapir, 1927, p. 137).

Interviewers are no exception to the above. They frequently are exposed to verbal messages that run concurrently with gestural expressions. If the two are discrepant, the interviewer will nearly always give the gesture greater credence than the verbalization. Thus, a 17-year-old boy sought treatment because of an abrasive, disturbing relationship with his father. In an early interview he spoke about an incident that had occurred the preceding day, in which he had approached father with a request for the use of the family car. "I wasn't angry at all when I started talking to him," he remarked. "I was calm and respectful." The verbal content was clear. But more compelling were the following gestures. As he denied any anger, the patient clenched his fists and drummed lightly on the arms of the chair. The boy appeared unaware of his clenched fists, only of the verbal content of his message. As for the interviewer, he heard the words but believed the gestures.

The practice of mental health interviewers to attribute greater authenticity to gestural rather than verbal communications, when the two conflict, is based on their assumption that the gestural channel is less distorted by defensive modification because it is under less conscious and deliberate control.

Facial Expression

As an instrument of communication, the major function of the face is the expression of emotion. Without deliberate self-prompting, a listener will tend to monitor the face of a speaker for signs of stress and relaxation and for patterns of muscular mobility that are associated with different emotions. Without specific instruction, an interviewer will normally scan the face of the interviewee for brief and intermittent intervals, searching for emotional signals.

Charles Darwin believed that facial expression in humans, and indeed in other primates, was biologically derived through the process of evolution and was therefore universal in character. A current author (Ekman, 1975) has presented considerable evidence to support the Darwinian view. His method has been largely that of showing photographs, preselected to depict six emotions, to college students in five literate cultures, with the request that they match photograph with emotion. "The great majority of observers in each country agreed on the emotion that each picture expressed, and observers in all five countries agreed with each other as well" (Ekman, 1975, p. 36). In two preliterate cultures Ekman used stories that were indigenous portrayals of the six emotions, rather than verbal labels. He asked the Ss to match facial expression with story. Again there was a high level of agreement, this time in the matching of the pictures with the stories.

The evidence is therefore persuasive that facial expression is employed universally as a means of expressing affect and, indeed, that there is cross-cultural agreement about the feelings expressed by specified patterns of facial display. Understandably, interviewers regard the face as an important nonverbal channel of communication.

Kinesics

Gesture and facial expression may well be regarded as subcategories of body movement. Known as kinesics, its study has been defined as the investigation "of those patterned and learned aspects of body motion which can be demonstrated to have communicational value" (Birdwhistell, 1963, p. 125).

Birdwhistell thinks of human communication as a multichannel system divisible into two major subsystems, one of which is "spoken" communication and the other, "body motion" language. Indeed, he regards body motion as having a structure analogous to that of spoken language. For example, he has isolated basic body motion units, which he calls kinemes and which he regards as the body language counterparts of the basic units of spoken language, called phonemes.

That the body motion of one participant in an interview may be "read" by the other, is evident in the following clinical anecdote.

A therapist was contemplating the termination of the interview while listening to his female client when she suddenly rose saying, 'I guess it is time to stop.' Trying to make sense of the client's behavior, the therapist analyzed his own behavior and discussed the incident with the client. It became evident that the client had inferred termination from observing the therapist's forward movement in his chair which was accompanied by the slow uncrossing of his legs. (Wiener & Mehrabian, 1968, p. 16)

Though meaningful, postures and body movements are more difficult to interpret than verbal messages, or even specific gestures. Nevertheless, the interviewer is attuned to the expressive signals sent out by the interviewee's body. For example, s(he) will note its rigidity or looseness, its immobility or activity, and the degree to which it may be leaning forward eagerly or slumping backward in apathy and withdrawal.

***

Having delineated a number of separate channels of communication, it is important to emphasize that any attempt to study the interview in a single channel would be excessively narrow and limiting. A group of authors carried out a highly detailed linguistic and paralinguistic analysis of the first five minutes of a psychiatric interview (Pittenger et al., 1960). Toward the end of the book in which they report their study, they remark that many channels were required to investigate the brief interview segment because human communication is typically a multichannel process. For this reason, there will be few investigations of the interview in the chapters that follow in which a single channel will be the focus of study.

Finally, the research reviewed will not be classified according to the verbal and nonverbal categories outlined above. Instead, it will be arranged to accord with the interview communication and relationship topics outlined immediately prior to the present digression.

Moreover, the research surveyed will be both clinical and experimental in character. In the clinical research, naturalistic interviews are recorded and analyzed by procedures that are prompted by the problems under investigation. For example, one may be interested in comparing the effects of interpretation versus exploratory prompts, both given by the same interviewers, in a clinic that is psychoanalytic in its theoretical orientation. A representative group of interviewers in the clinic would be asked to record a number of interviews at various stages in psychotherapy sequences. The verbatim transcripts of the selected interviews would be scored for interpretive and exploratory therapist remarks and the characteristic of immediately following interviewee responses would be determined (e.g., productivity, self-disclosure, hesitation, and resistiveness). Whatever the results, their applicability to interviews conducted by other interviewers, in other clinics, would be limited. The findings would therefore be of practical use only to interviewers who work within the same type of situation as those who actually conducted the interviews in the study.

The limited generality of application of findings in clinical studies is one problem. Another is the possible confounding of the selected variables with others which might be operating at the same time. The latter problem might be caused by uncontrolled variables that may be expected to occur in a clinical situation. Thus, it might become evident in the above example of a clinical study that interviewers use exploratory prompts more frequently when focusing on early family history, and interpretations more frequently when dealing with current interpersonal relationships. If this should be the case, it would be impossible to distinguish between the interpretation and exploration on the one hand and topical focus on the other as possible causes of the results obtained. To control for confounding variables, one might develop an interview analogue in which the interviewer is given a script to follow when conducting the interview. The script could control and balance out interpretive and exploratory remarks within the two topics. If one wished to extend the applicability of the findings of the study, one could select interviewers from a range of clinics, with different orientations and with varied personal attributes. The study would then cease to be a direct clinical investigation and would become an experimental analogue of the clinical interview - i.e., an experiment that simulates the clinical interview.

Both clinical and experimental studies will be reviewed. There is no intention here to make a simple value distinction between the two. Both have their assets and limitations. As indicated above, the experimental analogue eliminates error and distortion consequent on the confounding of variables. But, it also abstracts the findings - i.e., it takes them out of practical clinical situations. One is therefore left with some uncertainty about their relevance to a particular situation. One investigator puts this matter succinctly: "The point is that one should not expect to move directly from theoretical hypothesis to clinical application without prior information concerning the interaction of mediating variables such as personality, task, and setting. 'Bridging' steps are required between hypothesis and application" (Heller, 1969).

Clearly both types of studies are needed; the experimental, for the investigation of the effects of interview variables, and the clinical, for the generating of hypotheses and, later, for determining the practical applicability of hypotheses that survive experimental tests.

Finally, not all the research surveyed will necessarily apply directly to the interview. Many studies, particularly in the areas of communication and interpersonal attraction, may be judged to be relevant to issues in interview process, though they may not be studied in the interview situation. Whenever they are judged to be relevant, such studies will be included in the text.

REFERENCES

Beier, E.G. Nonverbal communication. How we send emotional messages. Psychology Today, October 1974, 8, 53-56.

Birdwhistell, R.L. Kinesic level in the investigation of emotions. In Peter H. Knapp (Ed.), Expression of the emotions in man. New York: International Universities Press, 1963.

Cautela, J.P. Behavior therapy. In Leonard Hersher (Ed.), Four psychotherapies., New York: Appleton-Century-Crofts, 1970.

Chapple, E.D., & Arensberg, C.M. Measuring human relations: An introduction to the study of the interaction between individuals. Genetic Psychology Monographs, 1940, 22, 3-147.

Ekman, P. Face muscles talk. Psychology Today, September 1975, 35-39.

Gill, M.G., Newman, R. & Redlich, F.C. The initial interview in psychiatric practice. New York: International Universities Press, 1954.

Goldman-Eisler, F. Individual differences between interviewers and their effect on interviewees' conversational behavior. Journal of Mental Science, 1952, 98, 660-671.

Heller, K. Effects of modeling procedures in helping relationships. Journal of Consulting and Clinical Psychology, 1969, 33, 522-526.

Lennard, H.L., & Bernstein, A. The anatomy of psychotherapy. New York: Columbia University Press, 1960.

Lewis, N.D.C. Outlines for psychiatric examinations. Albany: The New York State Department of Mental Hygiene, 1934.

Lounsbury, F.G. The varieties of meaning. In Alfred G. Smith (Ed.), Communication and culture. New York: Holt, Rinehart and Winston, 1966.

Mahl, G.F. Measures of two expressive aspects of a patient's speech in two psychotherapeutic interviews. In L.A. Gottschalk (Ed.), Comparative psycholinguistic analysis of two psychotherapeutic interviews. New York: International Universities Press, 1961.

Mahl, G.F. Gestures and body movements in interviews. In J.M. Shlien (Ed.), Research in psychotherapy. Vol. 3. Washington, D.C.: American Psychological Association, 1968.

Matarazzo, J.D. The interview. In B.B. Wolman (Ed.), Handbook of clinical psychology. New York: McGraw-Hill, 1965.

Mehrabian, A. Nonverbal communication. Chicago: Aldine-Atherton, 1972.

Miller, G.A. (Ed.), Communication, language, and meaning. New York: Basic Books, 1973.

Nemiah, J.C. Foundations of psychopathology. New York: Oxford University Press, 1961.

Pittenger, R.E., Hockett, C.F., & Danehy, J.J. The first five minutes. Ithaca, N.Y.: Martineau, 1960.

Pittenger, R.E., & Smith, H.L. A basis for some contributions of linguistics to psychiatry. In Alfred G. Smith (Ed.), Communication and culture. New York: Holt, Rinehart and Winston, 1966.

Pope, B., Blass, T., Siegman, A.W., & Raher, J. Anxiety and depression in speech. Journal of Consulting and Clinical Psychology, 1970, 35, 128-133.

Riesman, D., & Benney, M. The sociology of the interview. The Midwest Sociologist, 1956, 18, 3-15.

Sapir, E. The unconscious patterning of behavior in society. In E.S. Dummer (Ed.), The unconscious: A symposium. New York: Knopf, 1927.

Saslow, G., & Matarazzo, J.D. A technique for studying changes in interview behavior. In E.A. Rubinstein & M.B. Parloff (Eds.), Research in psychotherapy. Washington, D.C.: American Psychological Association, 1959.

Seeman, J. The case of Jim. Nashville: American Guidance Service, 1957.

Smith, A.G. (Ed.), Communication and culture. New York: Holt, Rinehart and Winston, 1966.

Sommer, R. Small group ecology. In Shirley Weitz (Ed.), Nonverbal communication. New York: Oxford University Press, 1974.

Sullivan, H.S. The psychiatric interview. New York: Norton, 1954.

Vetter, H.J. Language behavior and psychopathology. Chicago: Rand McNally, 1970.

Weitz, S. (Ed.), Nonverbal communication. New York: Oxford University Press, 1974.

Wiener, M., & Mehrabian, A. Language within language: Immediacy, a channel in verbal communication. New York: Appleton-Century-Crofts, 1968.

Will, O.A., & Cohen, R.A. A report of a recorded interview in the course of psychotherapy. Psychiatry, 1953, 16, 263-282.

II

Communication in the Interview

2 The Communication of Verbal Content

In the first chapter the interview was defined as a dyadic communication system with two major, interacting components - i.e., the communication and exchange of information and the relationship between the two participants. Communication refers to the transmission of information through verbal and nonverbal channels. Moreover, the concept of information is broadly defined. In the sense in which it is used here all of the following messages would be considered to be instances of the communication of information: a narrative of events in the interviewee's past life, an account of stresses in living which have brought the patient into treatment, a precise description of symptoms from which the patient seeks relief, self-disclosing statements about attitudes and feelings that the interviewee experiences about significant people in his/her life, and the expression of feelings experienced in the past or within the interview situation.

Relationship refers to a perceptual, attitudinal, or emotional interaction between the two participants in the interview that may be explicitly communicated in the interview or may remain implicit and not expressed by the interviewer and the interviewee. At any rate, whether public or private, explicit or implicit, relationship provides an interpersonal context for the communication that occurs. Certain qualities of relationship have been demonstrated to be supportive of the communication between the two members of the dyad; others, to be obstructive.

The concern in the present chapter and in the three that follow will be with communication. These will be followed by several chapters that focus on relationship.

The student beginning his training in interviewing takes a very basic view of communication in the interview. One of his fears is that he will not be able to sustain a conversation for the required or expected duration of the interview. Even more basic is the anxiety that somehow he will not know how to speak with the interviewee, that in place of the pleasant stimulation that one experiences when communication with another flows easily, he will feel the discomfort of an embarrassed silence.

The presence or absence of satisfactory communication in this basic sense is intuitively recognized whether one has or has not been trained as an interviewer. For example, can there be any doubt that the following excerpt from a psychotherapy interview is an instance of very bad communication?

EE: I wonder if it's my educational background or if it's me.

ER: Mhm.

EE: You know what I mean.

ER: Yeah

EE: (Pause) I guess if I could just solve that I'd know just about where to hit, huh?

ER: Mhm, Mhm. Now that you know, a way, if you knew for sure, that your, your lack, if that's what it is - I can't be sure of that yet.

EE: No.

ER: (continuing)...it's really so, that it, it might even feel as though, it's something that you just couldn't receive, that it, if that would be it?

EE: Well - I - I didn't, uh, I don't quite follow you - clearly.

ER: Well, (pause) I guess, I was, I was thinking that - that if you could be sure that, the uh, that there were tools that, that you didn't have, that perhaps that could mean that these - uh - tools that you had lacked - way back there in um, high school

EE: Yah.

ER: (Continuing)...and perhaps just couldn't perceive now and, of...

EE: Eh, yes, or I might put it this way, um (pause). If I knew that it was, um, let's just take it this way. If I knew that it was my educational background, there would be a possibility of going back.

ER: Oh, so I missed that now, I mean now, and uh...

EE: ...I'm really getting myself equipped.

ER: I see, I was - uh - I thought you were saying in some ways that, uh, um, you thought that, if that was so, you were just kind of doomed.

EE: No, I mean...

ER: I see.

EE: Uh, not doomed. Well, let's take it this way, um, as I said, if, uh, it's my educational background, then I could go back and catch myself up.

ER: I see.

EE: and come up.

ER: Um. (Truax & Carkhuff, 1967, p. 47-48)

In this example, the problem was the therapist's failure to understand what the interviewee had attempted to say. The result was his distortion of the interviewee's meaning and a consequent deterioration of the interviewer's speech. In fact, its saturation with speech disturbances made his remarks nearly incomprehensible.

Contrast the above example of blocked communication with the excerpt that follows, taken from an intake interview in a university counseling center. The interviewer had focused largely on the interviewee's academic adjustment and on her family relations. At the beginning of the excerpt, he summarizes some of the things that the interviewee had told him:

EE: Ahuh well the way I see the situation is that you are now kind of moving away from your home for the first time and you are dealing with things like establishing yourself on your own and choosing your kind of work you like to do in your life and you seem to be handling that very well from what you tell me.

EE: Oh I don't know.

ER: You don't know?

EE: I get really confused all the time.

ER: Yes.

EE: And -

ER: Like once in a while you might get a little overwhelmed - right - with the whole - like things might be too much for you to -

EE: Yes and I just it's like I 'cause you know when everything just doesn't go right and doesn't fit into place like you know then I don't know then I just get really upset, you know, but it's okay.

ER: When when you do get really upset how upset do you get? Does that affect your sleep or your eating? Does it get to be that bad?

EE: Uh oh it doesn't affect my eating. I don't think every - anything will affect my eating.

ER: Yeh.

EE: Uh when I get really upset I usually just I just, you can, I just don't talk or anything and I just, I don't know, I can't; I have to be alone when I'm really upset because if I hear too many people I e- I just have to be in a quiet place alone, because too many people if I had. Like the other day I was sitting in the cafeteria and I was really upset and I just had to get up and walk out and I just went for a walk and I usually go for a walk and just, you know, you know, get out in the fresh air and be alone and I go

down to the creek sometimes down there and just sit down there
and then usually I feel better 'cause I can't be around people
when I'm upset; cause -

ER: Do you find as as you look back at the - say, since you went to
college, do you find that you are making some progress in terms
of being able to master more things as you go along, like you
are learning and growing that way.

EE: Uh.

ER: Being able to cope with more things or improving them?

EE: Yeh I think - I don't like when people do something that's really
petty. I don't scream and, you know, jump at them. I'll sit and,
you know, and just don't let, it, I'll try not to let it bother me as
much, cause I re- like my roommates, if they do something
really annoying, you know, like w- when they wake up in the
morning they usually wake up earlier than I do and they leave a
light on all the time, you know, like I'll just kind of of hide my
head und- the usually, I would yell about it and say 'turn the
light off' or something, you know, and 'hurry up hurry up', and
now I'll just you know, hide my head under blankets or
something and and I'm taking more time to study now 'cause I,
and I'm getting a little bit better, not much, but a little bit
better...

In this excerpt the interviewer understands what the student is telling
him; in fact, he seems to resonate accurately with the feelings expressed by
her. His questions and comments are expressed empathically and readily
grasped by the student. While both speak with the hesitations and
nonfluencies that characterize spontaneous rather than rehearsed speech,
they are clear and comprehensible to each other. In all these respects the
communication in the second interview contrasts markedly with that in the
first. It is consistently free of the blocked communication that was the major
attribute of the first interview.

MULTIDIMENSIONAL CHARACTER OF
INTERVIEW COMMUNICATION

The global impressions of good and bad communication in the preceding
interviews were responses to complex processes.

Communication in psychotherapy relies heavily, but not exclusively, on verbal techniques. We come to know others not only by what
they say but also by the way they say it; by what they do not say, by
what they imply by their posture, their gesture and their dress; and by
every aspect of their behavior... The skilled therapist becomes
increasingly an interpretor of communication in many 'tongues.'

(Watkins, 1965, p. 1153)

The task of the interviewer would be relatively simple if the various "tongues" used by the interviewee all communicated the same messages. Unfortunately, this is not frequently the case. Speaking of the relationship between interviewee verbal content and gesture, Mahl, Danet, and Norton (1959) remarked that some "gestures have the same meaning as the concurrent verbal content, some betray contrary meaning, some anticipate later verbal statements, and some seem to be a direct function of interaction with the interviewer" (p.17).

VERBAL CONTENT

Topics and Associations

Of the various "tongues" used in the interview, the most evident is that of its verbal content. As mentioned above, uncertainty regarding what to talk about is a major source of anxiety for the novice interviewer. In teaching an undergraduate course in interviewing for the first time, the present author began his exposition of verbal communication in the interview with a survey of such interviewer dimensions as specificity-ambiguity, directiveness, interpretation, reflection, and others. The class appeared interested but increasingly tense as the time for practicum experience approached. In the end, a member of the class took it upon herself to explain to the instructor that the students appreciated the insight they were gaining into the verbal interaction that occurred in the interview. However, they would feel much more relaxed about their imminent, first attempts at conducting interviews if the instructor would be willing to give them some sort of topical outline, as a general guide. He did, and the students had an immediate sense of closure regarding the conversational exchanges confronting them.

In defense of his procrastination with his class, the present author has asserted to himself and to others that he was reluctant to impose his own biases upon the students regarding the relative importance or lack of importance of different topical areas. There is no general consensus among mental health interviewers about this matter. Each must determine "what to attend to in watching the client and in listening to him. There are myriad facts, after all, from the clients's age, to her hair color, to her mother's depression at age forty-one. Which facts matter? More precisely, which matter the most if one wishes to help her? We need a precise base for judging relevance" (Polansky, 1971, p.3).

This base is ordinarily provided by the theory that guides the interviewer in his work and, perhaps more pragmatically, by his clinical experience. Thus, the behavior therapist in the first chapter hunted for specific trigger stimuli for the headaches that the interviewee complained about. The psychoanalytic interviewer sought the dynamics of his patient's phobias, obsessions, and compulsions in the associational patterns of this patient's freely verbalized speech and the fantasies and memories that occurred to him. as he responded to the therapist's open-ended invitations to speak about his problems. Finally, the Sullivanian interviewer focused on the patient's style of communication and the mutual perceptions that both participants in the dyadic exchange had of each other. Each interviewer emphasized topical areas that he considered to be particularly relevant to his theoretical view of human behavior. Thus, the interviewer is an important determinant of the verbal content emphasized in an interview.

But there are other determinants as well. Whenever the interviewee is given the latitude needed to communicate, without excessive interviewer constraint, the associational patterns that emerge are richly informative about his/her psychological condition. The use of such associational patterns as bases for inferences about a patient is traditional in the clinical literature of psychoanalysis. Again, referring back to the psychoanalytic interview in the first chapter, the patient spoke about his anxieties, organizing them into associated clusters. Thus, he feared open elevator doors, visualizing himself as falling down elevator shafts; in a related manner, he feared sewer covers because of the phobia that if he were to step on one he would fall down the sewer. The dynamic interviewer assumes that such clusters of concepts or images relate to a common psychological theme. The theme or dynamic is not manifest in the cluster itself, but the associated concepts function as important directional guides for the inquiry conducted by the interviewer.

Verbal content in the interview is therefore informative in more than one way. Thus, an interviewee comment may be a direct response to a question by the interviewer and may provide an explicit informational input into the interview. Such inputs could be factual ("I have been married for 26 years") or experiential ("Whenever I visit my parents I have a feeling of being trapped, of never being able to escape from them again"). But verbal content may be informative in the associational manner referred to above. Clusters of concepts or images provide the interviewer with fertile sources of clinical inferences regarding the psychological dynamics of the interviewee.

Harway and Iker (1969) make the point that content categories may be defined by associative clusters.

The concept of content presented in this paper is based on an associative model. People, objects, attributes, events, actions, states, affects, which tend to co-occur in a person's speech define an area of content. In the clinical setting inferences are made as to the patient's perceptions and conflicts, not only as explicitly stated by him, but also from associations in his verbalizations which may or may not be in the range of the patient's awareness and consciousness." (p. 97)

The authors present a hypothetical example in which a patient uses the same terms in speaking about wife and mother. The occurrence of these two persons in the same associational cluster ordinarily would lead the therapist to inquire into the extent to which the patient may be transferring perceptions and feelings about mother to wife and the psychological conflicts that may relate to such transference.

Recently, the objective study of the patterning of verbal content in the interview has been facilitated by developments in computer technology. Indeed, Harway and Iker (1969) have reported an interesting example of a study of this kind. It is based on interviews 23-27 in the fully recorded psychoanalytic treatment of one patient. While the focus in the report is on the method rather than the clinical problem, some information about the patient is in order. He was a 27-year-old divorced salesman with the following presenting problems: poorly controlled outbursts of hostility, an unstable employment history, a brief and unsatisfactory marriage, and compulsive stealing. During the course of working with the patient, the therapist developed the following inferences about the dynamics of the patient's behavior: he experienced difficulty in developing a comfortable identity as a male because of marked heterosexual anxiety, and he was hampered in developing an independent style of life because of unresolved and conflicted dependency attachments to his mother.

The method of carrying out the computerized analysis of the patient's speech went as follows. First, each interview was recorded and transcribed in a verbatim manner. Then the frequency of occurrence of all words considered to be relevant to the analysis was determined (the criteria of relevance will be spelled out below). The units on which word frequency counts were based were five-minute time segments into which each interview was divided. Across the five interviews, there were 52 such time segments. The word frequencies across these time segments were intercorrelated and factor analyzed. All words significantly loaded on a factor were regarded as belonging to an associative cluster. The clusters that emerged were used to define content areas.

The above procedure would obviously be excessively cumbersome (because of the time required to carry it out) without the help of computer technology. In this regard, the authors remarked that they "rely heavily on the computer for the statistical analysis of the data - for frequency counts, correlations, factor analysis" (Harway & Iker, 1969, p. 98). But even the computer would be overloaded by a task of the magnitude described above without some procedure for reducing the number of words fed into it. Thus, only the words considered as most relevant to an investigation of the problem were retained by the authors. The number of different words were further reduced by 50% through a computerized reduction of each word to its root form. Thus, such grammatical variants as "asks" and "asking" were reduced to their root form "ask." Then all interstitial words (such as definite and indefinite articles, conjunctions, and prepositions) were dropped. Finally, the computer was instructed to reduce all words in four specified categories to one synonym in each instance. For example, all forms of the negative, such as "not," "nor," "none," "nothing," and others were changed into "no."

Twenty factors, designating 20 clusters of associated words in patient speech emerged from the factor analysis. Only those words with loadings of .50 and above on a particular factor were retained as markers of the verbal content area described by the factor. When examining a cluster of words occurring together, one is often tempted to jump to dynamic conclusions. For example, consider the following cluster of associated words: "affection," "cry," "mother," "help," "wake," "show," "job," "mean," and "remember." The authors had tentatively labeled this factor as designating Dependency. Another factor, marked by the words "neck," "far," "pet," "let," "touch," "few," "play," and "girl," was labeled as Sexual Play; and a third, marked by the words "watch," "ashamed," "put," "breast," "embarrass," "band," "kiss," "start," "pretty," "close," "business," and "bit," as Sexual Ambivalence.

The authors emphasized that such labeling is the least objective aspect of their analysis. They prefer to take the conservative position that the "factors reveal which words occur in conjunction with other specific words" (Harway & Iker, 1969, p. 101) in the speech of the patient. The only use that they are comfortable in making of the verbal clusters is their designation of the context in which two or more words may occur together. Thus, if "mother" and "wife" were to occur together, one would have some evidence that the patient has similar perceptions and feelings about the two. As it turned out, the two words occurred in different clusters in the present study. Clearly, this particular patient, at the moments in time encompassed by the five interviews analyzed, was not speaking about the two in the same associative context.

Regardless of an investigator's penchant to use or avoid specific values for the verbal clusters, they do appear to have an evident meaningfulness. To the extent that this is the case, they provide statistical and objective support for the clinician's assumptions that the associations between the occurrence of words in the unconstrained speech of the interviewee designate psychologically significant content areas. The use of a computer objectifies the support for the above assumption because the machine has no a priori theoretical bias programmed into it. It is not instructed to group together words that are related to such concepts as the Oedipal complex, oral dependency, and others. Instead, it selects out and groups words that occur in similar frequency patterns over the interview time segments used. It has been noted that the word clusters that have been extracted in several studies appear to make clinical sense (Laffal, 1965, 1968; Starkweather, 1969; Starkweather & Decker, 1964).

Verbal categories undoubtedly vary, both in content and salience, across different interviewees and, within the speech of a single interviewee, across different moments in time. In the type of patient communication that occurs in open-ended interviews, verbal content is individually defined and, in fact, may be variously defined by a single individual at different times.

In a linguistic sense the Harway and Iker (1969) study is characterized by its use of individual words as its primary data. Studies of interest to the interviewer, similarly based on individual words, have been carried out by other investigators (Laffal, 1965, 1968; Starkweather, 1969; Starkweather & Decker, 1964). A less objective method, but one which had led to psychologically meaningful results in the analysis of verbal content, was developed by Laffal (1965, 1968). He started with the assumption noted also in the work of Harway and Iker (1969) that all words that associate with each other in the speech of an interviewee, for example, may be further assembled into groups or clusters of words. Without specifying the complex steps followed by Laffal for deriving clusters of associated words, the application of his method to a well-known psychiatric autobiography will be reviewed (Freud, 1953). The patient was Daniel Paul Schreber, whose name has become associated with Freud's theory of the dynamics of male homosexuality (Freud, 1953). Dr. Schreber was a prominent German judge in the late nineteenth century, who developed a paranoid psychosis and then published an account of his delusions. Freud read this autobiography carefully and, without direct contact with the patient, developed a theory that related Dr. Schreber's use of paranoid projection to a condition designated as latent homosexuality. The word "sun" occurred frequently in the delusions expressed in Dr. Schreber's account. Freud assumed that "sun," "God," and "father" were symbolically related; in fact he hypothesized that "sun" and "God" were both father symbols. "Freud maintains in addition that Dr. Flesching, Schreber's physician, was the subject of the patient's homosexual longings, and that both God and Dr. Flesching stood as dominant male figures in relation to Schreber" (Laffal, 1968, p. 282).

Laffal tested these assumptions by determining how Schreber talked about God, male, female, sun, and how these words clustered with each other. Thus, if God were perceived by Schreber to be more male than female, God and male should cluster more closely than God and female. In fact, this is what Laffal found. In the same way Laffal determined that Schreber associated Flesching and male more closely than Flesching and female. Thus far, Freud's assumptions were vindicated. But the final assumption that "sun" and "male" would be more highly correlated than "sun" and "female" was not sustained; in fact, the reverse occurred. Thus, all the links required by Freud's hypothesis are not present in the verbal associative data provided by Laffal.

This study is not reported because of its relevance to the controversy around Freud's theory regarding paranoid psychosis and male homosexuality. Rather, it is included as an example of how the associations between words and verbal categories may be used for generating inferences regarding psychological dynamics. Stated somewhat more generally, it demonstrates one kind of use of verbal content in the mental health interview.

Finally, there is the method for the designation of verbal content areas, developed by Psathas and Arp (1966) and applied to interviewer rather than interviewee communications. The method used by these authors is one of a set of computer programs described in the work entitled The General Inquirer (Stone, Dunphy, Smith, & Ogilvie, 1966). Unlike the previous methods, the present one used the sentence rather than the individual word as the unit of linguistic analysis. But sentences were classified according to the presence within them of certain root words that had been selected because of their relevance to the mental health interview, and then arranged in a dictionary. The process of developing the dictionary is complex and will not be detailed here.

The study by Psathas and Arp (1966) was actually an application of the dictionary to an earlier experimental analogue investigation of the initial interview conducted by Heller, Davis, and Myers (1966). These authors had trained 12 interviewers to perform four different interviewer roles: that of the active-friendly interviewer, the passive-friendly interviewer, the active-hostile interviewer, and the passive-hostile interviewer. Each interviewer performed one role only. In the original study it was found that the active-friendly interviewers were best liked by the interviewees, and the passive-hostile interviewers were least liked. Of the four types of interviewers, the above two turned out to be polar opposite when the dimension of comparison was the interviewee's positive feeling for the interviewer.

It is therefore interesting to note that the active-friendly and passive-hostile interviewers again emerged as polar opposites when compared through the linguistic analysis of their verbal remarks, later conducted by Psathas and Arp (1966). Without specifying the details of the linguistic analysis, suffice it to say that the passive-hostile interviewer used verbal content that was congruent with his role; that is, he communicated a passive, nongiving attitude toward the interviewee through the use of such verbal categories as probing and direct urging. By contrast, the active-friendly interviewer gave verbal expression to a more active, supportive, and contributory attitude. The verbal categories he used most frequently were agreement and praise. The Psathas and Arp (1966) study is a good example of an inquiry into the correlation between verbal content and other dimensions (i.e., interviewer role) in a dyadic interaction. The next section deals with this matter.

Correlates of Verbal Content in the Interview

In the preceding study, interviewers asked to act out different interactional roles (but given no instructions about the specific remarks they were to make) were distinguishable from one another in the categories of verbal content that they used. Conversely, the members of a dyad may be expected to change their styles or expressive attributes of speech when they are prompted to move from one topic or content area to another. For example, an experienced interviewer is likely to anticipate some change in interviewee rate and fluency of speech when he moves from a low- to a high-anxiety topic, or vice versa.

Such was the case in the following brief interview conducted on a psychiatric ward as part of a sociometric study (Pope & Nudler, 1970). Each participating patient was asked by the second author to pick one person on his ward whom he liked most, and another whom he liked least. Shortly after he made his choices, the first author conducted a brief interview with the patient. One of these interviews follows:

ER: Mr. K. is the patient you like most. Tell me whatever you can, whatever comes to mind about Mr. K.

EE: He j- just seems to have a ah keen interest in what's going on around the hospital and is a very sincere person and st- that I like (Pause) and they this is the idea of his sincerity and having interest in what's going on means a lot to me cuz I have a respect for what the ah for the hospital and ah the people here so that's why he comes out on top.

ER: Well, tell me whatever else you can about what you like about Mr. K.

EE: Well not ah j- justa as a personal friend but rather pretty close ah I can talk to him pretty well. Things like that

ER: Alright. Now Mr. B is the patient you like least. Tell me about him.

EE: Well ah like ah even the opposite of the top I don't see a very
        keen interest in in the hospital (Pause), and ah j- just the other
        people you know on the hall from what I can see and I think
        there's a kind of prudism in a sense cuz I I consider myself kind
        of a sensitive person to what goes on around me and ah I don't I
        don't recognize this you know in him. I'm not saying it's good or
        bad; but to me I like to have a ah sensitive person as a friend
        and I don't see this

ER: Tell me whatever else you can about why you like Mr. B. least

EE: (Pause) Ah. It it's kinda hard for me to do. Becuz I can't say I
        really dislike him. If I had to put someone at the bottom it
        would just have to be my choice. That's all. Main reason that I
        discussed. Ah, most important. It's it's jus things tha I think I
        loaned him some money one time or something. Yah and ah ah I
        I had to ask for it back. I don't like to do that with people. I
        think if you owe them some money they should ah come to you
        and ah pay it back. It's just the idea of having to ask somebody,
        and jus these other things in general...

One would expect that it would be easier, in general, for a person to speak
about someone he has evaluated positively rather than one he regards in a
negative way. Similarly, it was expected that the interviewee quoted above
would speak about his sociometric choice with less stress than his sociometric
rejection. On several paralinguistic variables, the anticipated contrast in the
stressfulness of the two topics was borne out. At a later point, studies will be
summarized in which Ss are more verbose when they are anxious than when
they are relaxed. The patient in the present interview uttered 99 words in
speaking of his sociometric choice, 225 words in speaking of his sociometric
rejection. Additionally, it is evident that the patient's speech was less
flustered or disrupted when he spoke about his choice rather than his
rejection. Finally, this patient, in partial remission from a psychotic episode,
was not able to communicate in a coherent and comprehensible manner when
he was describing the patient he rejected. The fragile structure of his speech
broke under the stress of the content of his last two responses resulting in
some psychotic disruption of communication. While individuals may vary in
their manner of expressing anxiety, it is evident from the above interview
excerpt that for a given individual stressful content will be expressed in a
style that contrasts with that used for nonstressful content.

The correlation between verbal content and expressive attributes of
speech has frequently been investigated through the planned manipulation of
topic by the interviewer to vary interviewee stress or anxiety. In the above
excerpt from the sociometric study, the high-anxiety topic (the rejected
patient) elicited a higher level of productivity and more frequent speech
disturbances than the low-anxiety topic (the chosen patient). These results
appear to be contradictory, for high-anxiety topics seem to activate and
disrupt speech at the same time. Siegman and Pope (1966) offer a concise
statement of the view that anxiety may function as a drive, and of the
application of this view to the two apparently contradictory attributes of

anxious speech. "If anxiety is regarded as a drive state, then it is to be expected that with an increase in anxiety level there would be an increase in verbal output both in terms of number of words and rate of speech. Moreover, the activation of different response tendencies may also produce an increase of speech disturbances (such as corrections, repetitions, etc.)" (1966, p.530). The increase in number of words uttered requires no further explanation. The postulated increase in speech disturbance may not be quite as evident. Anxiety causes speech disruption by activating many thoughts and associations, some of which may not be compatible with others. Thus, a patient may remember a recent quarrel with his father after his failure to comply with a paternal request that he perform a specified house chore. The patient, anxious in his recollection of the event, begins to say, "I wouldn't do it." But, in his own defense, he thinks simultaneously of saying, "I couldn't do it." The result was: "I would-couldn't do it." This remark is clearly flustered, containing both a word incompletion and a sentence change. Without deliberate analysis, the interviewer intuitively recognized it as a signal of anxiety.

The studies that follow investigate the arousal of anxiety in the interviewee through the interviewer's focus on high- and low-anxiety topics, and the correlates of anxiety in expressive aspects of speech.

In one investigation (Siegman & Pope, 1966) the Ss were 50 junior and senior nursing students, all female, ranging in age from 20 to 22. Because the intention was to carry through an exploratory interview in two topical areas, one neutral (past school history) and the other anxiety-arousing (primary family relationships), the students were selected to ensure that the two topics would indeed be perceived by them in the above ways. Thus, only Ss without any reports of school or college maladjustment or anxiety were used. This selection procedure made it likely that the Ss would perceive past school history as a nonanxious topic. To ensure that family relationships would be perceived as stressful, by contrast, the interviewer preceded his questions in this area with the following remark: "You remember taking a number of personality tests last week? Several of the questions in the tests dealt with family relations. I am interested in talking about this area further with you, because we know from past experience that even when a person is not aware of problems in this area and therefore does not express them in her responses to the test, such problems may actually exist." In their responses to a post-interview rating scale, the Ss showed that they did indeed perceive the first topic as less stressful than the second. As expected, the anxiety-arousing topic did function as an activator of speech in the following ways: it elicited higher productivity - that is, more words per response than the neutral topic (Pope & Siegman, 1965); it tended to elicit a faster rate of articulation of words and fewer hesitations in the form of such expressions as Ah and other filled pauses (Siegman & Pope, 1965); and it increased the diversity of words used by the interviewee (i.e., the Type Token Ratio, a ratio of number of diverse words over the total number of words in a speech sample) (Siegman & Pope, 1966). But the same anxiety-arousing topic also functioned as a disruptor of language, noted in the higher ratio of flustered or disturbed speech (i.e., change of topic in the middle of a sentence, incomplete sentence, incomplete word, repetition of words and/or phrases, stuttering, intruding incoherent sounds, and tongue slips).

Others have investigated the effect of stressful interview topics on the interviewee's response with somewhat more variable results. In his first of two studies dealing with anxiety arousal by topic, Kanfer (1959) set out to determine whether one might partition topical anxiety into two components, one reflecting that which is common to a number of individuals in a homogeneous group, and the other reflecting that which is personal and individual. To the extent that all the members of a group view some topics as more anxiety arousing and other topics as less so, there should be group differences in anxiety response to topic. One would be led to expect such group differences from Jourard's (1971b) finding that a number of Ss agreed in classifying a range of interview topics into two clusters, one consisting of verbal content about which it is easy to speak openly and freely (tastes, attitudes, opinions, and work), and the other of verbal content about which self-disclosure is difficult (money, personality, and body). The preceding studies by Pope and Siegman (1965) and Siegman and Pope (1965, 1966, 1972) also seem to point toward such group differences.

Kanfer regarded anxiety as a drive state and therefore anticipated that verbal rate would increase with anxiety. His group of Ss was relatively homogeneous, consisting of 20 members, both male and female, from one of his classes in Abnormal Psychology. He conducted an open-ended interview with these Ss, covering the following five topics in the given order: family relationships, the interviewee's degree of confidence in self, his/her sense of competence and achievement, feelings of attractiveness to and confidence with the opposite sex, and feelings of emotional maturity.

No group differences were obtained; for the group as a whole, there were no differences in verbal rate between topics. However, when individual responses to the five topics were rated for anxiety, with a scale that was developed for this study, some correlations between the anxiety level in individual responses (as rated) and verbal rate did emerge. These correlations were significant in interviewee responses within the topical areas of family relationships and sexual adjustment only. Kanfer concluded that "the assumption of a culturally determined, universal anxiety-arousing effect of the various topics is not borne out" (Kanfer, 1959, p.309). Instead, the same topics differed in the anxiety that they aroused in different individuals.

Kanfer (1960) pursued his inquiry into the effect of topic in the interview in a second investigation. His Ss were married female patients, newly admitted to a psychiatric hospital. After a warm-up period, each S was asked to speak about the following four topics: her place of residence and her thoughts and feelings about it; her family and how she got along with its members; her success with and attractiveness to the opposite sex; and, finally, the trouble that brought her to the hospital. Whatever the varied personal meanings of the first three topics, it was anticipated that the last one would stir a common anxiety in all of the Ss, who were acutely ill and recently hospitalized for their illnesses. In fact, the last topic did elicit a higher verbal rate in the group as a whole than the other three. It would appear that when a topic is salient to an entire group of Ss, it is likely to evoke a common reaction from all the members of the group. In this instance the reaction was one of anxiety. When such group salience is lacking, the personal meaning of the topic becomes predominant. Thus, the anxiety effects of the topics in the previous Kanfer study varied from one S to another. Evidently, the topics used did not have a common salience for the college students who participated in the study.

The concept of salience in verbal content is clarified further in the next study (Manaugh, Wiens, & Matarazzo, 1970). The Ss were undergraduate college students asked to speak about family, education, and occupation in a standard interview. Although the initial experimental objective was to investigate the effect of deception on interviewee speech, the major finding was that the topic of education elicited longer utterances and quicker reaction times from the interviewees than the other two topics. The authors concluded that the topic of education was clearly the most salient one for a student population, with resulting enhanced productivity.

That topical salience varies from one group to another was evident in another study (Matarazzo, Wiens, Jackson, & Manaugh, 1970) in which the Ss were job applicants for the position of patrolman. With these applicants, the interviews were divided into three 15-minute periods, dealing with the topics of occupational background, education, and family history. In this instance the topic most salient to the group of Ss, within the context of their employment interviews, was that of occupational background. As expected, the interviewees spoke significantly more per utterance with significantly shorter reaction times in the occupational segment of the interview than they did in the other two segments.

None of these findings will surprise the experienced clinician. He knows that patient A may block and stammer when speaking about his mother, while patient B may do so when speaking about academic failure. He also knows that patient A may be less distressed when speaking about his mother at a later point in therapy. Moreover, the implications of the salience studies are also evident to him. For example, he will proceed more warily when exploring suicidal thoughts and feelings with an acutely depressed patient at the point of admission to a hospital, than he might with a college student seeking help because of minor academic difficulties. In a word, he has learned that verbal content defined as topic is a significant parameter in his conduct of the interview. Certainly he senses that he may vary the emotional tone of the interview, the level of anxiety that develops, and either the self-disclosure or the resistiveness of the interviewee, through the topics on which he chooses to focus.

Finally, some authors report findings that deal with certain evaluations that both interviewers and interviewees make of the verbal content that they communicate. In one investigation (Howard & Orlinsky, 1971) topical focus in psychotherapy sessions was correlated with judgments made by both patients and therapists about the satisfaction experienced. It was found that the most satisfying sessions focused on past and present intimate personal relationships and experiences, such as early family relationships, erotic attachments, and highly personal fantasies about self and others. Clearly, these are topics that are ordinarily not easy to talk about. Yet clients tend to understand and accept the importance of communicating about such "difficult topics." For example, Talland and Clark (1954) asked a number of clients to judge the therapeutic value of 15 topics which had been discussed in their counseling sessions. These clients achieved a high level of agreement about the relative value of the topics, but then, somewhat surprising, rated the more helpful topics as the more "disturbing" ones. For example, the topic designated "shame and guilt" was considered to be extremely upsetting, but its discussion, very helpful. Finally, the clients' judgments of the helpfulness of specified topics correlated at a high positive level with the "intimacy" rating made by psychologists of the same topics.

The research dealing with the correlates of verbal content alerts the interviewer to the possible consequences of a change in topic or a continuing focus on a topic under discussion. While the psychological impact of a topic may vary from one group to another (and, indeed, between individuals), there are certain general correlates of topic that call for the perceptive attention of the interviewer. Topics vary in anxiety arousal and in their salience to individuals and groups. They also differ in the degree to which interviewees feel good or bad about having dwelt on them, or the extent to which they feel they have been helped through talking about them. Some research has been prompted by values among mental health interviewers that have led to widely shared preferences for some forms or categories of content. For example, personal self-disclosure is widely regarded as a particularly desirable form of verbal communication. In the initial interview it is the process by which useful psychological information is communicated. In the therapy interview, it is regarded as a dynamic of therapeutic change. Yet the interviewee frequently experiences considerable resistance to speaking in an open and free manner. Some of the research dealing with interviewee self-disclosure and resistance to it will be reviewed in the sections that follow.

SELF-DISCLOSURE

The following excerpts are taken from two initial interviews with freshman college students who had volunteered to participate in an interview study. The first exemplifies a superficial level of interviewee response.

ER: How is your social life at college?

EE: At_____, well I don't date the boys that go to _____.
      I date a lot of boys I know that go to University of _____.

ER: Ahuh.

EE: In fact, I'm going there next weekend. So excited (Laugh). I I -
      I think it's so pretty there. People are nice.

ER: Did you meet them through your brother?

EE: Well the boy that I date that goes there; when we first went down there to take my brother to school it was my father and me and my sister; and my next door neighbor. When we were there there was this really loud music coming from the room next door. My brother said that he would close the door, so that dad would not get mad. So I said that if he would close the door I would go out into the hall.

The reader may be puzzled at what appears to be an arbitrary and abrupt end to an excerpt that has yet to develop a point. In fact, a close reading of all the remaining pages of the interview would fail to discover any remarks with greater psychological relevance than those already made. There is no introspection, no focus on thoughts, feelings, attitudes toward self and others; in fact, no psychological presentation of self.

Contrast the preceding excerpt with the one that follows:

ER: How has it been for you living say on campus as compared to commuting from home? Ah, can you talk a b- a little bit about that.

EE: Well, it's like a shock to me some of the things that go on. 'Cause ah well I'm from _____ county and that's where I commute from,

ER: Ahuh

EE: and out there the people are more or less narrow minded, you know. They have a lot of prejudice and things like that and you know they just saw it one way. They either liked this or didn't like that.

ER: Ahuh.

EE: And like now this semester like okay my roomate's gay and it just shocked me a bit. I just I don't know. It's taken me a long time to get used to it. I didn't know if I should leave or just you know get adjusted to it. 'Cause I don't know what my values are. So I just learned to accept at the _____. But there's a, I - I don't know, like I'm meeting so many different types of people, you know, people I've heard, you know, that do certain things, but I've never known the people themselves and I don't know, it's just like there's a conflict building up in me. 'Cause I don't know which values are right; which values I want to take.

ER: Well, I'm wondering just where you stand with all this you kn-- people at home feel one way -- or -- but when you come here and experience new things you find that you're not quite sure that you agree with what they're saying at home.

EE: Yeh

ER: Yeh

EE: Ahuh, and like I said something to my mother about my roommate and she got totally upset. She said, 'I'll call it in there and make 'em leave -- make you get a new room' and all this and like I got in a big fight 'cause I don't want her running my life, telling me what to do. You know, it was more or less my problem

ER: Ahuh

EE: for me to you know accept it or make my own decision about it
and it's kind of hard going back home now.

The second interviewee, with some support from the interviewer, was able
to disclose a very difficult and stressful recent experience, and introspect
about it, both in terms of her own values and her relationship with her
mother. She explored her conflicts about this experience and revealed her
strivings for independence and the achievement of a separate identity. If the
first excerpt illustrated superficial avoidance in the interviewee's speech, the
second is an example of personal self-disclosure.

The mental health interviewer is attuned to the occurrence of self-
disclosing remarks by the interviewee and intuitively discriminates between
such responses and others that have a nonpsychological focus. The latter are
designated as Superficial by Pope and Siegman (1968) and defined as
"objective, trivial, or factual, rather than psychological in orientation" (p.
589). The following are some examples of superficial interviewee remarks:
"My father is originally from Texas"; "I attended a public kindergarten"; "The
classes were fairly small"; "He lives near here." Such remarks may indeed be
necessary as structural links in a psychological narrative, but in themselves,
they are external in reference and lacking in psychological content.
Moreover, a high percentage of such remarks in a clinical interview would
signal a lack of psychologically focused self-expression on the part of the
interviewee (that is, a lack of self-disclosure) and would almost certainly
evoke feelings of discomfort and displeasure in the interviewer.

This displeasure would dissipate rapidly if the interviewee switched from
superficial to psychologically expressive communication. In the latter event
the interviewee might speak in a self-exploratory and/or self-evaluative
manner ("I'm more like my older rather than my younger brother"; "When I
was in my teens I was much closer to my mother, than I am now"). He might
examine himself, keeping in focus his thoughts and feelings about self, others,
and significant experiences ("I don't seem to be able to keep my cool when I
talk to my father") (Speisman, 1959). If he were to speak about others, he
would emphasize his relationship with them, avoiding simple description or
preoccupation with objective events. An interviewee's expression of feelings,
whatever their object, would also be considered self-disclosing ("I felt very
angry..."; "I was glad that she wrote me"). Finally, an interviewee would be
psychologically expressive if s(he) were to speak frankly about his/her own
deviations from the normal, and to acknowledge openly whatever problems
and deficiencies he/she might have ("I have no feeling for my brother"; "I
worry too much about what others think about me") (Ashby, Ford, Guerney, &
Guerney, 1957). *

---

* The examples of "superficial" and "psychologically expressive" communication have been provided by the author of the present book, not by the
authors to whose work reference is made - Ashby, Ford, Guerney, & Guerney,
1957.

A similar, but not an identical definition of personally expressive communication was given by Haymes (1970) in a scale that he developed for measuring self-disclosure in tape-recorded interviews. His four categories of response include expressions of emotions and emotional processes ("People like that really bug me"; "That gal really turns me on"; "For the last two weeks I've felt weighted down by a heavy burden of gloom"; and "I've been excited by the prospect of the new job"); expressions of needs ("I need a lot of support"; "I can't work at a subject unless I feel good about the teacher"); expressions of fantasies, strivings, dreams, hopes ("My daydreams are full of images in which others are applauding me enthusiastically"; "Ever since I can remember I've wanted to be a dancer"); and expressions of self-awareness ("My mind wanders hopelessly when I try to sit down to read"; "I get angry at myself whenever I remember how I treated my cousin").

The systematic study of self-disclosure as a dynamic force in psychotherapy is associated with the name of Jourard (1971a, 1971b) whose concise characterization of this form of communication gives point to the above two definitions: "To disclose means to unveil, to make manifest or to show. Self-disclosure is the act of making yourself manifest, showing yourself so others can perceive you" (Jourard, 1971a, p. 19). Much of Jourard's research aims to demonstrate that the outlook for a successful outcome of psychotherapy is very good indeed when both interviewer and interviewee are able to unveil themselves freely to each other.

However, ease of self-disclosure is, at least in part, culturally determined varying with the topic under discussion. Some are designated as high-disclosure topics and others, low-disclosure topics. Thus, openness of communication in high-disclosure topical areas would not be considered to be as significant as would openness in low-disclosure areas. On a clinical, common-sense basis, one would expect self-disclosure to be more difficult in topics that are highly personal and intimate rather than in topics that are impersonal and lacking in intimacy. Such a relationship has indeed been demonstrated by Jourard and his colleagues in a number of investigations (Jourard & Friedman, 1970; Jourard & Lasakow, 1958).

In many of these studies Jourard has not measured the process of self-disclosure in the interview directly. Instead he has used a questionnaire (Jourard's Self-Disclosure Questionnaire) to determine the willingness of a $\underline{S}$ to disclose himself in certain designated topical areas. The first questionnaire, described by Jourard and Lasakow (1958), consisted of 60 items - 10 items in each of six content areas. These included attitudes and opinions ("What I think and feel about religion"; "My personal religious views"; "My personal views on sexual morality - how I feel that I and others ought to behave in sexual matters"); tastes and interests ("My favorite foods, the ways I like food prepared, and my food dislikes"; "What I would appreciate most for a present"); work or studies ("What I find to be the most boring and unenjoyable part of my work"; "How I really feel about the people that I work for, or work with"); money ("How much money I make at my work, or get as an allowance"; "How I budget my money - the proportion that goes to necessities, luxuries, etc."); personality ("What feelings, if any, that I have trouble expressing or controlling"; "What it takes to hurt my feelings deeply"); and body ("How I wish I looked - my ideals for overall appearance"; "My feelings about my adequacy in sexual behavior - whether or not I feel able to perform adequately in sex-relationships").

The usual instructions for responding to the above questionnaire items require the S to indicate the degree to which he/she is willing to disclose himself/herself to certain designated individuals. The degree of disclosure, on each item is defined in the following terms, each given a different value:

o: Have told the other person nothing about this aspect of me.

1.   Have talked in general terms about this item...

2.   Have talked in full and complete detail about this item to the other person

o: Have lied or misrepresented myself to the other person...
                                        (Jourard, 1971a, p. 216)

The finding regarding the relationship between degree of self-disclosure and topic about which willingness to disclose was assessed, was based on data provided by white male, white female, black male, and black female students, selected from three Alabama college populations. The Ss, as a group, varied in self-disclosure according to topics. A "high-disclosure" cluster consisted of tastes and interests, attitudes and opinions, and work; and a "low-disclosure" cluster consisted of money, personality, and body. Thus, the Ss were more willing to disclose themselves in the less intimate group of topics than the more intimate group.

Another investigation (Jourard & Friedman, 1970) demonstrated the willingness of interviewees to speak at greater length about "high-disclosure" rather than "low-disclosure" topics. The Ss were both male and female college students from an introductory psychology course. In this instance each topic had already been rated for intimacy level by a previous group of students. All topics were then distributed into low-intimacy ("What are your views on the way a husband and wife should live their marriage?"; "What are your personal views on politics, the presidency, foreign and domestic policy?"), medium-intimacy ("What are your usual ways of dealing with depression, anxiety and anger?"; "What are the unhappiest moments in your life; why?"), and high-intimacy ("What are the actions you have most regretted doing in your life and why?"; "What are your favorite forms of erotic play and lovemaking?") groups. The E conducted an interview with each S, asking that answers to the questions be typed on a sheet of paper. The questions were selected equally from the three intimacy groups. The finding of the study that is relevant at this time pertains to the mean duration of interviewee speech at each intimacy level. It was found that high-intimacy topics produced significantly less disclosure than the medium or low topics. The combined results of the preceding two studies indicate a greater willingness of Ss to disclose themselves on a low- rather than high-intimacy topics, both when responding to questionnaires and in interviews.

Out of client-centered theory and practice (Rogers, 1957; Truax & Carkhuff, 1967) comes the concept of client self-exploration; very close in some ways to that of self-disclosure. First, a few comments about the difference between the two. The process of self-disclosure is primarily an interpersonal one. To be sure, there are intrapersonal changes that occur as a consequence of self-disclosure, but the act of self-disclosing is directed toward another person. By contrast, self-exploration is a dual process. In the first place it is literally a process of discovering oneself. The originators of a scale for measuring depth of self-exploration (Truax & Carkhuff, 1967) in the therapeutic interview acknowledge both the psychoanalytic and the client-centered lineage of the concept. In both therapeutic frameworks it is assumed that the patient must spend much time and effort in becoming acquainted with the beliefs, values, and motives that determine his behavior. "In the terminology of psychoanalytic theory, this process of self-exploration is described as the patient's becoming aware of and exploring unconscious material and distortion effects of the unconscious material upon perception of reality" (Truax & Carkhuff, 1967, p. 189). Using a somewhat different language, Rogers described the same process in the following terms: "Optimal therapy has meant an exploration of increasingly strange and unknown and dangerous feelings in himself. Thus he becomes acquainted with elements of his experiences which have in the past been denied to awareness as too threatening, too damaging to the structure of the self" (Truax & Carkhuff, 1967, p. 189).

Both the psychoanalytic and the client-centered definitions of self-exploration emphasize the internal focus, the process of exploring oneself introspectively to extend one's inner awareness. But self-exploration, in the sense in which Truax and Carkhuff (1967) use the term, implies the communication by the interviewee of the content of his/her introspective exploration to the interviewer. This communication is a self-disclosing process and is regarded as a crucial variable in psychotherapy (Truax & Carkhuff, 1967).

The excerpt that follows is taken from a client-centered therapy interview, and is presented here because it illustrates poignantly the process of self-exploration. First, there will be a brief summary of the patient's background, provided by the author:

> Jim was in his early twenties. For years he had had a speech handicap which affected his personality and behavior. He had made several attempts at speech therapy to correct his difficulty, without any pronounced effect. Jim came for counseling because of general unhappiness and feelings of inadequacy. Jim and the counselor understood from the first that this experience was to be one of personal counseling, rather than speech correction.
> (Seeman, 1957, p. 3)

The excerpt is taken from the eighteenth interview, when Jim, who had always been a quiet, unaggressive person, began to explore and express feelings with which he had been quite unfamiliar. The parts of the interview quoted below demonstrate with unusual clarity the process of self-discovery during a period of psychological change:

EE: Well ah, I've been th- thinking about my ag- aggression. - It's - I'm beginning to s-s-s well, I'm - not beginning to see more, I'm beginning to feel more that I might be showing a lot of aggression in my st- stuttering toward other people because I know now ah, the other person suffers even more than I do sometime. And it's, I don't know, I guess I am doing it to make the other person suffer. I mean this is something I could never - I could never admit before. I mean, I mean it would - if I just said it, it would just be a lie, but I'm beginning to see now maybe it isn't a lie, maybe I do have a lot of aggression in myself. That's the way I'm showing toward other people. I know I used to feel quite bad about my speech. But ah, it's it's something s-so new that I'm probably showing agression in my speech. I need to say it over and over again. It's, I'm just trying to work it through. I-It surprises me so much.

ER: It's an idea you have to keep close to you...

EE: I do.

ER: ... and play around with because it's new, and, it seems like it hits you rather strong too.

EE. Yes, it has. I didn't know, well, I mean, oh, I've read about it before. But I always want to hurry and get over to the next sentence, you know.

ER: That was for somebody else.

EE: Yes. That was for the other guy, that wasn't for me. But I'm beginning to see it, I guess it is for me. I rather enjoy talking now. And I can also be quiet and sort of enjoy it. (Slightly laughing) But before I didn't want to talk and I didn't want to be quiet either (very loud). <u>Boy, That was terrible!</u> (raising voice) I was completely licked.

ER: What a fight you were having your your speech; talking or no talking, it was still a fight.

EE: Boy, it was, it was a terrible fight. I never realized it. I guess it was too painful to admit that fight. I mean, it's, I mean, I'm just beginning to feel it, to feel it now. Oh the terrible pain. I mean it was terrible. I never realized how terrible it was. I'm just beginning to, I just have a little feeling now. I'm now just beginning to sort of get a hold of a small, small bit now, yeah, right now. How terrible it was. Man all these years I had to put up with that. Man, man, I don't see how I did it, I don't see how I did it. Whew, my goodness, I didn't realize it. I'm just trying to feel it now, trying to get hold of it here right now. It was <u>terrible</u> to talk, I mean you wanted to talk and then I didn't want to. M-hm.

ER: It hurt you so much all these years and you didn't really know that it hurt you that much.

EE: That's right. It's so painful, yet I don't feel depressed. It's tension, I don't know what it is now, I'm feeling (Pause). It's it's

I think I know, it's just plain strain, terrible strain, stress, oh that word stress, that's the word, just so much stress I've been feeling. I'm just beginning to feel it now after all these years of that. Gee I don't know what to do, I don't know what to do; it's terrible (pause) (Sigh). I can hardly, I'm having a time getting my breath now too, just all choked up inside.

ER: You've let yourself feel it so much....

EE: I'm all tight inside, I'm all tight in the lungs. I mean I don't feel like crying, I'm just tight! All this heavy burden I've been bearing. I just feel like I'm crushed. Like I've been hit by a truck. Never wanted to talk, just never wanted to say anything. You know, I, I, I, also never wanted to talk because I was afraid I would reveal myself. That's also.... Before I was - I didn't want to be a person. I didn't want to be a self. But I am now and the t-times that I feel bad now are when I do not become an individual. (Pause) Do you know, I just can't realize, I just can't realize that I had a lot of aggression in me. Gee, I mean it's so new yet. (sounds surprised) I mean I have to go back and talk about it again and again. It's just, boy! I'm aggressive. Even now, no I'm not agressive. Yes I am. I mean I just said I was, but I just don't want to quite accept it yet. I am agressive - or am I? I'm beginning to doubt. M-hm. That's also - gee, I though I'd be going out of here admitting that I was ag-ag-aggressive. But now I don't know whether I"ll be able to or not. You know - well, I mean - I could admit to you I was aggressive, OK, you moved up one, made some progress. But I'm not interested in making progress. Hm, I'm not interested in making progress. That's something new. Before, I thought gee, I wanted to make some progress in here, going to improve. That was important, I mean that was important for me to make progress in here, in therapy. But now it isn't. It isn't important. Hmm. That is also something new now that I'm feeling. That was something that sort of threatened me before, too. It sure was, whether I was going to make progress or not. Yeah, that was really something. Because if - I knew if I would not make any - well, gee, that was - I wouldn't want to like that. I wouldn't be able to accept that at all.

ER: It was one of your biggest fears ...

EE: Yeah, you know that (slightly laughing) was. I thought gee, I'm going to take therapy and I - boy, you'd better make progress, if you don't why you're screwy or something, you're nuts. Mhmm. Things are sure changing around, boy! Boy, I can't even predict my own behavior around here anymore (Laughing) - something I was able to do before. Now boy, I don't know what I'll say next. Man, it's a real - you know, that's quite a feeling. Not to be able to predict your own behavior; that is quite a feeling. Something I haven't been able to do before. I mean well, I'll just say, well, what I want to say. I, I thought I was doing that all along here. But I guess I wasn't. Hmm. Just let come what may. Really, let come what may. Are you really - Now I'm beginning to doubt that. I'm beginning to wonder whether -

ER: Can you be that free?

EE: Yes. Can I really be that free or am I sort of just kidding myself again that I am that free? I'm back again to where I'm beginning to wonder about this whole thing. By jove! Really something (softly) I'm begiinning to enjoy this now, I'm getting a big kick out of it. Before I used to get - it was work. Now, I'm beginning to enjoy this, now. It's adventure, happiness. Well, I'm joyful about it, let's say I'm joyful. Even about all these old negative things, I don't want to make progress, that I'm aggressive, I'm, I'm I'm, joyful with my agression. Sad and mo-mo- mournful, mournful about it (keeps repeating the word voluntarily). There the third time, why I'll do it, you just give me plenty of time (Laughs). That's something I wasn't able to do before; I would have just said mo-mournful once and hurried to something else. But -

ER: Now, you're saying to me, 'OK, so I'll let you know I have trouble with my speech and I'm going to keep on working, right in front of your face.'

EE: Right! That's right! I don't care what you think about it. Maybe I'm showing ag-ag-ag-aggression like that. Maybe I am. Maybe I'm, I'm just gonna make you hurt. (leans very close to therapist, voice raising) I'm just gonna hurt you all I can with this stuttering. That's some - hmm, I'm surprised I said that. I'm just going to hurt you all I can with my speech. I'm just gonna st-st-st-stutter all I c-c-c-can. (voluntarily imitates stutter) That wasn't an actual block, I imitated those, but I'm able to do it and I'm able to s-s-show ag-ag-aggression (real stutter) towards you like that. Gee! I showed quite a bit of aggression even toward my therapist, toward my therapist. Boy this is surprising.

ER: You never knew you felt that?

EE: I never knew I could do something like that. I'm surprised you're not klopping me on the head or something. 'Mustn't do that man, mustn't do that.' I'm surprised you're not rejecting me, you're not punishing me, I'm surprised.

ER: Surprised that I'm not giving....

EE: (Talking at the same time) I am, I'm terribly surprised (slightly laughing).

ER: Surprised that I'm not coming back at you.

EE: Yeah, that you're not. I can't believe it. (softly) I can't (slightly laughing) I can't, I can't believe it. (Laughing to relieve tension) You're not jumping all over me. You're not angry at me. You're not. (Laughing) For once somebody's not angry at me. I don't have to worry whether you feel angry at me or not. This is the first time I ever felt this. That you're not angry at me. It sur-surprises me. (Pause) All this aggression I've shown towards you. Yet I'm, showing it in my speech. That is the thing that is more surprising than ever. That's the thing that surprises me that I sh-showed aggression by my stuttering. By my stuttering I've showed aggression. Something I've tried to get rid of all the time. Something I didn't want to do all the time. I mean before this was - I never thought of this. It was just something, well, it just did-didn't exist.

ER: Of all the things you're doing with your speech is showing aggression.

EE: By - that is right! M-hm. That is really a revelation. That really surprises me. My goodness! Sure does, sure does.

ER: This is what speech meant to you. It rea-lly must surprise you.

EE: That is what speech means, to be aggressive. And I was proudly trying to hold it in. Sp- speech is aggression. Speech is aggression. When I'm - When I talk I'm being ag-ag- aggressive. Something I never wanted to be. Maybe that's the reason I didn't want to talk. Yeah, but yet when I was quiet, I didn't want to be that way either. (pause)

ER: Jim, let's stop for today.

EE: All right, let's do. (Seeman, 1957, pp. 10-15)

Attitudes and feelings previously denied were experienced for the first time. The interviewee trusted the interviewer enough to communicate the painful and exciting process of self-discovery openly to him.

Truax and Carkhuff (1967) have taken the position that self-exploration is not an all-or-none process but rather that it occurs to a greater or lesser degree. To measure the depth of self-exploration, they developed a 9-point scale, ranging from "no demonstrable intrapersonal exploration to a very high level of self-probing and exploration" (p. 195). Three equidistant points will be taken on this scale to illustrate the range of the continuum designated as Depth of Self-Exploration.

Stage O is characterized by an absence of "personality relevant" communication, illustrated in the following interview excerpts:

T: So you'll see Mrs. Smith about taking those tests? Have you got your slip?

C: Yeah.

T: As I mentioned earlier, I have to leave a little early today.

C: At ten?

T: Yes or a little bit after. (Truax & Carkhuff, 1967, p. 196)

Stage 5 does include personally relevant material discussed either "with feeling" or with "spontaneity," but not with both. Consider the following excerpt as an example of this level:

C: He's the only close relative I have. But he's wrapped up in his own family up there ... and he doesn't seem to ... to realize that this house is the type...it's clear to me...I don't want to sell it, it... I really don't.

T: But he wants to sell it.

C: ... He wants to sell it. He's eager to get rid of it because it's not worth keeping ... to him, ... (Truax & Carkhuff, 1967, p. 200)

Finally, stage 8 is achieved when the patient explores new feelings in himself and new aspects of himself. For example:

C: (She is relating experiences in Germany during World War II) I don't want to exaggerate but, why, you could have killed for some things...you'd steal carrots to eat because you were always so dreadfully hungry. There was no clothing, no fuel...and the cold... (voice soft, reflects a great deal of concentration).
(Truax & Carkhuff, 1967, p. 206)

Some Interview Correlates of Self-Disclosure

In a study conducted by Kirtner and Cartwright (1958) it was demonstrated that success in treatment was positively correlated with self-disclosing communication in the interview. Although the research evidence for this relationship is not voluminous, the belief has taken a firm hold in the psychotherapeutic community. This belief applies to the self-revelation of both the interviewer and the interviewee. The quotation that follows pertains to the interviewer's self-disclosure:

To be transparent to the client, to have nothing of one's experience in the relationship which is hidden...that is, I believe, basic to effective psychotherapy.... The therapist by being openly and freely himself, is ready for and is offering the possibility of an extensial encounter between two real persons.... (It) is these moments, I believe, which are therapeutic."   (Jourard, 1971a, p. 147)

With a focus on the interviewee, Truax and Carkhuff (1965) have asserted repeatedly that successful psychotherapy depends on the patient's willingness to reveal personal information about himself, and have demonstrated the association between self-disclosure and successful outcome of therapy in a number of investigations. Their research on individual psychotherapy with schizophrenics (Truax & Carkhuff, 1967) provided some of the evidence. There they found that patients who were high in self-exploration showed

significantly more positive personality change during the course of psychotherapy than patients who were low in self-exploration. The same two
authors (Truax & Carkhuff, 1967) have summarized a number of other studies
which demonstrated that interviewee self-disclosure increased over the
course of psychotherapy when its outcome was judged to be successful.

Thus, self-disclosure is treated as an index for predicting success in
therapy, and simultaneously as a dimension for measuring change in the
interviewee over the course of therapy. Jourard (1971a) provides the
following vignette of a patient's enhanced capacity for disclosing himself as
client-centered therapy proceeds:

> At first the patient is trying to manipulate the therapist's
> perception of him. But the latter listens and seems to avoid
> conventional responses to what is told him, such as scolding, shock,
> scorn, and moral indignation. Encouraged by the lack of expected
> censure, the patient may go on spontaneously to reveal all manner of
> things about himself. One gathers he had never before in his life told
> these things or expressed these feelings to anyone. In fact, in the
> therapy situation, the patient remembers things which surprise him; he
> experiences feelings that never before had he ever imagined. As time
> goes on he becomes remarkably free in expressing what is passing
> through his mind, and if late in therapy you ask him to describe
> himself, he would give a much more comprehensive picture of his
> wishes, feelings and motives than he might have earlier in the game.
> (p. 138)

Jourard portrays the delicate balance between the internal exploration of
experience and its communication to the interviewer. Both have reciprocal
effects on each other. The introspective exploration generates verbal
content; this content is communicated and, if received positively by the
interviewer, reinforces the interviewee's further self-exploration.

Self-disclosing communication therefore occurs within the context of the
interviewee's relationship with the interviewer. There is a series of
investigations in which interviewee self-disclosure occurs together with
feelings of trust and love toward the interviewer. Such strongly positive
feelings evidently provide the emotional climate in which the interviewee is
able to communicate openly and freely about intimate matters. Several of
Jourard's investigations deal with the relationship between the level of self-
disclosure of a person and the degree of positive feeling for the one with
whom he/she is communicating. In his own words: "Researches I have
conducted show that a person will permit himself to be known when he believes
his audience is a man of goodwill. Self-disclosure follows an attitude of love
and trust. If I love someone, not only do I strive to know him; I also display
my love by letting him know me" (Jourard, 1971a, p. 5). In one (Jourard,
1971b) of a number of studies in which Jourard tested the above assumption,
the eight members of a newly organized college of nursing, together with the
dean, served as Ss. The investigator conducted an interview with each S to
determine the extent to which she had disclosed herself to the others in the
past. She was asked to indicate to which of her colleagues she had
communicated about a number of personal information topics (undergraduate

extracurricular activities; town in which born; aspects of physical appearance would like changed; sports in which participated). Then each S produced a rank order of preference for her colleagues, with the criterion, "liked best as a close friend." Significant rank-order correlations occurred between the amount disclosed to each colleague and the degree of liking for her in seven out of the nine Ss. Therefore, in seven out of nine cases Ss disclosed most about themselves to those colleagues whom they liked most. A second investigation (Jourard, 1971b), followed the same procedures as the first. In the second instance, however, the Ss were nine male graduate students in Psychology. This time, significant rank-order correlations between the liking of a S for his colleagues and the amounts he had disclosed to them occurred in only two out of nine cases.

In a third study (Jourard, 1971b), there were two experimental groups of female undergraduates matched, by questionnaire, on past history of disclosure and on willingness to disclose in the present. The experimental procedure was complex and will be reported only briefly in the present summary. With the members of one of the experimental groups, the E spent 20 minutes in individual sessions, engaging in mutually revealing dialogue. She covered the same topics with the Ss of the second experimental group, this time limiting herself to a 20-minute exploratory interview, with no self-disclosure on her part. All Ss were then paired at random and asked to spend 20 minutes in any conversation that would help them become acquainted with each other. The rest of the data was obtained through the use of questionnaires. The Ss in the group to whom the E had revealed herself showed more trust in the E, were willing to take a greater risk in revealing themselves both to the E and to their conversational partners, and were more willing to disclose themselves on intimate topics both to the E and to their partners than the Ss with whom the E conducted a probing inquiry with no self-disclosure.

The evidence about the relationship between the trust a speaker feels in an addressee and her willingness to disclose herself is rather indirect in this study, but is nevertheless persuasive. When the interviewer discloses herself mutually with the interviewee, the interviewee feels a high level of trust in her and is prepared to speak openly and freely both with her and with peers. There will be further reference to this study, at a later point in the present chapter, when mutuality of self-disclosure or the "dyadic effect" (Jourard, 1971a, 1971b) is considered.

Finally, Friedman (1969) studied the relationship between interviewee self-disclosure and personal distance from the interviewer. It was anticipated that the greater the personal distance between the interviewer and interviewee, the less the willingness of the interviewee to speak freely about personal matters. The following were the four degrees of personal distance used, arranged in decreasing order: (1) The interviewer signaled the interviewee that he was listening but made no further response. (2) In addition to the above "listening" behavior, the interviewer touched the interviewee in the center of his/her back as he guided him/her to a seat before the beginning of the interview. (3) The interviewer spoke to each S about himself for about five minutes before seating him/her. (4) Both (2) and (3) were combined. As anticipated, Ss to whom the experimenter revealed something of himself disclosed themselves at greater length than did subjects to whom he did not so reveal himself. Touching the subjects in combination with the experimenter's self-disclosure, resulted in more disclosure from the subjects than either touching alone, or experimenter disclosure alone" (Jourard, 1971b, p. 149). Moreover, the positive feeling that the Ss had about the E, as measured by rating scales, increased as personal distance decreased. Again, self-disclosure by the interviewer had a positive effect on the attitudes of the interviewees toward him/her, and simultaneously enchanced their self-disclosing communication. In both of the preceding two studies, the evidence regarding the association between interviewee attitudes toward the interviewer and the interviewee's self-disclosure was indirect. An additional result in the second study, providing a more direct addendum to the basic finding, was a significant correlation (r) of .73 between the positive feeling and self-disclosure scores of the Ss.

The preceding group of studies investigates the association between certain attributes of the interviewer-interviewee relationship and self-disclosure by the interviewee.   The research that follows deals with situational aspects of the interview that affect the interviewee's readiness to speak about intimate matters. In the first of two experiments by Edelman and Snead (1972) the interviewer in the role of mental health professional was compared with the interviewer in the role of personnel manager; and the interview in which confidentiality was assured when compared with a second in which it was explicitly not assured; and with a third in which it was simply not mentioned. The interviewer in the role of mental health professional was significantly superior to the interviewer in the role of personnel manager in his/her capacity to elicit from the S a willingness to communicate intimate information. The Ss who were told that their communications would not be treated confidentially were not willing to reveal themselves as much as those who were either told that the information they disclosed would be kept confidential or were given no instructions about confidentiality.   In an additional experiment the same two authors (Edelman & Snead, 1972) found that a S who participates voluntarily in an interview will be more openly expressive than one who is compelled to take part.

The research summarized above provides a sketchy beginning to the task of mapping the interview conditions that sustain the communication of intimate content in a mental health interview. Interviewee trust and positive feeling for the interviewer are essential relationship attributes that promote the flow of self-disclosing communication. Situational conditions within the interview also govern the communication of personal content. Thus, such variables as the professional role of the interviewer, the confidentiality of the interview, and its voluntary or coerced nature, all affect the probability that interviewee self-disclosure will occur.

The Dyadic Effect in Self-Disclosure

Increasing emphasis has been given in the literature to the interviewer's willingness to communicate openly as a crucial factor in prompting the interviewee to do the same. This form of mutual response by the two participants in a conversational exchange has been referred to as reciprocity in self-disclosure or, alternatively, as the dyadic effect (Jourard, 1971a, 1971b). The contrast between the more ambiguous role of the traditional mental health interviewer on the one hand and a more personally expressive interviewer role is represented by the two fictional interview segments that follow. In the first, the interviewer pursues a psychological inquiry into the interviewee's problems by limiting himself to ambiguous questions, and without engaging in any self-revelation. In the second, he elicits interviewee self-disclosure by first speaking openly about himself.

A young man, aged 20, has been referred to the psychological clinic on the campus of a large, midwestern university, because of his depressed condition. The dean of students, who referred him, was prompted to see him in the first place because of his failing grades. The first interviewer, using an ambiguous style, attempted to elicit information from the student that would be relevant both to his depressive reaction and his present academic failure.

ER: I understand you've been feeling quite depressed.

EE: Yea. (Sighs)

ER: Can you talk about it?

EE: What is there to say? I feel depressed.

ER: Tell me more about the depression.

EE: (with impatience) I never feel like getting up in the morning. I'm not interested in my studies. I can't concentrate. I don't want to talk to any of my friends. Nothing seems to matter. That's it; the whole damned story.

ER: How long have you felt this way?

EE: Since the beginning of this academic year.

ER: How come this year is different from the previous ones?

EE: Well, I had to declare a major. My father has been pressuring me to prepare to go to law school, starting as far back as I can remember. That's not what I want to do. So we're at an impasse. And right now I just can't get myself going on anything.

ER: Tell me about your father

EE: Oh he's a nice guy. We get along on most things. But now we're at loggerheads about this one question.

ER: Go on.

EE: There's nothing more to tell.

The above information was all the student could muster. He resisted all further probes into his relationship with his father and made a successful effort to maintain the communication limits that he had imposed on the interview.

An interviewer who would have been willing to reveal himself, particularly when self-disclosure from the interviewee faltered, might have followed a different course. Instead of stopping after a limited inquiry into the interviewee's relationship with his father, he could have continued the interview in the following vein:

ER: I understand the predicament you're in, particularly since I had a similar struggle, with my mother, as it happened, when I was in college. My mother had been pressuring me to become a doctor. I went along with her plans when I was in high school. But it became clear to me in college that I couldn't get interested in a pre-med program. The subjects that turned me on were psychology, sociology, and political science. As my mother felt me slipping away from her plans for me, our relationship became very strained. We quarreled whenever I went home. In between home visits I received probing letters, and unpleasant telephone calls which I experienced as a nagging sort of pressure. I became increasingly upset, and started failing some exams. Finally I couldn't go on. So I took a year off, during which I worked as a teacher's aide. This year helped me get myself together. I also settled things with my mother although we were never again as close after this year, as we had been earlier. But, you see, I can understand your depression now, and your academic problems.

The student listened to the interviewer, at first with reluctant interest, and later with a more animated attentiveness than he had been able to manage earlier. The interview continued:

ER: Can you tell me more about how you get along with father?

EE: Well, we used to be real close. I'm the oldest in the family and, when I was younger, we were buddies. My father and I would go to baseball games, and sometimes the two of us would go off camping by ourselves.

ER: Are you saying you're not so close now?

EE: No, we're not, and we haven't been, since maybe my last year in high school. He didn't like my friends in high school. Occasionally, I'd go off to the ocean for a weekend with some of them. He never stopped me; but he'd be so damned unhappy about it. Come to think of it, I've been depressed in his company for years now. Nothing to say to him. Now it's worse.

ER: By the way, what does your father do?

EE: Oh, he's a lawyer.

ER: You see, it looks as though your depression and your academic problems are connected with an increasing crisis in your relationship with your father. I think you need some time to

review this relationship, and your problems in finding out what
you want for yourself, even though this may not be the same as
what father wants.

The immediate effect on the student, of the interviewer's self-revelation
was a decrease in his depressive resistiveness and a willingness to communicate more openly about his relationship with his father. Such a reaction
would be expected if the dyadic effect were indeed, operative. In Jourard's
words, there is "no way to force somebody to talk about himself. You can
only invite. The most powerful...invitation I could find was to share my
subjectivity with the other" (Jourard, 1971a, p. 14). The section that follows
will include a number of studies by Jourard and other investigators that
provide evidence in support of the dyadic effect, and others that trace the
limits of this effect.

Several of these studies have already been referred to above, in a
somewhat different context. The first two were discussed in the section
dealing with the association between trust in a person and willingness to
disclose to him/her. In the first (Jourard, 1971b, 108-113), female
undergraduate Ss, matched for previous history of self-disclosure, and self-
disclosure willingness in the present, were more willing to communicate about
intimate matters, both to the E and to other Ss with whom they had been
paired, after having participated in mutually revealing dialogue with the E,
than they were after having been engaged in a conventional exploratory
interview, with no interviewer self-disclosure. The second study (Friedman,
1969), also summarized earlier in the present chapter found that those Ss "to
whom the experimenter revealed something of himself disclosed themselves
at greater length than did the subjects to whom he did not so reveal himself"
(Jourard, 1971b, p. 149).

In the last study of the present group (Jourard, 1971b), each S was asked
to read one of three transcriptions of simulated psychotherapy sessions. In all
three transcriptions the client's responses were the same. However, there
were three different scripts for the therapist's comments. In one (No Self-
Disclosure) the therapist spoke in a conventional way, with no self-disclosure.
In the second (Warm Support) the therapist made the same nonrevealing
comments as in the first, but added warm, supportive remarks at several
points. In the third (Self-Disclosure) the therapist used the script of the
second interview, but added self-disclosing statements at intervals. Each S
was asked to complete a questionnaire indicating his/her willingness to speak
freely to the therapist in the transcription that he read. The Ss reading the
Self-Disclosure interview reported a significantly greater willingness to
disclose themselves to the interviewer than those reading the Warm Support
and No Self-Disclosure interviews. In all three of the preceding studies the
reciprocal or dyadic effect in self-disclosure was evident.

The dyadic effect has been traced above in a number of studies in which
findings about willingness or readiness for self-disclosure were based on
responses to questionnaire items. In the next two experiments, analogues of
mental health interviews were used to elicit actual interviewee responses.
The purpose of the first of these (Jourard, 1969) was to determine what
effect pairing with high-disclosing Ss would have on low-disclosing Ss. When

paired in this way, did the latter tend to increase their habitual levels of personal communication? The Ss were female Ss, half of whom were designated as high disclosers and half, low disclosers, on the basis of a questionnaire which assessed both past self-disclosing behavior and current readiness to communicate openly to a stranger of the same sex. In the first half of the study, high disclosers were paired with high, and low with low, and were asked to interview each other on 20 personal topics. The intimacy values of the communications of each S were then determined. Not surprisingly, the high dyads attained greater intimacy scores than the low. In the second session, highs were paired randomly with lows, and the members of the dyads again interviewed each other. The high self-disclosers in these pairs maintained their elevated levels of disclosure, while the low disclosers increased theirs significantly. The author concluded that in conversational dyads "open" members tend to increase the level of personal communication of "closed" members.

In the second experiment (Jourard, 1971b, pp. 118-119), female undergraduate students were assigned to two experimental groups, matched for previous self-disclosure. The Ss in both groups were interviewed about the same six topical areas. However, with the Ss in one group, the interviewer revealed himself on each topic before asking the S to speak about herself. There was no interviewer self-disclosure with the Ss of the second group. All interviews were tape-recorded and transcribed. Interviewee responses were all rated for degree of self-disclosure, with the use of a technique that was developed by Haymes (1970). The major finding was that the Ss with whom the interviewer was open about himself revealed significantly more about themselves than those with whom he was nondisclosing.

There is little doubt, then, that reciprocity governs the self-disclosing behavior of two persons engaged in an interview or some other form of communicational exchange. Not quite as evident is the reason for the occurrence of the dyadic effect. In their inquiry into why this effect occurs, Davis and Skinner (1975) considered two alternative explanations, one referred to as social exchange theory and the other as modeling. Social exchange theory implies that interviewer and interviewee exchange reinforcement of each other when they engage in mutual self-disclosure. The various studies that demonstrate mutual trust and mutual liking as mediating variables are consistent with social exchange theory. Thus, if A and B are conducting a conversation and A speaks freely about intimate matters to B, B will respond with positive feeling about A. He will both like and trust him. Such feelings will prompt B to speak freely about himself to A, evoking similar feelings in A and further self-disclosure from him/her. The two reciprocate self-disclosure because each experiences the communication of the other and his/her attitudes as reinforcing.

According to the modeling theory, one person may function as an exemplar, a model for the other, to be imitated (Bandura, 1969). A test of the relative applicability of the above two theories to interviewee self-disclosure required "a direct comparison between the facilitating effects of self-disclosure on the part of the interviewer and on the part of a model enacting the interviewee role" (Davis & Skinner, 1975, p. 216). If the former were more facilitating, the evidence would point to social exchange as the explanation; if the latter, then modeling would be favored.

The Ss, both male and female students, were told that they would participate in an interview of a "personal" nature. Prior to the interview, each S had been assigned to one of three experimental treatments. The first, known as the "interviewer disclosure" condition, required the interviewer, prior to the beginning of the interview, to make a full and frank self-disclosure about each topic to which the interviewee would later be asked to respond. The second, called the "model condition," exposed the S to an audiotaped model of an "interviewee" speaking about the same topics prior to proceeding with the interview itself. The third was the "control condition" in which there were no experimental treatments prior to the interview. In each of the three conditions the Ss were asked to speak freely about a series of preselected high-intimacy topics. The interviews were recorded and transcribed so that interviewee responses could be rated on a scale measuring degree of disclosure. Ratings turned out to be significantly higher in the interviewer disclosure condition than in the other two, which did not differ significantly from each other.

There will be a more extended consideration of the effect of modeling on the direction and control of verbal content in the interview in the next chapter. For the moment, it would appear that when interviewer self-disclosure and interviewee modeling are compared directly, the former is more effective in eliciting open interviewee communication than the latter. While this study cannot be considered conclusive, it does suggest that social exchange (that is, the mutual reinforcement of both members of the dyad) may be a better explanation of the dyadic effect in self-disclosure than modeling.

The case for reciprocity in self-disclosure has been extensively documented. It is now proposed to delineate some of the boundaries or limits of this effect. First, there will be a brief look at a study that deals with quantitative limits in the dyadic effect. Levin and Gergen (1969) had expected that a medium level of self-disclosure from one member of a conversational dyad would signal the other member that his partner wishes a closer relationship and that he is trustworthy. On the other hand, a high level of self-disclosure could indicate a lack of discretion and therefore of trustworthiness. One might therefore expect the second partner to respond by increasing his self-disclosure, as the first increased his from low to medium levels, but to decrease his self-disclosure as the first partner continued to increase his from medium to high levels. When the authors experimentally manipulated the first partner's self-disclosure from low to medium and then to high levels, the anticipated curvilinear pattern in the second partner's response did not, in fact, occur. What did happen was a succession of increases in the second partner's response, as the first went from low to medium to high levels. However, the increase between the medium and high levels was less than it had been between the low and medium levels. Transposing experimental into interview teams, one might expect interviewees to reveal more as interviewers increased their self-disclosure. However, a point would be reached at which the interview in interviewee self-disclosure would begin to lag behind that of the interviewer. This relationship may be due to a sense in the interviewee that the interviewer who reveals too much transgresses against norms of appropriateness in behavior.

That such norms influence the readiness of a person to reveal himself to another is strongly suggested in a sequence of studies conducted by Chaikin and Derlega (1974). The authors undertook their work because "little research has been conducted on the rules governing appropriate self-disclosure or on the norms, regulating when it is socially acceptable to divulge personal information about oneself to another" (Chaikin & Derlega, 1974, p. 588). The Ss were again the ubiquitous male and female undergraduate students. Each S read about a fictional encounter on an airplane between a discloser, named Joan, aged 19, and a target person, another female who happened to take the seat next to Joan. Joan was evidently troubled, and was in fact invited to speak about what was troubling her by the target person. Joan was actually troubled by a personal problem, which she disclosed to the target person in the prepared material given to one half of the Ss, and which she avoided disclosing in that given to the other half ("Flying makes me nervous"). In the experimental manipulation of the relationship between Joan and the other female, all Ss were asked to imagine that the target person was either a stranger, a casual acquaintance, or a close friend. Ss then rated Joan's communication to the other woman on a series of scales assessing its appropriateness. "The results indicate that disclosure of intimate information to anyone but a close friend is less appropriate and less socially desirable than nondisclosure" (Chaikin & Derlega, 1974, p. 590). Only when the target was a friend was the discloser seen as more appropriate than the nondiscloser. The difference in favor of the nondiscloser was particularly great when the target person was a stranger.

The procedure in the second study was the same as that in the first, with the exception that the experimental manipulation of the relationship between Joan and the target of her communications occurred along an age dimension. It will be recalled that Joan was 19 years of age. The age of the target person was alternately, 12, 19, 45, and 75. In every case, except when the target was a peer, disclosure was rated as less appropriate than nondisclosure. Repeating the above finding somewhat differently, disclosure to a peer was significantly more appropriate than disclosure to a target who is either younger or older than the discloser. Although the preceding two studies do not deal with the efficacy of interviewer self-disclosure in prompting openness in the interviewee, they suggest that there might indeed be many interview relationships in which the interviewee could judge his/her self-disclosure to be inappropriate. At any rate, this possibility deserves investigation.

In a later study the same authors (Derlega & Chaikin, 1976) demonstrated that norms regarding the appropriateness of self-disclosing behavior differ with the sex of the speaker. These differences were attributed both to the early learning of sex roles during childhood and to cultural expectations that operate during the adult years. As a child, the boy is taught to hide his feelings because their display is not a manly form of behavior. By contrast, girls are encouraged to show their feelings to others. Once such self-disclosing predispositions are built into people, they continue to be reinforced during adult years by culturally sponsored approval and disapproval. "Men who identify with the masculine role may fear being rejected or ridiculed if they violate expectancies of appropriate sex-typed behavior. Similarly, expressive behavior of women occurs because they continue to expect reinforcement and approval for such behavior" (Derlega & Chaikin, 1976, p.

377). Using methods similar to those in the preceding three studies, the authors obtained the following results: "The male stimulus person was rated as better adjusted when he failed to disclose than when he did disclose. The reverse trend occurred when a female stimulus person was being evaluated: She was seen as better adjusted when she disclosed than when she did not" (p. 378). Moreover, "the female was liked better under high disclosure than nondisclosure,...whereas the male tended to be liked about the same under either high disclosure or nondisclosure" (p. 379). Finally "high disclosure was given a higher femininity rating...than nondisclosure..., indicating that expressive behavior tends to be attributed to a feminine role" (p. 379).

The preceding studies tell us very little about how the situational norms studied might operate in the mental health interview. In general, the person who enters into a mental health interview does so with the expectation of speaking openly about the problems for which help is sought. But this is not always the case. When it is not, the interviewer must find a way to prompt the interviewee toward the type of personally open communication that the situation requires. If the interviewee is, nevertheless, resistant to revealing himself, the roots of this unwillingness to communicate openly may be sought in his past interpersonal experiences - that is, his resistance may be regarded as a manifestation of transference. However, the two studies just reviewed prompt us additionally to look at the situational characteristics of the interview. Is there an age discrepancy between the interviewer and the interviewee? Are there cultural and socioeconomic differences between them? What is the sex of each? The above studies alert us to the possible relevance of such variables to expressive communications in the interview. But these variables must be studied directly within the mental health interview if there is to be some assurance about their relevance. It would be hazardous to assume that one can apply the findings of questionnaire and rating studies of fictional, noninterview interactions directly to the dyadic exchange in the interview.

The impressiveness of the evidence for the occurrence of reciprocity between interviewer and interviewee self-disclosure is not diminished by the observation that high self-disclosure by the interviewer is not his/her only way of eliciting productive personal communication from the interviewee. The psychoanalytically oriented interview in Chapter 1 is a clinical example of a productive interview in which the interviewer utilizes an ambiguous form of inquiring into the patient's problems, quite lacking in any personal expressiveness. The research evidence for a positive correlation between interviewer ambiguity and interviewee productivity will be discussed in Chapter 4. In anticipation of this evidence, it can be said that interviewer self-expression is only one of many variables capable of evoking interviewee response. Moreover, interviewer expressiveness may be peculiarly suited to elicit one type of interviewee response and interviewer ambiguity, quite another. It would appear that the former interviewer style prompts a direct interviewee encounter with previously avoided attitudes and feelings. The latter style seems to invite an associative process of thought and verbalization that may help the interviewee to retrieve repressed thoughts and feelings, leading the interviewer to make interpretations and the interviewee to acquire related insights. These conjectures are offered tentatively. They suggest the desirability of a further consideration of various types of interviewer style, a task that will be pursued further in Chapter 4.

RESISTANCE

Theoretical Aspects

If self-disclosure is a style of interviewee communication that is generally approved by the mental health interviewer, interviewee resistance, its opposite, meets with a contrary reaction. It is disapproved because it frustrates the objectives of both the initial and the psychotherapeutic interview. In the former, it reduces the communication of psychologically focused information which the interviewer attempts to elicit. In the latter, it reduces the kind of self-exploration and communication that sparks the process of psychotherapy. Indeed, the term "resistance" implies that the interviewee is manifesting oppositional behavior. The precise way in which this oppositional behavior occurs and its causes need specification, for the concept of resistance varies a little, depending on the context in which it is used.

The term "resistance," in its modern psychotherapeutic sense, was first used by Freud in reporting some observations about the interview behavior of psychoanalytic patients. Thus, he remarked that "one comes across a resistance which opposes the work of the analysis and in order to frustrate it pleads a failure of memory" (Freud, 1957, p. 16). Freud was referring to the patient's inability to recall crucial information out of his past as a major manifestation of resistance. But the failure of memory is only one form of resistance. Other forms, to be specified below, contribute to a rather complex pattern or style of communication, designated as "resistive." To Freud, these forms were all equivalent because they all served to maintain the patient's repressions, the elimination of which the psychologist considers to be a central objective of his treatment efforts.

For example, a psychoanalyst might observe that whenever he invites his 23-year-old male patient to speak about childhood events in which he and his father participated together, there are long periods of silence. The silences are tense because the patient is in fact making an effort to remember the events about which his therapist had inquired. But, in spite of painful and protracted efforts, very little comes to mind. After a period of stressful introspection, the patient remarks with some embarrassment: "I can't seem to remember much." The analyst does not accept this response and continues to wait in demanding silence. Again there is a painful introspective search by the patient, with some shadowy results. He is able to muster a transient, half-image of himself and his father, on the seat of a train, enveloped in a haze of joy as the sunlight streaming in through the window is intermittently cut off by a succession of trees moving rapidly past on the outside. A happy flow courses through the patient as this image possesses him for a moment. Soon, however, it is displaced by another in which he sees himself, as a small child, firmly grasped by his father with one arm, as he is spanked vigorously by his father's free hand. The perception of the event is dreamlike because the child is facing downward toward the floor, which appears to be rising as it recedes from him. And in the background there is the sound of his baby sister crying with a terrifying abandon. The two scenes flash through the patient's mind rather quickly, and then fade. He cannot embellish them, or even bring them back with the momentary clarity that they assumed when he first remembered them. He relates the events to his therapist but is aware of their incompleteness. Why was his sister crying? Why does he experience a vague feeling of guilt, even dread, as he tries without success to answer this question? He can guess at the answer but cannot remember it. Further self-probing makes him feel frightened. Eventually the whole process of reminiscing comes to a halt as he feels increasingly confused and muddled.

While his abortive introspective efforts were in progress, he tried to communicate them to his therapist. The latter was, of course, aware of the long silences. Later the therapist heard the patient complain of the great difficulty he was experiencing in recalling any childhood events in which both he and father were jointly involved. The therapist noted the brevity, the patchy incompleteness with which the two events were recalled. He also observed that any further attempts to inquire into them simply blocked the patient; he could not add to, clarify, or enlarge on the events he had partially remembered. Moreover, the patient's style of communication became increasingly disorganized as he attempted to explore his memories and feelings. "My father and I were close when I was a kid." But a moment later, on further reflection: "No. I was really pretty scared of him." There was barely any statement he might make that he would not be impelled to negate almost immediately. In the end, even his speech became disrupted: "My father was a stric ... a stro ... well he had a temper that would scare the hell out of me."

The introspective process of the patient encountered the kind of inner obstruction to the recall and experience of painful thoughts and feelings that Freud had, quite early in his career, designated as repression. Repression is regarded as a mechanism for avoiding anxiety and thus for maintaining a kind of psychological equilibrium through the blanking out of thoughts and feelings related to anxiety-arousing events in the past. But repression is a construct. It is not overtly manifest. What the therapist does hear and observe is the patient's resistance. While repression is a silent inner process, resistance is an audible style of communication. Both, however, are continuous; in fact they are part of the same process.

Thus, in psychoanalytic theory, resistance is not an act of deliberate opposition to the expectations of the therapist. It is not "a conscious reluctance to reveal ideas of which one is aware, out of embarrassment or fear of censure; rather, resistance is motivated by unconscious anxiety, and it typically prevents the emergence of ideas into consciousness even while it is preventing their expression to the therapist" (Auld, 1968, p. 169).

If the effect of resistance is to reduce the interviewee's anxiety, then the various forms of resistance should be functionally equivalent. On this assumption, several resistance scales have been constructed. For example, Dollard and Auld (1959) developed a Resistance Scale for use in the content analysis of interview transcripts, consisting of nine major categories of verbal response. While the authors have demonstrated that the scale can be scored reliably, there is little intercorrelational data to support the assumption of equivalence between the different categories. Such as there is demonstrates the functional equivalence between resistance as silence (category nine of the scale) and resistant talk (all remaining eight categories). Using the Dollard and Auld (1959) scale for scoring transcribed psychotherapy interviews, Auld and White (1959) found that the probability was significantly greater that silence would follow a sentence scored as resistant rather than nonresistant. It was also found that silences are likely to be followed by resistant talk. Because there was a flaw in the design of the Dollard and White (1959) study, in that the scorers of resistant talk knew at what points silences occurred, Goldenberg and Auld (1964) repeated the investigation, eliminating the possible confounding of the two variables in the first study. The earlier findings were vindicated. Again, resistance followed silence with significantly greater frequency than it followed nonresistant talk, and silence followed resistant talk with significantly greater frequency than it did nonresistant talk.

These findings are of interest to the practicing interviewer because they alert him/her to certain emerging probabilities as the interview proceeds. If there is a palpable increase in the frequency of silence, he/she may take this as a signal that the interview is entering a resistant period. But the statistical significance of the above findings notwithstanding, the experienced interviewer knows that silence cannot be taken as an infallible signal of resistance. Certainly the level of probability in the results is not great enough to eliminate the possibility that the interviewee's silence may have other meanings as well. For example, the interviewee may have completed a train of associations in one topical area and may be struggling with inner uncertainty about what new direction to take. Or, in a more immediately interactional sense, the interviewer may have asked him a question couched in terms so ambiguous as to bring the interviewee to a momentary silent halt. In both of these instances, resistance is not the most accurate characterization of the interviewee's behavior.

Moreover, these investigations do not provide unequivocal support for the psychological assumption of the close relationship between repression and resistance. Indeed, much of the psychological research on resistance in an interviewee's communications does not concern itself with this assumption. Resistance is simply regarded as a process of avoiding or diminishing the self-disclosing communication requested by the interviewer because of its capacity to make the interviewee uncomfortable or anxious. For the purposes of investigating interview communication, it is considered sufficient to define resistance in terms of the forms or categories of verbal behavior of which it is composed. The possible relationship between resistance, as it occurs in communication, and the inner construct of repression will not be a major concern in the studies summarized below.

Resistance in Verbal Content

In their consideration of resistance as a style of communication, Watzlawick, Beavin, and Jackson (1967) depart briefly from the interview to a fictional encounter between two strangers seated side by side in an airplane. Passenger B wishes to carry on a conversation; passenger A would rather not. The authors then consider the options open to passenger A, caught in a situation which he cannot leave physically and which he would find extremely awkward to ignore. Note the similarity between the situation in which fictional passenger A and the resistive interviewee find themselves. While it is conceivable that the latter could walk out of the interview situation, or physically remain there in complete silence, both of the indicated courses would be socially uncomfortable to pursue.

If passenger A decides to stay in his seat and respond in some way to passenger B, he might choose one of the following courses:

1. He could bluntly inform B that he would rather not talk to him. However, the strain that would ensue would be difficult for both passengers to endure.

2. A more manageable option would be one in which A does enter into a conversation but maintains it at a totally superficial level. Thus, he might speak about the weather at the destination of his trip, about the long wait in the airport before boarding, and other banalities. At all costs, he avoids deviating into more personal disclosures, because he knows that once he begins to speak in a personal vein, it is difficult to limit or reverse the conversational tide.

3. A third course for A would be to speak in a manner that obscures or disqualifies what he says. "Disqualification covers a wide range of communicational phenomena, such as self contradictions, inconsistencies, subject switches... incomplete sentences... obscure style or mannerisms of speech" (Watzlawick et al., 1967, p. 76).

The types of "disqualifiers" referred to above tend to occur in communication in which the speaker is buffeted by contradictory wishes. On the one hand, he would like to maintain the conversation; on the other, he is impelled, usually by anxiety or some feeling of embarrassment to negate, diminish, block, or otherwise "disqualify" what he has said or is in the process of saying. The result is a choppy, disrupted flow of speech. Consider the following interview excerpt, as an example of "disqualified" or disrupted speech by an interviewee.

ER: How does it work out, Mr. R, with your parents living in the same town as you and your family?

EE: Well we try, uh, very personally I mean ... uh, I prefer that Mary (his wife) take the lead with them, rather than my taking the lead or what. I like to see them, but I don't try too much to make it a point to be running over to have them ... they know very definitely that ... oh, it's been always before Mary and I ever met and it was a thing that was pretty much just an accepted fact - in our family I was an only child - and they preferred that they would never, to the best of their ability, not ah, interfere. I don't think there is ... in any case I think there is always a - an underlying current there in any family, I don't care whether it's our family or any family. And it is something that even Mary and I feel when we ... both of us are rather perfectionists. And, ah, yet again, we're very ... we are ... we are st - rigid and ... we expect that of the children and we feel that if you got to watch out - I mean, if ah ... you can have interference with in-laws, we feel, we've seen others with it and we've just ... it's been a thing that my own family tried to guard against, but ah ... and uh, like here - why we've ... I wouldn't say we are standoffish to the folks. (Watzlawick et al., 1967, p. 77)

In brief, three basic forms of resistance in a dyadic communication situation have been presented: the blunt refusal to participate in a conversational exchange; the adherence to a banal, superficial line of talk; and, finally, a relatively complex form in which the speaker does engage in brief spurts of personal communication which he quickly tries to "disqualify" through the switch of a topic in the middle of a sentence, the aborting of a sentence leaving it dangling in an incomplete state, the disruption of speech, and the fracturing of a sentence to the point of blocking of speech.

The latter two strategies of resistance are very close to the two categories of resistance that Pope and his colleagues have termed Superficiality and Resistiveness (Pope, Blass, Siegman, & Raher, 1970; Pope & Siegman, 1968; Pope, Siegman, & Blass, 1970; Pope, Siegman, Blass, & Cheek, 1972).

When an interviewee is avoidant of personal or psychological expression, his/her speech is considered to be superficial. Clauses, such as the following, would be so classified: "My father is originally from Texas"; "I attended a public kindergarten"; "The classes were fairly small." These clauses are factual and objective in content, lacking the intraceptive quality of a personally self-disclosing expression. On the other hand, resistive clauses are similar to those designated by Watzlawick et al., (1967) as disqualifiers. An interviewee begins to speak in a disclosing way about thoughts, feelings, and relationships that bring on unpleasant feelings of anxiety, embarrassment, and, more generally, discomfort. To continue to communicate about these matters, which s(he) regards as the business of the interview, s(he) needs to transiently "disqualify" or modulate what s(he) has said (sometimes, what s(he) is about to say) through minimizing or excessively justifying it. A somewhat different category, also included in the Resistiveness scale, and possibly more directly related to repression, is blocking in the expression of personal matters. Some examples of each of the Resistiveness categories follow. Included in minimizing are statements that deny ("I don't think I'm really closer to one than to the other"), minimize ("She's not really that old"), and express doubt about ("I suppose my relationship with my mother is average") a self-disclosing remark. In the next category the interviewee seeks to justify thoughts or feelings, often by attributing blame to external events or other people ("I was unhappy then because I was just growing"; I don't like to visit my family because they act like I'm in the wrong"). Blocking is a basic inhibition of speech or verbal expression when the interviewee is attempting to make a self-disclosing statement. Speech disturbance may block such expression, taking on the form of incomplete sentences ("and ah Biology.... I s s I struggled through tenth grade"), retracing, rephrasing, and fumbling sentences ("Oh I had ah I don't know tenth grade I had I had well I never really made bad grades"). Blocking may also take on the form of a total inhibition of thought and memory ("Gee, it's hard to think ...").

The Superficiality and Resistiveness scales have been used as dependent variables in a series of studies (Pope, Blass, et al., 1970; Pope & Siegman, 1968; Pope, Siegman, & Blass, 1970; Pope, Siegman, et al., 1972), with a range of different goals and objectives. In each of these studies the Superficiality and Resistiveness scores were the percentages of clause units that fell into these two categories in the speech samples used. The most consistent finding in all of these investigations was the significant negative correlation between Superficiality and Resistiveness ranging from $-.66$ (Pope & Siegman, 1968) to $-.70$ (Pope, Siegman, & Blass, 1970). This negative correlation prompted the conclusion that resistance in interviewee speech is not a homogeneous category. Of the two forms of resistance, Superficiality appears to be the more complete because it is a means of totally avoiding psychological communication. On the other hand, the interviewee who manifests Resistive speech vacillates between self-disclosure and its disqualification or reduction. Even his moments of blocking give way to others of self-disclosure in passages that are categorized as Resistive.

If Superficiality is a means of avoiding self-disclosure, one would expect it to be associated with low rather than high anxiety. By contrast, one would expect Resistiveness to vary directly with anxiety. The former relationship is anticipated because superficial avoidance of personal expression is the most effective barrier against anxiety. It is a stable defense and therefore impermeable to infusion by warded off feelings. When Superficiality prevails, there is no self-disclosure. On the other hand, Resistiveness is a relatively unstable defense. Indeed, it functions intermittently to dampen the intensity of feelings, the openness of self-disclosure, during passages in which the interviewee is making an effort to express himself. It is therefore reasonable to expect that Resistiveness will occur when the interviewee is, in fact, expressing disturbing feelings.

The above contrast between the two forms of defensive speech was partially borne out in one study (Pope, Blass, et al., 1970), although the results were a little short of conventional significance. The Ss were six psychosomatic patients on a research ward of a psychiatric hospital, four females and two males, ranging in age from 17 to 39. The daily vicissitudes of anxiety in these six patients were rated by two nurses. On the same days for which the ratings were made, the patients taped daily 10-minute free speech monologues. The results for high- versus low-anxiety days demonstrate higher Superficiality on low- rather than high-anxiety days; higher Resistiveness on high- rather than low-anxiety days. However, only the latter difference had borderline significance at a $p < .10$ level.

In a later investigation (Pope, Siegman, et al., 1972) the Ss were male and female undergraduate psychology students who were divided into two similar groups, one experimental and the other control group. The Ss in both groups were interviewed twice with about a week intervening between the two interviews. Both groups were given accurate instructions before the first interview. The members were told that each would be interviewed for information about his/her educational history and family background. The control group was similarly instructed before the second interview. But the experimental group was misinformed at that time. It was told that the interviewer would inform each S about his or her performance on a battery of psychological tests taken before the first interview. However, according to the research design, the interviewer actually conducted a second information-gathering interview with the members of both groups. The members of the experimental group therefore experienced the second interview as one that was conducted along lines that were incongruent with their expectations. They had been led to believe that the interviewer would provide them with information. Instead, they were again requested to communicate information to him. Since the control group did not have this conflict of expectation induced in its members, their responses would provide sequential baseline data for the experimental group.

It had been anticipated that the conflict in the experimental group would prompt it to be less disclosing in the second rather than the first interview - that is, its members would be more Superficial and less Resistive in their interview communications. The control group would manifest neither change. As it turned out, there was both an increase in Superficiality and a decrease in Resistiveness in the experimental group, but only the Resistiveness result was significant. There were no changes in the control group.

Superficiality and Resistiveness in the above studies are very similar to the concepts of stable and unstable resistance as defined by Klein (1965). He reasoned that stable resistance protects the interviewee against anxiety, while unstable resistance, which permits the intermittent intrusion of anxiety-provoking thoughts into the interviewer's mind and speech, does not protect against anxiety nearly as well. In the Klein study the Ss were four women ranging in age from 17 to 43, diagnosed as psychoneurotic, in treatment with four different therapists. The source of data was 39 tape-recorded interviews divided into five-minute segments. Each five-minute segment was rated for stability of verbal defense and for number of GSR responses. The GSR response was the measure of anxiety. As predicted, for each of the four cases, there were more GSRs in periods of unstable rather than stable resistance.

Whether one utilizes the quantitative concept of relative stability of resistance or the qualitative one, which divides resistant speech into Superficial and Resistive categories, the interviewer must clearly respond differently to each. When he is subjected to superficial periods of communication, during which the interviewee is avoiding the self-disclosing type of communication requested by him, he is confronted with a much more formidable task of redirection of the course of the interview than he has when the interviewee alternates between periods of openness, and others during which he attempts to modulate the anxiety resulting from his openness by "unstably defensive" or "resistive" verbalizations.

The Multichannel Expression of Resistance

Until this point, resistance has been traced only in the verbal channel of communication. Thus, whether the interviewee is openly communicative or resistant has been noted both in the verbal content and in the style of his speech - that is, it has been sought in both linguistic and paralinguistic channels. With the advent of an increasing interest in nonverbal communication has come an awareness that verbal communication is much more susceptible to control and manipulation than its nonverbal counterpart. Consequently, the interviewer is more sensitively attuned to signals of resistance if he is simultaneously resonant with all channels of communication rather than with the verbal one alone. In order to explore the role of nonverbal communication in resistance, a digression will be necessary from the major focus of the present chapter on verbal content.

In the section of the first chapter dealing with the various channels of communication there was a brief reference to the interviewer's frequent experience of hearing discordant or contradictory messages from different communication channels. An example was given of a middle-aged school-teacher, depressed by the burden of her professional work but unable to accept or directly express this depression, who began a psychotherapy interview by speaking of the pleasure she had in a recent class discussion. The therapist, who both listened and observed, noted that her face wore a strained smile and that her hands gripped each other with great intensity even as she spoke about pleasure in the classroom. Without reflection, as though he were responding in a well-habituated way, the therapist discounted her verbal narrative and focused instead on the nonverbal signals that communicated tension. He perceived his patient as showing a depressive reaction to her work as a teacher.

Wiener and Mehrabian (1968) distinguish between more and less explicit channels. The verbal channel, in this instance, was more explicit than the nonverbal ones of facial expression and gesture. The interviewee, therefore, made an explicit statement verbally. It is not surprising that the explicit channel is the one that is used most frequently for resistant communications; it is, after all, the channel from which the speaker receives most feedback and over which he is able to exercise the greatest control. As a child grows up in a western culture, he is trained to regard language as the major mode of communication. If there is some awareness that something is also "said" by one's face and hands, for example, it is peripheral. Thus, a child is more likely to be told by his parents to hold his tongue than to control his hands or to stifle his smile. In fact, he learns to distort his thoughts and deny his feelings through his speech rather than through posture and gesture. When confronted with discordant signals, the interviewer of the schoolteacher assumed that the emotion communicated in facial expression and gesture was more authentic than that reported verbally. This assumption would accord with the view expressed by Wiener and Mehrabian (1968) that the verbal channel is more explicit in character than the nonverbal ones, and therefore more subject to deliberate control and manipulation.

The example that follows (Beier, 1966) illustrates a patient's expression of dependency feelings through posture and gesture while she is silent about them in her speech. Before each psychotherapy interview, a young adult female patient would stand next to her chair in the therapist's office until he would gently invite her to be seated. This sequence had become a ritual, to which the therapist had, at first, given no thought. Eventually his supervisor made him aware that through this behavior his patient was "saying" something to him, eloquently but silently. One day, after the supervisor had brought the possible meaning of the patient's behavior to the therapist's attention, he began the interview without the usual invitation to the patient to be seated. The patient responded with depressive feeling, tears, and eventually with some verbal content that helped to clarify the nonexplicit communication of dependency in her previous behavior. Evidently, this patient felt vulnerable about her dependency feelings and could not speak with her therapist directly about them. She therefore chose the indirect (more resistant) course of expressing her feelings through posture and gesture, while saying nothing about them explicitly.

Beier (1966) refers to the information transmitted through explicit verbal content as overt information, and that which is less explicitly expressed, as covert information. While others have spoken of resistance as a form of communcation which protects the speaker against impulses, feelings, and thoughts that are internally perceived as dangerous, Beier (1966) gives the concept an external referent. Consider the following examples. There is no trace of either internally or externally directed resistance in the angry instruction of one person to another to "go to hell!" Such uncomplicated directness contrasts sharply with the mincing, patronizing remark of a wife to her husband, as he nurses a throbbing hangover the morning after a party at which he had been a star performer: "Honey! You were cute last night. Everyone thought you were hilarious." This occasion may be one in a long succession of such occurrences. The wife may be angry and depressed by the incident. But she protects herself against any retaliatory anger from the husband by the distortions in the verbal content of her remark and its style of expression. Nevertheless, she may betray her true feelings to a perceptive husband by wringing her hands or tensely kicking off her shoe as she uncrosses her legs impatiently. If the beleaguered husband responds to the covert, or nonexplicit, feeling with anger to match her own, she can fall back on her literal communication as her defense and reproach him for being hostile without provocation. In Beier's (1966) view, resistant communication has both its self-protective and manipulative aspects. In his own words, almost "all messages are sent with the purpose of influencing the respondent. That is, a message is designed to create certain 'sets' in the respondent which, in turn, create predictable, expected responses" (p. 280).

The interviewer is frequently subject to this type of resistant manipulation. For example, an earnest, introspective young man, with a history of several psychotic episodes, is, at the moment, participating in an evaluative interview before members of the staff, shortly after admission to a state hospital. His interviewer is a young psychology intern, about his age. The patient speaks in the gentle cultivated tones of an intellectual who is experienced at communicating with others about troubled thoughts and feelings. With him, such conversations start with introspective promise but quickly dissipate into a schizoid vagueness. When asked to speak about the troubles that brought him to the hospital, he refers to much identity confusion related to his belonging to a number of different social groups. He designates some of these groups as gay. Then, in a voice that sounds pedantically expository, he remarks that he has certain tendencies and interests in a gay direction himself. Flatly with no cues of topical transition, he quickly moves on to speak of his recent psychotic experience, still in the manner of a person explaining an interesting phenomenon to which he was not personally related. When the interviewer attempts to inquire into the patient's perception of himself as a gay person, he is disregarded. When he persists, the patient becomes momentarily confused, pauses, remarks that the conversation has become confusingly esoteric, and then moves on to still another topic. Clearly, he wishes to display his homosexual identity briefly, for whatever reason, but does not wish to be made accountable for his remark by providing further information about it. However, in a covert way he never departs from the topic. He sits close to the interviewer; crosses his legs and swings one foot repeatedly in a manner that brings it very close to the interviewer's legs. The interviewer does not notice the body language, but others present at the evaluative interview do and they remark about it in the subsequent discussion.

In speaking of the task of the interviewer in responding to covert communication of the above kind, Beier made the following comment: "To recognize the meaning of these communications, the therapist must learn to use himself as an instrument and understand which of his feelings are due to the information conveyed to him by the patient" (Beier, 1966, p. 283). This injunction is relevant, but not always easy to implement. In the above instance, the interviewer admitted feelings of great discomfort to his colleagues during the ensuing discussion, but had no awareness of their probable cause in the patient's covert communications. Freud had alerted interviewers to the rich source of information transmitted nonverbally by the resistant patient in the following well-known quotation: "He that has eyes to see and ears to hear may convince himself that no mortal can keep a secret. If his lips are silent, he chatters with his fingertips; betrayal oozes out of him at every pore" (Freud, 1959, p. 94).

But the task of decoding the interviewee's nonverbal messages is fraught with ambiguity. The interpretation of verbal content is, to a considerable extent, independent of immediate context. Thus, rules governing syntax, sentence structure, and the semantics of the spoken word are widely shared by the members of a culture. Granting the nuances of meaning that may be contributed to verbal content by tone of voice, tempo of speech, speech disturbances, gesture, posture, and social context, the decoding of language remains a more specific and consensually shared undertaking than the decoding of communications in the nonverbal channels. There is an impression among clinicians that some are better at "reading" body language than others. Moreover, all of them tend to focus more intently on nonverbal clues when speech is either superficial or resistive. In part, this differential attending to nonlinguistic cues is prompted by a search for information wherever it may occur. If resistant talk chokes it off in the speech of the interviewee, the interviewer seeks it in other signals. Moreover, in his training, the mental health professional is sensitized to style of speech, facial expression, posture, and gesture as sources of the "leakage" of information deliberately withheld in speech content.

The process of withholding and distorting information verbally, while unwittingly "leaking" it through other channels, has been investigated and amplified in a series of studies using deception as a major experimental variable. Typically, the speaker is instructed to deceive the addressee about specified topics or during specified speaking intervals. While resistance, in its clinical sense, is not synonymous with conscious deception, the two processes have enough in common to permit one to illuminate the other.

Studies in Deception; Their Relevance to Resistance

The experimental manipulation of deceit in communication was hit on by several investigators (Ekman & Friesen, 1972, 1974a, 1974b; Mehrabian, 1972) as a means of exploring the processes by which an interviewee may avoid or distort the expression of distress, discomfort, or other affects and thoughts that make him/her feel vulnerable, in more explicit channels of communication, while unwittingly revealing them through less explicit channels. The basic assumption in the deception studies is that certain forms of "nonverbal behavior may escape efforts to deceive, may evade self-censoring, or may betray dissimulation" (Ekman & Friesen, 1974a, p. 269).

Ekman and Friesen (1974a) define two basic forms of deception, "alter-deception, where ego, the deceiver conceals information from the other interactant, alter; and self-deception, where ego is the object of his own deception, concealing information from himself" (p. 270). What Ekman and Friesen are referring to is the target of the speaker's deception. If the interviewee is the deceiver in an interview, the alter must be the interviewer. When the interviewee deceives himself, as he does in the classical psychoanalytic repression situation, the object of the deception is the ego. It is evident that the above two forms of deception cannot be independent of each other. The interviewee (ego) may deliberately mislead the interviewer (alter), or he may first deceive himself and, incidentally, deceive the interviewer (alter). Both of these are alter deceptions, the first a consciously manipulated, deliberate one, and the second, an unconscious alter deception, resulting from deception of self in the first place. The above distinction between the two aspects of deception has been useful in the design of research studies, and both may be assumed to be relevant to the clinical concept of resistance. Resistant behavior encompasses both.

The interviewee has two basic ways of implementing his/her deception. He may inhibit a response that would communicate information that he/she wishes to withhold. Thus, he may fall into silence, deliberately refusing or unconsciously blocking a response that would cause him anxiety or embarrassment. Or he may simulate a response, maintaining the communicative flow but avoiding the disturbing information. The latter may be accomplished through superficial talk that is avoidant of self-disclosure, or through the type of Resistiveness that Pope and his colleagues have investigated in studies, reviewed above.

A criminal during an interrogation in which he deliberately sets out to deceive his questioner exemplifies an uncomplicated form of alter deceit. By contrast, the young lady who was not able to speak to her therapist about her dependency feelings but acted them out unwittingly through standing until invited to sit, is an example of the unconscious deception of the interviewer, consequent on her own prior self-deception. The criminal sustained his deception through simulation; he lied about his involvement in a crime. The young lady stood in silence; she, therefore, sustained her deception through inhibition. However, she too may have needed eventually to resort additionally to simulation. The interviewer may have confronted her with her preinterview ritual of standing and waiting, compelling her to fabricate a reason for behavior which she herself did not understand.

A sensitive interviewer would be alerted to cues of deception (resistance) in conflicting messages from different channels of communication. Moreover, previously quoted examples notwithstanding, the incongruence between messages may not always occur between verbal signals on the one hand and those from all other channels on the other. Ekman and Friesen (1974a) note that there are differences in explicitness of communication between certain nonverbal channels as well, such as the face, hands, and feet. There would probably be little disagreement with the assertion by these authors that the face is the most explicitly communicative channel of the three referred to above. It is expressively flexible and can send emotional messages rapidly. There is a wide consensus regarding the meaning of a facial expression - that is, the emotion that is being transmitted by it. And lastly, the face is highly visible. By contrast, the feet and legs are the least explicitly communicative. Their messages cannot be sent with the speed of facial expression. Moreover, there is little agreement regarding the meaning of a leg or foot message. A young lady in a paraprofessional training program in mental health was chided by a supervisor for the hyperkinetic way in which she crossed her legs and swung one leg over the other as she talked. He implied that she was manifesting a sort of neurotic tension that she might well attend to as she trained for a career in mental health. But there was no consensus among faculty and the student's peers regarding the leg messages sent by this young lady. In fact, most of her peers would have perceived the message to be sexual rather than neurotically tense. The ultimate truth of this matter is not the point at issue but, rather, the ambiguity of the message sent through her lower extremities. Finally, legs and feet, often covered with clothing do not have the visibility of the face. Even if the screen imposed by the clothing were not there, feet and legs are positioned below eye level, sometimes hidden by furniture, and nearly always require the kind of obvious direction of gaze by the addresser that would usually be considered to be improper. "Anatomically, hands are intermediate between face and feet/legs, and this is also true of their sending capacity" (Ekman & Friesen, 1974a, p. 276). Most hand movements do not achieve the speed noted in mercurial changes in expression of which the face is capable. While the hands may match the face in the number of recognizable messages they are able to transmit, they are not quite equal to the face in visibility. Although not covered by clothing or obscured by furniture, they can be easily hidden.

The relative explicitness of the face renders it the nonverbal channel of communication that is most readily placed in the service of deception by a resistant interviewee. The basic reason for the availability of facial expression for deceptive communication lies in the interviewee's past experience with external and internal feedback to previous facial expressions. A female patient in her early 30s, in treatment for a post traumatic reaction to a car accident, had become subject to severe mood changes from one week to the next. To assess these quickly, before the beginning of each interview, her therapist had come to rely on a glance focused on her facial expression as she sat in the waiting room. Often, as she was being seated, he would remark in the following vein: "Things seem better this week"; or "You look a little down today." The patient usually confirmed his observation, without any feeling of surprise that he would know how she felt. As she grew up, she came to expect that others would notice her facial expression and would often provide her with feedback about it. This type of external feedback made her wary about what she might betray facially, when directly communicating with others or when she was aware that she was under scrutiny. She seemed to know, with considerable accuracy, when she appeared happy, when she frowned, when she looked angry, and particularly when others would notice a cloud of gloom that might be spread over her face. But external feedback and her inner awareness of her facial expression made it possible for her to control and manipulate messages from the face when she was impelled to deceive others by hiding or distorting her feelings.

She did not have the same level of awareness of the communications from her feet/legs, possibly because external feedback to these was never as rapid and/or explicit as it was to her face. Moreover, she did not have as detailed an internalized scheme for classifying foot/leg messages as face messages. Thus, she would have found it more difficult to manipulate her foot/leg messages for purposes of deception. In fact, such a possibility may never have occurred to her.

The patient referred to above wore her mood on her face, when sitting alone, but she did not always do so during the interview. She would often speak about frustrations in her recent life, particularly with a group of physicians who were dealing with many somatic consequences of her accident, with a fixed smile, but betraying a good deal of tension in the manner in which one hand would grasp the other, and frequently would tug at each finger of the other hand separately. Although the smile was deceptively deliberate the tugging on her fingers was not, and clearly "leaked" the tension about which she was not speaking.

Briefly, in the words of Ekman and Friesen, "sending capacity and external and internal feedback are greater for the face than for the hands and feet.... ego will attempt much less inhibition or dissimulation in the areas of the hands and the feet. Thus, the face is likely to be the major nonverbal liar" (1974a, p. 280).

The first two studies reported by these authors were clinical in nature and were regarded by them as preliminary. Their objective was to test their hypothesis that the leakage of withheld information would be much greater from the body (hands and feet/legs) than from the head/face during interviews in which hospitalized female patients were demonstrably deceptive.

The procedure was the same in the analysis of each of three clinical interviews studied. The interviews were selected because a group of clinical judges agreed that interviewee deception occurred in each. The judges were also in agreement about the nature of the deception. A silent film of each interview was shown to two different groups of observers, one viewing only the face and head, and the other, the body from the neck down. The interviewees were not identified to the observers as psychiatric patients, but rather as persons carrying on conversations. After viewing the film, each group of observers was asked to give its impressions of the interviewee by checking items on an adjective checklist. Deceptive behavior would be reflected in the ratings of the head/face and the leakage of hidden behavior in the ratings of the body.

The first patient studied was depressed on admission, with much overt expression of anger, screaming, and many suicide threats. About two and a half weeks after admission, she had begun to control the expression of her anxiety, anger, and depression. One of the films of this patient was taken about midway through her hospitalization, when the consensus of information about her indicated that she was making a strong attempt to conceal the disturbance that she still felt covertly, and to simulate a recovery from her emotional condition on admission. Under these circumstances, the authors anticipated that "observers who view the face/head cues, more than those who view the body cues, will miss concealed information about depression and agitation, and instead will pick up the simulated message about well being" (Ekman & Friesen, 1974a, p. 280). The results provided partial support for this anticipation. Thus, the observers who viewed the head messages only rated the patient as sensitive, friendly, cooperative, and self-punishing, an image of herself that the patient was believed to be simulating. By contrast, the observers who viewed the body messages only, rated the patient as tense, excitable, high strung, fearful, hurried, impatient, and rigid. It would be difficult to visualize these two sets of adjectives as pertaining simultaneously to the same person. The positive feeling conveyed by the face was deceptive, while continuing disturbance was leaked by the rest of the body. However, the clarity of the results was obscured somewhat by a third group of adjectives which occurred in the ratings of both groups of observers: anxious, emotional, confused, defensive, worrying, dissatisfied, and despondent. The evidence for resistance in this patient's nonverbal communication is good. But it would appear that both nonverbal channels participated to some degree in the leakage of the patient's covert feelings.

A second patient was actively hallucinating, and delusional with ideas of reference, when admitted to the same hospital. Nine days after admission, the acute psychotic symptoms disappeared. When asked, the patient would deny any continuing psychotic experiences. A filmed interview with her was recorded during this phase of her hospitalization. Both the interviewer and the attending psychiatrist agreed that the patient was still considerably anxious, confused, and deluded, in spite of her denials. Later, the patient herself attested to the accuracy of the clinicians' judgments.

The rating of the silent tape of the interview by the two groups of observers gave strong support to the predictions of the authors. Thus, those observers who viewed her head/face messages only, saw her in a consistently positive way: cooperative, friendly, cheerful, sensitive, affectionate, appreciative, pleasant, warm, kind, talkative, considerate, good-natured, and honest. The denial implicit in this facade, presented through facial expression by the patient, was offset dramatically by the condition leaked by the patient through other nonverbal clues, reflected in the following adjectives: tense, nervous, defensive, confused, cautious, and worrying. The three ratings made by both groups (active, changeable, alert) of observers did not diminish the contrast between them.

The above clinical studies provide some support for the theory that the face is more readily used to conceal, distort, and otherwise resist the expression of disturbing feelings than hands and feet/legs. The latter organs are less useful for deception and are more likely to permit the disturbed feelings to evade the censure of the interviewee, thus signaling his/her resistance to open communication and, indeed, providing the interviewer with some clues about the concealed message.

To augment the evidence supporting the above findings, Ekman and Friesen (1974b) supplemented their clinical study with one in which interviewee honesty and deception were experimentally manipulated. Their Ss were beginning female nursing students. The experimental manipulation of honesty and deception in communication was carried out by a carefully controlled but rather complex procedure. The interviewer, the same adult female for all Ss and across all sessions, conducted four brief seven-minute interviews with each S consecutively. The interviewer's task was to elicit an expression of feelings experienced by each S as she viewed a brief two-minute film, not visible to the interviewer. The interviewer continued to explore the interviewee's feelings about the film for the five minutes left in each session, after the end of the film. In sessions 1 and 2, the S saw pleasant films and was instructed to describe any feelings frankly. In sessions 3 and 4, the S saw stressful films dealing with amputations and the treatment of severe burns. In session 3, each S was instructed to deceive the interviewer by concealing unpleasant feelings and simulating continued enjoyment of another pleasant film. Finally, in session 4, the S, still viewing an unpleasant film, was told to speak honestly about the feelings she was experiencing. Instructions about deception or honesty were projected onto the screen during the showing of the film and were not visible to the interviewer.

The major finding pertained to the accuracy with which observers could judge a S's behavior as either honest or deceptive, when shown face tapes or body tapes alone. The expected differences in the accuracy of observers in judging deceptive and honest communications was obtained. Thus, the observers were significantly more accurate in judging whether the S was being honest or deceptive when viewing body messages rather than facial messages while the patient was under instructions to deceive. An analogous difference between the accuracy of observers' judgments about face and body was not significant when the S was under instruction to communicate honestly. These results confirmed the authors' hypothesis that when "observers are required to judge whether a person is honest or deceptive, more accurate judgments will be made from the body than from the face when deceptive behavior is considered; when honest behavior is considered, there will be little difference in accuracy between judgments of the face and the body" (Ekman & Friesen, 1974b, p. 289). In conclusion the authors have provided both clinical and experimental proof "that the face more than the body is subject to control and disguise during deception" (p. 297).

Another series of studies dealing with deceit in communication was conducted by Mehrabian (1972), emphasizing experimental procedures that were quite different from those used by Ekman and Friesen (1974a, 1974b). Although the results presented are taken from three investigations, the method will be outlined only for the first. The Ss were male and female undergraduates, paid to participate in the experiment. The design of the study required Ss to communicate both deceitfully and truthfully to different addressees. First, they were asked to give their opinions about the legalization of abortion, an issue extremely controversial at the time, and only those with strong feelings about the subject were selected. One-half of those picked favored abortion and the other half opposed it. The design of the study then called for each S to present one truthful communication about abortion, consistent with his/her views, and one that was deceitful - that is, inconsistent with his/her opinion. This was accomplished by having each S make a presentation to one judge advocating abortion, and one to another judge opposing it. The S was instructed to make both presentations (the truthful and the deceitful) in a way that would convince the judges of the truthfulness of the communication. Observers watched the S's behavior through a one-way mirror, scoring various verbal and nonverbal dimensions descriptive of it.

Mehrabian's choice of dependent variables was broad, not geared to testing specific hypothesis about a limited number of channels of communication (Ekman & Friesen, 1974a) but rather directed toward a comparative description over a wide spectrum of deceitful and honest communication. Because of the range of variables that he studied, Mehrabian gave the practitioner a little more to work with in coping with the applied clinical question of how an interviewer might recognize resistant or.deceitful interviewee communication.

Immediacy is a prominent variable in much of Mehrabian's research. "It has been defined as the degree of directness and intensity of interaction between communicator and his referents" (Wiener & Mehrabian, 1968, p. 4), and was measured in the first of the present group of studies through such nonverbal cues as distance between the speaker and his addressee, forward lean of the speaker, and eye contact. The more positively the speaker feels toward an addressee, the more his/her style of communication will be characterized by immediacy - that is, the closer he/she will position himself/herself to the addressee, the more forward lean he/she will manifest, and the more eye contact there will be. Mehrabian accepted the expectation that "a speaker is expected to exhibit a greater degree of negative affect toward the communication situation while being deceitful than while being truthful" (Mehrabian, 1972, p. 86). He therefore anticipated that honest communication would be associated with higher immediacy (less distance, greater forward lean, more eye contact) to the addressee than deceitful communication. His studies bore out this anticipation. An interviewer, aware of an increase in the distance assumed by the interviewee, the interviewee's shift from a forward to a backward leaning posture, and from eye contact to averted gaze, should read these cues as indicating the possible emergence of unpleasant feelings associated with resistance.

The research dealing with resistance in communication is highly salient to the work of the interviewer. He is alerted to the emergence of resistance if the person he is interviewing begins to speak superficially or with disqualifying passages that mitigate, deny, or excessively justify what he may already have disclosed about himself. Blocking and disruption of speech may also signal his inability or unwillingness to provide certain information. During periods of resistance, the interviewer may also become aware of conflicting signals between different channels of interviewee communication. Thus, deceit may prevail in the verbal content and the facial expression, but warded off feelings and thoughts may leak through hand gestures and movements of the legs and the body. Posture changes and nonverbal signs of decreased proximity of the interviewee to the interviewer may signal that there has been a drop in interviewee immediacy, another index of resistance.

There are other nonverbal messages that are also relevant. But the above will suffice to show how complex the perceptual task of the interviewer will be in sensing the presence of resistance. The task is complicated by the fact that none of the above clues are infallibly related to resistance. Instead, the relationship is a probabilistic one. The interviewer must therefore be sensitized to the indicated clues as possible signs of resistance, but must learn to keep himself ready to consider other possibilities at the same time. In Beier's words, quoted above, "the therapist must learn to use himself as an instrument" (1966, p. 283). Such learning occurs in a fairly long-term apprenticeship sort of training. It cannot result from the promulgation of a set of operational directions based on a point-by-point direct translation of research findings.

APPLICATION SUMMARY

In an intuitive sense, it is possible to distinguish satisfactory from unsatisfactory communication. Without specifying the attributes of the two, one can sense their differences. When communication between two people flows well, they understand each other without undue hesitation or flustering of speech. In experiential terms one may speak of the two communicators resonating with each other. The novice interviewer tends to be more concerned with the "feel" that communication is going well than with more remote worries about whether or not he/she has attained the goals of the interview.

In a more analytical vein, any communication between two people occurs in both verbal and nonverbal channels. But the first concern of the new interviewer is what to talk about, what verbal content to ask about, and how to evaluate it. These problems are particularly anxiety arousing to beginning interviewers because they lack the theory and the clinical experience on which to base decisions about verbal content. Not surprisingly, they may insist that a usually reluctant instructor provide a topical outline as a guide. Later the interviewers may dispense with such an outline, but at the beginning they are reluctant to proceed without it.

When the interviewers have acquired a measure of clinical experience and a sense of theoretically based direction, their initial anxiety will diminish. Instead of leaning on an externally acquired outline, the interviewers will derive some security from an awareness of their own internally programmed guidelines. Moreover, they may eventually be able to delay reacting to what is said until they have some sense of how the interviewee is organizing his/her associations, and which of these appear more crucial than others. The interviewer's interest in the interviewee's flow of associations is based on the assumption that it is expressive of his/her psychological condition. Clusters of concepts or images provide the interviewer with fertile sources of clinical inference regarding the dynamics of the interviewee.

The student of interviewing must be aware of the large element of subjectivity in such clinical inferences. Even if the clustering of interviewee words and images were accurately perceived by the interviewers, the psychological inferences that they make about these clusters are inevitably subjective in nature. But the interviewers' use of associations in the interviewee's verbal content may actually go astray at an earlier point in the process. When computerized methods are used to intercorrelate and factor analyze the relationships between the occurrence of key words or phrases, initial clinical impressions about the associations between them often turn out to be wrong. Since clinicians do not have available to them the instant correcting effect of a computer, they must learn to listen closely with as few preconceptions as possible, so that they might hear accurately and thus mitigate the kind of personal bias in perception to which all persons are subject. The skill that interviewers must develop is that of accurate interpersonal perception in the verbal channel. If they accomplish this interpersonal skill, they acquire a capacity to extract a rich supply of psychological information from the verbal content emitted by interviewees.

Much may be learned about a patient through relating his/her verbal content to other aspects of the communication. For example, style of speech may change as the speaker moves from one topical area to another, signaling changes in the speaker's psychological condition. Some topics may evoke rapid and flustered speech (high anxious); others, slower and less disrupted communication (low anxious). The experienced interviewer has learned to perceive changes in expressive style and to relate them to shifts in verbal content, when possible. Having learned to attend to changes in topic and style of expression, the interviewer has acquired the capacity to hear and use cues regarding topical areas that may require further exploration.

Each interviewer tends to value certain topics over others, on the basis of theoretical preference. While allegiance to a school of psychology - that is, a theoretical orientation - is inevitable, the interviewer must learn to place this in balance with a pragmatic openness to the signals coming from the patient. For with experience and training will come the awareness that a topic that arouses anxiety in one person, or in a particular group, may not have that effect at all on other individuals or groups. This variability may be a consequence of the salience of the topic in one situation, and its lack of salience in another. There is no instant formula for instructing a novice interviewer about such intergroup and interindividual differences. He/she learns to perceive them as he/she conducts interviews, particularly if there is an apprenticeship relationship with an experienced clinician.

Thus, interpersonal perceptions in the interview interaction are in large part individual; but not totally so. There are, in addition, certain values and attitudes about interviewee verbal content that are widely shared by mental health interviewers. The broadly accepted preference for personal self-disclosure over psychologically avoidant speech is one of these. In the initial interview self-disclosing communication is used as a source of psychological information; in the therapy interview it is regarded as a dynamic of personal change. The belief that both interviewer and interviewee openness are conducive to a successful outcome of psychotherapy is supported by the results of a number of research studies. While openness of personal expression is a process that is intuitively recognized, many researchers have translated the process into specified categories of verbal content. Through the various categories run two basic themes: the internal exploration of experience and its communication to the other member of the dyad.

The occurrence of interviewee self-disclosure is associated with certain qualities of his/her relationship with the interviewer. Only when the interviewee feels a high level of trust in the interviewer, with a sense of personal closeness, is he/she able to speak freely and openly about personally intimate topics. One of the conditions that helps to accomplish both of the above attitudes is the interviewer's willingness and ability to speak in a personally open manner to the interviewee. Finally, there are certain situational attributes of the interview that help to promote open and free communication. Two of these are the interviewee's belief in the confidential nature of the interview, and his/her voluntary rather than coerced partipation in the exchange. Some of these conditions can be introduced in a careful and deliberate manner by an interviewer who has acquired the necessary knowledge and skills. Thus, the interviewer may speak in an open manner and may arrange for both confidentiality and voluntary participation as matters of policy. His/her capacity to foster trust and personal closeness are less tangible matters, more dependent on extended training and on the inter-viewer's possession of certain personal attributes.

The evidence is now impressively in favor of the interviewer's willingness to speak openly and freely about himself if he wishes to encourage the interviewee to do likewise (the dyadic effect). But the principle of reciprocal openness between the two members of the dyad cannot be applied unconditionally. The nature of the interview, its primary purpose of eliciting information from the interviewee rather than the interviewer, and the role of the patient as the focus of treatment in a psychotherapy interview, are considerations that govern the degree of interviewer self-disclosure. Clearly, an interviewer should not make himself/herself the central referent of the mental health interview, displacing the interviewee from this position. These comments are not meant to diminish the effectiveness of interviewer self-disclosure in encouraging interviewee openness, but rather to emphasize that it be practiced with clinical judgment and restraint.

Indeed, there is considerable research that delineates the limits within which interviewer self-expression may be practiced. Some of these follow:

Excessive interviewer self-disclosure would be experienced as in-appropriate by the interviewee and would therefore diminish its effectiveness in prompting interviewee openness.

Interviewer self-disclosure is likely to be effective in evoking similar communication from the interviewee only if the interviewee views the interviewer positively as a friend and not as a stranger. Rapport and a positive relationship between interviewer and interviewee are required.

Extreme age differences between the interviewer and the interviewee will weaken the response of the latter to openness by the former. Thus, an interviewee would regard frankness in personal communication by an interviewer who is considerably older or younger than himself/herself as inappropriate.

The above cautions are clinical translations of experimental findings, some not directly related to the interview. They should therefore be used as tentative guides not as explicit directions. But they permit one conclusion about the interview that may be made with some certainty. If an interviewee is not able to speak openly, the cause may be sought not only in his/her inner-determined resistances but also in the situational attributes of the interview.

Since resistance, whatever its source, frustrates the purposes of the interview, its recognition is an important interviewer skill. In verbal communication it takes on three basic forms:

1. The interviewee may be blocked to the point of total silence.

2. The interviewee may keep up a flow of communication but limit what he/she says to nonpsychological banalities. Thus, the interviewee may comply superficially with the requirement that he/she speak, but, in effect, manage to do so by skating on the surface of the psychological content that might have evoked anxious or unpleasant feeling had he/she spoken more freely.

3. A third form of verbal resistance consists of disqualifying remarks and of speech that is symptomatic of blocking. This form of resistance is considered to be less stable than superficial avoidance because it occurs intermittently between self-disclosing remarks. Thus, an interviewee may admit some fault in himself or make a critical comment about another person. He/she may then experience the open remark as a lapse in control, which needs to be nullified by a statement of denial or of excessive justification. In other instances such slips may be followed by speech that is fractured, sometimes to the point of incomprehensibility. This form of resistance is less stable, more expressive, and tends to be associated with more anxiety than the avoidant superficiality discussed above.

The development of the kind of interpersonal perceptiveness that attunes the interviewer to the emergence of resistiveness cannot be directed to the verbal channel alone. Often resistive communication is signaled by conflicting messages from the verbal and nonverbal channels. The former are more explicit, more subject to deliberate control, and, therefore, more readily available for resistive purposes than the latter. Messages and emotions that are avoided or distorted by the interviewee's verbal communications are often leaked nonverbally. Such discordance alerts the trained interviewer to the occurrence of resistance.

Discordance, in the form of conflicting messages need not be limited to a clash between verbal and nonverbal messages. It may also occur between certain nonverbal channels, such as the face, hands, and feet. Of these modalities of communication, the face is the more explicit, and the hands and feet, the less explicit. Again, because of this difference, the face is a better instrument of resistant deception than the hands and feet. It is more readily used to conceal, distort, and resist the expression of disturbing feelings and thoughts.

Clearly, the perceptual task of the interviewer in sensing the presence of resistance is a complex one. Since the clues considered above are not always related to resistance but, rather, show this relationship only some of the time, the interviewer must "hang loose" before responding. He/she must become a sensitive instrument for processing messages that are often conflicting, a kind of development that occurs in an apprenticeship type of learning. The next chapter deals with the methods by which the interviewer may control and direct the content communicated in the interview.

REFERENCES

Ashby, J.D., Ford, D.M., Guerney, B.G., & Guerney, L.S. Effects on clients of reflective and leading types of psychotherapy. Psychological Monographs, General and Applied, 1957, 71 (453, Whole No. 24).

Auld, Frank. Vicissitudes of communication in psychotherapy. In John M. Shlien (Ed.), Research in psychotherapy. Washington, D.C.: American Psychological Association, 1968.

Auld, F. Jr., & White, A. Sequential dependencies in psychotherapy. Journal of Abnormal and Social Psychology, 1959, 58, 100-104.

Bandura, A. Principles of behavior modification. New York: Holt, Rinehard and Winston, 1969.

Beier, E.G. The silent language of psychotherapy. Chicago: Aldine, 1966.

Bundza, K.A., & Simonson, N.R. Therapist self-disclosure: Its effect on impressions of therapist and willingness to disclose. Psychotherapy: Theory, Research and Practice, 1973, 10, 215-217.

Chaikin, A.L., & Derlega, V.J. Variables affecting the appropriateness of self-disclosure. Journal of Consulting and Clinical Psychology, 1974, 42, 588-593.

Davis, J.D., & Skinner, A.E.G. Reciprocity of self-disclosure in interviews: Modeling or social exchange? In Gerald R. Patterson (Ed.), Behavior change 1974. Chicago: Aldine, 1975. Pp. 215-220.

Derlega, V.J., & Chaikin, A.L. Norms affecting self-disclosure in men and women. Journal of Consulting and Clinical Psychology, 1976, 44, 376-380.

Dollard, J., & Auld, F. Jr. Scoring human motives: A manual. New Haven: Yale University Press, 1959.

Edelman, R.I., & Snead, R. Self-disclosure in a simulated psychiatric interview. Journal of Consulting and Clinical Psychology, 1972, 38, 354-358.

Ekman, P., & Friesen, W.V. Hand movements. The Journal of Communication, 1972, 22, 353-374.

Ekman, P., & Friesen, W.V. Nonverbal leakage and clues to deception. In Shirley Weitz (Ed.), Nonverbal communication. New York: Oxford University Press, 1974a, 269-290.

Ekman, P., & Friesen, W.V. Detecting deception from the body or face. Journal of Personality and Social Psychology, 1974b, 288-298.

Freud, S. Psycho-analytic notes upon an autobiographical account of a case of paranoia (demented paranoides) (1911, Vol. 13). In J. Strachey (Ed.), The standard edition of the complete psychological work of Sigmund Freud. London: Hogarth Press, 1953.

Freud, S. On the history of the psychoanalytic movement (1914). S.E. XIV. Longon: Hogarth, 1957.

Freud, S. Fragment of an analysis of a case of hysteria (1905). In Collected Papers, Vol. 3. New York: Basic Books, 1959.

Friedman, R. Experimenter-subject distance and self-disclosure. Unpublished master's thesis, University of Florida, 1969.

Goldenberg, G.M., & Auld, F.J. Equivalence of silence to resistance. Journal of Consulting Psychology, 1964, 28, 476.

Harway, N.I., & Iker, H.P. Content analysis in psychotherapy. Psychotherapy: Theory, Research and Practice, 1969, 6, 97-104.

Haymes, M. Self-disclosure and the acquaintance process. Unpublished article, 1970.

Heller, K., Davis, J.D., & Myers, R.A. The effects of interviewer style in a standardized interview. Journal of Consulting Psychology, 1966, 30, 501-508.

Howard, K.I., & Orlinsky, D.E. Psychotherapeutic process. Unpublished paper, 1971.

Jourard, S.M. The effects of experimenter self-disclosure on subjects' behavior. In C.D. Spielberger (Ed.), Current topics in clinical and community psychology. New York: Academic Press, 1969.

Jourard, S.M. The transparent self. New York: Van Nostrand, 1971a.

Jourard, S.M. Self-disclosure, an experimental analysis of the transparent self. New York: Wiley-Interscience, 1971b.

Jourard, S.M., & Friedman, R. Experimenter-subject "distance" and self-disclosure. Journal of Personality and Social Psychology, 1970, 15, 278-282.

Jourard, S.M., & Lasakow, P. A research approach to self disclosure. Journal of Abnormal and Social Psychology, 1958, 56, 91-98.

Kanfer, F.H. Verbal rate, content, and adjustment ratings in experimentally structured interviews. Journal of Abnormal and Social Psychology, 1959, 58, 305-311.

Kanfer, F.H.   Verbal rate, eyeblink and content in structured psychiatric
    interviews.   Journal of Abnormal and Social Psychology, 1960, 61, 341-
    347.

Kasl, S.V., & Mahl, G.F.   The relationship of disturbances and hesitations in
    spontaneous speech to anxiety.   Journal of Personality and Social
    Psychology, 1965, 1, 425-433.

Klein, L.S.   Relation of physiological arousal to psychological resistance in
    psychotherapy.   Unpublished doctoral dissertation, Wayne State University,
    1965.

Laffal, J.   The contextual associates of sun and God in Schreber's
    autobiography.   Journal of Abnormal and Social Psychology, 1960, 61, 474-
    479.

Laffal, J.   Pathological and normal language.   New York: Atherton Press,
    1965.

Laffal, J.   An approach to the total content analysis of speech in
    psychotherapy.   In John M. Shlien (Ed.), Research in psychotherapy.
    Washington, D.C.:   American Psychological Association, 1968.

Levin, F.M., & Gergen, K.J.   Revealingness, ingratiation and the disclosure of
    self.   Proceedings of the 77th annual convention of the American
    Psychological Association, 1969, 4 (Pt. 1), 447-448.

Mahl, G.F., Danet, B., & Norton, N.   Reflection of major personality
    characteristics in gestures and body movement.   Paper presented at
    annual meeting, American Psychological Association, Cincinnati, Ohio,
    September 1959.

Manaugh, T.S., Wiens, A.N., & Matarazzo, J.D.   Content saliency and
    interviewee speech behavior.   Journal of Clinical Psychology, 1970, XXVI,
    17-24.

Matarazzo, J.D., Wiens, A.M., Jackson, R.H., & Manaugh, T.S.   Interviewee
    speech behavior under different content conditions.   Journal of Applied
    Psychology, 1970, 54, 15-26.

Mehrabian, A.   Nonverbal communication.   Chicago: Aldine-Atherton, 1972.

Orlinsky, D.E., & Howard, K.I.   The good therapy hour.   Archives of General
    Psychiatry, 1967, 16, 621-632.

Orne, M.T., & Wender, P.H.   Anticipatory socialization for psychotherapy:
    Method and rationale.   The American Journal of Psychiatry, 1968, 124,
    1202-1212.

Polansky, N.A.   Ego psychology and communication.   New York: Atherton
    Press, 1971.

Pope, B., Blass, T., Siegman, A.W., & Raher, J.   Anxiety and depression in
    speech.   Journal of Consulting and Clinical Psychology, 1970, 35, 128-133.

Pope, B., & Nudler, S.   Mental status, sociometric status and interviewee
    verbal behavior.   Unpublished manuscript, 1970.

Pope, B., & Siegman, A.W. Interviewer specificity and topical focus in relation to interviewee productivity. Journal of Verbal Learning and Verbal Behavior, 1965, 4, 188-192.

Pope, B.,& Siegman, A.W. Interviewer warmth in relation to interviewee verbal behavior. Journal of Consulting and Clinical Psychology, 1968, 32, 588-595.

Pope, B., Siegman, A.W., & Blass, T. Anxiety and speech in the initial interview. Journal of Consulting and Clinical Psychology, 1970, 35, 233-238.

Pope, B., Siegman, A.W., Blass, T., & Cheek, J. Some effects of discrepant role expectations on interviewee verbal behavior in the initial interview. Journal of Consulting and Clinical Psychology, 1972, 39, 501-507.

Psathas, G., & Arp. D.J. A thematic analysis of interviewers' statements in therapy - analogue interviews. In P.J. Stone, D.C. Dunphy, K.Y. Smith, & D.K. Ogilvie. The general inquirer: A computer approach to content analysis. Cambridge, Mass.: The M.I.T. Press, 1966.

Rogers, C.R. The necessary and sufficient conditions of therapeutic personality change. Journal of Consulting Psychology, 1957, 21, 95-103.

Seeman, J. The case of Jim. Nashville: American Guidance Service, 1957.

Siegman, A.W., & Pope, B. Effects of question specificity and anxiety producing messages on verbal fluency in the initial interview. Journal of Personality and Social Psychology, 1965, 2, 522-530.

Siegman, A.W., & Pope, B. The effect of interviewer ambiguity-specificity and topical focus on interviewee vocabulary diversity. Language and Speech, 1966, 9, 242-249.

Siegman, A.W., & Pope, B. The effects of ambiguity and anxiety on interviewee verbal behavior. In A.W. Siegman & B. Pope (Eds.), Studies in dyadic communication. New York: Pergamon Press, 1972.

Siegman, J.C. Depth of interpretation and verbal resistance in psychotherapy. Journal of Consulting Psychology, 1959, 25, 93-99.

Starkweather, J.A. Overview: Computer aided approaches to content recognition. In G. Gerbner, O.R. Holst, K. Krippendorf, W.J. Paisley, & P.J. Stone Eds.), The analysis of communication content. New York: Wiley, 1969.

Starkweather, J.A., & Decker, J.B. Computer analysis of interview content. Psychological Reports, 1964, 15, 875-882.

Stone, P.J. Dunphy, D.C., Smith, M.S., & Ogilvie, D.M. The general inquirer: A computer approach to content analysis. Cambridge, Mass.: The M.I.T. Press, 1966.

Talland, G.A., & Clark, D.H. Evaluation of topics in therapy group discussion. Journal of Clinical Psychology, 1954, 10, 131-137.

Truax, C.B., & Carkhuff, R.R.   Client and therapist transparency in the psychotherapeutic encounter. Journal of Counseling Psychology, 1965, 12, 3-9.

Truax, C.B. & Cardkhuff, R.R.   Toward effective counseling and psychotherapy. Chicago: Aldine, 1967.

Watkins, J.G. Psychotherapeutic methods.   In Benjamin B. Wolman (Ed.), Handbook of clinical psychology. New York: McGraw-Hill, 1965.

Watzlawick, P., Beavin, J.H., & Jackson, D.D.   Pragmatics of human communication. New York: Norton, 1967.

Wiener, M., & Mehrabian, A.   Language within language: Immediacy, a channel in verbal communication. New York: Appleton-Century-Crofts, 1968.

3 Control and Direction of Verbal Content in the Interview

The previous chapter has dealt with the correlates of verbal content in the interview and its evaluation by the interviewer. The present chapter will discuss the control and direction of interviewee verbal response. What are the methods available to the interviewer for eliciting some categories of verbalization and discouraging others?

The information-gathering diagnostic interview in psychiatry excerpted in Chapter 1 is an example of the interview as a sort of oral questionnaire. The interviewer proceeds down a list of specific questions that can be answered for the most part in brief, objective, and factual terms. The course of such an interview is highly predictable. Certainly it leaves no doubt about the method for the interviewer to follow in obtaining the prescribed information. It is a controlled, structured interview devoid of any ambiguity.

Yet it is not the kind of interview widely practiced in mental health. Most clinicians prefer the uncertainties of the relatively unstructured, ambiguous interview to the high predictability of the interview fashioned out of preformulated specific questions. The reason for this choice does not lie in an ingrained perversity found in clinicians who would appear to choose a difficult course, full of uncertainty, rather than a sure and simple one. It pertains rather to the kind of information desired, and the type of interaction that the interviewer wishes to foster. To be sure, some of the information that the interviewer needs is factual and specific. Thus, he/she will need to know the age of the interviewee, the time of onset of the problem, its duration, the patient's marital status, the location and conditions under which he grew up, and many other bits of historical and contextual information. For this type of information, questions that tend to be highly specific are appropriate. But most of the information needed by the clinician is of a more subjective character, consisting largely of self-disclosing messages. These include such verbal content categories as descriptions of one's problems, self-evaluative remarks, thoughts and memories about self and others, feelings, moods, and many others that are generated by personal introspection. Moreover, the interviewer "reads" the interviewee's style of communication, and receives an entire spectrum of nonverbal messages. Self-disclosing and expressive communication are fostered by interview conditions of sufficient ambiguity to permit a communicational interaction to develop.

Whatever the orientation of the interviewer, he must find a balance between enough ambiguity to permit the interviewee to speak freely and expressively and enough structure to conduct the communication into channels that are considered important by the interviewer. To accomplish this balance, he may choose to be more or less active, more or less ambiguous, and to proceed in a more or less interrogatory manner. These are stylistic matters and will be considered in the next chapter. In the remainder of this chapter, three rather specialized procedures for controlling verbal communication will be reviewed: the provision of a set of orienting instructions to the interviewee at the beginning of the interview; the modeling of the type of interview interaction and the categories of content desired by the interviewer, also usually at the beginning of the interview; and the conditioning of selected interviewee responses through reinforcement methods. The latter procedure differs from the former two in its occurrence within the interview interaction rather than at the beginning.

All three methods will be illustrated with partially fictionalized material developed from a recent interview study. The interviewer, in the example given below, was a male psychiatrist, about 50 years of age, who was asked to interview a female freshman student who had volunteered for the project. The interviewer was instructed to obtain enough information from the student about her educational history and adjustment and her primary family relationships to permit him to dictate a five-minute note. The interview was to last no less than 15 minutes and no more than 45.

The instructions to the interviewer were clear, but moderately ambiguous in the latitude that they left him for conducting the interview. Although preferring a moderate level of ambiguity in the body of the interview, the psychiatrist was quite explicit in his initial instructions to the interviewee:

> You have volunteered to participate in an interview study. To begin with, let me tell you a little about the topics that we shall be covering. I shall ask you to tell me what you can about the various schools that you attended, from your elementary grades right up until the present. I would hope that you would be able to speak in a personal vein. Tell me about your experiences as a student, how well you did in your studies, how you got along with the other students and with your teachers, and any problems that you encountered. We shall also talk about your immediate family and how you have gotten along with members of your family in the past; how you get along with them in the present. I would like you to talk about these two areas in your own way, starting with whatever topic you pick and just telling me whatever you remember and think about as it comes to you. For the most part I shall just listen, but I may have something to say from time to time as we go along, if there is a need. O.K.? Begin now wherever you would like ...

This type of induction of the interviewee into his/her role is not unusual, even among low-active interviewers. Indeed, for many it is the most active part of the interview. Lennard and Bernstein (1960) refer to such initial instructions as primary system references, including such topics as: "Who shall speak, how much, about what, and when?" (p. 154).

The induction of the interviewee in the early stages of the interview need not always take on the form of verbal instructions. Many authors report the use of some form of modeling to achieve the same end as the instructions (Marlatt, 1972). If the psychiatrist referred to above were inclined toward the use of a modeling procedure, he could have given the student a brief verbal introduction to the interview and then moved rather quickly toward playing a tape of one or more excerpts from an analogous interview that he had conducted with another student. In that event, he might have started in the following way:

In the interview we shall do presently, we shall talk about two topics, your educational history and adjustment, and your immediate family relationships, past and present. To give you more of an idea of the topics we shall discuss, and how I should like you to talk about them, I am going to play some taped excerpts from an interview I conducted with another student. This student has given me permission to use these taped segments in the present study. After listening to the tape we shall go ahead with the interview.

The following is one of the taped interview excerpts used by the psychiatrist, taken from the part of the interview that dealt with educational history and adjustment:

ER: You're a student at _____, and what year are you in?

EE: Freshman

ER: A freshman. So you've really just started.

EE: I'm just beginning.

ER: Where did you ah go to school before this?

EE: I went to - ah - two high schools. To _____ a Catholic high school, and then I went to _____, a public high school.

ER: How did you happen to go to two high schools? What was it? Did you move, or what?

EE: No, i- it was financial.

ER: I see, _____ was the ah private school

EE: Ah-huh.

ER: So you began at _____.

EE: for two years and I finished up two years at public school.

ER: Was there much difference between the two schools?

EE: Oh yeh. There's a lot. Ah well, for one thing public schools don't have nuns, right?

ER: Right.

EE: I was, I thought you learned more at the Catholic School. I thought it was harder I f- figured that if I went there I would be more prepared for college. But you know, the - going to the public school I s- I sort of slackened down. So now I'm not used to the work. I'm having a hard time.

ER: Tell me more about how things went for you at the two high schools?

EE: Well, I said that I had to leave the Catholic school because of finances. But I was getting to the point of wanting to leave it anyway. My grades were not good. I couldn't seem to st- concentrate on my studies. There was always too much to do; too many parties to go to. I was beginning to - to date quite a bit and I started getting my parents upset with my "attitude," as they always referred to it. So my, my attitude was rotten and I started getting into trouble with the nuns too. They remember- ed me as a good student, with a serious att- attitude when I started and suddenly I became wild, and I- lost lost interest in what I was supposed to be doing. So I was looking for some way out of the situation. My parents' financial problems came just in time.

ER: Yes

EE: I went to the public school for two years. (Pause)

ER: (Silence)

EE: But things g- got no better there.

ER: Mm hmm! (Nods)

EE: No. They didn't. There was ahm - there was less discipline and nothing to stop my spending a lot of ti- I would often hook school. My girl friend and I would go (Long silence)

ER: Yes. Go on.

EE: Well, we would go to the movies a lot. Once she and I (Pause)

ER: Mm. Hmm. (Nodding)

EE: We both had a boy friend. My my boyfriend had a car and we just took off one Friday afternoon to Ocean City. That was the worse - the worst thing we did in high school. I called my parents from Ocean City and told them where I was and what I had d- d- done. My mo- mother cried and my father yelled at me. And I just conti- kept acting in this wild way. I'm lucky I made it out of high sch- sch- school and into college. I just could- couldn't change my behavior. I did these crazy things but I wasn't hap- happy.

ER: Ah! You weren't happy, but -?

EE: But I couldn't stop. I was torn up. And I'm sorry about it now.

ER: Sorry? Go on.

EE: Well I don't know. I (Long pause).

ER: (Silence)

EE: I'm sorry because -

ER: Yes.

EE: because I feel like I've gone down and down since the ninth grade.

ER: Hm! Hm! Things have gone down hill.

EE: Yea! I haven't prepared myself well for coll- college, and I'm having trouble now

ER: I see.

EE: Yes. I wish I had more confidence in myself as a student. But I still can- can't concentrate. I can't sit- sit dow- down to study. And I'm getting worried about my gr- grade- grades.

There were other excerpts of this interview. But the above will illustrate the use of a selected segment of a taped interview to model content and style of interviewee communication. The assumption is that the interviewee would be prompted by this model to respond in the interview as the model did on the tape.

A third option available to the interviewer is to guide the interviewee's communication through the use of verbal conditioning in the actual interview interaction. The psychiatrist might have limited himself to a brief introductory remark, very much like that contained in the first sentence of his comments before playing the tape. Then he might have added: "Let's begin with your school experiences." The rest of his guidance would be contained within his reactions to the interviewee's remarks. In fact, verbal reinforcement as a means of directing the interviewee's communication is quite well illustrated in the previous taped interview segment. After the initial questions that the interviewer asked to structure the interview, his inputs were either brief reinforcing responses such as "yes," "Mm Hmm," "Yes. Go on." "Oh! You weren't happy," "I see," or nonreinforcing silent nonresponses. The former were used to encourage introspective narratives of high school experiences, accounts of rebellious behavior, and disturbed feelings - in a word, psychologically revealing communications. On the other hand, resistance, as noted in silence and such expression of denial as "I don't know," were greeted with nonresponsive silence from the interviewer.

The above semi-fictional excerpts exemplify three methods that may be used for directing the course of an interview. These include initial instructions to the interviewee, modeling of the interview, and verbal reinforcement. In the section that follows, the literature that defines, evaluates, and compares the three methods with each other will be reviewed.

INSTRUCTIONS TO THE INTERVIEWEE

All three methods share two basic attributes. They provide the interviewee with information about what is expected of him/her in the interview. They also strive to instigate or motivate him/her to communicate in a self-disclosing manner. Yet they are quite different in the operations pursued. Of the three methods, that of verbal instructions to the interviewee at the beginning of the interview incorporates the informational and instigational elements most explicitly. Thus, the psychiatrist's initial instructions to his student interviewee quoted above included information in rather specific terms of the desired verbal content and the obligations of the two participants in the impending interaction. The instigational aspect is noted in clauses such as the following, that are pervasive throughout the instructions: "I shall ask you to tell me"; "I would hope that you would be able to speak in a personal vein"; "I would like you to talk about"; and other expressions that impose specified obligations on the interviewee. In brief, the "instigational function of instructions is designed to initiate or facilitate intention to perform in a general sense (the 'this is what we want you to do' aspect). ....The directive function directs the subject's attention to stimulus conditions in the task and to specified performance responses required to engage in task behavior" (Marlatt, 1972, p. 340). Although Marlatt uses experimental rather than clinical terms, he is clearly referring to both the instigational (or motivational) and informational aspects of the kind of initial induction into interviewee role behavior that most interviewers employ to a greater or lesser extent.

While the research literature has something to say about the relative efficacy of instructions versus modeling and verbal conditioning as a means of directing the interview, there are very few studies that deal with the effectiveness of instructions considered alone. Some of these are reviewed later in Chapter 10 under the caption "Breaching the Communication Barrier Between Social Classes," and require only brief summary here.

Lennard and Bernstein (1960) spoke about initial instructions by the interviewer when they discussed primary system references. These are remarks made by the interviewer and questions asked by the interviewee about "reciprocal therapist patient role relations" (p. 92). These references to the primary system in the interview are considered later as means of reducing strain through clarifying role expectations, and, in fact, inducing the same expectations regarding interview roles in the interviewee as the ones already possessed by the interviewer. But remarks referring to the primary system, occurring characteristically early in the interview, or in a psychotherapy sequence of interviews, may also be regarded as instructional in nature, providing the interviewee with both information and motivation. Such instructions were found to be particularly useful with low socioeconomic patients, whose initial information about the interview process tended to be rather vague. The authors found that the interview dyads that showed least strain and produced most open communication were the ones in which there were most early primary system references - that is, the ones with most adequate instructions to the interviewees.

Some investigators have worked with a more formal kind of initial instruction, particularly with low socioeconomic patients (Hoehn-Saric, Frank, Imber, Nash, Stone, & Battle, 1964; Orne & Wender, 1968), referred to as a role induction interview. This interview is characteristically conducted by a research clinician (not the therapist) before the beginning of a psychotherapy sequence and has, as its objective, informing the interviewee about the topics that will be discussed in the subsequent therapy interviews, the style of communication expected of him/her, and what interviewer behavior the interviewee might expect to encounter. One of the findings was that patients given the preparation or instructional interview, in contrast to the ones who were not, exhibited more acceptable in-therapy communication as judged by the therapists.

MODELING

In the semi-fictional example of modeling given above, a taped segment of an interview was presented to the interviewee as a model of what she was expected to say and how she was to say it. The presentation of the model in tape, typescript, or even live, at the beginning of an interview is perhaps its most characteristic form in the research literature.   But this is not necessarily the only way in which modeling may be carried out.   In the literature on self-disclosure (Jourard, 1969, 1971) the interviewer may be open about himself/herself, in the course of interacting with the interviewee. In fact, the latter is possibly the most usual form in which modeling is likely to occur in naturalistic interviews. Thus, the openness of the interviewer in the Sullivanian interview in Chapter 1 may be taken as an instance of the form in which modeling is most likely to be encountered in the clinical interview.

But, whatever the type, there is a wide consensus that modeling, just as verbal instruction, functions through the provision of information to the interviewee regarding what is expected of him/her, and through instigating or motivating the interviewee to behave as expected. This process could not be one of simple imitation by the interviewee of specific bits of behavior, according to Marlatt (1972), because the interviewee does not usually repeat the model's behavior, point by point. Instead he/she seems to learn certain rules or principles which then govern his/her interview responses.   The student in the example of modeling given above may well have learned the following guiding principles:

"Speak about your school experiences in an open, personal way."

"Try not to hold back if something you remember is painful or embarrassing."

"Talk about problems as well as good experiences."

"The initiative in and responsibility for deciding the specific things you will talk about is yours."

In Marlatt's words "the subject must derive a general rule, based on his observation of the model's performance, which would define the criteria of the response class(es) accounting for the instance demonstrated by the model" (1972, p. 340). Having acquired directional information at the level of general rules or principles, the interviewee then proceeds to generate his/her own personal communications in accordance with the principles or rules learned. "Subjects exposed to a verbal model do not just mimic identical response items in a one-to-one correspondence with the model's performance. Rather, they appear to also produce unique response items that fall within the general response class which the subject assumes to govern the model's performance" (Marlatt, 1972, p. 341).

The interviewee's response to modeled information is most probable if the interview that he participates in is unstructured.   In that event the interviewee is particularly responsive to cues that reduce his/her uncertainty, particularly when the model is encouraged or reinforced for certain classes of response and not for others. Thus, the student exposed to the model earlier in the present chapter, must have noticed that the interviewer remained silent when the interviewee said "I don't know," but responded ("Yes"; "I see"; "Go on") when the interviewee spoke openly about problems she encountered in school. "Observation of a model who is 'encouraged' to discuss this same material may enable the observer to engage in a discussion of his own problems. In this sense, the behavior of the model may have a disinhibiting or response facilitation effect on previously learned responses by the observer" (Marlatt, Jacobson, Johnson, & Morrice, 1970, p. 105). The disinhibiting or response facilitating effect is, in fact, the instigating or motivating effect, earlier ascribed to verbal instruction, modeling, and to verbal reinforcement.

What follows is not a comprehensive review of modeling studies but, rather, a summary of a small number, selected because of their direct relevance to the clinical interview. In an interview analogue study conducted by Duke, Frankel, Sipes, and Steward, reported by Heller (1968), the objective was to demonstrate the efficacy of modeling for increasing the time a $\underline{S}$ spent talking about a topic that he/she had avoided before exposure to the model. The $\underline{Ss}$ were introductory psychology students who had volunteered to participate in two interviews one week apart.   The modeling experience for those assigned to experimental groups occurred between the first and second interviews.   All $\underline{Ss}$ were distributed randomly among two experimental groups and one control group.   The members of one experimental group were exposed to a taped model of an "interview"; those of the second read a typed manuscript of the same "interview"; and the $\underline{Ss}$ in the control group participated in two interviews, like the others, but with no intervening model to audit or read.   The modeled interview was recorded in three variants - one emphasizing the topic of family; the second, social aspects of a person's life; and the third, academic experiences.   For each experimental $\underline{S}$, a version of the modeled interview was selected which emphasized a topic which he/she had discussed least in the first of the two interviews.   The effectiveness of modeling was sought in its capacity to increase the time a $\underline{S}$ spent talking about a previously avoided topic.

Subjects in both experimental groups talked longer about their previously least preferred topics than did subjects in the control group, but the two types of modeling experience were equally effective in increasing topic talk time. Thus, even a relatively simple procedure such as reading a typescript is capable of providing direction and focus to an otherwise ambiguous interview.   (Heller, 1968, p. 254)

A somewhat more searching investigation of the use of modeling in overcoming interviewee avoidance or resistance was conducted by Sarason, Ganzer, and Singer (1972). In their study, resistance was evaluated both as a pattern of avoidance of personal communication in the interview and as a personality trait. The Ss were male undergraduate students enrolled in introductory psychology courses, selected so as to represent the high and low extremes on a defensiveness scale. They were assigned to three different experimental groups exposed to gradations of modeled self-disclosure and to one control group. One experimental group audited a tape at the low extreme of self-disclosing communication, called the "Defensive tape," on which the speaker described himself in neutral or positive terms only; a second audited the "Ambivalent tape," on which the model spoke with uncertainty, anxiety, and conflict about personal and emotional matters; and a third heard the "Expressive tape," on which the speaker was direct and open about positive and negative feelings and other personal matters. Ss in the control group were not exposed to any taped model. After the Ss in the three experimental groups had listened to the taped models, all were asked to spend 10 minutes describing themselves and speaking about what they thought and felt about themselves.

The Ss in the three experimental groups produced more statements - that is, were more productive than those in the control group - but only at a borderline level of significance. Thus, modeling did appear to facilitate the Ss' gross verbal output. In regard to positive self-references during the 10-minute interviews, only two of the modeling groups (Defensive and Ambivalent) were significantly higher than the control group. For negative self-references, the highest frequency was obtained by the Expressive modeling group, significantly different from both the Defensive modeling group and the control group.   Thus, "exposure to a model who willingly expressed his feelings, worries, and unfavorable facts about himself facilitated the subsequent expressions of Ss of negative self evaluation" (Sarason et al., 1972, p. 487).

In addition, anxiety statements were emitted by the four groups in the following increasing order: control, Defensive model, Ambivalent model, and Expressive model.   "Again, exposure to the expressive model seemed to facilitate the subsequent expression of anxiety related statements" (Sarason, et al., 1972, p. 487). Both of the preceding findings are congruent with each other since it may be assumed that negative self-references and expressions of anxiety would occur together.

In general, the S high on defensiveness as a personality trait tended to be low in the disclosure of unfavorable facts and attributes.   However, the pervasive defensiveness of this person could be breached by exposing him to an expressive model. There was a significant increase in the defensive S's negative self-evaluations after he listened to a model who willingly discussed personal problems.

In a study by Doster and Brooks (1974) the focus was on the interviewer as a behavioral model for interviewee self-disclosure. It had been anticipated that the interviewer would be a more effective model if he spoke positively rather than negatively about himself, because it was thought that negative self-reports would lower his/her status. Thus, there were two experimental groups, one exposed to a positively self-disclosing and the other to a negatively self-disclosing model. A third group (control) was not exposed to any model.

Again, the Ss were undergraduate male volunteers from an introductory psychology class, and were randomly assigned to the three groups designated above. All Ss received the brief instructions "to focus on himself and those aspects of his experience that would help the interviewer to understand him" (Doster & Brooks, 1974, p. 421). Then, all were asked to speak about their relationships with their fathers. With the members of the control group, the interviewer proceeded, as he had begun, with a relatively ambiguous, unstructured interview. He covered the additional topics of the Ss' relationships with their mothers, male friends, and female friends. After completion of the first topic (father), the members of one experimental group listened to a tape of the interviewer speaking openly, in positive socially desirable terms only, about his own relationships with the remaining three topic persons. The members of the second experimental group heard a tape of their interviewer speaking freely about his relationships with the same topic persons, but this time in negative or socially undesirable as well as positive terms.

As in the study by Sarason et al. (1972), both experimental groups were more verbally productive, without reference to content, than the control group. The interviewees generally talked more to interviewers who were willing to be open with them. Moreover, there was no diminishing of interviewer efficacy as a model for self-disclosing communication if he spoke in negative terms about himself and his relationships with the topic persons. "Clearly, the presence or absence of a model rather than the positive or negative disclosures of the interviewer had the strongest effect on self disclosure" (Doster & Brooks, 1974, p. 423). The modeling effect was particularly noticeable in the experimental interviewee's willingness to make negative admissions about himself and his relationships with significant others, in contrast to the control interviewee. The freedom to speak openly about problems in relationship was evident in the Ss exposed to both the positively and negatively self-disclosing interviewer model.

The next study dealt with the relative effectiveness of modeling under three different feedback conditions (Marlatt et al., 1970). Groups of interviewees were exposed to live modeling with positive, negative, and neutral feedback to the speaker after he had been openly communicative about personal problems. The Ss were the ubiquitous introductory psychology students, again male in this instance. They volunteered to participate in two interviews. Before the first interview, all Ss received the following brief instructions from the interviewer. "I am interested in getting an idea of how students think and feel about themselves. I'd like to know what you are like as a person. I believe the best way to accomplish this is simply to ask you to talk about and describe yourself" (Marlatt et al., 1970). A confederate of the E waited with each S for both interviews to begin, posing as another S. Prior to the second interview, the confederate talked at length about his problems to the E who paused in the doorway, on his way to the interview room. The response the confederate received from the E was sometimes positive and encouraging, sometimes negative and discouraging, and sometimes neutral, depending on whether the S was assigned to the positive, negative, or neutral feedback group. Control Ss waited in the company of the confederate but heard no conversation between him and the E.

Ss who were exposed to modeling with positive and neutral feedback demonstrated a greater increase in rate of problem admission between their first and second interviews than the Ss exposed to modeling with negative feedback and those with no feedback at all. It would appear that while modeling is effective in increasing open expression by the interviewee, there are some conditions which may reduce or negate its effectiveness. One of those is the condition in which the model receives negative feedback from the person to whom he/she is speaking.

A number of investigations dealing with the use of modeling as a means of facilitating low social class response to the clinical interview (Goldstein, 1973) is reviewed in Chapter 10, in the section entitled, "Breaking the Communication Barrier Between Social Classes." These need no detailed repetition here. Of the various findings of these studies, only one is relevant at this point. S exposure to a taped model of a highly self-disclosing interviewee prompted high S self-disclosure in interviews that followed.

VERBAL CONDITIONING

Most mental health interviewers, given to conducting unstructured or ambiguous interviews, resort to the direction of its verbal content through informal reinforcement procedures. Their initial instructions to the interviewee tend to be brief. Modeling is never very prominent, either in its formal sense, at the beginning of the interview, or in the interviewer's own self-expressive style during the interview. But he/she generally does provide the interviewee with a variety of cues reinforcing certain categories of verbal communication and certain forms or styles of expression during the interview interaction.

In the semi-fictional example earlier in the chapter, the interviewer encouraged certain categories of psychologically revealing communication with such reinforcing responses as "yes," "mm-hmm," "Go on," and "I see." He discouraged resistance, in the form of silence or such expressions of denial as "I don't know" with his own nonresponsive, nonreinforcing silence. In doing this he was controlling the interviewee's verbal behavior either through providing her with social reward or withholding it from her. In a word, he was informally applying operant conditioning procedures.

That the elements of the operant conditioning paradigm were indeed present may be noted in the following concise description of a series of early studies of the experimental conditioning of verbal behavior: "The studies follow this Skinnerian paradigm in that the dependent variables are the S's verbal behavior and the independent variables are generalized conditioned reinforcers intended to bring verbal behavior under the control of the examiner" (Krasner, 1958, p. 148). In an operational sense, "the S is asked to emit verbal behavior in terms of a given task, and the examiner attempts to reinforce a preselected class of his 'verbal behavior' by carefully controlled verbal or nonverbal behavioral cues" (Krasner, 1958, p. 148). These cues, when verbal, may range from brief responses such as "mm-hmm" to psychoanalytically derived interpretations (Krasner, 1966). Applying the operational language used above to the semi-fictional interview given earlier in the present chapter, one may speak of the interviewee's self-disclosing responses as the dependent variables, and the interviewer's brief reinforcing comments as the independent variables. In the form of conditioned reinforcers, these variables were used to bring the interviewee's verbal behavior under the interviewer's control and direction. The interviewee was asked to emit specified categories of verbal behavior - that is, communications about her school history and adjustment. Although not instructing her to speak in a self-disclosing way, he did, in fact, set out to reinforce this preselected class of verbal response with the various cues listed above.

That verbal conditioning does not occur in a therapy interview is implicit in an observation by Gill and Brenman (1948) that what the patient says and how he/she says it are subtly and often unconsciously controlled by the interviewer. Thus, the views that the interviewer holds influence the verbal content given by the interviewee. This influence occurs through reinforcers, such as verbal cues that the interviewer is attending (mm-hmm), head nods, approving glances, or the establishing of eye contact.

Without denying the efficacy of reinforcement as a means of directing the verbal content communicated by the interviewee, it may be asked what the advantage might be in resorting to the kind of indirect, sometimes manipulative conrol represented by the operant conditioning paradigm. Why not frankly instruct the interviewee in the content and style of communication desired, as the psychiatrist in the semi-fictional interview did? In reply, it should first be noted that reinforcement is not proposed as an exclusive form of controlling the interviewee's communications (instructions and modeling are clearly others). Even when explicit instructions are given, there is a naturalistic tendency to respond to the interviewee's communications with more or less reinforcement of specified topics or categories of verbal behavior. Most interviewers enter an interview with a set of preferences regarding the content they wish to hear. While it is true that some interviewers may impose their preferences more blatantly than others, even those who reject any intention of intruding their values into the interview in fact tend to do so, however subtly, through reinforcing cues. It therefore seems idle to speak about reinforcement as though one could choose whether or not to use it. In fact, it is an integral component of a communicational interaction between two people.

But it is not utilized equally by all practitioners of the interview and under all circumstances. The point has been made that verbal conditioning is most likely to occur in an interview when it is particularly ambiguous (Heller & Marlatt, 1969). Ambiguity may occur because there has been little initial instruction. In that event the interviewee will lack information about how he/she should proceed, and will be sensitively attuned to each reinforcing cue given by the interviewer. Or the interviewee may be asked to respond to an ambiguous instruction, like, "Tell me what you can about your father." Again, the interviewee, left with a great deal of uncertainty regarding how to begin, will be guided by the information provided by the interviewer's cues, however limited they may be. In fact, under conditions of great ambiguity, the more infrequent and selective the interviewer's responses, the more information they impart. Thus, the silent, inactive interviewer is not devoid of means of influencing the course of the interview. The more inactive the interviewer, the more likely it is that there will be a verbal conditioning effect. The more active he/she is, the more interactive, the more likely it is that information will be transmitted to the interviewee through direct instruction and modeling, and the less likely that conditioning will be the predominant source of guidance. In the words of Heller and Marlatt, "the less responsive the therapist and the more ambiguous the stimulus field in which the patient must operate, the more likely will the patient be to follow the few orienting cues that the therapist provides" (1969, p. 579). One is left with the amusing paradox that the interviewer most likely to oppose the notion of conditioning as an element in his direction of the interview - that is, the analyst who maintains a low verbal profile - is the one most likely to influence the interviewee through the process of verbal conditioning.

The early work on verbal conditioning did not deal directly with the interview. Instead, it attempted to "create an experimental situation to study verbal behavior that paralleled the operant conditioning conditions with infrahumans" (Greenspoon, 1962). Thus, it was committed to showing that verbal behavior may be controlled and changed by using the same procedures that had been effective in modifying the behavior of pigeons.

Greenspoon (1962) offers a concise summary of the pioneering effects in operant conditioning of verbal behavior. He himself had carried out the initial studies. First, college students were asked to emit individual words, being careful to avoid using phrases, sentences, or numbers. This is as ambiguous an instruction as one might find in the most unstructured of interviews. During the first 25 minutes, such cues as the brief comments "mm-hmm," a visual stimulus (a red light flash), and an auditory stimulus were used as reinforcers. The response class selected for conditioning was that of plural nouns. The above three stimuli used as reinforcers did indeed increase the number of plural nouns spoken, when the experimental groups were compared to a control group.

Other verbal conditioning, studies summarized by Greenspoon (1962), used a method developed by Taffel (1955). $\underline{S}$s were given white cards, on each of which were typed six pronouns and one verb. The $\underline{S}$s were instructed to select any one of the six pronouns and to form a sentence by combining it with the verb. The $\underline{E}$ set out to condition the use of the first-person pronoun, by saying "good" whenever members of the experimental group selected it. As expected, the $\underline{S}$s in the experimental group selected first-person pronouns with significantly greater frequency than those in the control group. The range of words selected for conditioning and that of the reinforcing cues were extended in later experiments. Thus, conditioning was demonstrated for nouns, adverbs, travel words, and references to living things, with the use of such reinforcing cues as "mm-hmm," "good," or the silent recording of the response.

As the investigation of verbal conditioning was applied increasingly to the interview, both the classes of verbal response selected for reinforcement and the reinforcers used became increasingly complex and more directly related to the verbal content and the interactional process of the interview. This progression may be noted in the following response categories that have appeared in verbal conditioning studies over the last two decades: affect words and statements (Hagen, 1959; Salzinger & Pisoni, 1958, 1960); positive and negative self-references (Rogers, 1960); patient verbalizations of moves toward independence (Murray, 1956); hostility and dependence statements (Bandura, Lipsher, & Miller, 1960; Varble, 1968; Winder, Ahmed, Bandura & Rau, 1962); early family memories (Quay, 1959); and nondelusional and nonbizarre verbalizations (Krasner, 1962; Rickard, Dignam, & Horner, 1960). A review of the research referred to above will mark the crossover from the experimental laboratory to the clinical interview of studies in verbal conditioning.

One of the earliest of these was an attempt "to examine the effect of reinforcement upon schizophrenics' output of affect responses in an interview" (Salzinger & Pisoni, 1958, p. 84). Both male and female schizophrenic patients were interviewed one week after admission to a psychiatric hospital. The patients had been assigned randomly to an experimental and a control group. Those in the experimental group were interviewed twice, for one-half hour on each occasion, with one day intervening between interviews. The first 10 minutes of each interview were used to determine each S's baseline frequency for emitting spontaneous affect responses. During the second 10 minutes, the interviewer reinforced affective verbalizations by immediately following each with expression of verbal agreement ("mm-hmm," "I see," "yeah"). Extinction occurred during the last 10 minutes when the interviewer discontinued reinforcement. There were no 10-minute segments in the single interview for members of the control group. In both the first and second interviews of the experimental group the greatest number of affect responses occurred during the middle (reinforcement) period. No analogous difference in frequency of occurrence of affect statements was found in the control group. Thus, the evidence was in favor of the conditioning of affect statements within an interview situation in the first study. In a later study (Salzinger & Pisoni, 1960) the same two authors extended the above findings by conditioning affect statements in a sample of normal individuals. The interviewer and conditioning procedures were the same in both studies, as indeed were the results. The normal group, just as the schizophrenic group before it, made the largest number of affect statements in the middle (conditioning) segment of the interview.

A third investigation (Hagen, 1959) used the same procedure as the preceding two, differing from them only in its selection of Ss. It employed two diagnostic groups of chronic undifferentiated schizophrenic and paranoid schizophrenic patients. The Ss who were reinforced for affect statements showed a significant increase over the control Ss. Although there was no significant difference between the diagnostic groups, there was a tendency for the undifferentiated schizophrenics to manifest a higher degree of conditioning than the paranoid schizophrenics. The evidence in the preceding three studies in favor of the verbal conditioning of affect statements in interviews is particularly persuasive because it occurs in both normal and psychotic groups of Ss.

Since a person's evaluation of himself, as it may be reflected in both positive and negative self-references, is widely accepted as an important aspect of his psychological adjustment, it was inevitable that someone would become interested in the susceptibility of self-referent remarks to conditioning within interviews or interview-like situations. Someone (Rogers, 1960) did. The Ss in the study conducted by Rogers (1960) were college students who volunteered to participate in a situation that resembled a clinical interview. Each S took part in six 10-minute open-ended interview sessions. Students who volunteered were randomly assigned to three groups, two experimental and one control. The members of one experimental group were reinforced by the interviewer with the usual "mm-hmm" for each positive self-reference; those of the second experimental group were similarly reinforced for each negative self-reference. The first experimental group did indeed make more positive self-references than the other two groups, but apparently because the frequency of positive self-references in the latter two groups decreased over the six interviews and not because there was an increase in the first group. One could assume that a tendency over time for positive self-references to decrease appears to have been counteracted by the use of reinforcement in the first group. However, such an assumption would leave the finding in some doubt. No such doubt mars the finding for negative self-references for there was a significant increase in this class of verbal response over the duration of the study.

An earlier investigation by Murray (1956) was not based on an experimental use of reinforcement. Instead it was a content analysis of a number of naturalistic psychotherapy interviews, from which it was evident that the therapist quite regularly approved certain patient verbalizations (interpreted as moves toward independence) and disapproved others (independence anxiety, intellectual defenses, and sexual statements). Expressions of movement toward independence tended to increase in frequency over time, and those of independence anxiety, intellectual defenses, and sex, tended to decrease. While this investigation is not a controlled study of verbal conditioning, it does present some interesting evidence about the informal operation of reinforcement in a clinical situation.

An early investigation of verbal conditioning in the psychotherapeutic interview was made by Bandura et al. (1960) who studied the effect of an interviewer's approach to or avoidance of the expression of hostility, on the interviewee's use of this verbal category. The data consisted of tape-recorded interviews of 17 parents who were undergoing psychotherapy at a parent-child clinic. The verbal expression of hostility by a patient was defined as any expression of "dislike, resentment, anger, antagonism, or of critical attitudes" (Bandura et al., 1960) to any one or more of six specified objects (spouse, children, parents, self, therapist, and others). It was assumed that the therapist's approach to an expression of hostility would be reinforcing and would encourage the patient to continue to speak in a hostile vein. On the other hand, the therapist's avoidance of an interviewee's expression of hostility was expected to discourage him/her from making further hostile statements. An interviewer approach to a hostile remark was defined in the following ways: approval of it, expression of interest in it through exploring it further, instigating further expression of hostility by shifting the discussion from a nonhostility to a hostility topic, and simply labeling the feeling expressed by the patient as one of hostility. Interviewer avoidance of patient hostility was defined as disapproved of it, changing from a hostility to a nonhostility topic, silent nonresponse, ignoring the feeling implicit in a hostility remark by focusing on a peripheral aspect of the content communicated, and mislabeling a hostile remark as nonhostile.

Since the interviews used were taken from naturalistic psychotherapy series, it was first necessary to determine what the actual responses of therapists were to patient expressions of hostility. The therapists as a group showed a greater tendency to avoid dealing with hostility when it was directed toward themselves than toward other objects. Hostility directed by patients in this manner therefore did not lead to responses that distinguish between different interviewers. But distinctions did occur when patient hostility was directed toward other objects. Therapists rated by their colleagues as capable of communicating hostility directly and as having a low need for the approval of others were more likely to approach patient expressions of hostility than their colleagues not able to express angry feelings directly and considerably dependent on the approval of others. These two subgroups of therapists had contrasting effects on the patient's communication of anxiety.

The unit of study was a triad of responses consisting of a patient statement, the therapist response, and the next patient statement. Each triad was labeled as either hostile or nonhostile depending on the first patient statement in the group of three. If the first statement was nonhostile, the triad was not studied further. If it was hostile, the therapist response was classified as one of approach or avoidance, and the second patient response as one that either continued or discontinued the communication of hostility begun by the first statement in the triad. The results showed that there was a significantly higher probability that a patient would continue his/her verbalization of hostility in the second response if the interviewer's response had been one of approach rather than avoidance.

In a later investigation, Varble (1968) replicated the above finding when he extended the study of the verbal conditioning of hostility expressions to the entire course of treatment rather than limiting it to the single interview. Over a psychotherapy sequence, a therapist's approach to expressions of hostility led to an increase of such expressions and his/her avoidance to a decrease.

Finally, another group of investigators (Winder et al., 1962) used the basic method of Bandura et al. (1960) to demonstrate that therapist approach led to a continuation of patient expression of dependency, and therapist avoidance to its discontinuation. In a further result with possible implications for the relationship between interviewer and interviewee, therapist approach to the patient's communication of dependency led to patient continuation of treatment and therapist avoidance led to patient termination.

A study by Quay (1959) based on an experimental analogue of the therapy interview used the interviewer's minimal reinforcement responses ("uh-huh") to condition the Ss verbalizations of early childhood memories. Such memories are frequent components of the content of the clinical interview. They are highly personal in character, emotionally charged, and psychologically complex. The Ss were university undergraduates enrolled in a class of introductory psychology. Each S was seated in a comfortable chair, facing away from E, and was instructed to recall events from early childhood as they came to mind. The experiment was divided into two half-hour sessions, about one week apart. The Ss were assigned to two experimental groups, one in which all memories concerned with family and individuals within the family were reinforced. The first 10 minutes of each half-hour session was the period during which the operant levels of the verbal categories later to be reinforced were determined. The interviewer listened but did not respond. During the remaining 20 minutes all "family" memories were reinforced in one group and "nonfamily" memories in the other group. As anticipated, the reinforced categories occurred with greater relative frequency (reinforced memories divided by all memories) during the 20-minute reinforcement periods than during the 10-minute operant periods. Thus, the type of subtle interpersonal influence that occurs in the work of low-activity interviewers is capable of influencing the production of complex, personal responses of the interviewee, highly relevant to the content of the psychotherapy interview.

The full measure of the transition from the early laboratory work in verbal conditioning (Greenspoon, 1962) to its later application to clinical communication may be noted in the studies dealing with the conditioning of nondelusional and nonbizarre speech of psychotic patients. The findings of these investigations are unsettling because they place the usual clinical diagnostic procedures under question. When first admitted to a psychiatric hospital, the diagnosis rests heavily on the initial interview. Moreover, the pathology that is evident in the patient's verbal communication is probably the single, most frequently used indicator of the presence or absence of psychosis. The studies, summarized below, show that the level of pathology in the patient's speech may be a consequence both of his/her clinical condition and the exchange between the interviewer and the interviewee. Under these circumstances, the interview in itself must be regarded as an insufficiently reliable procedure for determining the degree of pathology in the patient.

In one of the investigations referred to above (Rickard, et al., 1960) the amount of delusional speech in a 60-year-old man with 20 years of psychiatric hospitalization, was manipulated. In an effort to reduce this patient's delusional verbalizations, the interviewer smiled, nodded, or reinforced the patient verbally in some other way, whenever he made a nondelusional remark. After delusional responses, the interviewer turned away from him, gazed at the floor, or looked out of the window. A reduced rate of delusional speech was maintained in this way. However, when reinforcement of nondelusional speech was reduced, delusional speech increased again. Clearly, the pathology in the patient's speech is not a simple consequence of his internal psychological condition but a result of the interaction of this condition with the interviewer's response to it.

Krasner (1962) refers to a study related to the same problem in which the therapist turned away from the patient, opened his mail, or made a telephone call whenever the patient spoke in a bizarre fashion. But, when the patient spoke rationally, the therapist reinforced this speech by leaning forward, approving briefly by saying "mm-hmm," or nodding. Presently, irrational speech began to decrease and more time was spent by the patient in a realistic discussion of his illness.

Although reinforcement has been applied to increasingly complex interviewee content, there is only one study that has come to the attention of the present author in which the relative efficacy of reinforcement as a means of increasing the frequency of specified verbal categories has been assessed for responses of varying complexity (Waskow, 1960). The reinforcement in this investigation was Rogerian reflection. Feelings and attitudes were reflected in one group, content in a second, and feelings as attached to specific content in a third. The "content" group showed a significant increase as a consequence of reinforcement (reflection). The other two groups failed to manifest any increase in their reinforced responses (feelings and feelings attached to specific content). While it would be difficult to assume that feeling responses are necessarily more complex than content responses, such an assumption does appear justified for the feeling attached to specific content responses.

The use of reinforcement as a means of directing and controlling the communication of selected verbal content has been amply demonstrated in both a formal, experimentally controlled, and a less formal, clinical sense. It has been studied as a deliberately manipulated method in interviews or interview analogue situations. It has also been noted to occur casually, without deliberate intent. It would be difficult for an interviewer with an interviewee, a parent with a child, or two co-equals in a conversational exchange not to attend more closely to some topics than to others. Selective attention is one method of informally reinforcing some categories of verbal content and discouraging others. Other casual forms of reinforcement that occur in conversational exchanges are brief verbal responses (mm-hmm), head nodding, eye contact, and forward body leaning. In the section that follows the focus will move from the various classes of verbal response selected for reinforcement to the relative strength of selected forms of reinforcement.

Krasner (1962) places reinforcers of verbal behavior in four major categories. (1) the verbal reinforcer is the one most frequently encountered in the mental health interview. It includes minimal remarks that indicate the therapist is attending ("mm-hmm"), brief evaluative comments ("good," "right," "fine"), the paraphrasing or reflecting of previous interviewee communications, and interpretive statements. (2) Gestural reinforcers include head nodding, head shaking, smiling, and forward movement of the body. (3) Mechanical cues are found most frequently in the laboratory experiment rather than the interview. These include such stimuli as light flashes, the sound of a buzzer, a bell tone, or some device for delivering such primary reinforcers as pieces of candy. (4) Symbolic reinforcers, including poker chips and other tokens that can be exchanged for primary reinforcers like cigarettes and candy.

As Krasner (1966) implied, a review of verbal conditioning studies that relate to the interview does indeed demonstrate the predominant use of verbal reinforcers. In one (Powell, 1968), interviewee positive and negative self-referent remarks were the categories selected for reinforcement, and the following three types of interviewer response, the three reinforcers whose relative potency was investigated:

> (a) approval-supportive, statements designed to support the subject's self-reference; (b) reflection restatement, statements designed to paraphrase the subject's self-reference; and (c) open disclosure, statements designed to match the subject's self-reference with a statement from the experimenter about his thoughts, feelings, or experiences about the pertinent topic.   (Powell, 1968, p. 210)

The $\underline{S}$s were male undergraduate students who participated in 20-minute experimental analogues of the clinical interview. In the first 10 minutes the interviewer remained silent in order to establish the $\underline{S}$'s operant level of either positive or negative self-referent remarks, depending on the experimental group to which he was assigned. In the second 10 minutes, the selected response for each $\underline{S}$ was reinforced with one of the three methods described above.

> Honest disclosure from the interviewer was found to be maximally effective, in that this type of intervention influenced the output of both positive and negative self-references. Interviewer statements which reflected or restated subjects' statements were effective with negative but not with positive self-references. Supportive statements from the interviewer were ineffective in increasing the rate of emission of subjects' self-references.   (Powell, 1968, p. 213)

Interviewer self-disclosure has now occurred in studies demonstrating the effectiveness of both modeling and reinforcement as means of directing and controlling the verbal content produced by the interviewee. The inclusion of interviewer self-disclosure in the two categories of modeling and reinforcement may be regarded by some as an excess of definitional permissiveness. Actually there need be no such concern. A self-disclosing statement or series of such statements by an interviewer may be used as a model for the interviewee to emulate if it is given either live or on tape at the beginning of an interview or of a segment thereof. It may be used as a reinforcer if it is given after a specified, preselected interviewee response, and is contingent on the occurrence of that response. Therefore, it is not its content but the way in which it is used that determines whether it functions as a model or a reinforcer. Having made this distinction on the basis of experimental design, it must be admitted that in the flow of a clinical interview the same verbal response may simultaneously serve both as a model and a reinforcer.

The pellets of food that Skinner used to reinforce the behavior of his pigeons were unambiguous stimuli. The verbal cues that an interviewer may use to control the interviewee's speech will usually lack the predictable effect of the primary reinforcers used with the pigeons. Krasner (1962) made this point when he emphasized that "the same stimulus is not necessarily reinforcing under all conditions" (p. 71). He quoted experimental findings that indicated that the word "good" spoken by the interviewer effectively reinforced selected verbal responses in a college population but did not do so reliably with schizophrenic patients. One can conjecture about the reason for this difference. It seems likely that a strongly evaluative term such as "good" would evoke many highly individual associations in a schizophrenic patient, many of them unpleasant, because of difficult past relations with parents and other significant people. Normal students, on the other hand, are more likely to respond to the positive connotation of the work in its ordinary usage. Whatever the actual reason for the inconsistent findings, they serve to demonstrate the importance of situational context as a determinant of the strength of a reinforcer.

The two studies that follow deal with a major component of situational context - the $\underline{S}$ to be conditioned. Not all $\underline{S}$s are equally susceptible to the subtle influence of verbal reinforcement. In one investigation (Marlowe, 1966) the need for social approval as a personality trait affecting a $\underline{S}$'s responsiveness to verbal reinforcement was studied; in another (Slechta, Gwynn, & Peoples, 1966) the presence or absence of schizophrenia, was the focus again with reference to susceptibility to verbal conditioning.

In the Marlowe (1966) study, male and female undergraduates volunteered to participate in a 15-minute interview, which, they were told, was conducted "to learn what college students think and feel about themselves" (p. 427). All $\underline{S}$s were instructed to describe their personality characteristics and traits in the interview. Prior to the interview, each $\underline{S}$ completed a scale which served as a measure of his/her need for social approval. In brief, the purpose of the study was to determine whether the $\underline{S}$s who demonstrated a high need for approval would condition more readily than those who had a low need. The interviewer reinforced each positive self-reference with a "mm-hmm" stated in a flat monotone so that the reinforcing cue would be subtle and minimal. Of the four groups (high and low need for approval experimental and control groups), the high need for approval $\underline{S}$s who were reinforced for positve self-references produced a higher ratio of such responses than those in the three remaining groups. In addition, the first group was the only one of the four that increased the number of positive self-reference responses over the duration of the interview. The experimental group consisting of low need for approval $\underline{S}$s failed to demonstrate a conditioning effect. Thus, the verbal conditioning of positive self-reference was demonstrated, but only in $\underline{S}$s with a high need for social approval. "In this study the behavior of the high need for approval subjects may...be interpreted as reflecting the greater sensitivity and responsiveness of these subjects to social reinforcers as compared to individuals less strongly motivated to seek social approval" (Marlowe, 1966, p. 429).

The investigation by Slechta et al. (1966) compared the susceptibility to verbal conditioning of matched groups of schizophrenic and normal $\underline{S}$s. In the schizophrenic group there were three male and seven female patients, regarded as chronically ill, matched for age, sex, marital status, and years in school with the $\underline{S}$s in the normal group. Each $\underline{S}$ was given the following instructions: "I would like to have you tell two stories including you, me, and two other people as characters. Make them about five minutes long." (Slechta et al., 1966, p. 432). The $\underline{E}$ was silent and motionless during the narration of the first story. During the second, each $\underline{S}$ was reinforced by the $\underline{E}$ each time the story included some reference to the $\underline{E}$.

It is apparent that schizophrenic subjects, although increasing the percentage of their criterion responses slightly, did not change significantly from nonreinforcement to reinforcement, while normals changed significantly in both direction and magnitude. In other words, normals not only emitted a significantly greater percentage of criterion responses under reinforcement than did schizophrenics, but also in comparison with the hospitalized group, normals conditioned more thoroughly.   (Slechta et al., 1966, p. 434)

The chronically schizophrenic patient's reduced susceptibility to verbal conditioning would appear to be one aspect of a more general impairment of capacity to relate, communicate, and be influenced by others.

The application of the verbal conditioning paradigm to the interview has made it possible to take a fresh look at some widely-used categories of interviewer verbal response. Accurate reflection of feeling, as it is defined and used in Rogerian client-centered therapy, is regarded as a valuable device because it permits the therapist to communicate his empathic perception of the patient's feelings, thus establishing a positive relationship and a climate that fosters therapeutic change. What is not emphasized frequently is the reinforcing effect that reflection has on the patient's communication of feelings. By using reflection, the therapist directs his/her selective attention to the patient's feelings (Ivey, 1971). If instead the therapist had chosen to paraphrase the content of what the patient had communicated, he would have selectively attended to and probably reinforced the latter rather than the former. The following clinical example was offered by Ivey (1971) to demonstrate the consequences of the therapist's use of the above two forms of response.

Client: So I'm wondering if you can help find a new major.

Counselor: (Silence)

Client: I suppose if I did find one, I'd just bungle things again.

Counselor: You feel discouraged.

Or

You feel that it's pretty futile to try again.

(Ivey, 1971, p. 58)

Both of the alternative counselor remarks, given at the end of the above exchange, may be regarded as reflections of feeling. Both are used to direct the client into a further exploration of and communication about his feelings regarding the academic crisis in which he finds himself. Consider the consequences for the direction of the interview if the therapist had chosen to say the following instead: "You've given me an account of how you have gotten into your present predicament, your dissatisfaction with your present major, and some thoughts that you have about alternative majors" (assuming that the client has spoken about such alternatives). This paraphrase is cognitively oriented, and would have the effect of directing the client toward further cognitive explorations of his present predicament.

The preceding study and clinical example both deal with the use of verbal cues and some of their attributes as reinforcers. The investigation that follows compares the relative efficacy of verbal and nonverbal reinforcers (Stewart & Patterson, 1973). The verbal reinforcer was the word "good" uttered by the E whenever the S gave a criterion response. The nonverbal reinforcers, used after the same criterion responses were eye contact and forward body lean. A control group was also used. The Ss were male and female undergraduates asked to respond to five TAT cards. All thematic responses were reinforced (except in the control group). All other responses received no reinforcement. The results indicate that the mean number of thematic responses per card for verbal reinforcement was significantly greater than for the two nonverbal forms of reinforcement and for the control group. While eye contact did show a partial conditioning effect over the five cards, the most powerful effect was clearly produced by the verbal cue "good."

Finally, there is a study (Dustin, 1971) that demonstrates the reciprocal character of verbal conditioning. Reinforcement is more frequently considered to be an instrument in the hands of the interviewer for controlling the interviewee's verbalizations rather than an interviewee method for influencing the interviewer's remarks. However, the latter use of reinforcement is demonstrated in a study by Dustin (1971). The author trained a number of "clients" (students from undergraduate education classes) to reinforce beginning counselors (volunteers from a Master's program in counseling) every time they expressed understanding of client content and feelings. The "clients" used seven short reinforcers ("right," "that's right," "very much," "correct," "you've got it," "exactly," and "that is it") and two longer ones. Each counselor met with an untrained "client" once to establish his/her base rate for uttering understanding statements. Then he/she met for a sequence of four 25-minute sessions with a trained "client," interviewing him/her, but unwittingly being reinforced by the "client" for each statement of understanding. As anticipated, the percentage of understanding statements made by the beginning counselors rose steeply and significantly, more than tripling during the experiment.

It need not be assumed that the conditioning of interviewers by interviewees is limited to novice interviewers. Experienced interviewers are sometimes helplessly aware of their own vulnerability to manipulation by perennial interviewees who have developed considerable skill in coping with interviewers. Sociopathic patients and others with multiple hospital admissions become adept at eliciting understanding, sympathy, and support from those who will exercise a great deal of control over them during their stay in the hospital.

SOME COMPARATIVE STUDIES OF INSTRUCTIONS, MODELING, AND VERBAL CONDITIONING

Considerable research has been directed toward determining the relative effectiveness of the three methods of controlling and directing verbal content in the interview and other dyadic communication situations. Marlatt (1972) summarized one study that compared the effects of instructions, direct questions, and reinforcement on "the frequency of positive and negative emotional words given by subjects in a task similar to the Thematic Apperception Test (telling stories about stick figures)" (p. 345). For both the positive and negative words, instructions and direct questions were found to have the most facilitating effects, significantly greater than reinforcement alone. A significant degree of conditioning, nevertheless, did occur for positive affective words, but none was discernible for negative words, possibly because the operant level for negative affect words was too low to provide a basis for a conditioning effect.

In the investigation that follows (Kanfer, 1965), the experimental variables included modeling, reinforcement, and vicarious reinforcement within modeling situations. (Vicarious reinforcement occurs when models rather than the Ss in the study, are reinforced.) The criterion of verbal learning was the increase in the rate at which Ss used nouns with human content. The modeling was provided to all experimental Ss with acquisition tapes which recorded the increased use of nouns with human content by a previous group of Ss. In the vicarious reinforcement tape the previous Ss were reinforced with the word "good" spoken by the E every time they uttered a human noun. In the other tape there was no such reinforcement. Neither modeling nor reinforcement by itself resulted in a significant increase in the frequency which nouns with human content were given. The highest learning rates occurred in the Ss who had been exposed to the modeling with vicarious reinforcement tapes. Other Ss who demonstrated significant learning were those who were exposed to a modeling tape with no vicarious reinforcement but with subsequent direct reinforcement from the E. Kanfer (1965) summarizes his findings as follows: The results indicate that only those groups that were exposed to acquisition tapes and received either direct or vicarious reinforcement showed learning" (p. 259).

There is no clear learning resulting from either modeling or reinforcement when taken by itself in this study. However, modeling combined with reinforcement in either vicarious or direct form is a powerful procedure for controlling verbal response. It is interesting that a good deal of verbal learning can occur by listening to and observing others, particularly if they are rewarded for the behavior they are modeling. While the study itself provides no bridge from the laboratory to the interview, some relevance of modeling plus vicarious reinforcement to the interview may be assumed.

The relative efficacy of modeling and instructions has been given a good deal of research attention. It is the subject of the three studies that follow. In the first (Green & Marlatt, 1972), the Ss were undergraduate males distributed among one control and five experimental groups. All Ss were asked, rather ambiguously, to speak for 15 minutes "about areas which are of concern to people of your age." The Ss in two of the experimental groups received additional instructions. In one of these, Ss were told to speak about subjective feelings regarding specified topics (Feeling Instructions); in the other, they were directed to talk about objective and descriptive ideas concerning the same topics (Content Instructions). The members of a third experimental group (Model-No Instructions) were exposed to tape-recording of a previous "subject," speaking about the same topics that had been included in the instructions. The Ss in the remaining experimental groups were assigned to two combined instruction and modeling conditions. In one, the model was combined with feeling instructions; in the other, with content instructions. The Ss in the control group were simply signaled when to start and when to stop their 15-minute monologues. Each S's monologue was broken up into 10-second periods and scored for the presence or absence of both content and feeling statements.

The results for content units were equally significant for both modeling and instructions, when given separately or in combination with each other. All experimental groups were significantly higher than the control group, but did not differ among themselves. For affect units, the results clearly favored instructions. Those Ss who had received instructions produced more affect statements than the control group. No other experimental groups differed significantly from the control group. While both modeling and instructions provided some structure to an otherwise highly ambiguous situation, and probably served to instigate the S to communicate the specified classes of verbal content, instructions appeared to offer a slight advantage.

The second study (Doster, 1972) in the present triad adds role playing as a method of affecting verbal behavior to the previous two - instructions and modeling. Moreover, it approaches the actual interview situation a little more closely than the preceding one. Again, the Ss were male undergraduate college students who were informed that they would be participating in a study of psychotherapy. They understood that they would be questioned about their attitudes, feelings, and opinions on several topics. The members of the control group received only minimal instructions before the interview. Those in the other five groups received the following treatments: detailed instructions about the character of self-disclosing communications requested, exposure to a taped model of self-disclosing communication, role rehearsal based on the script of the taped model, a combination of detailed instructions and exposure to the taped model, and a combination of detailed instructions and role rehearsal. Of the three methods taken singly, only detailed instructions resulted in a significantly higher level of self-disclosure than that obtained from the control group. While the combined methods (instructions plus modeling; instructions plus role rehearsal) were also more evocative of self-disclosing communication than the control condition, both modeling and role rehearsal added nothing to the effect of specific instructions.

In the last of the three investigations (McGuire, Thelen, & Amolsch, 1975), the variable of time of exposure was added to those of direct instructions and modeling. Would a long set of direct instructions be more effective than a short set; a long exposure to modeling more effective than a short exposure? Is it possible that duration may have a different effect on modeling than on instructions? In fact, the authors (McGuire, et al., 1975) approached their study with the assumption that some of the inconsistencies in findings, comparing instructions and modeling as factors influencing the communication of verbal content, were a consequence of failure to control duration of exposure.

The Ss were the usual male undergraduate students, assigned, in this instance, to comparison groups, exposed to four ways of providing information about the character of self-disclosing information. Instructions were recorded on videotapes; one contained short descriptive instructions (two minutes); another, short modeling or demonstrative instructions (two minutes); a third, long descriptive instructions (25 minutes); and the last, long modeling or demonstrative instructions (25 minutes). After a $\underline{S}$ was exposed to one of the four tapes, the $\underline{E}$ gave him a set of 3 x 5 cards containing three topics, and asked him to speak about each, in a personally open way, for about four minutes. Self-disclosing communication was measured with a rating scale. The results showed that long exposure to taped models of self-disclosing speech was more effective than short exposure to such models, or short and long instructions. "It appears that on the Disclosure Rating Scale, $\underline{S}s'$ scores were increased by lengthening the demonstrative (modeling B.P.) instructions but not by lengthening the descriptive instructions, and that scores were higher following the long demonstration than the long description" (McGuire, et al., 1975, p. 356). Only when comparing the short modeling condition with the short instructional condition was there a borderline significant difference in favor of the instructional group.

Thus, one cannot speak of an advantage for either modality that would apply across all conditions. "If the level of self-disclosure is important, a relatively long demonstration of self-disclosure appears to be a more effective method of training than direct verbal instructions. However, when time is very short, perhaps simple verbal instructions would be more appropriate" (McGuire et al., 1975, p. 361).

Regarding the applicability of the above findings to the clinical interview, it should be noted that the interview in the second investigation, the monologue in the first, and the responses to the topics on cards in the third, were all unstructured, and in this respect analogous to the body of the open-ended clinical interview. The structuring provided the $\underline{S}$, whatever its form, always occurred at the beginning, resembling the initial induction of the interviewee, which provides him with orienting information and instigates him to follow the model of communication that will prevail in the interview. The facilitating effect of such initial structuring has been demonstrated in all of the preceding studies. As to the relative effectiveness of detailed instructions and modeling, neither appears to have a clear advantage over the other, across varying situations. It is possibly significant that the study that most clearly resembles the interview situation (Doster, 1972) finds detailed instructions to be adequate in themselves without the addition of modeling or role rehearsal. Fortunately, the imparting of specific instructions early in the interview is more congruent than the other methods, with the usual pattern of communication in the interview and the sequential changes that take place over its duration.

In the investigations that follow the emphasis is on the combined effect of both instructions and modeling rather than the comparison of their separate effects. In the first (McAllister & Kiesler, 1975), male and female undergraduate students distributed among two experimental and one control condition were

exposed by the experimenter to detailed instructions describing high self-disclosing behavior and one of two taped models exhibiting identical self-disclosing material. One model was the interviewer, and the other was identified as a colleague of the interviewer. Subjects in the control group were not exposed to a model but received only minimal verbal instructions. (p. 428)

Both experimental groups, in which combined instructions and modeling were used, were rated as significantly higher in self-disclosure than the control group. In another investigation (Doster & McAllister, 1973) combined instructions and modeling once again proved to be a significantly effective method for the initial structuring of an interview.

The last investigation (Marlatt, 1970) in the present chapter compares "the effects of vicarious and direct reinforcement upon the discussion of personal problems by subjects in an interview setting" (p. 695). Though the goal of the study is the comparison of two methods of verbal control, its discussion includes a consideration of the optimum combination of both.

Undergraduate students, both male and female, were assigned to four groups, three experimental and one control. All three experimental groups listened to taped models of college students discussiong personal problems. In one, the admission of problems by the student model was positively reinforced by such interview comments as "good" and "mm-hmm"; in another, the reinforcement was negative ("uh-uh," gestures of exasperation); in the third, it was neutral ("go on," "I see"). Thus, all three tapes included vicarious reinforcement. The control group received no tape. Each of the four groups was then subdivided into thirds during the interview that followed the initial modeling for different forms of direct reinforcement. One-third of each group was directly and positively reinforced for all problem admissions; the second, negatively; the last, neutrally. Conditioning occurred for both vicarious and direct reinforcement, both more strongly for the former than the latter. Thus, the positive vicarious condition elicited more problems than the positive direct conditon. The most effective combination turned out to be positive vicarious reinforcement followed by neutral direct reinforcement in the interview. Marlatt (1970) explains this finding by relating it to the ambiguity of the interview situation. Whenever the task requirements are highly ambiguous, he reasons, the use of a vicarious model at the beginning of an interview is equivalent to giving the interviewee task set instructions. He explains the relative superiority of detailed instructions over modeling, in some of the preceding studies, as a consequence of the failure to include vicarious reinforcement in the modeling procedures.

In the end, however, Marlatt (1970) remarks that both vicarious and direct reinforcement "could be used cojointly whenever the desired response has a low operant baseline: the application of vicarious reinforcement to the modeled response could serve an elicitative and directive function, while later administration of direct reinforcement could 'bolster' and maintain the response" (p. 702). Clearly, not enough is known at present about the relative effectiveness of different methods to warrant a definitive selection of one over the other. At some time in the future, there may be enough information about the differential effects of various forms of verbal content control, to permit the prescription of appropriate methods and their combinations for different interview situations (Marlatt, 1970). The goal would be the discovery of "an optimum combination of modeling procedures combined with vicarious reinforcement, verbal instructions, and selective use of direct verbal reinforcement for the elicitation and control of verbal behavior" (p. 703).

APPLICATION SUMMARY

Following the pattern established in Chapter 2, the summary for the present chapter and for those that follow will deal with the implications of research findings for the practice of interviewing. Chapter 3 presents a fairly extensive review of research on three basic methods of controlling interview content: detailed instructions, modeling, and verbal conditioning.

Instructions are used by clinical interviewers at the beginning of the interview to inform the interviewee about its purpose and to motivate him/her to produce specified verbal content in a style that is considered appropriate by the interviewer. When instructions by the interviewer are adequate, expectations of both participants become congruent with each other, and strain in the interview remains at a minimum. The length of the initial instructions and their detail will depend, in part, on the information that the interviewee has, a priori, about what and how he must communicate. Low socioeconomic interviewees, whose initial information about the interview process is particularly vague, receive crucial help when they are given adequate detailed instructions at the beginning of the interview. In fact, the role induction interview is an example of a formalized preinterview, before the beginning of a psychotherapy sequence, that has been particularly effective in making the client's in-therapy communication more appropriate than it would otherwise have been.

The effectiveness of the interview may also be enhanced through a demonstrative sort of instruction at the beginning of the interview, better known as modeling. The interviewee listens to a tape, reads a script, or observes a live interaction between an interviewer and a interviewee (or their surrogates in various experimental designs), demonstrating the content and style of expected communication by the interviewee. Although the insertion of modeling as a procedure early in the interview has proven effective both as a dramatized set of instructions and through its power to instigate behavior in the interviewee similar to that of the model, the method is more of an intrusion into the interview process than a set of verbal instructions would be. Nevertheless, research results have demonstrated the usefulness of modeling in increasing self-disclosing communication, enhancing the freedom with which the interviewee speaks about personal problems, and in helping the interviewee cope with his/her avoidance of and resistance to speaking about such problems. The power of modeling is increased if vicarious reinforcement is built into it - that is, if the model-surrogate of the interviewee receives positive feedback from the person representing the interviewer in the modeling situation.

Verbal conditioning, more than instructions and modeling, tends to occur informally in all dyadic conversational encounters. Thus, each participant is likely to attend to certain topics and to fail to respond to others. The research dealing with verbal conditioning has illuminated the character of the informal process, and the conditions under which it occurs, making it possible for the interviewer to use reinforcement in a deliberate way, for controlling interviewee verbal content. The process of verbal conditioning is most pronounced when the interview remains ambiguous, due to the passivity and silence of the interviewer.

A story that has reverberated through the years in the halls of psychiatry portrays the dramatic end of a psychoanalytic session that had been quite usual in other respects. The young man on the couch had been complaining bitterly throughout the session about his struggle with his homosexual impulses. As time went by, his complaints became more strident, alternating with a demand that the analyst tell him whether he should act on his insistent impulse to seek out a homosexual partner. From the analyst, he received only silence. His words seemed to die and disappear into a silent vacuum. Finally the patient screamed out his intention to leave the session in immediate search of homosexual experience. At this point the analyst said, in a ritually routine manner: "O.K. Our time is up." The patient heard the "O.K." as a cue of approval from the analyst and left the office in hot pursuit of a new kind of pleasure. It would be idle to deny that his misinterpretation of the analyst's remark was related to the wish that was consuming him increasingly during the analytic interview. But it seems equally evident that he would have experienced less reinforcement from the analyst's "O.K." if it hadn't loomed so large due to the complete silence during the rest of the session. Thus, interviewer ambiguity enhances the reinforcing impact of the few remarks that he/she may make, particularly if the interviewer is careless about the contingencies that may occur. The analyst seemed unaware of the contingency between his O.K. and the patient's stridently announced intention. Had he been knowledgeable about the verbal conditioning literature, he might have avoided the unintended reinforcement that occurred. Although the early laboratory experiments on verbal conditioning reinforced narrow categories of preselected words, the later studies have worked with verbal categories that are quite usual in the speech of interviewees in mental health interviews. Some of these are affect statements, positive and negative references to self, expressions of hostility and dependency, and early childhood memories. Moreover, the reinforcing responses available to the interviewer need not be verbal "pellets" that might intrude as alien sounds into the naturalistic communication of the interview. For example, the following verbal responses of the inteviewer are readily used as reinforcers: minimal verbal cues such as "mm-hmm," "good," "fine"; more complex verbal remarks such as the reflection of affect or the paraphrasing and summarizing of interviewee responses; and open self-disclosure by the interviewer. Also useful as reinforcers, but not quite as effective as verbal ones, are certain nonverbal interviewer responses such as forward lean and eye contact. Interviewer cues such as those enumerated above occur quite casually in a communication exchange between two people. But their deployment as reinforcers calls for their disciplined use, immediately following verbal categories that the interviewer wishes to encourage. At any rate, none of the above interviewer cues, that may be used as reinforcers, are artificial intrusions into the interview. No interviewer need feel that his resort to the subtle direction of interview content through reinforcement violates the normal flow of communication in the interview.

Finally, the practitioner of the interview must be aware that, in contrast to food pellets for pigeons, verbal reinforcers for humans are variable and dependent on the interview context. Even the word "good" cannot be accepted, a priori, as positively reinforcing to all interviewees. Some may suspect it because of their mental condition. Others may respond to it with varying intensity because they differ in their need for social approval. Clearly, the use of reinforcement as a method of directing and controlling verbal content does not liberate the interviewer from the need to make clinical judgments about specific interview situations. The reinforcers used and the categories of verbal response chosen to reinforce will vary with the interviewee and the goals of the interview.

Finally, not enough is known at present about the relative effectiveness of the different methods of controlling verbal content to make possible the prescription of one rather than another, with a high degree of certainty. Some investigative work has indeed focused on the efficacy of different methods, singly and in combination, for specific interview situations. Whatever the future may bring, for now the practitioner of the interview will probably need to place in balance both research findings and practical considerations about the feasibility of use of the different methods. An example of a practical consideration is the fact that detailed instructions are easier to arrange, in the normal course of a clinical interview, than modeling procedures.

REFERENCES

Bandura, A., Lipsher, D.H., & Miller, P.E.   Psychotherapists' approach-avoidance reactions to patients' expressions of hostility.   Journal of Consulting Psychology, 1960, 24, 1-8.

Doster, J.   Effects of instructions, modeling and role playing on interview verbal behavior. Journal of Consulting and Clinical Psychology, 1972, 39, 202-209.

Doster, J.A., & Brooks, S.J.   Interviewer disclosure modeling, information revealed, and interviewee verbal behavior.   Journal of Consulting and Clinical Psychology, 1974, 42, 420-426.

Doster, J.A., & McAllister, A.   Effect of modeling and model status on verbal behavior in an interview.   Journal of Consulting and Clinical Psychology, 1973, 40, 240-243.

Dustin, R.   Trained clients as reinforcers of counselor behavior.   Journal of Consulting and Clinical Psychology, 1971, 37, 351-354.

Gill, M.G., & Brenman, M.   Research in psychotherapy.   American Journal of Orthopsychiatry, 1948, 18, 100-110.

Goldstein, A.P.   Structured learning therapy.   New York: Academic Press, 1973.

Green, A.H., & Marlatt, G.A.   Effects of instructions and modeling upon affective and descriptive verbalization. Journal of Abnormal Psychology, 1972, 80, 189-196.

Greenspoon, J.   Verbal conditioning and clinical psychology. In A.J. Bachrach (Ed.), Experimental foundations of clinical psychology. New York: Basic Books, 1962.

Hagen, J.   The conditioning of verbal affect responses in two hospitalized schizophrenic diagnostic groups during the clinical interview. Unpublished Ph.D. dissertation, University of Washington, 1959.

Heller, K.   Ambiguity in the interview interaction.   In J.M. Shlien (Ed.), Research in psychotherapy. Washington, D.C.: American Psychological Association, 1968.

Heller, K., & Marlatt, G.A.   Verbal conditioning, behavior therapy, and behavior change. In C.M. Franks (Ed.), Behavior therapy, appraisal and status. New York: McGraw-Hill, 1969.

Hoehn-Saric, R., Frank, J.D., Imber, S.D., Nash, E.H., Stone, A.R., & Battle, C.C. Systematic preparation of patients for psychotherapy. I. Effects on therapy behavior and outcome. Journal of Psychiatric Research, 1964, 2, 267-281.

Ivey, A.E. Microcounseling. Springfield, Ill.: Thomas, 1971.

Jourard, S.M.   The effects of experimenter self-disclosure on subjects' behavior.   In C.D. Spielberger (Ed.), Current topics in clinical and community psychology. New York: Academic Press, 1969.

Jourard, S.M.   Self disclosure, an experimental analysis of the transparent self. New York: Wiley-Interscience, 1971.

Kanfer, F.H.   Vicarious human reinforcements. In L. Krasner & L.P. Ullman (Eds.), Research in behavior modification. New York: Holt, Rinehart and Winston, 1965.

Krasner, L.   Studies of the conditioning of verbal behavior.   Psychological Bulletin, 1958, 55, 148-170.

Krasner, L.   The therapist as a social reinforcement machine. In H.H. Strupp & L. Luborsky (Eds.), Research in psychotherapy.   Washington, D.C.: American Psychological Association, 1962.

Krasner, L.   Reinforcement, verbal behavior, and psychotherapy.   In A.P. Goldstein & S.J. Dean (Eds.), The investigation of psychotherapy: Commentaries and readings. New York: Wiley, 1966.

Lennard, H.L., & Bernstein, A.   The anatomy of psychotherapy.   New York: Columbia University Press, 1960.

Marlatt, G.A.   A comparison of vicarious and direct reinforcement control of verbal behavior in an interview setting. Journal of Personality and Social Psychology, 1970, 16, 695-703.

Marlatt, G.A. Task structure and the experimental modification of verbal behavior. Psychological Bulletin, 1972, 78, 335-350.

Marlatt, G.A., Jacobson, E.A., Johnson, D.L., & Morrice, D.J. Effect of exposure to a model receiving evaluative feedback upon subsequent behavior in an interview. Journal of Consulting and Clinical Psychology, 1970, 34, 104-112.

Marlowe, D. Need for social approval and the operant conditioning of meaningful verbal behavior. In A.P. Goldstein & S.J. Dean (Eds.), The investigation of psychotherapy. New York: Wiley, 1966.

McAllister, A., & Kiesler, D.J. Interviewee disclosure as a function of interpersonal trust, task modeling, and interviewer self disclosure. Journal of Consulting and Clinical Psychology, 1975, 43, 428.

McGuire, D., Thelen, M.H., & Amolsch, T. Interview self disclosure as a function of length of modeling and descriptive instructions. Journal of Consulting and Clinical Psychology, 1975, 43, 356-362.

Murray, E.J. The content-analyses method of studying psychotherapy. Psychological Monographs, 1956, 70, No. 13 (Whole No. 420).

Orne, M.T., & Wender, P.H. Anticipatory socialization for psychotherapy: Method and rationale. The American Journal of Psychiatry, 1968, 124, 1202-1212.

Powell, W.J., Jr. Differential effectiveness of interviewee interventions in an experimental interview. Journal of Consulting and Clinical Psychology, 1968, 32, 210-215.

Quay, H. The effect of verbal reinforcement on the recall of early memories. Journal of Abnormal and Social Psychology, 1959, 59, 254-257.

Rickard, H.C., Dignam, P.J., & Horner, R.F. Verbal manipulations in a psychotherapuetic relationship. Journal of Clinical Psychology, 1960, 16, 264-267.

Rogers, J.M. Operant conditioning in a quasi therapy setting. Journal of Abnormal and Social Psychology, 1960, 60, 247-252.

Salzinger, K., & Pisoni, S. Reinforcement of affect responses of schizophrenics during the clinical interview. Journal of Abnormal and Social Psychology, 1958, 57, 84-90.

Salzinger, K., & Pisoni, S. Reinforcement of verbal affect responses of normal subjects during the interview. Journal of Abnormal and Social Psychology, 1960, 60, 127-130.

Sarason, I.G., Ganzer, V.J., & Singer, M. Effects of modeled self disclosure on the verbal behavior of persons differing in defensiveness. Journal of Consulting and Clinical Psychology, 1972, 39, 483-490.

Slechta, J., Gwynn, W., & Peoples, C. Verbal conditioning of schizophrenics and normals in a situation resembling psychotherapy. In A.P. Goldstein & S.J. Dean (Eds.), The investigation of psychotherapy. New York: Wiley, 1966.

Stewart, D.J., & Patterson, M.L.   Eliciting effects of verbal and nonverbal
    cues on projective test responses.,   Journal of Consulting and Clinical
    Psychology, 1973, 41, 74-77.

Taffel, C.   Anxiety and the conditioning of verbal behavior.   Journal of
    Abnormal and Social Psychology, 1955, 51, 496-501.

Varble, D.L.   Relationship between the therapists' approach-avoidance
    reactions to hostility and client behavior in therapy.   Journal of
    Consulting and Clinical Psychology, 1968, 32, 237-242.

Waskow, I.E.   The effect of selective responding by the therapist in a quasi-
    therapy setting.   Unpublished Ph.D. dissertation, University of Wisconsin,
    1960.

Winder, C.L., Ahmad, F.Z., Bandura, A., & Rau, L.C.   Dependency of
    patients, psychotherapists' responses, and aspects of psychotherapy.
    Journal of Consulting Psychology, 1962, 26, 129-134.

4 Studies on Style in Interview Communication

The previous two chapters have dealt with verbal communication in the interview; the present chapter will review a wide range of studies dealing with interviewer style. First, a definition of interviewer style will be offered, and some effort will be made to draw the limits of the domain that will include studies on interviewer style. Kiesler (1973) refers to stylistics as a component of psycholinguistics applied to psychotherapy process studies. He goes on to characterize it as "the study of individual differences in the selection of words in various contexts" (p. 8). This aspect of verbal style was brought home to the present author recently when he was asked to review an article submitted to a psychology journal. Although the article was reviewed under the usual conditions of author anonymity, the identity of the author was apparent to the reviewer from the imprint of such aspects of verbal style as idiosyncratic preference for certain words and forms of sentence structure. One attribute of style is quite evidently its idiosyncratic character.

The linguist studies style in verbal communication only. But not all aspects of verbal communication serve equally well as vehicles of style. Mahl (1963) subdivides speech into its lexical and nonlexical aspects, and locates style not exclusively but most clearly in the nonlexical aspects. For Mahl, the most significant locus of style is not the verbal content of what is said but rather how it is said. The mode or style of communicating content is sought in nonlexical linguistic indices such as grammatical aspects of language and in nonlexical, extralinguistic aspects of speech such as rate of speech, duration of utterances, and speech disruptions.

It is in the nonlexical channels of verbal behavior that one hears the relatively uncontrolled expression of affect that the speaker may not intentionally wish to communicate. Thus, a therapist attuned to the emergence of anxiety in a patient is most likely to hear it in verbal rate and speech disruption rather than in the manifest content of the message. These are the modalities of speech which express affect directly. Such expressiveness is considered to be a second attribute of style, on a par with its idiosyncratic character.

129

The ambiguity of the term "style" becomes increasingly evident as one separates out its definitional ingredients. For example, what is meant, precisely, by the term "expressiveness"? Although the concept has thus far been applied to linguistic and extralinguistic aspects of speech only, Dittman (1963) speaks without hesitation about <u>expressive movement</u>. He postulates and partially demonstrates that movement expresses something inside the person like affect, mood, or tension. In this sense stylistic expressiveness (now attributed to both verbal and nonverbal communication) performs a discharge function; through expression there is a reduction in the level of tension or emotion within the organism. But discharge is not the sole function of expressiveness. By semantic definition, it refers to communication as well. Thus, when a person becomes agitated in an interview situation, he may express his psychological condition through elevated motility, increased verbal rate, and flustering of speech, and in doing so may be momentarily discharging the tension within. But, wittingly or unwittingly, he is simultaneously making his condition known to his dyadic partner - i.e., he is communicating it. In the process of communicating he is influencing the other person, evoking his support, or eliciting some other reaction. In an interpersonal sense, therefore, the interviewer's expressiveness performs an instrumental (Dittman, 1963) function as well. It need hardly be added that the three functions of expressiveness are by no means independent of each other. Thus, the discharge of tension may very well be facilitated by its communication to others. It is evident that the investigation of style does not bespeak a concern with the decorative or the trivial. Rather it is indicative of a focus on interactional process in the interview, and is therefore quite central to the communication that occurs.

The stylistic differences between proponents of different therapeutic schools have been considerably explored (Matarazzo, 1965). Without benefit of formal investigation, one may obtain an impression of stylistic contrasts by reading the verbatim transcripts of three of the interviews in Chapter 1 representing a psychoanalytic (Nemiah, 1961), a Sullivanian (Will & Cohen, 1953), and a Rogerian (Seeman, 1957) orientation. These interviews contrast markedly in the content elicited from the interviewee. Just as decided are the stylistic differences between the interviewers. The psychoanalytically oriented interviewer (Nemiah, 1961) let his patient tell his story in his own way. To grant the interviewee the latitude he needed to do so, the interviewer's questions were ambiguous in character. Although not passive, the interviewer was permissive, directing the course of the interview through selective attention rather than through a more directive form of guidance. The following words which describe the psychoanalytically oriented interview are stylistic references: "ambiguous," "permissive," but not "passive."

The words that describe the style of the Sullivanian interview (Will & Cohen, 1953) are somewhat different. The therapist was more "active" and "productive" than the first one, without being more "directive." Above all, he was more personally "expressive." In the Rogerian interview (Seeman, 1957) the therapist limited himself to "reflective" remarks, remaining moderately "productive" while expressing an "accepting" and "empathic" attitude.

The first group of studies below will be based on multidimensional systems of stylistic analysis. In these, the authors strive for comprehensiveness, for breadth rather than for the definitional specification of stylistic variables. These were the earliest investigations in therapeutic style, applied to the gross comparison of therapy schools. It was only later that investigators worked with single dimensions of style, more rigorously defined and directed toward nicer comparisons than those based on therapist school of allegiance.

MULTIDIMENSIONAL STUDIES

With the emergence of nondirective counseling in the early 1940s, psychotherapy research began to focus on interview process and particularly on the style of the therapist. While much had been said in the early 1940s about the principles and goals of nondirective therapy, it was not until somewhat later that investigators developed systems for describing the therapy process that could be used for characterizing the nondirective orientation and differentiating it from other approaches. The early studies in this area were contained within linguistic channels and were based on content.

The first Rogerian research to develop a content-analytic scheme for studying the process of psychotherapy was Porter (1943). Extending and modifying Porter's scheme, Snyder (1945) constructed one which achieved a greater utility and a much broader application, over a period of several years. Only his counselor categories will be presented in brief form at this point, including lead taking (structuring, forcing the client to choose and develop topic, directive questions which require the giving of factual information, nondirective leads and questions which encourage the client to enlarge on his communication), nondirective response-to-feeling (simple acceptance, restatement of content or problem, clarification or recognition of feeling), semi-directive response to feeling (interpretation), and directive counseling categories (approval and encouragement, giving information or explanation, proposing client activity, persuasion, disapproval and criticism).

The language designating the above categories is dated by now, but the focus of the scheme on the issues of counselor lead and directiveness remains currently relevant. The system was applied to typed verbatim transcripts of psychotherapy interviews. In his 1945 study, based on 48 therapy interviews obtained from six clients and four nondirective counselors, Snyder's purpose was to assess the relative efficacy of directive and nondirective therapist style. Some of his findings follow. His four counselors utilized clarification of feeling in approximately half of their statements. In reaction their clients expressed understanding and insight in 12% of their responses at the beginning of therapy, but increased this category to 30% at the end. The most frequent response to a nondirective lead by a counselor was the client's statement of his problem. On the other hand, the client was seldom induced to express his problems by the counselor's structuring of the interview, direct questioning or clarification of feeling, and almost never by interpretation, persuasion or disapproval and criticism. Although the results were not all congruent with principles of nondirective therapy, Snyder felt they were sufficiently so for him to conclude: "The facts of the present study clearly support the theory that it is the nondirective elements of this type of treatment which produce the favorable change in the client's behavior. What directive elements exist are unfavorably received" (Snyder, 1945, p. 203).

In the beginning, then, therapist style was demonstrated to relate to therapist orientation. Moreover, Snyder (1945) operationalized the directive and nondirective approaches and demonstrated the greater efficacy of the latter.

Five short years after Snyder's first study, Fiedler appeared to challenge his major thesis of a stylistic distinction between therapists adhering to different schools of orientation with his classic work on the ideal therapeutic relationship (Fiedler, 1950a, 1950b). First (1950a) he asked therapists from the psychoanalytic, Adlerian, and nondirective schools to describe their concepts of an ideal therapeutic relationship by means of a Q-sort assembly of 75 statements. What emerged was a high level of agreement among Ss from the various schools. A finding that Fiedler made much of was the higher level of congruence between experienced rather than inexperienced therapists, regardless of school of allegiance. Indeed, two experienced therapists from different schools were more likely to agree with each other than an experienced and inexperienced therapist within the same school.

In a second study (1950b) Fiedler asked analogous groups of therapists to use the same Q-sort as an instrument for rating recordings of actual therapist behavior. The results were essentially the same. Experienced therapists of the three schools evaluated therapist behavior in the same way, differing, however, from inexperienced therapists in their own schools. A subsequent factor analysis (Fiedler, 1951) yielded one general relationship factor out of the intercorrelations of the 75 items of the Fiedler Q-sort. This has been designated as an accurate empathy factor (Kiesler, 1973), on which the following items are some of those that were positively loaded:

"Is able to participate completely in the patient's communication."

"Comments are always right in line with what the patient is trying to convey."

Really tries to understand the patient's feelings."
(Kiesler, 1973, p. 341)

The inconsistency between the Snyder and Fiedler studies is not surprising since the two authors sampled different aspects of therapist behavior. The stylistic elements rated by Snyder related to directive and nondirective categories of verbal response. In fact, they were highly salient to the central element in nondirective practice. By contrast Fiedler's array of therapist behaviors emphasized general aspects of relationship not as likely to differentiate between the processes emphasized by the three schools investigated. Historically, the studies by Snyder and Fiedler are significant because they posed a central problem that researchers in the realm of therapy style and process grappled with for nearly two decades - the relative weights of therapist school of allegiance and therapist experience in determining style of therapist behavior. Most of the multidimensional studies reviewed below addressed themselves to this problem.

Strupp's work (1958, 1960) dominated the scene in the late 1950s. During this period, his efforts were directed toward the descriptive study of therapeutic style with an approach that was largely exploratory. His system consisted of two basic categories for classifying a therapist's communication: Type of Therapeutic Activity and Dynamic Focus. Under Type of Therapeutic Activity, Strupp included such major techniques as facilitating communication ("Go on"), exploratory operations ("Tell me what you can about your father"), interpretive operations ("You reacted to your teacher as you often have toward your father"), structuring remarks ("My practice will not be to intruct you how to conduct your life, but rather to listen to your thoughts and feelings and to respond when I feel I have something helpful to say"), direct guidance ("I don't think you should ask your wife to stay home from work whenever you think you may be catching a cold"), activity not clearly relevant to the task of therapy ("You can reach Annapolis by taking the Mountain Road"), and other responses not classifiable. (The examples are the present author's and not Strupp's). Dynamic Focus appears to consist of two, apparently compounded dimensions. One pertains to the therapist's tendency either to go along with the patient's topical focus through remaining silent, passive acceptance, reflecting of feeling, and nondirective questions, or, on the contrary, to take the iniative in changing the topical focus. The second dimension pertains to topical content, including such categories as asking for additional information about a topic under discussion, changing the focus to past events, present events, and the therapist-patient relationship.

In the first study based on this system reported by Strupp (1958) the therapist sample was a completely medical one. The procedure followed in gathering data went as follows. A film of an initial interview with a male phobic patient was shown to groups of Ss. At 28 points within the interview, the film was stopped and Ss were asked to respond to the question: "What would you do?" The Ss, all pyschiatrists, were requested to cast themselves in the role of the filmed patient's therapist, and write their response on a record blank provided them.

In the context of the initial interview the Ss, in general, tended to use responses that evoked information from the patient, avoiding highly inferential communications. As to the experienced-inexperienced distinction, the experienced rather than inexperienced psychiatrists asked fewer exploratory questions, gave more interpretation communications at a higher level of inference with a focus on interpersonal events in the patient's life, showed a higher level of initiative, and changed the focus of communication more. In general, with experience came a reduced emphasis on interrogatory remarks, an enhanced emphasis on interpretation, and an active approach.

Since experience may interact with the professional discipline to which a therapist belongs, the above findings for psychiatrists were compared with analogous ones for psychologists. The psychologists showed fewer stylistic differences with experience. In one of these, the more experienced psychologist more frequently communicated as an expert or an authority than his/her less experienced colleague. There was no similar finding for the psychiatrists.

Other comparisons between the two disciplines were made after they were equated for length of experience and personal analysis. In contrast to psychologists, psychiatrists asked a significantly larger number of exploratory questions, used less reflection of feeling in the Rogerian sense, and changed the focus of the interview more. The above differences appear to reflect a more marked Rogerian orientation among psychologists than psychiatrists.

To further clarify the stylistic character of Rogerian psychotherapy, with the discipline of the therapist kept constant, Rogerian therapists (all psychologists) were compared with psychologists who represented a psychoanalytic orientation. In general the Rogerian psychologists assumed a more positive attitude to the patient than those with a psychoanalytic orientation; a greater number of them judged the patient's prognosis with therapy to be favorable and rated their personal reaction to the patient as positive. The greater tendency of Rogerian rather than analytical psychologists to stay within the patient's frame of reference was noted in the more frequent reluctance of the former group to set up therapy goals or even direct the patient to specific topical areas. Rogerians were more frequently reluctant than analytical therapists to encourage specified patient attitudes or behaviors. By contrast, analytical therapists were more likely to prompt the patient to develop a sense of responsibility and increased socialization and to discourage such attitudes and behaviors as intellectualization, obsessive-ruminations, helplessness, and other symptomatic and maladaptive forms of behavior. Although there was no difference between the two groups on activity-passivity, the analytical therapists tended to recommend therapist firmness with the patient, a response lacking in the Rogerian group. In contrast to analytical therapists, few Rogerians paid attention to such clues as gestures, body movements, patient style of speaking, and interpersonal relationships with significant others. Instead, the Rogerians were preeminent in their attention to patient feelings and attitudes, without specifying the channels of communication through which such attitudes and feelings were to be expressed. Most pointedly, the client-centered group tended to emphasize the reflection and clarification of feeling, while the analytical group advocated interpretation, reassurance, and firmness.

None of the contrasts between the Rogerian and analytical groups of therapists comes as any surprise; all are congruent with the theoretical orientations and practices advocated by both groups. What Strupp has contributed is a carefully etched description of stylistic behaviors advocated by psychotherapists of both persuasions.

In an historical sense one may regard each therapy school as the proponent of one major stylistic variable or pattern of variables. Later in the chapter, research findings regarding such variables, taken one at a time, will be considered. At this time, the focus will be on a study by Frank and Sweetland (1966) dealing with a number of stylistic variables studied as part of a single scheme. The objective was not the comparison of different schools of therapy but rather the investigation of the effects of the variables themselves. A system for classifying therapist verbalizations was developed, the categories of which were correlated with patient response. As it happened, the four interviewers (all clinical psychology graduate students) were Rogerian in approach. The following verbal categories differed significantly from each other in interviewee response elicited: Forcing Insight I ("What do you think made you so disturbed, just at that moment?

What was going on?"); Forcing Insight II ("Is there any relationship between your headaches and your fear of people?"); Forcing the Topic of Discussion ("Tell me more about your mother."); Direct Questioning ("How long have your been married?"); Clarification of Feeling (Reflection) ("Over the last two weeks you've been feeling more and more angry"); and Interpretation ("You couldn't stand your English teacher because he sounded so much like your father").

Forcing Insight I remarks by the interviewer evoked statements of uncertainty by the interviewee ("I'm not sure why I got upset"), tentative striving ("Maybe I ought to work on becoming less disturbed"), and understanding and insight ("Yes, by God! I never thought of that. I nearly always get disturbed in that situation"). Forcing Insight II and Clarification of Feeling (Reflection) also led to interviewee statement of insight and understanding.   Direct Questioning led to an increase in interviewee statements about problems ("We've been married a long time and our marriage is full of problems").   By contrast, Interpretation was followed by interviewee remarks about understanding and insight, and a decrease in problem statements ("Come to think of it, my English teacher does sound like my father").

The above findings are not offered as general guides for the use of verbalization classes in eliciting specified responses from the interviewee. Later sections of the present chapter, dealing with separate stylistic variables, will proceed some distance in the above direction. But the present study does provide some general evidence that a relationship does occur between interviewer style and interviewee response.

Several authors have used multidimensional rating systems to distinguish between good and poor therapy hours.   For example, Orlinsky and Howard (1967) characterized good psychotherapy hours as "experiential" in manner. Such hours were "actively collaborative, genuinely warm, affectively expressive and humanly involving" (p. 631). Moreover, the manner of therapeutic work in the "good" therapy sessions was essentially symmetrical, that is, similar for both patient and therapist, rather than sharply differentiated.

Conceptualizing the psychotherapeutic interview as a dyadic communication system, Lennard and Bernstein (1960) compared those interviews in which patients felt communication flowed easily with those they rated as difficult, a comparison which is roughly analogous to that between good and poor therapy hours.   In the sessions rated as easy rather than difficult, therapist and patient verbal output was greater, the number of interactions between the two members of the dyad was greater, and therapists were somewhat more productive in relation to the productivity of the patients. Therapists asked fewer questions, and their statements were less ambiguous (i.e., more specific).   Patients tended to change the topic less frequently. Therapists communicated more affective statements both in absolute terms and relative to the number of affective expressions by the patients. In brief, patients preferred therapy sessions in which the therapist was active, productive, avoided a high level of interrogation and ambiguity, and was emotionally expressive.

It was inevitable that at some point in the use of multidimensional schemes in process research, questions would be raised about the comparability of dimensions similarly labeled and, indeed, about the meaning of the dimensions used. In an entire group of studies, factor analysis was used as a method of relating stylistic variables to each other and combining similar ones so that numerous redundant variables might be assimilated into a smaller number of more general stylistic dimensions. In an early study in the above-designated group (Sundland & Barker, 1962), the authors obtained responses from a large number of members of the American Psychological Association who were active in psychotherapy. They used the Therapist Orientation Questionnaire, consisting of items pertaining to therapist attitudes and methods which the Ss scored on a five-point Likert-type scale. The most illuminating finding was the emergence of a general, second-order factor which cut across the majority of scales, with one extreme labeled the analytic pole and the other, the experiential pole. The analytic pole is characterized by therapist "conceptualizing, the training of the therapist, planning of therapy, unconscious process, and a restriction of therapist spontaneity. The experiential pole de-emphasizes conceptualizing and unconscious process stressing instead the personality of the therapist, an unplanned approach to therapy, and therapist spontaneity" (Sundland & Barker, 1962, p. 205).

The above data were also used to test the familiar hypotheses that psychotherapist style would vary with school of allegiance and with experience. All respondents were assigned to one of three schools, designated Freudian, Rogerian, and Sullivanian. The greatest difference in attitude, as measured by the scale used, occurred between the Freudians and Rogerians. Limiting the report of findings to stylistic variables only, one notes that the Freudians emphasized the use of interpretation, the usefulness of conceptualizing causation, the therapist's impersonality and inhibited spontaneity. By contrast, the Rogerians placed a great deal more emphasis on spontaneity. With the Freudians and Rogerians as two poles of a continuum, the Sullivanians fell somewhere in between. They were closer to the Freudians than the Rogerians in stressing planning and conceptualization, and closer to the Rogerians in their preference for personal expressiveness. When experience was used as the basis of comparison, there was only one significant difference - the less experienced group espoused a self-actualizing theory of personal growth to a greater degree than the more experienced group did. The authors concluded: "In terms of the attitudes measured here the differences between therapists are clearly better accounted for by their theoretical orientation than by their amount of experience" (Sunderland & Barker, 1962, p. 208).

Another factor-analytic study of interviewer behavior (Mintz, Luborsky, & Auerbach, 1971) developed a polarity of style similar to that discovered by Sundland and Barker (1962). In the process the authors demonstrated that even when interviewers are selected from the same orientation (psychoanalytic) their actual behavior can be fully described only if one includes dimensions habitually attributed to other orientations. The data for the investigation were obtained from tape-recorded therapy sessions conducted by experienced, psychoanalytically oriented therapists. Three raters audited and scored the tapes on a large number of therapist and patient variables. Both therapist and patient scores were intercorrelated and factor analyzed with four factors emerging. Three are descriptive of therapist style and one, of the mental status of the patient. Of the former, the two designated as

Optimal Empathic Relationship and Interpretive Mode are reminiscent of the experiential and analytic poles of the general factor derived by Sundland and Barker (1962).

It is interesting that one can adequately describe the interview behavior of psychoanalytically oriented therapists only by including a dimension that has been characteristically associated with the client-centered orientation (i.e., the experiential dimension of empathic relationship). It would seem that, in an historical sense, various schools of therapy have emphasized and refined different communication and interaction dimensions. And, while the experiential dimension may be more central to the client-centered therapist and the interpretive dimension to the psychoanalytically oriented therapist, both are to some extent general, in all interviewer behavior.

In his work dealing with stylistic dimensions in psychotherapist behavior, Lorr (1965) used the perceptions of therapists by their clients. Borrowing from previous investigators (Apfelbaum, 1958; Fiedler, 1950a; Leary, 1957) Lorr constructed a questionnaire based on eight hypothesized dimensions. The instrument was administered to patients in individual therapy in over 40 veterans' clinics. In each response the patient indicated how often the therapist exhibited the behavior described (almost never, sometimes, usually, nearly always). The responses of the patients were intercorrelated and the following five orthogonal factors extracted, all descriptive of therapist style of relationship: understanding ("Seems to know exactly what I say"; "Seems to understand how I feel"; "Understands me even when I don't express myself well"); accepting ("Shows a real interest in me and my problems"; "Makes me feel that he is one person I can really trust"; "Shows a real liking and affection for me"); authoritarian ("Is full of advice about everything I do"; "Tells me what to do when I have difficult decisions to make"; "Seems to try to get me to accept his ideas and opinions"); independence encouraging ("Expects an individual to shoulder his own responsibilities"; "Encourages me to work on my problems in my own way"); and critical-hostile ("Becomes impatient when I make mistakes"; "Acts smug and superior as though he knew all the answers"; "Gives me the impression that he doesn't like me").

Later, Lorr and McNair (1966) reported several correlations between the above dimensions in therapist style and outcome variables. Thus, patient ratings of therapist understanding and accepting correlated positively with patient ratings of their own improvement; they also correlated at a somewhat lower level, but still significantly, with therapist ratings of patient improvement. On the other hand, patient ratings of therapists on the authoritarian and critical-hostile dimensions correlated negatively with patient self-ratings of improvement and satisfaction in treatment.

Reference was made above to the study of Apfelbaum (1958) dealing with the interviewee's perceptions of interviewer style of relationship. This investigation will be summarized briefly at this point because it resembles the Lorr (1965) study in two ways: (1) it is concerned with therapist style as it applies to his relationship with the patient; and (2) it is based on the patient's perceptions of the therapist's role. The author asked individuals seen in a university out-patient psychiatric clinic to Q-sort statements pertaining to patients' expectations, pretherapy, about the role behavior that they expected their prospective psychotherapists to manifest. Ratings for the various items were intercorrelated and then cluster analyzed with the following three types of therapist role behavior emerging:

1. The nurturant therapist is supportive, protective, and willing to guide the patient, actively helping him in his problem areas.

2. The model therapist is an interested, tolerant listener, tending to be permissive and nonjudgmental. While he is not prone to evaluate his patients or respond to them critically, neither is he particularly protective. Basically, he is perceived by his patients as well-adjusted, interested, but not highly responsive.

3. The therapist as critic is judgmental and expects his patients to show a high level of responsibility. Of the three types, the critic is least benign, largely lacking in permissiveness or supportiveness.

Apfelbaum's (1958) findings about the correlates of the patients' percep-tions of three styles of therapist relationship were not extensive. Moreover, the evidence he produced addressed itself to problems that were quite different from those with which the other studies in the present series were concerned. Thus, Apfelbaum (1958) found that those patients who expected a model therapist demonstrated lower dropout rates than the others who anticipated nurturant and critic therapists. On the other hand, those with nurturant expectations of the therapist, who remained in therapy, stayed longer than the others. Since all Ss had taken the MMPI, it was possible to obtain MMPI correlates of the three patterns of expectation. As it turned out, those with both nurturant and critic expectations started psychotherapy with higher maladjustment scores and more distress than those who expected their therapists to demonstrate model behavior.

Returning to the Lorr investigations, it is noted that Lorr and McNair (1966) developed an additional inventory, most of which was borrowed and modified from Sundland and Barker (1962). In this instance therapist style was investigated in the area of technique and communication rather than relationship. Three postulated factors included items descriptive of a psychoanaltyical style (A), an impersonal style (I), and finally an active, directive style (D). Respondents indicated degree of agreement or disagree-ment on eight-point scales, in response to the items in the inventory entitled AID. The Ss were male and female psychotherapists including psychiatrists, psychologists, and social workers. The responses to all items were intercorrelated and factor analyzed with the result that the three postulated factors were confirmed. Items loaded on the psychoanalytic factor A included the interpretation of unconscious motives and slips of the tongue, the analysis of resistance, and a focus on events in childhood. Those loaded on the impersonal factor I referred to an impersonal approach, an invariant unresponsiveness, and a greater evaluation of therapist technique than therapist personality. Directiveness D was characterized by a major emphasis on treatment planning, a downgrading of patient goals and an imposition of the therapist's own, an emphasis on the social adjustment of the patient, and the assumption of an active therapist role. Again, the later article by Lorr and McNair (1966) reported correlations of the above self-ratings of therapists with training and experience.

Each professional group exhibited distinct preferences for one or two of the patterns, suggesting a strong relation between therapeutic approach and training of therapist.... As expected, therapists who had some personal analysis were more likely to endorse...patterns characterized by high scores on the analytical factor. Experience of therapists was unrelated to the techniques they endorse. (p. 587)

In a novel study, Shostrom and Riley (1968) compared the interpersonal and communication styles of three well-known proponents of contrasting therapeutic approaches. They utilized a series of three films (Shostrom, 1966) recording the work of Carl Rogers (client-centered), Frederick Perls (Gestalt), and Albert Ellis (Rational-Emotive) with the same patient. In a series of two rating studies, Rogers scored highest on Caring ("The therapist's attitude of loving regard for the individual, whether expressed by unconditional warmth or aggressive critical caring") and feeling ("Helping the person to experience in a psychologically safe relationship, feelings which he has heretofore found too threatening to experience freely") (Shostrom & Riley, 1968, p. 629); Perls on encountering ("Providing the experience of encounter between person and therapist, each of whom is being and expressing his real feelings") (Shostrom & Riley, 1968, p. 629), feeling, and interpersonal analyzing (the therapist's analysis of the relationship between himself and the person he is interviewing, with a focus on the latter's perception of the relationship and manipulation of it), and Ellis on value-reorienting (the therapist focuses on the client's values directed toward self and others, and reorients them in a more adaptive direction). Thus, the three therapists were, in fact, stylistically different, although all parameters were relevant to the work of each.

A study by Rice, Gurman, and Razin (1974) provided additional data about therapist style in relation to level of experience and theoretical orientation and, additionally, included findings related to sex of therapist. A sample of therapists, of both sexes, contrasting levels of experience and theoretical preferences designated as analytic (Freudian, Adlerian, analytically oriented), phenomenological (client-centered, Gestalt, existential), and rational-behavioral (rational-emotive, behavioral) were asked to complete a "self-report therapist style questionnaire" borrowed from a previous study (Rice, Fey, & Kepecs, 1972). The questionnaire contained items descriptive of the respondent's style of response in a psychotherapy interview, including such attributes as talkative, supportive, guided by theory, critical, focusing on relationship, cautious, and others. The responses were intercorrelated and factor analyzed; eight orthogonal factors were extracted.

The results for therapist experience, theoretical orientation, and sex were given in terms of the eight factors. In the present summary, factor titles are replaced with the individual questionnaire items that are loaded on the factors, since these seem to be more descriptive of actual therapist behavior. Thus, experienced therapists rated themselves as more interested in history, more patient, more willing to wait for information, more interpretive, more variable in their interview behavior, and more affectively expressive than inexperienced therapists. As between the three above-designated psychotherapist orientations, those with an analytical bent emphasized history and interpretation; those with a phenomenological leaning underscored lack of anonymity and personal feelings; and those with a behavioral-rational orientation stressed high activity level, a cognitive and goal-directed focus. Women therapists described themselves as more variable than men in their psychotherapy behavior, less given to impersonal anonymity, and more judgmental.

From the studies in this section, it is evident that multidimensional systems of coding and describing style have effectively differentiated between subgroups and types of therapists - i.e., male and female, experienced and inexperienced, and therapists adhering to different theoretical orientations. The controversy about the relative salience of theoretical orientations versus level of experience has long since lost its point. Those systems that emphasize general aspects of relationship appear to differentiate level of experience more pointedly than they do theoretical orientation. Those that emphasize the parameters of behavior that are theory or school specific understandably differentiate between theoretical orientations.

A final study in the present section dealing with multidimensional systems is included because of the range of variables studied simultaneously, (Tourney, Bloom, Lowinger, Schorer, Auld, & Grisell, 1966). The actual therapy sessions of 10 psychiatric residents with both schizophrenic and psychoneurotic patients were observed by two experienced psychotherapists. Audiotapes of the sessions were later played back and rated on a number of therapist and patient variables, scored with a nine-point Likert-type rating scale. All patient and therapist variables were intercorrelated separately for the psychoneurotic and schizophrenic patients. Two of the therapist style variables were composites, one designated as errors of commission and one as errors of omission. Errors of commission were consequences of therapist overactivity, including excessive probing, interruption of patient, excessive questioning, inaccurate or untimely interpretations, inappropriate advice and direction, and provocation of the patient. Errors of omission were consequences of therapist underactivity, including insufficient questioning and failure to provide support when needed, to give appropriate interpretations, to express empathy and understanding. Clearly, these two composite categories of therapist style are highly evaluational in character. The following were the correlates of both forms of error. In the interviews with both groups of patients, errors of commission correlated positively with therapist anxiety and hostility. Only in interviews with schizophrenic patients did errors of commission correlate negatively with therapist depression. Thus, the errors of commission were a consequence of activating emotions in the therapist - i.e., anxiety and hostility. For both groups of patients, errors of omission correlated positively with therapist depression. The crucial contrast between the errors of commission and omission was the negative correlation of the former with therapist depression and the positive correlation of the latter, apparently supporting the authors' view of both types of errors as relating to an activity-passivity dimension.

The two kinds of errors correlated differentially with the responses of the two patient groups. To errors of commission, psychoneurotic patients responded with hostility (i.e., positive correlations between therapist errors of commission and patient resistance and hostility), and schizophrenic patients, with anxiety and withdrawal (i.e., a positive correlation with patient anxiety and a negative correlation with patient verbal productivity). In contrast to their reactions to therapist errors of overactivity, the two types of patients responded as follows to therapist errors of underactivity. The psychoneurotic patients tended to manifest an increase in verbal activity and anxiety at a significant but not a strong level. The schizophrenic patients also manifested an increase in verbal productivity, associated however with an increase in thought disorder and hostility to others, but a decrease in their own depression. The neurotic patient was less affected by errors of both types than the schizophrenic patients. The schizophrenic was more manifestly disorganized by errors of omission (i.e., by the therapist's underactivity) than by errors of commission (i.e., therapist overactivity).

The study investigated therapist style as expression of affect. One question it asked was how did patients react when the therapist was rated as anxious? Neurotic patients became angry with and resistive to the therapist; schizophrenic patients, more disorganized and anxious, less talkative and friendly. When the therapist was rated as hostile, neurotic patients reciprocated with hostility and negative feelings to the therapist; schizophrenic patients became silent, anxious, and paradoxically more friendly to the therapist. Clearly, the schizophrenic patients responded in a maladaptive and often an inappropriate manner. Depression in the therapist evoked both depression and negative feeling in the neurotic patients; in the schizophrenic patients, negative feeling, but most markedly, a thought disorder. In general, schizophrenic patients were more sensitive than neurotics to therapist style as the expression of affect. With therapist negative affect they became more withdrawn and disorganized. By contrast, with therapist positive affect they demonstrated a decrease in thought disorder, anxiety, hostility, and an increase in positive feeling. Neurotic patients responded to the therapist's positive feeling with similar feelings of their own. But in other respects they were not greatly affected.

Clearly, therapist style both as activity level (and its associated errors) and as affective expression are of marked clinical importance in the therapist-patient interaction. The sections that follow immediately deal with individual stylistic parameters, focusing on their effects in the interview.

STUDIES ON THE EFFECTS OF SOME ASPECTS OF THERAPIST STYLE

The Directive-Nondirective Dimension

It may appear unnecessarily redundant to begin the present section like the previous one, with a discussion of therapist directiveness, but the two sections approach the topic differently. In the previous section, composite scales were used to distinguish between therapy schools designated as directive or nondirective. In the present one, directiveness is studied as a dimension in the therapeutic interaction. What are its attributes? How does the client respond within the interview to therapist directiveness? To what client behavior does the therapist respond with directiveness? The methodology of research will move from content analysis in the previous section to the experimental analogue of psychotherapy in the present one.

Directiveness has been defined operationally in many of the early studies prompted by the client-centered orientation. Thus, Berdie (1958) developed a content analysis scheme for studying the counseling process which contained interviewer categories at varying levels of directiveness. The following may be assumed to exemplify low levels of directiveness: "nondirective leads: a request to the client to express himself, without the therapist specifying the topic" and "restatement of content or feeling: repetition of the idea expressed by the client which does not reorganize the statement in such a manner as to reveal more clearly the client's feeling or idea." By contrast, high levels of directiveness are exemplified by the following categories: "interpretation: therapist responses that either indicate relationship (one aspect must be inherent in the client's preceding statement) or respond to feelings that have not been expressed by the client" and "advice: recommending following a course of action" (Kiesler, 1973, p. 297). Bergman (1950) operationalized directiveness more concisely as structuring or interpreting, and nondirectiveness as simply the reflection of feeling. Although there is a drift in the definitional emphasis given directiveness as one moves from one study to another, most authors would agree that high therapist directiveness may be defined as high initiative and lead. It is characterized by the frequent use of inputs which arise outside of the client's frame of reference.

The contrast between directive and nondirective interviewer remarks is drawn through the use of several examples of alternative interviewer responses to a given client remark in a book that is designated as a guide to interviewing for health professionals (Bernstein, Bernstein, & Dana, 1974). This remark is made by a patient in a veterans' hospital, while being interviewed by a student nurse: "I tell you I hate that doctor of mine. . . I ask him about my diagnosis and he gives me the brush-off. . .It makes me feel so terrible I hate him so-especially when I have to count on him to get well. I- it worries me." (p. 31). The authors offer the following as an example of a nondirective response by the student nurse: "You're concerned about how sick you really are, and it worries you not to know for sure what the doctor thinks." They refer to this as an understanding response; it will be recognized as a reflection, the prototypical nondirective interviewer comment. The student simply demonstrates "that she is interested in understanding the patient's point of view, and in communicating that understanding to the patient" (Bernstein et al., 1974, p. 33).

With the above response as a nondirective baseline, consider the following examples of leading or directive responses that could have been made by the student nurse to the same patient remark. The first is evaluative in nature and could have taken on the following form: "You certainly must get this straightened out. There's no sense in hating your doctor. You'll find he'll treat you better if you just have more confidence in him." In this response the student nurse makes a critical judgment of the patient's feelings and advises him about how he ought to feel. An alternative, but still directive response by the student nurse could have taken on an active reassuring character. She might have said: "I guess most patients go through a period when they don't like their doctors. It's really not at all uncommon. I hear that from most patients. But things eventually settle down" (p. 32). Here she copes with the patient's disturbance by denying that he has a problem, and again implies that he should feel differently. Finally, the student nurse could have probed the patient's reaction intrusively: "Let's get at the root of your worry. Is there anything else your doctor has done to upset you besides not telling you your diagnosis?" (p. 32). There are other forms that interviewer directiveness might assume. But its essence is a move by the interviewer beyond the interviewee's immediate frame of reference, in which the interviewee is prodded or prompted to follow.

In some studies, therapist directiveness emerges as an independent variable with a unidirectional main effect, without interactional complications. Thus, Bergman (1950) found in the study referred to above, based on the content analysis of counseling interviews, that directive counselor statements (i.e., structuring or interpreting) discouraged client self-exploration and that nondirective statements (i.e., reflection of feeling) enhanced both self-exploration and insight.

A later and more complex investigation (Ashby, Ford, Guerney, & Guerney, 1957) studied the effects of therapist style on client behavior in a manner that allowed for an interaction between therapist and client variables. The therapists (six clinical psychology graduate students) were trained to use two contrasting therapy styles, designated as Reflective (restatement of content, reflection of feelings, nondirective leads and nondirective structuring responses) and Leading (directive leads, interpretations, directive structuring, information giving, and persuasion). The clients, all psychoneurotic, were randomly assigned to the six therapists and the two styles, each client continuing in treatment for a minimum of four sessions. In general, there was some support for the expectation that the two styles of therapy would have different effects on the clients. But the interaction between therapist style and type of client proved to be even more striking. Those clients who were more defensive before treatment behaved more defensively in treatment with a leading (i.e., directive) but not with a reflective (i.e., nondirective) therapist. Similarly, clients who were more aggressive pretherapy reacted more defensively in the leading rather than the reflective therapy. By contrast, clients who manifested a greater need for autonomy reported feeling less defensive in leading therapy. Thus, the two styles of treatment affected different types of clients differentially.

Although the next study (Abramowitz, Abramowitz, Roback, & Jackson, 1974) deals with group rather than individual therapy, it is reviewed here because it also found that directive versus nondirective therapy styles had differential effects on varying types of clients. The setting of the study was an interuniversity clinic serving two neighboring campuses. The patients were students who had responded to campus notices announcing the formation of groups with the objectives of improving personal adjustment and interpersonal relationship skills. The leader of the four groups formed was one of the authors, a clinical psychologist on the staff of the interuniversity clinic. Three of the groups were conducted along directive lines ("the

therapist was to structure sessions, steer discussions, and make interpretations"). In the fourth, designated a "problem discussion" group (the
nondirective group), the leader was less dominant, functioning as a
moderator. "Rather than to structure meetings, his prescribed role was to
encourage intermember discussion of presenting concerns" (Abramowitz, et
al., 1974, p. 850). To assess the possible differential effect of therapist
approach on different types of clients, all participating Ss were assigned to an
internal (I) or external (E) locus of control category (Rotter, 1966) depending
on whether they scored above or below the group median on the I-E variable.
The outcome scales to which the clients responded provided a means of
comparing the relative efficacy of directive and nondirective modes of
treatment for the internal and external Ss. As expected, the external Ss did
relatively better in directive rather than nondirective groups, while the
internal Ss did relatively better in the nondirective group. Since the
externals tend to believe that the events in their lives are determined by
outside forces, they are more responsive to group leaders who adopt an
active, powerful role. The internals believe in the efficacy of their own
initiative and are less responsive to external power and control. It is
therefore not surprising that they should find a less rather than a more active
and controlling leader more congenial.

A second study dealing with the interaction of therapist directiveness and
patient locus of control was conducted by Friedman and Dies (1974). These
authors arranged two forms of behavioral treatment (i.e., automated
desensitization and standard systematic desensitization) and nondirective
discussion-oriented counseling on a continuum of decreasing directiveness.
"The prediction was that internally controlled individuals would respond more
favorably to counseling in which they control the course of therapy, whereas
externals would react well to the more structured treatment in which control
of the therapy session is other determined" (Friedman & Dies, 1974, p. 921).
The Ss were introductory psychology students, selected because of high test
anxiety. One group of Ss, consisting of matched pairs scoring both at the high
and low extremes of the I-E Scale (Rotter, 1966), was assigned to discussion-
oriented counseling, another to systematic desensitization, a third to
automated desensitization, and a last group to a no-treatment control
condition. The focus of the study was not on outcome but on S perception of
and attitude toward the psychotherapy process. As expected, external Ss felt
that they retained too much control of therapy in both the discussion-oriented
counseling and systematic desensitization conditions. By contrast, internal Ss
felt that they had just the right amount of control in the counseling condition
with not quite enough control in systematic desensitization. In all three
conditions internal Ss would have "chosen more client control" with
significantly greater frequency then external Ss. Clearly, then, internal and
external Ss perceive and evaluate therapist directiveness in different ways.

In the 1970s, the inquiries of the 1940's into the relative merits of the
directive versus the nondirective schools seem remote and simplistic. Today
the focus in the study of the directive-nondirective dimension is on its
relative effectiveness for specific purposes, specific types of patients, and as
practiced by specified therapists. As in other areas of psychotherapy
research, the emphasis is less ideological and more pragmatic.

Therapist directiveness-nondirectiveness has been the subject of a number
of experimental analogue investigations. The objective of the first of these

was the experimental study of "the effects of therapist Leading and therapist Following on hypnotically induced repression and on neurotic interpersonal functioning" (Gordon, 1957, p. 406). Gordon proposed the following hypotheses: "Those who use Leading techniques tend to regard the lifting of repressions as the aim of therapy. Those who use Following techniques. . . focus instead on the improvement in the patient's present interpersonal functioning as the aim of therapy" (p. 406). Male college students who emerged as good hypnotic Ss in three screening and training sessions were retained for the study. The design called for the hypnotic induction of a traumatic experience, with repression of the experience consequent on the suggestion under hypnosis that the S would not be able to recall it when he awoke, but that he would be troubled by it. He was given leave, under hypnosis, to spend the subsequent interview in trying to determine what was bothering him. Because it was suggested that the hypnotically induced perpetrator of the trauma resembled the therapist, it was anticipated that a negative transference reaction (i.e., a hostile reaction) would develop to the therapist, during the posthypnotic therapy hours. The therapists, advanced graduate students in clinical psychology, were trained to conduct both Leading and Following interviews and, indeed, each therapist conducted one of each. As anticipated, the results indicate a tendency for Leading therapy sessions to be superior to Following sessions for the lifting of the hypnotically induced repression. Contrary to anticipation, there was no significant advantage for either form of therapy in the evocation of affect expression (i.e., transference hostility in this instance). A direct translation of these analogue findings into psychotherapeutic terms would prompt one to conclude that a directive (i.e., analytic) form of treatment is more effective than a nondirective form in uncovering repressions. By contrast, the asserted efficacy of nondirective treatment in evoking expressions of feeling and, therefore, in changing the patient's interpersonal functioning was not demonstrated.

In another experimental analogue, Wiener (1955) set out to determine the relative effectiveness of two verbal counseling techniques, designated as reassurance-interpretration (the interviewer reassured stress-induced Ss that their thoughts and feelings were quite normal; he also interpreted some reactions of the S as indicative of feelings not yet reported) and catharsis-reflection (the interviewer responded to similarly stress-induced Ss by a simple acceptance of their feelings and their reflection to encourage further expression of affect). The Ss were undergraduate college volunteers from advanced psychology courses. The experimental induction of stress was accomplished by the raising of some questions about the adjustment of each experimental S on the basis of a previously administered Rorschach examination. Utilizing a number of outcome criteria, the two treatment groups combined showed greater recuperation from the stress than two control groups, but there were no significant differences between the reassurance-interpretation (i.e., directive) and catharsis-reflection (i.e., nondirective) groups. .

While most process studies on psychotherapist directiveness have dealt with it as an independent variable, its role as a dependent variable is not without interest. Is directiveness as a form of therapist behavior evoked more frequently by certain types of clients rather than others and by certain forms of client behavior? The answer to both of these questions is in the affirmative in the studies that follow.

Parker (1967) found that male therapists' verbal behavior on a directive-nondirective continuum was significantly related to the sex of the client being interviewed. His therapists gave significantly more nondirective responses to female clients than to male clients. Heller, Myers, and Kline (1963) observed that client dependence evoked dominant (i.e., directive) interviewer behavior, and client dominance evoked passive (i.e., nondirective) interviewer behavior. The latter study was an experimental analogue of the initial interview in a university counseling center. Graduate students, in training as interviewers in the counseling center, were asked to interview "clients" applying for admission to the center. Actually, the "clients" were actors who were trained to portray four types of client roles: dominant-friendly, dominant-hostile, dependent-friendly, and dependent-hostile. The friendly-hostile client dimension is not relevant at the moment, but the dominant-dependent dimension is. Observers rating the interviews judged that "dominant client behavior... evoked significantly more interviewer dependence than was the case for dependent clients, regardless of condition of affect" (Heller et al., 1963, p. 120). If one can hazard translating interviewer dominance to interviewer directiveness, one can conclude that a dependent client is more likely to evoke directive interviewer behavior than a dominant client. The two preceding studies suggest that directiveness is not necessarily a stable invariant trait within the interviewer; it may well vary in response to type and behavior of interviewee.

Finally, in a further test of this impression, Bohn (1967) investigated the responses of students in a graduate psychology course on psychological counseling to three tape-recordings of simulated initial interviews. The tapes represented three client types, called "the typical client," "the hostile client," and "the dependent client." The procedure followed was similar to the one originally used by Strupp (1958). During selected silences on the tape, the S responded by selecting a counselor response from a group of four presented in multiple choice format. The alternatives had been scored for directiveness according to a system derived from Snyder (1945). The taped interviews were administered to the Ss before and after the course in psychological counseling. During both pre- and postcourse evaluations, the dependent client elicited a significantly higher level of directiveness from the interviewers than the "typical" client. The hostile client's evoked directiveness fell in between that of the dependent and "typical" client.

Interpretation

In the early investigation of directiveness, therapist interpretation tended to be assimilated into the directive-nondirective continuum, on the directive or "semi-directive" side (Snyder, 1945). As one would expect, interpretation was given a negative connotation in the client-centered value system. Thus, Rogers asserted: "It is always best to deal with attitudes already expressed.

To interpret unexpressed attitudes is definitely dangerous" (1942, p. 205). In direct contrast, interpretation is considered to be the major instrumentality of therapeutic movement in the psychoanalytic system.   According to Bernstein (1965), interpretation is used to make the unconscious conscious, to provide the patient with an insight or a solution, to allay anxiety, to provide support, to overcome resistance, to facilitate communication, to produce changes in extratherapeutic behavior, to inhibit acting out, and for many other purposes.   Clearly, then, for the psychoanalytically-oriented therapist, interpretation is a multipurpose instrument with a diversity of consequences. It need hardly be added that psychotherapists of other persuasions and many psychotherapy researchers disagree with several of the above claims for interpretation.   In this section the meaning or definition of interpretation, its attributes, and its sequellae in the interactional process of psychotherapy will be considered.

Snyder's (1945) definition of interpretation is characteristic of its operational description when it is consigned to the directive-nondirective continuum: "Responses in which the counselor points out patterns and relationship in the material provided.   The category is always used when causation is implied or indicated.   'You do this because....'   If the counselor attempts even vaguely to say 'why' the client does or feels something, it is considered interpretation" (Kiesler, 1973, p. 417).   Thus, in making an interpretation about the behavior of the patient, the therapist goes beyond the personal information communicated to him; he makes a causal inference about this information.

The analyst would not object to the designation of inference as an attribute of interpretation.   But s(he) would hasten to add that the inferences made pertain to motives, experiences, images, and thoughts beyond the patient's awareness.   Thus, the therapist as interpreter amplifies and translates the signals from the patient's unconscious.   S(he) knows that "the patient's utterances are frequently allusions to other things" and "endeavors to deduce what lies behind the allusions and at the proper time to impart this information to the patient."   S(he) considers that the task is "to infer what the patient has forgotten from what the patient tells him and to reconstruct the patient's past" (Bernstein, 1965, p. 1178).   In a word, interpretations are based on inferences directed toward experiences or cognitions that are beyond the patient's awareness.   In the terms of Dollard and Auld (1959) the therapist provides the patient with verbal labels for unconscious experiences, thus making them manageable.

The definition of interpretation may be clarified further if one were to relate it to two other categories of therapist style that happen to be close to but not synonymous with it.   One of these is reflection and the other is paraphrase of a patient response.   It will be recalled that the purpose of reflection is the extraction and communication to the patient of the feeling implicit in a comment or response made by him/her.   Consider the following example from a psychotherapy interview:

Client (with agitation):
              My wife and I had a fight last night after watching a
              sexually exciting movie.   I tried to make love and she
              rejected me again.

<u>Counselor</u>:   You're upset about and troubled about what happened.
(Ivey, 1971, p. 72)

The paraphrase differs in that it is simply a condensed summary of something said by the patient. For example, the interviewer might have responded to the above client remark with the following verbalization: <u>Counselor</u>: "Your fight followed a sexually exciting movie." Note that both the reflection and the paraphrase stay within the client's frame of reference. They condense and feed back to him/her either the content or the feelings s(he) has communicated.

The interpretation, however, goes beyond the patient's frame of reference. Drawing on past experience, theoretically and empirically based knowledge, and his/her perception of the patient's communication, the interviewer offers the patient a new frame of reference from which to view his/her problem. Again, with the above client's complaint about his wife as the stimulus, the interviewer could have responded as follows: "You've mentioned several times that you are interested in making love to your wife after some external sexual stimulation. You've never mentioned your wife as being sexually exciting" (Ivey, 1971, p. 72).

The studies that investigate the effects of the psychotherapist's interpretations on immediate patient responses, reflect the contradictory anticipations of adherents of the client-centered and psychoanalytic schools. This does not imply that all researchers were necessarily partisans of any one school but rather that they tended to deal with questions posed by the schools. Investigators have dealt with such matters as the impact of interpretation on client verbal productivity, self-exploration, resistance, and therapeutic movement.

Though not presenting themselves specifically as advocates of the client-centered school, the authors of the first study to be reviewed in this section (Kanfer, Phillips, Matarazzo, & Saslow, 1960) reported findings that were broadly congruent with the Rogerian view of the effect of interpretation on the interview process. They investigated the effect of interpretation as a therapist category, without reference to its content. Basing themselves on the opinions of previous authors (Auld & White, 1959; Speisman, 1959), they anticipated that the formal aspects of interpretation, regardless of its veracity or content in a particular instance, would affect the patient's interactional pattern in the interview. In their own words, "the basic hypothesis of the present study is simply that interpretations, as a global category of interviewer's behavior, differ from exploratory or information seeking statements in their immediate effect on the interviewee's verbal output, in time units, regardless of their differing content or their role in the interview strategy" (Kanfer et al., 1960, p. 529). The Ss were female volunteers from the nursing staff and student nurses at the University of Oregon Medical School. All Ss participated in a single initial interview which dealt with such topics as vocation, family, friends, and social and recreational activities. The nurses were subdivided into three experimental groups and two control groups. For all groups, the interviews were divided into three periods - the first of 15 minutes duration, the second and third of 10-minute duration each. In the control groups the interviewer (the senior author) utilized exploratory information-gathering questions in the three interview periods. In the experimental groups, the first and third periods were similarly exploratory and information-gathering; the second period was interpretive. The results clearly   point to a   significant drop in mean duration of interviewee utterance in the second (interpretive) period of the experimental interviews in contrast to the first and third periods (exploratory). No such drop occurred in the control interviews, which were exploratory throughout. Regardless of content, the effect of interpretive style was the inhibition of interviewee productivity.

Although the results of this study are striking, it should be noted that they say very little about the therapeutic effects over time of therapist interpretations.   Instead, they are limited to the immediate interactional consequence of this category of interviewer remark.   Indeed, after the end of the experiment, the authors (Kanfer et al., 1960) asked each S to recall the most vivid statement made by the interviewer.   The experimental Ss all mentioned an interpretation; the control Ss could not recall a single, most memorable statement. Moreover, the experimental Ss discussed the recalled interpretive statements as though they had unleashed a process of self-exploration.   Thus, interpretation appeared to have one effect on the immediate interviewee response but quite another in a more protracted sense. However, only the former was experimentally supported.

In the Kanfer et al. (1960) investigation, interviewer interpretation appeared to function as an inhibitor of speech, when measured in duration units.   It is therefore puzzling to note that in a series of three later investigations (Adams, Butler, & Noblin, 1962; Adams, Noblin, Butler, & Timmons, 1962; Noblin, Timmons, & Reynard, 1966) interpretation was used effectively as a reinforcer of preselected verbal responses. To be sure, the context for interpretation in the latter investigations was not an interview but a Taffel type of verbal conditioning experiment. In all three, hospitalized schizophrenic patients were the Ss. A standardized pack of cards was used, each card containing two pronouns at the top, one first person (I or we) and the other third person (he, she, they). At the bottom of each card, a sentence fragment was printed. A complete sentence could be formed by attaching one of the two pronouns to the sentence fragment below. The object of the experiment was to condition the S's use of the first-person pronoun.   The reinforcer was a psychoanalytically derived interpretive statement.   In the first two investigations (Adams, Butler, & Noblin, 1962; Adams, Noblin, et al., 1962) the interpretations were preselected to relate to the content of the stimulus sentences.   In both, the frequency of selecting the first-person pronoun was raised significantly when "correct" choices were followed by interpretations.

The third study of the series was designed to test the assumption that the content of the interpretation, particularly its "truth status," was crucial to its efficacy. A procedure was followed which scrambled the interpretations so that they were randomly related to the content of the sentences on the cards.

The learning curve for the Ss receiving 'shuffled interpretations' was quite similar to that of Ss who received the logically fitting interpretations following 'correct' responses. The data support the hypothesis that the 'truth status' or relevance of interpretations is not the central factor in whether interpretations lawfully modify verbal behavior in a verbal conditioning situation.

(Noblin, Timmons, & Reynard, 1966, p. 418)

From the preceding studies it would appear that interpretation as a stylistic category tends to inhibit verbal productivity in an initial interview, but paradoxically serves as a reinforcer of verbal learning in a verbal conditioning situation. More congruent with the first finding than with the second is the belief, derived from the client-centered school, that interpretation is likely to evoke client resistance. This belief was challenged by Auld and White (1959) who failed to find that therapist interpretations were followed by patient resistive remarks.

The psychoanalytic origin of interpretation as a process category has prompted an interest in depth as a major attribute of interpretation. In its psychoanalytic sense an interpretation is assumed to proceed beyond the current limits of awareness of a patient. "Depth of interpretation is a description of the relationship between the view expressed by the therapist and the patient's awareness. The greater the disparity between the view expressed by the therapist and the patient's own awareness of these emotions, the deeper the interpretation" (Raush, Sperber, Williams, Harway, Bordin, Dittman, & Hays, 1956, p. 44). Based on this definition a seven-point graphic rating scale of depth of interpretation had been developed (Harway, Dittman, Raush, Bordin, & Rigler, 1955) marked by the following items, among others, arranged in the order of increasing depth:

Therapist merely repeats the material of which the patient is fully aware.

Therapist connects for the patient two aspects of the content of the previous patient statement.

Therapist response deals with information about material completely removed from the patient's awareness. (Harway et al., 1955, p. 249)

Not necessarily in conflict with the above definition of depth of interpretation, but with a somewhat different emphasis, is another based on the concept of plausibility: "It was hypothesized that judgments relating to depth of interpretation are implicitly derived from (and hence should be correlated with) the rater's subjective estimate (i.e. prediction) of how 'plausible' the interpretation is to the patient: deep interpretations will be considered more 'implausible' than shallow interpretations" (Fisher, 1956, p. 249). In the study that follows, a number of therapist statements were selected because they met the author's criterion of interpretation and varied widely in depth. The raters were psychiatrists, psychologists, and psychology graduate students, organized into subgroups of 10, each instructed to rate each statement for either depth of interpretation or plausibility to the patient. The graduate students' plausibility ratings correlated .88 with psychiatrists' depth ratings. Therefore, depth and plausibility appear to refer to the same attribute of interpretation.

Whatever definition one accepts, the following two examples will illustrate contrasting extremes in depth of interpretation: The first is of zero depth and is very much like a simple paraphrase of what the interviewee has said:

Cl.   I've been awfully nervous and high-strung lately. It's hard for me to get to work and concentrate on what I have to do. I think it's pretty natural though. I had a pretty big operation not long ago, and I haven't really got my strength back yet.

Th.   You feel your nervousness and inability to work are just a natural aftermath of your operation.
(Shaffer & Shoben, 1967, p. 64)

Whether depth of interpretation is measured in terms of the disparity between the interviewer's remark and the patient's awareness or the plausibility of the remark to the patient, the excerpt that follows will be recognized as contrasting sharply with the one above, in the direction of greater depth:

Pt.   It's got so bad that I can't even drive over a bridge any more without feeling so scared it's all I can do not to leave the car and run away.

Th.   You....hate yourself for being so inadequate in your own eyes.... bridges symbolize the river in which you could drown this person whom you despise so, and every time you cross them, they arouse this urge to do yourself harm....
(Shaffer & Shoben, 1967, p. 65)

In general, the greater the depth of the interpretation, the greater the likelihood that the interpretation will not be accepted by the client. From this, Fisher (1956) is led to predict that "deep interpretations should be rejected by the patient more frequently than shallow interpretations" (p. 255). This anticipation accords completely with predictions based on the Rogerian approach, according to which deep interpretations are likely to be followed "(a) by a reduced frequency of insight and (b) by an increased frequency of rejection by the client of these therapist responses" (Collier, 1953, p. 329). This attitude is not discordant with the psychoanalytically based one that the premature "communication of interpretations may be wasted because they are unacceptable to the patient, or they may drive the patient out of treatment because of the resistances they evoke or because of the relief that results from the insight obtained" (Bernstein, 1965, p. 1179).

Basing himself on Fenichel's (1941) view of the role of interpretation, Speisman (1959) studied the proposition that "deep interpretations lead to the most resistance, moderate interpretations lead to the least resistance, and superficial interpretations fall between the other two levels as to their influence on resistance" (p. 93). Depth of interpretation was measured by an adaptation of the scale developed by Harway et al. (1955); resistiveness by two verbal categories, one designated exploration (a positive, nonresistive category) and the other opposition. Patient statements assigned to the opposition category expressed doubt, negativism, and denial toward the therapist or therapy. The data consisted of verbatim transcriptions of taped therapy interviews of psychoneurotic patients, rated by advanced graduate students and faculty members in clinical psychology. The original proposition was borne out. Both superficial and moderate interpretations were followed by more exploratory and fewer oppositional patient statements than were deep interpretations. Moreover there was less resistance after moderate rather than superficial interpretations. Following Fenichel (1941), the author concluded that moderate interpretations relate to experiences that are close to consciousness. They lead to new insights by the patient without evoking the kind of blocking or opposition that is prompted by deep interpretations. Speisman interprets his findings to be supportive of the position taken by Fenichel (1941) rather than Rogers (1942) - i.e., the therapist should go slightly beyond the preconscious level in his interpretations rather than limit himself to restating that of which the patient is already aware.

The next study dealing with the effects of interpretive versus noninterpretive interviewer remarks (Garduk & Haggard, 1972) seems to supply some support for each of the preceding investigators. Thus, like Kanfer et al. (1960), Garduk and Haggard (1972) found that patients spoke fewer words in response to interpretive rather than noninterpretive interviewer remarks. Along with reduced verbal productivity, there was also increased hesitation (longer reaction times and more periods of silence). In accordance with client-centered prediction, the patients in the Garduk and Haggard (1972) study were more oppositional and defensive in response to interpretive remarks, but at the same time, more expressive of understanding and insight. Finally, like Speisman (1959), Garduk and Haggard (1972) found that interpretations of moderate depth, were followed by less resistance ("more expressions of anger, hostility, and aggression") than were interpretations of greater depth.

These findings appear to be inconsistent in that they present paradoxically both resistive responses with reduced productivity and nonresistive expressions of understanding and feeling as consequences of interpretation. Yet it is plausible that the interviewee may respond in both ways when grappling with a painful interpretation. Resistive expressions, characterized by reduced productivity and increased silence may alternate with expressions of understanding related to the interpretations, associated with the release of feeling. This range of reaction may well explain the difference between the interviewee's response to moderate and deep interpretation. A moderate interpretation which the interviewee may be able to assimilate more readily is likely to evoke relatively more of the above positive responses to interpretation and few of the negative (resistive) ones. The opposite may be the case with deep interpretations.

Therapist Activity Level

Activity level is a third attribute of therapist style. Although it may be distinguished from the first two, directiveness and interpretation, it is by no means independent of them. Indeed, there is a good deal of overlap among the three. According to Murray (1973), active remarks include "all clearly interpretive, evaluative, and manipulative responses... Passive remarks refer to those remarks that are primarily designed to acknowledge that the patient is talking" (p. 148). Some subcategories of active remarks are instructions to the interviewee about content and style of verbalization, strong approvals, demands, and directions. Subcategories of passive remarks include mild probings, mild approvals, and simple acknowledgments by the therapist that s(he) is attending, such as "Mm-hmm."

In their definition of interviewer activity level, Howe and Pope (1961a) emphasize three components, which they designate as ambiguity, lead, and inference. A high-active therapist remark is low in ambiguity, high in lead and in inference. In this regard, consider the following three descriptions of therapist response:

1. Therapist gives a general, unfocused invitation to talk.

2. Therapist asks the patient to describe the occasion when a pattern of symptoms occurred.

3. Therapist explores the patient's feelings about something just reported by the patient.   (Howe & Pope, 1961a, p. 511)

As one proceeds through the above sequence of responses, ambiguity decreases, and both lead and inference increase. In a word, activity level increases. It should be noted that the above definition of activity level relates to certain lexical attributes of therapist style that have both informational (ambiguity and inference) and interactional (lead) implications.

Some of the studies that follow are based on the above definition of activity level. First, Howe and Pope (1961a) constructed two parallel 11-point scales for rating the activity level of therapist remarks. A number of board-certified psychiatrists were asked to rate descriptions of therapist verbal responses. Those items that were scored reliably were retained, and their scale values computed by averaging the ratings of all the Ss. The following three items occur at low, medium, and high points on the first of the two scales.

Therapist uses a single word or syllable to give a patient an invitation to continue.

Therapist focuses upon an objective, factual aspect of patient's life (age, job, salary).

Therapist suggests that what the patient has just said is inconsistent with certain other things said earlier by the patient.
                              (Howe & Pope, 1961a, p. 513).

With the use of the above scale, the authors (Howe & Pope, 1961b) investigated the dimensionality of the concept of therapist activity level. Experienced psychiatrists were asked to make semantic ratings of 10 therapist responses, representing the entire range of the Activity Level Scale. These ratings were based on bipolar adjectival scales, most of which were selected because they had some connotative reference to ambiguity, lead, and inference. Other adjectives were selected because thay had established relevance to the three semantic differential dimensions: Evaluation, Potency, and Activity (Osgood, Suci, & Tannenbaum, 1957). The first factor to emerge from the intercorrelation and factor analysis of the ratings was one of Professional Evaluation, marked by such bipolar adjectives as wise-foolish, acceptable-unacceptable, skillful-unskillful, and sensitive-insensitive. The concept of activity-passivity appeared only in a modest second factor, characterized by such adjectival variables as colorful-colorless, vibrant-still, precise-vague, strong-weak, and active-passive. The first factor accounted for 33% of the total variance; the second, 18%. It may be that ratings based on therapist categories lexically defined must contend with the ubiquitous presence of a primary evaluative factor, regardless of the specific dimension on which the ratings are made. At any rate, such a finding would be consistent with the position of Osgood and his colleagues (1957).

When a group of psychiatrists and clinical psychologists classified therapist responses (already independently rated for activity level) into five other therapist-response categories, these arranged themselves into the following sequence of increasing activity level: simple facilitation, exploration, clarification, interpretation, approval, and reassurance. Thus, there is a systematic association between activity level and a number of conventional categories of therapist response.

For the most part, studies that attempt to correlate interviewer activity level, as lexically defined, with interviewee response are disappointingly meager in their findings. With the initial diagnostic rather than the psychotherapy interview in mind, Finesinger (1948) regarded the interviewer's low activity level as a means of encouraging the patient to unfold his story spontaneously, following his own associative path. In a sense, low interviewer activity was thought to ensure the projective character of the interview, and thus its diagnostic usefulness. This expectation notwithstanding, the one study that attempted to establish a relationship between therapist verbal activity level and diagnostic utility of patient verbal response (Howe & Pope, 1962) obtained negative results. The experiment investigated the hypothesis that "discrete patient responses immmediately following low-active rather than high-active therapist responses, should be judged to carry greater diagnostic utility" (Howe & Pope, 1962, p. 149). The data for the study were based on the published verbatim transcripts of four psychiatric interviews. The activity level of each therapist remark was averaged across eight raters, as was the diagnostic utility of each subsequent patient response. These two sets of averaged scores were then correlated for each of the four interviews. In two of the four interviews significant negative correlations did indeed occur, only to be lost when the length of the patient response (i.e., number of clause units) was partialed out. A later study (Pope & Siegman, 1962) investigated the relationship between the activity level of each therapist remark and the productivity or length of each subsequent patient response (i.e., number of clauses) in 12 psychiatric interviews, again with negative results.

One might be led to conclude that content based or lexical measures of therapist style possess some flaw that dooms them to failure as instruments for illuminating communication interactions within the interview. Such a conclusion might be prompted further by the many positive results that are obtained in studies that utilize a direct, behavioral measure of activity (e.g., duration of speech or productivity). However, before dismissing lexical measures, the studies in the section dealing with therapist specificity should be examined. Meanwhile, a series of investigations based on activity level such as speech duration or productivity follows.

The utility of therapist activity level defined as gross productivity or output in the description of the interview will now be examined. Lennard and Bernstein (1960), both associated with Columbia University's Bureau of Applied Social Research, have made an important contribution in this endeavor. They have rather impressively applied concepts and methods from the social sciences to the process of psychotherapy, focusing on the verbal interaction between the interviewer and the interviewee. These authors have described their approach to the study of the psychotherapeutic interview in the following terms: "From the perspective of the social sciences, the focus in the study of therapy can be upon therapy as a system of action (verbal communication), upon therapy as a system of expectation, and upon the interrelations between communications and expectations" (Lennard & Bernstein, 1960, p.4). Although a dyadic communication system is channeled through many variables simultaneously, the present focus will be on therapist activity level as a single dimension within the system. The interviewer's activity level is an important referent in the anticipatory role expectations with which both patient and therapist approach the psychotherapeutic encounter. It is equally relevant to any examination of the verbal interaction between the two.

In the Lennard and Bernstein (1960) studies eight therapies (four therapists with two patients each) were recorded over a period of eight months, resulting in more than 500 therapy interview protocols. The two most frequently used indices of activity level as gross productivity were average number of clause units per session and therapist proportion of the total output of the session.

The authors broke down role expectations of both participants in an interview into the following components: "Who shall speak, how much, about what, and when?" (Lennard & Bernstein, 1960, p. 154). They found that nearly all the patients they studied anticipated that the interviewee would do most of the talking during psychotherapy; with this, the interviewers agreed. However, complementarity between interviewers and interviewees regarding level of activity was limited to the general premise stated above. With reference to specifics there is considerable disagreement. For example, interviewers and interviewees tended to have discrepant expectations regarding the role of each in the initiative for and control of communication during the interview. Disagreement about the content of communication (the subject matter to be covered) was similarly prevalent. The therapists and patients disagreed about the relevance of approximately one-half of the topics about which the investigation inquired. In general, patients tended to exclude certain topics from discussion, while the therapists were more broadly accepting.

Whenever dissimilarity with reference to activity level expectations arose, the therapist would attempt to reduce the resulting conflict of expectation by introducing into the interview a "primary system reference." This term refers to any remark by the therapist that has the aim of making the patient aware of what is required of him regarding both type and level of activity. Thus the patient is taught how to engage in a reciprocal role relationship as defined by the therapist.

The naturalistic movement of a dyadic communication system that remains viable is toward stability. Consider the following tendencies toward equilibrium found by Lennard and Bernstein (1960) and summarized by Matarazzo (1965).

1. The relative quantities of therapist and patient speech move toward a stable and fixed ratio, maintained over a psychotherapy interview series, but varying over different patient-therapist pairs. In the group of patients and therapists studied by Lennard and Bernstein (1960) the patients were four times as productive verbally as the therapists, when the interview as a whole was the unit. Single patient verbalizations averaged about five times the length of the preceding interviewer remarks. The generality of this ratio is noted in its occurrence in other studies conducted under different circumstances. Thus Matarazzo, Wiens, Matarazzo, and Saslow (1968) found patient to therapist duration of utterance ratios of 5 to 1 and 6 to 1 in a sample of initial interviews. These are average figures and do not necessarily remain invariant over time. In fact, Lennard and Bernstein found two contrasting patterns in the psychotherapy sequences they studied. In one the ratio of therapist output to that of total interview output did indeed remain constant, without fluctuation. In another there was a tendency for the ratio of the therapist output to fluctuate around an overall mean. When the ratio was below the mean during one session, it tended to rise above the mean in the next session. As in the motion of a pendulum, equilibrium in the interview was not static, but instead, a fluctuating or dynamic steady state over time.

2. Within the relative stability of each therapist's activity level, there were certain interactional fluctuations relative to the verbal output of the patient. When the patient increased his output, the therapist reduced his. Conversely, when the patient decreased his output, the therapist increased his. Thus, there was a tendency toward an overall constant level of verbal productivity for any given psychotherapy dyad. However, there are exceptions to this steady state model of the interview which will be considered below.

3. Some therapists demonstrated greater flexibility and greater capacity to vary their verbal activity level than others.

While the viability of a dyadic communication system is noted in its stability, equilibrium is by no means inevitable. Lennard and Bernstein (1960) found that strain in the interview was frequently a consequence of low therapist activity level. Thus, when they divided their four therapists into two who were more active and two who were less active, they noted that there were no broken appointments among the patients of the more active therapists and 10 broken appointments among the patients of the two less active therapists. In addition, there were frequent expressions of "situational dissatisfaction" by patients in the typescripts of the less active therapists and almost none in those of the more active therapists. No tests of significance of the preceding two impressions were given. However, the third body of evidence regarding the strain engendered by low therapist activity level was statistically documented and evaluated. Patients were asked to compare the ease and satisfaction of communication in any given hour with that which they experienced over the preceding two weeks. To a significant degree, they rated interviews in which the therapist was relatively active as the ones in which communication went more easily than those in which the therapist was relatively inactive. In general, the patients preferred those sessions in which the therapist spoke more frequently and at greater length. It may be assumed that they found the more highly active therapists more reinforcing than the more passive ones. The results of the following two studies provide some evidence as to why this should be so. Truax (1970) found a positive relationship between duration of therapist utterance and his independently rated accurate empathy. Similarly, Pope, Nudler, VanKorff, and McGee (1974) found a positive association between interviewer productivity (i.e., number of words uttered) and his independently rated warmth. It seems plausible that interviewees are likely to perceive their more active therapists in the same way that the raters did (i.e., as more empathic and warmer). These considerations are, of course, additional to the widely held impression that feedback to a participant in a dyadic exchange is, on its face, reinforcing.

In one investigation (Anderson, 1960) the results show that a high level of interviewer activity is associated with a positive reaction of the interviewer himself to the interviewee. In employment interviews conducted by army personnel officers, the interviewer was more verbally productive in interviews with applicants whom he accepted than with those he rejected. There is a hint that the interviewer might have felt better about communication in the interviews which he conducted with applicants whom he later accepted, since there was less time spent in silence in this group. Whether the higher level of interviewer activity in the acceptance interviews was a response to or the cause of the positive attitude that he had to the applicant is uncertain. But there is an accumulating body of evidence that interviewees feel better about interviews in which the interviewer is relatively active, and some evidence that in some interview situations the interviewer may also respond positively to his/her high activity level.

It should be noted that there is nothing here to justify the view that the long-term goals of psychotherapy are necessarily better served by high therapist activity. Rather, the evidence points only to lesser strain and the easier flow of communication with high rather than low therapist verbal activity. It is conceivable that a therapist may deliberately choose to increase the strain experienced by the patient within a particular therapy hour by maintaining a low level of activity.

Moreover, an increase in therapist activity level is not always associated with an analogous increase in patient activity. In some interview situations the synchrony model does indeed obtain; in others the communication model may be quite different. The results in the first investigation immediately below (Heller, Davis, & Myers, 1966) accord with the synchrony model. The purpose of the study, in the authors' words "was to examine the interaction of interviewer affect and activity level in a laboratory interview in which the behavior of the interviewer could be standardized and controlled" (Heller et al., 1966, p. 501). Each of 12 graduate students in speech and theater was trained to conduct one of the following four types of interviews: active-friendly, passive-friendly, active-hostile, and passive-hostile. The active interviewer spoke often and verbosely; the passive interviewer, infrequently and laconically. The interviewees (introductory psychology students) in the active conditions did indeed use the time available to them for speaking significantly more than those in the passive conditions. The most inhibiting condition for the interviewee was that of interviewer silence, the condition which produced least interviewee speech. The authors concluded that their findings were at variance with what they designated as "the nonresponding, noninteracting model presented by Freud and the early writing of Rogers" (Heller et al., 1966, p. 507) and agreed with those in the studies reported by Matarazzo (1965).

The interview used by Matarazzo and his group leading to their early synchrony findings was not a psychotherapy but rather an occupational interview with applicants for positions as policemen and firemen. Without marring its functional character, Matarazzo and his colleagues inserted an experimental analogue into the naturalistic interview. The interview was divided into three 15-minute segments. During the first period, the interviewer spoke in five-second comments; during the second period, he increased the duration of each utterance to 10 seconds; and during the third period, he reverted to five-second remarks. During these segments, the interviewees tracked the interviewer's pattern with average speech durations that increased significantly between the first and second segments and decreased again between the second and third segments. In a second study, the interviewer's pattern was reversed; he started with 10-second remarks, dropping their duration to five seconds in the second period, and increasing them again to 10 seconds in the third segment. Again the interviewees tracked the interviewer's pattern, with remarks that decreased between the first and second segments and then increased again in the third. The case for synchrony as the interactional model for the activity levels of both interviewer and interviewee appeared to be solidly established.

Synchrony between therapist and patient activity was demonstrated in an interesting manner in a study based on an experimental analogue of a single interview (Lindsley, 1969). The interviewer was a psychologist who had not been engaged in regular therapy with the interviewee. The interviewee was a young, chronic schizophrenic. The two members of the dyad did not face each other directly. Instead, they spoke to each other from separate rooms through an intercom system and looked at each other on television screens that were part of the intercom arrangement. The patient could look at the therapist by the repetitive pressing of a handswitch. If he stopped, the television image of the interviewer would fade out. The patient could also listen to the interviewer by operating a second handswitch. Again, the interviewer's voice would fade if the interviewee stopped pressing the second handswitch. The patient could speak to the interviewer through a suspended microphone. The patient's responsiveness in the three modalities of speaking, listening, and looking to three levels of therapist activity was recorded. When the therapist initiated and maintained the conversation, the patient responded with a high rate of talking, listening, and looking. When the therapist ceased initiating conversation, but merely responded to the patient's remarks, the patient's talking rate dropped. Rate of listening and looking did not change. Later, when the therapist lapsed into silence, the patient's responses dropped out in the following order: first speech and later listening. Looking was maintained throughout, although at a somewhat diminished level. Eventually the therapist resumed his initiative in conversation and the patient's high rates of talking, listening, and looking were restored.

Synchrony between therapist and patient activity level is demonstrated here between therapist speech and patient speech, listening, and looking, although the degree of synchrony is not equal across the three modalities.

However, the apparently ubiquitous character of the synchronous relationship between interviewer and interviewee activity level was placed under question by a naturalistic psychotherapy study later conducted by Matarazzo and his colleagues (Matarazzo et al., 1968). Seven uncontrolled psychotherapy sequences were tape-recorded and observed. Three of the four authors conducted the psychotherapies, two treating two patients each, and the third, three patients. In the studies discussed above, which manifested synchrony so strikingly, the interviewer's inputs were experimentally manipulated and considered to be the independent variables. The design was therefore a unidirectional one, with the action proceeding from the interviewer to the interviewee. In the psychotherapy interviews, the communication situation was quite different; the process was one of dyadic interaction in which the two participants reciprocally affected each other. The data used were the mean durations of patient and therapist utterances in individual therapy sessions. If synchrony were present, it would be reflected in significant positive correlations between therapist and patient mean durations across sessions. In fact, such positive correlations did not occur. Three of the correlations were near zero, and the other four were negative with only one significantly so. Thus, instead of synchrony, there appeared to be a tendency toward an inverse relationship. When the output of the patient increased, that of the therapist decreased; when the output of the patient decreased, that of the therapist increased. This inverse model would accord with what Matarazzo et al. (1968) referred to as a "therapeutic set" and what Lennard and Bernstein (1960) spoke of as balance or equilibrium in a dyadic communication system. It is also completely congruent with the finding by Heller et al. (1963) that dependent and passive interviewees evoked a relatively high level of activity from interviewers while dominant interviewees evoked interviewer passivity. They concluded that in an interactional psychotherapy situation, high patient output would be associated with low therapist output, and low patient output, with high therapist output.

It would appear that the occurrence of synchronous communication is governed by situational factors. Thus, in the above studies the unidirectional process in an experimental analogue of the initial interview promoted synchrony; the free interaction of the two participants in a psychotherapy exchange did not. Additionally, one might expect certain variables to be more responsive to situational factors than others. Thus, mean reaction time latencies and interruption behavior of both therapist and patient remained synchronously related in the seven psychotherapy series as they did in the earlier analogue studies (Matarazzo et al., 1968). It may be that verbal activity level is more situationally responsive than latency and interruption.

The situational responsiveness of interviewer and interviewee activity level (number of words uttered) was studied in another investigation (Pope et al., 1974) based on a replicated comparison of the interviewer behavior of professionals and complete novices. In each of the two component studies the interviewees were 16 female freshman students. Sixteen interviewers were professionals (psychiatrists and third-year resident psychiatrist) and 16 were novices (sophomore students with no training in interviewing). Each interviewer conducted only one interview, but each interviewee was seen twice, once by a professional and once by a novice. "It was anticipated that when students interview students, interviewer and interviewee productivity will be positively correlated, that is, will manifest synchrony. When professionals interview students, an inverse or reciprocal relationship should occur." (Pope et al., 1974, p. 682). The above prediction was based on the view of the "nonprofessional" interview as a communication system that is relatively nonrole differentiated, akin to a conversational encounter, with a spontaneous mutuality of response. By contrast, the "professional" interview would be governed by an operating principle that prompts the interviewer to say little when the interviewee is productive and relatively more when the interviewee's productivity flags. The results bore out the first prediction; there was one significant and one borderline positive correlation between interviewer and interviewee productivity for the two groups of "nonprofessional" interviews. The evidence for the inverse model in the "professional" interview was less consistent. There was indeed a highly significant negative correlation between interviewer and interviewee productivity for the first group of interviews, but a failure to replicate it in the second.

In conclusion, the studies based on therapist activity level, lexically defined, failed to produce significant results. By contrast, therapist activity level objectively defined as quantity of verbal output has proven to be an illuminating variable, with significant findings in both the therapeutic and initial diagnostic interviews, and for both experimental analogue and naturalistic investigations. The failure of the lexical approach to the study of activity level may be a consequence of its dependence on a variable that lacks unidimensionality. For example, it will be recalled that the Howe and Pope (1961a) definition of therapist activity level referred to three attributes or semantic dimensions - lead, inference, and ambiguity. In the section that follows, only the last dimension - therapist ambiguity (or specificity) - will be considered to determine whether a reduction in the dimensionality of a variable increases its utility in the investigation of the interviewer-interviewee verbal interaction.

Therapist Ambiguity-Specificity

Such would appear to be the case in a study (Pope & Siegman, 1962) to which brief reference was made in the preceding section on therapist activity level. The data consisted of the verbatim transcripts of 12 naturalistic psychiatric interviews. Its objective was to determine the relationship between both activity level and specificity in therapist remarks and such aspects of patient verbal behavior as productivity (clause units) and speech disturbances (Mahl, 1956) in immediately following patient responses. Therapist remarks were rated for activity level with the Howe and Pope (1961a) scale discussed above and for specificity with a scale developed by Lennard and Bernstein (1960). No significant findings for activity level occurred, but predicted negative correlations between therapist specificity and patient productivity were obtained in nine out of 12 interviews, and similar negative correlations between therapist specificity and patient speech disturbance in six out of eight interviews. Thus, therapist message or informational ambiguity (the converse of specificity) was positively associated with patient productivity (clause units) and with an index that purported to measure anxiety (Mahl's Speech Disturbance Ratio).

The positive association of therapist ambiguity and patient productivity accords with the psychoanalytically based concept of the projective interview. Thus, Bordin (1955) spoke about ambiguity in psychotherapy as fostering the type of associational flow that circumvents the patient's ordinary defenses (as it does in a projective device) bringing into the therapy interview "his major conflictual feelings no matter how unaware he is of them" (Bordin, 1955, p. 13). Perhaps a word of explanation about the "projective" character of the ambiguous interview is in order here. If a S were asked to respond to a specific question in a personality inventory, asking him to state explicitly what his current adjustment problems are, he might demur. His hesitation could be a consequence of some confusion that he might have about precisely what his problems are. Such a S might need a chance to talk in an unfocused, associative way, in order that he might retrieve whatever scattered information he might have about the matter. His hesitation might also be indicative of a resistive opposition to confiding painful, intimate information to a stranger. It is assumed that a projective device such as an inkblot as the stimulus, and the examiner's request that the S respond by giving his/her perception of and associations to the inkblot, might facilitate the type of personal communication that the S found so difficult to give in response to the more explicit question. Confusion about exactly what the current adjustment problems are would not obstruct him/her because the greater ambiguity of the stimulus would grant him/her the freedom to associate freely in the area of personal experience. It would not limit him/her to an answer that is relevant to a specific question. If the S is hampered in his/her response by a resistive opposition, s(he) will be challenged less by an ambiguous stimulus than by a focused question. A similar contrast between the effects of specific and ambiguous interviewer inputs may also be operative in the interview. The specific question, "What are your troubles with your father?" may evoke more hesitation and resistance from an interviewee than the more ambiguous invitation to "Tell me about your father." Thus, the greater productivity of the interviewee in response to ambiguous rather than specific interviewer questions or comments, accords with the psychoanalytically derived preference for the projective rather than the highly structured interview.

Nor would psychoanalytic theory find it inconsistent that patient productivity would be associated with anxiety under the condition of therapist ambiguity. Such an expectation "assumes that people try to defend themselves against anxiety associated with conflictual impulses by denying to awareness or distorting those stimuli associated with the impulse. Where the stimuli are ambiguous, the discriminative processes necessary for defense are hampered and greater anxiety will result" (Bordin, 1955, p. 13). Specific therapist inputs, such as narrowly focused questions would provide the patient with the discriminant stimuli needed to activate his defenses. Ambiguous inputs would lack such stimuli, and would therefore foster the expression of anxiety-arousing communication.

The Lennard and Bernstein (1960) model of the psychotherapeutic interview as an informational exchange system provides a different theoretical foundation for the positive association between therapist ambiguity and patient productivity. Lennard and Bernstein (1960) speak about a reciprocal relationship between the information put into the communication system by each member of the therapy dyad. The informational input of the therapist is determined by the ambiguity of his remarks. Thus, an ambiguous remark which does not restrict the options available to the interviewee for replying has low informational stimulus value; a specific remark has high informational value. The informational input of the interviewee is measured by his/her productivity. In accordance with the principle of informational reciprocity advanced by the authors, ambiguous therapist remarks (i.e., remarks with low informational stimulus value) should be followed by relatively long patient responses, and specific therapist remarks by relatively brief patient responses. The same principle of reciprocity and, indeed, the findings of Lennard and Bernstein (1960) would lead one to expect that unproductive patient responses would be followed by specific therapist communications, and relatively productive patient responses by ambiguous therapist communications. Pope and Siegman (1962) were only able to confirm the therapist-to-patient component of the reciprocal relationship; the patient-to-therapist component was not significant in their data.

In the immediately preceding relationships, only message or informational ambiguity is involved. This aspect of therapist ambiguity is a major stylistic dimension, germane to the therapist-patient verbal interaction. But it is by no means the only form in which ambiguity may occur in the interview. Bordin refers to interviewer ambiguity as a variable related to the degree to which an interviewer defines himself or the situation to an interviewee: "It is possible to conceive of three especially relevant areas in which these definitions can take place: (a) the topics it is appropriate to discuss with him; (b) the closeness and other characteristics of the relationship expected; (c) the therapist's values, in terms of the goals he assumes he and the patient should work toward (p. 10). The first and third area relate to informational or message aspects of ambiguity. Under (a), consider the contrast between the analyst who instructs his patient to speak of anything that occurs to him, and the behavior therapist who might ask his patient to give him a precise blow-by-blow account of a recent angry exchange with his wife. Under (c), compare the analyst who begins the therapy session in silence, with the practitioner of desensitization who tells the patient that the goal on a particular day is to complete training in deep muscle relaxation. Finally, under (b), contrast the mute psychoanalyst, seated behind the patient, with the practitioner of some form of experiential therapy, facing his client, and engaging in a spontaneous, "genuine," egalitarian exchange. It need hardly be added that in each of the above instances, the first example in each pair is the ambiguous one; the second, the specific one.

In developing their empirical scale for assessing therapist specificity (the converse of ambiguity) Siegman and Pope (1962) utilized the informational definition of specificity advanced by Lennard and Bernstein (1960). Messages sent by the interviewer to the interviewee differ in the degree to which they narrow the range of possible patient response. For example, the therapist remark, "Just start by saying anything that occurs to you" does not limit the patient's response to any specific subject matter area and may therefore be said to have low informational specificity (high ambiguity). By contrast, the question, "How old is your sister?" sets definite and specific limits on the range of possible alternatives for the patient's reply. It may therefore be said to have high informational specificity (low ambiguity). In the studies that follow the informational definition of ambiguity governs the investigations carried out.

One additional comment is needed about the Pope and Siegman (1962) study reviewed above. The second finding of the study - i.e., the positive association between therapist ambiguity and the early Mahl (1956) Speech Disturbance Ratio - was considered, tentatively, as evidence that therapist ambiguity promotes patient anxiety. However, speech disturbances as scored by Mahl were viewed as indicative of cognitive uncertainty rather than anxiety in a study by Brenner, Feldstein, and Jaffe (1965). These authors determined the occurrence of speech disturbances when subjects were asked to read passages varying in their approximation to written English. They found a negative correlation between a passage's level of approximation to written English and the level of speech disturbance it elicited. Thus, speech disturbance has been variously assumed to be indicative of either anxiety or cognitive uncertainty. The meaning of patient speech disturbance as a consequence of therapist ambiguity was therefore itself ambiguous. Both anxiety and cognitive uncertainty were thought to be possible sequellae of therapist ambiguity.

To further test the consequences of interviewer ambiguity and, more particularly, to clarify the role of interviewee anxiety and/or cognitive uncertainty in resulting verbal behavior, an experimental analogue of the initial interview was devised (Pope & Siegman, 1965; Siegman & Pope, 1965). Both interviewer specificity as measured by the Siegman and Pope (1962) scale and the anxiety-arousing effect of his topical focus, were independently manipulated in an experimental interview. (The latter variable is not of immediate concern). The $\underline{S}$s were junior and senior female students at a university-based school of nursing. Again, ambiguous rather than specific interviewer remarks were associated with high interviewee productivity (number of words spoken). Regarding the occurrence of either (or both) anxiety and cognitive uncertainty, it should be noted that Mahl no longer considered his first Speech Disturbance Ratio (1956) as an index of anxiety. He had removed the category termed Ah (the expression Ah and allied hesitation expressions) from the ratio, designating the remaining speech disturbances as components of the Non-Ah Ratio (Mahl, 1956). Ah, sometimes referred to as the Filled Pause Ratio, is on its face, an expression of hesitation. The Non-Ah Ratio has been assumed to be indicative of the flustered speech of anxiety. In the results of the second investigation, therapist ambiguity was associated with a high Ah Ratio, a slow articulation rate and silent pauses, but was not significantly related to the Non-Ah Ratio. In sum, therapist ambiguity was associated with both high interviewee productivity and the type of hesitation and caution (Ah Ratio, slow articulation rate, and silent pauses) that reflects interviewee uncertainty. Interviewee anxiety did not occur. In a second experimental analogue study (Pope & Siegman, 1968) dealing only in part with interviewer ambiguity, the preceding results were replicated.

The findings regarding interviewee productivity and hesitation were replicated later in quite a different kind of investigation (Pope, Blass, Cheek, Siegman, & Bradford, 1971) based on semi-naturalistic interviews. In this instance the Ss were not nursing students, but psychiatric in-patients, interviewed three times by the same interviewer, in one low-specificity, one high-specificity, and one uncontrolled interview. In respects other than interviewer specificity, the interviews were uncontrolled. The low-specificity (ambiguous) interviews did indeed evoke significantly greater productivity than high, with uncontrolled interviews falling between the two. Low-specificity interviews also evoked high interviewee hesitation and caution (long reaction time, high silence quotient, and slow rate of speech). Thus, the association between interviewer ambiguity and both interviewee productivity and uncertainty, as reflected in several indices of caution and hesitation, has been noted in experimental analogues of the interview, in seminaturalistic interviews and partially, in an early naturalistic psychotherapy study.

The finding that interviewer ambiguity leads to interviewee uncertainty is dependent, in part, on the acceptance of interviewee silent pauses and filled pauses (Ah) as paralinguistic indices of uncertainty. The evidence regarding this interpretation of the two forms of hesitation is found in a number of psycholinguistic studies not directly related to the interview. The results of one investigation (Maclay & Osgood, 1959) showed that both silent and filled pauses occurred more frequently before lexical rather than function words. Lexical words are substantive in character (e.g., nouns and verbs); they are the vehicles of the content of a communication. Function words such as prepositions, conjunctions, and auxiliary verbs relate the lexical words to each other. A speaker is less certain before the choice of a particular lexical word than he is likely to be before the choice of a function word, because his major decisions regarding what to say occur before the former rather than the latter. As to the speaker's preference for the silent pause or the filled pause to express his/her uncertainty, the choice is regarded by Maclay and Osgood as mainly one of individual style of speaking. The choice may also be a consequence of the length of the pause. If the pause is long, and the speaker becomes concerned that the person he is speaking to may "take the floor" from him, he will be prompted to utter something like "ah" in order to retain his/her right to continue speak.

The above findings were borne out in part by another study (Goldman-Eisler, 1972) based on quite a different method. Ss were shown cartoon sequences without captions and asked first to describe the content of the story represented by the cartoons and then to formulate the meaning or point of the story. The first task was the easier one because it was more concrete than the second; the second called for abstracting of the story and making inferences about it. One would therefore expect the second task to be associated with more uncertainty and hesitation than the first. In fact there were fewer pauses of shorter duration in the story descriptions than in the inferences about story meaning. Goldman-Eisler (1972) also produced some evidence to support the Maclay and Osgood (1959) finding that filled pauses occur after prolonged silences as a means of retaining control of the "floor."

A third investigation (Boomer, 1972) accepts the two forms of pauses as expressions of uncertainty and hesitation, but differs from the Maclay and Osgood (1959) position by demonstrating that the phonemic clause rather than the single word is the unit against which hesitation should be measured. Boomer found that both types of hesitations tend to occur at the beginning of phonemic clauses, and cannot be significantly related to individual words. Boomer's results do not conflict with Goldman-Eisler's, but are discrepant from those of Maclay and Osgood (1959). He reasons that when a person is uttering spontaneous speech, as in a conversation or an interview, he must select his units of communication as he speaks. Whenever he has a new selection to make there is the experience of uncertainty, accompanied by a hesitation, until the selection has been completed. But does the speaker select one word at a time? Or does he think in larger units? Boomer (1972) argues in favor of the latter process, in which "planning ranges forward to encompass a structured 'chunk' of syntax and meaning. As a given clause is being uttered the next one is taking shape and focus... If, however, the emerging clause has not yet been subjectively formulated, speech is suspended until the entire pattern is clarified. This suspension may be manifested as either a pause or a vocalized hesitation sound" (Boomer, 1972, p. 90).

The phonemic clause as the unit rather than the individual word is congruent with the experience of the mental health interviewer, because s(he) tends to be attuned to the topic as a segment of verbal content. Certainly, the clause is a more meaningful component of an interview topic than the individual card.

But, setting aside the problem of unit, it must be evident to the interviewer that both silent and filled pauses are important signals from the interviewee. They convey to the attentive interviewer that the interviewee is grappling with uncertainty about what to say next. The uncertainty may derive primarily from a linguistic impasse; for example, s(he) may be confused about how best to complete a sentence. It may be cognitive in origin, in the sense that the interviewee is simply uncertain about what to speak about next. This type of uncertainty occurs frequently in a highly ambiguous interview. Most intriguing to the clinician is the situation in which the interviewee may be blocked by a psychological conflict, creating uncertainty about communicating some information that occurs to him or about which he has been asked.

Pope, Siegman, and their colleagues distinguish between interviewee anxiety as reflected in flustered speech (Non-Ah Ratio) and cognitive uncertainty as noted in hesitation and caution (Ah Ratio, rate of speech, silence, reaction time). They considered only the latter to be a consequence of interviewer ambiguity. But their findings conflict with clinical impression and some findings of other investigations.

Sullivan (1954), for example, was emphatic in his observation about the capacity of therapist ambiguity to stir up patient anxiety. "Were any of us to be interviewed about a significant aspect of our living by a person who gave us no clues as to what he thought and how we were doing, I think we would be reduced to mutism within a matter of minutes" (p. 103).

Sullivan's clinical impression was supported by an investigation carried out by Dibner (1953), based on semi-naturalistic diagnostic interviews conducted at the point of admission to a psychiatric service in a general hospital. Four clinicians were instructed to interview half of the 10 patients each saw, ambiguously, and the other half, in a structured manner. The experimentally manipulated ambiguity of the interviewer was clearly informational in character, and would in fact rate at a low point on the Siegman and Pope (1962) Specificity Scale. Patient anxiety was measured with ratings of speech disturbance, GSR conductance level, introspective report by the patient, and global ratings of anxiety by a clinical judge who audited the interview tape-recordings. The ambiguity achieved by each interviewer was determined by a measure of the structure provided by the interviewer's verbalizations (objective index) and by the patients' ratings of their perceptions of interviewer structure. The four measures of anxiety correlated positively with the objective index of therapist ambiguity, and two of them correlated with the patients' subjective ratings. Thus, Dibner did indeed find a positive relationship between therapist ambiguity (the opposite of structure) and patient anxiety.

Another investigation (Boomer, 1963) which appears to support Dibner's finding was based on a series of one and one-half minute tape-recorded excerpts from psychotherapy interviews with one patient. A significant but low positive correlation was found between filled pauses (Ah hesitations and repetitions) and body movement. Without an external criterion of ambiguity, Boomer (1963) assumed that filled pauses were indicative of uncertainty and body movement was indicative of tension; he demonstrated that the two were positively correlated.

The Dibner position regarding therapist ambiguity and patient anxiety was contradicted by a later investigation again using GSR amplitude as a measure of anxiety arousal (McCarron & Appel, 1972). This study was based on two analyses. In one, a 21-year-old patient with a schizoid personality disturbance was studied across a series of 12 weekly psychotherapy sessions. His therapist was a psychiatrist with more than 10 years of clinical experience. In the second analysis based on an initial interview, the Ss were 12 patients with a variety of problems and their therapists, six male psychiatrists and six male medical students. The therapist remarks were distributed among four categories - designated reflection, interrogation, interpretation, and confrontation - arranged in the order of low to high specificity as defined by Lennard and Bernstein (1960). Both in the psychotherapy series and in the group of initial interviews, GSR amplitude in both patient and therapist was found to increase with the stimulus specificity of the therapist verbalizations. Clearly, specificity, and not ambiguity, as in the Dibner (1953) study, evoked anxiety in patient and therapist. Specificity appeared to impart a quality of stimulus potency to interviewer remarks. Both the Dibner (1953) and the McCarron and Appel (1972) investigations found significant associations between interviewee anxiety and interviewer ambiguity, although the direction of relationship in one study was the opposite of that in the other. Both investigations are in conflict with those by Pope and Siegman (1965, 1968) and Pope et al.(1971) in which no association between interviewer ambiguity and interviewee anxiety occurred.

As Bordin (1955) implied, the study of therapist ambiguity need not be limited to lexical or message aspects of the communication system. Situational or relationship ambiguity is the subject of the two studies that follow. In one (Siegman & Pope, 1972) situational or relationship ambiguity was created by placing a screen between the interviewer and interviewee. It was assumed that the barrier posed by a screen would indeed create a condition of relationship ambiguity because the "interviewer's feelings and attitudes about the interviewee are encoded primarily in such non-verbal cues as smiling, head nodding, and other body movements. By monitoring these non-verbal interviewer cues, the interviewee obtains information about the adequacy of his responses and the impression he is making upon the interviewer" (Siegman & Pope, 1972, p. 48). When such information is cut off by a screen, one may assume that a condition of interpersonal ambiguity results. The presence of the screen had the effect of significantly reducing the verbal productivity (number of words spoken) of experimental Ss below that of control Ss, decreasing the rate of speech, and increasing the Ah Ratio (filled pauses). Thus, unlike message ambiguity, relationship ambiguity decreased productivity; like message ambiguity, it increased verbal indices of hesitation and uncertainty.

In order to assess the possibility that the above results were artifactual consequences of the presence of the screen rather than sequellae of relationship ambiguity, the procedure was varied somewhat in a second investigation. In the second experimental condition the interviewees faced away from the interviewer, so that they could not see him, while he had an angular view of them. In this experimental analogue of the psychoanalytic situation, the interviewer's nonverbal reinforcing cues were reduced, as in the case of the interposition of the screen. In the control condition the interviewees faced the interviewer in the usual manner. Again, interviewee productivity was significantly lower and hesitation greater in the experimental than in the control condition. However, the significant indices of hesitation varied somewhat from those that were significant in the previous study. Thus, the Ah Ratio was again greater in the ambiguous rather than the control condition, but the speech rate difference dropped out, being replaced by a slower reaction time.

Thus, whether it occurs in the interviewer's messages, or in situational aspects of the relationship between himself and the interviewee, ambiguity is associated with interviewee hesitation and uncertainty. The drop in interviewee productivity under conditions of relationship ambiguity, but not message ambiguity, may be a consequence of the threat that the former poses to the communication system.

That the communication system is indeed weakened when relationship ambiguity is increased through the elimination of visual cues in the dyadic interaction was demonstrated in a much earlier study by Mahl (1968). Both male and female college students were interviewed in two contrasting conditions. In one-half of each interview, the two participants faced each other in the usual manner; interpersonal visual cues were thus evident to both the interviewer and the interviewee. In the other half the participants were in a back-to-back situation with no possibility of perceiving visual cues. The only significant difference between interviewee behavior under the two conditions was a decrease in the frequency of communicative gestures and an increase in the frequency of autistic gestures. Communicative gestures were defined as "common substitutions for verbal utterances; that is, actions with a meaning shared by sender and receiver. Examples: shaking head 'yes' or 'no', pointing, pounding with the fist, shrugging shoulders, illustrative motions" (Mahl, 1968, p. 30). Autistic actions are those "judged not to be common substitutions for verbal utterances... Examples: playing with jewelry, clothing; scratching, rubbing, random touching of various parts of the body" (Mahl, 1968, p. 30).

In brief, relationship ambiguity through the elimination of visual messages between the two members of a dyad reduces communication by decreasing communication gestures while increasing autistic ones.

The interviewer who attempts to evaluate the effects of message ambiguity on interviewee response is confronted with the paradoxical results in research studies of high interviewee productivity on the one hand, and hesitant uncertainty on the other. High interviewer productivity is quite generally regarded as desirable, but interviewee hesitation and caution may not be. The trainee in the practice of interviewing can accept the above contingencies between interviewer ambiguity and both interviewee productivity and hesitation as reliable, but any decision about their desirability will depend on the nature and goals of the interview, and the interviewer's theoretical and personal preferences.

The advantage of an ambiguous rather than a specific interviewer style has been asserted for the mental health interview as well as for those conducted in medicine (Bernstein et al., 1974). Bernstein and his colleagues take the position that a broad initial remark or question serves to open the area of discussion and prompt the production of a wide range of information.

When the patient has begun to explain what brought him to seek help, he should be allowed to continue, preferably without interruption... Of major interest will be the manner in which the patient formulates his complaints, how concerned he is about them, and whether he attempts to relate them to certain events in his life. The interviewee should also be alert to the sequence and order of events described. (p. 101)

The interview excerpt that follows demonstrates the limitations imposed on the interviewee by an overly specific interviewer:

Dr.:   What symptoms bring you here?

Pt: Last night I woke up with a terrific pain in my stomach - right here (points).

Dr.:   Ever had it before?

Pt: No, not that bad.

Dr.:   You had it before, but not so bad?

Pt: Not really, I've had mild stomach aches before but nothing like this.

Dr.:   Any other complaints?

Pt: No sir.   (Bernstein et al., 1974, p. 98)

Clearly, the initiative is in the hands of the physician who limits the interviewee's response to specifically defined areas and quantities of information, usually factual. The interviewee is not free to develop his/her story in his/her own way with reference to both the sequence of events and their association with each other.

The latter type of narrative is possible if the medical interview is carried out with more ambiguous questions and comments, as in the following excerpt:

Dr.:   I wonder if you could tell me something about why you've come to see me?

Pt: Well, like I told your nurse... I've been having these headaches. They started out about a month ago and they've been getting worse - to the point where I'm embarrassed about going to work. When one comes on at work, I have to hide the pain's so bad...
                    (Bernstein et al., p. 101)

Proceeding in this vein, the patient was able to tell the doctor about her pressures at work, her fear that she may have a brain tumor, her father's recent death of a brain tumor, mother's subsequent moving in, the tensions attendant on this move, and finally her discovery that she was pregnant. It's likely that a rapid-fire medical interrogation of the kind presented in the first of the two excerpts would have missed the sequence and the confluence of life events that the doctor would need to know about to begin to assess the patient's headaches.

Yet a conscientious physician might object to the second example, because the initiative taken by the patient may not touch all required information bases. In response to such an objection, Bernstein et al. (1974) admit that ambiguous open questions which characterize the open interview need to be supplemented by more specific follow-up inquiries. "Even in the most successful open interview, there will be areas about which information is needed. Direct questions will have to be asked. However, there is a vast difference between an interview limited entirely to a brief question, 'yes' or 'no' answer session, and one in which questions are asked after the patient has been permitted to give his own account of matters" (p. 103). The sequential principle is for the interviewer to proceed from general or ambiguous to specific questions or inquiries.

The above case made for an ambiguous interviewer style does not deal with its second, less desirable correlate - that of interviewee hesitation and uncertainty.   Whether interviewee hesitation is regarded positively or negatively by the interviewer depends, in part, on the character or goal of the interview. A psychotherapist engaged in exploring psychological experiences in depth will find ambiguous inputs particularly useful for the goal of the interview, and will be quite prepared to accept the patient's hesitations along with his/her productivity. By contrast, an employment interviewer inquiring into the past work history of an applicant, may phrase his/her questions specifically, and be quite discomfitted by hesitations in an interviewee response.

In addition, interviewers may have individual preferences in interviewee behavior.   These may be determined, in part, by personal differences. Interviewer A may be better able to tolerate interviewee hesitation than Interviewer B. Since it may be expected that interviewers will work within the limits imposed by their own personal traits and attitudes, one would expect Interviewer A to be less avoidant of an ambiguous style than Interviewer B. Finally, the theoretical orientation of the interviewer - that is, his overall goals - tend also to govern his/her choice of ambiguity level. A psychotherapist with a dynamic orientation is more likely to use an ambiguous style than a behavior therapist, in the process of specifying problem behaviors and the reinforcing contingencies that sustain them.

Whatever the goals of a particular interview, and the individual personal and theoretical preferences of an interviewer, s(he) will be helped by an awareness of the consequences of using inputs at varying levels of ambiguity. Moreover, all interviewers will do well to accept the dimensional character of ambiguity-specificity as a stylistic attribute that occurs at varying levels rather than in an all-or-none dichotomy. As ambiguity increases, interviewee hesitation and uncertainty increase too.   Clinical experience and research findings tend to point toward critical levels of ambiguity, beyond which interviewee uncertainty may become a serious impediment to communication. Although research findings regarding the anxiety-arousing effect of message ambiguity are conflicted, it seems likely that ambiguity, beyond certain critical levels, may well generate both cognitive uncertainty and anxiety. The latter eventuality might well disrupt communication and unduly disturb the interviewee.

In fact, the persuasive power of some therapists may well be a consequence of the high level of ambiguity they maintain and the anxiety that they arouse in this way (Frank, 1961). Such therapists maintain an aura of ambiguity about the goals of treatment; they imply that they know what the patient's problems are but that the patient can only benefit from treatment if he discovers them for himself. The patient is compelled to strive for an unspecified cure and lacks cues regarding his progress toward its attainment.

Since the patient remains dependent on the therapist for a reduction of stressful ambiguity, s(he) is highly susceptible to the therapist's influence. This picture may be somewhat overdrawn, but it is not a basically inaccurate description of the manipulation of ambiguity in some forms of traditional psychotherapy.

A trainee in the practice of interviewing may be taught, with comparative ease, how to recognize the ambiguity dimension in interviewer style and, indeed, how to use it in his/her interview behavior. Much more complex and less susceptible to specific prescription is the clinical judgment about when to use various levels of ambiguity. Certainly his/her own stylistic preferences will enter into such judgments. But beyond personal preference, there will be additional factors such as the goal of the interview, the interviewer's theoretical orientation, and an awareness of critical levels of ambiguity, beyond which both cognitive uncertainty and anxiety may attain levels that block and disrupt interviewee communication.

APPLICATION SUMMARY

The focus has now moved from verbal content, in Chapters 2 and 3, to those paralinguistic and nonverbal aspects of communication that are associated with its style. The term "style" refers not to what is said, but, very broadly, to how it is said. It may be noted in individual differences in the selection of words (lexical), in preferred grammatical forms (nonlexical, but verbal), in such aspects of speech as rate, duration of utterances, and speech disturbances (paralinguistic), in facial expression, posture, gesture, directness of bodily orientation, and body motility (nonverbal). Style imparts an expressive coloration to what is said. Thus, one person may speak dramatically; a second, stolidly; and a third, belligerently. Such expressive styles imply the display and discharge of certain emotions by the speaker.

It is evident, however, that style is not a process of the private discharge of emotion, but one which colors and affects interpersonal communication. The expression of affect will be the subject of Chapter 5. Chapter 4 has been concerned with the pragmatics of style (largely, but not entirely interviewer style) - that is, the effect on the course of the interview if the interviewer (in some instances, the interviewee) uses one stylistic dimension more than another.

The dimensions of interviewer style that have come to interest both clinicians and researchers are those that have emerged as critical variables, differentiating one school of psychotherapy from another. Thus the client-centered, the psychoanalytic, and the various experiential schools have asserted different positions for themselves on such therapist dimensions as directiveness-nondirectiveness, interpretation, activity level, and ambiguity-specificity. Out of the polemics between different schools regarding the above stylistic dimensions has come an awareness that interviewers in general tend to be more or less directive, more of less interpretive, active, and ambiguous. There has therefore been an increasing interest in the consequences of the greater and lesser use of these stylistic dimensions by representatives of all schools of therapy. Implicit is the assumption that all dimensions are required to adequately describe the interactions between two people communicating with each other.

After the years of research on the relative merits of the directive and nondirective approach, there is disappointingly little advice that can be given to the novice interviewer about the general use of this stylistic attribute. One study does find that directive counselor statements (structuring or interpreting) tend to discourage client self-exploration, while nondirective statements enhance both self-exploration and resulting insight. But more important than such general conclusions are the many recent findings that any stylistic attribute will have varying effects on different types of clients. The interviewer needs to ask himself how his/her directiveness will affect different types of interviewees; not whether it is better in general to be directive or nondirective. It has been noted, for example, that clients who were more defensive before beginning treatment behaved more defensively with a leading (directive) rather than a reflective nondirective therapist. Interviewees with an external locus of control were better able to respond to directive rather than nondirective interviewers, while those with an internal locus of control responded better to nondirective therapists. Because externals tend to believe that events in their lives are determined by external forces, they are more responsive to interviewers who adopt an active, powerful role. By contrast, internals are more self-directed and prefer the nondirective interview situation which provides fewer obstructions to their own initiative.

Part of the interviewer's development may be traced in his/her increasing sensitivity to individual differences in those s(he) interviews, and the skill with which s(he) is able to adapt his/her style to the idiosyncracies of the interviewee. One study demonstrates that, in fact, interviewers do tend to respond to the interpersonal behavior of the interviewee by modifying their style of communication. Thus a dependent client is likely to evoke directive interviewer behavior, while a dominant client, nondirective interviewer behavior.

One of the components of directiveness in the client-centered scheme of things is the interviewer operation known as interpretation. The interviewer responds to what the patient has told him/her by relating events, ideas, or attitudes to each other so that patterns emerge which permit a statement of causality. "You felt angry at your teacher because she reminded you of your mother." In arriving at this inference the therapist had related several associations of the patient to each other and to earlier or current experiences in the patient's life. The degree of inference implicit in the interpretation indicates that the therapist has had to go beyond the patient's present level of awareness. S(he) tells the patient something that the latter had not been able to think of on his/her own. In fact, the interpretation is likely to penetrate into experiences that the patient has resisted learning about because of the anxiety that they aroused.

In the early research comparing interview process in both the client-centered and psychoanalytic schools, the findings tended to run against the use of interpretation. Among client-centered therapists and the research prompted by them, a belief that has endured for many years is that interpretive remarks by the interviewer tend to evoke client resistance. Although not all studies support this belief, the major evidence in favor of it is the reduced productivity of the interviewee following an interpretation.

Thus, an experimental study demonstrated that interpretation by the interviewer reduced the gross productivity of the interviewee in an initial interview. But one cannot assume from this that an interpretive comment by the interviewer has no clinical utility whatever. Indeed, even the above study found, additionally, that Ss who were asked to recall the most vivid statement made by the interviewer all mentioned an interpretation. Moreover, a series of experiments in which interpretive remarks were used as reinforcers in a verbal conditioning procedure all demonstrated that significant verbal learning occurred.

The interviewer therefore, needs to know that when he is conducting an exploratory interview in which verbal productivity by the interviewee is crucial, he would be well advised to avoid interpretive remarks. But, if gross productivity is secondary to other goals, such as new self-understandings, interpretation may indeed be the stylistic mode for the interviewer to use.

The concept of interpretation originated in psychoanalytic practice. Out of this background came a technical view of the function of interpretation as a category of interviewer behavior that helps the interviewee become aware of thoughts, images, memories, and affects that had been relegated to the unconscious because of their anxiety-arousing capacity. There was, therefore, an early tendency to evaluate interpretation along a depth dimension. If it reaches into the unconscious, how deeply does it penetrate? Indeed, the depth attribute of interpretation is widely represented in much of the research that has investigated this stylistic dimension. Investigators turned from their inquiries into the effects of interpretation as a generality to others dealing with the effects of interpretation at varying depths. They have defined depth of interpretation either as the discrepancy between the interviewer's remark and the interviewee's awareness, or as the plausibility of the interpretation to the interviewee. Thus, if there is a great discrepancy between the interviewer's interpretation and the interviewee's awareness, or the interpretation seems highly implausible to the interviewee, it is regarded as a deep interpretation.

Most investigations find that the greater the depth of the interpretation, the greater the likelihood that the interpretation will not be accepted by the client. Yet the relationship is not linear. Thus, deep interpretations evoke resistance. But the least resistance is evoked not by the most shallow interpretations, but by those that are moderate in depth.

These findings would imply that the interviewer whose goals are furthered by interpretive remarks needs to avoid those of excessive depth. If interpretive remarks are excessively distant from the interviewee's awareness, and seem implausible, they will be resisted by him/her. Just as important, however, is the view taken by many therapists that the interviewer should go a little beyond the present level of awareness of the interviewee in his/her interpretations rather than limit himself/herself to the simple restatement of that which the interviewee already knows.

The third stylistic dimension dealt with in the present chapter is that of activity level. Significant research findings relate chiefly to activity level, defined as gross productivity. Moreover, studies have focused equally on both interviewee and interviewer activity level rather than on that of interviewer alone, as in the case of the other variables of style considered in the present chapter.

In several investigations, interviewees have expressed a preference for interviews in which the therapist was relatively active over others in which s(he) was passive. In general, patients prefer psychotherapy sessions in which the therapist speaks more frequently and at greater length over those in which his/her speech is sparse. It has been assumed that patients find the more highly active therapists more reinforcing than the passive ones. There is some additonal evidence that active therapists are regarded as warmer and more empathic than their passive counterparts.

Since interviewees feel more positively about active interviewers, it may well be asked why interviewers tend to pull back from a high level of activity. In part this reticence may be due to value preferences deriving from both the client-centered and psychoanalytic schools of therapy. The former regard high interviewer activity as akin to directiveness and reject it on this basis; the latter view it as a form of interviewer behavior that reduces the projective character of the interview. When the interviewer is verbose, s(he) impedes the interviewee from communicating his/her associations as they occur, thus depriving the interviewer of a rich source of clinical information, and the interviewee of an experience in self-discovery.

As noted above, many investigators report findings in which interviewees express a preference for active rather than passive interviewers. But research studies do not provide a blanket endorsement of high interviewer activity level in all situations and in all types of interviews. A number of investigations, carried out as experimental analogues of the initial interview, discovered what has come to be known as a synchronous relationship between interviewer and interviewee activity level. In segments of the interview in which duration of interviewer utterances increase, duration of interviewee remarks do likewise. When interviewer utterances decrease in duration, those of the interviewee follow suit.

But synchrony does not always occur. The same authors who found synchrony between interviewee and interviewer activity level in experimental analogues, failed to find it in several psychotherapy series of interviews. In fact, in the psychotherapeutic situation an inverse relationship occurred. When the output of the patient increased, that of the therapist decreased; when the output of the patient decreased, that of the therapist increased.

What guidance do such varying findings provide the interviewer? To begin with, it is clear that the occurrence of synchrony will depend on situational factors, such as the type of interview conducted and, indeed, the character of the relationship. The latter was evident in a study in which synchrony occurred in an interview exchange between two equals, but failed to appear when there was a considerable status difference between interviewer and interviewee.

The occurrence of synchrony between the activity level (i.e., verbal productivity) of both members of a dyad in some situations and its absence in others, provides the interviewer with cues regarding the appropriate use of high and low activity. In a first encounter with an interviewee, when a prominent goal is the maintenance of a high level of productivity from the latter, the interviewer often finds that s(he) cannot allow his/her own activity to lag. If it does, that of the interviewee does too. To avoid a protracted drop in interviewee productivity, the interviewer becomes more active, prompting a similar increase in activity from the interviewee. In interviews of this kind the interviewer maintains the productivity of the interviewee through sustaining his/her own.

But the situation is quite different in a viable, continuing therapy relationship. The therapist may find that the relationship with the client and the momentum of the therapeutic task are enough to support patient productivity over significant periods of time. When this happens, the therapist is generally content to remain attentively silent. Only when the patient's communication runs down is the therapist likely to activate himself/herself, and thus begin the cycle again. In such a case, the balance between therapist and patient activity level may take on an inverse pattern.

What message is there in these findings for a novice interviewer regarding the most desirable activity level to follow? Clearly, the answer will depend on the kind of interview being conducted, the level of activity of the interviewee and, indeed, the character of the relationship that exists between the two participants. Thus, what one could tell the interviewer is riddled with contingencies. But s(he) can depend on one basic principle: to activitate the interviewee's verbal productivity one's own must be elevated.

When the interviewer makes a decision about verbal productivity level at which to speak, s(he) quickly encounters the need to make related choices regarding other stylistic dimensions. Should s(he) decide to raise the activity level of his/her utterances, s(he) may then be compelled to choose between directive or nondirective comments, interpretive or exploratory ones, and finally in the present chapter, specific or ambiguous remarks. The dominant value system among clinicians appears to favor the open-ended interview - that is, the one in which the interviewer's remarks are ambiguous rather than specific. At issue, at this time is ambiguity as it applies to verbal messages, and not as it might pertain to the relationship between the two members of the dyad, or to other aspects of the interview situation.

The necessity of choosing between ambiguous and specific inputs burdens the interviewer at almost any point in the interview. For example, s(he) might open an intake interview on the admission service of a psychiatric hospital by simply asking the patient: "What brings you here?" Alternatively, s(he) could begin with the following comment: "I have spoken to your doctor who tells me you've been depressed. How long have you felt this way?" The ambiguity of the first question may give the patient pause, but will also leave him/her more options for responses than are left by the second question. In reply to the first question an oppositional patient, or a schizophrenic one, might say, "I was brought here by a taxi." The former may be deliberately avoidant of the content requested by the interviewer; the latter may be derailed by the word "brought" because s(he) has a tenuous hold on the conceptual framework within which the interviewer speaks. A third patient could give the doctor considerable detail about the experiences leading up to the hospital admission. Such varied responses were permitted by the ambiguity of the question. An ambiguous question or comment is considered to have low informational value because it imposes few limits on the alternative responses that may be made to it. The second question is, of course, quite different. It leaves very few options to the interviewee. A specific question or comment is regarded as possessing high informational value because it imposes strict limits on the alternative replies that might be made to it.

How should the beginning interviewer be advised to proceed with reference to the ambiguity-specificity dimension of style? The research findings are quite uniform in pointing to a positive association between interviewer ambiguity and interviewee productivity. Thus, in most instances, the question: "What brings you here?" will be followed by longer replies than: "How long have you felt this way?" The principle that operates is that of a reciprocal relationship between the information provided by each participant. An ambiguous question from the interviewer (a low informational input) will usually elicit a productive response from the interviewee (a high informational input). On the other hand, a specific question will elicit a brief response from the interviewee.

The following are two instances of situations in which interviewee ambiguity is frequently effective. The first pertains to interview segments in which the interviewee maintains a flow of productive speech. In this circumstance the interviewer ensures the continuation of the flow of communication by the use of high ambiguity (low specificity) remarks. A second occurs at the beginning of the interview or at a later point when the interviewer wishes to open up a new area of communication, and is interested in both the content that the interviewee chooses to present and the associational sequence of the interviewee's reply. Thus, the above doctor conducting the intake interview, might have learned that the patient was either resistive or schizophrenic if the reply indeed was, "I came by taxi." He might have learned a good deal more if a cooperative (or more rational) patient spoke at some length about the death of a parent and a falling out with a spouse as events that preceded the depressive breakdown. It is clear that the highly specific question quoted above could not in itself have produced the same quantity and variety of information.

But there are limits to the usefulness of the ambiguous question. The inverse relationship described above (reminiscent of a similar inverse relationship for activity level in certain types of interview situations) is obtained as long as the flow of interviewee communication is maintained. If it falters - if long periods of silence threaten the communication system of the interview - the interviewer must "prime the pump" by more specific questions, just as s(he) did above, by elevating his/her activity level. If the interviewer is successful, the cycle begins again and a return to more ambiguous questions and remarks is presently possible.

A second limitation on the use of the ambiguous question is its frequent failure to elicit specific content desired by the interviewer. In such an event the interviewer's ambiguous leads may have to be followed by more specific follow-ups to produce the precise information required. Thus, a patient might reply to the first question quoted above by saying rather vaguely, that there had been a falling out with some members of the family. Continuing ambiguously, the therapist would say, "Go on," to which the patient would add that there had been much conflict over several months. To complete the inquiry, the therapist may need to narrow the focus considerably by asking, in specific terms: "With whom has this conflict occurred?"

A final and rather potent limitation on the usefulness of ambiguous questions may be the patient's refusal to respond to them. Such refusal is often a consequence of the uncertainty imposed on the interviewee by an ambiguous question and, indeed, the anxiety associated with it. The research that has so consistently demonstrated the positive relationship between interviewer ambiguity and interviewee productivity has also shown a similar positive association between interviewer ambiguity and interviewee hesitation in speech (filled and silent pauses). Hesitation, in the form of the above paralinguistic indices, is assumed to be indicative of cognitive uncertainty. The interviewee is uncertain about what to say next, either because s(he) has not been given specific instructions about how to proceed, or because s(he) cannot choose, for whatever reason, which of the available options to communicate.

Some investigators have drawn a line between cognitive uncertainty and anxiety, recognizing the former as a consequence of interviewer ambiguity, but not the latter. This position is taken because these investigators have found that ambiguity is followed by verbal expressions of hesitation (Ah and silent pauses) but not by expressions of anxiety (speech disturbances). This separation of uncertainty and anxiety has not been found by several other investigators. Whatever the ultimate resolution of this inconsistency in research results, it seems reasonable at the moment to assume that both uncertainty and anxiety do occur when an interviewee is asked to speak but given few guidelines for response. And some interviewees are not able to tolerate both the uncertainty and the anxiety that they experience in such situations. Clearly, as a clinician, the interviewer has the task of sensing the tolerance of the interviewee for ambiguity and adapting the ambiguity-specificity of his/her remarks and questions to what s(he) perceives.

REFERENCES

Abramowitz, C.V., Abramowitz, S.I., Roback, H.B., & Jackson, C. Differential effectiveness of directive and non-directive group therapies as a function of client internal-external control. Journal of Consulting and Clinical Psychology, 1974, 42, 849-853.

Adams, H.E., Butler, J.R., & Noblin, C.D. Effects of psychoanalytically derived interpretations: A verbal conditioning paradign. Psychological Reports, 1962, 10, 691-694.

Adams, H.E., Noblin, C.D., Butler, J.R., & Timmons, E.O. The differential effect of psychoanalytically-derived interpretations and verbal conditioning in schizophrenics. Psychological Reports, 1962, 11, 195-198.

Anderson, C.W. The relation between speaking times and decision in the employment interview. Journal of Applied Psychology, 1960, 44, 217-268.

Apfelbaum, B. Dimensions of transference in psychotherapy. Berkeley, Calif.: University of California, 1958.

Ashby, J.D., Ford, O.H., Guerney, B.F., Jr., & Guerney, L.F. Effects on clients of reflective and a leading type of psychotherapy. Psychological Monographs, 1957, 71 (24 Whole No. 453).

Auld, F., & White, A.M. Sequential dependencies in psychotherapy. Journal of Abnormal and Social Psychology, 1959, 58, 100-104.

Berdie, R.F. A program of counseling interview research. Educational and Psychological Measurement, 1958, 18, 255-274.

Bergman, D.V. The relationship between counseling method and client self exploration. Unpublished master's thesis, University of Chicago, 1950.

Bernstein, A. The psychoanalytic technique. In Benjamin B. Wolman (Ed.), Handbook of clinical psychology. New York: McGraw-Hill, 1965. Pp. 1168-1199.

Bernstein, L., Bernstein, R.S., & Dana, R.H. Interviewing: A guide for health professionals. New York: Appleton-Century-Crofts, 1974.

Bohn, M.J. Therapist responses to hostility and dependency as a function of training. Journal of Consulting Psychology, 1967, 31, 195-198.

Boomer, D.S. Speech disturbance and body movement in interviews. The Journal of Nervous and Mental Disease, 1963, 136, 263-266.

Boomer, D.S. Hesitation and grammatical encoding. In S. Moscovici (Ed.), The psychosociology of language. Chicago: Markham, 1972.

Bordin, E.S. Ambiguity as a therapeutic variable. Journal of Consulting Psychology, 1955, 19, 9-15.

Brenner, M.S., Feldstein, S., & Jaffe, J. The contributions of statistical uncertainty and test anxiety to speech disruption. Journal of Verbal Learning and Verbal Behavior, 1965, 4, 300-305.

Clore, G.L., Wiggins, N.H., & Itkin, S. Judging attraction from nonverbal behavior: The gain phenomenon. Journal of Consulting and Clinical Psychology, 1975, 43, 491-497.

Collier, R.M. A scale for rating the responses of the psychotherapist, Journal of Consulting Psychology, 1953, 17, 321-326.

Dibner, A.S. The relationship between ambiguity and anxiety in a clinical interview. Unpublished dissertation, University of Michigan, 1953.

Dittman, A.T. Kinesic research and therapeutic process: Further discussion. In Peter H. Knapp (Ed.), Expression of the emotions in man. New York: International Universities Press, 1963. Pp. 140-160.

Dollard, J. & Auld, F., Jr. Scoring human motives: A manual. New Haven, Conn.: Yale University Press, 1959.

Fenichel, O. Problems of psychoanalytic technique. Psychoanalytic Quarterly, 1941 (Albany, New York).

Fiedler, F.E. The concept of an ideal therapeutic relationship. Journal of Consulting Psychology, 1950a, 14, 239-245.

Fiedler, F.E. A comparison of therapeutic relationships in psychoanalytic, nondirective, and Adlerian therapy. Journal of Consulting Psychology, 1950b, 14, 435-436.

Fiedler, F. Factor analyses of psychoanalytic, nondirective, and Adlerian therapeutic relationships. Journal of Consulting Psychology, 1951, 15, 37-38.

Finesinger, J.E. Psychiatric interviewing: Principles and procedure in insight therapy. American Journal of Psychiatry, 1948, 105, 187-195.

Fisher, S. Plausibility and depth of interpretation. Journal of Consulting Psychology, 1956, 20, 249-256.

Frank, G.H., & Sweetland, A. A study of the process of psychotherapy: The verbal interaction. In A.P. Goldstein & S.J. Dean (Eds.), The investigation of psychotherapists: Commentaries and readings. New York: Wiley, 1966.

Frank, J.D. The role of influence in psychotherapy. In M.I. Stein (Ed.), Contemporary psychotherapists. New York: The Free Press of Glencoe, 1961.

Friedman, M.L., & Dies, R.R. Reactions of Internal and External Test-Anxious students to counseling and behavior therapies. Journal of Consulting and Clinical Psychology, 1974, 42, p. 921.

Garduk, E.L., & Haggard, E.A. The immediate effects on patients of psychoanalytic interpretations. Psychological Issues. 1972, 7, No. 4 (Monograph 28).

Goldman-Eisler, F. A comparative study of two hesitation phenomena. In S. Moscovici (Ed.), The psychosociology of language. Chicago: Markham, 1972.

Gordon, J.E. Leading and following psychotherapeutic techniques with hypnotically induced repression and hostility. Journal of Abnormal and Social Psychology, 1957, 54, 405-410.

Harway, N.I., Dittman, A.T., Raush, H.L., Bordin, E.S., & Rigler, D. The measurement of depth of interpretation. Journal of Consulting Psychology, 1955, 19, 247-253.

Heller, K., Davis, J.D., & Myers, R. A. The effects of interviewer style in a standardized interview. Journal of Consulting Psychology, 1966, 30, 501-508.

Heller, K., Myers, R.A., & Kline, L.V. Interviewer behavior as a function of standardized client roles. Journal of Consulting Psychology, 1963, 27, 117-122.

Howe, E.S., & Pope, B. An empirical scale of therapist verbal activity level in the initial interview. Journal of Consulting Psychology, 1961a, 25, 510-520.

Howe, E.S., & Pope, B. The dimensionality of ratings of therapist verbal responses. Journal of Consulting Psychology, 1961b, 25, 296-303.

Howe, E.S., & Pope, B. Therapist verbal activity level and diagnostic utility of patient verbal responses. Journal of Consulting Psychology, 1962, 26, 149-155.

Ivey, A.E. Microcounseling. Springfield, Ill.: Thomas, 1971.

Kanfer, F.H., Phillips, J.S., Matarazzo, J.D., & Saslow, G. Experimental modification of interviewer content in standardized interviews. Journal of Consulting Psychology, 1960, 24, 528-536.

Kiesler, D.J. The process of psychotherapy. Chicago: Aldine, 1973.

Leary, T. Interpersonal diagnosis of personality. New York: Ronald Press, 1957.

Lennard, H.L., & Bernstein, A. The anatomy of psychotherapy. New York: Columbia University Press, 1960.

Lindsley, O.R. Direct behavioral analysis of psychotherapy sessions by conjugately programmed closed-circuit television. Psychotherapy: Theory, Research and Practice, 1969, 6, 71-81.

Lorr, M. Client perceptions of therapists. Journal of Consulting Psychology, 1965, 29, 146-149.

Lorr, M., & McNair, D.M. Methods relating to evaluation of therapeutic outcome. In L.A. Gottschalk & A.A. Auerbach (Eds.), Methods of research in psychotherapy. New York: Appleton-Century-Crofts, 1966. Pp. 573-594.

Maclay, H., & Osgood, C.E. Hesitation phenomena in spontaneous English speech. Word, 1959, 15, 19-44.

Mahl, G.F. Disturbances and silences in patient's speech in psychotherapy. Journal of Abnormal and Social Psychology, 1956, 53, 1-15.

Mahl, G.F. The lexical and linguistic levels in the expression of the emotions. In Peter H. Knapp (Ed.), Expression of the emotions in man. New York: International Universities Press, 1963. Pp. 77-105.

Mahl, G.F. Gestures and body movements in interviews. In J.M. Shlien (Ed.), Research in psychotherapy. Washington, D.C.: American Psychological Association, 1968.

Matarazzo, J.D. The interview. In Benjamin B. Wolman (Ed.), Handbook of clinical psychology. New York: McGraw-Hill, 1965. 403-450.

Matarazzo, J.D. Wiens, A.N., Matarazzo, R.G., & Saslow, G. Speech and silence behavior in clinical psychotherapy and its laboratory correlates. In J.M. Shlien (Ed.), Research in psychotherapy, Washington, D.C.: American Psychological Association, 1968.

McCarron, L.T., & Appel, V.H. Categories of therapist verbalizations and patient-therapist autonomic response. In Psychotherapy 1971, An Aldine Annual. Chicago: Aldine Atherton, 1972.

Mintz, J., Luborsky, L., & Auerbach, A.H. Dimensions of psychotherapy: A factor analytic study of ratings of psychotherapy sessions. Journal of Consulting and Clinical Psychology, 1971, 36, 106-120.

Murray, E.J. A content analysis method for studying psychotherapy. In D.J. Kiesler (Ed.), The process of psychotherapy. Chicago: Aldine, 1973.

Nemiah, J.C. Foundations of psychopathology. New York: Oxford University Press, 1961.

Noblin, C.D., Timmons, E.O., & Reynard, M.C. Psychoanalytic interpretations as verbal reinforcers: importance of interpretation content. In A.P. Goldstein & S.J. Dean (Eds.), The investigation of psychotherapy. New York: Wiley, 1966. Pp. 416-418.

Orlinsky, D.E., & Howard, K.I. The good therapy hour: Experiential correlates of patients' and therapists' evaluations of therapy sessions. Archives of General Psychiatry, 1967, 16, 621-632.

Osgood, C.E., Suci, G.J., & Tannenbaum, P.H. The measurement of meaning. Urbana: University of Illinois Press, 1957.

Parker, G.V.C. Some concomitants of therapist dominance in the psychotherapy interview. Journal of Consulting Psychology, 1967, 31, 313-318.

Pope, B., Blass, T., Cheek, J., Siegman, A.W., & Bradford, N.H. Interviewer specificity in seminaturalistic interviews. Journal of Consulting and Clinical Psychology, 1971, 36, p. 152.

Pope, B., Nudler, S., VonKorff, M.R., & McGee, J.P. The experienced professional interviewer versus the complete novice. Journal of Consulting and Clinical Psychology, 1974, 42, 680-690.

Pope, B., & Siegman, A.W. The effect of therapist verbal activity level and specificity on patient productivity and speech disturbance in the initial interview. Journal of Consulting Psychology, 1962, 26, 489.

Pope, B., & Siegman, A.W. Interviewer specificity and topical focus in relation to interviewee productivity. Journal of Verbal Learning and Verbal Behavior, 1965, 4, 188-192.

Pope, B., & Siegman, A.W. Interviewer warmth in relation to interviewee verbal behavior. Journal of Consulting and Clinical Psychology, 1968, 32, 588-595.

Porter, E.H. Jr. The development and evaluation of a measure of counseling interview procedures. Education and Psychological Measurement, 1943, 3, 105-126, 215-238.

Raush, H.L., Sperber, Z., Rigler, D., Williams, J., Harway, N.I., Bordin, E.S., Dittman, A.T., & Hays, W.L. A dimensional analysis of depth of interpretation. Journal of Consulting Psychology, 1956, 20, 43-48.

Rice, D.G., Fey, W.F., & Kepecs, J.G. Therapist experience and "style" as factors in co-therapy. Family Process, 1972, 11, 1-12.

Rice, D.G., Gurman, A.S., & Razin, A.M.   Therapist sex, "style", and theoretical orientation. Journal of Nervous and Mental Diseases, 1974, 159, 413-421.

Rogers, C.R.   Counseling and psychotherapy.   Boston: Houghton Mifflin, 1942.

Rotter, J.B.   Generalized expectancies for internal versus external control of performance. Psychological Monographs, 1966, 80 (Whole No. 609).

Seeman, J.   The case of Jim.   Nashville: American Guidance Service, 1957.

Shaffer, L.F., & Shoben, E.J.   Common aspects of psychotherapy.   In B.G. Berenson & R.R. Carkhuff (Eds.), Sources of gain in counseling and psychotherapy.   New York: Holt, Rinehart and Winston, 1967.

Shostrom, E.L.   Three approaches to   psychotherapy.   Santa Anna: Psychological Films, 1966.

Shorstrom, E.L., & Riley, C., M.D.   Parametric analysis of psychotherapy. Journal of Consulting and Clinical Psychology, 1968, 32, 628-632.

Siegman, A.W. & Pope, B.   An empirical scale for the measurement of therapist specificity in the initial psychiatric interview. Psychol. Rep., 1962, 11, 515-520.

Siegman, A.W., & Pope, B.   Effects of question specificity and anxiety arousing messages on verbal fluency in the initial interview. Journal of Personality and Social Psychology, 1965, 4, 188-192.

Siegman, A.W., & Pope, B.   The effect of interviewee ambiguity-specificity and topical focus on interviewee vocabulary diversity. Language and Speech, 1966, 9, 242-249.

Siegman, A.W. & Pope, B.   The effects of ambiguity and anxiety on interviewee verbal behavior. In A.W. Siegman & B. Pope (Eds.), Studies in dyadic communication. New York: Pergamon Press, 1972.

Snyder, W.U.   An investigation of the nature of nondirective psychotherapy. Journal of General Psychology, 1945, 33, 193-223.

Speisman, J.C.   Depth of interpretation and verbal resistance in psychotherapy. Journal of Consulting Psychology, 1959, 23, 93-99.

Strupp, H.H.   The psychotherapist's contribution to the treatment process. Behavioral Science, 1958, 3, 34-67.

Strupp, H.H. Psychotherapists in action. New York: Grune & Stratton, 1960.

Sullivan, H.S.   The psychiatric interview. New York: Norton, 1954.

Sundland, D.M., & Barker, E.M.   The orientation of psychotherapists. Journal of Consulting Psychology, 1962, 26, 201-212.

Tourney, G., Bloom, V., Lowinger, P.L., Schorer, C., Auld, F., & Grisell, J.   A study of psychotherapeutic process variables in psychoneurotic and schizophrenic patients. American Journal of Psychotherapy, 1966, 20, 112-124.

Truax, C.B.   Length of therapist response, accurate empathy, and patient improvement. Journal of Clinical Psychology, 1970, 26, 539-541.

Wiener, M.   The effects of two experimental counseling techniques on performances impaired by induced stress. The Journal of Abnormal and Social Psychology, 1955, 51, 565-572.

Will, O.A., & Cohen, R.A.   A report of a recorded interview in the course of psychotherapy. Psychiatry, 1953, 16, 263-282.

5 Expressive Communication in the Interview

In defining style in communication at the beginning of Chapter 4 reference was made to its expressive attributes. Expressiveness in communication performs a discharge function; it reduces the level of tension or emotion in the organism. It was noted, however, that discharge of emotion or tension does not occur independently of the communication of emotion to others. Angry speech may, in time, reduce the anger of the person speaking. But the person being addressed hears the anger and is influenced by it. If the anger is directed toward the addressee, the latter may recoil with anxiety and fall silent. Or s(he) may reciprocate the anger and presently there may be an altercation. In either case, the addressee has been influenced by the expression of anger and has responded to it. The exchange indicates that there usually is no discharge of emotion without some instrumental consequences.

The research reviewed in Chapter 5 will indicate that the release of psychological tensions is only one of the functions of expressiveness in interview communication. Others include the display and communication of emotion, the eliciting of resonant emotional responses from the other participant in the interview, and other effects on its course.

GENERAL EXPRESSIVENESS

Later in the chapter studies dealing with the communication of specific emotions will be reviewed. First, however, there will be a summary of the results of research dealing with general aspects of expressiveness in the interview. Such expressiveness may occur in both linguistic and paralinguistic components of speech, but possibly more in the latter than the former. It may also occur in other aspects of nonverbal communication.

Expressiveness in language will first be examined in an excerpt from a mental health interview and then in a number of research investigations. The interview was conducted with a hospitalized psychotic patient, whose silence

184

and unresponsiveness posed a frustrating challenge to the interviewer. In an attempt to evoke some response from him the therapist unleashed a burst of feeling expressing his personal frustration and empathy with the hopelessness felt by the patient.

T: I was just thinking, I'd be responding so differently to you.

C: What do you mean? I don't know what you mean.

T: Well, that I'd wade into the ...messiness of it, the scariness of it. I'd wade right smack into the center of it... I'd say things like, Well, of course you're thinking of committing suicide; what the hell do you have to live for? Really!... You're flunking out of school... holed up in some you know...holed up on X street.... What friends do you have? You don't think anybody likes you - you cordially hate them.

C: Why not kill myself, right?

T: No, I - no, I'm not saying that, but I'm saying it, it makes sense to me that you would think that way... I'm not suggesting that you kill yourself, but, of course you've suggested it to yourself, you know how many times during the past several weeks? (Pause - C. doesn't answer).

T: Hmm?

C: (almost inaudible) Oh... on some days, not too....

(Seeman, 1965, p. 1221)

The interview went on in this vein with an eventual response from the client. In this example there is no record of paralinguistic and nonverbal elements in the interviewer's expressive communication. The transcript leaves us with the lexical content of the communication only and with an impression of the kind of breakdown in communication and relationship that might prompt an interviewer to speak in the above manner.

In the two studies that follow expressiveness again occurs in language only. Lennard and Bernstein (1960) gave considerable attention to the therapist's linguistic references to affect in the psychotherapeutic interview, and how they articulated with those of the patient. Basing themselves on eight psychotherapeutic dyads (four therapists with two patients each) over their first 50 sessions they found that the therapists increased the frequency with which they inquired into patient feelings as the therapy proceeded. Congruently, the patients increased the frequency with which they spoke about their feelings. When Lennard and Bernstein (1960) divided their psychotherapy protocols into three successive time intervals, they noted an increasing synchrony over each successive interval. Thus, the correlation between percentage of patient and therapist propositions dealing with affect was .23 over the first two sessions, .43 over the fifth and sixth sessions, and .70 over two sessions from the third and fourth months.

With the division of individual sessions into three 15-minute segments, the authors found that there was an increase in communication about affect between the first and second segments, and a drop again between the second and third. The drop was probably a consequence of the tendency of communication to veer in the direction of arrangement-type talk about such matters as fees and appointment time as the end of an interview approaches. The sequential pattern within the interview was more marked for the therapist than for the patient.

Another therapy process study (Isaacs & Haggard, 1966) investigated the relationship between therapist interventions containing affective words and the meaningfulness of patient response. Therapist and patient statements were classified into those containing affect words (directly expressing joy, sadness, love, hate, loneliness), emotionally toned words (either mixtures or amalgams of affective and cognitive elements or such ambiguous emotions as worry, upset, disturbance), and nonaffective words. A meaningfulness scale for patient responses was developed by submitting patient statements to experienced therapists for rating on a five-point scale tracing a meaningfulness dimension. On relating the affect and nonaffect groups of therapist interventions to the immediate responses of patients, as scored on the meaningfulness scale, the affect group was found to be more evocative of meaningful patient response than the nonaffect group. Additionally, the similarity of the present and the preceding study regarding the interviewer-interviewee synchrony in the communication of affective words is striking. There was a rho of .80 between interviewer and interviewee overall level of affective statement across interviews in the work by Isaacs and Haggard (1966).

The two preceding studies were randomly selected and cited at this point as examples of linguistic approaches to the study of the communication of emotion in the interview. The ones that follow illustrate the possibility of both communicating emotions and receiving communications about emotions, with significant accuracy, through the use of paralinguistic and other nonverbal channels. Some implications for the interview are considered. The two studies that follow examine vocal tone as a modality for transmitting feeling, and the next two - facial expression.

As early as 1959, Davitz and Davitz (1974) demonstrated that vocal tone may, in itself, communicate recognizable emotions. Communicator Ss were asked to express 10 feelings (anger, fear, happiness, jealousy, love, nervousness, pride, sadness, satisfaction, and sympathy) vocally, by saying the alphabet. The emphasis, in the instruction to each S was on the vocal expression of feeling without reference to verbal content. Other Ss, given the task of identifying the emotion in each message, were able to do so at a level considerably in excess of chance.

But not all emotions are recognized with equal accuracy. If one listens to vocal tones associated with specific emotions, in pairs, one notes that some pairs are easier to discriminate than others. Davitz and Davitz (1959) reasoned, and indeed they found, that those pairs of emotions that were subjectively similar were harder to tell apart through vocal tone than those that were dissimilar. For example, anger and impatience were more difficult to discriminate than anger and sadness.

Evidently people can communicate feelings accurately to each other through vocal tone alone, without resorting to verbal content. The interviewer is quite aware of this. However, s(he) is equally aware, as a rule, that the level of accuracy of this type of communication of feeling is not sufficiently high to eliminate an appreciable level of error. Fortunately for the interviewer, s(he) will almost never have to interpret vocal tone by itself. Instead, s(he) will hear it in the context of words spoken as well as other nonverbal signals.

Facial expression is a silent channel for the communication or display of emotion. Thompson and Meltzer (1964) were interested in determining the degree to which "expressors" could convey specific emotions to student judges, using facial expression alone. In each instance the judges were given the task of selecting the emotion portrayed by an untrained expressor, from a list of 10 affects (happiness, love, surprise, fear, determination, disgust, contempt, suffering, anger, and bewilderment). In a significant percentage of the trials the expressors were successful in communicating the emotions intended. To be sure, some emotions were easier to express than others. Thus, the rate of success for contempt was considerably lower than that for happiness. Moreover, there were individual differences between expressors in capacity to communicate emotions. Some were consistently more accurate than others.

The transmission of affect in nonverbal communications, as these relate to the situations in which they occur, was studied by Frijda (1953, 1958) and summarized by Dittman (1973). Frijda worked with facial expression as the vehicle for the communication of feeling. He made motion picture records of the faces of two young women in response to a number of stimulus situations, such as hearing an explosion, smelling hydrogen sulfide, remembering a personally disagreeable event, receiving a slight electric shock, listening to a poem, talking thoughtfully, and many others. These films, not including the stimulus situations, were shown to Ss who were asked in each instance to identify the emotion being expressed and the situation to which the young woman on the film was responding. Most Ss described the stimulus situation as they imagined it to be, and then named an emotion that was congruent with both the situation that they envisaged and the facial expression of the young woman.

Frijda's Ss needed both the message (facial expression) and the context within which it occurred to identify the emotion transmitted. In a later study (Frijda, 1969) the focus was on the balance between facial expression and situation in the communication of emotion. "In all cases, expression was the dominant cue, especially when the expressions and situation descriptions were incompatible, but the situations were never without influence, and usually the influence was strong" (Dittman, 1973, p. 50).

Other students of nonverbal behavior have noted its role in the communication of relationship as well as affect: "Nonverbal behavior can be considered a relationship language, sensitive to, and the primary means of signaling changes in the quality of an ongoing interpersonal relationship" (Ekman & Friesen, 1968, p. 180). For example, a therapist may invite a patient to speak about his/her mother. The invitation ("Tell me more about your mother") is a verbal expression of interest immediately belied, however, by contradictory messages from the therapist, expressed through body language. No sooner does the patient begin to provide the therapist with the requested information than the latter slumps back in the chair, averts his/her gaze from the patient, yawns, and begins to scratch one hand with the other. On observing this nonverbal response, the initial impetus with which the patient began to speak is quickly extinguished. If the clinician, in this instance, were insufficiently aware of his/her own nonverbal messages, he might have attributed the deterioration of relationship in this instance to the patient's resistance rather than his/her own boredom.

Nonverbal communication as relationship language was the object of an interesting investigation by Beier (1974). More specifically, his goal was the study of the closeness of relationship between two people, as it might be reflected in body language. First, a number of couples, married for only a few weeks, were rated for relative closeness, stability, and harmony of relationship. A videotape was then made of an interview with each couple to obtain a record of the silent, nonverbal messages that passed between the two participants.

The author and his colleagues found that "nonverbal cues express a person's feelings very accurately. The happy couples would sit closer together, look more frequently into each other's eyes, would touch each other more often than themselves" (Beier, 1974, p. 55). By contrast, gestures and postures signaled the presence of a gap between the less happy couples. "They tended to cross their arms and legs, had less eye contact, and touched themselves more frequently than they touched each other" (Beier, 1974, p. 55).

The assumptions that both affect and relationship may be communicated nonverbally is supported by considerable clinical and research evidence. Both therapist and patient may be expected to respond to the expressive signals emitted nonverbally by the other. From these, each participant in the interview learns something about the emotions and relationship attitudes experienced and communicated by the other. In the ensuing investigations, originating within the client-centered orientation, the channels for expressiveness for the most part are paralinguistic. The objective of the first (Duncan, Rice, & Butler, 1968) was to determine whether patterns of paralinguistic variables might distinguish between effective and ineffective psychotherapist behavior. In the words of the authors the goal was to determine "the relationship between the therapist's designation of therapy hours as either peak or poor and his voice quality during these hours" (Duncan et al., 1968, p. 566). They had assumed that when voice quality and content were not congruent the listener gave greater credence to the former than the latter. Each of a number of experienced therapists was asked to select a peak interview from his first 20 sessions (all taped) with one patient, and a particularly poor interview from his first 20 sessions (also taped) with another patient. Thus, the basic data consisted of nine peak sessions and nine poor sessions, selected on the basis of the therapists' own criteria of excellence and inferiority. From the various paralinguistic categories outlined by Trager (1958), the following were chosen because they were considered to be particularly germane to the psychotherapy process: (1) intensity of voice including such gradations as overloud, normal, and oversoft; (2) pitch height encompassing overhigh, normal, and overlow pitches; and (3) vocal lip control (i.e., control of vocal cords) which may range from overtight to open, the latter associated with softness and warmth of tone. In addition, three types of verbal nonfluencies were used, including unfilled hesitation pauses, filled hesitation pauses (Ah), and repeats.

Through a process of factor analysis, three paralinguistics interview types emerged, the first associated with peak interviews and the remaining two, with poor hours. The peak interviews were characterized by such attributes of interviewer speech as oversoft intensity, oversoft pitch, open vocal cord control, unfilled hesitation pauses, and repeats. In this type of interview the therapist would sound "serious, warm, and relaxed. In those moments when open voice was present, the therapist would sound especially close, concerned, and warm" (Duncan et al., 1968, p. 569). Two paralinguistic patterns were associated with poor hours. In one the major characteristic was a forced overloud intensity together with overhigh pitch at some times and oversoft intensity at other times. "In this type of interview the therapist's voice would sound dull and flat, rather uninvolved. When his voice took on more energy, he would seem to be speaking for effect, editorializing" (Duncan et al., 1968, p. 569). The third pattern, also associated with poor hours, included all three nonfluencies, but predominantly filled pauses.

The authors concluded that groups of paralinguistic variables, rather than the variables taken singly, distinguish between effective and ineffective psychotherapist behavior. In addition they remarked: "It may prove highly profitable to take non-verbal behaviors of this nature into account in evaluating the reinforcement characteristics of any interpersonal interaction, whether it be social, therapeutic, or experimental" (Duncan et al., 1968, p. 570).

Finally, there is an important group of studies within the client-centered framework (Butler, Rice, & Wagstaff, 1962; Rice, 1965) that uses both linguistic and paralinguistic variables to investigate therapist and client expressiveness. The rationale of the authors is that an expressive therapist has a stimulating impact on a client, evoking a strong response from him and thus prompting him into new experiences. "The effect of a stimulating therapist is to arouse or re-arouse within the individual more associations, images, trains of thought, etc.... It seems obvious that the stimulus (therapist communication and behavior) with the greatest connotative range, with the most far-reaching reverberations within the organism, results in a maximum of satisfying experience" (Butler et al., 1962, p. 188). The authors imply that a stimulating therapist style is an important condition for therapeutic change.

In one of the studies of the present group (Rice, 1965) the author set out to develop and test a process language, both lexical and vocal, for describing therapist style. The system she designed consisted of three categories:

1. Freshness of words and combinations. Fresh, connotative words have "a metaphorical quality with high imagery, auditory and kinaesthetic as well as visual" while ordinary language consists of commonplace words and phrases.

2. Voice quality. An expressive voice manifests high energy which is controlled but not constricted. There is a wide range of pitch, emphatic and appropriate to the communication. A usual voice demonstrates a moderate level of energy and a limited pitch range. A distorted voice shows marked

pitch variation with a declamatory emphasis which connotes a speaking for effect rather than for the spontaneous expression of meaning.

3. <u>Functional level</u>. This refers to the "expressive stance" of the therapist. If it is one of inner exploring, the focus is on the client's immediate <u>inner experience</u>. If it is an <u>observing</u> stance, it prompts the therapist to join the client in "observing and analyzing the self as an object." In an <u>outside focus</u> the therapist responds to something outside the client, but from within the client's frame of reference.

The data on which the study was based consisted of taped interviews of client-therapist pairs, all selected from the files of the University of Chicago Counseling Center, a clinic with a Rogerian orientation. Advanced graduate students audited the tapes (two students for each tape) and rated therapist responses in consecutive sequences selected from equal thirds of the interview. Through a process akin to factor analysis (Butler et al., 1962), three interview types were separated out, each characterized by a different pattern of therapist expressive behavior. In Type I the therapist style was ordinary, characterized by commonplace words and phrases, a usual voice quality, and an observing functional level. Type II interviews were, again, noted for commonplace (not fresh) language and a self-observational functional level. However, their most prominent attribute was a distorted voice quality. Finally, Type III interviews were characterized by fresh, connotative language, an expressive voice quality, and a functional level of inner exploration. The third type of interview in contrast to the first and second was considered to be the most stimulating and was expected to be most evocative of positive therapeutic change. One measure of change was based on a questionnaire completed by the therapist at the termination of therapy. The other four were client measures, including a questionnaire paralleling the therapist's, a client change measure based on a Q-sort, and two MMPI-based client change measures - the Taylor Manifest Anxiety Scale and the Barron Ego Strength Scale. Type II interviews were negatively associated with successful outcome on three of the five outcome measures. By contrast, Type III interviews were positively correlated with successful outcome on three of the five outcome measures. The author concluded that "style of participation is related to. . .favorableness of case outcome" (Rice, 1965, p. 160). The expressive style of the interviewer most conducive to positive therapeutic change (i.e., Type III) was an active one, marked by fresh, connotative language, expressive voice quality, and a focus on inner exploration.

Using the same basic procedure and the same interview sources of data as Rice (1965), Butler, Rice, and Wagstaff (1962) had earlier obtained results for the client that were very much like those that Rice (1965) obtained for the therapist. Thus, the client expressiveness factor that was found to be most conducive to success in therapy was described as energetic, expressively open, and directly communicative. It will be recalled that two of the terms used to describe the expressive style of the most successful type of interviewer were "active" and "expressive voice quality." By contrast, the client's expressive style least likely to lead to a successful outcome of treatment was found to be "self-avoidant" and "nonparticipating."

Though the language used in classifying both client and therapist style is impressionistic, "the results of the analysis as viewed through the perspectives of the classification system employed, suggest that there are causal relationships between client expressiveness, therapist expressiveness, the process of psychotherapy, and the outcomes of psychotherapy" (Butler et al., 1962, p. 203). In brief, a stimulating style of expression by the therapist and an open, active, and direct style of expression by the client are both prognostic of a favorable therapeutic outcome.

In a later investigation, still maintained within the client-centered framework, Rice and Wagstaff (1967) extended their classification system for describing style of client communication (Butler et al., 1962) to include additional vocal and lexical categories. The descriptive categories that they developed for both the vocal and lexical components of their system were particularly relevant to the client-centered therapy, because the former were formulated as attributes of "self exploration in an interpersonal context" and the latter, as dimensions that are derived from a form of therapy in which both participants stay within the client's internal frame of reference.

Through a type of factor analysis (Butler et al., 1962), two contrasting client types emerged. One epitomized a "productive" therapy process and was characterized by a focused voice quality (a quality of voice that was energetic, but in which the energy is turned inward in an exploring fashion) expressed in verbal content that is directed both to an objective analysis and description of outside events, and to immediate subjective reactions with a focus on inner feelings and experiences. The other, representing the client style of expression associated with minimal progress in therapy was characterized by a limited voice quality of low energy, a narrow pitch range, and an even tempo. "The general impression one gets is that of limited involvement, of distance from what is being expressed" (Rice & Wagstaff, 1967, p. 558).

Granted the limitation of these findings to client-centered therapy, the correlation between client expressive style and outcome of therapy has certain more general implications as well. Clearly, the therapist must be attuned both to verbal content and to vocal expressiveness, because both have prognostic implications for the client's ultimate response to the treatment.

Since both therapist and client expressive style are related to therapy outcome, it may be asked whether the two have any effect on each other. Because an inexpressive client with a flat voice and a tendency to use dull, lifeless words is likely to be an unsuccessful client, the authors of one investigation (Wexler & Butler, 1976) have asked what the therapist can do to modify an inexpressive client style. In their view the "inexpressive client is problematic for he/she typically does not provide the therapist with the informational substrate that is necessary for the ongoing therapeutic enterprise. Moreover, from an interactional standpoint, his/her uninvolved style of participation tends to dampen the responsiveness of the therapist" (Wexler & Butler, 1976, p. 262).

The problem posed by Wexler and Butler (1976) was whether a highly expressive intervention by the therapist could significantly raise the expressive level of the client's response, and thus improve the therapeutic climate. Their study is based on a single psychotherapy sequence with an inexpressive client. Expressiveness for both members of the dyad was defined in both vocal and lexical terms, as proposed by Rice and Wagstaff (1967). Using pitch, range, tempo, loudness, and stress as the vocal criteria, and both activity and vividness of words as the lexical criteria, Wexler (1975) had developed a scale for the measurement of client and therapist expressiveness. The design of the research called for a therapist high expressive intervention in the eighth interview, after an unbroken sequence of interviews in which both members of the dyad had been quite inexpressive. Ratings of both client and therapist verbalizations before, during, and after the eighth interview demonstrated the effect of the therapist's intervention. The therapist was indeed more expressive in the eighth interview than in the previous ones. The effect was to produce a significant increase in the client's expressiveness in the ninth interview, an increase which was maintained at least up to the twentieth interview.

The findings suggest that a therapist's attempt to be highly expressive with an inexpressive client can produce a significant increase in client expressiveness. The fact that the client maintained his increased expressiveness in Interviews 9 and 20 despite the fact that the therapist was no longer being more expressive than the client is consistent with the idea that the client's expressiveness was intrinsically reinforcing. (Wexler & Butler, 1976, p. 264).

In the light of the present investigation, the positive correlation between therapist expressiveness and outcome of treatment (Rice, 1965) may well be mediated by the tendency of high therapist expressiveness to evoke high client expressiveness. Whether or not such mediation will be proven, there is little doubt about the beneficial effect on the course of an interview of an expressive therapist style. Some attention to the development of such a style needs to be paid in the training of clinical interviewers.

As to the possibility of improving an interviewer's sensitivity to nonverbal clues of emotion, Davitz (1966) has the following to say: "We do not know the particular aspects of training which are most effective, and we cannot define the generality of the effects produced. But we do know that practice in expressing and receiving emotional communications results in higher scores on a subsequent test of sensitivity" (p. 474). To be sure, this conclusion rests on a single study and is therefore not very securely based. But it is congruent with our knowledge of the trainability of other communication skills and, for this reason, it is credible.

As one might expect, the susceptibility of interviewers to training in sensitivity to nonverbal emotional expression is subject to limitations imposed by individual differences between them. That such differences occur to a significant degree was demonstrated by Beldoch (1964) in a study that compared the accuracy of untrained men and women students in recognizing 10 different emotions, expressed in three different nonverbal modalities. The 10 emotions were: admiration, amusement, anger, boredom, despair, disgust, fear, impatience, joy, and love. The modalities of expression were vocal tone (speakers expressed the emotions vocally, through speaking a paragraph with unrelated, neutral verbal content), abstract graphic respresentations, and short musical compositions created by musicians to express the selected emotions.   The Ss were asked to identify all 10 emotions as expressed vocally, graphically, and musically.   The accuracy with which the Ss identified the emotions in the three modalities correlated positively, demonstrating a significant level of consistency within individuals and a range of differences between them.

Moreover, the sensitivity of the individual as a receiver of the vocal communication of feeling is matched by his/her accuracy as a sender of vocal messages (Levy, 1964).   A group of Ss manifested a significant positive correlation between accuracy in identifying the 10 emotions used by Beldoch (1964), when expressed by others through vocal tone, and in expressing the same emotions themselves. It may therefore be expected that an interviewee who is sensitive in recognizing emotions expressed nonverbally by others is likely also to be a sensitive nonverbal communicator of such emotions.

Findings such as these do not diminish the role of training in the development of clinical skills.   But, inasmuch as individual differences in communication skills appear to occur before the beginning of training, the careful selection of applicants for admission to clinical training programs must include a consideration of their sensitivity in the receiving and sending of emotional messages.

It is likely that both individual differences and the consequences of training are reflected in the results of an investigation that compares the sensitivity of psychotherapists and trained dancers to facial and bodily expression of emotion (Dittman, Parloff, & Boomer, 1965).   Both groups of judges, the psychotherapists and the dancers, demonstrated the capacity to distinguish reliably between pleasant and unpleasant feeling as recorded in a silent film of a female interviewee during a psychotherapy session. The study inquired further into the relative contributions of the face and the rest of the body to the expression of feeling, and the relative sensitivity of the two groups of judges to the two modalities of nonverbal communication. "Facial cues were the easier for the judges to use, but when they were precluded judges were remarkably consistent in appraising feelings expressed in bodily cues. Yet although bodily expression yields information, the groups of judges differed in their ability to respond to it" (Dittman et al., 1965, p. 243). The dancers were more accurate in their interpretation of body cues than the psychotherapists.

One would expect dancers to be particularly perceptive of body messages because they are trained to use their bodies for communication and to observe body communication in others.   It is also possible that a naturalistic process of selection is at work; those who choose careers in dancing may be particularly sensitive to body expression before their formal training begins. By contrast, the major instrument of the psychotherapist is his/her verbal interchange with the patient.   Before the beginning of formal training, an aspiring psychotherapist may well be a person who is biased toward verbal and against body messages.   Even if such individual differences were to be associated with choice of vocation, there seems little doubt that the interviewer's responsiveness to body communication could be enhanced if his/her training were to emphasize it adequately.   At present, there is a good probability that psychotherapists as a group tend to miss significant emotional messages of their patients because they are insufficiently responsive to body cues.

Finally, a particular kind of perceptiveness of body language is deserving of some mention - the sensitivity of the interviewer to his/her own nonverbal messages. For example, an interviewer may disapprove of something that the interviewee has said, but may be particularly vigilant in his/her avoidance of expressing the disapproval. There is the probability, however, that the interviewer's linguistic silence may not be matched by a similar reticence in body language. In fact, psychoanalysts appear always to have been aware of the risk of unwittingly communicating an attitude or feeling to the patient that might derail the flow of the patient's associations, or introduce an actual expression of relationship that would block the patient's expression of transference. For these reasons, they avoid being "read" by their patients through simply placing themselves behind the couch on which the patient rests. Short of blocking the patient's perception of him/her, the interviewer must risk exposure of his/her implicit nonverbal signals to the gaze of the interviewee. If there is risk in such exposure, there is also potential benefit, in the enhanced opportunities for the interviewer to learn about the interviewee through the entire range of expressive modalities. Therefore, the student of interviewing has much to gain from training that teaches him/her to monitor his/her own nonverbal messages and to "read" those of the interviewee.

THE EXPRESSION OF SPECIFIC EMOTIONS

The extensive literature dealing with the verbal expression of specific emotions focuses on the interviewee, for the most part, rather than the interviewer. This need surprise no one since the communication of such feelings as anxiety, hostility, or depression by the patient is considered to be central to the psychotherapeutic process. By way of introduction, there will be a look at a study that ranged over three specifically designated affects - i.e., anxiety, anger, and depression in tape-recorded interviews of a patient in intensive psychotherapy (Eldred & Price, 1958). Avoiding the technical specifics of a microlinguistic analysis of their data, the research group pursued an impressionistic clinical course. After the four auditors participating in the study listened, both privately and as a group, to many psychotherapy interviews, they developed "the hypothesis that passages which communicate certain kinds of feeling states to the auditors have over-all vocalization patterns in the rest of the interview" (Eldred & Price, 1958, p. 116). The groups selected the following paralinguistic variables as the channels in which they listened for the above designated affects:

1. Alterations of pitch (overhigh pitch and overlow pitch).

2. Alterations of volume (overloudness and oversoftness).

3. Alterations of rate (overfastness and overslowness).

4. Break up (much break-up or little break-up...). (Eldred & Price, 1958, p. 116)

The last variable pertains to the disruption of the smooth flow of speech. Later in this section, similar variables will be designated as pauses and speech disruptions.

The four auditors listened to the 15 tapes as a group, following on typescripts, and characterizing interviewee passages agreed upon as expressive of specific emotions, with the above parameters. Following this impressionistic procedure, they arrived at a consensus about the paralinguistic features of three basic emotions and two additional emotional variants.

Anxiety was always marked by increased break-up (i.e., flustering) of speech. In other respects it varied over time. Sometimes, patient anxiety was associated with overhigh pitch, overloudness, and overfastness; at other times, the opposite characteristics were found. Suppressed anger had a pattern of overhigh pitch, overloudness, overfastness, and high break-up. Overt anger was similar to suppressed anger in its overhigh pitch, overloudness, and overfastness. But, unlike suppressed anger, it lacked a high level of break-up for the patient spoke fluently, without disruption. The patient's passages designated as suppressed depression were characterized by overlow pitch, oversoftness, and overslowness, associated with increased break-up. In overtly depressed passages, the patient's communication was similarly marked by overlow pitch, oversoftness, but without the increased break-up of suppressed depression. Although this study is intuitive and qualitative rather than rigorously controlled and quantitative, it presents in a vivid way some strikingly discernible paralinguistic differences between specified emotions in the patient's speech.

Anxiety

Because of its central role in personality theory and in communication, anxiety is the affect that has received most intensive scrutiny in psychotherapy research. The literature on the expression of anxiety reflects rather clearly the two basic and sometimes contending approaches to the study of affect in speech - i.e., the linguistic and the paralinguistic routes. Gottschalk and his colleagues (Gottschalk & Gleser, 1969) have pursued the former course and Mahl (1959) followed by others (Siegman & Pope, 1972), the latter.

Gottschalk and his group (Gottschalk, Winget, Gleser, & Springer, 1966) based their advocacy of the use of linguistic content for the assessment of transient feelings such as anxiety and hostility, on the following assumptions:

1. "The relative magnitude of an affect can be validly estimated from the transcript of the speech of an individual, using solely content variables" (Gottschalk et al., 1966, p. 96).

2. From verbal content alone, it is possible to assess the strength of a transient feeling. This strength varies directly as (a) the relative frequency of the verbal themes that are related to specific affects, and (b) the weight assigned to each. "Higher weights have tended to be assigned to scorable verbal statements which communicate affect that, by inference, is more likely to be strongly experienced by the speaker" (Gottschalk et al., 1966, p. 67). The more directly the statement relates the affect to the speaker, the

more intensely he is assumed to experience it. Additionally, a greater personal involvement is weighted more than a lesser one (e.g., an unmodulated statement about a feeling is given greater weight than a statement followed by its denial). An ordinal measure of the magnitude of the affect is calculated by obtaining the product of the frequency of occurrence of specified categories of verbal statements and the weights assigned to them.

The Anxiety Scale developed by Gottschalk and his colleagues for scoring transcripts of interviews and other verbal communications was based on the above assumptions. The thematic categories in the Anxiety Scale include death anxiety ("It all began when my mother died"; "How would you explain it to the child's parent if you were the one responsible for the child being drowned?"), mutilation ("She's afraid that she might hurt him"), separation, ("I was so scared I could hardly stand it when my husband put me away in the hospital"), guilt ("Please tell me when I step out of line"), shame ("They laugh at my awkwardness"), and diffuse or nonspecific anxiety ("I was lying on the beach, and suddenly, with no warning, this panic came over me").

This Anxiety Scale is a sophisticated example of the use of linguistic content in the assessment of affect.

Verbal samples to which the scale is applied "are usually obtained by asking the subject to speak for five minutes, with as little interruption as possible, about any interesting or dramatic personal life experiences.... For spoken verbal samples, the subject speaks into a tape recorder and the material is later transcribed verbatim by a secretary. The typescript is then scored by one or two trained technicians" (Gottschalk et al., 1966, p. 100).

Some of the research with the Anxiety Scale was directed toward demonstrating that when a speaker produces a verbal sample with anxiety content that s(he) is actually experiencing the feeling of anxiety - that is, that the scale is a valid measure of anxiety. In one validity study (Gottschalk & Gleser, 1969), clinical judges rated five-minute samples of taped speech for the magnitude of anxiety expressed. These tapes had been previously scored for anxiety with the Gottschalk-Gleser verbal content analysis scale. The correlation between the two anxiety scores was significantly positive, demonstrating that professional judgment led to the same assessment of anxiety in the taped speech excerpts as verbal content analysis. Additional evidence about the validity of the verbal content scale was provided by investigations in which the scale significantly discriminated between population groups known to differ in anxiety level. Thus, the scale yielded significantly higher scores for a group of hospitalized psychiatric patients than for a group of people healthy in both a medical and psychiatric sense. Finally, the above hospitalized psychiatric patients were rated on a clinical scale of anxiety by two resident physicians just prior to the time each patient gave a five-minute verbal sample. The resident physicians made their judgments about anxiety level on the basis of a clinical rating scale using motor and sensory signs of anxiety, physiological symptoms, and the direct observation of anxiety in behavior and communication. Again, this composite clinical assessment of anxiety correlated positively with the scaling of anxiety in verbal content (Gottschalk & Gleser, 1969).

In assessing the feeling expressed by an interviewee, the interviewer cannot afford to overlook any source of information. Anxiety may be read in linguistic content; it may be heard in vocal tone and other paralinguistic attributes of speech, and it may be seen in nonverbal signs. The interviewer need not be concerned about the overlap of this information, for its very redundancy reduces the uncertainty with which s(he) normally operates.

The preceding studies exemplify a linguistic approach to the study of anxiety; the ones that follow - a paralinguistic course. On the basis of clinical observation, Sullivan (1954) remarked that "much attention may profitably be paid to the telltale aspects of intonation, rate of speech, difficulty in enunciation." In this observation, Sullivan anticipated the later research emphasis on paralinguistic cues of emotion in patient speech. Thus, Mahl (1963) listed such extralinguistic variables as rate of speech and its duration as vehicles of affective expression. But the categories that were by far of greatest interest to him were those indicative of speech disturbance. (See previous reference to his Non-Ah Ratio in the discussion of therapist ambiguity.) His first Speech Disturbance Ratio included the following categories: filled pauses (i.e., Ah and allied hesitation expressions); sentence changes that interrupt the flow of speech and alter either the form or content of the utterance; superfluous repetition of one or more words; stutters; omission of parts of words, usually occurring during sentence change and repetition; sentence incompletion in which a partial sentence is left dangling without correction; tongue slips including neologisms; the transposition of a word from an appropriate to an inappropriate position in a sentence; the substitution of an unintended for an intended work; and intruding incoherent sounds. Initially, all of the above forms of speech disturbance were assumed to be indicative of anxiety (Mahl, 1956). Later, Mahl (1959) concluded that Ah and similar expressions of hesitation were not related to the expression of anxiety. Since all other categories continued to be associated with anxiety in speech, his verbal index of anxiety came to be known as the Non-Ah Ratio.

In an early study (Mahl, 1956) based on a single psychotherapy series, the therapist acting as judge divided six psychotherapy interviews into high- and low-anxiety segments. In order that his judgments might not be contaminated by the attributes of speech that were to be the dependent variables, all speech disturbances, silences, and other hesitations were removed from the typescripts. Speech disturbances, scored independently by another person, were significantly more frequent in the high- rather than the low-anxiety segments of patient speech. In a later, follow-up experimental analogue study, Kasl and Mahl (1958) assessed the speech disturbance levels of 25 experimental Ss, all male college students, during two successive interviews, the first functioning as a control for the second, which was an experimentally manipulated "anxiety" interview. Ten additional control Ss, also male college students, were given two successive control interviews. The rate of speech disturbance increased significantly during the "anxiety" interview.

One attempt to replicate Mahl's (1956) findings ended up inconclusively (Boomer & Goodrich, 1961). When the therapists of two patients divided four interviews into high- and low-anxiety segments, a positive association between speech disturbance and high-anxiety segments occurred for one patient but not for another. When independent judges similarly divided the same recorded interviews into high- and low-anxiety segments, the correlation between anxiety and speech disturbance could not be demonstrated. The association between interviewee anxiety and speech disturbance therefore occurred in only one out of four tests. Later investigations, to be reviewed below, tended to vindicate Mahl's view of the expressive role of speech disturbances.

Mahl (1963) regarded flustered speech as a stylistic or expressive variable marking the discharge of feeling. He contrasted this discharge function with certain resistive linguistic expressions such as "I don't know..." and "I can't...," and noted that speech disturbances and such verbalizations as the above were likely to occur together in an interview, but the functions of the two were not the same. The former served to reduce emotion or drive and the latter to express a conscious sort of verbal resistance. Thus, he maintained a distinction between the expressive function of paralinguistic variables and the consciously controlled, frequently defensive functions of linguistic variables.

But a close reading of the Mahl Non-Ah Ratio dispels the notion that Non-Ah is purely an expressive index. Part of it does indeed appear to channel the discharge of anxiety as affect or drive - i.e., repetition, stutter, tongue slip, and intruding incoherent sound. Other speech disturbance categories appear to play the role of censor or editorial revisionist of what has already been or is in the process of being said - i.e., sentence incompletion, omission, and sentence correction. Actually, Mahl and Schulze (1964) accepted this dual function of speech disturbances in their later work, emphasizing both the direct effect of anxiety noted in some categories of speech disturbances and the defense against the experienced anxiety noted in other categories. This distinction was given formal definition by Boomer (1963) when he divided the Mahl speech disturbance categories into articulation errors (stutter, tongue slip, incoherent sound) and editorial corrections (omission, sentence change, incompletion).

Siegman and Pope (1972) took the position that anxiety may be regarded as a drive that would tend simultaneously to activate and disrupt speech. This view seemed to encompass in a parsimonious manner a number of paralinguistic findings that might otherwise appear contradictory. Thus, Kanfer (1958, 1960) had found that verbal rate accelerates in response to shock-conditioned tones and anxiety-arousing interview topics. Basing themselves on this finding and the view of anxiety as drive in the experimental literature, Pope and Siegman (1965; Siegman & Pope, 1965) predicted that an increase in anxiety level would bring an increase in verbal output both in terms of words uttered and rate of speech. Simultaneously, the activation of competing response tendencies would result in an increase in speech disturbances. These predictions were tested in an experimental analogue study based on the initial interview already discussed in the section on therapist specificity-ambiguity (Siegman & Pope, 1965). The Ss were female nursing students, all interviewed by one of the authors, who followed a standard interview outline. Eight questions pertained to the topic of school experiences, and eight other questions, to family relationships. For the population studied, the former topic was demonstrated to be neutral in character, and the latter, moderately anxiety arousing. That anxiety did indeed function as a drive was noted in the greater productivity of the interviewee (number of words uttered), greater vocabulary diversity as measured by the Type Token Ratio (Siegman & Pope, 1966), higher speech rate and shorter reaction time associated with the anxiety-arousing rather than the neutral topic. The last two findings were only at a borderline level of significance. Simultaneous with anxiety's function as an activator of speech was its additional function as a disruptor of speech. This was noted in the higher Non-Ah Ratio occurring in interviewee speech in the anxiety-arousing rather than neutral segment of the interview.

The activation effect of anxiety was noted in another investigation by Sunshine and Horowitz (1972). Contrary to what they expected, they found that speech elicited under stress conditions was more productive and diverse than that obtained under nonstress conditions. Undergraduate college students were divided equally into "stress" and "nonstress" groups. All $\underline{Ss}$ were asked to speak ionto a tape recorder, with the $\underline{E}$ in the room, about a poem each had been given to read. The results indicated that stressed $\underline{Ss}$ (i.e., more anxious $\underline{Ss}$) spoke at greater length than nonstressed $\underline{Ss}$ and with a higher percentage of words repeated fewer than five times. The authors concluded that both the greater productivity and verbal diversity of the stressed rather than nonstressed $\underline{Ss}$ were consequences of the activation effect of anxiety.

The basic paralinguistic pattern associated with interviewee anxiety, noted above, was observed in a further study by Pope, Blass, Siegman, and Raher (1970), in which anxiety and depression in speech were investigated in a series of brief monologues taped by a number of psychosomatic patients. The daily vicissitudes of anxiety and depression in the patient sample were determined by two nurses with research training using a rating method described by Bunny and Hamburg (1963). For each of the patients, eight high- and eight low-anxiety days were selected, and eight high- and low-depression days. Several paralinguistic attributes of speech in the monologues taped on the selected days were scored and analyzed. (Note that the monologues were taped daily over an extended period of time without reference to the days selected later for the study.) The activation effect of anxiety was observed in the higher speech rate and the lower silence quotient on high-rather than low-anxiety days; its disruptive effect was evident in the higher Non-Ah Ratio on high-anxiety days.

There is further evidence for the validity of patient speech disturbance as an index of anxiety. This was provided by a study in which the skin resistance response was used as a measure of autonomic arousal and, therefore, presumably of conflict and anxiety (McCarron, 1973). The skin resistance responses of a number of patients were monitored during initial interviews which were later transcribed. The analysis of the verbatim transcripts of the interviews, with reference to points of occurrence of skin resistance responses, demonstrated that there was a higher rate of speech disturbance when the amplitude of the skin resistance response was high rather than low. Speech was therefore likely to be disrupted when autonomic arousal rose. That a rise in the skin resistance response was related to anxiety was suggested by a content analysis of patient-therapist interactions, which showed that "uncertainty about discussing a particular problem with the therapist and ambivalent, confused feelings concerning the topic being discussed were associated with high levels of skin resistance response and speech disturbance" (McCarron, 1973, p. 229). The author concluded that the training of psychotherapists should include an emphasis on the paralinguistic features of interviewee speech as possible signals of anxiety and conflict.

Further evidence for the use of speech disturbance as an index of anxiety (Smith, 1976) was found in a study with a primary focus on the effect of dyadic communiction of a form of exchange called the double bind. The double bind has long been considered an attribute of communication in families of schizophrenic patients. However, the goal of Smith (1976) was not to investigate the double bind as a cause of schizophrenia but rather to test its capacity to arouse anxiety in normal Ss. He therefore developed an experimental procedure for applying the double bind in a dyadic communication situation and measured its effect on the speech of the Ss to whom it had been applied.

The double bind is particularly relevant to the interview because it is a form of expression that is often found in the communication of a person in authority speaking to a subordinate. The following is an example of how a mother might place a son in a double bind. The son, a young man of 18, is getting ready to leave the house on a Saturday night to spend the evening with a group of friends. The mother, a divorced woman in her mid-50s, has come to depend on the presence of her son to provide her with company and to banish loneliness. On noticing the son's imminent departure she says: "Please stay home tonight. I'm not feeling well and need you." After some hesitation, the son, with exasperation, tears off his coat, throws it down on a chair, and with an angry sigh throws himself down into another chair, tight lipped and silently angry. Whereupon the mother adds: "If you feel this way, you don't need to stay home. How come you're so weak-kneed and give in to me whether you want to or not?" This complex communication from the mother is composed of contradictory messages, "Please stay!" and "Why are you so weak that you need to stay when I ask you to?" Moreover, both messages are punishing - the first because it deprives the son of his Saturday night fun and the second, because it denigrates him when he gives in to his mother's request.

Smith (1976) asked female undergraduate student volunteers to respond to taped messages designated as coming from a "mother" to a "daughter." (The female Ss were asked to put themselves in the place of the daughter.) There were four comparison groups of Ss, one that received double-bind messages on tape with the subsequent punishment of those of their responses which were judged to be wrong (the punishment was a three-second blast of white noise, and fictitious feedback from the E implying that nearly all other Ss were able to give correct responses); one with punishment but no double-bind messages; one with double-bind messages but no punishment; and a control group with neither punishment nor double-bind messages. As expected, the first group (both punishment and double-bind message) demonstrated a significantly higher Mahl Speech Disturbance ratio than the other three groups, and the last group (no punishment and no contradictory message) a significantly lower ratio than the other three groups. The remaining two groups (punishment with no contradictory messages; contradictory messages but no punishment) fell in between the first and last groups but did not differ from each other. Thus, the Ss that received both the punishment and the contradictory message of the double bind were the ones that manifested the highest levels of anxiety as expressed in their disrupted speech.

The cumulative evidence shows that the interviewer may rely on disrupted interviewee speech as a signal of anxiety. Moreover, the point of emergence of an increased rate of disrupted speech provides him/her with important information. For example, s(he) may find that a change from a neutral to an anxiety-arousing topic was the point at which speech flustering increased. Or the increase may have occurred after some remark that the interviewer made. The double bind is not the only kind of disturbing input that an interviewer can make, but it is one whose noxious effect has been demonstrated. Whatever the cause in a particular instance, the interviewer is more likely to determine what it might be if he hears the interviewee's style of expression, particularly such storm signals as a pointed increase in the flustering of speech.

The preceding studies deal with paralinguistic indices of anxiety in the speech of patients and other interviewees. Analogous studies dealing with anxiety in the speech of interviewers are considerably fewer in number. In one investigation (Pope, Nudler, VonKorff, & McGee, 1974) the major purpose was a comparison of the interviewer behavior of complete novices and experienced professionals when conducting initial interviews. Anxiety was only one of 10 variables on which the two groups of interviewers were compared. The novices were male and female sophomore students who were about to begin their training as mental health workers but who had neither experience nor training as interviewers at the time the investigation was carried out. The experienced professionals were staff psychiatrists and third-year psychiatric residents in a private psychiatric hospital, matched with the novices for sex. The interviewees were female freshman college students. Under the circumstances of the study, one would have expected the novice interviewers to be more tense and anxious than the experienced interviewers. That they were perceived by the interviewees as more tense was evident in their post-interview ratings of the interviewers. The differential perception of the two groups of interviewers by the interviewees may indeed have been based, in part, on each group's expressive style, because there was a significantly higher level of speech disturbance (Non-Ah) for the novice rather than the professional interviewers.

In a study by Russel and Snyder (1963) the behavior of the client was the independent variable, and counselor response was the dependent variable. The goal was the investigation of the relationship between client hostility and interviewer anxiety in an experimental analogue of the counseling interview. The "clients" were two male actors selected from an undergraduate course in theatre arts, and carefully trained to perform two "client" roles, one friendly, positive, and helpful, and the other, hostile and negative. The counselors were graduate students in counselor training. There were four criteria of counselor anxiety. The first two, palmar sweating and eyeblink rate, were physiological in nature and not particularly relevant to the current discussion of therapist expressiveness. However, the third and fourth were more congruent with the stylistic variables under examination in the present chapter. At the end of each interview, the "client" completed a 60-item scale rating counselor anxiety. Finally, the authors developed a composite scale containing a number of criteria for assessing verbal anxiety. Six experienced counselors listened to the taped interviews recorded by the counselor Ss and judged the verbal anxiety level of each with the use of the scale. The most frequently occurring criteria in the verbal anxiety scale were speech disturbances, such as unfinished sentences, repetition of words and phrases, stuttering, and blocking. Others were "tone of voice" variables such as poor voice quality and tremulousness. The remaining criteria included both inept interactions (interrupting, premature interpretations, unnecessary reassurance) and counselor avoidance of "client" content (changing the subject and not responding to the "client's feelings"). On three of the four criteria, hostile "client" behavior evoked greater counselor anxiety than friendly client behavior. Two of these are relevant to the present discussion. Thus, in their postinterview ratings of the counselors, the "clients" perceived greater counselor anxiety in "hostile" rather than "friendly" interviews. However, the sharpest discriminations between the two types of interviews occurred in the ratings of verbal anxiety, with the highest counselor anxiety again occurring in the "hostile" interviews.

Evidence of the occurrence of anxiety has been found in both lexical content and certain paralinguistic attributes of speech. It has also been noted in other nonverbal behaviors such as frequency of body movement. Sainsbury (1955) devised an experimental analogue of an interview to determine whether anxiety experienced during an interview might result in increased motor response. The beginning and end of the interview was emotionally neutral, but the middle was anxiety arousing. As expected, more body movement occurrered in the middle segment than in the other two.

Boomer (1963), too, provides some evidence of the relationship between anxiety and body movement. One and one-half minute speech excerpts were tape-recorded from a sequence of psychotherapy interviews with one patient. These excerpts were scored for two of Boomer's categories of speech disturbance - articulation errors (stutter, tongue slip, incoherent sound) and editorial correction (omission, sentence change, incompletion). Speech disturbances were then correlated with frequency of body movement with the result that both editorial corrections and articulation errors correlated positively, but only the former at a significiant level.

The evidence is consistent that muscle tension and resultant body movements are indicative of anxiety. Since both muscular tension and body movement are readily visible to the interviewer, they are useful and available cues of the emergence of anxiety.

Two additional studies deal with emotions that are akin to anxiety, but designated more generally as "distress" or "stress." They are included here because they deal with anhedonic or unpleasurable emotions and may therefore be grouped with anxiety although many authors might wish to make a distinction between the two.

Leventhal and Sharp (1965) demonstrated regular changes in facial indicators of emotion with increases in stress. Their study focused on the facial expression of stress by women in sequential stages of labor. "The investigation, which was conducted in an obstetric unit of a major hospital, was motivated in part by the desire to obtain empirical evidence that observable changes in the patient's facial reactions would prove to be valid indicators of stress" (Leventhal & Sharp, 1965, p. 297). The authors anticipated that as labor progressed the expectant mothers would show increasingly frequent facial signs of distress and less frequent signs of comfort. Moreover, women who were habitually anxious and tense were expected to exhibit more facial signs of stress and fewer of comfort, than low-anxious mothers.

For all Ss, the entire period of labor was divided into four successive intervals. Only cues emitted by the forehead, brows, and eyelids differentiated significantly between these intervals. Thus, there was a significant decrement in signs of comfort (e.g., smooth forehead, no ridge or depression between or over either brow, eyelids motionless with no creases in upper lid if eye closed) as delivery approached and a significant increase in signs of discomfort (e.g., horizontal or vertical depression in forehead, V formation between brows and depression over one or both brows, fluttering of upper eyelids). When the Ss were later assessed for habitual or predispositional anxiety with a scale derived from the MMPI, it turned out that high-anxiety Ss had manifested significantly fewer brow and eyelid signs of comfort and more forehead, brow, and eyelid signs of discomfort than low-anxiety Ss.

Whether one labels the emotion expressed by the faces of the Ss specifically as anxiety or, more generally, as distress, the face has expressed the negative affect rather eloquently. Since anxiety and the more general emotion of distress are frequently encountered in mental health interviews, so should their facial signs.

Both facial expression and body posture were used as sources of cues that enabled untrained judges to discriminate between stressful feeling and its cathartic release, in a study conducted by Ekman (1965). The data used consisted of time-sampled still photographs of the faces and bodies of both interviewer and interviewee in a standard interview that had been divided into stressful and cathartic segments. The judges were untrained college freshmen, asked to discriminate between photographs selected from the two segments. About the stressful segment, the judges had been told that "the Examinee became hostile and challenging, disagreeing with everything the Subject said, and continually interrupting him" (Ekman, 1965, p. 401). During the cathartic segment "the Examiner explained.... that it had been part of the research to try to provoke the Subject and study his reactions to stress. In this final period, the examiner attempted to reassure the Subject, and generally bring about a release of tension" (Ekman, 1965, p. 401).

The success of the judges in identifying the photographs of the two interactants in both the stressful and cathartic phases of the interview showed that it was possible accurately to communicate both stress and its release through the use of such nonverbal cues as body posture and facial expression. If such cues of positive and negative feeling are available to the interviewer, it is well for him/her to remember that they are also available to the interviewee. Nonverbal communication of affect may flow in both directions within a dyad.

Mehrabian (1972) used the term "tension" rather than "stress" in his integrative summary of the results of a number of studies dealing with nonverbal cues of emotion. Thus, a seated person experiencing tension is likely to hold his/her arms in a controlled, symmetrical way, pressed tightly against the body, while the body is stiffly erect, leaning neither to the right nor the left, and the legs are maintained in a vertical, closed position. The relaxed person, on the other hand, may hold his/her arms in an asymmetrical position, with the seated body in a sidewise lean, arms open, and legs positioned asymmetrically.

These cues are familiar to the clinical interviewer, and indeed to the interviewee too, for each tends to scan the other for postural signs of tension or relaxation. Indeed, each is likely to form an impression of the predominant mood or affect of the other, even before speech begins, from nonverbal cues such as those above.

Depression and Elation

If anxiety may be viewed as an activator of speech, depression may be regarded as a retarder. This view was borne out in the lower speech rate and higher silence quotient on the high rather than low depression days in the monologue study conducted by Pope, Blass, et al. (1970), to which reference had been made earlier in this chapter. The characteristics of depressive speech are seen even more clearly if communication during a depressive period is compared with speech during its clinical opposite, a manic or hypomanic episode. A group of researchers (Harway, Warren, Leibowitz, Tinling, & Iker, 1973) set out to test the assumption that a patient in a manic or hypomanic condition will manifest activation of speech in the form of an increase in the rate and amount of speech (as in Anxiety) and in a "flight of ideas" (not usually present in Anxiety).

The Es obtained speech samples from a group of hypomanic and manic patients, and a matched group of nonpsychiatric Ss. Speech samples were obtained from the patients on their admission to a psychiatric hospital and prior to discharge, and for matched time intervals in the normal control group.

The speech of the patient in contrast to the control group clearly showed the traces of pathological activation. The patients spoke more prolifically and rapidly than the controls, on admission, but decreased their verbosity and rate of speech dramatically during their treatment period. "While control Ss showed a slight, statistically insignificant increase in verbal productivity from the first to the second examination, patients revealed a marked decrease" (Harway et al., 1973, p. 447). Just prior to discharge, the treated patients were significantly less verbal than the controls. As to the "flight of ideas," a change in the verbal content of patients over the treatment period was noted. The number of different nouns they used decreased between admission and discharge. Since the number of nouns used may be taken as an index of diversity of topics discussed, the patients showed a decrease in their flight from one topic to another as their manic activation decreased. This index actually increased for the controls.

The mental health interviewer must be attuned to excessive activation of speech as a signal of either Anxiety or excitability. Speech disturbances may also occur in both conditions but has been investigated primarily as an index of anxiety.

The contrast between manic and depressive speech has been drawn in clinical terms by Vetter (1970). He refers to the manic patient "as talking rapidly and incessantly. He tends to be telegraphic in his style and the rapidity of his speech frequently produces mispronunciations. He flies from topic to topic, with little concern for his listener; many connective constructions are omitted in his speech" (p. 5). For the depressed patient "speech of any kind seems as if it were a crushing burden to bear... The patient speaks slowly, with monotony, and exhibits little variety of voice, tempo or subject matter" (p. 5).

In an earlier study by Davitz (1964), a similar contrast between low- and high-activation emotions was drawn. The low-activation affect was called "sadness" and the high-activation affect "joy." Thus, Davitz (1964) spoke in normal rather than pathological terms. But the contrasts made between "sadness" and "joy" when spelled out in paralinguistic attributes of these emotions resembled the differences found between depressive and manic conditions in the two studies reviewed above (Harway et al., 1973; Pope, Blass, et al., 1970). Davitz (1964) used a large number of paralinguistic variables. Of these, only loudness, pitch, and rate of speech will be considered here. Sad speech was rated by judges as soft, low, and slow in rate; joyous speech as loud, high, and fast. The difference between the two is apparently one of emotional activation, with the softness, even pitch, and slow rate of sadness signifying low activation, and the loudness, high pitch, and fast rate of joy, high activation.

In the three preceding studies speech has been the primary vehicle for the expression of depression and elation. In the one that follows depression is sought in nonverbal messages (Ekman & Friesen, 1968). The study is exploratory rather than definitive; it is clinical in nature, lacking in strict experimental controls, but richly productive in the information generated for subsequent verification. The data are limited to the changes in one patient, a female, admitted to a psychiatric hospital with serious depressive complaints. On the basis of viewing a silent, eight-minute film of this patient, at the point of admission and shortly before discharge, college sophomore judges attained a significant level of agreement in describing her with an adjective checklist. At the time of admission, the following adjectives were used to portray her silent, nonverbal behavior: despondent, worrying, dissatisfied, fearful, self-pitying, sensitive, unstable, complaining, disorderly, gloomy, and moody. Depression and, secondarily, anxiety are the major emotions. The picture had changed at the time of discharge, as reflected in the following adjectives: friendly, talkative, active, impulsive, immature, cheerful, cooperative, energetic, feminine, and informal. Depression had given way to behavior that could be described as moderately excitable or hypomanic. These adjectival ratings, based on nonverbal behavior in two brief, silent films of interviews, accorded well with self-ratings by the patient and ratings by the patient's doctor. In a research-oriented clinical sense, one may accept the above judgments of nonverbal emotional expression as valid.

However, Ekman and Friesen (1968) did not let the matter rest there. They proceeded to "show that specific acts (movements distinguished in terms of their visual appearance) have distinctive psychological meaning: they are systematically related to the patient's psychological functioning, occur regularly with specific verbal content themes, and communicate specific messages to observers" (Ekman, & Friesen, 1968, p. 198). The specific acts referred to above were hand gestures.

The following hand gestures and motions occurred predominantly during the depressive period at admission. The meaning of each was determined by examining the verbal content associated with it.

Hands toss. "One or two hands are thrown up to shoulder or head area space and fall or hang down" (p. 202).

The most frequent verbal theme associated with hands toss was a lack of control, a helpless inability to stop crying, to articulate, and to accept responsibility. In a secondary theme the patient expressed ambivalent feelings about other members of the family. The authors interpreted both the hand act and the related verbalizations as expressing "frustrated anger" and "desperation, aimed primarily at self."

Hand shrug rotation. "One or two hands rotate palm down to up in space" (p. 202).

Verbal expressions of uncertainty ("I mean"; "It's as if"; "I guess") and confusion ("I'm mixed up"; "Don't know") were the most frequent verbal accompaniments of the hand shrug rotation. Both the shrugging gesture and the associated verbal messages express uncertainty and confusion.

Eye cover. "Fingers or palm of one hand rub, pick or hold eye" (p. 202).

The patient would always cry as she covered her eyes, simultaneously complaining that she should not be in the hospital or denigrating herself for her aggressive impulses. Her verbal remarks, her weeping, and the covering of her eyes all appear to express depression and shame.

In the predischarge interview, when the patient's mood was moderately elevated and anxiously agitated, there were different hand gestures and movements:

Open hand reach. With the "palm up the hand reaches out laterally and out toward the interviewer" (p. 202).

This act was noted when the patient was attempting to answer a direct question or to complete an answer she was able to give only partly before blocking. During the period of blocking, there would be such expressions of uncertainty as "probably," "I mean," "I suppose." Both the verbal remark and the act were appeals to the interviewer for help.

Hand-rub hand. "Finger only or finger and palm, hand folded or partly closed or on top of each other" (p. 202).

This gesture was associated with remarks about fear of the future, conflicts and anxieties about decisions she must make, and difficulty in sitting still or staying in one place. The hand gesture appears to be part of a multichannelled expression of nervous agitation and self-administrered comfort through massage.

Microphone-wire play. The patient tosses, waves, twitches, or coils the wire.

Two verbal themes occurred during wire play - that of being "upset" and the need to be "active" or keep moving. Both the hand movements and the verbalizations are congruent, expressing a sort of agitated restlessness.

The findings, though preliminary, are provocative. The same hand gestures may not always communicate the same emotional meaning but the interviewer must learn to read such nonverbal signals within the broader context of the messages that are simultaneously being transmitted through other communication channels. What is the interviewee saying at the same time? What can one read in his face, his posture, and body lean? When the focus is on a specific feeling being expressed, the interviewer will be tuned into all channels through which the emotion is transmitted. But he may find that one happens to be more salient than the other. Thus, an anxious plea for help may be discerned in the patient's verbalizations, facial expressions, and open hand reach. However, this interviewee may give verbal expression to the plea in a muted, grudging manner. S(he) may reveal it only dimly in facial expression. But it may be brought to a dramatic focus with the open hand reach.

Anger

In contrast with the relatively extensive treatment of the expressive communication of anxiety and depression, anger will be considered only briefly. Along with anxiety, anger is regarded as an activator emotion. Thus, Dittman (1962) found more body movement in an interviewee during an angry than a depressed mood. A more focused study (Loeb, 1968) dealt with the expressive meaning of one specific hand gesture, a fist formation, and its association with angry content. This gesture was selected because of its frequent recurrence in a film of a psychotherapy session with a 27-year-old white, female patient. The hand motion under study was noted in both normal and slow speed playbacks of the film. It was defined as the gesture that emerged every time the patient closed either hand. "The hand must be empty; either the fingers must all touch the palm and the thumb must touch the fingers or the thumb must approximate the palm and the fingers must touch the thumb" (Loeb, 1968, p. 612). The method consisted of examining the verbal context in which the gesture occurred, to determine whether there was a reliable association between the verbal expression of some meaning and the fist formation. The verbal contexts in which the fist gesture occurred were direct expressions of anger ("I - keep trying my best not to - show - blow up too much for _____(her son)"); the patient's frustrated wish to contact her therapist during a period prior to a scheduled therapy session ("and I kept thinking I wanted to... I kept thinking I wanted to call you and then I thought no"); and the patient's fear that she might have killed her son (more specifically, one night she feared that she had overdosed her son with barbiturates to put him to sleep and out of the way). The content "anger" was literally evident in the first of the above three classes of verbalization and was inferred to be present in the latter two categories. By this type of contextual analysis, the author established the expressive meaning of the fist-like gesture as that of anger. Although controlled experimental evidence for the conclusion is lacking, Loeb has embellished the ordinary perceptual and associative methods of the clinical interviewer with the precision of the film recording of body motions and a rather careful content analysis of associated verbal responses.

Finally, there is a study (Milmoe, Rosenthal, Blane, Chafetz, & Wolf, 1974) that provides some indirect evidence of the communiction of anger through vocal tone. The authors suggest, but do not prove conclusively, that the persuasiveness of a doctor's recommendation to a patient is related inversely to the anger that the patient may hear in the doctor's tone of voice. The investigation was carried out on the emergency service of a large New England hospital. A number of resident physicians had occasion to refer alcoholic patients who sought help on the emergency service to the alcoholic clinic conducted by the hospital. At a later date, each of the resident physicians participated in an open-ended interview about his experiences with the patients he had referred to the alcoholism program. A segment of each interview was passed through a filter modifier, eliminating the top decibels needed to recognize the words spoken. A group of judges then rated the filtered tapes on four emotions. Only the emotion of anger was significantly correlated, in a negative direction, with the number of alcoholic patients who accepted the residents' recommendations. The authors concluded that the patients resisted the recommendations of those physicians whose vocal tone registered anger. "The relationship between an 'angry' tone of voice and lack of effectiveness with alcoholic patients who may be especially sensitized to rejection accords with clinical and anecdotal accounts of doctor-alcoholic patient encounters" (Milmoe et al., 1974, p. 120). Although the evidence is not direct, there is an implication that the patients heard the doctor's anger in his tone of voice and resisted persuasion because of what they heard.

Research on the expression of negative feelings such as anxiety, depression, and hostility will now give way to that dealing with positive affects. First there will be a review of several studies on the nonverbal communication of pleasant feeling, liking, and other positive interpersonal attitudes. This will be followed by a summary of research on the effects of therapist warmth and permissiveness on interviewee response. However, the review of studies on the Truax-Carkhuff facilitative conditions will be deferred to Chapter 8 in which therapist attributes of relationship are considered.

Pleasant Feeling

The first two investigations in this section deal with the general hedonic tone of expressed feelings - that is, their pleasantness-unpleasantness. One of these (Buck, Savin, Miller, & Caul, 1974) is a demonstration of the capacity of the face to transmit affect on a pleasant-unpleasant dimension. Both male and female college students were the Ss; some played the role of senders of emotional messages and the others, observers. Each sender was shown a number of color slides with content of varying pleasantness which s(he) first observed and then discussed, describing his/her emotional responses. Each sender then rated his/her reactions on two scales, one assessing them on a pleasant-unpleasant dimension, and the other, on a strong-weak dimension. Sender facial responses to the slides were communicated without sound to paired observers in another room through closed circuit television. Using the two scales on which the senders had rated themselves, observers rated the senders' facial expressions for pleasantness-unpleasantness and strength-weakness. The averaged correlations for both male and female sender-observer pairs were significantly positive for scaled pleasantness but not for strength of emotional response. Thus, pleasant-unpleasant emotion could be accurately transmitted through facial expression alone.

A study (Dittman, et al., 1965) reviewed earlier in this chapter is relevant at this point, because it investigated the transmission of pleasant-unpleasant feeling through facial and bodily cues. The two objectives in the study included the demonstration of the capacity of S̲s to discriminate between pleasant and unpleasant feeling transmitted nonverbally (facially and bodily) and the determination of the relative weight assigned to each of the modalities of expression by S̲s judging the feelings displayed. The stimulus material consisted of short segments of silent movie film of a woman during an interview. In one-third of the segments the woman's expression was considered by the three authors to be pleasant in face and body; in another third, her expression was considered to be unpleasant in both modalities; and in the last third her face expressed pleasant feeling and her body, unpleasant feeling.

> Pleasant facial expression consisted of smiling and laughing, the head usually up, looking directly and openly at the interviewer. Unpleasant facial expressions included frowns and drawn, tight expressions, with the head often looking down. Bodily expression is more difficult to characterize as pleasant or unpleasant. In other excerpts, relaxed posture with little movement was regarded as pleasant, and obvious muscle tension or fidgety, nervous activity as unpleasant.
> (Dittman et al., 1965, p. 240)

The segments were shown to the S̲s, who were asked to rate the affect communicated on a pleasant-unpleasant scale. As a group, the S̲s discriminated significantly and correctly between the pleasant and unpleasant expressions. All judges were influenced more by the face than the body.

In one sense the results of this study are fortunate for the interviewer. Since the face is less obstructed than the body, s(he) has readier access to the modality that provides the greater flow of emotional information. However intermittently one member of a dyad looks at another, the face of the other is easily available for visual scanning.

Liking

In the preceding study the face has demonstrated greater transparency than the body in the display of pleasant feeling. The next investigation (Mehrabian, 1968a), dealing with one person's expression of liking for another, again selects the face as the primary vehicle for communicating positive feeling, followed by vocal tone and verbal content, in the given order of importance. The author asserts that "the verbal part of a spoken message has considerably less effect on whether a listener feels liked or disliked than speaker's facial expression or tone of voice" (p. 53).

Later, Mehrabian (1968a) adds to facial expression and tone of voice other nonverbal modalities for the communication of positive feelings and attitudes of one person toward another. These include a high rate of speech, infrequent speech disturbance, a relaxed posture, and a complex of attributes of communication which he designates immediacy. Immediacy may be noted in direct rather than indirect verbal content, eye contact, physical and psychological closeness, and directness of inclination, of one person to another.

In one investigation (Mehrabian & Ferris, 1974) the facial and vocal communiction of liking were compared with each other to determine the relative clarity and strengths of each. The Ss who were asked to make judgments about the affect expressed both facially and vocally were female undergraduate students. The vocal communication of an attitude of liking or disliking toward another was recorded by two female speakers. To keep content neutral, they were asked to express positive and negative attitudes through the repetition of the single word "maybe." Facial photographs were also made of two models expressing the same contrasting interpersonal attitudes. In the experiment each taped vocal expression of a positive or negative attitude was matched with each facial expression. The Ss were given the following instructions: "You will be shown photographs of different facial expressions and at the same time you will hear a recording of the word 'maybe' spoken in different tones of voice. You are to imagine that the person you see and hear (A) is looking at and talking to another person (B). For each presentation, indicate on the scale what you think A's attitude is toward B." (Mehrabian & Ferris, 1974, p. 295). The Ss rated the attitude of the fictional communicator to the one she was addressing on a scale with "like" at the positive pole and "dislike" at the negative pole.

Both facial expression and vocal tone were effective carriers of positive and negative interpersonal attitudes. Each functioned independently for there was no interaction between them. But facial expression had a somewhat stronger effect than vocal tone. According to this study, an interviewer would receive a more informative signal about how well the interviewee liked him/her, if s(he) watched the interviewee's face rather than listened to his/her tone of voice. However, both face and voice would provide information.

Vocal tone has been studied, both in its own right and in comparison with verbal expression, as a conveyor of interpersonal attitudes (Mehrabian, 1968a). In research on vocal tone an electronic filter is used to eliminate the higher frequencies of recorded speech to the point at which words become unintelligible but vocal qualities are identifiable. Ss, asked to judge the degree of liking communicated by the filtered speech, achieve a significant level of agreement.

Mehrabian summarized some research that demonstrated the greater weight given to vocal rather than verbal communication when identifying the affect expressed in a communication. One group was asked to judge the degree of liking communicated by a verbal transcription of a message. A second group was asked to judge the vocal component of the message, and a third group - the combined vocal and verbal component. Whether the message was one of liking or disliking, it was judged to convey a higher level of emotion when the two components were presented simultaneously, and they both agreed with each other, than it did when only one component was given. But when the verbal and vocal components, presented simultaneously, disagreed, the vocal component was more influential in the identification of the emotion expressed than the verbal component. Thus, the interviewer who is greeted by a patient with the remark "I've really had a good time this week", rendered in a thin, forlorn, wistful tone, is not likely to feel that the patient has completly surmounted a depressive episode.

As noted above, the liking of one person for another is observed additionally in the immediacy or directness with which s(he) communicates with the other. "We use more distant forms of communication when the act of communicating is undesirable or uncomfortable" (Mehrabian, 1968a, p. 54). Thus a nonassertive interviewer who wishes to confront a patient with his/her repeated tardiness, may use an indirect way of conveying the point: "Sometimes, when one is dissatisfied with a situation one tries to avoid it through tardiness," rather than a more direct form, such as: "You've been late repeatedly now for a month. We'd better talk about this behavior."

Directness may be expressed physically as well as in verbal content. A person is likely to assume a position of greater distance from one s(he) dislikes rather than likes. "The more you like a person, the more time you are likely to spend looking into this eyes as you talk to him. Standing close to your partner and facing him directly (which makes eye contact easier) also indicates positive feeling" (Mehrabian, 1968a, p. 54).

To be sure, an interviewee may not be able to easily alter his/her physical distance from the interviewer because of the manner in which the interview room is arranged. But s(he) may be able to express dislike or anger by turning the body away, leaning back instead of forward, and avoiding eye contact.

The studies that follow investigate the relationship between various aspects of immediacy or directness in the communication of one person with another and the attitudes expressed. Mehrabian (1968b) asked the Ss in one study to infer the degree to which a fictional person liked or disliked them from the distance this person stood from them and from other postural cues. Additionally, he asked the same Ss to act out the distance they would stand from fictional persons whom they liked and disliked and to demonstrate other aspects of their nonverbal behavior toward these persons. In the first study the Ss expected that a person who liked them would stand close to them and would lean toward them, and one who disliked them would stand at a distance and lean away. The Ss themselves would stand close to others whom they liked. Two additional findings varied with the sex of the S. Thus, the male Ss would establish more eye contact with persons they liked than with those they disliked. The female Ss would favor those they liked with an arms open posture, which would be absent when they communicated with those they disliked.

Several authors (Argyle & Dean, 1965; Exline & Winters, 1965) have studied the communication of positive affect through the face, particularly the eyes. These authors draw a distinction between gaze and eye contact; the former is a unidirectional process in which A looks at B; the latter is mutual, in that both A and B look into each other's eyes simultaneously. They find that there is more gaze from A to B if A likes B; less gaze, if there is tension in the relationship. Hess (1965) has found that emotional arousal leads to an enlargement of the pupils, and that men tend to be attracted to woman with enlarged pupils, even though they may not be aware of the cue to which they are responding (Exline & Winters, 1965).

The above relationship between the positive feelings two members of a dyad have for each other and their willingness to look into each other's eyes is further evident in two interview experiments conducted by Exline and Winters (1965). In one the Ss, all male college students were distributed among three groups. All were given a brief baseline interview in which the E elicited information about leisure time activities. Later they were briefly interviewed again about travel interests. The two mini-interviews were open-ended and sustained by reinforcing remarks from the interviewer on a fixed schedule. In between the first and second interviews the E induced positive feeling toward him in one group, negative feeling in a second group, and neutral feeling in a third (control) group. In the positive affect group there was a small increase in duration of eye contact by the interviewee between the first and second interviews; in the negative affect group, a sizable decrease; and in the control group, no change.

In another Exline and Winters (1965) investigation each S was interviewed simultaneously by two interviewers of his/her own sex. Midway through the interview, the S was removed from the presence of the interviewers by the E, and asked to state which of the two s(he) found more likable. When the interview was resumed, both male and female Ss increased eye contact with the preferred interviewer, and decreased it with the other.

If an interviewer finds that the person s(he) is interviewing is grossly avoidant of eye contact, s(he) may well become concerned about the status of the relationship. The findings of the above studies would imply that an interviewee who avoids eye contact feels negatively about the interviewer. However, there is at least one author (Sullivan, 1954) who would take exception to this interpretation. In Sullivan's (1954) view, direct eye contact is so painful and difficult for most patients, he is prompted to advise interviewers to avoid gazing at the interviewee beyond an initial quick usual reconnaissance.

This apparent conflict between Sullivan's view and the above immediacy findings may be more apparent than real. To begin with, the Ss in the immediacy studies are students who lack the anxiety and vigilant sensitivity about being scrutinized that Sullivan's patients undoubtedly possessed. Moreover, it is evident from studies dealing with gaze and eye contact, that no two people, however sturdy, look at each other constantly during a conversational exchange. The interviewer's excessive gaze at a patient would undoubtedly "spook" him/her and arouse anxiety. On the other hand, the complete avoidance of looking by the interviewer would impair the relationship and close off a rich source of information about the immediate interaction.

That an anxious and sensitive interviewee may tolerate the gaze of an interviewer less than one who is lacking the above vulnerabilities is suggested by a study (Ellsworth & Carlsmith, 1968) that investigates the interaction between eye contact and verbal content in an interview. The findings indicate that the association between eye contact and positive feeling is mediated by the verbal context in which it occurs. "If the topic of conversation is neutral to generally positive, subjects like the interviewer more when she looks them in the eye.... But in a conversation which is indirectly but persistently critical of the subject, this relationship is reversed" (Ellsworth & Carlsmith, 1968, p. 18). There is a parallel between the interviewee who breaks off eye contact whenever s(he) feels criticized by the interviewer and the patient who feels generally vulnerable and therefore needs to avoid eye contact most of the time.

Other Positive Interpersonal Attitudes

Since both participants in an interview are likely, part of the time, to seek approval of one another, the experimental study of approval-seeking and approval-avoiding behavior (Rosenfeld, 1966) has some important implications for the manner in which each may go about the construction of a positive relationship with the other. In a study by Rosenfeld (1966) some $\underline{S}$s were instructed to seek approval from their addresser's, and others, to avoid approval. The following are some of the results of the study:

At the nonverbal level, AS (approval seeking - B.P.) subjects emitted a significantly higher percentage of smiles and a significantly lower percentage of negative head nods than did the AA (approval avoiding - B.P.) subjects.... AS men were significantly higher than AA men in percentage of positive head nods....

At the verbal level, AS subjects emitted significantly lengthier speeches and utterances than the AA subjects."

(Rosenfeld, 1966, pp. 600-601)

There is no surprise in the finding that a person who wishes to gain the approval of another, particularly when seeking to open up or maintain communication, should smile at him/her rather than frown, nod positively rather than negatively, and speak freely rather than sparingly. Yet many clinicians take the view that an interviewer must avoid the open and free expression of a positive attitude toward the interviewee. Other clinicians and researchers (Jourard, 1971; Lennard & Bernstein, 1960) have challenged this practice of interviewer austerity in self-expression and, indeed, provided data to show that interviewees respond more productively and openly when the interviewer feels free to do likewise.

Finally, there is a study (Katz, 1964) dealing with an interviewer variable which the author designates as the "understanding posture," a body configuration recognized with a high level of agreement by observers. First, a group of judges was asked to rate a number of filmed interviewers on the presence or absence of the "understanding posture." Then the films were stopped at preselected points and judges were requested to rate the interviewers on such nonverbal parameters as frequency of glances at the interviewee, frequency of smiles, head activity, and body slant toward or away from the interviewee.

Katz (1964) found that interviewer "understanding posture" was characterized by head activity signifying attending to the interviewee and body tilt toward the interviewee. To distinguish it from empathy, the author emphasizes the expression of an understanding of the interviewee's experiences as the hallmark of empathy. Empathy must therefore have a considerable lexical component. An "understanding posture" lacks the semantic specificity that one might find in an empathic statement, but it helps to create a climate of understanding within which empathy may flourish.

Research on the nonverbal communication of positive feelings has been, for the most part, experimental in nature. Yet the implications for communication in the clinical interview are evident. Nonverbal channels are utilized widely by persons with and without clinical training, as sources of information about affect and attitude.

> Untrained adults and children easily infer that they are liked or disliked from certain facial expressions, from whether (and how) someone touches them, and from a speaker's tone of voice. Other behavior, such as posture, has a more subtle effect. A listener may sense how someone feels about him from the way the person sits while talking to him, but he may have trouble identifying what his impression comes from.   (Mehrabian, 1968a, p. 53)

When a member of a dyad appears to know that the other likes or dislikes him but is unable to identify the source of his knowledge, the impression tends to be attributed to intuition. But the terrain on which intuition stands erodes steadily, as subtle, implicit channels of communication are identified and studied. Thus, much that had been regarded as intuition in clinical communication and perception is now recognized as a product of sensitization to such nonverbal channels as facial expression, tone of voice, eye contact, and a complex of body reactions grouped together in the concept of immediacy or directness. As the role of intuition recedes, there may be some loss in the sense of poetic wonder about the subtleties of dyadic communication but an undoubted gain in the capacity to enhance, through training, the interviewer's sensitivity to many signals of emotion and interpersonal attitude, that may have gone unheeded before such training.

Warmth

Personal warmth has long been lauded as a desirable trait for a mental health interviewer or therapist to have. Yet it cannot be said that there is a reliable way of distinguishing between warmth and other positive feelings toward others. In the literature dealing with the nonverbal communication of positive feelings the concepts of warmth toward and liking for another are well nigh interchangeable. Thus, smiles (Reece & Whitman, 1962), eye contact (Exline, Gray, & Schuette, 1965; Exline, & Winters, 1965); and forward lean toward the interviewee (Reece & Whitman, 1962) are frequently offered as the primary nonverbal indices of the communication of warmth. It will be recalled, however, that the same indices were used to designate the communication of liking for another.   It might be argued that the definitional distinction of warmth from other feelings is without practical significance. If it can be demonstrated that positive feelings have certain effects on the course of the interview, does it matter whether they are labeled as liking for or warmth toward one's dyadic partner?   But it is precisely at the point of definition that the difficulty occurs.   Studies pertaining to the effects of interviewer warmth have produced contradictory findings. Without a definition of warmth, there can be no certainty that interviewers behaving warmly in different studies are, in fact, behaving in the same way. If interviewers are inconsistently warm from one investigation to another, can one expect interviewee responses to be any more consistent?

Earlier definitions of warmth have not been couched in terms of specific forms of communication behavior but rather in terms of motivation and style within an interpersonal framework. In their definition of warmth Raush and Bordin (1957) speak of three components, which they designate as commitment, effort to understand, and spontaneity.   A therapist's commitment to a patient may be noted in many ways. He assigns a specified time to the patient, and an undisturbed place to meet. In addition "he commits his skills and his efforts at understanding and aiding the patient; he also commits to the patient a relationship in which the patient's needs and interests are dominant, and in which the therapist's personal demands are minimized" (Raush & Bordin, 1957, p. 360). A therapist's commitment is most poignantly evident when he is working with a seriously handicapped patient, whether the handicap be of a long-term character as in chronic schizophrenia, or of an acute but transient nature, as in acute anxiety or depression. Warmth, as commitment, may be noted in these instances in the active support and assistance that the therapist will offer.

As an aspect of warmth, the therapist's effort to understand is not independent of his commitment to the patient. Nor does it lack some overlap with the concept of empathy. However, empathy includes both process and its end result - i.e., the accuracy with which the therapist perceives the patient. In a discussion of warmth, it is only the process that is of interest - i.e., the therapist's effort to understand, which may be communicated to the patient "by attentive and unintrusive listening, by questions indicative of interest, by sounds of encouragement, by any of the verbal or nonverbal cues which say in effect, 'I am interested in what you are saying and feeling - go on'" (Raush & Bordin, 1957, p. 360).   The third ingredient of warmth (i.e., therapist spontaneity), appears to be similar to the kind of general expressiveness that Rice (1965) and her colleagues associate with positive psychotherapy outcome. Central to therapist spontaneity is his readiness to be emotionally expressive in the interview situation.   Raush and Bordin assume that "a more spontaneous therapist will... interact with more expression of affect than will a less spontaneous one" (p. 362).

In their definition of therapist warmth, Strupp, Fox, and Lessler (1969) followed a more empirical course.   Their discussion of warmth occurred within the context of a study which elicted from former patients ratings of their impressions of both the psychotherapy process and of their former therapists.   In the words of the authors "we asked the patients to speak for themselves and to assess the over-all value of their experience" (p. xv). This the patients did by indicating the degree of their agreement with a number of questionnaire statements descriptive of psychotherapy and psychotherapists as these might apply to their erstwhile therapists. Their responses were then intercorrelated and factor analyzed, with two of emerging factors of particular relevance to the present discussion. Indeed, one was designated as therapist warmth and the other as therapist interest, integrity, and respect. The two factors correlated positively with each other (r = .55) demonstrating a considerable degree of overlap. Moreover, the therapist traits associated with the two factors correlated positively and significantly with the patients' own judgments about the positive therapeutic change that they experienced.

The warm therapist was "always keenly attentive ... having a manner that patients experienced as natural and unstudied, saying or doing nothing that decreased the patient's self-respect, at times giving direct reassurance ... and leaving no doubt about his 'real' feelings" (Strupp, et al., 1969, p. 80). Although Strupp et al. followed an empirical course, the definition that emerged in their study is similar to that developed by Raush and Bordin (1957), on clinical and speculative grounds.

It would be safe to assume that there would be a broad consensus among clinicians that warmth is a positive force within the interview. Researchers, however, do not attain the same level of agreement. Several authors have found that interviewer warmth does indeed facilitate interviewee communication in the forms of gross productivity, speed of response, and verbal fluency (Allen, Wiens, Weitman, & Saslow, 1965; Pope & Siegman, 1972; Pope et al., 1974; Reece & Whitman, 1962). However, several other authors have questioned the assumption that interviewer warmth necessarily promotes meaningful communication (Ganzer & Sarason, 1964; Heller, 1972; Heller, Davis, & Myers, 1966; Sarason & Winkel, 1966).

In the Pope and Siegman (1972) research the Ss were junior and senior female nursing students with ages ranging from 20 to 22, each given two interviews, one warm and the other cold. The interviewers were two female clinical psychology interns, in their mid-20s. Each interviewer conducted both warm and cold interviews. The warm-cold manipulation was achieved by arousing contrasting warm and cold interviewee expectations regarding the interviewers before the two succeeding interviews and by varying the interviewers' behavior to accord with interviewee expectations. As predicted, warm interviews evoked a significantly higher productivity (i.e., mean number of words per response) than cold interviews. However, the warm-cold effect interacted with warm-cold sequence. Thus, the greater productivity associated with warm rather than cold interviews held only when the warm interview was the first in a sequence of two. When the cold interview was first, its inhibiting effect continued into the second (warm) interview, eliminating the productivity difference between the two. In a later study by Pope et al. (1974) in which experienced interviewers were compared with novices, interviewer warmth, as scored with the Non-Possessive Warmth Scale (Truax & Carkhuff, 1967), correlated positively with interviewee productivity (i.e., number of words spoken), but only in the interviews conducted by the novices.

A research study conducted by Reece & Whitman (1962) investigated the effect of interviewer warmth and coldness on verbal productivity when the S was asked to free associate. The authors specified interviewer warmth in terms of frequent smiling, the absence of fidgety finger tapping, considerable eye contact with the S, and forward body lean. Defined in this way, interviewer warmth was positively associated with the number of words spoken by the S.

In an earlier investigation Allen et al. (1965) had failed to obtain a positive relationship between interviewer warmth and interviewee speech duration (i.e., productivity). The method, however, was different in several respects from the procedure followed by Pope and Siegman (1972). The Ss were men applying for civil service positions as policemen or firemen who were given employment interviews. The interviewer's behavior was not included in the warm-cold manipulation. The latter was based entirely on the creation of warm and cold sets, in random order, but equally distributed among the Ss. The warm-set Ss read a paragraph descriptive of the interviewer they were to meet shortly, identical in content to the one read by the cold-set Ss, with the exception that the words "very warm" were used to characterize the interviewer rather than the words "very cold." As indicated above, there was no difference in average length of interviewee utterance as between warm and cold interviews. However, the average interviewee reaction time, between the completion of the interviewer's utterance and the beginning of the interviewee's responses, was significantly shorter for the Ss, given a warm rather than a cold set indicating a readier interviewee responsiveness. Finally, returning to the Pope and Siegman (1972) study, cold interviews elicited higher Non-Ah speech disturbance ratios from the interviewees than the warm interviews, but only in high rather than low specific segments of the interviews. Thus, under certain circumstances the warm interviews elicted greater interviewee fluency. The evidence thus far tends in the direction of greater productivity, more rapid reaction time, and greater verbal fluency in response to warm rather than cold interviewers.

For the most part, these results are not directly challenged by the research reviewed below, but the negative findings of the studies that follow do create a climate of skepticism about the earlier positive ones. The first study is clearly relevant to the interview interaction, although it was designed in a verbal conditioning format (Ganzer & Sarason, 1964). The Ss were male undergraduate students selected from an introductory psychology class. All Ss were put through an interview-like procedure in which they were told that the interviewer was interested in learning how students think and feel about themselves. One-half of the Ss was both greeted and later instructed in a hostile manner by the E; the other half was treated in a friendly way. In the interview analogue that followed all Ss were reinforced for making negative self-references. As it turned out, those who were given the hostile treatment by the E were more self-disclosing in their more frequent use of negative self-reference than those treated in a friendly manner - i.e., they demonstrated a greater amount of conditioning. One may assume that the interview analogue in the Ganzer and Sarason study resembled a verbal conditioning experiment more than an interview. Yet it is difficult to avoid the possible implications of this experiment for interviewee self-disclosure. Is it conceivable that a cold interviewer rather than a warm one is more likely to promote the self-disclosure of negative psychological information? That such may be the case was suggested by Sarason and Winkel (1966) who found that the less favorably an interviewee rated an interviewer (i.e., more hostile), the more likely he was to speak to him in a personally revealing manner.

Partly as a consequence of these findings, Heller (1972) developed the hypothesis that moderately stressful interviews were more likely to evoke more self-disclosing communication than nonstressful interviews, particularly when an interviewee's defensive style permits him to be openly communicative about personal matters.

In one of his studies (Heller et al., 1966) each of a number of male interviewers was trained to play one of four experimentally controlled roles - i.e., that of an active-friendly, passive-friendly, active-hostile, or passive-hostile interviewer. Additionally, there was a group of interviewers that remained completely silent after they gave the Ss initial instructions. The Ss (interviewees) were introductory psychology students, both male and female. The effect of therapist activity-passivity in this study has been considered at an earlier point in the present chapter. With reference to the friendly-hostile dimension, the results were unambiguous. There was a clear preference by the Ss for friendly rather than hostile interviewers. This preference was determined by asking each S to complete an inventory giving his reaction to the interview and the interviewer immediately after the completion of the experimental interview. The best-liked interviewers were the active-friendly ones; and the least liked, the passive-hostile ones. The silent interviews evoked preference scores that fell in between those for the hostile and friendly groups. However, there was no relationship between interviewer warmth and interviewee verbal behavior. Unlike Pope and Siegman (1972), Heller et al. (1966) failed to obtain a significant association between interviewer warmth and interviewee productivity (speaking time). Nor did they find any correlation between warmth and interviewee self-disclosure of pathology. The authors concluded that "there was no indication that verbal behavior during the interview changed in any way as a result of friendliness" (Heller et al., 1966, p. 506).

These findings were largely negative with reference to interviewer warmth, but they neither negated nor supported Heller's concept of the optimum, moderately stressful interview. Actually, his later work uncovered an interaction between type of interviewee and the degree of stress in an interview, as will be evident in the next three studies.

In the first, Heller and Jacobson (1967) selected male and female Ss on the basis of their high and low dependency scores on the EPPS and asked them to talk about themselves in 30-minute personal interviews. There were three interview conditions. In the friendly condition the interviewers were trained "to appear friendly, expressive, and encouraging by smiling appropriately, nodding, leaning toward the subject, and maintaining eye contact" (Heller, 1972, p. 18). In the reserved condition they did not smile, were nonexpressive, leaned away from the subject and maintained minimum eye contact. In the no-interviewer condition subjects were given initial instructions to talk about themselves, after which they were left to respond to a tape recorder, with no other person present in the room. As in previous studies, friendly interviewers were best liked by all Ss. However, the verbal responses of Ss to the different interview conditions varied with the interviewee type. High-dependent males talked about themselves most often and their problems -

i.e., they were most self-disclosing in the reserved condition. By contrast, low-dependent (i.e., independent) males talked about themselves least in the reserved condition, a finding that contradicted the anticipations of the investigators. Similarly, independent females made their fewest problem references in the reserved condition. These findings do not offer strong support for Heller's hypothesis. There was, indeed, evidence that one group of Ss was prompted most toward self-disclosure by reserved interviewers, but the investigators had incorrectly predicted the specific group of Ss that would react in this way.

The contrast between the responses of varying interviewee types to friendly and reserved interviewer styles was more emphatically evident in a later investigation (Heller, Silver, Bailey, & Dudgeon, 1968). Friendly and reserved interviewer styles were structured into single interviews so that style sequence followed a friendly-reserved-friendly (FRF) pattern in one group of interviews and a reserved-friendly-reserved (RFR) pattern in another group. There were two groups of interviewees, college students and patients, both encouraged to speak about themselves. The two groups of Ss responded to the two interviewer style sequence patterns in sharply contrasting ways. The college students were more verbally productive in the RFR sequence than in the FRF sequence, and were less disturbed than the patients by the reserved condition, when it came first. The degree to which they were able to speak in a self-disclosing manner about themselves or their problems was not affected by the changes of interviewer style within interviews. The patient group was more productive and more self-disclosing in the FRF rather than the RFR sequence. In this instance the moderate stress of a reserved interviewer style stimulated the verbal responsiveness of one group of interviewees, inhibiting that of another.

Finally, there will be a brief reference to an investigation of the effect of therapist permissiveness on a patient's galvanic skin response (Dittes, 1957). It is selected as the concluding study of the chapter because it provides an intra-organism view of the psychological effect of interviewer warmth on the interviewee.

Dittes' (1957) definition of interviewer permissiveness overlaps considerably with the Raush and Bordin (1957) concept of warmth. Thus, the permissive therapist is attentive, attempts to understand the patient, and does not intrude or force his opinions on the patient. Therapist permissiveness is characterized by the absence of critical, punishing behavior that often occurs in stressful interpersonal relationships. The typed transcript of the final 43 hours of therapy with a 36-year-old male neurotic patient was rated on a four-point permissiveness scale defined in terms of therapist understanding, gentleness, and overall acceptance. Therapist permissiveness showed a significant negative relationship with frequency of galvanic skin response. As therapist permissiveness increased within and across interviews, the patient's GSR frequency decreased and, thus, presumably his tension. Moreover, the therapist's permissiveness helped the patient to mitigate his embarrassment or anxiety whenever he communicated self-disclosing information that tended to arouse such feelings. Thus, embarrassing sex statements were accompanied by a GSR more frequently in hours that were scored low on permissiveness than in other hours scored high. The Dittes (1957) study is an intensive investigation of a single individual. It does not address itself to the kind of interactional problem raised by Heller and his colleagues. It does, however, demonstrate the psychological impact of warmth or permissiveness in one person, regardless of the ultimate view that will be taken of the interaction of this variable with different interviewee types.

APPLICATION SUMMARY

When either member of a dyad speaks expressively, one of the outcomes is likely to be the release of inner tensions. Certainly, there can be no doubt that a discharge function occurs when the interviewer or interviewee expresses such high activation emotions as anxiety, anger, or elation. Discharge occurs to a lesser extent when activation is not as decided an attribute of the emotion; for example, when one member expresses a liking for or warm feeling toward the other. However, when the emotion is inherently low active in character as in the case of depression, discharge of tension may not occur at all.

But the discharge of tension is only one of the functions of expressiveness. Others are noted in the effect of general expressiveness, or the expression of specific emotions, on the interaction between the two participants in an interview. For example, a number of studies have investigated interviewer general expressiveness as it relates to interview process. Such expressiveness is recognizable, though not easy to define. It is inadequately described by the communication of anxiety, anger, warmth, or any of the specific emotions taken singly, although all of these feelings may contribute to the overall impression of expressiveness. In the research literature general expressiveness is usually described by such characteristics of communication as colorfulness, stimulation, and reinforcing quality.

Expressiveness may occur in both linguistic and paralinguistic components of speech, but possibly more in the latter than in the former. It may also occur in nonverbal communication. But whatever the channel of communication, interviewer expressiveness is a more frequent subject of investigation than that of the interviewee, because the former is viewed as a more crucial determinant of the course of the interview than the latter. Thus, it has been demonstrated that interviewer speech that is affective in content evokes more meaningful patient response than nonaffective interviewer speech.

Several research studies had as their objective the determination of the specific attributes of interviewer expressiveness that were associated with both effective communication and positive outcome of psychotherapy. In one (Duncan et al., 1968) peak therapy hours were contrasted with poor hours conducted by the same therapists. In the former, interviewer speech was characterized by oversoft intensity, oversoft pitch, open vocal cord control, unfilled hesitation pauses, and repeats. The impression was that of a serious, warm, and relaxed voice. In another study (Rice, 1965) favorable outcome of treatment was associated with an expressive style that was active, marked by fresh, connotative language and a focus on inner exploration. The analogous style of expression of the client, also associated with successful outcome of treatment, was energetic, open, and direct. In brief, a stimulating style of expression by the therapist and an open, active, and direct style by the client are both prognostic of favorable therapeutic results. Findings such as these give the interviewer leave to be openly expressive rather than mute, or dull and retentive.

One might argue with some justification that the above expressive attributes, as indices of therapeutic success, are relevant to client-centered therapy, but not to other forms of treatment since they have been found largely in the former context. But there is a more general implication in these findings. The therapist must be attuned both to verbal content and vocal expressiveness since both have an effect on the interviewer-interviewee interaction and on the outcome of treatment.

Because the interviewer tends to be engaged primarily with the content of the interviewee's communications, s(he) may be unresponsive to the vocal tone of the interviewee. The present findings should prompt him/her to attend to vocal expressiveness as well as content. Moreover, the interviewer is not without means of elevating the interviewee's expressiveness if it tends to sag. In most instances a deliberate increase in the stimulating quality of the interviewer's speech will suffice since it has been demonstrative that a therapist can produce a significant increase in client expressiveness through increasing his/her own. The interviewer in training should be sensitized to the sounds of expressiveness in the interviewee, and rehearsed in the use of such sounds.

Unfortunately, little is known at present about the specifics of training an interviewer to speak expressively. But the provision to the student of interviewing a model and an opportunity to rehearse the style of expression that is modeled have been demonstrated to be effective, very much as they are in the coaching of an actor.

If the interviewer has been the major recipient of the researcher's attention in studies of general expressiveness, s(he) takes a second place in research on the expression of specific emotions. This is not unexpected since the communication of such feelings as anxiety, hostility, and depression by the patient is quite central to the psychotherapeutic process. Of all the specific emotions, anxiety has received the most extensive scrutiny because of its important role in personality theory and in communication. Anxiety may be read in linguistic content; it may be heard in vocal speech tone and other paralinguistic attributes of speech; and it may be noted in nonverbal messages.

When examining lexical content for traces of anxiety, one attends to references by the speaker to death, body injury, and mutilation, the insecurity associated with separation from familiar people, guilt and the anticipation of punishment, and diffuse or nonspecific anxiety (Gottschalk & Gleser, 1969). When listening for anxiety in paralinguistic aspects of speech, one learns to note points in the interview when the productivity of the speaker increases, tempo becomes faster, reaction time is reduced, and speech becomes flustered and disrupted (Pope & Siegman, 1965; Siegman & Pope, 1965). When observing the speaker for nonverbal signals of anxiety, the interviewer's attention will be arrested by sudden increases in body movement (Sainsbury, 1955), clear traces of discomfort in the face - i.e., depression in forehead, creases between the brows and fluttering of upper eyelids (Leventhal & Sharp, 1965), and certain postural rigidities, such as arms held tightly pressed against the body, body stiffly erect, and the legs maintained in a vertical, closed position (Mehrabian, 1972).

The interviewer will hear the interviewee clearly when s(he) expresses anxiety openly in the lexical content spoken. But the interviewee will often defer the direct expression of anxiety for some time after it intrudes into his/her thoughts and feelings, if indeed s(he) does not avoid it altogether. A sensitive and skilled interviewer may hear it nevertheless in the increased tempo and productivity of speech, and in the enhanced frequency of speech disturbance. S(he) may note it in the rise of body tension and activity, in the traces that it leaves in facial expression and in postural rigidities.

Anxiety and depression have contrasting effects on speech, with anxiety functioning as an activator and depression as a retarder. In contrast to anxiety, depression lowers the rate of speech and increases the frequency and duration of silence (Pope, Blass, Siegman, & Raher, 1970). The retarding effect of depression is particularly evident when one compares it with manic or excited speech. Manic patients speak rapidly and prolifically in contrast to normal controls. The rapidity of manic speech is noted not only in rate but in the quick tempo of change of content, known as "flight of ideas" (Harway et al., 1973). In each of the above three respects, the depressive patient differs markedly from the manic. The depressive labors under a crushing burden when s(he) attempts to say anything at all. Speech is slow, limited in quantity and monotonously uniform in content (Vetter, 1970). Two additional attributes of depressive speech are softness of volume and lowness of pitch. The difference between depressive speech on the one hand and manic speech on the other is mainly one of emotional activation, with the softness, low pitch, and slow rate of depression signifying low activation, and the loudness, high pitch, and fast rate of elation, high activation.

Reference has been made to verbal content and paralanguage as two channels in which marked contrasts between anxiety and elation on the one hand (activator emotions) and depression on the other (retarder emotion) have been noted. Contrasts between these emotions may also be found in other nonverbal channels. For example, very specific hand gestures have been associative with depression ("hands toss," "hand shrug rotation," and "eye cover") and others with moderate elation and anxiety ("open hand reach," "microphone wire play," "hand rub hand") (Ekman & Friesen, 1968).

When tuned into the emotion being expressed by the interviewee, the interviewer will monitor all channels of communication. At any given moment, however, one may be more salient than the others. Thus, the patient may express an anxious plea for help in what s(he) says in facial expression and through an "open hand reach" (Ekman & Friesen, 1968) gesture. The patient's verbal plea may be spoken weakly. S(he) may ask for help with somewhat more forcefulness in facial expression. But the plea may be brought to its clearest focus on the "open hand reach."

In the many investigations dealing with the expression of affect there is a bias in the direction of a more frequent focus on the interviewee when the emotions are painful and unpleasant (anxiety and depression), and on the interviewer when the emotions are hedonic, or at the least, pleasant. The reason is evident. The interviewee as patient usually seeks relief from some distress associated with painful feeling. The interviewer as therapist tends to support the patient in treatment through the expression of pleasant feeling and, more specifically, through personal warmth.

In the communication of positive feeling the various channels assume a rank order of importance very similar to that noted for unpleasant feeling. The means by which one person expresses liking for another are primarily the face, followed by vocal tone and finally by verbal content. In the words of one author "the verbal part of a spoken message has considerably less effect on whether a listener feels liked or disliked than a speaker's facial expression or tone of voice" (Mehrabian, 1968a, p. 53). Cutting across the various modalities of expression, Mehrabian and Ferris (1974) refer to immediacy or directness as the major signal sent by one person to another to express liking or affection. Immediacy may be noted in verbal content characterized by directness of expression, eye contact, physical and psychological closeness, and directness of inclination of the body of one toward the other.

The interviewer who tells his/her client that s(he) would like to hear about the latest fight between her and her oldest son, but utters this remark with a stony face and a drab, strained voice, is not likely to encourage the client to say very much about the event. The client will say even less if the interviewer gazes away from the client as s(he) makes the request, slumping back in a chair which s(he) swivels away from the client as s(he) prepares to be bored.

As indicated above, eye contact is one of the components of immediacy in the communication between two people. An interviewer who looks into the eyes of the interviewee intermittently is said to express positive feeling toward him/her. On the other hand, the interviewer who avoids eye contact altogether is said to dislike the interviewee. Yet it would be foolhardy to instruct an interviewer to follow an intermittent schedule of eye contact with all patients under all circumstances. Sullivan (1954), who worked with acutely disturbed patients, frequently diagnosed as schizophrenic, recommended against any eye contact at all beyond an initial visual reconnaissance. This rather extreme attitude may well be a consequence of the acutely anxious and vigilantly sensitive patients with whom Sullivan worked. Additionally, it is well known that one person can "spook" another, regardless of how healthy the latter may be, by gazing at him/her in a fixed, unrelenting way. The findings of the immediacy studies may be translated into guidelines for interview practice only after a careful review of all interactions between the interview variables investigated. For example, an interviewee will probably respond favorably to eye contact with an interviewer when the topic of conversation is positive to neutral. But the favorable response may turn sharply negative if the interviewer continues to maintain eye contact as s(he) begins to criticize the interviewee (Ellsworth & Carlsmith, 1968).

In the preceding section the focus has been on the means used by a person in expressing his liking for another when the two are engaged in direct communicaton with each other. It may now be asked how one participant in a dyadic situation elicits the "liking" response or the approval of the other. Stated otherwise, what signals does one person transmit to the other when s(he) seeks to construct a positive relationship with him/her? One investigator (Rosenfeld, 1966) found that a person who wishes to gain the approval of another, particularly when opening up or sustaining communication, should smile rather than frown, nod positively rather than negatively, and speak freely rather than sparingly. This model of spontaneous, open, and expressive communication does not accord with the view of interviewer style held by many clinicians, who think that their communication should be spare, austere, and minimally expressive. The style of interviewing that is chosen will depend, in part, on the theoretical orientation of the clinician. But the trend of the evidence over the last decade, showing that interviewees respond more openly when the interviewer feels free to do the same (Jourard, 1972; Lennard & Bernstein, 1960) presents a challenge to all mental health interviewers, whatever their school of allegience.

Both clinical tradition and the literature that sustains it, assumes that interviewer warmth is a stimulating force within the interaction, fostering a positive relationship and promoting a flow of productive, self-disclosing communication from the interviewee. But the research investigation of this assumption has run a troublesome and contradictory course. Part of the difficulty lies in definitional ambiguities. Thus, interviewer smiles, eye contact with, and forward lean toward the patient have all been offered as indices of warmth. Unfortunately, they have also been used as signs of liking, and perhaps more general, undifferentiated positive feelings. In an early study (Raush & Bordin, 1957) interviewer warmth was defined in terms of commitment to the patient, effort to understand the patient, and spontaneity of expression. The last attribute in the above three overlaps with general expressiveness, considered earlier. The first two involve a high level of inference and would be difficult to operationalize in an experimental study. Because of this, most investigations tend to deal with interviewer warmth as general positive feeling and liking for the patient. The difficulty of operationalizing interviewer warmth may indeed be the basic reason for the contradictory findings of different studies. In one (Pope & Siegman, 1972) consistent with traditional expectation, warm interviewers evoked significantly higher productivity (i.e., number of words spoken) than cold interviewers, while cold interviewers elicited higher speech disturbance rates (i.e., higher anxiety) than warm interviewers. Another group of researchers (Heller et al. 1966) found that friendly interviewers (assumed to be the same as warm interviewers) were those who were best liked by the interviewees. But they did not elicit more communication from the interviewees than the hostile (i.e., cold) interviewers. However, before dismissing warmth, or friendliness, or positive feeling as a desirable interviewer trait one should note that a later study by Heller and his colleagues (Heller et al., 1968) demonstrated a differential response to interviewer warmth by two contrasting groups of Ss. College students were more verbally productive, and more self-disclosing in response to interviewer reserve (i.e., coldness) than a group of hospitalized psychiatric patients. The patients, on the other hand, were more productive and more self-disclosing in response to interviewer friendliness (warmth). Moderate stress from the interviewer stimulated the responsiveness of the students, but inhibited that of the patients.

It is certain that the last word has not yet been spoken on this matter. But the message for the clinician from the Heller et al. (1968) investigation is clear. Before deciding whether to stress the interviewee into self-disclosure, or gently to encourage such self-disclosure through the expression of warm interest, the interviewer would need to form an impression of the kind of person s(he) is speaking to.

REFERENCES

Allen, B.V., Wiens, A.N., Weitman, M., & Saslow, G. Effects of warm-cold set on interviewee speech. Journal of Consulting Psychology, 1965, 29, 480-482.

Argyle, M., & Dean, J. Eye contact, distance, and affiliation. Sociometry, 1965, 28, 289-304.

Bandura, A., Lipsher, D., & Miller, P.E. Psychotherapists' approach-avoidance reactions to patients' expressions of hostility. Journal of Consulting Psychology, 1960, 24, 1-8.

Beier, E.G. Nonverbal communication. How we send emotional messages. Psychology Today, October 1974, 8, 53-56.

Beldoch, M. Sensitivity to expression of emotional meaning in three modes of communication. In J. Davitz (Ed.) The communication of emotional meaning. New York: McGraw-Hill, 1964.

Boomer, D.S. Speech disturbance and body movement in interviews. The Journal of Nervous and Mental Diseases, 1963, 136, 263-266.

Boomer, D.S., & Goodrich, D.W. Speech disturbance and judged anxiety. Journal of Consulting Psychology, 1961, 25, 160-164.

Buck, R.W., Savin, V.J., Miller, R.E., & Caul, W.F. Communication of affect through facial expressions in humans. In S. Weitz (Ed.), Nonverbal communication. New York: Oxford University Press, 1974.

Bunny, W.E., & Hamburg, D.A. Methods for reliable longitudinal observations of behavior. Archives of General Psychiatry, 1963, 9, 280-294.

Butler, J.M., Rice, L.N., & Wagstaff, A.K. On the naturalistic definition of variables: An analogue of clinical analysis. In H.H. Strupp & L. Luborsky (Eds.), Research in psychotherapy. Washington, D.C.: American Psychological Association, 1962. Pp. 178-205.

Davitz, J.R. The communication of emotional meaning. New York: McGraw-Hill, 1964.

Davitz, J.R. The communication of emotional meaning. In A.G. Smith (Ed.), Communication and culture. New York: Holt, Rinehart and Winston, 1966.

Davitz, J.R., & Davitz, L.J. Correlates of accuracy in the communication of feelings. Journal of Communication, 1959, 9, 110-117.

Davitz, J.R., & Davitz, L.J. The communication of feelings by content-free speech. In S. Weitz (Ed.), Nonverbal communication. New York: Oxford University Press, 1974.

Dittes, J.E. Galvanic skin response as a measure of patient's reaction to therapist's permissiveness. The Journal of Abnormal and Social Psychology, 1957, 55, 295-303.

Dittman, A.T. The relationship between body movement and moods in interviews. Journal of Consulting Psychology, 1962, 26, 480.

Dittman, A.T. Interpersonal messages of emotion. New York: Springer, 1973.

Dittman, A.T., Parloff, M.B., & Boomer, D.S. Facial and bodily expression: A study of receptivity of emotional cues. Psychiatry, 1965, 28, 239-244.

Duncan, S. Jr., Rice, L.N., & Butler, J.M. Therapists' paralanguage in peak and poor psychotherapy interviews. Journal of Abnormal Psychology. 1968, 73, 566-570.

Ekman, P. Communication through nonverbal behavior: A source of information about an interpersonal relationship. In S.S. Tomkins & C.E. Izard (Eds.), Affect, cognition, and personality. New York: Springer Press, 1965.

Ekman, P., & Friesen, W.V. Nonverbal behavior in psychotherapy research. In J.M. Shlien (Ed.), Research in psychotherapy. Washington, D.C.: American Psychological Association, 1968.

Eldred, S.H., & Price, D.B. A linguistic evaluation of feeling states in psychotherapy. Psychiatry, 1958, 21, 115-121.

Ellsworth, P.C., & Carlsmith, J.M. Effects of eye contact and verbal content on affective response to a dyadic interaction. Journal of Personality and Social Psychology, 1968. 10, 15-20.

Exline, R., Gray, D., & Schuette, D. Visual behavior in a dyad as affected by interview content and sex of respondent. Journal of Personality and Social Psychology, 1965, 1, 201-209.

Exline, R.V., & Winters, L.C. Affective relations and mutual glances in dyads. In S.S. Tomkins & C.E. Izard (Eds.), Affect, cognition, and personality. New York: Springer, 1965.

Frijda, N.H. The understanding of facial expression of emotion. Acta Psychologica, 1953, 9, 294-326.

Frijda, N.H. Facial expressions and situational cues. Journal of Abnormal and Social Psychology, 1958, 57, 149-154.

Frijda, N.H. Recognition and emotion. In L. Berkowitz (Ed.), Advances in experimental social psychology. Vol. 4. New York: Academic Press, 1969.

Ganzer, V.J., & Sarason, I.G. Interrelationships among hostility, experimental conditions and verbal behavior. Journal of Abnormal and Social Psychology, 1964, 68, 79-84.

Gendlin, E.T. Client centered developments in psychotherapy with schizophrenics. University of Wisconsin Psychological Institute Bulletin, I (7), 1961.

Gottschalk, L.A., & Gleser, G.C. The measurement of psychological states through the content analysis of verbal behavior. Berkeley: University of California Press, 1969.

Gottschalk, L.A., Springer, M.J., & Gleser, G. Experiments with a method of assessing the variations in intensity of certain psychological states occurring during two psychotherapeutic interviews. In L.A. Gottschalk (Ed.), Comparative psycholinguistic analysis of two psychotherapeutic interviews. New York: International Universities Press, 1961. Pp. 115-138.

Gottschalk, L.A., Winget, C.M., Gleser, G.C., & Springer, K.J. The measurement of emotional changes during a psychiatric interview: A working model toward quantifying the psychoanalytic concept of affect. In L.A. Gottschalk & A.H. Auerbach (Eds.), Methods of research in psychotherapy. New York: Appleton-Century-Crofts, 1966.

Harway, N.I., Warren, S., Leibowitz, G., Tinling, D., & Iker, H. Some aspects of language style of manic patients. Proceeding of the 81st Annual Convention. Washington, D.C.: American Psychological Association, 1973.

Heller, K. Interview structure and interviewer style in initial interviews. In A.W. Siegman & B. Pope, Studies in dyadic communication. New York: Pergamon Press, 1972. Pp. 9-28.

Heller, K., Davis, J.D., & Myers, R.A. The effects of interviewer style in a standardized interview. Journal of Consulting Psychology, 1966, 30, 501-508.

Heller, K., & Jacobson, E.A. Self disclosure and dependency. The effects of interviewer style. Unpublished research, 1967.

Heller, K., Silver, R., Bailey, M., & Dudgeon, T. The interview reactions of patients and students to within-interview changes in interviewer style. Unpublished research, 1968.

Hess, E.H. Attitude and pupil size. Scientific American. 1965, 212, 46-54.

Isaacs, K.S., & Haggard, E.A. Some methods used in the study of affect in psychotherapy. In L.A. Gottschalk & A.H. Auerbach (Eds.), Methods of research in psychotherapy. New York: Appleton-Century-Crofts, 1966.

Jones, E.E., & Thibaut, J.W. Interaction goals as bases of inference in interpersonal perception. In R. Tagiuri & L. Petrullo (Eds.), Person perception and interpersonal behavior. Stanford: Stanford University Press, 1958.

Jourard, S. Self disclosure. New York: Wiley-Interscience, 1971.

Kanfer, F.H. Effect of a warning signal preceding the noxious stimulus on verbal rate and heart rate. Journal of Experimental Psychology, 1958, 55, 73-86.

Kanfer, F.H. Verbal rate, eye blinks, and content in structured psychiatric interviews. Journal of Abnormal and Social Psychology, 1960, 61, 341-7.

Kasl, S.V., & Mahl, G.F. Experimentally induced anxiety and speech disturbance. American Psychologist, 1958, 13, 349.

Katz, R. Body language: A study in unintentional communication. Unpublished Ph.D. thesis, Department of Social Relations, Harvard University, 1964.

Lennard, H.L., & Bernstein, A. The anatomy of psychotherapy. New York: Columbia University Press, 1960.

Leventhal, H., & Sharp, E. Facial expressions as indicators of distress. In S.S. Tomkins & C.E. Izard (Eds.), Affect, cognition, and personality. New York: Springer, 1965.

Levy, P.K. The ability to express and perceive vocal communications of feeling. In J.R. Davitz (Ed.), The communication of emotional meaning. New York: McGraw-Hill, 1964.

Loeb, F.F. The microscopic film analysis of the function of a recurrent behavioral pattern in a psychotherapeutic session. Journal of Nervous and Mental Disease, 1968, 147, 605-618.

Mahl, G.F. Disturbances and silences in patient's speech in psychotherapy. Journal of Abnormal and Social Psychology, 1956, 53, 1-15.

Mahl, G.F. Exploring emotional states by content analysis. In I de S. Pool (Ed.), Trends in content analysis. Urbana: University of Illinois Press, 1959. Pp. 89-130.

Mahl, G.F. The lexical and linguistic levels in the expression of the emotions. In P.H. Knapp (Ed.), Expression of the Emotions in Man. New York: International Universities Press, 1963. Pp. 77-105.

Mahl, G.F., & Schulze, G. Psychological research in the extralinguistic area. In T.A. Sebeok (Ed.), Approaches to semiotics. The Hague: Mouton, 1964.

McCarron, L.T. Paralanguage and autonomic response patterns in psychotherapy. Psychotherapy: Theory, Research and Practice, 1973, 10, 229-230.

Mehrabian, A. Communication without words. Psychology Today, September 1968a, 2, 53-55.

Mehrabian, A. Inference of attitude from the posture, orientation and distance of communicator. Journal of Consulting and Clinical Psychology, 1968b, 32, 296-308.

Mehrabian, A. Nonverbal communication. Chicago, Aldine Atherton, 1972.

Mehrabian, A., & Ferris, S.R. Inferences of attitudes from nonverbal communication in two channels. In S. Weitz (Ed.), Nonverbal communication, New York: Oxford University Press, 1974.

Milmoe, S., Rosenthal, R., Blane, H.T., Chafetz, M.E., & Wolf, I. The doctor's voice: Postdicter of successful referral of alcoholic patients. In S. Weitz (Ed.), Nonverbal communication. New York: Oxford University Press, 1974.

Orlinsky, D.E., & Howard, K.I. The good therapy hour: Experiential correlates of patients' and therapists' evaluations of therapy sessions. Archives of General Psychiatry, 1967, 16, 621.

Pope, B., Blass, T., Siegman, A.W., & Raher, J. Anxiety and depression in speech. Journal of Consulting and Clinical Psychology, 1970, 35, 128-133.

Pope, B., & Siegman, A.W. Interviewer specificity and topical focus in relation to interviewee productivity. Journal of Verbal Learning and Verbal Behavior, 1965, 4, 188-192.

Pope, B., Siegman, A.W., & Blass, T. Anxiety and speech in the initial interview. Journal of Consulting and Clinical Psychology, 1970, 35, 233-238.

Pope, B., & Siegman, A.W. Relationship and verbal behavior in the initial interview. In A.W. Siegman & B. Pope (Eds.), Studies in dyadic communication. New York: Pergamon Press, 1972.

Pope, B., Nudler, S., VonKorff, M.R., & McGee, J.P. The experienced professional interviewer versus the complete novice. Journal of Consulting and Clinical Psychology, 1974, 42, 680-690.

Raush, H.L., & Bordin, E.S. Warmth in personality development and in psychotherapy. Psychiatry, 1957, 20, 351-363.

Reece, M.M., & Whitman, R.N. Expressive movements, warmth and verbal reinforcement. Journal of Abnormal and Social Psychology, 1962, 64, 234-236.

Rice, L.N. Therapist's style of participation and case outcome. Journal of Consulting Psychology, 1965, 29, 155-160.

Rice, L.M., & Wagstaff, A.K. Client voice quality and expressive style as index of productive psychotherapy. Journal of Consulting Psychology, 1967, 31, 557-563.

Rosenfeld, H.M. Approval-seeking and approval-induction functions of verbal and nonverbal responses in the dyad. Journal of Personality and Social Psychology, 1966, 4, 597-605.

Russel, P.D., & Snyder, W.U. Counselor anxiety in relation to amount of clinical experience and quality of affect demonstrated by clients. Journal of Consulting Psychology, 1963, 27, 358-363.

Sainsbury, P. Gestural movement during psychiatric interview. Psychosomatic Medicine, 1955, 17, 458-469.

Sarason, I.G., & Winkel, R.   Individual differences among subjects and experimenters and subjects' self descriptions.   Journal of Personality and Social Psychology, 1966, 3, 448-457.

Seeman, J.   Perspectives in client-centered therapy.   In B.B. Wolman (Ed.), Handbook of clinical psychology.   New York: McGraw-Hill, 1965.

Siegman, A.W., & Pope, B.   Effects of question specificity and anxiety arousing messages on verbal fluency in the initial interview.   Journal of Personality and Social Psychology, 1965, 4, 188-192.

Siegman, A.W., & Pope, B.   The effect of interviewer ambiguity-specificity and topical focus on interview vocabulary diversity.   Language and Speech, 1966, 9, 245-249.

Siegman, A.W. & Pope, B.   The effects of ambiguity and anxiety on interviewee verbal behavior.   In A.W. Siegman & B. Pope (Eds.), Studies in dyadic communication.   New York: Pergamon Press, 1972.

Smith, E.K.   Effect of the double bind communication on the anxiety level of normals.   Journal of Abnormal Psychology, 1976, 85, 356-363.

Strupp, H.H., Fox, R.E., & Lessler, K.   Patients view their psychotherapy. Baltimore: The Johns Hopkins Press, 1969.

Sullivan, H.S.   The psychiatric interview.   New York: Norton, 1954.

Sunshine, N.J., & Horowitz, M.K.   Differences in egocentricity between spoken and written expression under stress and non-stress conditions.   In S. Moscovici (Ed.), The psychosociology of language.   Chicago: Markham, 1972.

Thompson, D.F., & Meltzer, L.   Communication of emotional intent by facial expression.   Journal of Abnormal and Social Psychology, 1964, 68, 129-135.

Truax, C.B., & Carkhuff, R.R.   Toward effective counseling and psychotherapy.   Chicago: Aldine, 1967.

Vetter, H.J.   Language behavior and psychopathology.   Chicago: Rand McNally, 1970.

Wexler, D.A.   A scale for the measurement of client and therapist expressiveness.   Journal of Clinical Psychology, 1975, 31, 486-489.

Wexler, D.A., & Butler, J.M.   Therapist modification of client expressiveness in client-centered therapy.   Journal of Consulting and Clinical Psychology, 1976, 44, 261-265.

III
Relationship
in the Interview

6 Relationship Within the Interview

The communication of information within the interview has been dealt with in preceding chapters. The next topic of major importance is that of the interviewer-interviewee relationship, the central dynamic of the interview. Although the term "relationship" tends to evoke an intuitive recognition, its study is impeded by a high level of definitional ambiguity. Consider, for example, the following excerpts from two interviews that have been utilized as illustrations of relationship. The first interview was conducted by a public health nurse with an 18-year-old girl who had delivered an illegitimate child in her home two months previously. The child was born with a club foot. Earlier attempts to interview this girl had been made by another public health nurse who had repeatedly tried to learn about the parentage of the child, with very little success. There was a complete failure to gain rapport with the client. The second public health nurse approached the girl while she was hanging clothes in the back yard early one morning. She introduced herself but obtained no response while the girl continued to hang clothes.

Nurse: I'd like to see if the two of us, together, can work out a plan whereby your child can get good medical care for his bad foot.

Girl: Well, if it won't bother you to see a lot of dirty clothes I suppose we could talk about it in the basement. The house is full upstairs.

Nurse: I don't think it would - except it may remind me of the pile I have to wash at home.

Girl: (with vehemence): My baby has to be all right! He has to get a decent start in life. This is the only thing that matters to me! If he can't grow up right there is just no - no sense to anything!

Nurse: That is just why we like to call on all mothers - to help them decide on ways to get their babies off to a good start.

233

Girl: Nurse, can you - is there any way that Jimmy's - I call him Jimmy - leg can be fixed?

Nurse: Have you talked it over with your doctor?

Girl: He said I'll have to take him to a specialist, but there are none here, and I don't know how I can leave - take him somewhere else, I mean! I've been thinking and thinking! And I can't find an answer.

Nurse: Have you heard about the Crippled Children's Clinics?

Girl: No.

Nurse: Every year the best specialists from the University go out to different counties all over the state and set up clinics where anybody can come to see if a physical handicap can be corrected. It's free of charge.

Girl: When are they having one of these clinics near here?

Nurse: I just got a notice the other day telling about such a clinic in L.... Now that's only ten miles from here. Is there any way that you can make arrangements to get there? It will be next Wednesday.

Girl: Maybe I could get my brother to drive me over in his truck. Sometimes he gets jobs over there.

Nurse: Would you like to talk this over with your brother tonight? Then I will call tomorrow and see how we can plan further?

Girl: That'd be swell. I have lots of other things I want to ask, but well, I'm pretty busy today and I'd sort of like to get this clinic business straightened out first. After all, that's most important!   - you will come back tomorrow, then, Nurse, I'll show you the baby!

Nurse: Yes, I'll see you tomorrow. I'm anxious to see that young son of yours. Goodbye.

Girl: Goodbye, Nurse. And thanks a lot.

                                                        (Fenlason, 1952, p. 286)

This brief interview came after a series of unsuccessful attempts to establish contact with the client. It was possible to initiate communication on the present occasion because the worker's approach facilitated the easy establishment of rapport. It would appear that the worker succeeded because she was able to circumvent the client's previous suspicions by addressing herself immediately to a painful need, a currently unresolved problem. Whatever the method, it is usual to refer to this type of initiation of relationship as the establishment of rapport.

The excerpt that follows is also taken from an initial interview, this time in a university counseling center. This interview is remarkable for the depth and intensity of feeling that it evokes in the interviewee, particularly since it is only the first in a psychotherapy sequence. It is used to demonstrate another aspect of relationship quite different from the one designated above as the establishment of rapport. The student began by telling the therapist that he was glad to have liberated himself from excessive parental control over him. Very soon after this remark, and quite early in the interview, he began to speak about his feelings toward the therapist, and as he did so he started to develop a "chill" and a "shiver." He explained that this reaction occurs whenever he talks to a "high authority" figure. A portion of the interview follows.

S: I'd like to talk about something that's happening now. I notice that as I'm talking I'm getting a chill, a sort of physical shivering. This has happened before in a situation where there is an adult present; an adult whom I view as having a certain amount of authority over me, or authority in general. As I begin to talk I begin to shiver more.

T: What did you mean by a 'person in authority'?

S: I'm not sure whether I'm transferring this from your other role but you have the power to injure me. (The student is referring to the fact that the therapist is also the professor in one of his psychology classes.)

T: You're finding yourself anxious about what I would find out about you.

S: The intellectual part enters in; in other words, I made an evaluation, and I'm expecting a certain amount of difficulty in relating to you.

T: Why do you think that is?

S: I notice now that this physiological reaction is getting much stronger. I made an evaluation of you like everyone else, and...

T: It's hard to talk about anything else, when that bothers you. Actually I don't think you need to feel too concerned or too anxious about it. I think it's understandable that you might.

S: Actually, I'd like to some day talk about the situation; it's more than just the situation as such; I think it touches on something deeper. Just to say the way I feel it is now, and this makes me feel pretty nervous...it's the authority you represent.

(Snyder & Snyder, 1961, p. 51)

A little later the therapist referred to the student's earlier mention of a previous personal encounter similar to the one he was experiencing in the ongoing interview.

T: Did you want to tell me about that time when it came up pretty intensely?

S: Yea, that might help. (The student goes on to describe an event involving a male teacher whom he perceived as a 'nice guy' but on his terms. He could crack a joke, but he had the self-confidence that many physicists have, a sort of authoritarian person.) There was a certain sense of relief after I'd spoken to him. I assume the relief was due to the fact that here I was coming into contact with authority, and getting approval in terms of doing something which he would think was a good thing to do. But it might have entered into it that I had expected this punishment, and it hadn't occurred to me before, that element of it. In this case, I was asking for approval; it might have been that I was afraid I wasn't going to get it. Maybe I was afraid of some kind of disapproval; he had this sort of attitude, that we are sort of little boys, just seniors and juniors.

T: And you wanted approval, and you were somewhat afraid that you might get disapproval, might be rejected.

S: Once the feeling gets going there is nothing I can do to stop it.

T: What do you have to do, wait for it to wear itself out?

S: Well, I have to leave the situation; it won't wear itself out in the situation.

T: Are you still feeling it now?

S: No, if it is it is just a very little bit, the edges of it. It's gone away. I'd like to try to talk about you again. I think I'd like to wait. (The therapist gives him leave to talk now or to postpone the discussion.) Well, let's try again. You see, it's an evaluation of your abilities, in a sense and this strikes home in terms of, you're an authority. I had seen you in terms of an administrator, a very efficient administrator, and I used within myself the analogy of you having to control a lot of external things. And so, therefore, you had little depth, in a sense. In other words, there is only a certain amount of volume, and if, say it's a ball and you have flattened the ball in order to take into account a certain amount of circumstances, then there is only a limited amount of depth. And so I felt that I wouldn't care to work with you in therapy.

T: You were wondering whether I could possibly go very deep, or have very much understanding, because I might be spread so thin, in a sense, with all the administration front that I couldn't think very well about, couldn't be very much interested in an individual person.

S: Yea, that's part of it. Another thing, I have this idea that certain people can feel things, and certain people can't, and I found that those people who can't feel things are very good at organizing the world; they have this ability to conceptualize, whereas some of the other people who are always aware of all the nuances of feeling, but they can't control and they can't conceptualize too well.

(Snyder & Snyder, 1961, p. 53)

After this first interview the therapist thought about the patient's response to him - i.e., his relationship with him. The student had, in fact, communicated considerable content regarding this relationship which the therapist interpreted in the following manner. He perceived the student as experiencing his chills in the presence of "high authority figures." This suggested an emotional reaction which had its roots in the patient's earlier relationship with his own father. Later developments in the psychotherapy of this patient substantiated this early interpretation. Clearly, the therapist in this instance went a good deal further than simply establishing rapport with the patient. He became involved with the patient's early transference to him. Transference in this case is the patient's pattern of transferring the feelings, the perceptions, and the interpersonal behaviors that developed in the first place in relationship with his father to other males whom he perceives to be in authority positions.

If we may think of gradations of relationship, we might place rapport at a point of minimum depth - i.e., the beginning, the point of initiation of a relationship - and transference at one of greater depth. Transference is an interpersonal behavior pattern which the patient brings into the interview situation. It is a resultant of earlier relationships with significant people, particularly his/her parents. Rapport implies a point of contact between the two participants in the interview. It is generally assumed that the onus for establishing this contact is on the interviewer. The terms "rapport" and "transference" are not systematically associated with each other. They are selected out of the total language with which one speaks of relationship in the interview because they contrast in significant ways. Any further inquiry into relationship will require, first, some effort at definition and description of the interaction between the two people composing a dyad (a group of two).

But before this is done, there are some further thoughts about rapport. Its characterization as an aspect of relationship that is more superficial than transference is not meant to denigrate it. In actuality, rapport refers to the interaction that occurs at the sensitive interface between two persons who are beginning to move toward a relationship. That the establishment of rapport may be exquisitely difficult and painful for some people is evident in the following account of the first tentative steps taken by a clinical interviewer and a schizoid patient toward a relationsip (Polansky, 1971). The interviewer's account follows:

When I came out to get him, the young man was lolling in the waiting room, and holding a magazine. His response to my greeting was silence - not aggressive, not obviously frightened, just bland and noncommunicative silence. Of course, I already knew something about him. He had a severe upset in college and had to withdraw in his freshman year. Since then, he had been surviving a marginal sort of existence at home, and was neither productive nor happy with his idleness. Pressure from his parents had brought him to our hospital, and to me. About me, he knew practically nothing; it would be months before he would admit curiosity if, indeed, he had any.

(Polansky, 1971, p. 160)

The interviewer's account continues:

> In the office, he stood dumbly waiting to be asked to be seated, took the preferred chair, and finally yielded a passing smile. He began the interview by staring at a spot three feet, two and a third inches beyond my right metatarsal arch. Later, he shifted his gaze to a point four miles and seventy-six yards out of the window. He evaded eye contact and, in fact, appeared never to look at me. Yet I soon discovered that he was preternaturally alert to my inflections, expression, general demeanor. Evidently, he was an acute observer of feelings, in his darting fashion.   (Polansky, 1971, p. 162)

This schizoid young man found it painful and difficult to develop any rapport with the therapist, who was initially a stranger to him. Having learned to protect himself by retiring into a bastion of private, self-imposed isolation, he scanned the defensive barriers he had thrown up between himself and others with a suspicious, alert vigilance. Thus, the schizoid person, who seems so bland, so flat in his emotional responses to others, and so unaware of his surroundings, is actually poignantly attuned to events around him. It is not his perception of others that is deficient, but rather his will and capacity to respond. It is evident that a schizoid patient's blunting of interpersonal responsiveness presents a serious block to a new interviewer attempting to enter into rapport with him.

Polansky (1971) then reviewed the psychological barriers that separate a schizoid person from others. Some of these are referred to here because they characterize the obstacles to the development of a relationship between any two people, however normal, although they may come to their clearest focus in the experience of the seriously withdrawn person.

Burdened with feelings of futility about the possibility of experiencing any balm, any comfort from human contact, the schizoid defends himself against hurt through detachment. Although assuming a posture of distance from others may help him/her to avoid extremely noxious feelings, s(he) pays an exorbitant price for this relief in the form of a serious inhibition in the capacity to experience emotion. "The patient does his best literally to feel nothing.... Not to feel and not to care gives rise to enormous emptiness and a numbness with awesome connotations of death. It is a bleak and hopeless state of mind" (Polansky, 1971, p. 164).

Others are discomfitted and challenged by the schizoid's "spooky" lack of feeling and paralysis of personal response. They try to crash through by pressing him/her to relate to them. This the schizoid person perceives as a threatening intrusion against which he/she defends through a stubborn resistance and an impressive negativism. Even the most persistent efforts to establish rapport generally founder.

The concept of relationship is highly inferential and difficult to define. But the schizoid person's opposition to interpersonal entanglements provides us with a negative, a converse impression of the experience of relationship. At later points, there will be further attempts to conceptualize what is meant by relationship. For the moment, it is important to note that relationship, as it is considered in this chapter, has the interview as a major point of reference and is inferred largely from the communication between its two participants.

COMMUNICATION AND RELATIONSHIP

Chapters 2 and 3 have dealt with the communication of verbal content - that is, the transmission of information. As a matter of convenience, one often speaks about the exchange of information in the interview as though it were a topic, distinct from that of relationship. But in fact, the two are closely connected. While listening to the content of the interviewee's speech, the interviewer may become aware of distinctive elements of style and expressiveness in what s(he) is hearing. Neutral words, impersonal in content, may be the bearers of anxious or angry feelings, more readily related to the interviewee's attitude toward the interviewer than to the content of the speech. Communication thus reflects some aspects of relationship, even when the content transmitted appears to be quite independent of the immediate interaction.

Often a trivial remark can be understood only if one discounts its semantic content and considers its instrumental role in an exchange between two people. For example, a patient may enter his/her therapy hour in a tensely retentive mood. S(he) is seated for five long minutes of thunderous silence, and then remarks thinly: "It's been cold all week." Is this patient intent on providing his/her therapist with some crucial meteorological information or has silence become so intolerable that a casual way needs to be found for terminating it? The remark about the weather fills the void and possibly may start an exchange between the two. Thus, one may speak of the semantic aspect of human communication ("It's been cold all week") and its pragmatic aspect (the change in the relationship between the two brought about by the remark).

"In face to face communication it is quite possible to talk without conveying any real information about the outside world, but it is not possible to talk without saying something about the relationship between the participants in the communication situation" (Danziger, 1976, p. 27).

When the balance of emphasis in a particular communication is on the transmission of information about the external world, it is said to be representational in character; when it is more subjective with the relationship between communicators as the primary referent, it is said to be presentational (Danziger, 1976). An example of the former is an expository lecture about some external naturalistic phenomenon, such as the aurora borealis (to continue in a meteorological vein). An example of the latter would be a personal remark made by a patient during a psychotherapy session expressing a feeling or attitude about the interviewer.

The communication channel for the representational remark is usually linguistic; for the presentational remark, there is usually a mix of several channels. For example, the lecturer on meteorological phenomena will use language in a precise manner so that the meaning conveyed will be consensually shared by his listeners. To be sure, his scientific messages may be rendered more or less dramatically, with varying color and expressiveness. But such stylistic responses to the lecture room situation are secondary. The essence of the message is contained in its semantic content.

Compare the communication of the lecturer with that of a young female psychotherapy patient who was attending her third session with a male therapist whom she had already likened to her father during the initial interview. She spoke about an earlier treatment experience during which she had frequently asked the male therapist with whom she was working many personal questions about himself. This therapist was quite willing to oblige her by speaking at length about himself. (Note the implicit reproach to the present therapist for being less self-revealing.) With a seductive smile and bright eyes she probed the therapist searchingly: "You can tell me anything. For example, are you married?" (To this the therapist replied with a neutral "yes.") "Do you have children? Are you happily married?" As her personal inquiries escalated, the therapist became less and less responsive. After this one-sided communication ran a course of about three minutes the patient rose abruptly and asked to be shown to the toilet. (Actually she knew quite well where the toilet was located.)

Without attempting to unravel the intricate dynamics of this interaction, it is readily recognized as a presentation (rather than a representation) of a transference relationship theme. The referents would appear to be father and the relationship between father and mother. Moreover, the relationship is presented through facial expression, eye contact, and the pragmatics of the verbal content of her questions (i.e., the context in which she asked her questions, their timing, and their urgency). In this regard Danziger (1976) remarks that "bodily movements of approach or withdrawal, gestures symbolizing incorporation or rejection, voice qualities expressing domination or compliance, facial expressions of positive or negative affect are such an important part of the presentation the patient directs at the therapist that nonverbal behavior has sometimes been considered the 'relationship language' par excellence" (p. 106).

While communication, in all its channels, may be regarded as an instrument of relationship, it is equally true that communication between two people is unlikely, unless it is sustained by a relationship between them. For example, a minimal condition for A's communication with B would be an awareness by A that B knows of his/her presence and is willing to listen. Stated otherwise, A must have some feeling of confirmation (Buber, 1957) by B.

The following interaction between a married couple and a psychiatrist from whom the couple had sought help, portrays the kind of void in relationship that stifles communication.

Dr.:   So what you are saying is that you don't get the clues from your husband that you need, to know if you are performing well.

Wife: No.

Dr.:   Does Dan criticize you when you deserve criticism - I mean, positive or negative?

Husband: Rarely do I criticize her...

Wife: (overlapping) Rarely does he criticize.

Dr.:   Well, how - how do you know....

Wife: (interrupting): He compliments you. (short laugh) You see, that is the befuddling thing... Suppose I cook something and I burn it - well, he says it's really 'very, very nice.' Then, if I make something that is extra nice - well, it is 'very, very nice.' I told him I don't know whether something is nice - I don't know whether he is criticizing me or complimenting me. Because he thinks that by complimenting me he can compliment me into doing better, and when I deserve a compliment, he - he is always complimenting me - that's right...so that I lose the value of the compliment.

Dr.:   So you really don't know where you stand with someone who always compliments...

Wife: (interrupting): No, I don't know whether he is criticizing me or really sincerely complimenting me.

                    (Watzlawick, Beavin, & Jackson, 1967, p. 87)

If the husband in the above excerpt were to be critical of his wife, he would, in fact, be telling her that she ought to do things differently. However unpleasant it might be to hear this from one's spouse, it would at least have confirmed the presence and existence of the wife as a person. What did occur was the husband's undifferentiated praise. The words directed toward her therefore lacked meaning, since they made no distinctions between the behaviors to which they were offered as responses. This undifferentiated use of words is a type of subtle nonresponse and bespeaks an absence of relationship.

Whether relationship is attenuated in a subtle manner like the one above, or in a gross physical sense (the interviewer's absence from the room), a reduction in relationship reduces the flow of communication. A relationship, whether positive or negative, is needed as a supporting structure for communication between two people. This principle has been variably demonstrated in a number of different investigations.

Colby (1960) studies the effect of the presence or absence of an interviewer on the free associations of $\underline{S}$s (male medical students) during a sequence of interviews over a three-week period. He found that the presence of the interviewer had an activating effect. The $\underline{S}$s spoke at greater length about persons with whom they had significant relationships during the interviewer's presence than his absence.

Another investigation (Martin, Lundy, & Lewin, 1960) compared interviewee response to interviewers who manifested three degrees of involvement with those they were interviewing. In the first group there was a zero level of involvement; no interviewer was present. The $\underline{S}$s simply talked into a tape recorder. In the second group the interviewer was physically present but was permitted, by experimental instruction, to make only nonverbal response. And in the third group the interviwer responded normally, in a client-centered manner. Each $\underline{S}$ was seen for five interviews during which his/her speech was continually recorded. The group that talked to a fully response interviewer (the third group) spoke at greater length than the other two, about emotionally important material and, indeed, increased its productivity markedly over the five interviews. The group with no interviewer present (the first group) manifested a slight drop in productivity in emotionally important areas over the same interview span. And the group with nonverbal contact only between interviewer and interviewee (the second group) fell between the two others.

In an experimental study, Lindsley (1969) varied degree of relationship in a novel manner. He used a chronically psychotic adult male as the interviewee. There were two interviewers who were alternated in the experiment; one was a second chronically psychotic patient and the other was a psychologist. On the assumption that the capacity of the two psychotic patients to communicate and to attend to the communication of the other would be fragile and unreliable, Lindsley (1969) anticipated less interviewee response when the interviewer was the second patient rather than the psychologist. In fact, the results supported this anticipation.

The interviewer and interviewee did not face each other in the same room. Instead, they communicated between two separate rooms through a rather complex audiovisual system. The patient could speak to the interviewer through a microphone, and be heard and seen by the interviewer through a speaker and a television screen. He was able to control the time he wished to attend to the voice and the image of the interviewer through the speaker and television screen in his room by pressing a button that controlled each channel.

Whenever the second patient became the interviewer, the interviewee's talking time dropped significantly, followed by a drop in his listening time, and finally in viewing time. When the psychologist would become the interviewer, the time during which the interviewee talked to, listened to, and looked at the interviewer increased markedly.

This experiment demonstrates the interactional character of dyadic communication. If both members of the dyad have impaired capacities for relationship, the flow of communication between the two is considerably blocked. If only one of the participants is an interactionally impaired person, the blocking of communication occurs to a lesser degree. This blocking would be least if neither participant had an interactional disability. In brief, there is a positive association between degree of relationship and productivity in communication. If relationship is diminished either through external manipulation, or internally through some form of psychological debility, communication is reduced as well.

GOOD AND POOR RELATIONSHIPS

In the studies reviewed above, relationship was present or absent; if present, it was there to a specifiable degree. But it may be demonstrated that the effect of relationship on communication and, indeed, on the outcome of treatment, is a consequence not only of the degree of relationship, but also of its quality. To the clinician, there are good relationships and poor relationships. In fact, there is a widespread consensus among them about the attributes of relationship that are considered to be positive. "The characteristics most frequently cited as desirable are the therapist's warmth, acceptance, permissiveness, respect for the patient, understanding, interest in the patient, and liking for the patient" (Gardner, 1964, p. 426). To be sure, there would be some differential emphasis on these attributes, depending on the interviewer's theoretical school of allegiance. But, by and large, these are virtues in the clinical value system.

The character of a relationship may be specified through the use of a range of operational procedures. One of these is a rating device known as the Q-sort, which was used by Fiedler (1950), when he applied his concept of the ideal therapeutic relationship to recordings of actual therapist behavior. The study has been referred to in Chapter 4. At the moment it need only be repeated that the basic factor in the ideal relationship has been described by others (Kiesler, 1973) as accurate empathy. The following items descriptive of therapist behavior, taken from the Fiedler Q-Sort, exemplify this dimension of relationship:

Is able to participate completely in the patient's communication.

Comments are always right in line with what the patient is trying to convey.

Really tries to understand the patient's feelings.

Much later a scale developed by Anderson and Anderson (1962) and summarized by Kiesler (1973) described the counseling relationship in terms of the concept of "ideal rapport." After a careful process of item selection, those that remained were evenly divided between items that represented good and poor rapport, and further divided into those describing client and counselor behaviors and attitudes. Some examples follow. Positive Client Rapport: "The client feels accepted as an individual"; "The client can talk freely about his innermost feelings." Negative Client Rapport: "The client distrusts the counselor"; "The client feels frustrated and blocked in his attempt to relate to the counselor." Positive Counselor Rapport: "The counselor creates a feeling of 'warmth' in the relationship"; "The counselor's tone of voice conveys the ability to share the client's feelings." Negative Counselor Rapport: "The counselor had a condescending attitude"; and "The counselor acts cold and distant."

In one investigation (Parloff, 1956) the Fiedler Q-Sort describing an ideal therapeutic relationship was used to assess the quality of relationships that two group therapists established with individual members of their therapy groups. An independent observer attended the group meetings and judged the interaction between the group leader and each group member with the Fiedler Ideal Therapeutic Relationship Q-Sample. These Q-Sorts were then correlated with the Fiedler Ideal Therapeutic Relationship Sort to determine how closely each resembled the description of the ideal relationship. A high correlation was indicative of a close resemblance; a low correlation, a lack of resemblance. To obtain an independent measure of the capacity for relationship of each therapist, twelve mutual acquaintances of both were interviewed. They all agreed that one therapist achieved better social relationships than the other. It was then found that the one rated as establishing the better relationships with friends came closer to the ideal therapeutic relationship in his interactions with his patients. In this study, two procedures were used to evaluate the quality of relationship that a therapist achieves with patients and with friends. The one who relates better in one context does so in the other as well.

Having found that the quality of relationship for two therapists is consistent across friendship and group psychotherapy situations, Parloff (1961) then demonstrated that there was a positive association between quality of relationship and treatment outcome. Two small groups of patients were treated by two therapists. The quality of the relationship between the therapist and each patient in his group was determined in the same manner as that in the preceding study. Observers used the Fiedler Q-Sort to describe the interaction with each patient. Each actual relationship was then correlated with the Fiedler Q-Sort description of the ideal relationship with the resulting correlation serving as the index of the quality of the relationship. These indices were correlated with a number of criteria of improvement, and several of these correlations turned out to be significant. Parloff concluded: "Patients who established better relationships with their therapist tended to show greater improvement than those whose relationships with the same therapist were not as good" (Parloff, 1961, p. 37).

Other investigators (Lorr, 1965) obtained results that pointed to the occurrence of several dimensions or types of relationship rather than a single monistic pattern. Lorr relied on patient reports of actual therapist behavior, given at selected points during a psychotherapy series. Ratings of therapist behavior were made by male patients, drawn from a large number of V.A. outpatient clinics. The ratings were intercorrelated and factor analyzed. The resulting factors were then correlated with patients' ratings of improvement and satisfaction, and with therapists' ratings of improvement, to separate the good attributes of relationship from the bad. Therapist attitudes of understanding, accepting and independence encouraging were positively correlated with favorable outcome criteria. On the other hand, authoritarian and critical-hostile attitude among therapists were negatively correlated with outcome.

Four Rogerian attributes of relationship are contained within a single Relationship Inventory developed by Barrett-Lennard (1959) and discussed by Kiesler (1973). The relationship attributes are empathic understanding, positive regard, unconditionality of regard, and congruence. These traits will be discussed at greater length in Chapter 8. At this point, the four relationship traits, so characteristically Rogerian, will be conceptually clarified with the results of the Barrett-Lennard (1959) study. The author based his scale on the assumption that "a client is most directly influenced, in the relationship with his therapist, by what he experiences and perceives his therapist's response to him to be. From this point of view it appeared most meaningful to employ client perceptions as the basic data from which to assess the effective therapeutic quality of a relationship" (p. 1). The scale was therefore used by the clients to describe the relationship behavior of their therapists.

In the section that follows the four variables of relationship are defined and illustrated with scale items.

Empathic understanding is considered to be a process by which "one person is conscious of the immediate awareness of another... an active process of desiring to know the full present and changing awareness of another person, of reaching out to receive his communications and meaning, and of translating his words and signs into experienced meaning that matches at least those aspects of his awareness that are most important to him at the moment" (Barrett-Lennard, 1959, p. 2). Two items that are used to assess this variable follow: "He nearly always knows exactly what I mean"; "He appreciates exactly how the things that I experience feel to me."

Level of regard refers to the total quantity of feeling, both positive and negative, expressed by one person to another. Thus, one person may speak to another with excitement, with color, with intense feeling. Or, by contrast s(he) may speak in a wooden, flat manner. An item descriptive of a positive emotional response to the client by the therapist is illustrated by the following item: "He is friendly and warm with me." A negative emotional response is noted in the next item: "At times he feels contempt for me." But, whether the feeling is positive or negative, the sum total of items like the preceding two is an index of level of regard. In brief, what is meant by level of regard is the degree or intensity of feeling that one person has for the other.

Unconditionality of regard refers to the constancy of one person's regard or feeling for another. If A feels warmly disposed toward B, regardless of what B says or how B acts, his/her regard for B is considered to be unconditional. Total unconditionality probably never occurs, for if it did, one might question whether A and B were truly responding to each other. In the mental health interview, however, unconditionality may be approached if the interviewer warmly confirms the interviewee as a person, even though s(he) may not approve of particular attitudes, feelings, or actions of the person. However, if the interviewer responds positively or negatively to the interviewee, depending on the attitude or feeling that the interviewee expresses, or the behavior that s(he) reports, the regard of the interviewer would be clearly conditional. An example of an unconditional interviewer response is given in the following item: "Whether I am feeling happy or unhappy with myself makes no real difference to the way he feels about me." By contrast, the next interviewer response is a conditional one: "Depending on my behavior he has a better opinion of me sometimes that he has at other times."

Therapist congruence occurs when the therapist is at one with himself. If s(he) gives verbal expression to an interest in the client's story, but emits nonverbal signals of boredom, s(he) is lacking in congruence. If the therapist invites the client to speak about his/her hostile feelings, but reacts to a narrative about violent behavior with anxiety and discomfort, s(he) is conflicted or incongruent in his/her relationship behavior. Therapist congruence is found in the item: "He is comfortable and at ease in our relationship"; and incongruence in: "Sometimes he is not all comfortable but we go on, outwardly ignoring it."

In concluding this section on good and poor relationships, it is evident that it is difficult to speak about the interaction between two people in nonevaluational terms. Thus, one may refer to a positive relationship, a negative relationship, one that is good, bad, ideal, or mediocre. Researchers have correlated relationship with interviewee productivity and therapy outcome and found that some attributes facilitate communication and favorable outcome, while others do not.

Orlinsky and Howard (1967) studied the qualities of relationship that are associated with good and poor therapy hours, as judged separately by female out-patients and their therapists. The data were obtained from a questionnaire called the Therapy Session Report, to which both patients and therapists responded immediately after each psychotherapy interview. The therapists and patients judged those sessions in which both participants were emotionally involved as good therapy hours, and others in which such involvement was lacking, as poor. The reciprocal expression of positive feeling was characteristic of good sessions. By contrast, those in which patients felt irritable, frustrated, and inadequate, were judged by the patients to be bad sessions. On this, the therapists disagreed because they believed that such negative patient feelings might well need to be experienced and expressed for therapeutic reasons.

The literature reviewed in this section does not permit the operational prescription of good relationship behavior. Instead, it presents the clinician with certain clearly delineated models of interactional behavior, evaluated as either good or bad by consensus among clinicians, or more pragmatically, by correlation with volume of communication and with positive outcome of treatment.

RECIPROCITY IN RELATIONSHIP

The attributes of a relationship, whether good or bad, cannot be spelled out in terms of the subjective experiences of one participant only, or of the two members of a dyad, taken singly. The interaction between the two must be captured in some way if one is to deal with the essence of relationship. In the view of several authors this essence is best defined as reciprocity in the exchange between two people. Reciprocity as an interchange of affective attitudes is the central concept in the following definition of relationship:

"As we see it, the therapy relationship is best described as the reciprocity of various sets of affective attitudes which two or more persons hold toward each other in psychotherapy. The form of behavior we wish to include in the concept of relationship is limited to attitudes, which of course, include affect" (Snyder & Snyder, 1961, p. 270).

In the Snyder & Snyder (1961) studies, the reciprocal attitudes and feelings held toward each other by interviewer and interviewee were assessed with scales devised to measure the feelings of the therapist and client toward each other. The scales are known as the Therapist's Affect Scale and the Client's Affect Scale. They were usually filled out by clients and therapists immediately after selected psychotherapy interviews. In one study (Snyder & Snyder, 1961) the responses to both scales obtained at several representative points across a number of psychotherapy sequences were factor analyzed. Only two major item groupings appeared in each scale - a positive cluster and a negative one. Some items that express positive postinterview client attitudes toward the therapist follow:

Today I was pleased with my counselor's interest and attention.

My counselor's attitude gives me hope I can get something out of this.

Today I have a very warm feeling toward my counselor.

Other items express postinterview negative client attitudes:

Today I felt that my counselor and I are strangers in many ways.

Today I felt a certain amount of contempt for my counselor.

Today my counselor just didn't seem to understand what I was talking about.

The next three items, from the therapist scale, are examples of positive attitudes of the interviewer toward the client:

Today I felt that we had a pretty relaxed, understanding kind of relationship.

Today I hoped the therapy session with this client would not end soon.

Today I felt more comfortable in the therapy sessions with this client than with most others I've had.

Finally, the items below express negative therapist attitudes toward the client:

Today I wonder if another therapist might not get further with this client than I.

The hour seemed to be dragging with this client today.

Today I resented the client's attitude.

The scales provide a descriptive language for characterizing the therapeutic relationship. The bipolar clustering of relationship items into positive and negative groups demonstrate that statements about relationship, as indicated in the preceding section of this chapter, are strongly evaluational in character. But of greater importance at the moment is the use that Snyder and Snyder (1961) has made of the scales to demonstrate the concept of relationship as a reciprocal interaction of the emotional attitudes of the therapist and client. He obtained an overall correlation of client and therapist positive attitudes toward each other of .70, and concluded: "When client and therapist are properly matched, they can develop an effective interpersonal and therapeutic relationship which is quite reciprocal in character, and which grows increasingly positive, making an effective therapeutic outcome probable" (Snyder & Snyder, 1961, p. 367).

This definition of relationship is reminiscent of the principle of reciprocal affect (Truax & Mitchell, 1971), as it operates in a therapeutic interview. For example, the introduction of positive affect into an interview by a therapist is likely to elicit a positive response from the patient. That this reciprocity of feeling does indeed occur was demonstrated in an experimental analogue study (Heller, Myers, & Kline, 1963). The "patients" were actors who simulated the roles of both friendly and hostile interviewees. The therapists were graduate students in clinical training. Reciprocal affect was demonstrated when the therapists responded in a more friendly fashion to friendly "patients" and in a more hostile fashion to hostile "patients."

However reciprocity between the two members of a dyad may be defined in other ways, too. One author (Rosen, 1972) thinks of a positive relationship between two people as an interaction in which the speaker receives feedback from the person being addressed, telling him/her that the message has been heard and understood and that it is relevant to the communication in progress. When this occurs the speaker feels confirmed or reinforced. Such confirmation is needed to sustain the flow of communication, and to ensure that the two interactants will feel positively about each other. In Rosen's (1972) view, a member of a dyad, who receives the kind of feedback from the other member that informs him/her that s(he) has been heard, understood, and found to be speaking about matters that are congruent with the thematic content of the conversation, is likely to talk more, and express more positive feeling to the other member than s(he) would if such feedback were not given. Moreover, both members of the dyad are responsive to the type of feedback described. "The outcomes and satisfactions that clinicians derive from their treatment relationship are just as affected by patients' interactive responses as are the patients by the clinicians' responses" (Rosen, 1972, p. 335). Reciprocity therefore emerges as a significant aspect of a positive relationship, whether it is defined as an exchange of feelings and attitudes or as mutual feedback between the two partners in a dialogue in response to the messages communicated.

RELATIONSHIP AS ATTRACTION

An additional definition of relationship will be discussed in the present section - that of the attraction of one person to another. Attraction as a relationship concept is devoid of emotional and attitudinal content. One does not ask whether A feels friendly or hostile toward B, or whether A dominates B when they interact with each other. One simply determines whether A is attracted toward B; that is whether A seeks B out when s(he) happens not to be in his/her company, whether A chooses to remain in B's company and to communicate with B when both are together, or whether A chooses B over others when the situation calls for an expression of preference. In all these situations A is psychologically impelled toward B, that is A is attracted to B. The meaning of a concept, as lacking in subjective content as attraction is specified by the operations used in assessing it.

The Libo Pictures Impressions Test (Libo, 1969) is a TAT-like instrument designed to measure "the strength (attractiveness) of the patient-therapist relationship by capitalizing on the oft-noted sensitivity of projective techniques to the social situation in which they are administered" (Libo, 1957, p. 36). Libo (1957) defines the patient's attraction to the therapist as his/her psychological movement toward or away from the therapist. Such movement is "the resultant of forces acting on the patient to maintain his relationship with the therapist" (Libo, 1957, p. 35).

The Picture Impressions Test consists of four cards with black and white sketches portraying therapy-like situations. The interviewee is asked to tell a story about each, very much as s(he) would in response to TAT cards. However, the test is given to the S when s(he) is in a therapy or initial interview situation. Moreover, when possible, the test is administered by the interviewer. It is therefore expected that the congruence between the content of the sketches on the cards and the context in which the test is administered, will serve to enhance the influence of the immediate situation on the projective responses of the S. A scoring manual was developed to assess the strength of the psychological locomotion of the patient toward the therapist - that is, the strength of his/her attraction. In an early study with his test Libo (1957) found a significant relationship between the strength of patient attraction toward the therapist in an out-patient clinic after the initial interview, and his/her subsequent return for treatment.

Several other investigators have used the Picture Impressions Test to study the effect of interviewee attraction to interviewer on interview process and on therapeutic change over time. In one of these (Heller & Goldstein, (1961) the authors explored the correlation between client pretherapy attraction to the psychotherapist and both client pretherapy dependency and movement toward independence over therapy. The clients were undergraduate university students who had applied for psychotherapy at a university psychology clinic. The therapists were clinical psychology graduate students who had completed their predoctoral training in psychotherapy. Client-therapist attraction was measured by the Libo Picture Impressions Test, administered before the beginning of therapy. Client dependency was measured in two ways, a self-descriptive assessment based on the client's responses to the Edwards Personal Preference Schedule and a behavioral assessment (overt dependency) based on a role playing situational test. "Those individuals who wrote stories to the Picture Impression Cards indicating that they anticipated positive gratification from therapy, described themselves before therapy as more dependent according to the EPPS, and also acted more dependently on the Situation Test of Dependency" (Heller & Goldstein, 1961, p. 373). In addition, the results showed that pretherapy client attraction to the therapist was positively correlated with the client's movement toward self-descriptive independence over the course of treatment. Even before their first contact with the therapist, more dependent clients anticipate a greater attraction to the therapist than less dependent clients. These clients also feel that they move further in the direction of greater independence as therapy progresses.

Another investigation (Pope & Siegman, 1966) studied the association between interviewee attraction to interviewer and interviewee style of communication. In this research the focus was on the attraction to the interviewer experienced by the interviewee during the course of an initial interview. To assess this, Ss were given the Libo Picture Impressions Test immediately before and after the interview. The first administration provided a measure of anticipatory attraction; the second, of postinterview attraction. The subtraction of the first from the second resulted in an index of increase or decrease in attraction as a consequence of the interview experience. One of the four pictures was used for the preinterview test, and another, for the postinterview test. The Ss were female junior and senior nursing students; the interviewer was one of the two authors. It had been anticipated that those Ss who showed the greater increases in attraction to the interviewer would be more verbally productive and less hesitant in speech than those who showed lesser increases in attraction. The anticipated difference in productivity was not obtained, but that in hesitation (Ah ratio, reaction time, silence quotient) was. Thus, the more attracted Ss spoke with fewer filled pauses, less silence, and faster reaction times than the less attracted Ss. If hesitation in speech may be taken as an indication of uncertainty and possibly resistiveness, the more attracted Ss were evidently less uncertain and resistant than the others.

In the third study with the Libo Picture Impressions Test (Pope & Siegman, 1968) interviewee attraction to interviewer was a minor variable. Yet the results provided an element of construct validation of the concept of attraction and will therefore be reviewed briefly. The major purpose of the research was the experimental manipulation of interviewer warmth to determine its effect on interviewee communication. Again, the interviewees were junior and senior female nursing students. The interviewers were two female clinical psychology interns, in their last predoctoral year. To determine the effectiveness of the warm-cold manipulation, two steps were taken. In the first, all interviewees rated their interviewers on 10 semantic differential-type, bipolar scales, describing interviewer affect and attitude toward interviewee. In the second, the interviewees responded to the Libo Picture Impressions Test, altered to depict the interviewer as a female rather than the male in the Libo pictures. The ratings attested to the success of the warm-cold manipulation. The Ss perceived the interviewers in the warm condition to be significantly warmer, more accepting, more understanding, pleasanter, more responsive, friendlier, and more interested than those in the cold condition. They liked the interviewers in the warm condition better, felt they were liked better by them, and were considerably happier at the prospect of their interviewers becoming their therapists. In addition, there was a finding at a borderline level of significance that interviewees were more strongly attracted to warm rather than cold interviewers. The congruence between interviewee attraction to interviewer and her positive perception of him provides some validation data for the concept of attraction.

Relationship, conceptualized as attraction, has lent itself to experimental manipulation in a number of studies reviewed by Goldstein (1971). On the whole, the experimental investigation of attraction has not been highly rewarding. The findings are scanty and variable, possibly because the operations by which attraction has been manipulated have differed from one group of studies to another. The point had been made that the concept of attraction lacks psychological content. Its meaning is therefore derived considerably from the operations used in its investigation. When these operations differ, however subtly, the results obtained are likely to vary.

The following are some of the methods that have been used in the experimental manipulation of attraction. In an early investigation Back

(1951) used a design that called for the grouping of his Ss into pairs. Some pairs perceived a high attraction induction; the others, a low attraction induction. The Ss were college student volunteers. At the outset they were asked a number of questions which ostensibly were to be used to select their mates. Some of the Ss were led to expect that they would be strongly attracted to their partners because of the closeness of their match on the questions they had been asked. Others were led to anticipate a weak attraction to their partners because of a poor match.

The success of the attraction induction was checked against a sociometric measure of the frequency with which one partner would choose the other, if both were free to select or reject each other. The sociometric measure did indeed show that those Ss led to expect strong attraction actually picked their partners more frequently than those with the anticipation of weak attraction.

The next experiment (Sapolsky, 1960) used a method roughly similar to the first but different in a number of specifics. Instead of the questions that were used for pairing Ss in the first study, the Ss in the second, all female freshman students, were told that they would be matched with experimenters congenial to themselves. To achieve this matching, each S was asked to respond to the FIRO-B Scale (Schutz, 1966), a measure of three basic dimensions of interpersonal behavior. Having thus expressed her preference for certain forms of behavior in social situations, the S was led to believe that she would be given an E who was compatible with her preferences. Actually there was only one E for all Ss. Those assigned to the High Attraction group were simply told: "Usually we can't match people exactly, but in your case this will be possible." By contrast, those in the Low Attraction group were told: "Usually we can match people quite well, but in your case we're going to have some trouble. It's going to take too long to locate somebody for you, so I'm assigning you to Miss C. She may irritate you a little, but do the best you can." No mention is made in the report of the Sapolsky study of any effort to determine the success of the structuring of attraction. In both investigations the manipulation of attraction was attempted through the induction of certain expectations.

In the third and fourth studies of the present group (Davidoff, 1969; Goldstein, 1971) the method of manipulation was again similar to that used by Back (1951). The Ss were patients in a university counseling center (Goldstein, 1971) and a V.A. psychiatric hospital (Davidoff, 1969). In both studies patients were induced to anticipate high and low attraction to their therapists, whom they had not yet met. Later, after the completion of the initial interview, patients and therapists completed questionnaires which assessed the level of negative, positive, and mixed feeling that each had for the other. The algebraic sum of positive and negative items was assumed to be an index of attraction. Unlike the Back (1951) study, the Goldstein (1971) and Davidoff (1969) experiments failed to vary degree of attraction with the manipulation used. Those Ss who received the high induction did not manifest greater attraction than the others with the low induction.

The fifth and sixth studies (Liberman, 1970; Orenstein, 1969) used a modeling procedure as the method of structuring attraction. In the Orenstein investigation the Ss were female students in an Introductory Psychology class;

in the Liberman study they were male alcoholic in-patients in a state hospital. In the first investigation all Ss were asked to listen to taped segments of a psychotherapy session. Actually there were two tapes, identical in therapist verbalizations, but partially different in patient speech. In the High Attraction tape a number of patient remarks expressed positive feeling toward the therapist, and in the Low Attraction tape, an analogous number expressed negative feelings. Immediately after listening to the tapes, all Ss responded to a questionnaire measuring positive and negative feelings toward the therapist. Those exposed to the High Attraction tape did indeed feel more positively toward the taped therapist than those exposed to the Low Attraction tape. Thus, the prediction that "subjects hearing a model (taped patient) display high attraction toward a taped therapist would themselves report significantly higher attraction toward the therapist than subjects hearing a model who expressed negative feelings" (Goldstein, 1971, p. 106) was borne out.

But the efficacy of modeling as a means of enhancing attraction may well vary with the type of patient, because negative results for modeling were obtained when the patients were lower class alcoholic in-patients in a state hospital (Liberman, 1970). It should be added that the criteria for the efficacy of the manipulation of attraction were also different. Basically the same type of modeling procedure used by Orenstein was employed. But the procedure in the second study differed in one basic respect. The taped modeling of high and low attraction was followed by an individual intake-like interview, during which the interviewee was asked the same questions he had heard from the taped interviewer. Each S's attraction to the actual interviewer was then measured by the postinterview questionnaire referred to above. In the Liberman study, no significant differences in attraction to the interviewer emerged.

The evidence for the efficacy of the experimental manipulation of interviewee attraction to interviewer is not as strong as one would like. In only two of the preceding six studies is there direct evidence of its success. However, indirect evidence is implicit in some of the results that pertain to the effects of attraction on other aspects of the dyadic interaction.

Two of these studies investigated the role of attraction on the influence that one member of the dyad might have on the other. It will be recalled that Back (1951) had arranged his Ss into high and low attraction pairs. These were compared on a joint story writing task, devised to measure the influence that the two members of a pair exerted on each other. Results showed that members of high-attraction pairs demonstrated considerably more mutual influence than members of low-attraction pairs.

In the Sapolsky (1960) investigation, each dyad consisted of the E and a S who underwent a verbal conditioning procedure. It was hypothesized that Ss in whom a high attraction toward the E had been aroused would demonstrate a greater conditioning effect than those in whom low attraction had been induced. Ss were reinforced by the E for selecting "I" or "We" from groups of pronouns in a sentence construction task. Those Ss who were in the high-attraction condition did indeed learn to use "I" and "We" with greater frequency over the duration of the experiment than those in the low-attraction condition. The author concluded that the high-attraction Ss were more susceptible to influence by the E̱ than low-attraction S̱s. Thus, attraction between two persons interacting with each other enhances the influence each has on the other. Although neither of the above two experiments deals directly with the interview, the association between attraction and influence is undoubtedly relevant to the interview interaction.

Although the experimental manipulation of attraction failed in the studies by Goldstein (1971) and Davidoff (1969), naturalistically occurring individual attraction of patient and therapist to each other did correlate with certain variables in the interviewee's communication. Thus, both pre- (Picture Impressions Test) and post- (questionnaire) interview attraction of the interviewee to the interviewer correlated negatively with two measures of resistance (Goldstein, 1971). The more attracted the interviewee was, the less resistant and the more communicative (i.e., the less silent) s(he) was. This finding is very similar to that by Pope and Siegman (1966) in which interviewee attraction was negatively correlated with hesitation in speech.

Finally Davidoff (1969) obtained a result that was reminiscent of the principle of reciprocity in relationship, considered at an earlier point in the present chapter. As in the case of the Goldstein (1971) study, the experimental manipulation of attraction yielded negative results. However, both therapist and patient attitudes toward the other had been recorded in the questionnaires that they filled out immediately after the initial interview. The two sets of scores correlated positively with each other "thus indicating that patients who are more attracted to the interviewer are in turn more attractive" (Goldstein, 1971, p. 35) to the interviewer.

The findings in this group of studies are of considerable interest to the interviewer, supporting the clinically based impression that a positive relationship does indeed affect the course of the interview positively. A condition of high attraction increases the influence that the interviewer has on interviewee verbal communication. It reduces and increases verbal productivity (reduces silence). In view of the above, it is helpful to know that high attraction in one participant of a dyad appears to beget high attraction in the other.

DIMENSIONS OF RELATIONSHIP

Many authors have gone beyond the attempt to develop a condensed definition of relationship to a more empirical effort to uncover underlying dimensions of social interaction. Thus, they do not ask whether relationship in the interview is best defined as rapport, transference, or attraction. Instead, they inquire into the presence of a small number of dimensions of relationship that determine or describe a broadly representative range of interpersonal behaviors. Two-dimensional and three-dimensional schemes are the most frequent and are generally derived by intercorrelating a large number of ratings of interpersonal behavior, factor analyzing the correlation matrix, and labeling or defining the factors that emerge.

Danziger (1976) presents a three-dimensional scheme in his book on Interpersonal Communication. The first dimension, called status, refers to the "differences in the degree of prominence, control," and influence that one person has over another with whom he is interacting. "The second dimension involves the factor of solidarity, pulling together to achieve a common goal or maintain a common commitment.... Finally, the commonly recognized third dimension has to do with person-to-person social-emotional satisfaction, which involves relative closeness or intimacy rather than distance and impersonality" (Danziger, 1976, p. 49).

It has become customary to represent these three dimensions on coordinate axes drawn in what is metaphorically referred to as social space. The status aspect of a relationship may be represented by a vertical axis, along which one person may be represented as above or below another. Solidarity and intimacy may be represented by two horizontal axes, both bisecting the status axis and each other at right angles. Each axis may be divided into units that represent degrees of status, solidarity, and intimacy.

Consider the position in social space of the relationship between a dean of students in a college and an undergraduate student being interviewed by the dean because of recent academic failure. Since the dean would be regarded as possessing higher status than the student, the difference between the two could be represented at a selected point on the vertical (status) axis above its midpoint. (We shall assume that a status difference in which the dean is higher than the student will be a positive difference.) In a similar manner the degree of solidarity, if positive, would fall on the positive side of one of the horizontal axes and, if negative, on the negative side. Intimacy would be similarly positioned on the second horizontal axis. We may assume negative solidarity and negative intimacy in the above example of the dean and the student. Perpendiculars drawn from the three selected points on the three axes into the proper quadrant would intersect at a single point representing the locus of the relationship in social space. In the case of the dean and the student, a single point would be located which would represent a positive status difference (dean status - student status), and both negative solidarity and negative intimacy.

The position in social space of the relationship between two friends engaged in a spontaneous conversation would be quite different. We shall assume a lack of status difference between the two friends and shall therefore locate their relationship at the zero point on the vertical (status) axis. Since the conversation is both congenial and close, the relationship will be positioned on the positive side of the solidarity axis and on the positive side of the intimacy axis.

The following interviewer-interviewee interaction will exemplify a status differential between the interviewer and interviewee.

ER: Good morning, I am Dr. Hedlig. What is your name?

EE: Sue.

ER: Sue, and your last name.

EE: Witlock.

ER: How old are you, Sue?

EE: Eighteen.

ER: You are a freshman student?

EE: Ahuh.

In this fictional exchange, the interviewer introduces himself as a doctor and quickly establishes the age and freshman identity of the student. There is no doubt that the superior status of the interviewer was defined and established at the outset of the interview.

The following brief exchange between one student interviewing another, represents a high level of solidarity.

ER: Well, I've really enjoyed talking with you.

EE: Yes, it's really been good.

Finally, a high level of intimacy is represented by the following communication between a therapist and a patient, at the close of an initial interview:

EE: I feel as though I've known you for a long time.

ER: Good.

EE: I think it'll be easy for me to talk to you.

In a book which presents a theory of dyadic and group interactions Schutz (1966) begins by quoting three remarks that he made to his three-year-old daughter, each of which exemplifies a dimension of relationship. Thus, "I said go to bed!" is an instance of control; "No, Laurie, you can't come down and join the company," an example of negative inclusion; and "Yes, I still love you; I was just angry at what you did" (Schutz, 1966, p. 1), an expression of affection. It will be noted that these three dimensions resemble the ones designated above as status, solidarity, and intimacy. Since Schutz (1966) perceived these dimensions as descriptive of the interactions between individuals in dyadic and larger groups, he used both the attitudes and feelings expressed by one person to another and those which the person wished to receive from the other. With a scale that he developed to assess each of these dimensions of relationship, Schutz was able to describe and measure the attitudes and feelings that flowed from A to B, and back again, through social space. In a word, he was able to assess the relationship between the two persons.

Rather than defining the dimensions, they will be illustrated with a sampling of items from the Schutz questionnaire entitled "Fundamental Interpersonal Relations Orientation-Behavior (FIRO-B)." The expression of control by a person over others may be noted in the following items, to which the S responds with a six-point scale extending from the positive extreme ("usually") to the negative extreme ("never"):

I try to be the dominant person when I am with people.

I try to influence strongly other people's actions.

I take charge of things when I'm with people.

The wish of this person for control by others is noted in the next three items:

I let other people decide what to do.

I let other people strongly influence my actions.

I am easily led by people. (Schutz, 1966, p. 63)

A person's expression of an effort to achieve <u>inclusion</u> with others is heard in another group of items:

I try to be with people.

I try to include other people in my plans.

I try to avoid being alone.

The items that follow portray the converse - that is, the need of the same person to be included by others:

I like people to include me in their activities.

I like people to ask me to participate in their discussions.

(Schutz, 1966, pp. 61-62)

The need to behave affectionally toward others is evident in two other questionnaire items:

I try to be friendly to people.

I try to get close and personal with people.

Finally, a person's wish to receive affection from others is explicit in the last two items:

I like people to act friendly toward me.

I like people to act close and personal with me.

(Schutz, 1966, p. 64)

The broad consensus about basic dimensions of relationship is impressive, in view of the diversity of data on which it is based. Although the majority of studies favor a two-dimensional rather than a three-dimensional scheme, the two dimensions that recur will be readily recognized as components of the three-dimensional models already reviewed. Thus, one of these is variously designated as status (Pope & Siegman, 1972), dominance-submission (Leary, 1957), individual assertiveness (Borgatta, 1960), and control-autonomy

(Schaefer, 1959); and the other, love-hostility (Leary, 1957), warmth-coldness (Pope & Siegman, 1972), solidarity (Brown, 1965), and sociability (Borgatta, 1960).

Many of the studies dealing with the above two dimensions of human interaction have been summarized by Carson (1969). In one of these investigations the author (Borgatta, 1960) asked college men and women, meeting together in newly formed small discussion groups, to rank the other members of their groups on a number of trait and behavior variables. A similar factor structure emerged for each sex, consisting of two dimensions, designated as individual assertiveness and sociability. However, individual assertiveness was more salient for the men than the women.

Working in a completely different relationship situation, that is, the behavior of mothers toward their children, Schaefer (1959) obtained two similar dimensions, which he labeled control-autonomy and love-hostility. Schaefer's data consisted of ratings made by trained observers of the behavior of mothers toward their children during testing sessions and other ratings from written notes of the interaction of mothers with their children during home visits.

In a factor analysis of interviewee postinterview ratings of the interviewer carried out by Pope and Siegman (1972), two factors analogous to those referred to above were found. These were called warmth and competence or status. The positive pole of the first factor describes an interviewer perceived as warm, sympathetic, understanding, and pleasant; the positive pole of the second, an interviewer who is competent, confident, strong, comfortable, and intelligent.

Another attribute of the two-dimensional model for describing relationship is the tendency for the separate variables that give rise to the dimensions to correlate with each other in such a manner as to trace a circle with the two dimensions, forming two diameters of the circle, at right angles to each other. The circular ordering of variables is termed a circumplex. The circle is divided into four quadrants which are useful for the location in social space of single interactions, or single perceptions of the interpersonal behavior of each of the participants in a relationship.

In a summary of a widely ranging program of research, Lorr and McNair (1966) produced considerable evidence supporting a two-dimensional circumplex model of interpersonal behavior. They used a device called the Interpersonal Behavior Inventory for the rating of several groups of psychotherapy patients by their therapists and, additionally, for the rating of nonpatients by psychology students who were familiar with them. In all these instances, the focus of the ratings was the interpersonal behavior of the Ss. Lorr and McNair (1966) labeled the vertical diameter of their circumplex dominance-submission and the horizontal diameter, affiliation-aggression. The items of the inventory yielded 15 categories of interpersonal behavior, which arranged themselves in the following circumplex, clockwise order, starting with dominance (12 o'clock); exhibition, sociability, affiliation (3 o'clock); nurturance, agreeableness, deference, succorance, submissiveness (6 o'clock); abasement, inhibition, detachment, mistrust, aggression (9 o'clock) recognition, and back to dominance.

Some comment is now in order, about the types of data used in interactional studies. It is difficult to conceptualize the essence of relationship without resorting to abstractions that cannot be operationalized readily. Relationship is, after all, more than the separate cumulative sums of the perceptible behaviors of two persons responding to each other. A split-screen television projector could provide one with such cumulative sequences of behavior, when each participant is recorded separately. Even if the viewer knows that the two persons in the split halves of the screen are talking to each other, the relationship between them, as a unitary process, somehow eludes him/her, as s(he) views the split screen. One might think of relationship as a process that occurs in social space at a hypothetical interface between two or more persons. Because it is difficult to represent, observe, and measure such an hypothetical event, most investigators deal with more tangible components or correlates of the interaction. Thus, if one cannot represent the essence of an interaction between A and B, one may report observable or ratable behaviors of A or B or both A and B, that are assumed to be associated with, or expressive of, relationship. For example, Bales (1973) and Borgatta (1960) used measurable personality traits that predispose a person to certain patterns of relationship; Schaefer (1959) and Lorr'and McNair (1966) rated interactional behaviors recorded separately for the two partners; and Pope and Siegman (1972) employed the rated perceptions of interviewers by interviewees.

Leary (1957) also limited his focus to the participants in an interaction, taken singly. But he differed from the preceding authors in his conceptualization of levels on which relationship relevant responses might occur. Thus, Level I included the publicly observable behaviors of the persons interacting with each other; Level II, the perceptions by the interactants of self and others. Level I data may be obtained through ratings of a patient's behavior in an interview made by trained personnel or from sociometric ratings made, for example, by fellow patients. In either case, the resulting data describe the observations of a given S's overt behavior made by another. The ratings are based on descriptions of interactional behavior arranged in a circumplex which is divided into quadrants by dominance-submission and love-hate axes. Level II data are obtained from the S himself/herself, through the use of an interpersonal checklist, or the content analysis of the S's verbalizations in an interview or a group interaction situation. The interpersonal traits and attitudes included in the checklist items or content analysis categories correspond precisely to the observed behaviors rated at Level I.

One other aspect of the Leary system brings it very close to the interactional center of relationship. He included two sets of variables, one that describes the behavior of a given S, and the other, the corresponding behavior of the person or persons with whom the S is interacting. To accomplish this, he developed a theory of relationship that specified the most probable behaviors in others that the S's interpersonal behavior is likely to elicit. For example, at Level I there is a high probability that a S whose behavior in an interpersonal situation is characterized by managing, directing, and leading will provoke or elicit obedience from the person or persons with whom s(he) is interacting. Similarly, S behavior designated as "help, offer, and give" is likely to elict "trust" from another; "affectionate and friendly" acts will evoke love; and asking for help and trust should bring help.

At this point, the Leary framework becomes an interpersonal theory of behavior, with its roots deeply embedded in the concepts advanced by Sullivan (1953). Sullivanian theory becomes very much engaged with the problem of why a particular behavior of A is likely to elicit a specified behavior by B. For example, how might one understand the clinical commonplace that inverviewee dependent behavior will probably evoke a nurturant response from the interviewer? Sullivan (1953) would regard both behaviors as complementary to each other. The tendency toward agreement derives from the view that interpersonal interactions are basically security operations. Certainly, the dependent behavior of A will leave him/her in a state of anxiety unless B responds, in a complementary way, with help. The dependent behavior of A is therefore both the expression of a need and the demand for a complementary response from B. Both are essential components of the security operation. Similarly, if A leaves a psychotherapy interview with the anxious awareness that s(he) is not able to solve his/her problems alone, s(he) may presently experience a complementary awareness that the therapist may be a source of help. The mental health interviewer learns to sense the security demands implicit in much of what the interviewee says and does.

Consider the patient who delivers long, fluently articulated, insightful expositions of his problems. Whenever the therapist intrudes with a comment, the patient listens with a strained sort of tactful, but discernibly impatient, attention. After a decent interval during which s(he) tolerates the therapist's intrusion, s(he) returns to his/her intricately spun narrative. For whatever reasons in past personal history, this patient needs to communicate his/her intellectual virtuosity to the therapist. He also needs to control the interaction so that his/her programmed narrative is not disrupted. A complementary response from the therapist would somehow express an appreciation of the patient's intellectual abilities. This s(he) might do by communicating in the same intellectual idiom and style as the patient, but keeping such reply in low key so that the patient might not perceive it as threateningly competitive. Certainly the therapist would avoid wresting control of the floor from the patient. That is, the therapist would observe these rules of complementarity if s(he) wanted to help the patient complete the security operation implicit in his/her style of communication. Of course, the therapist might decide that the security operation itself is a suitable object of inquiry and might therefore avoid the complementary behavior sought by the patient, risking the ensuing anxiety.

But a persistent patient might train the therapist to observe the rules of complementarity, because they are reinforcing to both participants. If the therapist in the above example had been effectively trained by the patient, certain interactional patterns might ensue. Whenever the patient was verbally dominant, the therapist would remain submissively silent. Under the seduction of the patient's elegantly phrased verbalizations, the therapist might also lapse into decorative language. The basic reinforcer for both participants is the avoidance of anxiety. The patient's anxiety about loss of control of the communication situation and the therapist's anxiety about the possible expression of anger and disapproval or competitiveness with the patient are both stilled. An interviewer who does not tolerate anxiety in the person s(he) is interviewing, may learn to avoid it by assuming a passive role, reciprocal to the interviewee's activity, and a friendly role, corresponding to the positive feeling expressed by the interviewee.

The present section on dimensions of relationship will be concluded with a review of research dealing with status or control in the interview relationship. There has already been a summary of studies on warmth and coldness (positive and negative feeling) in Chapter 5. Earlier in this chapter status has been defined as the "differences in the degree of prominence, control," and influence that one person has over another with whom he is interacting. If A is superior in status to B, A has power, influence, and control over B. Moreover, if A and B are partners in an interview situation, the unequal status between A and B will be reflected in the kind of communication that develops between them. Thus, if A is the person of superior status, s(he) is likely to assert his/her dominance in the situation, and B will be prompted to assume a more submissive posture. This type of relationship is sometimes referred to as complementary* in contrast to the symmetrical relationship that obtains when A and B are of equal status (Watzlawick et al., 1967).

Carson (1969) had related complementary (reciprocal in Carson's terms) behavior to the dominance-submission dimension of relationship, and symmetrical (corresponding in Carson's terms) behavior to the love-hate (warm-cold, friendly-hostile) dimension. Watzlawick et al. (1967) made a similar distinction between relationships based on equality between the two interactants and those based on a status difference.

Perhaps the extreme in a status differentiated interview (i.e., complementary rather than symmetrical) occurs when A interrogates B under circumstances in which A's power over B is great. Danziger (1976) gives an interesting account of the interrogation of political prisoners in South Africa, who had been arrested because of active opposition to the apartheid regime, when such opposition had been declared illegal.

In accordance with the usual South African practice in such cases all the persons in the interviewed sample had been kept in solitary confinement during the intervals between the interrogations, although in the end all were released without any formal legal charges made against them. This study was conducted at a time when the use of physical torture against the political prisoners was far less usual than it subsequently became, and in fact none of the persons interviewed was subject to such treatment. The interrogators of the political police were therefore relying essentially on their exceptional powers to manipulate the interpersonal relationships of their prisoners who

---

* Note that the term "complementary" has a somewhat different connotation here than the one it had in the preceding discussion of Sullivanian theory. Complementary behavior, in its present sense, refers to a reciprocal or inverse interaction between two persons. In the Sullivanian sense it referred to whatever one person had to do to complement the behavior of the other in order to complete his security operation.

were deprived of their rights to consult lawyers, see relatives, communicate with other prisoners, and so on for indefinite periods of time. In many, though not in all, cases these techniques were effective and provided the police with some of the information they were after. (p. 15)

There can be no doubt that the interrogation interview occurred under conditions of marked status difference between the interrogator and the prisoner. The power of the interrogator was absolute. He enhanced it by isolating the prisoner, exercising control over the conditions under which s(he) lived, and permitting human contact and communication only when the prisoner submitted to the conditions imposed upon him. This submission was facilitated by the interrogators who frequently tempered their coercive behavior with a measure of feigned personal sympathy.

One of two officers had obviously specialized in this technique and would regularly appear on the scene at what was considered to be an appropriate moment. Suddenly the prisoner would be confronted with a strong supportive fatherly figure who would lament over his undeserved fate by putting a protective arm around him and even producing a discreet tear or two. He would promise to intercede for the prisoner, but somehow a promise of greater cooperation was delicately worked into the act. These were strong pressures to resist for anyone indefinitely isolated from genuine sources of interpersonal support.   (Danziger, 1976, p. 16)

The above operation, involving two interrogators and one prisoner, could be placed a little to the right of the top of the dominance axis in the Leary circumplex, and characterized sometimes by "dominate" and "boss," and at other times by "guide" and "advise." In later recalling their experiences many prisoners were astonished at their failure to feel appreciable hostility to their captors. Several remembered with incredulity some positive feeling for their jailors. Coming out of isolation, where they had been deprived of human contact, they had a range of reactions which subsequently seemed inappropriate to them. Frequently they attempted to joke and engage in pleasantries with their interrogators; often they would use a variety of ruses to prolong their interviews. Most puzzling to many prisoners after their release was their recollection of a wish for positive feedback from their captors, for expressions of approval and esteem. In a word, under conditions of the sometimes punitive and sometimes benign manipulation of dominance in interrogation interviews, the interviewees responded with a range of compliant and submissive behaviors.

Contrast status and dominance as they were manipulated in the interrogation interview with the symmetrical relationship advocated by many client-centered and other humanistic interviewers. In an article entitled "Equalizing the Counseling Relationship" (Boy & Pine, 1976), the authors made the following case for a nonstatus differentiated interview:

The mission of the counselor, then, is to create a counseling environment in which the relationship with a client, or group of clients, is equalized; a relationship in which each of the participants equally contributes to the goals, process, and outcomes of the relationship; an association in which the counselor significantly contributes to equalizing the relationship by not controlling or manipulating either the relationship or the client. (p. 20)

The implication of the above is that both a submissive response by a client to a dominant counselor, or rebellious resistance to him/her are likely to vitiate the counseling process. The preference is clearly for a nondominant, noncontrolling role for the counselor.

A reinforcement interpretation of symmetrical or nonstatus differentiated relationships on the one hand, and others based on dominance-submission or high and low status (Patterson & Reid, 1970) provides an explanation of how two such contrasting types of interaction are maintained. In a symmetrical relationship A and B reinforce each other at equalized or symmetrical rates. Thus, A's brevity is matched by that of B. But if A becomes more communicative, speaking with less hesitation, B is likely to be prompted to increase his/her productivity and readiness to respond. In a dyadic exchange in which the status difference between A and B is minimal, the productivity of each is positively reinforcing to the other. But if A is clearly dominant over B, whether such dominance occurs in a police station or a medical clinic, A's questions are either openly or implicitly punitive. If B fails to respond, s(he) may be subject to legal sanctions or medical rejection. In either case an aversive condition is created, which can be terminated only by B's communication of the information demanded. B's response will be positively reinforcing to the interrogator, but will have negatively reinforcing consequences for himself/herself. That is, ·the interviewee's responses will be maintained or coerced by the cessation of the aversive condition. Noncompliance is punished, and compliance reinforced, often simply through the termination of the punishment.

Until this point, status has been depicted as an aversive stimulus or condition. An unequalized interview in which there is a marked status difference between interviewer and interviewee has been portrayed as one in which the interviewer is inevitably coercive or dominant. Yet, it must be evident that such a picture is overdrawn. Status as a dimension is an abstraction. In actuality, different interviewers are likely to combine varying levels of status with different degrees of warmth or affection. Thus, some status roles and some components of status may be more benign than others. For example, the experienced mental health interviewer may evoke more trust and confidence from the interviewee than the novice interviewer. This is probably the case because experience in conducting a mental health interview is assumed to be associated with skill and competence. Status is therefore not always perceived in terms of control, dominance, and threat; it may also been seen as expertise. There is a widely shared body of opinion that people are more willing to communicate with an interviewer whom they perceive as a competent expert rather than an unskilled beginner.

In a study reported by Pope and Siegman (1972) it had been anticipated that high-status interviewers would elicit greater interviewee productivity, fluency, and less resistiveness than interviewers of low status. The Ss were junior and senior nursing students, all female, who were paid for participation in the experiment. Contrasting expectations were aroused in the Ss before the two interviews in which they participated, leading them to anticipate that one of the interviewers would be an experienced psychologist, and the other, an inexperienced trainee. To maintain the two induced expectations, it was necessary to place a screen between the interviewee and the interviewer, in order to eliminate visual cues which would have confounded the status manipulation in many ways. The words spoken by the interviewer were the same across both conditions.

The results indicated clearly that the high-status (experienced) interviewer commanded more productive (greater mean number of words per response) and readier (shorter average response time in seconds) responses than the low-status (inexperienced) interviewer. One is therefore tempted to conclude that interviewees do show greater trust and readiness to speak about personal matters to an experienced interviewer than to a novice. However, two additional borderline results raise some doubt about such a clear-cut conclusion. The average duration of interviewee silence within responses (Silence Quotient) was greater for the experienced interviewers at a borderline level of significance, as was interviewee Resistiveness (blocking, denial, excessive justification). The latter was a sequence effect. It occurred in both the high- and low-status interviews for those Ss who were given the high-status interview first. The suggested pattern of interviewee response to the experienced rather than the novice interviewer seemed to be one of quick and verbose compliance, associated, however, with little open self-disclosure (i.e., much silence and resistiveness).

In a later investigation (Pope, Nudler, Norden, & McGee, 1976; Pope, Nudler, VonKorff, & McGee, 1974) the experienced professional interviewer was again compared with the novice - this time, in a' more naturalistic context. In the first study, status, as experience, was experimentally manipulated through a preinterview induction. In a sense, experienced versus inexperienced status was an abstraction, because the interviewees were prevented from seeing the interviewers by a screen. In the present study the interviewees were female college student volunteers. The experienced interviewers were staff psychiatrists in a private psychiatric hospital and third-year psychiatric residents; the inexperienced interviewers were undergraduate students beginning their sophomore year, with no prior training in interviewing. Both experienced and inexperienced interviewers were matched for sex. Each volunteer student interviewee was interviewed once by a student and once by an experienced interviewer. The sequence of experienced and novice interviewers was counterbalanced across interviews.

In this investigation interviewer status was regarded as a two-component variable, the effect of which would be determined by the interviewee's perception of the two components within the interviewer. To the extent that the interviewee regarded the experienced interviewer as the one with greater expertise, it was expected that the advantage would go to him/her over the novice. To the extent that the interviewee perceived him/her as socially more distant and more dominant, the advantage would go to the novice.

Predictions about results were therefore not specific, since they rested on an uncertain balance between the two aspects of interviewer status.

Using 10-point rating scales, the interviewees recorded their perceptions of each interviewer immediately after the completion of the interview. They rated the novice interviewers as more sympathetic and accepting than the experienced interviewers. On the other hand, they perceived the experienced interviewers as more relaxed, skilled, and indeed, experienced. These postinterview ratings lend some support to the concept that interviewer status is not a unitary dimension, and that it may have both facilitative and inhibiting components. Certainly there is evidence that the interviewees perceived their peers, as interviewers, more benignly than they did a number of experienced and presumably skilled mental health professionals.

The initial comparison of experienced and novice interviewers was followed by two others (Pope et al., 1976), carried out as the erstwhile novice interviewers proceeded through a three-year mental health worker (paraprofessional) training program with an explicit emphasis on the development of interview skills. The student interviewers, no longer novices, interviewed a second group of female student volunteers one year later, and a third group, two and one-half years later, just before graduation. No longer were they perceived as less relaxed and less skilled than the professionals. Although they were still rated as less experienced, their level of experience, as rated by successive groups of student interviewers, rose significantly. The increase in relaxation and skill attributed to the student interviewers over the three-year training period may have been a consequence of their lowered verbal anxiety. In the first round of interviews, novice interviewers manifested more speech disturbances (incompletions, sentence changes, stutters, intruding incoherent sounds) than the professionals. In the subsequent two interviews this difference in speech disturbance rate between student and professional interviewers had disappeared. Thus, their discomfort decreased and their visible expertise increased. But there was no coincidental increase in social distance. The student interviewers continued to perceive them as more sympathetic and accepting than the professionals.

What were some of the correlates and consequences of the interviewee status differences in the present study? To the extent that relationship could be assessed, it favored the student interviewers. Thus, the students were rated by independent observers as higher than the professionals on the Truax-Carkhuff facilitative scales of warmth and genuineness.

As anticipated, the pattern of verbal interaction differed between "professional" and "student" interviews. Since the students were much closer to the interviewees in status, it was expected that the mode of communication in interviews that they conducted would be more symmetrical, more equalized, than that in interviews conducted by professionals. Synchrony between interviewer and interviewee should, therefore, occur more prominently in "student" rather than "professional" interviews. For example, there should be a positive correlation between interviewer and interviewee productivity (number of words uttered) in "student" interviews, but not in "professional" interviews. Such was indeed the case. One may conclude that there is a greater resonance between the two participants in interviews that lack status differentiation. Communication is more equalized; it resembles a conversation more than the role differentiated patterns that occur in the "professional" interviews.   If A emits a burst of conversation, B is likely to respond in kind.   If A becomes terse, there is a tendency for B to become similarly brief.

Finally, there are the payoff variables, interviewee productivity and self-disclosure.   One might assume that expertise and experience should have the power of eliciting the kind of trust that would permit the interviewee to speak in a free and open manner.   And this may indeed be the case in many situations.   For example, a person who seeks help because of disabling depression or confusing anxiety may indeed be quite prepared to communicate openly to an interviewer whom he perceives as a potential source of expert help.   But in the context of the present study, an outpouring of self-disclosing communication to the professional interviewer did not occur.   In fact, the significant differences tended in the opposite direction.   There were no differences in interviewee productivity.   However, self-disclosure as inferred from the level of Resistiveness in interviewee communication favored the student   interviewer;   that   is,   the   student   interviewer   elicited   less Resistiveness in the interviewee than the professional interviewer.

The studies by Pope and Siegman (1972) and Pope et al. (1974, 1976) do not permit a facile generalization about the matching of interviewer and interviewee on the status dimension.   The first investigation used an experimental manipulation of experience and obtained a more productive response from the interviewee to the more experienced interviewer.   But the latter two naturalistic studies favored the inexperienced (novice) interviewers.   It would appear that the social proximity between interviewer and interviewee may be more salient in some situations than the expertise and experience of the interviewer.   Recent impressions gained in work with clients of low socioeconomic origin suggest that the matching of status of interviewer and interviewee may be particularly important when the latter is a low-status person (Goodman, 1969; Guerney, 1969; Rappaport, Chinsky, & Cowen, 1971).   In this case status is associated with such aversive attributes as social distance and dominance.   For this reason the social proximity of nonprofessional mental health workers to low-status clients is often a facilitating asset. The adjustment and control of the social distance between the two participants in an interview is managed through the matching of the two.   The remainder of this chapter will review the literature dealing with matching.

THE MATCHING OF INTERVIEWER AND INTERVIEWEE

Research on the matching of interviewer and interviewee has led to few general guidelines for the selection of partners who are optimally matched for the development of a positive relationship. Nevertheless most clinicians would concede that informed matching could be important, because they know that they work better with some patients than with others. But very few have learned to identify the types of patients with whom they are likely not to be effective. "Most of us have been trained to 'universalize' ourselves, to behave as though we could be of decisive benefit to almost any patient with whom we happen to be doing psychotherapy" (Berzins, 1977).

Although the research on the matching of therapists with patients has yielded tentative and contradictory findings, it has reinforced the quest for guidelines that will permit the fitting of a therapist with a patient, so as to ensure a favorable result. However rudimentary the general guidelines for matching might be, certain patterns have recurred with sufficient frequency to provide some direction to the practitioner of the clinical interview. Of these, two basic ones may be characterized by the following two aphorisms: "It takes one to know one" (similarity) and "Opposites attract" (complementary) (Meltzoff & Kornreich, 1970). These two principles for matching the participants in a dyadic communication situation, are, at first glance, contradictory. The first implies that the interviewer and interviewee should be similar for optimum results; the second, that they should be sufficiently varied so that one complements the other. Although different, one need not assume that these two matching principles are incompatible. The literature surveyed in the preceding section demonstrated that therapist-patient similarity may indeed be facilitative on some dimensions (e.g., on the love-hate variable), and complementarity, equally facilitative on other dimensions (e.g., dominance-submission). Thus, expressions of love by A tend to evoke similar expressions of love from B. Hate also tends to evoke hate. But the rule of similarity does not govern relationships on the dominance-submission axis. On the contrary, dominance tends to evoke submission. Similar socioeconomic status may enhance communication in a psychotherapeutic interview, and dissimilar status, inhibit it. But, by way of contrast, a therapist who interviews a patient with neurotic conflicts similar to his/her own, may encounter greater difficulty in communicating and responding to the patient than s(he) might when interviewing a patient with neurotic problems that are quite different.

The matching studies reviewed below are by and large relevant to psychotherapy outcome rather than the interview process as such. The criterion, in most instances, is success versus failure in therapy. In one instance, however, self-disclosing communication in the interview is the dependent variable. The two studies that follow (Persons & Marks, 1970; Snyder & Snyder, 1961) deal with similarity in personality traits as though it were a linear dimension. The first one (Persons & Marks, 1970) obtained positive findings indicating that similarity between interviewer and interviewee had a facilitating affect on the interaction; the greater the similarity the greater the facilitation. The second study (Snyder & Snyder, 1961) produced negative results.

The major purpose of the first investigation in the present group "was to ascertain what interaction of personal attributes of interviewer and interviewee make it possible for the severely antisocial interviewee to be self disclosing" (Persons & Marks, p. 389). The $\underline{S}$s were inmates from a state reformatory for men, white, of normal intelligence, and 18 to 22 years of age. All $\underline{S}$s were selected because they had taken the MMPI and fitted one of three two-point profiles; 4-2 (Psychopathic Deviate-Depression), 4-8 (Psychopathic Deviate-Schizophrenia), and 4-9 (Psychopathic Deviate-Hympomania). Inter-viewers were selected who matched the interviewees on the three MMPI profiles. Thus, two interviewers had 4-2 profiles; two, 4-8 profiles; and two, 4-9 profiles. Each interviewer conducted an interview with an equal number of Ss from each of the three MMPI profile groups, one-third from his own profile group, and the remaining two-thirds from the other two profile groups. The object was to determine whether interviewees would be more self-disclosing when speaking to interviewers of their own profile types rather than different profile types. Such was the case. Five of the six interviewers elicited more self-disclosing responses from Ss of their own personality type.

In the second study (Snyder & Snyder, 1961) similarity between interviewer and interviewee did not turn out to be a significant influence on patient improvement. A single therapist worked with clients, all but one of whom were graduate students in psychology. The one who was not was a young faculty member from an allied department. The therapist described the type of treatment he conducted as ego building based on an application of learning theory. With the scales of the Edwards Personal Preference Schedule as measures of personality traits, he found that precisely one-half of the clients became more like the therapist over the course of treatment, on the EPPS scales, and the other half, less like him. Four of the clients who were most like the therapist on EPPS scores at the beginning of treatment were the least successful cases, and four others, who were least like the therapist, were the most successful. Even when comparisons were based solely on the eight EPPS scales that are most concerned with interpersonal relationship, there was no significant similarity between therapist and the clients, whether they belonged to the successful outcome or the unsuccessful outcome group.

The first two studies have investigated the hypothesis of a linear relationship between interviewer-interviewee similarity on personality traits and either psychotherapy outcome or communication within the interview. It was assumed that the greater the similarity, the better would be the results. The findings provided only partial support for the hypotheses.

Other investigators departed from the assumption of linearity, but continued to predict a significant relationship between similarity and both outcome and process. Thus, a number explored the possibility of a curvilinear relationship, according to which a medium degree of therapist-patient similarity would be conducive to better results than either high or low patient-therapist similarity (Meltzoff & Kornreich, 1970).

The first study in a series that dealt with a possible curvilinear relationship was carried out by Carson and Heine (1962). They reasoned that "psychotherapeutic success depends upon the therapist's being able to achieve an optimum balance between empathy and objectivity in dealing with his patient, ...with very high similarity the therapist might be unable to maintain suitable distance and objectivity, whereas in the case of great dissimilarity, he would not be able to empathize with or understand the patient's problems" (Carson & Heine, 1962, p. 38). The optimum relationship would therefore be one of moderate similarity, with therapeutic success falling away as one moved toward either extreme.

The therapists were senior medical students; the patients both male and female were selected from admissions to the psychiatric out-patient clinic of a medical school. The determination of similarity between patient and therapist was based on the MMPI profiles of both. The criterion for the outcome of treatment was a composite of several outcome ratings made by the psychiatrist who supervised each psychotherapy case. As predicted, moderate similarity between therapist and patient was associated with the highest level of success, while the extremes of the similarity dimension, with least success.

In a study by Cook (1966), the relationship between patient-therapist similarity in values and changes in patient self-concept was investigated. Medium patient-therapist similarity was associated with more positive change in self-concept during therapy than either high or low value similarity.

The curvilinear hypothesis has seductive appeal to the practicing clinician because of its commonsense plausibility. Unfortunately its initial success was not long sustained. An investigation (Lichtenstein, 1966) designed along lines that closely resembled those followed by Carson and Heine (1962) failed to replicate their findings. The therapists were medical students treating out-patients under supervision. The MMPI was again used to assess similarity between therapist and patient. The criterion of success in treatment was the same composite of several outcome ratings used by Carson and Heine (1962). But this time there was no relationship of any kind between the measures of similarity and success.

The retreat from the first positive findings was completed in a second replication study (Carson & Llewellyn, 1966), which followed the design of the Carson and Heine (1962) investigation. For the second time, there was no systematic relationship between personality similarity and outcome. The authors explained their failure in the following way: "In particular, we are no longer convinced at this stage of development that global personality similarity is either very fruitful or very workable as a concept, and would recommend that future investigators in this area consider its abandonment in favor of more precise, analytical procedures" (Carson & Llewellyn, 1966, p. 458).

Another matching investigation (Mendelsohn & Geller, 1965) demonstrates that the need for specificity of definition applies equally to the criteria of outcome success. Some outcome criteria may demonstrate the curvilinear relationship, while others may not. In the study by Mendelsohn and Geller (1965) the Ss were students who came to a university counseling center for assistance, with educational, vocational, and personal problems. The interviewers were permanent, full-time, professional psychologists. Global similarity between clients and counselors was assessed with the Myers-Briggs Type Indicator, a self-report personality inventory. A questionnaire filled out by the clients, several months after the completion of counseling, dealing with client attitudes toward the counseling experience was used as the source of outcome criteria. The items of this questionnaire were intercorrelated and cluster analyzed, with four resulting clusters. Three of these were designated evaluation ("I am well satisfied with my counseling experience"), comfort-rapport ("The counselor gave me the feeling that I was more than 'just another student' "), and judged competence ("The counselor tended to jump to conclusions"). For the evaluation cluster, a curvilinear relationship with client-counselor similarity appeared with medium similarity producing the highest scores. Comfort-rapport scores were also highest for the medium similarity condition, but only with the older students (nonfreshmen). Freshmen students in the high similarity group provided the highest comfort-rapport scores. The _evaluation_ finding is the more important because it is the most salient measure of the achievement of counseling objectives.

It seems reasonable to conclude that there is some research support for the curvilinear hypothesis, but it may be obscured by global measures of personality and outcome. The task of further research will be the specification of personality variables, outcome criteria and population groups, so that the predictive data accumulated will have sufficient precision to permit the clinical matching of patient with therapist.

In addition to studies on interviewer-interviewee similarity based on the personality traits and attitudes of both members of the dyad, a number of other matching variables have been investigated. Similarity of race and social class are considered at some length in Chapter 10. However, very brief reference will be made here to two studies that will serve as a bridge between the present discussion of matching and the survey of investigations dealing with race and social class that occurs in Chapter 10. One was conducted by Holzman (1962) with out-patients. He found that the ability to succeed on the job, to achieve independence of one's parents, and to enter into social relationships was significantly improved when the therapist and patient were of similar socioeconomic background and had similar values.

In a somewhat later study (Carkhuff & Pierce, 1967), which obtained its data from an initial interview rather than a psychotherapeutic one, similarity between interviewer and interviewee on both race and social class was significantly related to interviewee depth of self-exploration. Depth of client self-exploration has been found to be significantly associated with outcome in psychotherapy. There were four interviewers in the study, including one upper class white, one upper class black, one lower class white, and one lower class black. Each interviewer worked with an equal number of patients from the four socioeconomic and ethnic groups designated above. Taped segments of the interviews were then rated for depth of self-exploration. As it turned out, in the interaction between interviewer and interviewee, race and social class were significantly related to interviewee depth of self-exploration. It was found that "the patients most similar to the race and social class of the counselor involved tended to explore themselves most, and the patients most dissimilar tended to explore themselves least" (Carkhuff & Pierce, 1967, p. 634).

In the preceding studies on matching, interviewer and interviewee have been fitted on the same variables. Berzins (1977), however, reports an extensive investigation of what he calls asymmetrical matching, in which pairing is based on one set of variables for the therapist, and quite a different set for the patient. This asymmetrical approach is based on the assumption that some variables are more salient for therapists, and others, for patients.

Berzins' (1977) study, known as the Indiana Matching Project, developed and evaluated a therapist-patient matching procedure in a college clinic that practiced a short-term, crisis intervention type of psychotherapy. The investigators did not set out to formulate or confirm any general interpersonal theories for the optimal pairing of interviewers and inter-viewees. Instead, their goal was the development of a schema that could be used in one specific clinic with its unique patient population. En route, of course, the principles of similarity and complementarity were encountered.

But the emphasis was not on these principles as general laws of interaction. Instead, these and other findings were used as rules for the assignment of patients to therapists, in the hope that good results would be maximized and poor results, minimized. If the method were successful it could then be adapted to and used by other agencies. The work of the project moved through two basic steps. In the first, the rules for matching patients and therapists in the university clinic were developed empirically. In the second, the rules were applied in the assignment of patients to therapists and the effect of the matching assessed.

The patient variables studied were derived through factor-analytic procedures. They included "avoidance of others" (interpersonal anxiety), "turning against self" (depressive and somatic complaints), "dependency on others" (approval- and advice-seeking) and "turning toward others and self" (audience- and relationship-seeking). For the therapists, the selected variables were impulse expression, ambition, acceptance, dominance, caution, and abasement. The combining of patient and therapist variables to determine which pairs would predict successful treatment was accomplished through the correlation of the various pairings with the combined patient-therapist criterion of improvement.

Complementarity on a dominance-submission axis readily emerged as an important principle of pairing. Favorable matches occurred for both sexes when submissive, passive, patients were brought together with dominant, expressive, active therapists. The investigators noted additionally that "improvement in brief psychotherapy was facilitated by pairing patients with therapists whose personalities embodied ingredients that complemented the patients' needs, deficits, expectations or interpersonal stances" (Berzins, 1977, in press).

Another predictive matching cue applied to male dyads only. It specified that "given an interpersonally anxious patient, the appropriate match is a therapist who is at least moderate in acceptance; given a patient low in interpersonal anxiety, it does not matter whether the therapist is accepting or rejecting" (Berzins, 1977, in press).

The above two results exemplify an entire set of matching instructions applied by the clinical administrator to patients and therapists in the agency under investigation. Using these instructions, certain therapist-patient pairs were placed in an "assign" category, because the matches of variables on which they were based were found to be highly predictive of good outcome in the first part of the matching investigation. Other therapist-patient pairs were placed in "assign if necessary" and "do not assign" categories because they were based on combinations of variables that did not predict successful outcome as well. In the second part of the investigation, it was found that optimal ("assign") pairs showed higher improvement scores than the less than optimal pairs. Briefly, the objective of the study was the use of empirical procedures with one group of patients and therapists to determine how they might be matched in a specific clinical situation (clinic, agency, hospital) to ensure optimal therapeutic results, and then to test out the accuracy of the matching criteria. It is an exciting demonstration of the use of an empirically based matching procedure, developed to suit a specific agency or clinic, for the improvement of treatment outcome. While the matching rules that were useful in the clinic where the study occurred might not be valid in another agency, the technology would be transferable.

In addition to similarity and complementarity the concept of compatibility has also been used as a basis for matching interviewer and interviewee. Compatibility is a central component in a psychological theory of relationship developed by Schutz (1966). He defined compatibility as an attribute of relationship in which two persons coexist in harmony and work well with each other. "Compatibility does not necessarily imply liking. It is probable that often liking and compatibility are linked, but it is rather simple to recognize dyads (two people) who work well together without any particular liking, and dyads who like each other but don't work well together effectively" (Schutz, 1966, p. 106).

The scale discussed by Schutz to measure compatability between two persons, entitled FIRO-B has already been presented at an earlier point in this chapter. It will be recalled that it measures three dimensions of relationship, called Inclusion, Control, and Affection. Each dimension has two subscores, one assessing the S's expressed behavior, and the other, the behavior wanted from others. Thus, the subscale measuring expressed Inclusion is represented by the statement, "I initiate interaction with people"; that measuring wanted Inclusion, by "I want to be included." The subscale for expressed Control may be exemplified with the remark, "I control people"; that for wanted control, with "I want people to control me." Finally, the subscale dealing with expressed affection may be represented by the sentence, "I act close and personal toward people"; that with wanted affection, by the sentence, "I want people to get close and personal with me."

The two members of a dyad each complete all sections of the FIRO-B Scale, obtaining six subscores. From these scores, a number of compatibility indices are derived. Without dwelling on the scoring intricacies of the FIRO-B Scale, brief reference will be made to a few of the several compatibility concepts. The concept of reciprocal compatibility refers to a situation in which each participant achieves an optimal relationship between the behavior s(he) wants from the other person and the other person's expressed behavior in each need area. "By comparing A's description of how he likes to be acted toward with B's description of how he likes to act toward people, and vice versa, a measure of mutual need satisfaction emerges" (Schutz, 1966, p. 107).

A second form is called originator compatibility. For example, people who actively initiate inclusion in social groups and activities work best with those who have a more passive need to be asked to participate, to be invited to join. This is known as originator compatibility because one person is the originator and the other the receiver, and it is based on complementary behavior patterns of the two participants. A third form of compatibility occurs when both persons wish to actively express a specific need, or conversely apathetically to avoid it. Thus, two interactants may both express a preference for close personal relations, or conversely they may both wish to maintain considerable social distance from each other. Both the high interaction and the low interaction relationships are compatible ones.

Compatibility may be disrupted in various ways. When both members of a dyad have similar originator needs they may find themselves in competition with each other. Both A and B compete in their efforts to enter into a group, or to initiate an activity. When both have contrasting needs in the interaction, compatibility may be similarly disrupted. A may reach out affectionately toward B, but B may only wish to be left alone. Thus, incompatibility in the first instance results from similarity of needs between the two persons, and from contrasting needs, in the second instance.

Schutz (1966) gives compatibility a central place in his concept of the kind of relationship that promotes harmonious coexistence and productive co-operation. His is, in a way, a work-oriented, production-oriented theory of relationship. The studies that follow investigated the effect of compatibility in a number of different interactional situations.

An investigation conducted by Sapolsky (1960) dealt with verbal conditioning rather than the type of verbal exchange that occurs in an interview. Yet, its manipulation of compatibility between E and S and its focus on the control of verbal response makes it quite relevant to the interview. Es and Ss were both selected from undergraduate college classes, and matched so that half of the E-S pairs were compatible on the FIRO-B Scale, and the other half, incompatible. The E used "mm-hmm" to reinforce the use of "I" or "We" in sentence construction tasks given the S. It was found that the compatible group increased its use of reinforced pronouns to a greater degree than the incompatible group. Clearly, in this verbal conditioning study, the Es who were compatible with Ss were able to exercise greater influence over them than those that were not.

The next investigation by Sapolsky (1965) was more directly related to the psychotherapy interview. A number of voluntarily hospitalized female patients were treated by three psychiatric residents. Compatibility between the patient and doctor was again assessed with the FIRO-B Scale. A significantly positive correlation was found between patient-doctor compatibility and supervisors' ratings of patient improvement. The author concluded that compatibility of interpersonal needs are positively related to the outcome of treatment. "Highly compatible patients showed greater effects of their doctor's influence than did low compatibility patients" (Sapolsky, 1965, p. 73). Some mediating links between the FIRO-B measure of compatibility and outcome were found. With the use of a semantic differential device it was demonstrated that highly "compatible patients were more likely to feel that a similarity existed between themselves and their doctors and that their doctors understood them. Low compatibility dyads resulted in those patients feeling that a dissimilarity existed between themselves and their doctors and that their doctors did not understand them" (Sapolsky, 1965, p. 75). Moreover, feelings of being understood were related to favorable outcome. Thus, compatibility, as determined at the beginning of treatment is predictive of relationship attitudes that evolve during treatment (patient perception of doctor similarity to self; patient perception of being understood by doctor) and outcome.

Not all studies of compatibility between a counselor and a client, however, demonstrate the full range of the above positive findings. In one investigation (Mendelsohn & Rankin, 1969) compatibility was a poor predictor for male Ss, but a good one for females. The Ss were male and female clients in a university counseling center offering help with vocational, educational, and personal problems. Both clients and counselors took FIRO-B before the first interview. After the conclusion of the series of counseling interviews an evaluation questionnaire was filled out by each client. The results were for the most part disappointing. No significant correlations occurred between compatibility scores and evaluation of outcome by male clients, but a number did for female clients. However, the results for females were confusing. Compatibility on the Control dimension did correlate positively with the clients' evaluations of outcome, but compatibility on the Inclusion and Affection dimensions correlated negatively. The finding for the Control dimension suggests that the direction and control of the counseling process should be shared by both participants. But what is to be said of the negative correlations for Inclusion and Affection, both pertaining to the affective aspects of relationship? Is this an instance of the curvilinear relationship between client-counselor similarity on personality and attitudinal traits (Carson & Heine, 1962) as the authors contend, so that excessive similarity between client and counselor lead to an overidentification of the latter with the former's problems with consequent poor results? Possibly, but the argument does not seem very persuasive.

In a later study (Gassner, 1970) the results were somewhat more favorable to the compatibility hypothesis. The therapists were theological students engaged in pastoral counseling with largely psychotic in-patients. Three groups of Ss were selected for the study, one consisting of compatible pairs, one of incompatible pairs, and a third of no treatment controls. At three and 11 weeks of therapy, compatibly paired patients evaluated the therapy relationship more favorably than did incompatibly paired patients.

The concept of compatibility holds considerable promise. It penetrates into the center of relationship, encompassing both members of a dyad in a single process. It goes beyond such variables as similarity and complementary to a higher level of interpersonal inference. Though the results of various studies of compatability are not completely consistent, they are sufficient to suggest a positive relationship between compatibility, certain attitudes and perceptions of the interviewer by the interviewee, and the outcome of psychotherapy.

The present section on the matching of interviewer and interviewee will be concluded with a brief reference to its theoretical antecedent in the interpersonal psychiatry of Harry Stack Sullivan, (1965). In his summary of selected aspects of Sullivanian theory, Berzins (1977) refers to its emphasis on the dyadic interaction as an interpersonal situation "integrated" by the needs that each participant brings into the situation. It is therefore not the separate needs of the two individuals but their interaction which determines whether the "integration" that results will be "conjunctive" or "disjunctive" - that is, whether they bring people together or drive them apart. In Sullivan's language, conjunctive tendencies are associated with needs that are complementary; disjunctive tendencies, with needs that are antagonistic.

Indeed, Sullivan was very much concerned with the processes by which two persons might be attracted to or repelled from each other. In his day, the body of research literature dealing with similarity, complementarity, and compatibility as defined in the present chapter had not yet come into being. Yet Sullivan was very actively engaged in the clinical study of the matching of therapists and patients so that a "conjunctive" relationship would develop, facilitating a favorable outcome. "For example, he not only delimited his own therapeutic interactions largely to young, male, 'reactive' or catatonic schizophrenics but he also surrounded such patients with preselected aides on the rationale that their needs should not aggravate those of the patient even in casual interactions on the ward. Sullivan, thus seemed informally aware of which personal-social characteristics of therapists would facilitate or hinder therapy with these patients" (Berzins, 1977, p. 224).

Matching of patient and therapist or patient and hospital aide is clearly advocated in Sullivan's works. But matching cannot always be accomplished in practical clinical situations because of the press of work and staff limitations. Thus, an interviewer, sensitized to his/her own needs and the types of clients with whom s(he) experiences particular difficulty, may not be able to avoid clinical encounters with such individuals.

Nevertheless, some guidance may be obtained from the matching studies, since they deal not only with the pairing of individuals but with the matching of interpersonal behaviors. For example, the interviewer may anticipate the situations in which his/her friendly behavior will be facilitative and when it may be disruptive. While most patients will respond positively to an interviewer's friendly approach, paranoid patients may feel it to be intrusive. It may prompt them to withdraw further into their protected and very private enclaves. In addition, there will be clinical situations in which the interviewer may need to modulate or even reverse the interpersonal styles that may be habitually his/her own. Consider the interviewer who tends to be assertive, actively directive, or even dominant in social interactions. S(he) may need to be particularly sensitive to interview situations in which such patterns, however usual for himself/herself, may be disruptive of the interaction. A competitive encounter between two assertive, dominant, individuals is not conducive to the growth of a stable, positive relationship. On the other hand, an assertive, directive interviewer style may complement the passive self-subordinating style of an interviewee and lead to a "conjunctive" relationship.

But a word of caution is needed about the transposing of findings of matching studies into clinical practice. In terms of the preceding example, complementarity between the interviewer and interviewee in dominant behavior may indeed facilitate the growth of a positive relationship and productive communication between the two participants. But the interviewer may choose to trade off temporarily these advantages against another consideration to which s(he) may give higher priority. S(he) may sense as early as the initial interview in a psychotherapy sequence, that the passivity of the interviewee will become a central focus in the treatment to follow, and may therefore wish to avoid reinforcing it with his/her own initiative even at the outset. Considerations such as this one do not negate the value of the findings about the complementary character of the interaction between two people on the dominance-submission dimension. However, the actual deployment of the interviewer's dominant behavior may not always be determined by the need that the interviewee brings into the interview. The interviewer may choose to risk, for a time, some uncertainty of relationship in order to move the interviewee to a more dominant (less passive) point on the dimension. Thus, the application of research finding to a specific clinical situation is frequently a complex process for which there may be few guidelines in the research itself.

APPLICATION SUMMARY

Although clinicians accept the term "relationship" as code for an aspect of the interview which they intuitively recognize, it is difficult to inquire into the management of relationship without some definitional specification. The problem of definition was exemplified at the beginning of this chapter with the use of the two terms, rapport and transference. These were regarded as contrasting sharply in the depth of relationship to which they refer. Rapport is used to designate the beginning of the process of the integration of a relationship between two people. Transference, with its roots in psycho-analytic theory and practice, is a response of one person to another (A to B), determined only in part by B's attributes as a person and equally, or perhaps more, by A's relationships with significant people in his early years, particularly parents. Thus A transfers onto B the positive and negative feelings for and perceptions of parental and other significant persons.

The discussion by Polansky (1971) of the barriers to relationship and communication experienced by a schizoid person provides a rather striking example of a set of personality and attitudinal traits that seriously obstruct the development of rapport. The schizoid person's withdrawal from contact and communication is a pathological pattern, but it represents a kind of impediment to communication experienced to a lesser extent, by many people who are essentially normal. The pain and difficulty the young man felt when he found himself in a situation that required him to establish personal contact with an interviewer and to enter into a communicational exchange are not rare in the general population. The protective pattern of self-imposed isolation, to the point of inhibition of emotional response, is a basically human reaction. The attempts of some interviewers to crash through the protective barrier of self-imposed withdrawal is perceived as a threatening intrusion by the schizoid person. It nearly always fails as a method of developing rapport, violating, as it does, the principle of compatibility that Schutz (1966) has so clearly delineated. By contrast, Polansky's nonintrusive-ness, a good example of interchange compatibility (Schutz, 1966), creates the conditions for the gentle growth of rapport, a process more likely to succeed with the defensively withdrawn type of person he was interviewing

How does each participant in a dyadic exchange experience relationship? What is the instrumentality through which it is conveyed? Danziger (1976) provides a succinct answer when he remarks that two people communicating with each other may "talk without conveying any real information about the outside world, but it is not possible to talk without saying something about the relationship between the participants in the communication situation" (p. 27). In a word, relationship is conveyed through communication.

The interviewer learns to read the communication for its semantic content and, in a more pragmatic way, for what it conveys about relationship. The two aspects are frequently not congruent with each other. Thus, the patient who remarked after a period of silence that it has been cold all week might have been accused of making trivial small talk, if the lexical content of the remark were the sole consideration. But the remark, taken within the context of the preceding silence, was a poignant signal to the interviewer that the patient was inhibited in his/her presence. Unable to tolerate the audible silence and therefore driven to fill the void between herself/himself and the interviewer, the patient made the reported remark. From the comment, the interviewer must have learned considerably more about his/her relationship with the patient than about the weather.

Relationship may also be communicated in nonverbal channels. Consider the case of the patient described in a previous chapter who remained standing beside her chair at the beginning of each interview, waiting for the interviewer to invite her to be seated. It will be recalled that this patient was communicating a timid, self-subordinating sort of dependency. The perceptive interviewer listens to the words spoken by the interviewee, and scans his/her nonverbal behavior for what it may communicate about the interviewee's feelings and attitudes about the interviewer.

While communication may be regarded as an instrument of relationship, it is also seen as one of the consequences of relationship. A will not be able to speak or otherwise communicate with B unless there is a minimal relationship between the two. At the least, A must feel that B is aware of his/her presence and is willing to listen. A, as a person, must receive some measure of confirmation from B before being prompted to communicate.

In the folklore that abounds in the clinical field, the initial psychoanalytic interview emerges as the most difficult of all communication situations. The present author's brush with this type of interview has remained indelibly etched in his memory, undimmed by the passage of one quarter century. The analyst already ensconced in his unseen confessional cabinet, acknowledged the entrance of the patient in a perfunctory, barely visible manner. He pointed to the couch and lapsed into a ritual silence. The patient felt totally unrelated to this strangely inexpressive person. After some random delaying motions, he positioned himself on the sofa and promptly fell into a chilly silence. There he would have stayed if there were not two light knocks on the office door. Out of his invisible confessional stumbled the analyst and, with some muttered imprecations, he opened the door a crack just wide enough to admit two high-pitched piping voices that were clearly heard to say: "Trick or treat!" If it were not for the happenstance that this first analytic session occurred on Halloween night, the initial silence would undoubtedly have continued the full 50 minutes. What the patient lacked was some sense of confirmation by the analyst. Without a modicum of relationship there seemed nothing to say.

The studies dealing with this matter demonstrate that an interviewee will say more when talking to a live interviewer than to a tape recorder. Similarly, the interviewee will speak more fully if the interviewer is free to use all channels of communication, instead of being restricted to a secondary one only. When the objective of the interviewer is to prompt communication, a genuine, natural style of relationship is the one most likely to succeed.

Because relationship is so essential an aspect of a human interaction, it is not possible to speak about it in nonevaluational terms. One of the first questions that occurs when one is observing an interview through a one-way screen, for example, is whether the relationship is good or poor, positive or negative, ideal or mediocre. Clinicians and researchers have correlated relationship with interviewee productivity and therapy outcome and found that some attributes facilitate communication and favorable outcome, while others do not.

There will be no attempt in this summary to operationalize good and poor relationship behavior. Even if there were unanimity about the character of a desirable relationship, the behavioral elements that compose it are not yet adequately specified. The approach will therefore be one of a sort of verbal modeling. The types of desirable relationship behavior about which there is wide agreement will be described (that is, verbally displayed).

The following are some attributes of interviewer relationship that receive extensive approval among clinicians: "Warmth, acceptance, permissiveness, respect for the patient, understanding, interest in the patient, and liking for the patient" (Gardner, 1964, p. 426).

Nearly three decades ago a concept of the ideal relationship behavior was developed by Fiedler (1950). This pattern was later designated by others as expressive of accurate empathy. The Rogerians have proceeded further than others in characterizing the type of immediate interaction between two persons that is conducive to positive therapeutic change. Several Rogerian relationship dimensions are incorporated in a scale developed by Barrett-Lennard (1959). Three of these pertaining to therapist behavior will be presented here.

Empathic understanding is a process by which one person resonates with another to the point of an acute consciousness of the other person's subjective experiences - that is, his/her changing awareness, the personal meaning in his/her communication, and the feelings conveyed.

Unconditionality of regard refers to the constancy of one person's regard or feeling for another. In the mental health interview, unconditionality may be approached if the interviewer warmly confirms the interviewee as a person, even though not approving of particular attitudes, feelings, or actions of the person.

Therapist congruence occurs when the therapist is at one with himself. S(he) is genuine in the sense that his/her inner feelings and overt communications are consistent with each other. S(he) does not feel one thing and say another. There is no facade in conflict with underlying feeling.

The attributes of a relationship, whether good or bad, cannot be spelled out in terms of the subjective experiences of one participant only, or of the two members of a dyad taken one at a time. Instead, the interaction between the two must be captured in some way. Several authors define relationship in the interview as a reciprocal exchange between the two participants, because they regard reciprocity as the central principle governing the interaction. Indeed, Snyder and Snyder (1961) has found an overall positive correlation between client and therapist attitudes over a psychotherapy sequence. And a somewhat later experimental analogue (Heller et al., 1963) demonstrated that therapists responded in a more friendly fashion to friendly "patients" (actually actors simulating the roles of friendly and hostile interviewees), and in a more hostile manner to hostile "patients." The findings about attitudinal reciprocity in the interview should prompt an interviewer to communicate with the interviewee in a friendly manner if s(he) wishes to elicit a positive, cooperative response.

Reciprocity may also be defined as the feedback that one member of a dyad receives from the other. A positive relationship is seen as an interaction in which each speaker receives feedback from the other, informing him/her that his/her message has been heard and understood, and that it is relevant to the communication in progress. Each speaker feels confirmed by the other under these circumstances, responding with both high verbal productivity and a positive attitude toward the other. These findings underscore the importance of the interviewer's response to the interviewee. The latter needs feedback from the interviewer telling him/her that s(he) has not been speaking into a void, that in fact s(he) has been heard and understood. Lacking such feedback, the interviewee's communication is likely to wilt; the interviewee may eventually withdraw from the interaction.

Relationship is often defined as the attraction of one member of a dyad to the other. Most studies dealing with this definition of relationship focus on the attraction of the interviewee to the interviewer and investigate the correlates of this attraction. Thus, an interviewee who is strongly attracted to an interviewer tends to perceive him/her as warm, accepting, understanding, pleasant, responsive, friendly, and interested. Moreover, the interviewee speaks less hesitantly to an attractive rather than an unattractive interviewer, because s(he) feels less uncertain and resistive. Finally, a client who is attracted to a therapist is certain to be more susceptible to the therapist's influence than a client who is repelled. Since positive interviewee responsiveness to the interviewer is enhanced by the attraction of the former to the latter, one may ask what guidance there may be in research studies about the course the interviewer might follow to elicit interviewee attraction. In the studies reviewed in the present chapter there are only two findings bearing on this matter. One suggests that interviewer warmth is more likely to arouse interviewee attraction than interviewer coldness. The other derives from the conclusion that "patients who are more attracted to the interviewer are in turn more attractive" (Goldstein, 1971, p. 35) to him/her. It may be expected that the converse of the above is also true. Thus, interviewers who are attracted to an interviewee are likely to be more attractive to him/her. While it would be difficult to write a set of operational rules for an interviewer to follow in attaining a sense of attraction to an interviewee, there are nevertheless certain implications in the above conclusion, for the matching of clinician and client. When circumstances permit a choice, the clinician might well heed his/her own inner promptings regarding potential clients, avoiding those whom s(he) finds strongly repellent.

Much of the empirical research dealing with dyadic and small group interaction has been related to the recurrent finding that interactional behavior rests on two orthogonal dimensions. One, usually represented in a vertical position, has reference to the status, dominance, control, or power aspect of relationship. The other dimension, usually drawn in a horizontal position, represents the affective aspect of the relationship. It is variously referred to as the warm-cold, friendly-hostile, or love-hate axis. Many authors speak of complementarity (Sullivan, 1953) or reciprocity (Carson, 1969) as principles of relationship that operate to help the two participants avoid the experience of anxiety. This is indeed the case on the dominance-submission axis of relationship (Carson, 1969). Thus, therapist dominance complements patient submissiveness and, conversely, patient dominance, therapist submissiveness. By contrast, the interaction on the love-hate (warm-cold) dimension tends to be symmetrical. Love engenders love; hate arouses hate. There is nothing in the relationship between two people that makes the above interactional principles inevitable. Yet there are strong forces that activate these principles. In part, the dyadic system compels the above contrasting interactions on the two dimensions. If the system is to remain viable, if it is not to disintegrate, reciprocity on the status dimension and symmetry on the warm-cold (love-hate) dimension are evidently required. Clearly, two dominant people are likely to enter into a destructive competition with each other. But two affectionate people may well be attracted toward each other. Perhaps of greater interest to the mental health interviewer is the extension by Carson (1969) of Sullivan's (1953) concept of the security operations implicit in much of a person's social behavior. For example, a verbally active person who dominates a social exchange has learned to banish anxiety with this pattern of behavior. The interviewer who is sensitive to the security implications in the patient's verbal activity will tend to respond to it with nondominant behavior. To be sure, the interviewer may behave quite differently if s(he) wishes to challenge the patient's mode of achieving security. If complementarity occurs on the dominance-submission axis to modulate anxiety, similarity is the manner in which feelings of security are maintained on the love-hate axis. Each member of the dyad will answer love or warmth from the other person, with his/her own love or warmth. Both participants tend to respond to the other in these matters because the avoidance of anxiety is strongly reinforcing to both communicants.

However, interview situations vary radically, and the spontaneous pattern of interaction sketched out above may be changed by the context in which two people are interacting. Consider, for example, the role of the interviewer in an interrogation (legal, medical, employment) in which the control or dominance axis is more salient than the love-hate axis. The interviewer has real power over the interviewee and is quite willing to manipulate dominance. Whether s(he) does it with bluster and threat, or with the subtle promise of forgiveness, there is the deliberate arousal of anxiety in the interviewee, and the simultaneous arousal of hope that anxiety will terminate if the interviewee behaves submissively. Reciprocity functions in a unidirectional way in the interrogation. The dominant participant (the interrogator) has no need to reciprocate, because s(he) does not himself/herself experience anxiety. S(he) is therefore free to manipulate his/her dominance at will and place the onus for a reciprocal response entirely on the interviewee. The interviewer is positively reinforced by the interviewee's submission. S(he) is gratified when the interviewee, who had been silent, begins to talk. Simultaneously, the interviewee is negatively reinforced, because the anxiety that threatened him/her during the period of silence is reduced when s(he) begins to speak.

Contrast the status-differentiated relationship in the interrogation interview with the symmetry in a humanistic type of counseling interview (Boy &
Pine, 1976). The practitioner of this type of interview differs from the
interrogator in every respect. S(he) sets out deliberately to equalize the
relationship, avoiding any sort of manipulation or control. The aversive
aspects of an unequal relationship are absent. The dynamic of the interview
is now found in the symmetry that governs the interactions between the two
participants. If the interviewer speaks with brief responses, the interviewee
does likewise. The interviewer does not compel longer responses from the
interviewee, but elicits them by longer, self-disclosing communication of
his/her own. In this type of exchange, the responses of both participants are
positively reinforcing to each other. Negative reinforcement does not occur.

The above contrast between the status differentiated and equalized
interview is extreme. Generally, interview situations vary on both relationship dimensions at the same time. There are many in which status and warmth
occur simultaneously in the behavior of the interviewer. Thus, the
experienced mental health interviewer, with a commitment to help, may
evoke more trust and confidence from the interviewee than a less
experienced counterpart. Status is therefore not always perceived in terms
of control, dominance, and threat; it may also be seen as expertise in helping.
One experimental analogue (Pope & Siegman, 1972) that manipulated
interviewer status as expertise and experience did indeed obtain greater
verbal productivity and a quicker reaction time from the interviewees when
they perceived the interviewer as an experienced professional rather than an
inexperienced trainee. Certainly one would expect such a result when the
interviewee is highly motivated to seek help because of a strong need, such as
acute anxiety or profound depression. In such instances, the patient's
emotional condition renders him/her subordinate to a potential helper, to
whom s(he) is willing to ascribe the benign status implicit in professional skill
and expertise.

But there are limits to the power that a client is willing to tolerate in a
potential helper. In two later studies, Pope et al. (1974, 1976) assumed that
interviewer status was not a unitary variable, but, instead, consisted of two
components - professional expertise and social distance. The perception of
interviewer expertise was thought to be associated with a productive and
positive response from the interviewee, and that of social distance, with an
inhibition of response. The relative weight of each component is determined
by the match between interviewer and interviewee in each case. Thus, when
mental health professionals and student novices both interviewed freshman
college students, the latter perceived their student interviewers as more
sympathetic and accepting than the professionals. They judged the latter to
be more relaxed, skilled, and experienced. As it turned out, the benign
aspects of relationship associated with social proximity were the more salient
in this situation. Thus, the student interviewers were rated as higher than the
professionals on warmth and genuineness. Moreover, there were no
differences in interviewee productivity when responding to the two groups of
interviewers, and some evidence that students were more self-disclosing with
student interviewers than with mental health professionals. Finally, the
"student" interviews were more equalized than the "professional" interviews.

Synchrony governed the productivity of both participants; this interactional pattern was lacking in the "professional" interviews.

These findings have many implications for the practice of interviewing. Whether one follows an equalized or status-differentiated approach depends in part on the character of the interview. It is assumed, of course, that the interviewer is able to exercise an option. Having learned to play active and passive roles, and to behave with more and less dominance, the interviewer may, to a degree, decide when he wishes to function as a mental health interrogator and when as a participant in an equalized exchange; when s(he) prefers the active helping role of an advisor or counselor and when that of participant in an egalitarian exchange. In part, such a choice will depend on the interviewer's reading of the clinical problems presented by his/her patient and, indeed, the patient's interpersonal patterns and security operations. The choice will also be determined by the theoretical predispositions of the interviewer. A behavior therapist zeroes in actively and specifically on the contingencies that reinforce undesirable behavior patterns; a client-centered therapist exchanges feelings, attitudes, and perceptions with his client in an open and equal way.

But there are situational constraints that may limit the choices available to him/her. For example, the two groups of interviewers in the studies by Pope et al. (1974, 1976) were perceived quite differently by the interviewees, whatever the individual behavior of each interviewer might have been. Student interviewers close to the ages of the student interviewees were seen as socially less distant than the older professional interviewers, a difference that overshadowed any others that might have occurred. One may assume that social distance is a particularly salient variable when the interviewees are low-status individuals. Recent mental health work with low socioeconomic clients in the community would suggest that the aversiveness with which many underprivileged persons perceive high-status professional experts is a consequence of the great social distance that separates the client from the therapist. The optimal adjustment of the social distance between the interviewer and the client is a problem in matching, a topic that shall be considered in the remainder of this summary.

Two basic and rather general rules govern the matching of interviewer and interviewee. These are expressed concisely in the following two aphorisms: "It takes one to know one" (similarity) and "opposites attract" (complementarity) (Meltzoff & Kornreich, 1970). These apparently contradictory principles are not incompatible because they apply to different dimensions of relationship. Matching on the love-hate dimension follows the principle of similarity; on the dominance-submission dimension, that of complementarity.

The matching of individuals is basically a procedure for the clinical administrator, who has the responsibility of assigning staff to clients. The Indiana Matching Project (Berzins, 1977) should therefore be of considerable interest. It is an impressive example of the application of an empirical matching technology to the needs of a specific agency, with its own special staff and patient population. While the principles of pairing that were predictive of good outcome of treatment in the college clinic where the study was carried out might not be valid for a different agency, the technology for matching has a general applicability. After the rules for matching were derived empirically from the data provided by one group of patients and therapists, they were applied predictively to patients and therapists in another group, with significantly positive results. The study is particularly promising because it demonstrates the use of empirically derived principles of matching, developed for a unique patient and therapist population, in the successful assignment of patients to therapists.

To the two principles of matching discussed above, entitled similarity and complementarity, may now be added a third, called compatibility. This principle is derived from Schutz's (1966) theory of relationship and defined by him as a condition in which two persons coexist in harmony and work well with each other. Compatibility assumes that each person participating in a relationship is impelled both by behavior that s(he) acts out himself/herself, and behavior that s(he) wants from others. Thus, the item on Schutz's (1966) FIRO-B Scale, "I control people," is indicative of S's expressed behavior on the control dimension and the item, "I want people to control me," of wanted behavior from one's partner, on the same dimension. Actually Schutz (1966) works not with one, but with several compatibility scores. One of these, called reciprocal compatibility, is defined as follows: "By comparing A's description of how he likes to act toward people, and vice versa, a measure of mutual need satisfaction emerges" (p. 107). Thus, compatibility prevails if one member needs to control others and the other likes to be controlled. Such compatibility would be dissipated in a competitive struggle if each member needed to control the other, or would languish in an atmosphere of passive nonrelationship if each member needed to be controlled by the other.

The studies carried out with compatibility between therapist and patient as the central variable in relationship demonstrated its positive correlation with successful outcome of treatment and with certain positive attitudes and perceptions of the interviewer by the interviewee. Compatible patients feel that there is a similarity between themselves and their doctors and that their doctors understand them.

By now it is evident that the clinical administrator has at least three principles that he may follow in matching interviewers with clients; those of similarity, complementarity, and compatibility. In addition, there is the technology for empirically determining the matching principles that would be predictive of therapeutic success in a specific agency and clinic and, indeed, the procedures for assigning clients to therapists on the basis of these principles.

Even when matching is a luxury not permitted by the reality of limited staff, some guidance may be obtained by the individual clinician from the findings of the matching studies. S(he) may find it useful to apply the principles for the matching of individuals to the matching of his/her behavior with that of the interviewee. For example, the interviewer may anticipate the situations in which his/her friendly behavior will be facilitative (e.g., during an interview with a neurotically anxious patient), and when it may be disruptive (during an interview with a paranoid patient). But s(he) may encounter difficulties in switching from one style of relationship behavior to another. Thus, an interviewer who is normally quiet, passive, and unassertive in his/her social behavior, may find it hard to assume a directive, assertive stance with a passive patient. For this type of switch, there is no substitute for interviewer self-awareness and clinical training that will prepare him/her to assume assertive roles when needed. Finally, it must be emphasized that the interviewer may deliberately disregard compatibility considerations when they conflict with therapeutic goals. Even as early as the initial interview s(he) may, for example, perceive a major therapeutic objective to be that of nudging a passive patient in the direction of greater activity and initiative. In that event s(he) would avoid assuming an active role (compatible with the patient's passivity) and would instead assume one of low activity. The patient would then tend to be stressed out of his/her submissive stance by its incompatibility with the low activity of the therapist.

REFERENCES

Anderson, R.P., & Anderson, G.V. Development of an instrument for measuring rapport. Personnel Guidance Journal, 1962, 41, 18-24.

Back, K.W. Influence through social communication. Journal of Abnormal and Social Psychology, 1951, 46, 9-23.

Bales, R.F. Communication in small groups. In G.A. Miller (Ed.), Communication, language, and meaning. New York: Basic Books, 1973.

Barrett-Lennard, G.T. The relationship inventory: A technique for measuring therapeutic dimensions of an interpersonal relationship. Paper read at the Annual Conferences of the Southeastern Psychological Association, St. Augustine, Florida, 1959.

Berzins, J.I. Therapist-patient matching. In A.S. Gurman & A.M. Razin (Eds.), Effective psychotherapy: An empirical assessment. New York: Pergamon Press, 1977.

Borgatta, E.F. Rankings and self-assessments: Some behavioral characteristics replication studies. Journal of Social Psychology, 1960, 52, 297-307.

Boy, A.V., & Pine, G.J. Equalizing the counseling relationship. Psychotherapy: Theory, Research and Practice, 1976, 13, 20-25.

Brown, R. Social psychology. New York: Free Press, 1965.

Buber, M. Distance and relation. Psychiatry, 1957, 20, 97-104.

Carkhuff, R.R., & Pierce, R. Differential effects of therapist race and social class upon patient's depth of self-exploration in the initial clinical interview. Journal of Consulting Psychology, 1967, 31, 632-634.

Carson, R.C. Interaction concepts of personality. Chicago: Aldine, 1969.

Carson, R.C., & Heine, R.W. Similarity and success in therapeutic dyads. Journal of Consulting Psychology, 1962, 26, 38-43.

Carson, R.C., & Llewellyn, C.E. Similarity and therapeutic dyads. Journal of Consulting Psychology, 1966, 30, 458.

Colby, K.M. Experiment on the effects of an observer's presence on the image system during psychoanalytic free-association. Behavioral Science, 1960, 5, 197-210.

Cook, T.E. The influence of client-counselor value similarity on change in meaning during brief counseling. Journal of Counseling Psychology, 1966, 13, 77-81.

Danziger, K. Interpersonal communication. New York: Pergamon Press, 1976.

Davidoff, L.L. Schizophrenic patients in psychotherapy. The effects of degree of information and compatibility expectations on behavior in the interview setting: An operant conditioning analogue. Unpublished doctoral dissertation, Syracuse University, 1969.

Fenlason, A.F. Essentials in interviewing. New York: Harper and Row, 1952.

Fiedler, F.E. A comparison of therapeutic relationships in psychoanalytic, nondirective, and Adlerian therapy. Journal of Consulting Psychology, 1950, 14, 435-36.

Gardner, G.G. The psychotherapeutic relationship. Psychological Bulletin, 1964, 61, 426-437.

Gassner, S.M. Relationship between patient therapist compatibility and treatment effectiveness. Journal of Consulting and Clinical Psychology, 1970, 34, 408-414.

Goldstein, A.P. Psychotherapeutic attraction. New York: Pergamon Press, 1971.

Goodman, G. An experiment with companionship therapy: college students and troubled boys - assumptions, selection and design. In B.G. Guerney (Ed.), Psychotherapeutic agents: New roles for non-professionals, parents, and teachers. New York: Holt, Rinehart and Winston, 1969.

Guerney, B.G. (Ed.) Psychotherapeutic agents; New roles for non-professionals, parents, and teachers. New York: Holt, Rinehart and Winston, 1969.

Heller, K., & Goldstein, A.P. Client dependency and therapist expectancy as relationship maintaining variables in psychotherapy. Journal of Consulting Psychology, 1961, 25, 371-375.

Heller, K., Myers, R.A., & Kline, L.V. Interviewer behavior as a function of standardized client roles. Journal of Consulting Psychology, 1963, 27, 117-122.

Holzman, M.S. The significance of value systems of patient and therapist for outcome of psychotherapy. Dissertation abstracts, 1962, 22, 4073.

Kiesler, D.J. The process of psychotherapy. Chicago: Aldine, 1973.

Leary, T. Interpersonal diagnosis of personality. New York: The Ronald Press, 1957.

Liberman, B. The effect of modeling procedures on attraction and disclosure in a psychotherapy analogue. Unpublished doctoral dissertation, Syracuse University, 1970.

Libo, L.M. The projective expression of patient-therapist attraction. Journal of Clinical Psychology, 1957, 13, 33-36.

Libo, L.M. Manual for the Picture Impressions Test. Palo Alto, Calif.: Consulting Psychologists Press, 1969.

Lichtenstein, E. Personality similarity and therapeutic success: A failure to replicate. Journal of Consulting Psychology, 1966, 30, 282.

Lindsley, O.R. Direct behavioral analysis of psychotherapy sessions by conjugately programmed closed-circuit television. Psychotherapy: Theory, Research and Practice, 1969, 6, 71-81.

Lorr, M. Client perceptions of therapists: A study of therapeutic relation. Journal of Consulting Psychology, 1965, 29, 140-149.

Lorr, M., & McNair, D.M. Methods relating to evaluation of therapeutic outcome. In L.A. Gottschalk & A.H. Auerbach (Eds.), Methods of research in psychotherapy. New York: Appleton-Century-Crofts, 1966.

Martin, B., Lundy, R.M., & Lewin, M.H. Verbal and G.S.R. responses in experimental interviews as a function of three degrees of "therapist" communication. Journal of Abnormal and Social Psychology, 1960, 60, 234-240.

Meltzoff, J., & Kornreich, M. Research in psychotherapy. New York: Atherton Press, 1970.

Mendelsohn, G.A., & Geller, M.H. Structure of client attitudes toward counseling and their relation to client-counselor similarity. Journal of Consulting Psychology, 1965, 29, 63-72.

Mendelsohn, G.A., & Rankin, N.O. Client-counselor compatibility and the outcome of counseling. Journal of Abnormal Psychology, 1969, 74, 157-163.

Orenstein, R. The influence of self-esteen on modeling behavior in a psychotherapy analogue. Unpublished master's thesis, Syracuse University, 1969.

Orlinsky, D.E., & Howard, K.I. The good therapy hour. Archives of General Psychiatry, 1967, 16, 621-632.

Parloff, M.B., Some factors affecting the quality of therapeutic relationships. Journal of Abnormal and Social Psychology, 1956, 52, 5-10.

Parloff, M.B. Therapist-patient relationship and outcome of psychotherapy. Journal of Consulting Psychology, 1961, 25, 29-38.

Patterson, G.R., & Reid, J.B. Reciprocity and coercion: Two facets of social systems. In C. Neuringer & J.L. Michael (Eds.), Behavior modification in clinical psychology. New York: Appleton-Century-Crofts, 1970.

Persons, R.W., & Marks, P.A.   Self-disclosure with recidivists: Optimum interviewer-interviewee matching.   Journal of Abnormal Psychology, 1970, 76, 387-391.

Polansky, N.S.   Ego psychology and communication.   New York: Atherton Press, 1971.

Pope, B., Nudler, S., Norden, J.S., & McGee, J.P.   Changes in nonprofessional (novice) interviewers over a 3-year training period.   Journal of Consulting and Clinical Psychology, 1976, 44, 819-825.

Pope, B., Nudler, S., VonKorff, M.R., & McGee, J.P.   The experienced professional interviewer versus the complete novice.   Journal of Consulting and Clinical Psychology, 1974, 5, 680-690.

Pope, B., & Siegman, A.W.   Interviewer-interviewee relationship and verbal behavior of interviewee in the initial interview.   Psychotherapy: Theory, Research and Practice, 1966, 3, 149-152.

Pope, B., & Siegman, A.W.   Interviewer warmth in relation to interviewee verbal behavior.   Journal of Consulting and Clinical Psychology, 1968, 32, 588-595.

Pope, B., & Siegman, A.W.   Relationship and verbal behavior in the initial interview.   In A.W. Siegman & B. Pope (Eds.),   Studies in dyadic communication.   New York: Pergamon Press, 1972.

Rappaport, J., Chinsky, J.M., & Cowen, E.L.   Innovations in helping chronic patients (college students in a mental institution).   New York: Academic Press, 1971.

Rosen, A.   The treatment relationship: A conceptualization.   Journal of Consulting Psychology, 1972, 38, 329-337.

Sapolsky, A.   Effect of interpersonal relationships upon verbal conditioning. Journal of Abnormal and Social Psychology, 1960, 60, 241-246.

Sapolsky, A.   Relationship between patient-doctor compatibility, mutual perception, and outcome of treatment.   Journal of Abnormal Psychology, 1965, 70, 70-76.

Schaefer, E.S.   A circumplex model for maternal behavior.   Journal of Abnormal and Social Behavior, 1959, 59, 226-235.

Schutz, W.C.   The interpersonal underworld.   Palo Alto, Calif.:   Science & Behavior Books, 1966.

Snyder, W.U., & Snyder, B.J.   The psychotherapy relationship.   New York: Macmillan, 1961.

Sullivan, H.S.   The interpersonal theory of psychiatry.   New York: Norton, 1953.

Sullivan, H.S.   Collected works.   New York: Basic Books, 1965.

Truax, C.B., & Mitchell, K.M. Research on certain therapist interpersonal skills in relation to process and outcome. In A.E. Bergin & S.L. Garfield (Eds.), Handbook of psychotherapy and behavior change: An empirical analysis. New York: Wiley, 1971.

Watzlawick, P., Beavin, J.H., & Jackson, D.D. Pragmatics of human communication. New York: Norton, 1967.

7 Expectation and Interpersonal Perception in Relationship

To a considerable extent relationship is shaped by the expectations that the participants bring into an interactional situation. Consider, for example, the varied receptions meted out to a government census taker. If he knocks on the door of an affluent middle-class home in the suburbs, he is likely to be greeted in a friendly manner. The person whom he interviews may be well informed about the value of the census for government planning and for social research, and will be "set" to provide the census taker with all the information he needs to complete his inquiry. How differently he might be received in an inner-city house, occupied by a recent arrival from another state, who is receiving welfare, but whose welfare eligibility, in view of brief residency, is under question. However unrelated the census taker's questions may be to the interviewee's welfare eligibility, the latter is likely to be suspicious, guarded, resentful, and uncommunicative.

Much has been written (Goldstein, 1962) about the role of expectation in relationship. What forms of behavior does each member of a dyad anticipate of the other? What personal attributes and attitudes does he expect to encounter? It has been repeatedly demonstrated that a person's anticipations regarding an impending relationship are correlated in many ways with the relationship that actually develops. This association is particularly evident in the interpersonal perceptions that occur within the relationship.

In this regard, Asch's (1946) historic study, though well-known, bears summary here. Asch gave each S in two groups of students a list of adjectives that could be used to describe a person. Between the groups, the lists varied in only one respect. For one group, the list contained the word "warm" at a seriatim midpoint; for the second, the word "cold." In all other respects the adjectives were identical. Each S was asked to write a sketch of a fictional person described by the list of adjectives given him/her, and to select from a checklist of pairs of opposite traits those that best fitted the impressions formed of this person. In spite of the identity of the two lists (with the exception, of course, of the two contrasting terms, "warm" and "cold") the two groups of subjects differed decidedly in their impressions.

288

Thus, a change in one essential quality produced a marked difference in the resulting total impression of the fictional person. To the "warm" group, the fictional person was wise, humorous, popular, and imaginative, while to the "cold" group s(he) appeared in a much less favorable light. It is important to note that such radically different impressions would not have resulted if the contrasting adjectives were less crucial in the perception of persons. Thus, when Asch substituted "polite" and "blunt" for "warm" and "cold" in a later study, the differences in person perception was less marked.

Asch's study is of decided importance to the interviewer because it demonstrates the determining impact of expectation on interpersonal perception. And the interviewer knows that the interviewee's perception of him/her and his/her perception of the interviewee have a great deal to do with the relationship that develops. In fact, both participants in an interview are very much preoccupied with their expectations of each other during the first few minutes of an encounter.

> The client will relate his unspoken questions about the counselor to the kinds of problems that have brought him to counseling. If he is feeling helpless, he may be looking to see whether the counselor is the kind of person he can lean on. If he has certain feelings that bother him but that he is also ashamed of, he may be interested in how this counselor is likely to react to his disclosing such feelings. The counselor, meanwhile, will be concerned about his professional adequacy. Is he talking to someone he will be successful in helping? What does this person want of him? Will he be able to meet this need effectively? (Bordin, 1968, p. 49)

The expectation or set that a person brings into an interview situation may be a good deal more than a transient or situationally determined phenomenon. Thus a client who has been consistently rejected by parents may come to regard himself/herself as an undesirable person, who is, for example, stupid, ugly, lazy, and angry. This perception of himself/herself prompts certain attitudes regarding the behavior that s(he) expects from others. S(he) may indeed demonstrate the type of vigilance that one often observes in a person who has come to feel that others will perceive him/her as unattractive and undesirable. This person's aggressive defensiveness "will be anticipatory and thus self-concepts will be reinforced rather than denied or extinguished, since these anticipatory behaviors will be responded to, by and large, in such a manner as to confirm them" (Butler, 1952, p. 371).

Interviewee Expectations

The expectations of the above client have resulted from the personal relationships that have been experienced. Frequently interviewee expectations are a consequence of group membership rather than individual history. In this regard, consider the following fictional cases.

Mr. A is a dock worker, aged 45, whose job consists of unloading fruit ships. He spends much of his time trundling carts loaded with fruit from freighters to the warehouses across the street from the docks. He has two sons, both of whom were in the Army. One had been killed in Vietnam, and the other, soon to be discharged, had written recently telling his parents that he is in an Army detoxification unit, attempting to rid himself of a heroin addiction. In addition to his worries for his two sons, there has been strain in the marital relationship. By tacit but mutual consent, sexual encounters with his wife have been reduced to the vanishing point.

For the last six months Mr. A has not been well. One day while on the job he strained his back. The doctor put him to bed and treated him with both medication and heat applications. The muscular strain had been alleviated but his back continued to trouble him. Finally, his doctor, frustrated with his patient's lack of response, decided that the ailment had become "functional." He told the patient that he had no further medical problem and that whatever remained was "in his head." Then, with some irritation, he referred him to a hospital psychiatric clinic in the inner city because Mr. A could not afford private treatment. The doctor told him that one of the psychiatrists in the clinic might be able to help him, but that there was nothing further that could be done medically. In fact, he reiterated that Mr. A no longer had a real medical problem.

Mr. A is puzzled. He cannot visualize any relief to his back from conversations with a psychiatrist. His doctor had led him to expect that the treatment would consist of interviews and talk but no medication, and probably no further heat applications. Moreover, he has been discomfitted, even a little angered, by his doctor's peremptory remark about the locus of the problem "in his head." Was he suggesting that Mr. A was abnormal, crazy?

Mr. A is also troubled by thoughts about the reaction of his friends and even members of his own family. Will they begin to wonder about his sanity? Will they question his good judgment for expecting that talk with a psychiatrist will alleviate the pain in his back? Will they wonder whether he is placing his trust in a "fake" doctor who does little himself except listen and talk, without prescribing rest, some form of manipulation of his muscles, or medication?

Mr. A's reluctance to seek help in the clinic appears justified to him as he finds that he must wait in a long line before he can see the receptionist who will assign him to a doctor. It is not that the shabby character of the streets and the old clinic building put him off; he barely notices these familiar elements. But he is uncertain about how right a psychiatric clinic is for him. And a long wait to be seen by a young doctor (Did someone say he was a medical student?) puts him off a little more.

The doctor (or medical student) is patient, interested, and quite complete in his inquiry. In part, it is a familiar medical investigation. But there are many subjects Mr. A is asked to speak about that baffle him. He is questioned about mental illness in his family, previous episodes of mental illness in his own life, and many feelings and experiences of his own about which he is not able to form an impression. His interviewer wishes to know how frequently and intensely he feels anxious and depressed. If he had been asked about rough periods in his life, when jobs were scarce, and later when, for example, the war destroyed one son and alienated another, he would have been able to speak at length with involvement. But when asked to speak about thoughts and feelings, he is left cold. The urgencies of life have left little time for this kind of self-indulgence.

So he is now leaving the doctor's office in a cloud of gloomy uncertainty. Should he return to the clinic? He liked the doctor, even though he was puzzled by many of his questions which lacked a specific focus (e.g., "Just tell me what comes to mind about that"). Moreover, his back is now extremely painful and he feels that he has reached the "end of the road." There is no place else to turn, but he cannot arouse any enthusiasm, any hope, any trust or faith in the kind of help the clinic is holding out to him. Now he has a full week to trouble himself about the next appointment and to decide whether or not he should keep it.

Mrs. B is a housewife, aged 45, who lives in a comfortable part of the city, in a renovated old home with a large porch, set in a well-tended, sweeping open yard with many trees and rather carefully cultivated flower beds. She had been an elementary schoolteacher before marriage and for three years after marriage, until her first child was born. Her husband is a successful lawyer. Family income has always been adequate for a comfortable middle-class standard of life. There was no pressure for her to return to work even after the children were sufficiently grown to permit such a return. Mrs. B felt that she had been more than satiated with schoolteaching and, lacking any other vocational skill or drive, directed her energies toward gardening with an organic orientation and executive activity in the neighborhood improvement association.

Her life did not, in general, lack color and zest. However, about three years ago she began to experience a lassitude, a lack of interest in her usual activities and social contacts, and ultimately periods of gloom and depression with tearful episodes. Mrs. B responded to these changes in her life with vigorous introspective effort, and has been able to relate them both to external and internal influences.

The external stresses, although disturbing, were not unusual within her social milieu. Her two sons evoke anxieties that are not typical within the neighborhood in which she lives. The older son is completing his freshman year in college. His academic standing in high school had been good, but attained with much conflict within the family because of his opposition to parental pressure toward achievement. In college his grades have dropped, and he has turned rather heavily to marijuana as a source of weekend pleasure, with the frequently reiterated challenge directed toward his parents about the pointlessness of an achievement-oriented life. He taunts them with the chill constriction that they are placing on their own lives by not permitting themselves to experience the ultimate fruits of leisure found in the extension and alteration of one's consciousness with drugs. In fact, if it were not for the threat of draft, he would probably not return to an educational system in which he feels alienated. The second son is not nearly as rebellious by temperament. He is a very high academic achiever. But Mrs. B worries a little about him too because of his reserve, limited circle of friends, his current lack of interest in girls (while friends of his are already dating) and a tendency toward depressive moods.

Mrs. B thinks about these matters and relates them to her depressive periods. She is aware too of a drift in her relationship with her husband, a sort of mutual withdrawal, silent lull when they sit at the table after dinner, and a considerable decrease in   sexual interest in each other. She has attributed the latter to menopause, but she cannot shake off the depressive awareness that old bonds with her husband are being weakened.

A few months ago she had been working in the garden, perhaps a little too vigorously, had picked up a shovel full of sod, and felt a painful wrench in her back. Her internist had ordered her to bed, prescribed heat treatments and medication, reexamined her twice and eventually pronounced that her strained muscles had returned to their normal condition. The acute pain was gone but a pervasive discomfort in the lower part of her back had remained, and in fact intensified. Mrs. B's internist told her that he thought that the refractory character of the pain was functional. He reviewed her increasing depression with her and the recent stresses that she has been experiencing within her family, and ended by recommending psychotherapy. After obtaining her agreement, he called a prominent psychiatrist in the city, who happened to be a close friend of his, and arranged for an appointment.

Many of Mrs. B's friends have been in psychotherapy, and some in psychoanalysis. In general, they have spoken positively about the experience, and, even when left with unresolved problems, felt that their lives had been enriched. The referral of Mrs. B for psychotherapy came at a time when she was highly receptive to the idea.   As she has thought about her recent problems, she has encountered increasingly a sort of internal recognition that there are many segments of her life, particularly relating to early experiences with her parents and her sister, that need exploration. She has found introspection to be sometimes calming, and occasionally informative; indeed, she is now looking forward with positive anticipation to her first interview.

The psychiatrist's office is in a relatively modern structure in a renovated section of the city. He shares a waiting room with two colleagues. Mrs. B's appointment was for midafternoon and when she arrived she found another woman, about 10 years her junior, seated in one of the Danish modern chairs in the waiting room. This woman had undoubtedly been there before because she seemed comfortable and quite ready to strike up a conversation. Mrs. B, at first reticent and mildly embarrassed, warmed to the situation and presently found herself animatedly engrossed in the process of getting acquainted with a person with whom she felt congenial. Time passed quickly until she was invited into the doctor's office.

In the consulting room the interview went well. The psychiatrist's manner was warm and interested. Although not having experienced psychotherapy before, Mrs. B knew that he would want her to speak about her current problems, her early history, and about her feelings and thoughts regarding current family and other personal relationships. She also anticipated that he would invite her to speak about these matters but would leave much of the initiative to her. In fact, his questions pointed in certain directions but remained quite ambiguous.

Now, as she leaves the psychiatrist's office, she wonders why she has avoided psychotherapy until the present stressful period in her life. She found it very satisfying to explore her thoughts and feelings under the doctor's direction. She is looking forward to her next appointment with great hope and optimism, and a conviction that she is now, at long last, coming to grips with the present turn of events in her life.

The above sketches, although fictional, demonstrate an important determinant of the relationship that develops between the interviewer and the interviewee - that of the interviewee's expectations. Even before the two participants in the interview encounter each other, the interviewee approaches the event with a complex of anticipations. Some are fostered by society and, more particularly, by the socioeconomic culture in which the interviewee lives. Not independent of the socially fostered expectations, but somewhat separate, are those that arise out of the manner in which the referral is made, the intake procedure that ensues, and the idiosyncratically personal expectations about help that each individual brings to the initial interview. Clearly, the prognosis for Mr. A's therapy is not good; for Mrs. B, it would appear to be excellent. An important reason for the difference in outlook may well be found in the contrasting expectations that precede the initial interview for both patients.

Much of the material presented below pertains to psychotherapy rather than to the initial interview per se. Nevertheless, it is included because it is relevant to the relationship that develops even in the single interview. In the above examples it is evident that social groups foster varying expectations regarding psychotherapy and the therapist. But some expectations are quite general and tend to be pervasive in our society. In seeking out a psychotherapist the patient anticipates help because s(he) looks for it where society has indicated it might be found (Schofield, 1967). Through the dissemination of mental health education, society engenders a readiness for help in the patient and some faith that it will be forthcoming. Over the last several decades, there has been an institutionalization of both the process of psychotherapy and its symbols with a resulting increase in the status of the therapist and the power of suggestion and persuasion implicit in the role of therapist. Most clients approach the therapy situation with mixed feelings. Internalized anxieties are undoubtedly activated by this approach. But these may be mitigated a little by the socially fostered expectation that the therapist will be accepting, noncritical, and nonpunitive.

This system of institutionalized expectation regarding the behavior of the therapist places a certain obligation on him. He may, indeed, disapprove of the behavior of his patient; in fact, he may be socially outraged by it. Yet, within the context of his role as a therapist he is expected not to give vent to such judgmental reactions, but to be warm and accepting of the patient, at least within the confines of his office and the therapy process. Since the therapist is trained to behave in this manner, the patient's expectations of the therapist are closely associated with the therapist's actual relationship behavior.

Because society is not homogeneous but socioeconomically divided, there is a differentiation of expectation on the part of interviewees who come from varied social classes. Psychotherapy has tended to be a middle-class enterprise. Members of the middle class are therefore most likely to approach a psychotherapist with the expectations described above. Not surprisingly, they are the ones most likely to benefit from therapy.

Certainly, the initial interview would be easier for them than for members of other socioeconomic groups who would tend to arrive with expectations that are not particularly congruent with those of the therapist.

It is not that members of lower socioeconomic groups experience less emotional distress to have less faith in the doctor or in medicine. But they tend to expect to doctor to behave in an authoritarian manner, to prescribe for them, to manipulate them therapeutically, and to approach them as though they had physical ailments. In a word, they tend not as yet to be assimilated into the psychotherapy culture. Frank (1961) puts it especially well, when he states:

> Many forms of psychotherapy, having been devised by middle-class psychiatrists, attribute considerable healing power to self-knowledge and, to this end, require the patient to verbalize his inner feelings and personal problems. This activity may be totally unfamiliar to lower-class persons, and they cannot perceive that it is treatment. Nor do they attach any value to increased self-understanding. (p. 119)

In a questionnaire study (Yamamoto & Goin, 1965) directed toward lower-class patients who had entered a psychiatric out-patient clinic for the first time, the following expectations regarding psychotherapy were elicited. More than half of the patients indicated a desire to gain "self-understanding." However, further inquiry indicated that the expectation of "self-understanding" as a goal of therapy did not refer to insight into internal conflicts, but rather to the tangible resolution of specific external problems. "How, for example, could a patient stop drinking too much, or taking narcotics or beating his wife or children... How could he prevent his wife from leaving him?" (Yamamoto & Goin, 1965, p. 269). Moreover, the anticipated time for the attainment of the above specific goals averaged 4.7 sessions. It is evident that the expectations of this sampling of lower-class patients would differ from those of middle-class patients, and from those of the clinic psychotherapists.

Goldstein (1971) refers to the same matter when he speaks about his Yavis and non-Yavis patients. The former are Young, Attractive, Verbal, Intelligent, and Successful; the latter possess none of these traits. The former get along very well with psychiatrists and are responsive to them; the latter do not because they tend to expect an authoritarian attitude from the psychiatrist and the willingness on his part to prescribe for them. If non-Yavis patients get into treatment, they tend not to remain long. Their high psychotherapy mortality is due, not only to their own resistance to the process, but to the psychotherapist's unwillingness to respond to their expectations. One might designate the first of the two fictional cases described above, that of Mr. A., as an example of a non-Yavis type of patient; and that of Mrs. B, in most respects, as a Yavis type.

In spite of the findings that under ordinary circumstances members of low socioeconomic groups tend to approach psychotherapy with doubt and lack of trust, and therefore with a limited prospect of success, one need not assume that such a condition is inevitable. In one study (Goldstein & Shipman, 1966) a number of psychoneurotic out-patients, both male and female, with an average age of 34, all of lower socioeconomic origin, were treated by senior medical students within a medical school context. The authors demonstrated that there was a significant difference in confidence in the clinic expressed by the patients, depending on the source of referral. The patients were divided into two groups, representing favorable versus neutral and unfavorable referrals to psychotherapy, depending on the referral source. Favorable referral sources included psychiatrists, psychologists, social workers, and self-referrals; neutral and unfavorable referral sources included general medical practitioners, nonpsychiatric medical specialists, parents, and friends. As it turned out, those patients who were referred to the clinic by mental health sources felt more positively about the clinic as a means of help with their problems than those who were referred by other sources. The implication is that the degree of hope and optimism expressed by the referral source is transmitted to the patient, and that such a transmission is effective whatever the socioeconomic origin of the patient. One might also surmise that lower socioeconomic patients are ordinarily caught in a system of referral that does not arouse much faith or optimism in them regarding psychotherapeutic treatment.

Moreover, the intake procedure picks up where the mode of referral leaves off. Frank (1961) discusses this matter in the following terms:

The psychiatrist...often must take measures to acquaint the patient with the true nature of psychotherapy and, implicitly, to impress him with his authority and competence. This process may begin even before he meets the patient. Private practitioners urge their referring sources to prepare the patient properly for the psychiatric consultation by carefully informing him of its purpose and what it will be like. Clinics usually put the patient through some sort of intake procedure. Traditionally this consists of one or more interviews with a social worker, the purpose of which is to determine the patient's suitability for psychotherapy and prepare him/her for it. Implicitly intake may also enhance the importance of the psychiatrist and psychotherapy in the patient's eyes by taking on the aspect of a probationary period. In this sense it may not be too far-fetched to liken the intake procedure to the preparatory rites undergone by supplicants at faith-healing shrines, with the social worker in the role of acolyte and the psychiatrist as high priest.

Once in the presence of the psychiatrist, the patient's image of him as a help-giver and authority figure is reinforced by certain culturally established symbols. The clinic or hospital office automatically is identified with the healing activities of the institution. The private office of the psychiatrist who keeps his identity as a physician contains all the trappings with which the patient is familiar: the framed diploma and license, examining table, stethoscope, opthalmoscope, reflex hammer, doctor's white coat, and so on. ...Thus, the intake procedure and the therapeutic setting viewed from a sociocultural standpoint, implicitly or explicitly combat the patients' unfavorable attitudes and enhance their expectations of help. (Frank, 1961, p. 129)

It is evident that the preceding discussion of the effect of expectancy would be equally relevant to the interview as a single encounter and to psychotherapy as a sequence of interviews.

And now, a brief digression into a realm of medicine that has always intrigued behavioral scientists because it deals with nonspecific, relationship-engendered cures of somatic conditions. This form of cure is known as the placebo effect. A placebo is an inert pharmacological substance which has no inherent curative power, but which in effect facilitates the healing process when it is administered in a healing situation by a physician whom the patient trusts. There are no more precise words than faith and trust to describe the attributes of the patient's attitudes toward the physician, considered to be prerequisite for the placebo effect. The term "placebo" implies that the substance is used to placate the patient but that it is not a genuine form of treatment. Nevertheless

> placebos can have deep and enduring effects. The most commonplace example is the treatment of warts by painting them blue, or muttering incantations, or using other rituals. This phenomenon has been investigated quite thoroughly by dermatologists with good controls, and those who have done large series of cases claim that the cure of warts by suggestive methods is just as frequent as by any other method, and it is better than by spontaneous remission. A wart is a virus disease, not a psychogenic phenomenon. Apparently in certain patients, the belief that they are being helped can produce changes in the physiology of the skin which tips the balance so that the wart virus can no longer thrive. (Stein, 1961, p. 37)

Stein (1961) cites another instance of somatic improvement through the administration of an inert chemical, although he cautions the reader that the supporting evidence is not explicit. He refers to a study carried out in a municipal hospital in Budapest with two groups of patients suffering from bleeding peptic ulcers. The doctor injected one group with sterile water but told them that he was giving them a new medicine which would bring them relief. The very same sterile water was given to the second group, however this time by nurses who told them that they were receiving an experimental medicine of uncertain effectiveness. Seventy percent of the placebo group demonstrated excellent improvement, while only 25% of the nonplacebo group showed similar remission.

At issue here is not the traditional miracle cure, the religious ritual followed by dramatic results. Instead, the procedures followed are more modulated, more closely akin to regular medical procedures, and the changes are not as dramatic as those claimed by miracle cure workers. But it is not at all certain that the psychological process is different in these two instances. The elements of trust and faith would appear to be operative in both.

In one study described by Frank in 1961,

> a patient's expectations have been shown to affect his physiological responses so powerfully as even to reverse the pharmacological action of a drug. For example, the drug Ipecac is an emetic, which normally causes cessation of normal stomach contractions shortly after

ingestion. The patient experiences this as nausea. By having a patient swallow a balloon, which is inflated in the stomach and hooked to the proper equipment, these changes of stomach motility can be directly observed. A pregnant patient suffering from excessive vomiting showed the normal response of cessation of stomach contractions with nausea and vomiting after receiving a dose of Ipecac. When the same medication was given to her through a tube, so that she did not know what it was, with strong assurance that it would cure her vomiting, gastric contractions started up at the same interval after its administration that they would normally have stopped, and simultaneously the patient's nausea ceased. (p. 67)

This is strong medicine indeed, except that the effect of the medicine in this case is counter to its normal physiological impact. One can only attribute the reversal of pharmacological effect to expectation engendered by the doctor.

Shapiro (1971) raises a very provocative question about the character of the efficacy of drugs used by physicians through the ages. He refers to the fact that for centuries physicians have prescribed drugs known now to be useless, and even dangerous, because the scientific basis of pharmacological treatment is, in historical terms, a recent development. Yet, it is known that physicians have helped their patients in the past. Shapiro offers the opinion that their effectiveness is due not to the chemical nature of the medication, but to the placebo effect. "Since almost all medications until recently were placebos, the history of medical treatment can be characterized largely as a history of the placebo effect" (p. 442). The author is evidently suggesting that the physician's effectiveness during the prescientific period was based on psychological factors deriving from his relationship with the patient. In essence, the placebo effect demonstrates the efficacy of favorable patient expectation in reducing symptoms and distress. The point here is the curative power, not of a specific therapy procedure, but, in a general sense, of the interviewer-interviewee relationship.

The term "placebo effect" has its specific meaning in medicine. In the area of mental health it is used in a more metaphoric sense to refer to the role of patient expectation, faith and trust in the therapist, and in the treatment process. One study demonstrates in an interesting manner the relationship between the placebo effect in its original medical sense and the responsiveness of patients to psychiatric care (Hankoff, Friedman, & Engelhardt, 1958). The Ss were schizophrenic patients who were being followed in a clinic subsequent to their discharge from a state hospital. Immediately after discharge they were given placebos for three weeks. Their responsiveness to the placebo treatment turned out to be an extremely good prognostic sign of their capacity to remain out of the hospital. Not a single patient among those who had to return to the hospital in 30 days responded favorably to the placebo; of those who remained out of the hospital for a longer period of time 80% registered improvement after receiving the placebo. It may be assumed that the trust and faith shown by the patients in the clinic doctors were the effective elements in enabling the positive responders to avoid rehospitalization.

It may now be asked to what extent a client's or patient's responsiveness to an initial interview and to a psychotherapy sequence may be a sort of placebo effect - i.e., a consequence of attitudes of faith and trust in the therapist, the therapy, the institution in which it occurs, and the complex of expectations associated with such attitudes. One interesting study provides some information relevant to the foregoing question, at least with reference to psychotherapy (Rosenthal & Frank, 1956). If the efficacy of psychotherapy is the result of the specific technique used, we might expect that different techniques would yield different results. On the other hand, if it is a consequence of the relationship, and particularly that aspect of the relationship which we designate as the placebo effect, then techniques will be relatively less important than the interaction between doctor and patient. To test out this assumption, the authors used three different methods of treatment: individual therapy in which patients were seen for one hour a week, group therapy in which groups of five to seven patients were seen for one and one-half hours a week, and minimal contact therapy in which they were seen only one-half hour biweekly. The study was carried out in the Phipps Clinic of the Johns Hopkins Hospital. The patients, all seen in an out-patient clinic, were randomly assigned to the three types of treatment. The therapists were all second-year psychiatric residents. In order to equalize the effect of the individual therapist, each had six patients in each form of treatment. According to the design of the study, each patient was to receive six months of treatment. Actually, this goal was not quite attained. Each patient was assessed for increased comfort and increased social effectiveness at three times - at the end of the experimentally prescribed six months of treatment, after 18 months, and after five years. It was found that the degree of improvement in social effectiveness was related to the amount of treatment contact, and that the average decrease of symptomatic discomfort did not vary among the three forms of treatment. Moreover, those patients who dropped out of treatment within the first month demonstrated as much symptomatic relief as those who stayed in treatment for six months. Surprisingly, too, the relief from discomfort persisted over a five-year follow-up period, at least for the group as a whole. The authors conclude that the prompt occurrence of symptom relief is a demonstration of the effects of patient expectation and trust. In fact, it is evidence of the placebo effect within psychotherapy. To draw the analogy between the placebo effect and improvement with psychotherapy, the authors selected 12 patients from the original group who had shown considerable reduction in their distress, but later slipped back somewhat. These were given a two-week trial on a placebo during a routine follow-up between two and three years after the beginning of the research project. They showed as much reduction of discomfort after the administration of the placebo as they did after six months of psychotherapy. One of the authors concludes from the results of this experiment that "the healing power of all forms of psychotherapy lies in their ability to mobilize the patient's hope of relief" (Frank, 1961, p. 72).

Although the digression into a consideration of the placebo effect appears to have removed us somewhat from the discussion of the interview as a dyadic encounter, it was taken because it illustrates rather dramatically the power of patient or interviewee expectation as one aspect of relationship.

It is now proposed to consider the role of patient prognostic expectation in more specific terms. Do patients who expect symptom relief do better than those who do not have this expectation in psychotherapy? Are they more responsive and less defensive in the initial interview? In one study (Friedman, 1966) a population of neurotic out-patients was investigated in order to determine the correlation, if any, between their expected reduction of symptom intensity and the reduction that they were actually able to report after a single evaluation interview. It was hypothesized that the effect of expectancy as an influence in symptom reduction would be felt early, in fact as early as the first interview. There was a mixed population of American and English out-patients, with a mean age of 30.4 years. The patients responded to a self-rating questionnaire on which they scored a number of common psychological and physical symptoms on four-point scales of severity. Each patient responded to the questionnaire three times over a two-hour period, twice before the beginning of the initial interview, and once after the completion of the interview. During the first administration of the scale, the patient was asked to fill it out in terms of how s(he) felt at the moment; during the second, s(he) was asked to respond in terms of how s(he) anticipated feeling after six months of treatment; and during the third administration, s(he) was again asked to fill out the questionnaire in terms of how s(he) felt at that particular moment. The first score was a measure of initial level of discomfort; the difference between the first and the second scores constituted a measure of expected reduction of symptom intensity; and the difference between the initial and the final scores yielded a measure of reported reduction in symptom intensity. The results of this study indicated that "patients reporting marked improvement tended to have a high level of expectancy significantly more often than those reporting little improvement" (Friedman, 1966, p. 313). The author concludes: "that patient expectancy of help is activated at the first physician-patient contact and accounts for the reported decrease in discomfort after the initial interview" (p. 316).

If patient expectation of improvement leads to changes during the first encounter between the patient and the therapist, one might expect that those with high expectation of improvement would in fact behave differently during the interview than those with low expectation. Such a finding did occur in a study that initially had a different objective, but in which some of the evidence was relevant to the present issue. Thus, the author was able to conclude: "that high levels of patient expectation of gain in psychotherapy are associated with high levels of openness and low levels of guardedness in initial interview behavior. Furthermore, the greater the patient's confidence in the treatment center, the more he talks, the more open his verbalizations, and the less covertly resistive he is" (Goldstein, 1971, p. 26). Thus, an attitude of positive expectation before the initial interview results in greater verbal productivity and less resistiveness in the interview.

The intake worker in a clinic (the person who conducts the initial interview) must be very much concerned with the system of expectations brought to the clinic by a client or a patient. Does society, in fact, prepare the applicant for treatment to accept the values and procedures that will govern the therapy that he receives? One investigation (Garfield & Wolpin, 1963) carried out in the Outpatient Service of the Nebraska Psychiatric

Institute shows that when one minimizes socioeconomic distinction by selecting a group of patients representative of a broad range of social classes, one finds that patients arrive with expectations that are quite congruent with the predominant values among mental health professionals. The Ss in this study were over 16 years of age (mean age = 29.5), with education ranging from eighth grade to college graduation, and with occupations encompassing the entire spectrum from professional to unskilled work. The following are the specific expectations of the therapy process that the applicants for treatment expressed in responding to a questionnaire:

"In essence...a large majority of subjects expect that most personal matters may be discussed in therapy, that the patient should not withhold such information, and that psychotherapy is not to be compared to someone's prying into their affairs" (Garfield & Wolpin, 1963, p. 357).

Most of the applicants anticipated that the therapist would accept their feelings, even their angry feelings, without criticism. The applicant tended to expect that the therapist would listen primarily but would also frequently talk to the patient, although a few were quite prepared for the therapist to spend nearly all his/her time listening with very little talk. There was a distinct tendency for aspiring patients to accept the active role of the patient both with reference to verbal productivity and the choice of topics for discussion. Yet, there was an element of ambivalence regarding this matter, for "if given their choice most patients would prefer to be given advice rather than to be helped in developing understanding of their problems" (Garfield & Wolpin, 1963, p. 358). Nearly all of the applicants expected the therapist to be interested in their problems and to be truly understanding of them. While most of the patients did not literally attribute mind-reading ability to the therapists, about 40% of them did feel that they had perceptive abilities distinctly above the level of ordinary people.

Seven years later, another sampling of out-patients produced results congruent with, but not literally the same as, those above (Begley & Lieberman, 1970). A questionnaire was sent out to clinic applicants inquiring into the expectations that the prospective patients had about psychotherapy. There was a consensus among the applicants that the therapist would start by taking a history. Then s(he) would invite the patient to say whatever comes to mind. Intermittently there would be probing personal questions. There was a rather pervasive belief that patient and therapist would get along in a natural, easygoing manner with the therapist expressing attentive interest and acceptance. But the onus would be on the patient to decide what to say and what problems to present.

However, it may be anticipated that patterns of expectancy will vary with the sampling of Ss. If Ss are selected to be broadly representative of clinic patients in general, the expectancy picture is very likely to be a consensual one. But if there is a division of a sampling into subgroups that vary in some way that has a bearing on expectation regarding therapy, the result will be two or more contrasting expectation patterns. Such was the case in a study (Heine, 1962) that investigated the relationship between interviewee expectation and termination in psychotherapy. The therapists were senior medical students. Patients were divided into terminators (those who came for 12 or fewer interviews) and continuers (those who attended 13 to 18 interviews). More terminators than continuers expected specific advice on their problems in the first therapy interview. By contrast, more continuers than terminators expected a permissive attitude on the part of the therapist. The continuers had expectations that resembled those of the therapists to a greater degree than the ones entertained by the terminators. The contrast between the expectations of the terminators and continuers may be drawn in another way; the former did not distinguish between psychiatrists and other medical doctors, while the latter did. Those who left therapy expected to be treated by their psychotherapists in the directive, advice-giving manner of a medical practitioner. Clearly, their expectancies must have conflicted with the relatively passive permissiveness that they encountered in the psychotherapy interview.

In an earlier investigation (Heine & Trosman, 1960) the expectations of terminators and continuers had been related more explicitly to the attitudes of the therapists. The hypothesis advanced by the authors was "that patients and therapists may entertain expectations which are not complementary and, hence, are particularly disruptive in the early stages of a therapeutic relationship" (p. 275). In the views of the authors, the large dropout rate in clinic psychotherapy is not an indication of the untreatability of the patients, but is rather a sign of the failure of psychotherapists to adapt their procedures to the expectations and needs of the patients. The authors studied patient expectancies by asking them to respond to questionnaires that explored their reasons for seeking psychiatric help, their anticipations about the kind of help they would receive, and how this help would be given. Continuers differed from terminators in two basic respects: (1) they expected to play an active collaborative part in their treatment rather than one of passive cooperation; (2) their aim in seeking treatment included some awareness of a behavior problem and was not limited to a demand for medicine or diagnostic information. The authors concluded that the continuers remained in treatment because there was a "mutuality of expectation" between patient and therapist. Therapist expectations were expressed in the following terms:

1. The patient should desire a relationship in which he has an opportunity to talk freely about himself and his discomforts.

2. The patient should see the relationship as instrumental to the relief of discomfort, rather than expecting discomfort to be relieved by an impersonal manipulation on the part of the therapist alone.

3. Hence, the patient should perceive himself as in some degree responsible for the outcome. (Heine & Trosman, 1960, p. 278)

The preceding studies have dealt with patient expectations of therapist values and of the behavior that might be expected of each participant in the interview. Actually prospective patients relate some of their expectancies to basic demographic attributes of the therapist. One study (Boulware & Holmes, 1970) was carried out to determine the types of therapists to whom college students are attracted and the expectancies that the students have of them. The demographic characteristics of the therapist selected for investigation were sex and age. "In this study, male and female Ss were shown the faces of four potential therapists: older male, older female, younger male, and younger female. The Ss indicated how much they would like to talk to each therapist if they had a personal or vocational problem. The Ss also indicated their expectancies about what type of therapist and what type of person each pictured individual would be" (Boulware & Holmes, 1970, p. 270).

For both types of problems, the Ss in general preferred male therapists over female therapists, older therapists over younger ones. A rank ordering of preference arranged itself as follows: older male, younger male, older female, and younger female.

These findings for therapist preferences provided the context for the expectancy results. The older male had the most positive expectancy scores on seven out of 11 variables (understanding, advice giving, ability to handle his own problems, helping experience, familiarity with recent information regarding the resolving of patient problems, liking for patient, patient liking for him). Thus, the Ss had the most positive expectancies about the most preferred therapist type. The younger male received the most positive scores on each of the remaining four significant expectancy variables (Would not "take charge" and decide what patient would talk about; would not make a moral evaluation of patient's behavior; has experienced the same problems as patient; has interests and attitudes like the patient's). Thus, the expectancies that were primarily relevant to therapy favored the older male therapists; those that suggested an equality of status and a similarity of interest favored the younger male therapists. The expectancy results for the female therapists were all less favorable. The older female was expected to be the least like the students, and the younger female therapist was considered to be the least competent.

The expectations reviewed here do not relate to the values or behaviors of the therapists. They are not imbedded in the socioeconomic origins of the interviewees. Instead, they appear to derive from general stereotypes. There is no good evidence that older males are necessarily better therapists than older females, or that younger males resemble the college student population from which Ss for the study were drawn more than younger females might. (The Ss were both male and female.) Instead, these expectations were beliefs widely shared by the student Ss and, if put to the test, would probably affect the therapy relationships that developed, at least within their early stages.

That interviewee expectation is in fact related to interviewee behavior in the initial interview was demonstrative in an experimental investigation (Wilson & Rappaport, 1974) that studied the association between the interviewee's expectations about his/her self-disclosing behavior in an interview with a stranger and the actual self-disclosing behavior that ensued. Ss were white male students in an introductory psychology class, selected because they had extreme scores on the Jourard Self-Disclosure Questionnaire (JSDQ). Thus, they demonstrated either a strong readiness or a strong disinclination to speak openly about themselves to an interviewer whom they had not met before. The scale was taken to be a measure of general expectation. By contrast, specific expectation was experimentally manipulated by telling one-half of each general expectation group that disclosure of personal information to a strange interviewer would be easy, and the other half, that it would be difficult. Each S was subsequently interviewed by one of four interviewers. It was found that "when subjects were asked to anticipate their own self-disclosure in a specific situation (talking to a strange interviewer) there were significant differences in actual personal discussion between subjects who scored high and low on the JSDQ" (Wilson & Rappaport, 1974, p. 906). Similarly, there were positive results for the manipulation of specific expectations. "There was more personal discussion when subjects were led to believe that personal disclosure was easy for them rather than difficult" (Wilson & Rappaport, 1974, p. 907). Actually, there was an interaction between the above two effects so that Ss with a general expectation for high self-disclosure on personal topics, who were told that they would find it easy to talk to their interviewer, were indeed the ones who were the most self-disclosing in the interview that followed. In brief, those Ss who expected to speak frankly about personal matters were the ones who did so in the interview that followed.

Interviewer or Therapist Expectations

It will be recalled that Mr. A, a middle-aged dock worker, had a much less positive set of expectations regarding psychotherapy than Mrs. B., a middle-aged, middle-class housewife. As a result, the prognosis for the treatment of Mr. A - indeed, the likelihood that he would stay in treatment - was much less favorable than that for Mrs. B. One may assume that the therapist, too, would have analogous expectations to those noted in the patient. The therapist's attitude to Mrs. B would probably be expressed succinctly in the judgment that she is a good candidate for psychotherapy; his judgment about Mr. A would be much more "guarded," possibly negative. If both patients were to present themselves to the same therapist and to enter into treatment, would the contrasting therapist attitudes in the two cases make a difference? The research evidence which follows answers this question in the affirmative. If a therapist is more optimistic about one patient's prognosis than about another's, and if s(he) feels more positively about him/her, the outcome will be more favorable. Additionally, there is a high probability that the former patient will respond more productively in an interview than the latter.

A study by Goldstein (1960) deals directly with the relationship between therapist prognostic expectation regarding a patient and patient improvement. He divided his experimental groups of patients into two subgroups, one consisting of individuals who rated themselves as having improved over the course of 15 psychotherapy sessions, and the other of individuals who felt that their problems had intensified. When the initial prognostic expectations of the therapists for these two patient subgroups were compared, it was found that significantly more of the "improved" subgroup therapists were optimistic about outcome than of the "unimproved" subgroup.

The potency of the therapist's prognostic expectations is understandable when one considers their central role in a whole complex of attitudes that must surely influence the therapist-patient relationship. In one investigation of the present problem, Strupp (1958) used a sound film of an initial interview in which the two participants were a neurotic patient and a psychiatric resident. At selected points throughout the film, he introduced pauses during which Ss in his experiment, viewing the film, were asked to respond by stating what they would have said to the patient at that particular instant. The film was shown to psychologists and psychiatrists who were asked to assume the role of vicarious interviewer. After the film, all Ss completed a questionnaire in which they were asked to give their diagnostic and prognostic impression and other attitudes toward the patients. In general, there was a positive correlation between the favorableness of the S's (vicarious interviewer's) prognosis, and his/her attitudes toward the patient in other important respects. Thus, those "interviewers" who tended to be optimistic about the patient's prognosis, tended also to see him as less disturbed, and tended to give the patient fewer "cold" responses than did those who were pessimistic about the patient's prognosis. Clearly, if one expects the patient not to respond well to therapy, and as a consequence one tends to be "cold" toward the patient, the relationship that ensues is not likely to be conducive to effective psychotherapy.

To what extent might initial therapist expectation be a consequence of bias rather than simply the vicissitudes of professional judgment? In reviewing the findings of a number of authors, Goldstein (1971) summarizes the data with reference to this issue in the following way. He notes that the therapist who tends to be high on ethnocentrism also tends to avoid treating ethnic-minority patients; if he does undertake to treat such patients, he tends to see them for fewer sessions. In a word, therapist expectations may be determined in part by their biases; these may have much to do with the therapist's selection of patients for treatment and the differential treatment given different types of patients.

That personal bias may operate in the kind of selectivity a therapist shows when expressing a preference for one patient over another is strongly implied in a study by Goldman and Mendelsohn (1969). The authors asked a random sample of psychiatrists, clinical psychologists, and psychiatric social workers to respond to an adjective checklist describing their conceptions of a preferred male patient. The description that emerged was that of "imaginative, sensitive, curious, well motivated, but anxious person." There is little in this description to indicate the presence of pathology. In fact, if the adjective "anxious" were removed, the preferred patient would appear to be an unusually gifted and productive person. The preference of therapists for a patient of this kind is understandable. Since communication is the heart of psychotherapy, is there any wonder that the therapist would select a patient who communicates fluently, in a language code that is naturally congenial to the therapist? To be sure, this understandable preference is the factor that leads many to characterize psychotherapy as a middle-class enterprise and to designate the preference, however understandable, as a social-class bias.

If therapist bias is a discouraging phenomenon, one may derive some solace from the finding that with experience comes some mitigation of the effect of bias. For example, Chance (1959), in working with six therapists of whom three were experienced and three relatively inexperienced, found that the former demonstrated considerably less rigidity in their anticipations than the latter. To begin with, she noted that therapists demonstrated a significant level of consistency in their anticipations regarding patient behavior across the various patients with whom they worked. This finding would be consistent with the view that bias and personal inclination tend to determine the kinds of expectations that therapists have of patients. However, she did observe that the element of consistency across the patients was significantly stronger for the inexperienced therapists. Chance attributes this difference to the anxiety of inexperienced therapists and their need to develop stereotyped anticipations. She noted further that experienced therapists tended to be generally more optimistic about the capacity of their patients to change with therapy. And, finally, she noted that the three experienced therapists were, indeed, more effective and more successful in the results they obtained with their patients. This study lends support to the general finding that therapist prognostic expectation is positively related to therapy outcome. Additionally, it is encouraging in its indication that bias and stereotype in expectation tend to be reduced and controlled with experience.

In the two studies to be summarized, there is evidence that interviewer expectation is not only felt over a psychotherapy sequence, it also has an immediate effect on the course of the first interview. In one investigation, partially discussed earlier (Goldstein & Shipman, 1966), the therapists used were all senior medical students who conducted psychotherapy as part of the curriculum requirement in psychiatry. The patients they saw in this particular investigation consisted of male and female psychoneurotic outpatients with a mean age of 34. Since the interviewers were all medical students, their commitment to and interest in psychiatry actually varied considerably. Each was asked to fill out an Attitudes Toward Psychiatry Scale. The resulting score was a measure of each interviewer's favorable or unfavorable attitude toward psychotherapy. It may be assumed that those who obtained favorable scores on this scale had positive expectations regarding psychotherapy, while those who obtained unfavorable scores had negative expectations. The measure used for the efficacy of the first interview was a symptom-intensity inventory, filled out by the patient before and after the interview. The difference between the two symptom-intensity scores was a measure of the relief that the patient obtained from the interview. In fact, a significant but moderate positive correlation was obtained between favorableness of therapist's attitude toward psychotherapy and degree of symptom reduction. Thus, even during the course of a single interview, therapist expectation was related to reduction of intensity of patient symptomatology, at least as perceived by the patient.

That an interviewer's expectations will affect both his postinterview perception and evaluation of the interviewee is evident in the results of an additional investigation (Kumar, 1965). It will be recalled that interviewers who were led to expect friendly clients actually perceived them to be even more friendly than anticipated when their expectations were congruent with actual client behavior. When the interviewer's anticipations were not confirmed, his perception of the client was determined more by the actual behavior observed than by the anticipations. However, expectation continued to have a discernible effect on the resulting perception of the client. A second question asked whether the interviewer's expectations made any difference in his ultimate evaluation of the client. The results provide an affirmative answer to this question. Thus, when the interviewer perceived the client as friendly, he also reported, postinterview, that he liked the client, that he perceived the client as liking him, that he would be inclined to see the client again in counseling or therapy, that he felt that he helped the client, and that he would be adequate as a counselor in his work with this client. Clearly, the interviewer's initial anticipations are noted in a broad spectrum of attitudes and evaluations of the interviewee. Their effect on the subsequent relationship and the course of therapy must therefore be quite considerable.

If the interviewer's anticipations are as potent in the relationship that ensues as the preceding research would suggest, it becomes a matter of utmost importance that the interviewer become aware of the values and expectations that he brings to the treatment situation. Such an awareness does not come easily. It may be attained through personal therapy and the kind of supervision that is provided in clinical training. Stein (1961) argues strongly for this type of awareness when he advises the aspiring clinician to cultivate self-awareness lest his own biases affect his clinical work in a manner that is beyond his control.

> First the therapist must have had enough experience within himself, preferably through personal therapy, so that he can recognize his own needs in therapy and distinguish between an interest in helping the patient and more power-oriented motives. He must be aware of his own value judgments in order to check whether certain suggestions or advice arise from the patient's needs or from his own wish to espouse a cause. (Stein, 1961, p. 258)

Finally, one may again invoke the note of optimism implicit in the discussion of this subject by Chance (1959) in which she reports that with clinical experience comes the capacity for the interviewer to modulate and control the effect of initial expectation.

ROLE EXPECTATIONS

It is evident by now that both the interviewer and the interviewee enter the interview situation with a priori expectations regarding each other. Now it may be asked what it is that each expects and perceives in the interview relationship. Does each perceive an unorganized assembly of discrete traits and actions in the other? Or does each perceive an organized pattern of behavior that may be broken down into discrete roles?

In Sarbin's terms (Sarbin, 1954) the interviewer and interviewee may both be assumed to occupy certain positions vis-a-vis each other, commanding certain mutual expectations, and anticipating certain actions from the other person. These mutual expectations lead inevitably to a reciprocal pattern of behavior composed of interacting roles. Thus, one may speak somewhat ambiguously of the interviewer role and the interviewee role, or somewhat more specifically of an active interviewer role or a passive interviewer role. For possible roles are defined with great clarity in an experimental study (Heller, Davis, & Myers, 1966) in which the investigators speak about an active-friendly interviewer role ("This interviewer led the interview by encouraging verbalization but did not direct the content of the discussion. He was sympathetic, friendly, and considerate of the interviewee. He was supportive and helpful. He spoke often, tended to be verbose, and used non-verbal signs of approval"); a passive-friendly interviewer role ("This interviewer allowed the interviewee to lead the interview. He was agreeable, friendly, and interested. He was laconic but agreed readily when he did speak. He used non-verbal signs of approval"); an active-hostile role ("This interviewer led the interview by requesting verbalization but did not direct the content of the discussion. Although not in extreme form, he showed disdain, disapproval and lack of appreciation for the interviewee's approach to the task. He spoke often, tended to be verbose and used non-verbal signs of disapproval"); and a passive-hostile interviewer role ("This interviewer allowed the interviewee to lead the interview. He was aloof and showed lack of interest. He was laconic, but voiced skepticism or disapproval when he spoke. He used non-verbal signs of disapproval") (Heller, Davis, & Myers, 1966, p. 502). In another related study (Heller, Myers, & Kline, 1966) four standardized interviewee roles were designated as dominant-friendly, dominant-hostile, dependent-friendly, and dependent-hostile.

In an investigation previously discussed in another context, three rather clearly delineated patterns of patient expectation regarding therapist roles manifested themselves (Apfelbaum, 1958). The author asked each of 100 individuals seen in a university out-patient psychiatric clinic to Q-sort statements pretherapy that described expectations about the personality of a prospective psychotherapist. The Q-Sort scale was broadly descriptive of a range of therapist behaviors. Ratings for the various items were intercorrelated and then cluster analyzed with the following three clusters of patient role expectations emerging:

1. Nurturant - The patients who give high ratings to items that fall in this cluster tend to expect a therapist who will be supportive, protective, and willing both to guide them and actively give them whatever help they may need. He does not make appreciable demands on his patients to assume responsibilities; nor is he ever likely to be critical.
2. Model - The patients who contribute to this cluster expect a therapist who is primarily an interested, tolerant listener. He tends to be permissive and nonjudgmental. While he is not prone to evaluate his patients or respond to them critically, neither is he particularly protective. Basically, he is perceived by the patients as being well adjusted, interested, but not highly responsive.
3. Critic - Those patients whose expectations are primarily reflected in the third cluster anticipate that the therapist will be critical and will expect his patients to show a high level of responsibility. The therapist that they perceive is possibly the least benign of the three. He will not be gentle and certainly not permissive or supportive.

Clearly, then, patients bring into the interview situation varying expectations of the roles that their therapists or interviewers will play. Some of these expectations are socially and culturally determined; others are rooted in their own early interpersonal relationships within their families. But whatever their source, they are operative at the moment that the interviewee makes his/her move toward the first interview. One may ask whether these expectations make any difference in the patient's response to psychotherapy. Apfelbaum (1958) does find some positive evidence for such a difference. Thus, in his own data, those patients whose expectations led them to anticipate a model therapist demonstrated lower dropout rates than the others who anticipated either nurturant or critic therapists. On the other hand, those patients who remained in therapy with nurturant expectations of the therapist tended to stay in therapy longer than the two other groups. Since all Ss in this study had taken the MMPI, it was possible to obtain MMPI correlates of the three patterns of expectation. As it turned out, those with both nurturant and critic expectations started psychotherapy with higher maladjustment scores and more distress than those who expected their therapist to demonstrate model behavior.

In another investigation (Goldstein & Heller, 1960) both client and therapist expectations were evaluated on the basis of questionnaires devised to measure Apfelbaum's three expectations clusters. These cluster measures were then correlated with the clients', therapists', and supervisors' independent assessments of the quality of the client-therapist relationship within the interview. The latter was achieved through questionnaires that the three groups were asked to fill out. As it turned out, client and therapist expectancy scores did not correlate with relationship indices. However, therapist model expectancy with reference to his/her own behavior did correlate in a significantly positive manner with supervisor relationship ratings, while therapist nurturant expectancy regarding his/her own behavior correlated in a significantly negative manner with the same supervisor ratings. Additional correlations obtained in this study throw some further light on the kinds of therapists who are likely to expect to behave in a model and in a nurturant manner. Thus, the nurturant expecters tended to score relatively high on the Depression Scale of the MMPI, while critic expecters scored low in the Depression Scale and generally lacked in empathy. The model expecters were the ones who obtained the highest scores in empathy and the most positive ratings from their supervisors. Therefore, if one has a choice, one would select the interviewer who expects his/her own behavior to follow model lives as the one most likely to be empathic as a therapist.

The Apfelbaum study (1958) investigated patient conceptions of therapist roles. Thirteen years later, another study (Berzins, Herron, & Seidman, 1971) dealt with therapists' conceptions of patient roles. Using V.A. installations, university clinics and departments, and private out-patient clinics and hospitals, a nationwide sample of male therapists was obtained, of whom 63% were psychologists, 22% were psychiatrists, and 15% were social workers. Each therapist filled out a scale for rating patient behavior twice, once for the "typical" patient and once for the patient with whom the therapist had experienced the greatest success. The dual rating made it possible to evaluate patient behavior. That which rated higher for the successful than the typical patient was considered to be preferred because it was prognostic of therapeutic success; that rated higher for the typical than the successful patient was regarded as negatively valued. The therapists' ratings were intercorrelated and factor analyzed with three major factors representing three patient roles emerging:

The Deferent-Subordinate Patient Role was reflected in such patient behaviors as, "places you on a pedestal," "tries to elicit value judgments," "treats you as his teacher," "exudes 'niceness,' 'correctness.'"

The Expressive-Egalitarian Patient Role was characterized by items that were quite different from those in the first cluster. Some of these follow: "displays freedom of expressiveness," "loose, casual, few airs or pretensions," "engages in emotional give and take with you," "behaves as though you were 'equals.'"

Finally, the Self Reliant-Dominant Patient Role was traced in such items as "generally initiates the conversation," "leads the way in introducing topics," "controls the selection and direction of topics," "relaxed posture."

When the therapists were divided into experienced (four years or more in individual therapy) and inexperienced (three or fewer years) subgroups, it was possible to evaluate the patient roles in the following ways: "the Expressive-Egalitarian patient role is valued positively by both EXP and INEXP therapists; the Self-Reliant-Dominant patient role is especially important in the prognostic estimates of the INEXP therapists; and both groups agree that Deferent-Subordinate patient role behaviors have negative prognostic implications" (Berzins et al., 1971, p. 130).

The authors designated the Deferent-Subordinate Patient role as complementary to Apfelbaum's (1958) Nurturant or Critical patient expectancies regarding therapist roles, and the Self-Reliant-Dominant Patient role as complementary to that of the Model therapist. In essence both Apfelbaum (1958) and Berzins et al. (1971) deal with patient and therapist expectancies regarding the roles of their partners, permitting the development of a schema for determining the complementarity between the two sets of role expectancies.

Until this point, the discussion has amplified the significance of both interviewee and interviewer expectations. The problem now to be considered is whether it is important that these two sets of expectations be congruent with each other. In the two fictional examples given above, there was the implicit assumption that Mr. A, the dock worker, would demonstrate less congruence in his attitudinal set with his therapist than Mrs. B, the middle-class housewife, with hers. Mr. A could not see how mere talk would alter his condition. He was frustrated by the fact that his therapist was not willing to prescribe medication or other procedures for him. His therapist's anticipation that the patient would take the initiative in communicating about himself in the interview situation was not at all consistent with the kind of experience that Mr. A had had in the past with doctors. Moreover, the interviewer's request that he speak about feelings and emotional events in his life appeared strange and irrelevant to Mr. A. In a word, there was little mutuality in the role expectation held of each other by Mr. A and his therapist. By contrast, Mrs. B's expectations of therapy were completely complementary to those of her therapist. It was assumed that this difference in congruence between the expectations of the two patients and their respective therapists augured well for Mrs. B's prognosis in therapy and poorly for Mr. A's. Some evidence in favor of the assumption that congruence between the expectations of interviewer and interviewee is facilitative in an interview, and its lack, obstructive, will now be presented. Most of the findings that follow pertain to communication and relationship within a single interview rather than the long-term progress of psychotherapy.

Lennard and Bernstein (1960) offered, as one of their major assumptions, that the interview was a small social system, in fact, a dyadic system, which tended toward a state of balance. Whenever this balance is upset, an element of stress is introduced into the situation and measures have to be taken to alleviate the stress. Thus, they assumed, and demonstrated, that when therapist and patient had attitudes that were incongruent with reference to such matters as therapist activity or topical focus that the interview would be thrown into a state of imbalance. Both participants would feel the strain of this imbalance and would respond to it. Since the interviewer assumes the major responsibility for the direction of the interview, most of the corrective actions were undertaken by him.

The authors (Lennard & Bernstein, 1960) broke down the role expectations of both participants in an interview into the following components: "Who shall speak, how much, about what, and when?" (p. 154). The first two questions pertain to a dimension of "activeness." Both the interviewer and the interviewee have certain expectations regarding their own "activeness" and the "activeness" of the other member of the dyad. The authors then specify the behavior involved in expectations regarding activeness:

(1)   Who should take the initiative in communication?;

(2)   How frequently should they speak?;

(3)   To what extent should the therapist direct the patient as to what he should talk about?;

(4)   How "directive" should the therapist be with reference to the patients' activities outside of therapy?;

(5)   Should the therapist give advice and counsel?;

(6)   How much explanation about therapy should the therapist provide? (Lennard & Bernstein, 1960, p. 154)

Some of the findings with reference to mutual role expectations will be summarized here. It should be noted, however, that although Lennard and Bernstein (1960) were concerned with the interview as an entity, they worked with eight psychotherapy sequences rather than initial interviews. Their data were obtained from four therapists, each working with two patients over a period of eight months, recording more than 500 sessions. They found that nearly all the patients they studied anticipated that the interviewee would do most of the talking during psychotherapy; with this the interviewers agreed. However, complementarity between interviewer and interviewee regarding "activeness" was limited to the general premise stated above. With reference to specifics, there was considerable disagreement. For example, interviewers and interviewees tended to have discrepant expectations regarding the role of each in the initiative for and control of communication during the interview. Disagreement about the content of communication (i.e., the subject matter to be covered) was similarly prevalent. The therapists and patients did not agree on the relevance of approximately one-half of the topics about which the experimenters inquired. In general, patients tended to exclude certain topics from discussion, while the therapists were more broadly accepting.

Whenever dissimilarity with reference to activity level expectations arose, the therapist would attempt to reduce the resulting equilibrium by introducing into the interview a "primary system reference." This term refers to any sort of remark by the therapist that has the aim of making the patient aware of what is required of him regarding type and level of activity. Thus, the patient is taught how to engage in a reciprocal role relationship as defined by the therapist. S(he) might learn not to expect the therapist to speak about himself/herself, or to issue explicit orders and directions. S(he) may come to expect the therapist to select the topics for discussion, but to prompt their exploration with ambiguous rather than specific questions and comments. In these ways, a priori expectations of the interviewee are adapted to those of the therapist.

Changes in interviewee expectation occur only with difficulty. The interviewee does not readily give up his/her wish for a relatively high level of interviewer activity. Previous experience with communication in social situations has led him/her to expect a measure of reciprocity. Hence the patient starts with a preference for an active rather than an inactive interviewer, one who speaks in specific rather than ambiguous terms. This initial preference must be modified, in most instances, if a condition of complementarity between the two participants in the interview is to be achieved.

Incongruity between expectations may stress an interview whether the incongruity occurs between the expectations of the two participants in the interview or within one of the participants. The latter condition would obtain if, for example, the interviewee were to enter into the interview situation with a set of expectations about the interviewer's role, and find that the actual role of the interviewer was quite different. In one study (Pope, Siegman, Blass, & Cheek, 1972) this problem was investigated through an experimental manipulation of the interviewee's role expectations. The Ss of this study were undergraduate psychology students (sophomores, juniors, and seniors), both male and female. One-half of the Ss were assigned at random to a control group, and the other half to an experimental group. In a preinterview session attended by all the Ss the experiment was described as a study of personality and vocational interest, with the use of both tests and interviews. Then the short form of the Taylor Manifest Anxiety Scale (MAS) and the Strong Vocational Interest Inventory were administered. Later, each S was interviewed twice with an interval of about a week between the two interviews. Interview questions were prescribed in advance in order to keep content constant and related to two topics - family background and school experience. All Ss in the control group were given the same instructions before both interviews; they were informed that the interviewer would ask them questions about family relations and school experience. The Ss in the experimental group were given the same instructions before their first interview. However, before the second interview, they were told that the interviewer would tell them about their results on the personality question- naire and the vocational interest inventory and, indeed, would interpret the results. Expectational incongruence developed when the Ss of the experiment group entered the second interview and found that instead of telling them about test results, the interviewer again asked them further questions about school experience and family relationships. Clearly, then, the members of the control group experienced no conflict between their expectations regarding interviewer behavior and his actual behavior; such a conflict was quite pointed, however, with the members of the experimental group during the second interview. The resulting strain on verbal communication within the interview was noted in reduced verbal productivity on the part of the Ss in the experimental group, reduced rate of verbal articulation, and a tendency to resist communicating in a psychologically meaningful manner by speaking about superficialities. Thus, when conflicted by expectations that were incongruent with actual interviewer behavior, interviewees became less productive and more psychologically avoidant (i.e., resistive), in the content that they communicated than other Ss who did not experience this incongruence.

Many authors report a variety of measures taken to overcome the consequences of discrepant expectations. Goldstein (1971) makes brief reference to this literature. He refers to one investigation (Hoehn-Saric, Frank, Imber, Nash, Stone, & Battle, 1964) in which the authors gave a brief verbal induction to patients before the beginning of therapy about the role that they might expect their therapists to play. This induction apparently reduced expectational discrepancies and improved the course of psycho- therapy. He makes further reference to other studies which have demon- strated that middle-class therapists tend to overcome expectational discre- pancies on the part of lower socioeconomic patients if they become interested in working with them, thus improving therapeutic success rates. And in another investigation psychotherapy with "blue-collar" patients met with considerable success when the therapist proceeded with full knowledge of the assumptions that such patients have regarding the nature of emotional disturbance. Finally, Goldstein (1971) refers to the present movement toward the use of paraprofessional, nonprofessional, or indigenous psychotherapists as a further example of "discrepancy reduction by innovation."

> Here, similarity of ethnic or community background and lifestyle provides a nondiscrepant therapist-patient pair who share the same values, basic assumptions and levels of communication. As this and several other dimensions of the community mental health movement continue to expand and develop, our field can anticipate a growing variety of means for effectively reducing therapy-patient discrepancy of the types we have been discussing." (Goldstein, 1971, p. 61)

(These studies will be considered at greater length in Chapter 10.) In brief, if expectations on the part of patients like our fictional Mr. A, which are discrepant with those of traditional psychotherapists, tend to block the effectiveness of psychotherapy for many socioeconomic groups below the middle-class level, new approaches to these neglected segments of the population must be made. In some instances it has been demonstrated that they can utilize presently available psychotherapy if their expectations are modified by some preliminary preparation or induction. One may also consider modifying the actual behavior of the therapist (that is, his interviewing style) when he works with members of lower socioeconomic groups in order that communication might be more congruent with the patient's anticipations.

INTERPERSONAL PERCEPTION

Expectation and Interpersonal Perception

In the preceding part of this chapter the concept of expectation has been reviewed as it pertains to relationship within the interview. The aspect of relationship to which it is most relevant is that of interpersonal perception. This is not surprising since its connection with interpersonal perception is a special instance of its association with perception as a more general process. Consider, for example, the following brief conceptualization of the perceptual process:

The perceptual act is shaped, in part before the appearance of the stimulus; it is anticipated by the subject's expectations or set. Thus, casual perceptions may well express the personal biases and interests of the perceiver. For example, if one were to ask a husband, a wife, and three-year-old child to report what they see in and around a neighbor's house, the wife might speak of the color and texture of her neighbor's draperies, the husband might notice the neighbor's new car, and the child might observe a dog wagging his tail as his master approaches. All these observations could be accurate enough, but quite evidently would be differently focused. What one attends to and subsequently perceives is therefore not fortuitous, but a consequence of one's expectations or set. One sees what one looks for. In this sense expectation serves to select the stimuli to which one attends out of the welter impinging on a person at a given moment... In brief, a percept is a complex resultant of many antecedent conditions including the properties of stimulus, and the state of the organism, i.e., its set, motivation, past experience, and more generally personality.
(Pope & Scott, 1967, p. 133)

To be sure, with relationship as the present point of reference, the focus is on interpersonal perception rather than perception as a general topic in psychology. Reference has already been made to an early experimental study (Asch, 1946) in which two groups of Ss were given contrasting inductions, one to expect a warm person, and the other, a cold person. Actually there were no real interpersonal encounters; the two individuals described in this contrasting way were fictional. In a later study (Kelley, 1950), a real rather than fictional person was the interpersonal stimulus. The $\underline{S}$s in this study were students who were asked to rate a real instructor whom they met after they were given an experimentally manipulated induction. In the author's words, the purpose of the study was the measurement of the effect of the "expectation of the stimulus person which the observer brings to the exposure situation" (Kelley, 1950, p. 431). Undergraduate psychology students were used as $\underline{S}$s. Each class was told that their regular instructor was out of town. Out of an interest in determining how various classes react to different instructors, each student was to be asked to fill out a questionnaire about the new instructor at the end of the class. Under the guise of a written introduction, one-half of the students were led to expect a "warm" instructor and the other half, a "cold" instructor. The stimulus person then appeared and led the class in a 20-minute discussion. In the questionnaires filled out after class by each student, the "warm" $\underline{S}$s perceived the instructors as more considerate, more informal, more sociable, more popular, better natured, more humorous, and more humane than did the "cold" students, even though they were together in the same class. There was also a tendency for a larger proportion of those who were given the "warm" induction to participate in class discussion than of those given the "cold" induction. Thus, the manipulation of expectation affects the perception of the person described, whether it be a fictional individual or one who is live and interacting with the $\underline{S}$s.

A much later study (Greenberg, Goldstein, & Gable, 1971) dealt with the same problem in a therapy analogue context. It tested the hypothesis "that information given prior to a $\underline{S}$'s exposure to a therapy session can change his perception of that session and render him more attracted...to the session's therapist" (Greenberg et al., 1971, p. 423). In more specific terms it "was expected that overall, $\underline{S}$s would be more attracted to the therapist when he was structured as being warm rather than cold" (p. 424). The $\underline{S}$s were male and female normal high school students, and "disturbed" $\underline{S}$s from a children's treatment center. All $\underline{S}$s were asked to listen to a tape of a simulated counseling session, presented to them as a recording of an actual counseling interview. A group of psychologist judges had previously listened to the tape and rated the tone of the counselor as neutral with regard to the warm-cold dimension of relationship. Yet, one-half of the $\underline{S}$s were told that the counselor's friends regarded him as a warm person; the other half, that they viewed him as cold. Following the presentation of the tape, the $\underline{S}$s were asked to fill out a questionnaire which measured their attraction to the interviewer. It may be assumed that a successful induction would lead those $\underline{S}$s who expected the interviewer to be warm, to actually perceive him in this way and, as a consequence, report a greater attraction toward him than those $\underline{S}$s who expected him to be cold. The results did indeed show that the $\underline{S}$s who had received the "warm" induction were more attracted to the taped interviewer than those who were given the "cold" induction. The authors drew two conclusions: (1) "Normal and disturbed high school adolescents were more attracted to a therapist previously described to them as warm rather than cold" and (2) "the attraction results serve to underline the possibility that pretherapy messages regarding a therapist's characteristics may affect patients' initial perceptions of therapy" (Greenberg et al., 1971, p. 426).

Again, the manipulation of expectation has affected the perception that Ss have of a target person. The context in which this expectation effect was demonstrated was a therapy analogue situation.

The next investigation (Langer & Abelson, 1974) dealt with the biasing effect of interviewer expectation on his/her perception of the interviewee. Interviewer expectation was manipulated in two ways. (1) A videotaped interview was presented to one-half of a group of clinician Ss as a session with a job applicant, and to the other half, as a meeting with a patient. (2) One-half of the clinician Ss selected were psychologists with a behavioral orientation; the other half, with a traditional psychoanalytic orientation. Both the use of the patient versus job applicant label and the selection of Ss with contrasting theoretical orientations may be assumed to be associated with different interviewer expectancies regarding the interviewee. Moreover, it may be anticipated that the two expectation variables would interact. Thus, it was predicted that "(a) when the interviewee was labelled 'patient' he would in general be perceived as a more disturbed individual than when he was labelled 'job applicant' and (b) this labelling bias would be less for the behavior therapists than for the traditional therapists" (Langer & Abelson, 1974, p. 5).

The two groups of psychologists did not differ appreciably in their adjustment rating of the interviewee presented as a job applicant. But their difference was substantial when he was presented as a patient. Traditional clinicians perceived a significantly greater adjustment difference between job applicant and patient than the behavioral clinicians did.

It is evident that a priori set or expectation has a decided influence on the perception of a person. Thus, if the traditional and behavioral orientations function as filters through which the "label" used to designate the interviewee might be passed, the perceptions that emerge from both are likely to be quite different. The behavioral clinicians saw him pretty much in the same way, regardless of label applied. They perceived him as "realistic," "unassertive," "fairly sincere, enthusiastic, attractive appearance," "pleasant, easy manner of speaking," and "responsible in interview." As a job applicant the analytic clinicians saw him as "attractive and conventional looking," "candid and innovative," "ordinary, straightforward," "upstanding, middle-class citizen type, but more like a hard hat," and "probably of lower or blue-collar class origins." As a patient, however, they saw him quite differently: "tight, defensive person... conflict over homosexuality," "dependent, passive-aggressive," "impulsivity shows through his rigidity," "considerable hostility, repressed or channeled."

Clinicians may also manifest bias in their perceptions of patients by consensually shared sets about different types of people. For example, they are prone to perceive lower social class patients as more seriously disturbed than middle or upper class patients. This was demonstrated in an experimental investigation carried out by Lee and Temerlin (1970). A professional actor was trained to portray a mentally healthy person. One of the authors audiotaped a diagnostic interview with this person in which the "interviewee" portrayed himself as happily married, sexually well adjusted, warm, friendly, and relaxed. However, he did admit some differences of opinion with his wife about the management of the children, the war in Vietnam, and the role of church attendance in the family. But none of these differences were seriously disruptive of the marriage. A group of psychiatric residents audited the tape, after assignment to one of three experimental groups and one control group. The three experimental groups listened to the tape after being given one of three socioeconomic case histories which were constructed to depict the interviewee as belonging to an upper, middle, or lower socioeconomic group. The control group received no socioeconomic case history. After listening to the tape, all Ss rated the mental helath and prognosis of the taped interviewee. The results showed that "the group which heard the lower socioeconomic history diagnosed the patient as mentally ill with a fair prognosis, while the controls diagnosed him as normal with an excellent prognosis. There were no significant differences between the control group and the middle and upper class groups" (Lee & Temerlin, 1970, p. 183). The prognostic ratings were similarly biased against the low social class condition.

The social class manipulation in the study was successful only because the clinicians approached the diagnostic task with biased a priori expectations about the relationship between social class and mental illness.

An additional experimental manipulation of expectation is more directly relevant to the actual interview situation. This investigation (Kumar, 1965) had the following objective: "An experiment was designed to test the proposition that a counselor's prior set toward his client influences his evaluations subsequent to the initial interview" (Kumar, 1965, p. 57). Ss in this study were male and female graduate counseling students who were given the task of conducting intake interviews. The Ss understood that these were regular intake interviews in a university counseling center. In actuality the "clients" were two student actors, one male and one female, who were trained to ad-lib with credibility the two roles of a "friendly" and a "hostile" client. Other aspects of their interview behavior were controlled and kept constant. Thus, they dwelt on the same personality problems in each interview, observing specific instructions about how each personal problem was to be communicated to the counselor-subject. In brief, each counselor was confronted in the interview with either a friendly or a hostile client. Moreover, an expectation of working with either a friendly or hostile client had been induced before the beginning of the interview. The design of the study is therefore based on four conditions: friendly expectation in the counselor and friendly behavior by the client; hostile expectation in the counselor and hostile behavior by the client; friendly expectation in the counselor and hostile behavior in the client; and hostile expectation in the counselor and friendly behavior in the client. On the basis of descriptive questionnaires filled out by each counselor after the end of the interview, it was possible to determine the impact of expectancy on interpersonal perception, particularly as expectancy interacts with the actual experience that the counselor had with the "counselee." Thus, it was found that the interviewers who expected friendly clients actually perceived them to be even more friendly than anticipated when their expectation was reinforced by congruent behavior of the client. Similarly, those counselors who expected hostile clients perceived them to be even more hostile than anticipated when in fact the client's behavior was hostile. When the counselor's anticipations were not confirmed, his perception of the client was determined more by the client's actual behavior than by expectation. However, expectation tended to mitigate to a discernible degree the effect of actual client behavior and therefore still had an effect on the ensuing interpersonal perception.

Other data relevant to the effect of expectation on interpersonal perception may be found in sociometric studies that deal with interpersonal attraction and rejection. One question that may be asked pertains to the extent to which individual A who likes or is attracted to individual B will tend to perceive individual B as reciprocating his attraction. If A's perception of mutuality or reciprocation were accurate (without distortion), there would be no evidence that expectation or set (i.e., A's attraction toward B) might be affecting his perception of B. If, on the other hand, one encounters the perception of mutuality more frequently than its actual occurrence, then there would indeed be evidence for the effect of expectation. In one investigation dealing with problem (Tagiuri, 1958), observations were made on a large number of well-acquainted groups of a variety of kinds that existed for reasons other than the research that was carried out. Some of the findings follow:

Undoubtedly the most powerful relationship encountered among our variables is that of congruency - the tendency, correctly based on experience, to perceive a person's feelings for us as congruent with our feelings for him...that is, with respect to both choice and rejection, members of groups over-estimate the extent to which their feelings are reciprocated. Interestingly enough, although there is actually greater mutuality of choice than of rejection, members feel just as reciprocated in their dislikes as they do in their preferences.

(Tagiuri, 1958, p. 322)

In brief, this finding would indicate that if one person likes or is attracted toward another, he tends to be "set," to perceive this other person as liking or being attracted to him. At least in some of the instances investigated, this set or expectation is not based on an actual reciprocation of choice or preference; it is in this sense autistic. But it does demonstrate the impact of attraction as a form of expectancy in one's perception of the other person.

Interpersonal Perception in the Interview

Interpersonal perception is an inseparable component of relationship. There can be no relationship between two people if they do not perceive each other in some way. For this reason it is quite usual to assess relationship in an interview by asking each participant for his/her perceptions of the other. These are generally recorded immediately after the completion of an interview, either in narrative form or in response to a questionnaire.

For example, in an experimental manipulation of interviewer warmth (Pope & Siegman, 1968) each interviewee was asked to complete a postinterview rating scale recording her perceptions of the interviewer. In this investigation one-half of the interviews were "warm" and one-half, "cold." The warm condition was created experimentally through the arousal of an anticipation of warm interviewer behavior in the interviewee, and through the actual perception of interviewer warmth; similarly, the cold condition was experimentally manipulated. Interviewees' postinterview ratings were compared for both the warm and cold conditions to determine whether, in fact, the experimental manipulation was successful. On 10 semantic-differential type bipolar scales, the rating differences were all significant. The interviewees perceived the interviewers in the warm condition as significantly warmer, more accepting, more understanding, pleasanter, more responsive, friendlier, and more interested than those in the cold condition. They liked the warm interviewers better, felt that they were liked better by them, and were considerably happier at the prospect of the interviewers becoming their therapists.

In this instance, differential perception of interviewer warm and cold behavior was undoubtedly an important aspect of the relationship that obtained during the interview. However, differences that are as neat and schematic as the ones just reported are generally obtained only in experimental analogues of interviews. In naturalistic interview situations, the relationship between expectation and actual interviewer behavior is never as precise or as controlled as it was in the above experiment. Thus, the interviewee's immediate perception of the interviewer may not be at all what s(he) expected before entering the interview situation, or may resemble what s(he) expected to varying degrees. Moreover, first impressions may be considerably modified during the course of the interview.

Consider now a third fictional interview. Mr. C, a young man of 38, had been residing in the United States for seven years, coming to this country to escape a repressive regime in Europe. In order to obtain permanent residence, he had falsified some data about previous political associations in his country of origin. As soon as he was legally able, he applied for American citizenship. However, his application appeared to have been passed over, consigned to an inactive limbo, while many friends who came to America with him had already been naturalized. At long last, he received a request to appear at Immigration for an interview with reference to his petition for naturalization.

What are the expectations with which Mr. C approaches the interview? He feels guilty and anxious because of his failure to disclose past associations. He anticipates an austere, punitively judgmental interrogator who will confront him with inaccurarcies in his past information, and is periodically panicked at the possibility that he will be castigated and, indeed, punished for this inaccuracy by the interviewer, possibly through deportation.

Mr. C arrived 10 minutes before the appointed time and precisely on schedule was invited into the interview room by an outer office secretary. It had not escaped his notice that the secretary was attractive, friendly, and seemed interested in chatting with him as he waited. Dare he hope that the secretary's behavior toward him might be a happy omen? So it seemed when he entered the interview room and immediately felt an atmosphere of relaxed informality. His interviewer, though neatly dressed and wearing a tie, was in his shirt sleeves. His secretary poised with pen and notebook, was friendly, again attractive, and mini-skirted. The interviewer greeted him in a warm manner, shook his hand with just the right degree of vigor to convey a welcome, and graciously asked him to be seated. In fact, the interviewer was not a formidable person at all. A little short in stature, slight in build, with a smooth, soft, youngish appearing face, he looked very much like a moderately self-effacing, gentle person. The change in Mr. C's emotional state was dramatic. He had approached the meeting with the resolve to defend himself by covering previous inaccuracies with further plausible, self-exonerating falsehoods. Now this resolve drained out of him. He felt impelled to reach out to his interviewer in warmth, friendship, and completely self-disclosing frankness.

When the interview began, the atmosphere chilled, but subtly and not decisively. After establishing his identity and obtaining some general personal data from him, the interviewer suddenly, with no prodromal cues, confronted Mr. C with his previous misinformation. When Mr. C hesitated to admit that he had indeed avoided giving the specific information now requested, the interviewer became transiently sharp, momentarily accusatory. All the previous anxiety flooded back into Mr. C, this time associated with a state of moderate confusion. He could no longer remember his well-prepared defense, and was already "set" to throw himself on the mercy of this erstwhile warm, benign person who had aroused transient hopes of a happy outcome.

The confrontation lasted only about a minute. Mr. C admitted to his earlier misinformation, and his interviewer quickly reverted to his previous warmth and gentleness. The rest of the interview was an unbroken sequence of complete self-disclosure on the part of Mr. C, communicated in a dependent, self-abasing way, and responded to by the interviewer with sensitivity, approval, and reassurance.

At the moment of leaving the interview, Mr. C felt grateful to the interviewer. He had been helped to unburden himself of a guilty weight and could not for the moment imagine that his softly smiling interrogator could feel anything but good will toward him. Later on he again began to worry and ruminate about his status. In particular, he was haunted by the conviction that he had revealed much more than he had intended, that he had been "psyched" into communicating what he had intended not to say before he arrived. But for a period he was buoyed by the perception of a benign man, just a little older than himself, who brought him great relief by a warm, forgiving attitude.

Although Mr. C's exchange with the Immigration interviewer took place in a single encounter, the relationship between the two participants in the interview was quite central to its course. Moreover, the interviewee's perception of the interviewer was an important aspect of the relationship. A priori expectations had a considerable impact on the first impressions that were formed, in this instance, through their dramatic contrast with the interviewee's early perception of the interviewer. The concluding impression that Mr. C had of the interviewer as he left the office was a cumulative resultant of a priori expectation, early perception of the interviewer, and the subsequent interaction between the two.

Attributes of Interpersonal Perception

The assumption that perception is a central component of relationship has its roots in a more general role ascribed to perception in an organism's adjustment to the environment. It is not necessarily the objective behavior of the two participants in an interview dyad that determines the relationship that ensues, but rather the perception that each has of the other. Thus,

the situational component of the determinants of behavior are operative only as they are perceived by the person. Organisms do not directly apprehend the external environment; various forms of energy which impinge on the sensory receptor apparatus do not contain information in a form that is always immediately useful. Rather it is the case that we are all very elaborate, but very imperfect, computing devices when it comes to making "sense" out of the information provided to our senses by the so-called objective environment. This means that there is considerable possibility of slippage occurring between what is "out there" and our experience of it, as is readily demonstrated in visual illusion. It also means that our behavior, insofar as it is determined by the environment is a product only of what we perceive the environment to be - not of what it is. (Carson, 1969, p. 11)

From the preceding quotation, it may be inferred that interpersonal perception is subject to the same phenomenological laws as other forms of perception. We may be accurate in what we perceive (i.e., veridical); or we may be inaccurate (i.e., autistic). But whatever our level of accuracy, our perception of the environment, personal or impersonal, is an important mediating link between the environment as stimulus and our responses.

Having indicated the similarity in a basic way between perception of persons and perception of objects and things, it is now necessary to refer to some of the differences. Thus, one perceives an unbroken succession of objects and things as one drives down a street in a car. Most of the incoming stimuli are perceived in time and place but do not command a high level of attention. On the other hand, if one proceeds down the street in the car with the intention of finding a mailbox because one has an important letter to mail, a red and blue object seen at a distance may take on both the contour and the positioning of a mailbox. It will certainly be perceived with more vividness under these circumstances than under others when one has no letter to mail. The mailbox in this instance becomes a means-end instrumentality. Thus, in thing perception objects have physical and spatial attributes as well as functional properities. "In contrast to things, persons are rarely mere manipulanda; rather they are action centers, they can do something to us, they can benefit or harm us intentionally, and we can benefit or harm them. Persons are perceived as having abilities, as acting purposefully, as having wishes or sentiments, as perceiving or watching us. They are systems having representations, they can be our friends or our enemies, and each has his characteristic traits" (Heider, 1958a, p. 22). Moreover, person perceptions vary considerably along a time dimension. If one enters an interview situation one may indeed form an instant impression of the interviewer from a quick look at his/her face and body posture. But this impression will be modified over time as one perceives his behavior during the interview. This is not to deny the role of change over time in thing perceptions; but the time dimension is usually not as crucial for the achievement of a thing or object percept as it is for that of a person.

It would appear justified to designate person perception as more complex than thing or object perception. In all forms of perception the organism seeks to achieve a stable environment. Thus, after a minimal level of maturation a person will always see a chair as a chair. To be sure, he may later come to differentiate between one type of chair and another, but the basic category of chair is constant. This constancy brings with it an element of economy in perception and adjustment to the environment. The organism does not have to start de novo every time a chair enters its visual field. There is an act of instant recognition. But constancy is not as easily achieved with people. Color, form, structure, position within environment, and potential utility to the perceiver, are the determinants out of which thing and object constancy develop. How much more complex was the task of Mr. C in achieving some sort of perceptual stability with reference to his interviewer. He perceived his interviewer as young and gentle. These are traits which one person may attribute to another. This attribution is based on his past experience with other people. He has come to associate certain physiognomic cues with youthfulness. Constancy and economy are achieved through a process based on experience with people. In the case of Mr. C inference went beyond the attribution of certain character traits to the interviewer. Mr. C also made a number of rather high level inferences regarding the intentions the interviewer had toward him. For the moment, if not later, he perceived the interviewer as helpfully disposed toward him. To be sure, the stability of this perception was not great because Mr. C began to doubt it after some time had elapsed postinterview. Both the percept and the doubt were complex resultants of his immediate perceptual experience and previous expectation.

However, it is not enough to characterize person perception as more complex in character than object or thing perception. The role of person perception in the relationship between two or more persons gives it a particularly unique character as a form of perception. The example that follows pertains to the dominance-submission aspect of relationship. Every child knows that if he wishes to stay beyond the range of patental control, the thing to do is to stay out of sight. Once he comes into the view of a parent, he knows that he has entered the zone of parental dominance. Thus, a two-year-old boy became fascinated with a wristwatch worn by a visitor. On several occasions, he had attempted to remove the watch from the visitor's hand and had been told rather emphatically that this particular action was not permitted. Once, when the wristwatch was casually put down on an end table in the livingroom he moved quickly toward it but was again prevented from picking it up. Considerably later during the same day, his parents and the visitor became aware of a regular thumping sound coming through the ceiling of the livingroom. His mother knew that her son's bedroom was immediately above and eventually became curious about the activity going on overhead.

When she entered the boy's bedroom she found him on the floor with the visitor's wristwatch in his hand rhythmically thumping it against the planks of the floor. The fate of the wristwatch is not our concern at this point. Our interest rather is in the awareness of this two-year-old boy that he could only indulge his interest in the wristwatch in some place beyond the controlling range of parental vision.

The role of perception in interpersonal control is stated clearly in the following quotation:

> If person A sees person B, he first of all knows where B is which gives him a much greater possibility of acting on B. If A does not see B and does not know where B is, then B is out of the range of the physical power of A who does not know how to get hold of B. Therefore, B may hide from A by making it difficult for A to perceive B, if he is afraid A might harm him. B then prevents A's action by placing himself in a region which is unstructured for A. (Heider, 1958b, p. 30)

In an interview it is of course not possible for the interviewee to remove himself from the field of vision of the interviewer. However, an interviewee who fears control or harm from the interviewer may find other means of reducing his "visibility." Several modes of hiding his feelings, attitudes, or intentions from the interviewer are available to him. He may, of course, reduce or terminate any form of verbal communication. This method is extreme, and not in itself necessarily effective because the interviewee may still betray some affect through facial expression, body posture, and movement. When an interviewee is particularly resistive, one notes silence associated with a "frozen" lack of facial or kinesic expressiveness. In many cases when periods of extreme resistiveness have been overcome, it is possible to determine from the interviewee that verbal and visual inexpressiveness were motivated by a need to mitigate or reduce the interviewer's control over him. In such periods the interviewee is perceptually vigilant but inexpressive. There may be the anticipation that any evidence of feeling, whether it be anger, anxiety, or even warmth, attachment and dependency, is likely to evoke either rejection or punishment from the interviewer. In that event, the experience of being looked at by the interviewer may be highly anxiety arousing for the interviewee. Sullivan (1954) shows a sensitive awareness of this reaction when he reports that he looks closely at a patient only once, at the beginning of the initial interview, as the patient enters the consulting room. Then he shows the patient where to sit down and never again stares directly at him.

But visual contact is by no means always aversive. For example, in an interview that is going well both participants may frequently engage in eye contact. One may regard mutual eye contact as an index of a reciprocal interaction with a minimum of conflict over dominance-submission and few barriers to emotional expression. With reference to eye contact, one sociologist has the following to say:

> Of the special sense organs, the eye has a uniquely sociological function. The union and interaction of individuals is based upon mutual

glances. This is perhaps the most direct and purest reciprocity which exists anywhere. . . . This mutual glance between persons, in distinction from the simple sight or observation of the other, signifies a wholly new and unique union between them...by the glance which reveals the other, one discloses himself. By the same act in which the observer seeks to know the observed, he surrenders himself to be understood by the observed. The eye cannot take unless at the same time it gives. (Simmel, 1921)

Investigators interested in the interview process have long been aware of the importance of eye contact as a sign that the relationship is positive and communication is unimpeded. There are few interpersonal exchanges that are more mutual, more reciprocal, than a moment of eye contact in which the interviewer and the interviewee are simultaneously both the perceivers and the perceived. (Eye contact as a channel of communication has been discussed in Chapters 4 and 5.)

The present chapter has dealt with certain psychological processes that occur in a relationship between two people. In the two chapters that follow, the focus will be on relationship as viewed separately, from the vantage point of interviewer and interviewee.

APPLICATION SUMMARY

When two people meet for the first time in an interview their relationship has already been determined, in part, by past experiences. Thus, each enters the situation with certain expectations about the behavior, personal attributes, and attitudes of the other. These expectations have a great deal to do with the initial perceptions that the two participants have of each other and the relationship that follows. The interviewer will find it expedient to learn as much as s(he) can about the interviewee's expectations as early as possible. Indeed, the interviewer may find it necessary to modify the interviewee's expectations at the outset, if the interview is to proceed without obstruction.

Interviewee set may be idiosyncratic. Thus, an angry, sensitive, vigilantly defensive person will approach the interview in a guarded way, expecting to be criticized or attacked, and poised to ward off the hostility that is anticipated. This stance may be a consequence of the personal history of the interviewee.

But set may also be a result of experiences shared with other members of groups to which the interviewee belongs. For example, the two fictional cases (Mr. A and Mrs. B) presented at an early point in the present chapter, exemplify contrasting, group-engendered expectations that are certain to affect the relationships that develop, and indeed the prognoses for psychotherapy. Mr. A brings with him a complex of negative reactions to the style of communication and the treatment approach of the psychiatrist. His past experiences, shared with low socioeconomic relatives and friends, fill him with doubt about the efficacy of "talk" as a form of treatment. In fact, his own medical doctor has reinforced these doubts by implying that his inability to respond to conventional medical procedures has somehow tainted him. Referral to a psychiatrist was, in itself, a recognition of the patient's failure in treatment. His anticipations of censure from and possibly rejection by friends and relatives for seeking help from a "head" doctor filled him with apprehension and shame. Moreover, the failure of the doctor to prescribe for him, the ambiguous character of the inquiry he carried out, and his prompting of Mr. A to engage in personal introspection, all were discordant with the patient's usual set regarding a visit to a doctor's office.

Mrs. B approached her initial interview with a contrasting set of anticipations. To begin with, her referral was made in quite a different manner from that experienced by Mr. A. Her doctor spoke as though there were no barrier between the professional realm that he occupied and that of the psychiatrist; in fact, they seemed to be friends. The location of the psychiatrist's office, its furniture and appointments, were familiar and congenial to a member of the middle class. Her encounter with a person like herself in the waiting room, and the process of becoming acquainted with this patient served to support her in her approach to the interview. Moreover, the psychiatrist's invitation to Mrs. B to speak introspectively about early history and her thoughts and feelings about current relationships, in and outside of her immediate family, did not threaten her, as it had Mr. A. In fact, introspection and conversation about psychological experiences were quite usual forms of exchange between Mrs. B and some of her friends.

The above two instances demonstrate the role of the socioeconomic culture in which the interviewee lives in fostering the anticipations with which s(he) approaches the mental health interview. Clearly, the middle-class applicant for psychotherapy (Mrs. B) found the initial interview an easier experience than the applicant from the working class (Mr. A). In part, the relative ease that she experienced was a consequence of her familiarity with the concepts and the communication style she encountered in the initial interview. In part, it was a result of the congruence of her expectations with those of the interviewer. It is relevant at this point, to recall the distinction made by Goldstein's (1971) Yavis and non-Yavis patients. The former are Young, Attractive, Verbal, Intelligent, and Successful; the latter have none of these attributes. Most of the Yavis traits are found in middle-class patients; most are lacking in patients of lower class origin.

A lack of congruence between the expectations of the interviewer and interviewee places a strain on the interview and, indeed, may lead to an early termination of psychotherapy. Thus, terminators in treatment differ from continuers in a number of ways: they expect specific advice for their problems and medication for their ailments; their attitude to the therapist is one of passive cooperation rather than active collaboration. These expectations are in conflict with those entertained by the therapist, who tends to believe that the patient should be motivated to seek a relationship in which he is given the opportunity to talk openly about himself and his ailments; the patient should look to his/her relationship with the therapist as the instrument for the resolution of his problems. Consistent with the preceding two expectations of the therapist is his/her attitude that the patient should perceive himself as responsible, to a degree, for the outcome of therapy.

To mitigate the strain resulting from the dissimilarity between interviewer and interviewee expectations, the interviewer may first inquire into the set with which the client enters the initial interview. Who has referred him/her? What has the referring person told the client about the interviewer and the agency? Has the process of referral been demeaning, as it was with Mr. A., or was it personally enhancing, as it was with Mrs. B? Was the referral made in a manner that aroused hope and optimism in the client, or was it made with exasperation, as an act of last resort? How supportive was the intake procedure? How long did the client have to wait for the interview, and under what conditions? The entire passage of the client from the referral source to the initial interview itself is fraught with conditions for the arousal of positive or negative expectations. These are situationally aroused, in contrast to those that are of such long duration in the interviewee and so idiosyncratic as to be regarded as predispositional.

The work of Lennard and Bernstein (1960) is particularly helpful in the assessment of interviewee and interviewer set about the style of communication in the interview and, indeed, the topics that are suitable for discussion. Both the interviewer and the interviewee have certain expectations regarding their own "activeness" and the "activeness" of the other member of the dyad. In this regard, Lennard and Bernstein (1960) propose the following questions as guides for the evaluation of the expectations of both participants:

(1) Who should take the initiative in communicating?; (2) How frequently should they speak?; (3) To what extent should the therapist direct the patient as to what he should talk about?; (4) How 'directive' should the therapist be with reference to the patients' activities outside of therapy?; (5) Should the therapist give advice and counsel?; (6) How much explanation about therapy should the therapist provide? (Lennard & Bernstein, 1960, p. 154)

These questions provide the interviewer with a framework for assessing the degree of mutuality of expectation that exists between himself/herself and the interviewee. The probability is high that some differences will occur regarding the relative activity level of each, the topics to be discussed, and the active help that the client might expect from the interviewer. Having determined the expectations of the interviewee as they bear on relationship and communication within the interview, the interviewer then chooses the measures to be taken to reduce any disagreements between himself/herself and the client. There is an extensive and growing literature on the prescription of interview and treatment techniques to meet the expectations of low socioeconomic and other non-Yavis clients. Some of this literature will be reviewed in Chapter 10. For the present, the emphasis will be on the things the interviewer might do to prepare the interviewee for participating in a normative type of mental health interview.

Discrepant expectations are dealt with early in the interview, through measures designated as primary system references (Lennard & Bernstein, 1960). Such references include remarks by the therapist about the type and level of activity required of the patient. In effect, the patient is trained to engage in a reciprocal role relationship. For example, s(he) might learn not to expect the therapist to speak about himself/herself, or to issue explicit orders and directions. On the other hand, s(he) may be led to expect the therapist to select the topics for discussion, but to prompt their exploration with ambiguous rather than specific questions. As one would anticipate, the frequency of occurrence of primary system references decreases rapidly as the interview progresses.

Fortunately for the interviewer, a large proportion of applicants for psychotherapy have been reasonably well prepared by society for their first encounter with a mental health clinician. Many of them already know that the onus for personal self-disclosure will be on them. They expect that the interviewer will be nonjudgmental, accepting both positive and negative feelings without criticism. They anticipate an empathic interviewer with a supportive level of personal warmth. For these patients, a foundation already exists for any further structuring of expectation that might be needed.

While the interviewer is modifying a client's expectations, s(he) may simultaneously be adapting his/her own. For it has been demonstrated that the prognosis of a patient depends both on the patient's expectations and on those of the interviewer. If a therapist is more optimistic about the prognosis for one patient than for another, the evidence points to a more favorable outcome for the former. It also points to a more productive response of the former in the interview situation. The potency of the therapist's prognostic expectation is understandable when one considers its central position in a whole complex of attitudes that must surely influence the therapist-patient relationship. Optimism about the outlook for a patient is associated with feelings of warmth toward the patient and a tendency to minimize his/her degree of disturbance.

Many investigations have shown that the attitude of an interviewer to a patient is only partially based on clinical evaluation. In part it is a resultant of a priori biases. Thus, the interviewer is likely to prefer a Yavis type of patient to a non-Yavis type, a middle- or upper-class patient to one from the lower class, an educated patient to one of limited education. Such preferences have much to do with the kinds of relationships that subsequently develop.

However discouraging the presence of therapist bias may be, there is some comfort in the repeated finding that experience and training tend to reduce its effect. It may be assumed that over time the interviewer develops an awareness of the values and expectations that s(he brings into the interview situation. Such an awareness does not come easily. It may be attained through personal therapy and the kind of supervision that is provided in clinical training. Once attained it is a crucial instrument in the hands of the interviewer for the development of rapport with a client and the fostering of those aspects of relationship that sustain a single interview or a psycho-therapy series.

A central aspect of the experience of relationship is the perception that one has of the other person. Thus, an interviewer may decide, very early in a meeting with an interviewee, that s(he) is speaking with a warm or cold person, a friendly or hostile person. These early impressions are experienced as perceptions. If asked on what his/her judgment is based, the interviewer may simply assert that the interviewee has the appearance of the type of person described. It may well be that many instant or early perceptions are impressively accurate. But many are not, and the interviewer's clinical experience and training should alert him/her to the possibility of error in early interpersonal perceptions.

Several experimental investigations demonstrate the vulnerability of interpersonal perception to the manipulation of expectation. The study by Asch (1946) will be recalled in which a fictional person was perceived in widely divergent ways by two groups of Ss, because the adjective "warm" was inserted in a list of adjectives that described him to one group and the adjective "cold" was inserted in precisely the same list of adjectives when describing him to another group. Later, Kelley (1950) carried through a similar manipulation of warm-cold expectations with a class of college students meeting a new instructor for the first time. In this instance, the person perceived was real, not fictional, but the results were the same. Those students given the "cold" induction perceived the instructor much less favorably than those given the "warm" induction even though both groups of students attended the same class at the same time. In an additional investigation (Greenberg et al., 1971) those Ss who were told that a counselor in a taped counseling session was regarded by his friends as warm, were more strongly attracted to him than those who were told he was considered to be cold. In some instances manipulated expectation leads to blatant bias in interpersonal perception. One-half of a group of clinicians was told that the interviewee in a videotaped interview was a job applicant; the other half, that he was a mental patient (Langer & Abelson, 1974). Those who were told that he was a patient perceived him as significantly more disturbed than those to whom he was described as a job applicant. In response to an audiotape of an actor portraying a mentally healthy person (Lee & Temerlin, 1970), psychiatric residents who were told the speaker was of low socioeconomic origin regarded him as mentally ill; the others, to whom he was identified as a person of the middle or upper class, perceived no mental illness in him at all.

The warning should be emblazoned in every clinic, on every admission service of a psychiatric hospital, and in every private office of a mental health clinician. The early perception that a clinician has of a patient is subject to the biasing effect of expectation. Though clinicians are often exhilarated with their virtuosity in quick diagnostic assessments, they should allow for the possibility that they may be misled by their own a priori sets. Though the rush toward early closure in the perception of a new patient is frequently hard to resist, a deliberate effort should be made to remain open to new impressions throughout the evaluation period.

Clinicians are well acquainted with the inner experience of dissonance resulting from a clash between the anticipations about a prospective client that may have been aroused in them by a referral note, or even the verbal communication of a referral, and their early perceptions of the patient whom they later meet. The fictional case of Mr. C portrays an analogous experience for an interviewee, possibly a little more dramatic than it is likely to be in a clinical situation. In the end, Mr. C's view of the interviewer was a complex resultant of the clash between his expectation of a punitive interrogator and the benign perception of him in the actual interview.

The earlier warning to clinicians to keep themselves open to impressions that may not be congruent with initial expectations was not meant to imply that they tend, in general, to be nonreceptive to new perceptions that differ from earlier ones. In fact, a study by Kumar (1965) showed that both expectation and perception of ongoing client behavior contributed toward the ultimate evaluation of the client. When the interviewer's anticipations were not confirmed by the client's behavior, the latter weighed more heavily than the former.

Although the interviewer's perception of a patient is an important source of information about him/her, the act by which the former perceives the latter is fraught with clinical risk. Sullivan's (1954) observations about this matter have been quoted frequently. His practice was to look closely at the patient, only once, at the beginning of the initial interview and then to refrain from gazing directly at him/her again. To be sure, Sullivan worked with schizophrenic patients who are particularly sensitive to finding themselves the objects of scrutiny. For other interviewees, it is difficult to be precisely prescriptive. There is no doubt that the character of the interviewer's gaze makes a difference. Does s(he) scrutinize the patient as though s(he) were looking with curiosity or cold analytical interest? Or is there an element of mutuality in an exchange of glances between the two members of the dyad? In the former case, the interviewer's gaze is a blatant exercise of power and control. In the latter, mutual eye contact is a reciprocal exchange between two people, usually associated with positive feeling.

REFERENCES

Apfelbaum, B.   Dimensions of transference in psychotherapy.   Berkeley: University of California Press, 1958.

Asch, S.E.   Forming impressions of personality.   Journal of Abnormal and Social Psychology, 1946, 41, 258-290.

Begley, C.E., & Lieberman, L.R.   Patient expectations of therapists' techniques. Journal of Clinical Psychology, 1970, 26, 113-116.

Berzins, J.I., Herron, E.W., & Seidman, E.   Patients' role behaviors as seen by therapists: A factor analytic study.   Psychotherapy: Theory, Research, and Practice, 1971, 8, 127-130.

Bordin, E.S.   Psychological counseling.   New York: Appleton-Century-Crofts, 1968.

Boulware, D.W., & Holmes, D.S.   Preferences for therapists and related expectancies.   Journal of Consulting and Clinical Psychology, 1970, 35, 269-277.

Butler, J.M.   The interaction of client and therapist.   Journal of Abnormal and Social Psychology, 1952, 47, 366-378.

Carson, R.C.   Interaction concepts of personality.   Chicago: Aldine, 1969.

Chance, E. Families in treatment. New York: Basic Books, 1959.

Frank, J.D. Persuasion and healing. Baltimore: The Johns Hopkins Press, 1961.

Friedman, J. Patient-expectancy and symptom reduction. In A.P. Goldstein & S.J. Dean (Eds.), The investigation of psychotherapy. New York: Wiley, 1966.

Garfield, S., & Wolpin, M. Expectations regarding psychotherapy. The Journal of Nervous and Mental Diseases, 1963, 137, 353-362.

Goldman, R.K., & Mendelsohn, G.A. Psychotherapeutic change and social adjustment: A report of a national survey of psychotherapists. Journal of Abnormal Psychology, 1969, 74, 164-172.

Goldstein, A.P. Therapist and client expectation of personality change in psychotherapy. Journal of Counseling Psychology, 1960, 7, 180-184.

Goldstein, A.P. Therapist-patient expectancies in psychotherapy. New York: MacMillan, 1962.

Goldstein, A.P. Psychotherapeutic attraction. New York: Pergamon Press, 1971.

Goldstein, A.P., & Heller, K. Role expectations, participant personality characteristics, and the client-counselor relationship. Unpublished manuscript, August 1960.

Goldstein, A.P. & Shipman, G. Patient expectancies, symptom reduction and aspects of the initial psychotherapeutic interview. In A.P. Goldstein & S.J. Dean (Eds.), The investigation of psychotherapy. New York: Wiley, 1966. Pp. 307-311.

Greenberg, R.P., Goldstein, A.P., & Gable, R. Influence of background similarity and trait structuring on the perception of a taped therapist. Journal of Consulting and Clinical Psychology, 1971, 37, 423-427.

Hankoff, L.D., Friedman, N., & Engelhardt, D.M. The prognostic value of placebo response. American Journal of Psychiatry, 1958, 115, 549-550.

Heider, F. Perceiving the other person. In R. Tagiuri & L. Petrullo (Eds.), Person perception and interpersonal behavior. Stanford: Stanford University Press, 1958a.

Heider, F. Consciousness, the perceptual world and communications with others. In. R. Tagiuri & L. Petrullo (Eds.), Person perception and interpersonal behavior. Stanford: Stanford University Press, 1958b.

Heilbrun, A.B., Jr. Effects of briefing upon client satisfaction with the initial counseling contact. Journal of Consulting and Clinical Psychology, 1972, 38, 50-56.

Heine, R.W. (Ed.) The student physician and psychotherapist. Chicago: The University of Chicago Press, 1962.

Heine, R.W., & Trosman, H. Initial expectations of the doctor-patient inter-action as a factor in continuance of psychotherapy. Psychiatry, 1960, 23, 275-278.

Heller, K., Davis, J.D., & Myers, R.A. The effects of interviewer's style in a standardized interview. Journal of Consulting Psychology, 1966, 30, 501-508.

Heller, K., Myers, R.A., & Kline, L.V. Interviewer behavior as a function of standardized client roles. In A.P. Goldstein & S.J. Dean (Eds.), The investigation of psychotherapy. New York: Wiley, 1966. Pp. 398-403.

Hoehn-Saric, R., Frank, J.D., Imber, S.D., Nash, E.H., Stone, A.R., & Battle, C.C. Systematic preparation of patients for psychotherapy. I. Effect on therapy behavior and outcome. Journal of Psychiatric Research, 1964, 2, 267-281.

Howard, K.I., Orlinsky, D.E., & Hill, J.A. Affective experience in psychotherapy. Journal of Abnormal Psychology, 1970, 75, 267-275.

Kelley, H.H. The warm-cold variable in first impressions of persons. Journal of Personality, 1950, 18, 431-439.

Kumar, U. Client and counselor responses to prior counselor expectancies and to an initial interview. Unpublished doctoral dissertation, Ohio State University, 1965.

Langer, E.J., & Abelson, R.P. A patient by any other name...clinician group difference in labeling bias. Journal of Consulting and Clinical Psychology, 1974, 42, 4-9.

Lee, S.D., & Temerlin, M.K. Social class, diagnosis, and prognosis for psycho-therapy. Psychotherapy: Theory, Research and Practice, 1970, 7, 181-185.

Lennard, H.L., & Bernstein, A. The anatomy of psychotherapy. New York: Columbia University Press, 1960.

Pope, B., & Scott, W.H. Psychological diagnosis in clinical practice. New York: Oxford University Press, 1967.

Pope, B., & Siegman, A.W. Interviewer warmth in relation to interviewee verbal behavior. Journal of Consulting and Clinical Psychology, 1968, 32, 588-595.

Pope, B., Siegman, A.W., Blass, T., & Cheek, J. Some effects of discrepant role expectation on interviewee verbal behavior in the initial interview. Journal of Consulting and Clinical Psychology, 1972, 39, 501-507.

Rosenthal, D., & Frank, J.D. Psychotherapy and the placebo effect. Psychological Bulletin, 1956, 53, 294-302.

Sarbin, T.R. Role theory. In G. Lindzey (Ed.), Handbook of social psychology. Reading, Mass.: Addison-Wesley, 1954. Pp. 223-258.

Schofield, W. Some general factors in counseling and therapy. In B.G. Berenson & R. R. Carkhuff (Eds.), Sources of gain in counseling and psychotherapy. New York: Holt, Rinehart and Winston, 1967.

Secord, P.F. Facial features and inference processes in interpersonal perception. In R. Tagiuri & L. Petrullo (Eds.), Person perception and interpersonal behavior. Stanford: Stanford University Press, 1958.

Shapiro, A.K. Placebo effects in medicine, psychotherapy, and psychoanalysis. In A.E. Bergin & S.L. Garfield (Eds.), Handbook of psychotherapy and behavior change. New York: Wiley, 1971. Pp. 439-473.

Simmel, G. Sociology of the senses: Visual interaction. In R.E. Park & E.W. Burgess (Eds.), Introduction to the science of sociology. Chicago: University of Chicago Press, 1921.

Stein, M.I. (Ed.) Contemporary psychotherapies. New York: The Free Press of Glencoe, 1961.

Strupp, H.H. The performance of psychiatrists and psychologists in a therapeutic interview. Journal of Clinical Psychology, 1958, 14, 219-226.

Sullivan, H.S. The psychiatric interview. New York: Norton, 1954.

Sullivan, H.S. Clinical studies in psychiatry. New York: Norton, 1956.

Tagiuri, R. Social preference and its perception. In R. Tagiuri & L. Petrullo (Eds.), Person perception and interpersonal behavior, California: Stanford University Press, 1958. Pp. 316-336.

Wilson, M.N., & Rappaport, J. Personal self-disclosure: Expectancy and situational effects. Journal of Consulting and Clinical Psychology, 1974, 42, 901-908.

Yamamoto, J., & Goin, M.K. On the treatment of the poor. American Journal of Psychiatry, 1965, 122, 267-271.

8 Interviewer Attributes in Relationship

Professional psychotherapists tend to attribute success in treatment to the technical or procedural aspects of their work. Patients, on the other hand, tend more frequently to attribute whatever gains they make in treatment to the personal qualities of the therapist or the relationship that develops. This contrast is noted in the following summary Frank (1961) makes of one investigation (Blaine & McArthur, 1958) dealing with this matter:

> Both psychiatrists stressed insight into the correlations of childhood experiences with current symptoms, and the bringing to awareness of unconscious feelings as the sources of therapeutic gain. That is, they attributed their success to their therapeutic method. Neither patient mentioned these. Instead, both stressed the psychiatrists' indirect reassurance (in one case by granting an emergency interview and in the other by offering factual information as to the non-dangerous nature of the patient's symptoms) and the encounter with an authority figure who was both firm and completely accepting. These findings are highly tentative, being based on only two cases, but as far as they go they confirm that emotional support, kindly guidance, and the feeling of being accepted by the psychiatrist - qualities related to the psychiatrist's personality rather than his technique - are therapeutically important. (Frank, 1961, p. 132)

Frank's (1961) message is clear. Technical training and specific skill may be less important for the effective conduct of an interview or psychotherapeutic interaction than certain facilitating attitudes and personality attributes of the interviewer. He appears to be talking about factors affecting interviewer-interviewee relationship.

In a study previously referred to in Chapter 6 (Barrett-Lennard, 1962), five therapist relationship dimensions were correlated with outcome in therapy. A questionnaire was designed to yield measures of each variable based on client and therapist perceptions, and was administered to the clients and therapists at four points during the psychotherapy series. Most of the correlations are based on the ratings made by therapists and clients after the first five sessions. One objective of the study was to determine whether each of the measured qualities of relationship significantly predicted therapeutic improvement. Since the therapist attributes measured in the present study have been defined in Chapter 6, they will simply be designated by name at this time. They were empathic understanding, level of regard for the patient, unconditionality of regard, congruence or genuineness of therapist, and his willingness to know. Two measures of positive therapeutic change were used, both based on ratings by the therapists. The Ss were clients in the University of Chicago Counseling Center, with ages ranging from 19 to 45 years (most were in their 20s and 30s), 60% male, 50% college graduates. When clients were divided into two subgroups on the basis of the two criteria of change, one designated as "more changed" and the other as "less changed," it was found that the first four therapist attributes distinguished significantly between the two subgroups. Clients who were "more changed" were treated by therapists with higher levels of empathic understanding, level of regard for patient, unconditionality of regard, and congruence or genuineness, than clients who were "less changed." However, it was further noted that the association between measured relationship and change was always stronger when it was based on the clients' ratings of therapist attributes rather than the same ratings by the therapists. "This appears to be particularly compelling evidence of the primary relevance to therapeutic change of the client's perception of the relationship rather than the therapist's actual experience" (Barrett-Lennard, 1962, p. 15). Much of the rest of the chapter deals with interviewer attributes that enhance or diminish relationship.

INTERVIEWER WARMTH

In Chapter 6 relationship behavior has been dichotomized into its affective and dominance-submission dimensions. Warmth is, of course, included in the former. This interviewer attribute has already been considered at some length in Chapter 5. However, some reference to it will be included here because of its topical relevance to the content of the present chapter. A few studies, not previously mentioned in Chapter 5, will be added. But to a considerable degree, the present discussion of interviewer warmth will be theoretical and clinical in character.

A definitional analysis of warmth by Raush and Bordin (1957) was reviewed in Chapter 5. Because this analysis will be helpful in the present discussion, it will be given again in condensed form, taken this time from a later work by Bordin (1968). He designates three aspects of warmth as commitment, effort to understand, and spontaneity. By commitment, Bordin refers to the interviewer's dedication to the interviewee and his/her willingness to become involved with and to help him/her. When he speaks about effort to understand, Bordin does not allude to the therapist's intellectual grasp of the patient's problems but to a kind of emotional rapport, an attempt to put himself/herself into the patient's frame of reference, and to resonate with the patient's experience. Finally, there is the element of spontaneity, a quality of expressiveness which is the antithesis of the impassive mien and the inhibition of gesture characteristic of traditional psychotherapists with a psychoanalytic background. A therapist with a spontaneous style of communication avoids posture, facial appearance, and vocal tone that are deliberately rigid and blank, assuming instead an expressiveness that is genuine.

Bordin's definition of interviewer warmth is an inclusive one, assimilating into itself a range of positive attitudes toward the interviewee. Truax and Carkhuff (1967) preferred to deal with Bordin's three components of warmth separately, as though they were three dimensions. Thus, his effort to understand is analogous to Truax and Carkhuff's accurate empathy; spontaneity to therapist genuineness or self-congruence; and commitment to nonpossessive warmth, sometimes referred to as unconditional positive regard. Truax and Carkhuff define the latter as a dimension that "ranges from a high level where the therapist warmly accepts the patient's experience as part of that person, without imposing conditions; to a low level where the therapist evaluates the patient or his feelings, expresses dislike or disapproval, or expresses warmth in a selective or evaluative way" (1967, p. 58). They impart a rather specific meaning to nonpossessive warmth, derived largely from client-centered theory and practice. Thus, they speak about valuing the patient as a person in a way that is separate and distinct from any evaluation that the interviewer may make of the patient's behavior. Ideally, the attitude that they define would be similar to that expressed by a parent who has occasion to tell a child that he loves him but does not love a specific act or behavior of his. In a similar vein Truax remarks that Unconditional Warmth "involves a nonpossessive caring for the patient as a separate person who is allowed to have his own feelings and experiences; a prizing of the patient for himself regardless of his behavior" (Truax & Carkhuff, 1967, p. 60).

The authors actually go beyond the conceptualization of a dimension; they offer a scale for operationalizing this dimension and the other two designated above. Their concept of Nonpossessive Warmth becomes a little more explicit when one examines some examples that they provide to illustrate both the low and the high extremes of the Warmth Scale. Thus, at the low end of the five-stage scale, the "therapist is actively offering advice or giving clear negative regard. He may be telling the patient what would be 'best for him,' or in other ways actively approving or disapproving of his behavior. The therapist's actions make himself the locus of evaluation; he sees himself as responsible for the patient" (Truax & Carkhuff, 1967, p. 60). By contrast, at the upper end of the five-stage scale

the therapist communicates warmth without restriction. There is a deep respect for the patient's worth as a person and his rights as a free individual. At this level a patient is free to be himself even if this means that he is regressing, being defensive, or even disliking or rejecting the therapist himself. At this stage the therapist cares deeply for his patient as a person, but it does not matter to him how the patient chooses to behave. He genuinely cares for and deeply prizes the patient for his human potentials, apart from evaluations of his behavior or thoughts. He is willing to share equally the patient's joys and aspirations or depressions and failures. The only channeling by the therapist may be the demand that the patient communicate personally relevant material. (Truax & Carkhuff, 1967, pp. 66-67)

The literature abounds with experiential definitions of warmth. Indeed, the recognition of warmth in another person may be so complex a process as to lend itself best to experiential criteria. But some attempt has been made to separate out perceptible cues that may be used, by the interviewee for example, as signals of warmth in the interviewer. Vocal tone is perhaps the most generally recognized of these. It is undoubtedly the one that may be used by the interviewer most deliberately. While it lacks the directness of a verbal declaration of positive feeling or warmth, it is a little more credible. Other nonverbal cues for positive or warm feeling for the interviewee include a relaxed posture, a forward lean of the trunk toward the interviewee, and the reduction of the distance from him/her (Mehrabian, 1973). To be sure, the interview, like other interactions governed by social norms, has certain built-in ranges of appropriateness for expressive behavior. These would be operative in the expression of warmth.

The desirability of interviewer warmth has been accepted as axiomatic. Yet, it is incumbent on the investigator concerned with interviewer behavior to demonstrate that interviewer warmth does make a difference in the effectiveness of the interview. Research findings support the Truax and Carkhuff (1967) Principle of Reciprocal Affect. Warmth in one person evokes warmth in others with whom s(he) may be interacting; similarly, coldness or hostility evokes coldness or hostility. Warmth in the interviewer fosters positive feeling in the interviewee, and a cold attitude in the interviewer, negative feelings. Both the principle and its application to the study of interviewer warmth have been discussed in Chapter 5. Thus, Heller, Davis, and Myers (1966) found that interviewees preferred and were attracted to warm rather than cold interviewers in an experimental analogue investigation. Dittes (1957) demonstrated that interviewer permissiveness (very much like warmth) reduced interviewee tension and anxiety as reflected in GSR responses.

While agreement in studies pertaining to the effect of interviewer warmth on interviewee verbal response is not as great, it is still quite impressive. Several investigators found higher interviewee verbal productivity in response to interviewer warmth rather than coldness (Heller, Silver, Bailey, & Dudgeon, 1968; Pope, Nudler, VonKorff, & McGee, 1974; Pope & Siegman, 1972; Reece & Whitman, 1962); while two others were not able to replicate this finding (Allen, Wiens, Whitman, & Saslow, 1965; Heller et al., 1966). One study (Heller et al., 1968) produced a positive association between interviewer warmth and interviewee self-disclosure; another (Heller et al., 1966) failed to support this result, while yet another (Sarason & Winkel, 1966) produced a negative association. Two additional positive associations occurred between interviewer warmth and short interviewee reaction time (Allen et al., 1965); interviewer warmth and interviewee fluency (low Non-Ah Ratio) (Pope & Siegman, 1972).

The burden of the evidence in the foregoing studies supports the view that interviewer warmth facilitates a positive relationship with the interviewee and a productive and fluent verbal response from him/her.

Some additional studies not summarized in Chapter 5 will be added to the present review of interviewer warmth. In one naturalistic investigation (Hiler, 1958) therapists rated by staff psychologists as warm were more successful than those rated as cold in their efforts to keep unproductive patients in treatment. In another (Barrett-Lennard, 1962) there was evidence that therapists who were given high ratings in dimensions included in the concept of warmth tended to be more successful in fostering improved adjustment in their patients than those with low ratings. And in a third investigation (Strupp, Wallach, & Wogan, 1964) there was a positive relationship between therapist warmth and patient-perceived positive outcome.

In a later study (Greenberg, 1969) university undergraduates were asked to respond to a taped interview and to make certain ratings on the basis of what they heard. In essence, they were asked to place themselves vicariously in the roles of interviewees and to indicate how they would react to the particular session that they heard. The Ss were subdivided into four subgroups on the basis of two expectation dimensions - warm-cold and experienced-inexperienced. Thus, one-quarter of the Ss were led to expect that the interviewer whom they would listen to in the tape was an experienced and warm person; another quarter that he was an experienced and cold person. A third quarter expected him to be inexperienced and warm, and a fourth quarter, inexperienced and cold. The results pertaining to the experienced-inexperienced dimension will be discussed later. For the moment, the focus will be on the warm-cold dimension. On the basis of the postinterview questionnaire, it was found that Ss who were given a warm rather than a cold induction were more attracted to the therapist, more receptive to his influence, and more persuaded by the interviewer's ratings of the patient recorded in the tape when they were given an opportunity to compare their own ratings with the interviewer's. Moreover, a significantly larger number of Ss who perceived the interviewer as warm were willing to meet him in person than those who perceived him as cold. In a word, Ss who were cast in the role of vicarious interviewees were more strongly attracted to warm interviewers than to cold, and were more easily influenced by them.

Frequently the clinical relevance of studies based on the use of university students rather than patients is brought under question. With this type of objection in mind, there was a replication of the preceding study (Greenberg, Goldstein, & Parry, 1970). On the second occasion, the Ss were male psychiatric in-patients at a Veterans Administration psychiatric hospital, with a mean age of 43. In other respects, the experimental procedure was the same. Again the patients who were given a warm induction expressed a greater attraction to the taped therapist than did those in a control group. Although the basic procedure in the second investigation was the same as that in the first, a fifth group was added (i.e., a control group) in which there was no arousal of any kind of expectation regarding the therapist, neither warm nor cold. Unlike the first study, however, this second one yielded no significant differences for openness to persuasion. Thus, the results are not quite as general in the second investigation as in the first. Nevertheless, they do indicate that psychotic patients as well as normal students are more attracted to warm rather than cold interviewers.

One investigator (Rosenfeld, 1973) manipulated interviewer approval rather than warmth; yet it is evident that the two concepts were closely related. Smiles, positive head nods by the interviewer, and spontaneous gesticulation are widely recognized as communicating approval (warmth) through nonverbal channels; frowns and negative head nods, disapproval (coldness). The interviewees were male and female students ranging from 14 to 16 years of age. Two interviewers were used, one male and one female, with a balanced distribution of Ss of both sexes among the two interviewers. The interviews consisted of brief five-minute inquiries and follow-up probes into events in the daily lives of the Ss, conducted under four experimental conditions. In the approving condition the interviewer followed each utterance made by a S with a blend of approval responses, including smiles, positive head nods, gesticulation, and brief verbal signals of attention. In disapproving interviews the interviewer used a blend of contrasting responses such as frowns, negative head nods, and short disparaging comments. In the mixed condition there were approving responses in the first half of the interview and disapproving ones in the second half; and in the nonresponsive condition, the interviewer neither approved nor disapproved, remaining as nonresponsive as the interview situation permitted.

The major finding was that interviewer approval (warmth) elicited interviewee approval. Thus, interviewee smiles and positive head nods were significantly more frequent in the approving periods of the interviews than in the disapproving or nonresponsive periods. This result is reminiscent of the Truax and Carkhuff (1967) Principle of Reciprocal Affect. Two additional results characterize the interviewee's response to disapproval (coldness) from the interviewer: increased self-manipulations, previously found to function as an irritant to the dyadic partner, and an increase in the Mahl Non-Ah Ratio, an index of anxiety. The last finding is similar to one reported by Pope and Siegman (1972). Thus, interviewer warmth is reciprocated by interviewee warmth in specified nonverbal channels. Interviewer coldness results in nonverbal signs of self-involvement on the part of the interviewee, and in other responses indicative of tension and anxiety.

A unique series of studies investigating the efficacy of interviewer warmth (Morris & Suckerman, 1974, 1975) showed that this interviewer attribute was necessary for the success of systematic desensitization. The results of these investigations are particularly striking because many authors emphasize the conditioning procedure as the effective ingredient in desensitization, with relationship playing an insignificant role. In their first study Morris and Suckerman found that "therapist warmth is an important factor in effecting positive behavior change using systematic desensitization" (1974, p. 148). To apply a more stringent test to their hypothesis that therapist warmth was an important element in desensitization, they decided to manipulate warmth within an automated desensitization procedure.

The Ss were snake phobic female undergraduates recruited from an introductory psychology class. In the automated desensitization method, the relaxation and the desensitization instructions were both given by a taped voice. One-third of the Ss were assigned to a group that listened to a voice rated as "soft, melodic and pleasant" (warm group); another third was assigned to a group that listened to a taped voice that was "harsh, impersonal, and businesslike" (cold group); and the third was a no-treatment control group. Of the three groups, the "warm" one showed the largest drop in phobic response. The warm automated therapist was significantly more effective than the cold therapist. In addition, members of the warm group achieved significantly more desensitization than those in the control group. The cold and control groups did not differ. The authors concluded that "therapist warmth, operationalized in terms of the therapist's voice quality, is an important variable in producing positive change using automated systematic desensitization" (Morris & Suckerman, 1975, p. 259). It would appear that a warm therapeutic relationship plays a significant role in the reduction of phobic behavior, even when it is used in as highly technical a procedure as desensitization.

Warmth is generally accepted as a highly valued attribute in an interviewer. Moreover, both clinical experience and research demonstrate that interviewer warmth contribute significantly toward the success of an interview. One would therefore expect that experienced interviewers would possess this attribute to a generous degree. Unfortunately, one investigation (Strupp, 1961) places such an assumption under question. Strupp studied the interview responses of 126 psychiatrists. He presented to them a filmed interview which he interrupted at certain critical points, asking the $\underline{S}$s to indicate how they would respond to the interviewee at the moment of interruption. Only 4.6% of the responses that he obtained were judged to communicate any degree of warmth. Later when asked to indicate their attitudes toward the patient, less than one-third of the therapists could be rated as having a positive or warm attitude, while more than one-third were judged to be clearly negative or cold in their attitude. When he compared psychiatrists with psychologists who were matched on the basis of length of experience, the psychologists failed to present a picture that was significantly different from that presented by the psychiatrists. Still later, when submitting a questionnaire to a large group of therapists representing psychiatric social workers, psychologists, psychiatrists, and psychoanalysts, interviewer warmth turned out to be similarly infrequent for all subgroups; less than one-third of the respondents could be judged as warm, while more than one-third clearly gave cold responses.

Data such as that obtained by Strupp pose a challenge to all who are involved in the enterprise of psychotherapy and the conduct of clinical interviews. Interviewer warmth is an important variable, in short supply, even among experienced clinicians. Since warmth is a personal attribute it must be regarded as an important criterion in the selection of persons to be trained to conduct interviews and practice psychotherapy.

Empathy

While the concept of interviewer empathy overlaps considerably with warmth, it is by no means synonymous with it. The following definition is offered by Fenlason (1962).

<u>Empathy</u> is the capacity of an individual to identify himself with another in terms of the way the other would feel and act. It is the essence of understanding, the <u>why</u> of another's attitudes and behavior.

A rudimentary example of empathy is found in an apocryphal tale of Jason, a lost donkey. The whole village joined Jason's distressed owner in his futile search for the animal, but it was a feebleminded boy who triumphantly led the donkey into the village square. 'Where was he?' 'How did you find him?' cried the villagers, as they crowded around. 'Oh, it was simple,' was the laconic response. 'I just thought of where I'd go if I was Jason, so I went to the glen and brought him home.' (p. 204).

Fenlason may well refer to the above example as rudimentary. The village boy who found the donkey had to identify himself with the animal regarding one action only - i.e., the donkey's disappearance. Consider how much more complex an interviewer's empathy must be if he is to experience the interviewee's thoughts, associations, feelings, and behavior as the interviewee does. In a previously discussed study (Fiedler, 1950) the relationships established by experienced therapists were significantly distinguished from those of inexperienced therapists on the basis of certain traits assessed by three judges who used a Q-Sort instrument for making their ratings. A number of the traits that favor the more expert rather than the less expert appear to refer to the interviewer's empathic understanding of the interviewee:

The therapist is usually able to get what the patient is trying to communicate.

The therapist is well able to understand the patient's feelings.

The therapist always follows the patient's line of thought.

The therapist's comments are always right in line with what the patient is trying to convey.

The therapist is able to participate completely in the patient's communication.

The therapist's tone of voice conveys the complete ability to share the patient's feelings.

Fiedler appears to be describing a therapist who is quick to understand a patient's thoughts and feelings and is able to communicate to the patient in a manner that assures the patient that he is being understood.

Truax and Carkhuff (1967) referred to the present interviewer dimension as <u>accurate empathy</u> and operationalized it through the development of a nine-point scale for its rating. This scale is based on the concept that Accurate Empathy "involves more than just the ability of the therapist to sense the client or patient's 'private world' as if it were his own. It also involves more than just his ability to know what the patient means. Accurate

Empathy involves both the therapist's sensitivity to current feelings and his verbal facilities to communicate this understanding in a language attuned to the client's current feelings" (Truax & Carkhuff, 1967, p. 46). A comparison of Stage 1 in the scale (i.e., the low-empathy extreme) with Stage 9, the high-empathy extreme, may be of interest at this point. Stage 1 is defined as follows: "Therapist seems completely unaware of the most conspicuous of the client's feelings; his responses are not appropriate to the mood and content of the client's statements. There is no determinable quality of empathy, and hence no accuracy whatsoever. The therapist may be bored and disinterested or actively offering advice, but he is not communicating an awareness of client's current feelings" (Truax & Carkhuff, 1967, p. 47). Contrast this lack of empathy with the following high level: "The therapist in this stage unerringly responds to the client's full range of feelings in their exact intensity. Without hesitation, he recognizes each emotional nuance and communicates an understanding of every deepest feeling. He is completely attuned to the client's shifting emotional content; he senses each of the client's feelings and reflects them in his words and voice" (Truax & Carkhuff, 1967, p. 56).

Interviewer empathy is of course not possible if s(he) cannot concentrate completely without distraction on the interviewee's communication, both verbal and nonverbal. If the interviewer is preoccupied, if there are periodic lapses of attention during the course of the interview, if personal thoughts and fantasies intrude into the interview situation so that concentration digresses from a total focus on the interviewee, s(he) will not be able to achieve the kind of resonance with the interviewee's communications that would be truly empathic. To begin with, the interviewer must hear and remember what the interviewee says. But s(he) must also be aware of other cues coming from the interviewee. Thus, the interviewee may speak about feeling sorry for behavior on the previous day, but his/her tone of voice may betray an actual lack of concern. Such a conflict in communication should not escape the interviewer. Other types of nonlexical occurrences that might well engage the interviewer's attention might include discernible changes in tempo of interviewee speech, or fluency, or both. Thus, an interviewee may speak at a fairly slow tempo with a low, modulated volume. Suddenly, the tempo increases and the speech becomes flustered by frequent disruptions. Although these nonlexical changes in speech may not be reflected in its content, they generally communicate something significant to the interviewer, such as the emergence of anxiety or some other form of arousal. The perceptive interviewer has learned to note and store the observation of such an event, even if s(he) chooses not to respond to it immediately. The interviewer must also be alerted to postural, gestural, or other kinesic cues from the interviewee. These might include a forward movement in the chair, a tensing of the body, a strain toward the interviewer. Whether such nonverbal signals convey an angry upsurge of feeling, an urgent appeal for help, or a warm eruption of good feeling, the postural changes will not escape the experienced interviewer.

If a sensitive perceptiveness of the person with whom one is conversing is one aspect of empathy, a supportive level and style of responsiveness is another. One author (Mehrabian, 1972) reports a study in which a group of Ss, already rated for empathic capacity, were requested to characterize themselves and their emotions using a semantic differential scale. The one significant effect was a positive association between empathic tendency and responsiveness to emotional events. The more empathic the $\underline{S}$, the stronger were his/her ratings of experienced emotions. At issue, however, is not only the level of emotional responsiveness, but also its style. The empathic interviewer's style of expression is resonant with the interviewee's communication. If the interviewee is sad and restrained, the interviewer will modulate both tempo and volume of speech in a manner that will convey to the interviewee that s(he) is aware of his/her feelings and respects them. If a paranoid interviewee speaks in cold, brittle, sarcastic tones which communicate distrust and the desire for distance, the interviewer will not crowd him/her. S(he) will not invade the psychological stockades that the interviewee has thrown up. To be sure, the interviewer may, in some instances, deliberately decide to alter his/her style of communication in a manner that may appear to be incongruent with the style of the interviewee. Thus, a female patient in a state hospital came into a conference room where she had agreed to be interviewed before a number of staff professionals and, not waiting for the interview to begin, exploded into an excited, chaotic, sexually blatant, essentially manic recital. It would have been easy for the interviewer to be prompted into increasing his tempo of speech in order to keep up with that of the interviewee. Instead, he spoke in a slowed down, measured tempo in order to attempt to modulate the speech of the excited, disorganized patient. In this instance he met with a small degree of success. If the patient had been a little more excited and disorganized, this strategy may not have worked at all. In any case, it is mentioned to indicate that empathy on the part of the interviewer does not imply that s(he) necessarily is in step with every aspect of the patient's behavior. However, it does require that the interviewer be in touch with all the parts of the patient's world that have an immediate bearing on the interaction.

The relationship between interviewer style of expression and empathy is evident in different ways. It may be noted in the interviewer's attempt to bring his/her style of communication into synchrony with that of the interviewee. It may also be noted in certain expressive cues of empathy that may be generally recognized as signals of this attitude. A number of studies have investigated the correlation between interviewer productivity (total talk time, mean duration of response, proportion of talk time taken by interviewer, or number of words spoken) and his/her empathy as rated independently by observers. In one (Strupp & Wallach, 1965) psychiatrists and psychiatric residents were asked to view two psychotherapy films. The $\underline{Ss}$ were given the task of dictating their own verbal responses to the patient's last remarks at several preselected points at which the film was interrupted. The $\underline{E}$ recorded the duration of each $\underline{S}$'s dictated responses, his/her reaction time (time elapsed between interruption of film and the beginning of dictation by $\underline{S}$), and frequency of silent nonresponse by $\underline{S}$. The content of the dictated responses was scored independently for empathy. At the moment, the only finding to be considered is the correlation between interviewer empathy and total talk time. As it turned out, the correlation was significantly positive. In a second study, based on the interaction between actual therapists and their patients (Truax, 1970), there was a positive relationship between therapist empathy, as measured by the Truax and Carkhuff (1967) Accurate Empathy Scale, and both duration of therapist utterances and his/her proportion of talk time.   And again, in a third investigation (Pope et al., 1974), novice interviewers, but not experienced professionals, demonstrated a highly significant positive correlation between the productivity of each interviewer (number of words spoken in an interview) and the independently rated empathy of the interviewer, with the use of the Accurate Empathy Scale.   In a fourth study (Hargrove, 1974) based on tape-recorded psychotherapy sessions, there was a positive correlation between interviewer empathy and mean duration of each response, but it did not quite attain an acceptable level of significance.   Finally, an investigation by Wenegrat (1974) failed to obtain a positive association between interviewer empathy and productivity. The study was based on interviews between clients and therapists in a university psychology clinic.   Though the above findings are not completely consistent, they do indicate a strong trend for inter-viewers who are relatively productive to be perceived also as empathic.

If high verbal activity on the part of the interviewer signals empathy, one would expect that frequent silences would cause the interviewer to be perceived as nonempathic.   Indeed, this result occurred in several investi-gations (Pierce & Mosher, 1967; Staples & Sloan, 1976; Strupp & Wallach, 1965).   In the Pierce and Mosher (1967) study, a psychotherapy analogue, Ss were assigned to both "appropriate" and "inappropriate" interview conditions. The content of the two groups of interviews was the same; the interview duration was 15 minutes in both instances.   In the "appropriate" condition the standard questions were spoken with a warm and empathic vocal coloration. In the "inappropriate" condition the first five minutes resembled the appropriate condition.   In the second five minutes the E interrupted the S frequently, and in the last five minutes E responded only after uncomfortably long silences.   The results showed "that Ss in the appropriate interview condition perceived E as more empathic than did Ss who were interrupted and left in silence" (Pierce & Mosher, 1967, p. 101).   The other two studies referred to above (Staples & Sloan, 1976; Strupp & Wallach, 1965) agree with Pierce and Mosher (1967).   All three show that empathic interviewers are unlikely to respond to interviewees' comments with silence.   Moreover, this negative relationship applies not only to silence as a total response to the interviewee, but also as reaction time (the time period between the end of an interviewee's comment and the beginning of the interviewer's response) (Hargrove, 1974).

Finally, it comes as no surprise that interviewers who interrupt (overtalk) their clients are not likely to be perceived as empathic (Hargrove, 1974; Pierce & Mosher, 1967).   In brief, an interviewee tends to perceive an interviewer who is verbally active as empathic, and one who is given to silence, long reaction times and interrupting overtalk, as nonempathic. Empathy does therefore correlate significantly with selected aspects of the interviewer's verbal behavior.

Does it relate to more enduring aspects of the interviewer as well, such as any of his/her predispositional personality traits?   In this regard, only one limited study has come to the present author's attention (Hekmat, Khajavi, &

Mehryar, 1975). The $\underline{S}$s were not practicing clinicians but, instead, male and female undergraduate students who were rated on an empathy scale and asked to respond to a psychological screening inventory. The objective was to determine whether empathy as a general personality trait might correlate with other attributes of personality, within an untrained nonprofessional group of $\underline{S}$s. "Results, in general, support that high-empathy persons were significantly lower in signs depicting neurotic and psychotic disturbance as compared with low-empathy persons....The present study suggests that anxiety, general maladjustment, and a propensity toward psychotic pathology are associated with low levels of empathy" (Hekmat et al., 1975, p. 89). In brief, the findings of one correlational investigation would lead one to conclude that maladjusted persons tend to be nonempathic. One additional finding associates empathy positively with extroversion.

In a clinical context empathy is often regarded as a trainable skill rather than a basic personality trait. If this point of view is tenable, one might expect empathy to increase with training and experience. Two studies that address themselves to these questions will now be considered. In one (Strupp, 1958) the technique (well known by now) was used of playing a film of an initial interview to a clinical audience, interrupting the film at preselected points and asking the clinical $\underline{S}$s to respond at the points of interruption as though each were to continue the interview with the filmed patient himself/herself. The $\underline{S}$s in the present study were psychiatrists and psychiatric residents. For each, a global empathy rating was based on the protocol resulting from written responses at the points of interruption. There was no statistically significant relationship between years of experience of the $\underline{S}$s and their empathy ratings. However, personal analysis (a form of training) for the $\underline{S}$s was related to their empathy ratings; the analyzed group was significantly more empathic than the group with no analysis.

In a second study (Pope, Nudler, Norden, & McGee, 1976) there was again a failure to obtain any evidence of a relationship between experience and empathy. The $\underline{S}$s were female freshman students; the interviewers were sophomore students, both male and female, with no previous training in interviewing (the novices) and members of the psychiatric staff of a private psychiatric hospital (the experienced professionals), matched for sex with the novices. There were no significant differences between the professional and novice interviewers in empathy on the Truax-Carkhuff Accurate Empathy Scale, at three separate times. The first comparison occurred before the novice interviewers had any training at all; the remaining two comparisons, after the novices had one and two and one-half years of clinical training, respectively. Nor was there any significant increase in empathy scores within the novice group over the duration of their training. In brief, the results for experience are negative; those for training are mixed. It should however be noted that personal analysis is an intense and very special form of training that, in fact, aspires to restructure personality. The above data are therefore inconclusive. But, if one were compelled to decide on the basis of the information provided whether empathy is to be regarded as a personality trait or a trainable skill, the former would appear to be more likely.

The research evidence that interviewer empathy is a significant relationship variable is at least as consistent and impressive as that pertaining to

interviewer warmth; possibly more so. In summarizing a number of studies
pertaining to this variable, Bergin (1967) concluded that both the direct
analysis of recorded therapist behavior and the analysis of ratings made by
clients of their therapists have evoked consistently positive correlations
between interviewer's empathic understanding and favorable outcome of
treatment. A study by Cartwright and Lerner (1963) is particularly relevant
at this point. The Ss were patients at the counseling center at the University
of Chicago. One-half were male and one-half female, with ages ranging from
19 to 43 and a mean of 27.7. The only variables in this study that need
concern us in the present discussion are those pertaining to interviewer
empathy and outcome of psychotherapy. Interviewer empathy was measured
by determining the similarity between the patient's rating of himself/herself
on 10 personality scales selected for individual Ss because of their idiosyncratic relevance to them and the interviewer's predictions of the patient's
ratings on these 10 scales. These sets of ratings were obtained both after the
second interview and after the end of psychotherapy. In addition, the
therapist provided three measures of change and one rating of outcome of
therapy after the end of the psychotherapy sequence. The predicted
relationship between the therapist's empathic understanding of the patient
and the patient's degree of improvement was not borne out for the first set of
ratings obtained after the second interview, but was significantly supported
after the end of psychotherapy. The authors concluded that "at the close of
therapy the therapists understood the self-image of the improved patients
significantly better than they did those who were unimproved" (Cartwright &
Lerner, 1963, p. 140). In an additional study (Bergin & Solomon, 1963) there
was further evidence that accurate empathy was significantly related to
outcome in psychotherapy. The Ss in this instance were out-patients who
were seen in treatment by fourth-year graduate students in clinical
psychology.

In a somewhat earlier study (Truax, 1962) dealing with schizophrenic
rather than neurotic patients, the results were described as preliminary.
However, they appear to confirm those of the two preceding ones and
somewhat extend their generality. The Ss were eight psychotic patients, four
of whom showed improvement on psychological tests over a period of
treatment and four, deterioration. Samples selected from recordings of
therapy interviews with these patients were rated for degree of accurate
empathy. Improving patients received consistently more accurate empathy
than did those not improving. These results were considered preliminary
because the treatment had not yet been completed at the time of the
analysis.

The effect of interviewer empathy may be traced in its immediate impact
on the verbal behavior of the interviewee, as well as in its more protracted
influence on the outcome of treatment. Two of the studies reviewed above
(Pope et al., 1974; Staples & Sloan, 1976) found that interviewees were more
productive in response to empathic rather than nonempathic interviewers.
One (Staples & Sloan, 1976) showed additionally that interviewees responded
more rapidly (lower mean reaction time) to empathic interviewers. Thus,
interviewer empathy has a facilitating effect on interviewee communication.
Further data about this matter will be included below in the summaries of a
number of investigations that evaluate the effects of combined facilitative
conditions.

Interviewer Genuineness or Self-Congruence

The third interviewer attribute is referred to in the Truax and Carkhuff (1967) literature as genuineness or self-congruence. It may be assumed that each person has his own style of communication under ordinary circumstances. Thus, one individual may speak at a rapid tempo, with few pauses, and with a moderately excited emotional coloration in his voice. He may generally lean forward in his chair when he is addressing another person and frame his speech with broad, manual gestures, sweeps of the arm, and frequent changes of posture. Another person may speak softly, deliberately, with an even, modulated tone, essentially lacking in emotional color. The second person may ordinarily sit bolt upright in his chair when addressing someone with his hands holding the arm rests rather firmly and his body relatively immobile. Although these two styles of communication are quite different, each is authentic for the person described. To be sure, no person has a single style of communication. It may be expected that mode of expression will change from one situation to another and from one role to another. Thus, the first person may speak in the manner indicated when he is comfortably ensconced in a soft chair conversing with a friend in his livingroom. The description given above may pertain in particular to his expressive style in a situation that is relatively unstructured and informal. If it turned out that this individual were a high-school teacher of history and one were to observe him addressing his class, one would find him different in the classroom than he had been in his own livingroom. He might then prefer not to sit but to stride about in front of the class, speaking in an excited, loud voice, gesturing emphatically, approaching the blackboard, and punctuating his remarks with the staccato of chalk striking the blackboard, and moving about the classroom toward certain individuals rather than simply leaning toward them from a chair. The second person might show similar differences if he were removed from the comfort of his livingroom to a classroom. Let us assume that he too is a high-school teacher of history. He too prefers to remain erect in the classroom rather than be seated. But he does not move about as does the first teacher; instead he takes his station midway between his desk and the first row of students, and there he remains throughout much of the class session. His volume is, of course, greater in the classroom than it was in the livingroom. His speech is more emphatic but still measured, slow, with frequent pauses, and still essentially lacking in emotional color. If he has to illustrate a point on the blackboard, he moves toward it deliberately and writes slowly with the chalk as though each stroke of the hand were a modulated, measured movement fraught with significance. If he wishes to address individuals, he does not move toward them as did the first teacher, but fixes his gaze on them from his station at the front of the classroom. Although the two individuals described vary somewhat from one situation to the other, from one role to another, anyone listening to them, observing them, and rating them on a scale of genuineness, would consider that both are performing in a self-congruent manner in both situations.

What might one expect if both these individuals were to be observed conducting an interview? If they were prompted to communicate in a manner that is natural for themselves, one might note certain differences between the two that are analogous to the differences observed in the previous two situations. Thus, while the first individual, now an interviewer, might speak with his habitual emotional emphasis, with his usual rapid tempo, and might gesture expressively as he did in the other situations, he would do all these things in a manner that was consistent with his role as an interviewer. He would be considerably more restrained than he was in his livingroom, certainly a great deal more restrained than he was in front of his class. He would permit the interviewee a great deal more time than he himself preempts in the dyadic exchange that takes place. A friend, observing the interview, might remark that he performs the role of an interviewer well without in the least mitigating his genuineness as a person within the interview situation. How different this friend's remark would be, however, if this individual, now an interviewer, completely abandoned his usual mode of relating and communicating, and instead acted out a stilted, imitative, stereotyped role. He might assume an impassive facial expression, speak very briefly, in fact in little more than grunts, placing the entire burden of communication onto the interviewee. If he were impelled at any time to make some comments to the interviewee, he might do so in the manner of a Hollywood parody of a Viennese psychiatrist. Thus, in the first instance he would communicate with a high level of interviewer genuineness or self-congruence; in the second, genuineness would be at a very low level.

Many authors refer to interviewer genuineness simply as honesty (Snyder, 1961) and demonstrate that it is present to a greater degree in good than in poor therapists.

Along with interviewer <u>warmth</u> and <u>accurate empathy</u>, Truax and Carkhuff (1967) designate interviewer <u>genuineness</u> as a major relationship dimension.

> There is no real alternative to genuineness in the psychotherapeutic relationship. Even if he were a skilled, polished actor, it is doubtful that the therapist could hide his real feelings from the client. When the therapist pretends to care, pretends to respect, or pretends to understand, he is fooling only himself. The patient may not know why the therapist is 'phony' but he can easily detect true warmth from phony and insincere 'professional warmth.'
>
> (Truax & Carkhuff, 1967, p. 34)

To be sure, a person is most truly himself in a spontaneous encounter where there is no role differentiation between the participants. When s(he) is performing the role of interviewer, s(he) is assuming an institutionalized pattern of behavior, either as an information gatherer or a helper. S(he) cannot be spontaneous in a completely untrammeled sense. Therefore one does not speak about absolute but about relative degrees of genuineness, consistent with the role of interviewer.

For this dimension Truax and Carkhuff (1967) have developed a five-point scale which helps both to define and to quantify an observer's judgment about the genuineness or self-congruence of an interviewer. At the low end of the scale, the interviewer's behavior is clearly defensive in the interaction, and there is explicit evidence of a very considerable discrepancy between what he says and what he experiences. There may be striking contradictions in the therapist's statements, the content of his verbalization may contradict the voice qualities or nonverbal cues (i.e., the upset therapist stating in a strained voice that he is 'not bothered at all' by the patient's anger). (p. 69)

At the high end of the scale the therapist

is freely and deeply himself in the relationship. He is open to experiences and feelings of all types - both pleasant and hurtful - without traces of defensiveness or retreat into professionalism. Although there may be contradictory feelings, these are accepted or recognized. The therapist is clearly being himself in all of his responses, whether they are personally meaningful or trite. At Stage 5 the therapist need not express personal feelings, but whether he is giving advice, reflecting, interpreting, or sharing experiences, it is clear that he is being very much himself, so that his verbalizations match his inner experiences. (p. 72)

Bierman (1969) explains the positive effect of interviewer congruence on interviewee communication in the following way: "High levels of therapist genuineness would be expected to remove much of the ambiguity in therapy and to provide a behavioral model of undefensive openness for the client to imitate" (p. 344). The genuine therapist speaks without resorting to stereo-typed styles of expression. S(he) is perceived by the interviewee as open, transparent, prompting a reciprocal openness and transparency from the interviewee. Indeed, several investigators have found a significant positive correlation between the therapist's self-congruence and the interviewee's depth of self-exploration. One study (Truax & Carkhuff, 1965b) obtained this correlation with hospitalized patients in both individual and group therapy. Another (Van Der Veen, 1965), in which hospitalized schizophrenic patients were used, again found a positive correlation between therapist congruence and patient self-exploration. The same author (Van Der Veen, 1967) later obtained a borderline positive relationship between therapist congruence and a composite outcome score for the treatment. If the results of the above three investigations are sustained, one might conclude that a genuine open interviewer style is associated with open interviewer communication, and positive change with treatment.

In a paper presented at an American Psychological Association Symposium in St. Louis, 1962, Truax (1962) summarized some of the research completed at that time on the three interviewer relationship variables. The data presented included some evidence regarding the significance of interviewer genuineness or self-congruence. Applying the rating scale pertaining to genuineness to several hundred tape-recorded psychotherapy samples, he found that therapists in improved cases were rated significantly higher in self-congruence during the therapeutic interactions than therapists in nonimproved cases.

It is now proposed to examine some investigations in which the three relationship scales were used together. In these studies therapy cases rated high on all three conditions are compared both with control patients receiving no therapy and with therapy cases rated relatively low on the three conditions. In one such investigation (Truax, Liccione, & Rosenberg, 1962) schizophrenic patients treated in psychotherapy were matched with similar control patients with no therapy. Approximately one-half of the psychotherapy patients were judged to have received relatively high levels of interviewer warmth (i.e., unconditional positive regard, accurate empathy and genuineness), and one-half were judged to have received relatively low levels. A test battery was administered to all patients before and after therapy and to all control patients with a similar time interval elapsing between the two examinations for the control group as for the therapy groups. It was found that the patients receiving high levels of accurate empathy, warmth, and interviewer genuineness showed a general gain in psychological functioning, while patients who received relatively low levels showed a loss of psychological functioning. Control patients demonstrated only moderate gains. In a second study by the same authors, similarly designed, but depending on the use of an Anxiety Reaction Scale rather than a psychological battery as the measure of patient change, those receiving low conditions showed an increase in anxiety level while those receiving high conditions showed a decrease; there was no significant change for the controls. These results when first reported caused a considerable stir. It had been assumed that not all therapists were equally effective. However, it was felt that even those who did not obtain positive results did not, in fact, do any psychological harm to their patients. One can no longer find solace in such an assumption. In this investigation and in others by the same author, it has emerged that interviewers who are not able to maintain high levels of relationship behavior may in fact increase the anxiety experienced by their patients and lead to a worsening of their psychological condition. It therefore becomes important that potential therapists be selected for their capacity to achieve high levels of relationship behavior, and be trained to achieve such high levels.

The power of the facilitative conditions in determining the clinical course of long-term psychiatric patients was evaluated in a study conducted at Mendota State Hospital (Rogers, Gendlin, Kiesler, & Truax, 1967). Hospital records were examined and evaluated for the selected patients, extending over an 18-year period, nine years pretherapy, and nine years posttherapy. There were three groups: a therapy group receiving high conditions from its therapist, one receiving low conditions, and a control group. Over the nine-year period following the therapeutic intervention, the high-condition group was able to stay out of the hospital for a larger number of days than the control group and the low-condition group.

In a study reported by Welkowitz and Kue (1973) the possible correlation between the relationship conditions and certain interactional patterns of commmunication was investigated. The dyads studied were conversational partners of equal status; they were not interviewers and interviewees. Both male and female Ss were selected from introductory psychology classes and were randomly paired in same-sex dyads. The Ss were asked to converse for 45 minutes on any topic that interested them. The tape-recordings of the conversations were later scored for three temporal variables in the speech of both dyadic partners. Independent ratings of the warmth, empathy, and genuineness of the two conversational partners were made. Only the warmth of the two partners in the dyads correlated with synchrony or congruence between them on one of the temporal variables, referred to as switching pauses. "A switching pause is an interval of silence bounded on one end by a vocalization of one speaker and on the other end by a vocalization of the other speaker, which is assigned to the speaker whose vocalization it follows" (Welkowitz & Kue, 1973, p. 472). If speaker A has made a remark, the switching pause assigned to him/her is the duration in seconds for which s(he) will pause, while waiting for speaker B to begin his/her utterance. According to the results of this study, the greater the warmth between the two dyadic partners, the greater the congruence or synchrony between them in the time that one will wait at the end of his/her utterance for the other to begin speaking. Warmth therefore appears to introduce an element of mutuality into the communicational interaction between the two.

Both warmth and empathy from the interviewer appear to have an immediate affect on interviewee depth of self-exploration, according to the results of an experimental investigation (Truax & Carkhuff, 1965a). Interviews were conducted with three psychotic patients in a state hospital. During the first 20 minutes of each interview, the interviewers maintained high levels of warmth and empathy. During the second 20 minutes, they deliberately lowered the levels of both conditions. Finally, during the last 20 ιninutes, the interviewers' normally high levels in the two relationship variables were reestablished. The authors were interested in determining the effect of the experimental lowering of relationship variables during the middle segment of the interview on the patient's depth of self-exploration. As anticipated, patient self-exploration decreased when the interviewer became less warm and empathic. Thus, within the context of a single interview it was possible to demonstrate that both interviewer warmth and empathy have an immediate effect on the patient's willingness to communicate his/her inner experiences, feelings, and associations.

If the results of the preceding studies are supported, one might conclude that therapists able to relate in a warm, genuine, and empathic manner are likely to evoke open interviewee communication, synchronous on certain temporal variables with their own, and attain positive results in their treatment efforts.

There are, of course, some negative findings regarding the relationship between outcome and the three therapeutic conditions. One well-executed study (Garfield & Bergin, 1971) failed to obtain a single positive correlation between empathy, warmth, and congruence and a variety of measures of outcome. The investigation was carried out in a university psychology clinic. The therapists were advanced graduate students in clinical and counseling psychology who described themselves as eclectic in approach. Taped excerpts of therapy sessions were rated with the Truax and Carkhuff (1967) scales for Accurate Empathy, Warmth, and Genuineness. A large number of therapeutic change ratings were made of the clients, including client self-ratings, therapist ratings, and therapist supervisors' ratings of client change. None of these and other measures of change correlated significantly with any one of the three therapy condition scales. In considering the conflict between their negative results and the positive ones so widely reported in the literature, the authors noted that their interviewers were not followers of the client-centered orientation. In this respect they differed from those in most other investigations in the present area, prompting the speculation that the therapist conditions might have a parochial relevance to the client-centered approach. "Since the constructs and the scales used on their appraisal were derived from this framework... it does not appear that their utility or meaningfulness is related to client-centered therapy. These conditions, as defined operationally, may be more or less specific to one type of therapy and apparently do not have the same meaning or significance when applied to other forms of therapy" (Garfield & Bergin, 1971, p. 112).

While this study reduces the generality of the three therapist conditions, it does not diminish their significance within the client-centered approach. It seems reasonable that warmth, empathy, and genuineness, as measured by the Truax and Carkhuff (1967) scales may be significant variables within the context of one style of interaction, but may somehow lack this significance in other interactional styles.

In the above discussion there has been an implicit assumption that levels of relationship behavior are stable properties of different interviewers very much like predispositional traits. Thus, one may speak of the interviewer as possessing in some degree the capacity to understand the interviewee in depth and to communicate this understanding in a manner that is completely congruent with the interviewee's mood and thoughts. One may also speak about the interviewer as though s(he) were always able to respond with warmth and genuine emotional expressiveness, whoever the interviewee might be. But increasingly it has been asked whether an interviewer, however facilitative, is likely to manifest his/her interpersonal skills in all situations, with all interviewees. Since the kind of interview under consideration here is an emergent dyadic exchange, is it not possible that warmth, genuineness, and empathy are resultants of the interaction of two people rather than invariant properties of one? The answer is not an unequivocal "yes" or "no." There is undoubtedly some variation in the behavior of even the experienced interviewer from one interviewee to another. By and large, however, the evidence points to the interviewer as the most important determinant of the three facilitating variables. In one investigation dealing with this problem (Truax & Carkhuff, 1967) the patients residing on a single ward in a state hospital were all treated by eight different therapists on a demand basis. The research design called for the selection of taped samples from interviews in which the same eight therapists saw the same eight patients. Using therapist accurate empathy as the dependent variable, significant differences between therapists were found, but not between patients. "The therapist-offered level of accurate empathy appeared independently of the clients. The ability to empathize seemed to be part of the therapist's makeup and not contingent upon the client's makeup. In sharp contrast, different patients did not receive significantly different levels of accurate empathy when interacting with the same therapists" (Truax & Carkhuff, 1967, p. 101). The same patterns emerged for therapist nonpossessive warmth and genuineness.

In an additional study (Truax, Wargo, Frank, Imber, Battle, Hoehn-Sarik,

Nash, & Stone, 1966) patients were assigned randomly to each of two screening interviewers. It was found that the two interviewers differed from each other significantly on accurate empathy and self-congruence, but not on nonpossessive warmth. In the same study, other patients were randomly assigned to four different therapists. Again, there were different levels of accurate empathy and genuineness; in this part of the study, however, nonpossessive warmth also distinguished significantly between the four therapists. While the findings of this study do not necessarily imply that there are no differences between the patients, it is clear that patient differences are significantly overbalanced by therapist and interviewer differences.

The effect of the client on interviewer facilitating behavior has been investigated in several experimental studies in which client behavior has been manipulated. The purpose of these studies was the determination of the kinds of changes in client behavior likely to affect interviewer warmth, empathy, and genuineness. A second objective was the exploration of a possible differential reaction to such client changes by interviewers who are high and low on these conditions. In one of the investigations (Alexik & Carkhuff, 1967) a single "client" (an experimental accomplice) was instructed to engage in deep self-exploration during the first and last third of each hour with two therapists, but to drop to a low level of self-exploration during the middle third. One of the therapists was rated high on warmth, accurate empathy, and genuineness, while the other low. The high levels of the three conditions in the first interviewer were not altered during the middle third of the interview, but the low levels of the second therapist were significantly depressed. The difference in response of the two types of therapists to more and less self-exploring communication was made even more explicit in a second experiment similar to the one above. In this instance (Carkhuff & Alexik, 1967) there was a larger sample of each type of therapist. In addition to replicating the above results, there were two additional ones. The high-facilitative therapists tended to become even warmer, more empathic, and genuine when the client's communication became less self-exploratory. By contrast, the low-facilitative therapists dropped the levels of their conditions and were unable to return to their initial levels once the client returned to his earlier level of self-exploration. It would appear that interviewers with high levels of warmth, empathy, and genuineness are not as responsive to the deterioration of the interviewee's communication as are interviewers with low levels.

Training for High Levels of Relationship Behavior

Since the interviewer's input is crucial for the course of the interview, it may well be asked how one obtains interviewers with the capacity for high levels of relationship behavior. If empathy, genuineness, and warmth were predispositional personality traits not susceptible to significant modification by ordinary clinical training, the emphasis would have to be solely on selection; training would be secondary. It becomes important, therefore, to inquire into the evidence that training can be effective in raising a trainee's levels of relationship behavior.

Since Truax and Carkhuff (1967) have been more explicit than others in their discussion of forms of training and in their evaluation of training efficacy; their frame of reference will be maintained in the section that follows. To be sure, in doing this one must accept the limitation of a single point of view. Thus, the objectives of their training program are couched largely in terms of the three ingredients already discussed. With the selection of trainees in mind, Carkhuff (1969) refers to two basic skills that can be assessed before training begins. One he designates as discrimination ability and the other, communication ability. The former refers to the capacity to recognize high and low levels of relationship in tapes and actual interviews that one may audit; the latter refers to the capacity to communicate at high levels within an interview. Apparently a person may be skilled at making discriminations without necessarily being highly facilitating in the communications that he makes. Discrimination is a cognitive ability; communication pertains more to interpersonal interaction. Discrimination can be taught through the use of the usual didactic procedures; communication can be acquired only through supervised experience.

That the two are partially independent of each other is evident in the following research findings. In one investigation (Carkhuff, Collingwood, & Renz, 1969) undergraduate seniors were given a didactic course with the objective of training in discrimination. They rated standard interviews before and after the course, demonstrating significant improvement in this skill. Moreover, the degree of improvement pre- to posttraining was positively correlated with discrimination ability at the beginning of the course. It is significant, however, that there was little transfer from discrimination to communication. Carkhuff and his colleagues demonstrate in other studies that high-level communicators will improve their communication as a consequence of training in discrimination. This is, however, not the case with low-level communicators. If they are exposed only to a didactic emphasis on discrimination, without supervised experience in communication, the changes they will manifest will be noted only in discrimination. Stated otherwise, the above results would indicate that a didactic course would help initially high-level communicators improve their communication; it would have no such effect on initially low-level communicators. In an additional study (Carkhuff, Kratochvil, & Friel, 1968) an integrated didactic and experiential program for beginning graduate students was evaluated. Pre- and posttraining communication and discrimination assessment devices were administered to determine the predictive capacity of both instruments. The course led to improvement in both discrimination and communication among the students. Once again, initial communication level was positively related to final communication level, and initial discrimination level was related to final discrimination level. However, initial discrimination level did not predict to final communication level.

The message appears to be that while there is some usefulness in didactic training, the major contribution to the development of skill in communication derives not from the didactic aspects of a training course, but from the experiential ones. Carkhuff (1969) cites a number of investigations to demonstrate that whenever the training is given an experiential emphasis and the trainers themselves are able to demonstrate high levels of facilitative behavior in the interview, the trainees show significant improvement in communication. When an experiential emphasis is lacking and the trainers do not themselves possess high facilitative levels, one tends not to find significant improvement in communication among students. This general finding applies across training programs whether they be directed toward nonprofessionals, undergraduate, or graduate students. In fact, there is a tendency for graduate programs to be less effective than lay programs because of their mixed emphasis on science, research, and practice. Lay programs are likely to be a good deal more practice oriented. In brief, if the objective is to improve the practice of interviewing, it can be attained most economically when the emphasis in the training program is on practice.

For example, in the Bergin and Solomon (1963) study previously cited for evidence regarding a positive correlation between accurate empathy in the interviewer and client outcome, the Ss were postinternship graduate students at a major training institution for clinical psychologists. When these students were rated on the accurate empathy scale after the end of their training, they ranged from 1.91 to 3.84 (the scale ranges from 1 to 9 in the order of increasing accurate empathy) all placing below intermediate levels in Accurate Empathy. In this graduate training program for clinical psychologists, recognized widely as one of good quality, the actual level of Accurate Empathy of the trainees correlated -.17 and -.16 respectively with practicum and academic grades given the students. Clearly then, the students were graded on the basis of elements other than interview skills. One may surmise that grades were based more on conventional academic achievement than on the capacity to relate and communicate in an interview. This investigation has a bit of additional evidence pointing to the crucial importance of the supervisor himself in fostering the development of communicational skills. Thus, there were six supervisors working with the psychology graduate students, only one of whom made an explicit attempt to train his students along empathic lines. The students working with this supervisor averaged 3.8 on the Accurate Empathy Scale; the others averaged only 2.1. A second study by Melloh (1964), using postpracticum counselor trainees as Ss, determined on the basis of tape-recorded interview sessions that the average level of Accurate Empathy obtained was 2.46, again below median levels of relationship. Significantly, and in replication of the Bergin and Solomon (1963) study, there was no relationship between practicum grades and levels attained on the Accurate Empathy Scale.

The reason for the relative failure of graduate programs to help students develop high levels of interview behavior is suggested by another investigation (Baldwin & Lee, 1965) in which interview relationship behavior was taught by two procedures; one based on instruction with the use of a programmed teaching machine and the other based on an informal, combined didactic and group therapy experience. The Ss were undergraduate college students. The relative success of the two programs was determined by Accurate Empathy ratings of tape-recorded interview sessions produced by the students both before and after training. The students who had participated in the teaching machine approach to training showed no change in rated Accurate Empathy; the students who received the combined didactic and group therapy training showed significant improvement, advancing from an average level of 2.4 to one of 3.2. This research evidence supports the impression that practicum experience, particularly when directed by supervisors with high levels of relationship behavior, is much more effective as a method of developing relationship skills than a conventional didactic approach in itself.

It is relevant to note that experienced professionals tend to forget their earliest attempts at interviewing. If the screen of oblivion could be pierced, they might recall that shortly before their first interview assignment they may have spent many tense hours scanning and intensively reading the interview literature. However effective this method may have been in helping them cope with their anticipatory anxiety, such "boning up" was certainly of little assistance once they found themselves in the interview situation.

What then are the components of an effective preparation for interviewing? Some of the general principles are considered above. It is now proposed to examine in some detail the approach followed by Truax and Carkhuff (1967) as one example of a balanced didactic and experiential approach. Matarazzo (1971) provides an excellent and concise summary of the various elements in the Truax and Carkhuff program:

(1) Students were given an extensive reading list followed by a 'theory' examination.

(2) They completed twenty-five hours' time listening to taped individual and group psychotherapy sessions to increase their response repertoire.

(3) They rated excerpts from their tapes on the scales of 'Accurate Empathy,' 'non-possessive Warmth' and 'genuineness.' Some of the excerpts had already been rated by 'experts,' so that the student could obtain feedback (consensual validation) in the accuracy of his ratings.

(4) They practiced making responses to tape-recorded patients' statements (especially empathic responses). This was done in a group, competitively, and students were called upon randomly to assure vigilance and develop facility in verbalizing as well as in understanding. Training in warmth of tone was added as soon as empathy level was satisfactory.

(5) Outside of class, pairs of students alternated playing 'therapists' and 'patients' roles in sessions which were recorded and brought to supervisory sessions. Parts of the tapes were played back and rated on the therapeutic conditions scales by the supervisor and trainees, as a group, providing feedback for the individual student-therapist.

(6) After achieving minimal levels of therapeutic conditions, the students had single interviews with real patients, with the goal of establishing 'a good therapeutic relationship' and facilitating deep self-exploration. The interviews were tape-recorded and samples were played back for rating by the student, his peers, and the

supervisor, to promote the students' learning what specific behaviors contributed to or detracted from his therapeutic relationships.

(7) After the students achieved minimal levels of therapeutic conditions in single interviews, patients were assigned for continuing therapy. Sessions were tape-recorded, periodic samples were evaluated in the supervisory session.

(8) In the 6th week of the program quasi-group therapy was initiated with students who met for two hour sessions once a week.
(Matarazzo, 1971, p. 901)

The first three steps as outlined by Matarazzo (1971) include the didactic aspects of the training course - i.e., the development of the capacity to make discriminations between taped interview behavior of others. Steps 4 to 7 then provide the student with a graded sequence of experiences under the supervisory guidance of the instructor and the student's peers. Thus, the student first provides interview responses to tape-recorded patients' statements within the context of the group. In effect s(he) gets immediate peer feedback regarding his/her own relationship behavior in response to bits of recorded interviews. This first step toward the achievement of interpersonal skill within the interview is followed by a second in which s(he) is called upon to role play larger interview segments. At this stage, the student is given the opportunity to assume the roles of both patient and interviewer. Again, both the supervisor and peers judge his/her success. At the end of this stage, the student is ready to begin therapeutic work with actual patients. The beginning of actual therapy signals the introduction of the quasi-group therapy experience. In brief, the experiential aspects of the program include both a graduated approach to the conduct of an interview with a patient and the kind of learning that develops through one's interaction with a supervisor and with peers. Although the quasi-therapy group resembles a usual therapy group in its exploration of student thoughts and feelings, it differs in its constant focus on the student's experience in interviewing as its major point of reference. In the quasi-therapy group the stresses, dilemmas, anxieties, and tensions that the student may experience are dealt with both by the supervisor and the group. The student is both supported and therapeutically confronted with his/her own problems in developing relationship skills.

What evidence do Truax, Carkhuff, and their colleagues provide regarding the efficacy of their approach? In one study (Carkhuff & Truax, 1965) 12 advanced graduate students in clinical and counseling psychology and five lay counselors were the subjects of investigation. Both groups attended classes which met twice weekly over a 16-week semester period, for two-hour sessions. In both student groups the auditing of tape-recordings of therapy interviews was an assigned exercise. At the end of the semester, the students provided raters with six four-minute excerpts from taped interviews. These excerpts were all rated for empathy, warmth, and genuineness, as well as client depth of self-exploration. Similar ratings were made of taped excerpts of interviews conducted by 15 highly experienced counselors and psychotherapists. The graduate students provided with 100 hours of training along the Truax and Carkhuff lines approximated the level of therapeutic conditions communicated by experienced psychotherapists. Even the lay counselors, largely hospital attendants, did not differ significantly from the experienced therapists in the level of Accurate Empathy or of Nonpossessive Warmth attained. They did, however, score significantly lower on the dimension of genuineness. Additionally, this 100-hour training program rendered both the graduate students and the lay counselors superior in facilitative levels attained by the advanced graduate students in the previously quoted Bergin and Solomon (1963) and Melloh (1964) studies.

Even more provocative is the evidence generated by still another study (Berenson, Carkhuff, & Myrus, 1966) in which student volunteers for training as undergraduate dormitory counselors were the Ss. Thirty-six student volunteers were randomly assigned to an experimental group and two control groups. The experimental group received the full Truax and Carkhuff training approach. One of the control groups spent the same number of hours in training as the experimental group, without utilizing the three relationship scales as didactic instruments, nor the quasi-group therapy as an experiential component of the training. The second control group had no specific training in therapeutic work. Along all three dimensions the students who received the full training program were superior to the students in the two control groups.

Since the evidence appears to be impressively consistent, one caveat is needed. The above evaluative work was largely undertaken by the same people who formulated the relationship concepts, operationalized them through the development of scales for their measurement, and then designed a teaching procedure embodying both didactic and experiential aspects. It might be argued that the relationship dimensions had not been adequately tested with interviewers and therapists who utilized theoretical referents other than the nondirective derivatives that guide the work of Truax, Carkhuff, and their colleagues. It might also be asserted that it is easy to demonstrate improvement in scores based on specific scales when these scales are used as didactic instruments in a teaching program. Additionally, one is given pause by Rosenthal's (1963) findings that an investigator committed to a body of theory or practice may unintentionally shape the results he obtains through the provision of cues to his Ss. In fact, it would be easy to question the extent to which the findings of preceding studies may have been biased by the Rosenthal Effect. These studies are therefore not offered as the last word, the definitive body of evidence about the efficacy of a combined didactic and experiential approach in the training of interviewers. Nor do they present the final verdict regarding the "teachability" of relationship skills. But, in an area that is characterized by vagueness of impression, they represent instances of clarity in the formulation of hypotheses and the development of instruments for the measurement of results. There can therefore be no doubt about their practical usefulness at this time for trainers and trainees in the art of interviewing.

The skepticism expressed above about the limited generality of the evidence for the teachability of Warmth, Accurate Empathy, and Genuineness is reduced somewhat when one examines the experiences of others in the same area. In a book on interviewing directed toward health professionals (Bernstein, Bernstein, & Dana, 1974) some studies on the susceptibility of nurses and medical students to training in the use of an understanding attitude when conducting an interview were reported. The authors defined an understanding response as "one in which the health professional attempts to comprehend the patient's view and to communicate that comprehension to the patient" (Bernstein et al., 1974, p. 110). In the view of the authors, understanding is further characterized by a type of acceptance, which does not necessarily imply agreement with the attitudes and behaviors of the patient, but rather respect for the right of the patient to differ from the interviewer, even in ways that the latter considers crucial. By now, it will be evident that this type of understanding as a relationship variable contains components of both Accurate Empathy and Warmth.

The research summarized below set out to determine whether understanding as a form of relationship behavior in the interview could be taught. In one investigation a group of nurses participated in a series of weekly training sessions in which the basic techniques that nurses use in responding to patients were evaluated, and actual samples of the nurses' interactions with patients were discussed. There were two groups - a training group and a control group. Both took the Nurse-Patient Situation test before and after the time interval during which training occurred. Each item in this test consisted of a nurse-patient incident followed by five possible responses by the nurse, including one that was evaluative, hostile, reassuring, probing, and understanding. The last was, of course, the criterion response. The nurses who participated in the training group more than quintupled their understanding responses, while those in the control group showed no significant increases.

The authors posed the same challenge to their own findings that was directed above to those of Truax and Carkhuff. They asked whether the Nurse-Patient Situation Test might not function simply as a direct measure of the content of the course and not as a means of assessing more basic changes in underlying attitudes. To check such a possibility they used some additional pre- post measures of relevant attitudes that were not nearly as closely related to the content of the course. Thus, the training group but not the control group became more democratic in their attitudes as measured by the F Scale (Adorno, Frenkel-Brunswik, Levinson, & Sanford, 1950), and more sensitive to psychosocial aspects of a case history rather than somatic aspects only.

A similar study was carried out with medical students. The assessment instrument in this instance was the Physician-Patient Situation Test, analogous to the Nurse-Patient Situation Test. The training program focused on supervised bedside interviewing of patients. In this instance, too, the training group showed a highly significant increase in the number of understanding responses selected on the test over the training period. In a manner that was reminiscent of the distinction made by Truax and Carkhuff between discrimination ability and communication ability, the authors found that a sampling of these students actually used more understanding responses in posttraining interviews than they did in pretraining interviews.

Finally, two related studies (Goldstein & Goedhart, 1973) demonstrated the efficacy of structured learning as a means of enhancing empathic responses in nurses, attendants, and activity therapy personnel working in two psychiatric hospitals, one in Holland and the other in America. Structured Learning is a combined behavioral approach to training including elements of modeling, role playing, and social reinforcement. Two forms of a Hospital Training Questionnaire were used to measure the degree of empathy in each S's responses before and after training.

In the first study the Ss were student nurses employed in a public psychiatric hospital near Amsterdam, Holland. The questionnaire consisted of 30 common interactional situations between nurses and patients, to which the nurses were asked to respond. Their responses were then rated on the Carkhuff (1969) empathy scale. The training included a didactic presentation of the meaning of empathy, the modeling of empathic responses to the 30 situations contained in the questionnaire by the authors and the role-playing empathic responses to the same 30 situations, by the Ss. When the role-played responses were empathic, the feedback to the S was a form of social reinforcement; when they were not, the feedback was more modeling. The second form of the questionnaire contained the original 30 interactional situations plus 15 new ones. As anticipated, the nurses in the training group increased their empathy scores significantly more than the nurses in the control group. Because the first 30 items in the questionnaire were used in the training situation, the two groups were also compared on the 15 items added in the second form of the questionnaire but not used in the training operations. On these 15 items, too, the training group displayed significantly higher levels of empathy than the control group. In a one-month follow-up the higher empathy scores of the training group were sustained.

With one exception, the above study was replicated in a large American State Mental Hospital. In this instance the Ss were staff nurses, attendants, and activity therapists. Again, Structured Learning was an effective approach in the enhancement of empathy in the above categories of hospital personnel. In the second study there was an additional training group that emphasized the transfer of empathy from the training sessions to actual interactions that occurred on the ward between Ss and patients. The Ss were observed on the ward and then given feedback about their interactions in subsequent brief sessions with their observers. As in the basic training procedure, if their relationship behavior was empathic the Ss received social reinforcement; if it was not, an alternative empathic response was modeled for them. Transfer of training, as assessed with a special questionnaire reflecting actual staff-patient interactions on the wards on which observations were carried out, was significant.

The evidence about the trainability of empathy, warmth, and genuineness is moderately persuasive. The investigations carried out by Bernstein et al. (1974) and Goldstein and Goedhart (1973) extend the generality of the evidence beyond the inbred parochial limits that appeared to obtain in the work of Truax, Carkhuff, and their colleagues. The three therapist conditions are indeed teachable.

INTERVIEWER STATUS

In a factor analysis of interviewee ratings of the interviewer (Pope & Siegman, 1967) two dimensions descriptive of interviewer relationship behavior were obtained.   The first, an affective one, was designated as warmth; and the second, as competence or status.   The various interviewer attributes discussed in the present chapter all relate to the affective dimension.   It is now proposed to consider others associated with interviewer status or competence.   Some attention has already been paid this variable in the section of Chapter 6 dealing with dimensions of relationship.   Several studies not summarized in the previous discussion of status will now be considered.   Moreover the frame of reference will shift slightly, from status as an abstract dimension of relationship, to status as an interpersonal attribute of one of the participants in a dyadic exchange.

At the outset, one may ask whether the interviewee experiences status as an element in the interview situation.   Returning to our first fictional interviewee, Mr. A, it will be recalled that as a longshoreman he perceived a considerable social chasm between himself and his interviewer.   He thought of him as a professional person who occupied a higher social class level than he himself did.   This perception of elevated status was mitigated somewhat by two additional observations.   First, Mr. A noted that his interviewer was young; and second, he had heard that his interviewer might very well.be a medical student.   These additional observations tended to reduce the feeling of threat that the interviewer's relatively high social status held for him, but tended also to place under question the confidence that Mr. A could feel in his interviewer.

Mrs. B approached her interviewer as she might an equal.   Belonging to the comfortable middle class herself, many of her neighbors were medical people of a variety of kinds, including some psychiatrists.   Thus, she tended to experience her interviewer as warm and sensitive, but did not think of him at all in status terms.   If any thought of status occurred to her at all, it was simply that she saw him as an equal.

Mr. C approached his interview with the Immigration examiner apprehensively, tending to think of him, in a sense, as a punitive, authority figure who would judge him.   Thus, before he saw him he expected him to be dominant and threatening in the interview situation.   And, indeed, there was no question about the interviewer's dominance.   Mr. C's feeling of relief during the interview derived from the benign manner in which the interviewer manipulated his dominance; but the dominance remained.   If Mr. C were able to verbalize his feelings about the interviewer's status, he might have said the following: Here is a man who could do me a considerable amount of harm. Yet, he does not bludgeon me with the control that he could actually exercise over my life.   Instead, he desists from any sort of punitive talk or behavior, and in fact behaves in a kind and gentle manner.

In the study by Pope and Siegman (1967) status attributes of interviewer behavior were characterized by such adjectives as "strong," "comfortable," "confident," on the one hand and "intelligent" and "competent," on the other. These two adjectival groupings suggest two ways of speaking about interviewer status, one pertaining to dominance or power within the relationship and the second, to competence or experience.   In general, the research literature has supported the impression that an experienced interviewer is likely to inspire more trust in a patient and achieve greater success in therapy than an inexperienced interviewer.   Basing himself on a number of empirical studies

Bergin (1967) arrived at the following summary conclusion: "With regard to the much debated variable of therapist experience, it may be asserted that, in general, more experienced therapists are more effective and successful" (p. 142). Bergin's assertion pertains to the relationship between therapist experience and the effectiveness of a psychotherapy sequence. Maccoby and Maccoby (1954) refer to the interview as a separate entity rather than a unit in a psychotherapy sequence when they emphasize role as an important element in a relationship situation, and status as a significant dimension of role. They remark:

> In general we know that people are more anxious to communicate to those above them in the hierarchy than to those below them...while upper-class respondents feel they have little to gain by expressing their opinions to an interviewer, lower-class respondents are pleased to be consulted. The content of the communication, of course, will be affected by the status relationships: the person of lower status will be motivated to present himself in a favorable light to someone who might be in a position to influence his future. (1954, p. 462)

From the preceding quotation, it must be apparent that there are some hazards in attributing too much generality to the dimension of status as a facilitator of interviewee communication. The interviewee may indeed be more willing to cooperate with a high-status rather than a low-status person. But he may, at the same time, be more guarded, more concerned with making a good impression. If the content of that which he is willing to communicate is likely to be affected by the status of the interviewer, it is to be expected that the precise character of the status differential will be an important factor. Thus, a person living in a slum area in the inner city being interviewed by a graduate student in the School of Social Work will be both reinforced and inhibited in different content areas than a graduate student interviewed by a senior member of the faculty. The slum dweller may be quite willing to tell the interviewer about the deplorable conditions in the neighborhood schools, and within this context speak freely about the difficulties that his children may be experiencing in their studies. The graduate student may not be quite as eager to speak about his academic difficulties when communicating with a senior member of the faculty. This kind of distinction regarding the particular content areas in which communication is likely to flow freely and those in which it may be inhibited would probably obtain even if both interviewers played no part in the immediate power structure within which the interviewee lives.

The three studies that follow all point to the positive effect of interviewer experience on the establishment of a constructive relationship in the psychotherapy situation and, indeed, on the achievement of a successful outcome. In one (Cartwright & Lerner, 1963) the findings indicated that more experienced therapists tended to be more successful than inexperienced therapists. This investigation and others like it establish a positive association between experience and effectiveness in therapy. They do not, however, clarify the mediating variables. The next two investigations do attempt such a clarification in a small way. The first (Fiedler, 1950), reviewed earlier in the present chapter, provided evidence to demonstrate that the expert rather than the inexpert therapist had a greater capacity to establish a positive relationship with patients. Level of experience rather than adherence to a particular school of psychotherapy was the significant factor. The second study, also discussed earlier in the present chapter (Barrett-Lennard, 1962) found that more expert interviewers (i.e., those who were older) with more experience and with more personal therapy rather than less expert interviewers were given higher ratings by their clients on the following four personal attributes significantly related to outcome: empathic understanding, level of regard for the patient, unconditionality of regard, and congruence or genuineness of the therapist. In brief, the two foregoing studies produce evidence indicating higher levels of relationship behavior in more experienced rather than less experienced therapists.

A verbal conditioning study (Binder, McConnell, & Sjoholm, 1957) is included because it addresses itself to a number of problems that are particularly relevant to the present discussion of interviewer status. The class of S response reinforced in this experiment was that of "mildly hostile" words and sentences made up the by Ss and the reinforcing stimulus by the two experimenters was simply the response "good." The authors indicate that they chose the class of mildly hostile words because of the particular relevance to the psychological interview of this verbal category. The groups of Ss were freshmen volunteers from an introductory psychology course. The first group was conducted by an attractive, gently spoken, socially reserved young woman. The second group was led by a decidedly masculine, large aggressively mannered male. Although the male was actually 12 years older than the female, the age differential appeared to be much greater because the young lady could have passed for a high-school sophomore, and the male experimenter was frequently taken to be a faculty member. With experimenter status in mind, it was anticipated that the reinforcing word "good" would carry more weight when spoken by the powerful male rather than the slightly built, retiring female. As expected, both groups increased significantly in their use of mildly hostile words. Contrary to expectation, however, the increment was greater for the female experimenter than for the male. In reviewing this unexpected finding, the authors concluded that the female "provided a less threatening environment, and the Ss consequently were less inhibited in the tendency to increase their frequency of usage of hostile words" (Binder et al., 1957, p. 312). The results of this study provide the student of the interview with a caution regarding the effect of interviewer status. Interviewer status as experience may have one effect; interviewer status as dominance, and therefore threat, may have completely different results. The differences may indeed be reflected in the content areas emphasized by the interviewees. Clearly, when status is associated with threat certain content areas will tend to be minimized or avoided by the interviewee, as was the case in the preceding conditioning study. This finding is reminiscent of the assertion by Maccoby and Maccoby (1954) that the content of the interviewee's communication will be affected by the character of the status relationship.

Sociometric studies have demonstrated that a person's status is positively related to his attractiveness. In an interesting investigation (Pepitone &

Wallace, 1955) the Ss were presented with a script describing a purportedly real conversation between two people on the subject of economic aid to Liberia. The topic itself was not likely to evoke a strong personal reaction from any of the Ss. In the fictional dialogue that was enacted and tape-recorded, one of the participants was designated as a student. The other participant was identified at increasing status levels: in a control group as a student; in one experimental group as a "Dr. Brown, a high official in the State Department, African Plans and Programs Division"; and in a second experimental group as another "Dr. Brown, an occupant of the R.S. Van Heusen Chair of Political Science at Harvard, a highly paid consultant to the State Department's African Plans and Programs Division," considered to be "one of the finest minds of the generation." The same taped exchange was played to the three groups (i.e., the control group and the two experimental groups). The first speaker, always designated as a student, was self-effacing and naive. The second speaker, designated as a student for the control group and at two increasing status levels for the two experimental groups, was conceited, condescending, and generally tended to ignore what the first speaker said. All the Ss, therefore, listened to an unpleasant communication from a fictitious person whose attractiveness they were asked to rate. In this study there was a general assumption that the Ss would identify with the student, and would vicariously take part in the conversation. The results of this study were completely unequivocal. Even though the verbal communication from the second speaker was identical in all three experimental conditions, the Ss found him more attractive as his status increased.

Two experimental analogue studies, previously discussed in the section on interviewer warmth, will be scanned once more for their findings on interviewer status. The first (Greenberg, 1969) assigned a number of university undergraduates to four subgroups differing from each other in the specific expectations that were induced in them regarding the warm-cold and experienced-inexperienced attributes of the interviewer in a taped interview. They were asked to audit the taped interview, and to make certain ratings on the basis of what they heard. One-quarter of the Ss were led to expect that the interviewer they would hear was an experienced and warm person; another quarter that he was inexperienced and warm; a third, that he was experienced and cold; and a fourth, that he was inexperienced and cold. The findings on the warm-cold dimension have already been examined. On the experienced-inexperienced dimension, it was found that Ss who were given an experienced rather than an inexperienced induction were more attracted to the therapist. In this sense, the element of experience had the same effect as that of warmth. Unlike the Ss who were given the warm induction, however, those who were given an experienced induction did not prove to be more susceptible to the influence and persuasion of their interviewers than those given an inexperienced induction. Nor did they demonstrate a greater willingness to meet the therapists. Thus, the effect of warmth was more pervasive than that of experience.

The second investigation on interviewer experience level has also been discussed previously with reference to interviewer warmth. In this investigation (Greenberg, et. al., 1970) male psychiatric inpatients at a V.A. psychiatric hospital with a mean age of 43 served as Ss. The experimental procedure was the same as the one in the preceding study, with the one exception that a fifth group was added. This was a control group in which there was no arousal of expectation regarding the therapist on either a warm-cold or an experienced-inexperienced dimension. In the present study the findings of the Greenberg (1969) study were diminished considerably both with respect to warmth and experience. On the second variable there was a significant difference only on receptivity to influence as between the "experienced" and control groups. No other experienced-inexperienced effects emerged. Thus, one is left with the impression that experience as an interviewer attribute, though significant, does not have the generality, the pervasiveness, of warmth.

The investigation by Pope and Siegman (1972), already dealt with in Chapter 6, does not require detailed repetition here. Interviewer status, as experience, commanded a high level of productivity from the interviewees, interrupted however by long periods of silence expressive of caution and uncertainty. This paradoxical result is a consequence of both the reinforcing and punishing aspects of status. As experience and competence, interviewer status is reinforcing; as dominance or control, it is aversive. One additional finding is of interest. The standard interviews used in the Pope and Siegman (1972) study were based on two topics - school experiences and family relationships. The obtained results were due primarily to differences between high- and low-status interviewers in the topic of school experience, but not family relations. It will be recalled that Maccoby and Maccoby (1954) remarked that "the content of the communication will be affected by the status relationship" (p. 462). The experienced or high-status interviewer was presented as a senior faculty person; the inexperienced or low-status interviewer, as a student enrolled in a training program in interviewing. It is possible that status, in the sense of senior faculty position, would have greater relevance to an undergraduate student's discussion of school experience than family relations.

This paradoxical effect of interviewer status on interviewee response was noted in two other studies (Pope et al., 1974; Pope et al., 1976) reviewed at some length in Chapter 6. Female freshman students were interviewed by sophomore students with no previous training in interviewing (novices) and by staff psychiatrists in a private psychiatric hospital (experienced professionals). The interviewees perceived the professonals as more experienced and skilled, but viewed the novices as more sympathetic and accepting. Moreover, the student interviewers were rated as warmer and more genuine on the Truax-Carkhuff facilitative scales. There were no differences between the two groups of interviewers in the interviewee productivity elicited, but a significant difference in favor of the novices in interviewee self-disclosure. The advantage that one would expect with the greater experience of the professional interviewers appeared to have been nullified by the aversive effect of the social distance between them and the freshman student interviewees. In brief, status as experience and competence is reinforcing through the trust and confidence it inspires. But status as dominance and social distance presents a threat, particularly to low-status interviewees, which may well erase the advantage of experience.

This section will be concluded with a review of selected studies dealing with the communication of status in a dyadic situation. How does one talk to a person one perceives to be of higher status than oneself; of lower status? How does one respond to such persons? Much of the work done in this area has been concerned with nonverbal forms of communication. Such variables as eye contact, distance from the other person, posture, and relaxation are studied in both the communicator and the addressee when status difference is manipulated. Status in these investigations applies not to experience but to dominance, power, and social distance. The investigations do not deal with the interview but with experimental dyadic communication situations. But their relevance to the interview is evident. They point to some of the nonverbal signals that the interviewer may use as feedback from the inter- viewee, who perceives the interviewer aversively as powerful, dominant and controlling.

Eye contact between the two members of a dyad who differ in status has been intensively investigated. In summarizing his own work and that of others in this area, Mehrabian (1972, 1973) has found more eye contact with a high-status than a low-status addressee. In one study to which he makes reference (Mehrabian, 1972, p. 23) college freshmen addressed both seniors and other freshmen. The higher status seniors received more eye contact than the lower status freshmen. In a study of his own, which he called an encoding experiment, Mehrabian (1973) investigated several factors, one of which was the status of the person being addressed by the S. The Ss were university undergraduates, both male and female, asked to engage in an imaginary conversation with specified types of fictional addressees. In the instructions the S was told that s(he) would "be told different things about the sex, status, and your attitude toward this imaginary person in each part of the experiment. After the imaginary person is described, your task is to stand the way that you would if you were really talking with the person" (Mehrabian, 1973, p. 107). To emphasize that facial expression was not to be included in the expressive variables each S was given a mask to wear. Observers recorded eye contact, distance from addressee, orientation, arm position, and relaxation cues when the S engaged in imaginary conversation with several different types of addressees. The ones of immediate interest are high- and low-status persons of both sexes. The eye contact finding referred to above indicated more eye contact with high-status addressees than with those of low status.

In another study of eye contact between two persons of unequal status (Exline, 1974) the relative power of each participant was manipulated. The author assumed that when individuals are aware of the difference in power which defines their role relationship "we would expect that in a face-to-face interaction in which outcomes are in quesiton, the person in the less powerful position would have a greater need to monitor the expressive behavior of the other" (p. 76). The low-status person, subject to the greater power of the other, exercises a sort of watchful vigilance. Exline therefore predicted "that in a dyad marked by different power positions, the less powerful person would, everything else being equal, look more into the line of regard of the other" (p. 76).

A number of pairs of male Ss were instructed to arrive at agreed-upon solutions to assigned problems through discussion. The differential power positions of both members of a dyad were manipulated through the division of 10 chips between the two at the end of each problem solution. The chips were placed in the control of the high power (HP) member, who was instructed to divide them in specified ways, always disadvantageous to the low power (LP) member. The basic finding was summarized by the author as follows: "It is clear that, over all periods and experimental conditions, the less powerful person looked more at the powerful person than vice versa.... This was the case for looking while listening and tended to be the case for looking while speaking" (Exline, 1974, p. 78). In brief, one may assume that an interviewee who spends much of his/her time in gazing vigilantly at the interviewer while speaking, and particularly while listening, is probably very much aware of the superior power and status of the interviewer.

Other nonverbal cues regarding the relative status of two communicators emerged from the Mehrabian (1973) study in which undergraduate students were asked "to stand the way that you would if you were really talking" (p. 107) with higher and lower status fictional persons. Two results indicate a greater directness of posture when speaking to a high-status than to a low-status addressee. This directness was noted both in an upward tilt of the head and in a direct shoulder orientation toward the addressee. The interviewer may assume from these results that an interviewee who looks up at him/her and faces directly is perceiving him/her as a person of superior status and power. By contrast, a speaker who stands with his/her arms akimbo while speaking to another is probably perceiving the addressee as a person of lower status. Finally, the more relaxed the posture of a communicator and the greater the distance s(he) takes from the addressee, the more likely it is that s(he) is addressing a person of lower status.

In brief, the interviewer may assume that his/her superior status is an appreciable, possibly aversive element in the interview, if the interviewee demonstrated a high level of eye contact (vigilance), a head tilt that is close to the horizontal or above rather than hanging down, directness in facing the interviewer, an element of tension in body posture, and a decrease in distance through a forward rather than a backward lean.

Interviewer attributes have been demonstrated to have a significant impact on interviewee response, whether these attributes happen to be distributed along an effective dimension (i.e., warm-cold) or a status dimension (i.e., experienced-inexperienced). Of the two categories of attributes, however, the affective ones appear to have greater impact and more generality than the status ones. The precise character of status needs to be specified for a particular interview situation. More particularly, one has to be concerned with the power or dominance-submission and social distance aspects of status on the one hand, and interviewer experience, on the other. The two are likely to have different effects, and to be reflected in different content areas.

INTERVIEWER PERSONALITY

The preceding sections have dealt with interviewer attributes as separate parameters of relationship behavior. The approach now will be a more integrative one in which the two participants in an interview develop inferences about each other as persons. An inference may be something as basic as: "I like him" or "he's a cold and forbidding person." It may be one that is easily communicated and shared with another person, or it may be difficult to formulate, possibly autistic. For example, a paranoid patient may closely scrutinize every new person he encounters to determine whether he belongs to the "Divine Host" or to the "Devil's Minions." In using this primitive taxonomy of persons, he may deviate so grossly from others as to be readily recognized as psychotic. In fact, relationship and communication with others who do not share his delusional typology of people may be extremely limited, if not totally absent. But this paranoid patient may well persevere in using his classification scheme for whatever internal reasons, and indeed may base much interpersonal behavior on this monolithic division of people into two contrasting forces.

The interviewee draws on his cumulative experience with others, his a priori expectations of the interviewer, and his interaction with him to generate his inferences about him as a person. Consider the following employment interview in which a young psychologist, seeking his first position, was interviewed by the superintendent of a state hospital. Ordinarily, the psychologist referred to here would have been tense and anxiously apprehensive during an interview in which he was being evaluated. But in this instance the interview came at the end of a long day in which there had been two previous evaluational encounters. The earlier ones did not go badly but no specific job opportunities resulted. The next interview with the superintendent was in a section of the city remote from the location of the second interview. As the psychologist sat in the taxi transporting him to the third and last meeting of the day, he felt fatigued, irritated, and discouraged about the prospect of a job resulting from his next meeting.

In spite of his tardiness the psychologist was greeted warmly by the superintendent. Both sat down in a pleasant office. To the psychologist the superintendent appeared to be a comfortable person, thoughtful as he pulled on his pipe, gentle in manner, and hovering somewhere on the borderline between warmth and a sort of quiet reserve. He was interested and empathic as he tactfully guided the psychologist through a narration of his training, experience, and current employment interests. The superintendent ended the interview with a firm job offer. The psychologist demurred, promised to decide within a week, and walked away from the interview with an image of the superintendent as a "nice guy," "a guy I could work with," even though his warmth was subtly interwoven with a disappointing aloofness.

At issue here is not the validity of the image that the psychologist had of his interviewer; as yet he did not know if others would perceive the superintendent in the same way that he did. He was in the throes of a first impression. Yet he knew that he was about to make an important decision based, in part, on this impression of his interviewer as a person. While many decisions in life are based on such initial perceptions of others, research in this field aspires to greater objectivity than that ordinarily achieved through informal impression. Measures of personality or instruments for typing personality may be used to assess the other person - in this instance, the interviewer - and data may be collected in accordance with accepted principles of research design for subsequent statistical analysis. The objective is to correlate measures of the interviewer as a person with the interview process, interviewee response, and the outcome of the interview.

In a series of investigations at the Phipps Psychiatric Institute (Betz & Whitehorn, 1956; Whitehorn & Betz, 1954, 1960) two types of psychotherapists were distinguished on the basis of differential success in the treatment of hospitalized schizophrenic patients. The authors scanned clinical notes, treatment records, and used indirect observation to characterize the difference between these two groups of psychotherapists. On the basis of the descriptive data compiled, the high-success group turned out to demonstrate more active personal participation with their patients than the low-success group. Among psychometric instruments only the Strong Vocational Interest Blank was able to discriminate. At first, there were four scales in the SVIB that significantly differentiated the first group of therapists (Type A) from the second group (Type B). In the end the authors developed a 23-item scale based on the Strong Vocational Interest Blank which was able to discriminate reliably between the Type A and the Type B therapists. The SVIB characterized the interests of the Type A therapists as similar to those of persons who follow careers involving considerable close contact with others, the ability to understand them readily, and resourcefulness in responding to their interests. The Type B therapists tended to be more routinized, less imaginative, and more impersonal in their relationships with others.

A somewhat more detailed description of the Type A and the Type B therapist is provided by Rogers (1961):

> The physicians in the A group tended to see the schizophrenic in terms of the personal meaning which various behaviors had to the patient, rather than seeing him as a case history or a descriptive diagnosis. They also tended to work toward goals which were oriented to the personality of the patient, rather than such goals as reducing the symptoms or curing the disease. It was found that the helpful physicians in their day-by-day interaction, primarily made use of active personal participation - a person-to-person relationship. They made less use of procedures which could be classed as 'passive permissive.' They were even less likely to use such procedures as interpretation, instruction or advice, or emphasis upon the practical care of the patient. Finally, they were much more likely than the B group to develop a relationship in which the patient felt trust and confidence in the physician. (p. 98)

In Rogers' view the Type A therapist demonstrates a capacity for the kind of relationship that facilitates therapeutic progress. Moreover, he does not limit the efficacy of Type A therapists to schizophrenic patients, as Betz and Whitehorn did. Rogers' view, however, is not supported by other research conducted with Type A and Type B therapists. In one investigation (McNair, Callahan, & Lorr, 1962) the findings suggest that Type A and Type B therapists are successful with contrasting kinds of patients. Twenty Type A and 20 Type B male therapists were selected out of a large number treating patients in seven out-patient clinics. The patient sample was quite different from the one used in the Betz and Whitehorn studies, consisting of male, veteran psychiatric out-patients, under age 51, and all considered to be good candidates for intensive psychotherapy. The criteria of therapeutic success were more objective than in the preceding studies including Taylor's Manifest Anxiety Scale, Barron's Ego Strength Scale, a Symptom Checklist which was in fact an inventory of 21 common neurotic symptoms and complaints; a Severity of Illness Measure, and a measure of Interview Relationship Changes. Contrary to expectations, the patients of the Type B therapists in this study reported greater changes in the direction of improvement than those of Type A therapists. There was an increase in ego strength as measured by Barron's Ego Strength Scale, a decrease in manifest symptoms as noted on the Symptom Checklist, a drop in anxiety as indicated by the Taylor Manifest Anxiety Scale, and a decrease in severity of illness. The most provocative conclusion from this study, when considered together with the previous Whitehorn and Betz investigations, is that Type A therapists are more successful with hospitalized schizophrenic patients, and Type B therapists, with neurotic out-patients. The authors offered this interpretation tentatively, emphasizing that it required confirmation in a controlled study designed to test the specific hypothesis.

The possibility that therapists could be divided into two personality types, each suited to a different diagnostic group of patients, seemed like a breakthrough in the matching of therapist and patient. There followed then a number of therapy-analogue studies with results that were similar to the preceding clinical ones. In two of these (Berzins & Seidman, 1968, 1969) the therapists were totally untrained undergraduate male students separated into A and B types on the basis of their scores on the A-B Scale of the Strong Vocational Interest Blank. It was assumed that the A-B distinction would apply not only to male therapists, but more generally to male personality types. Moreover, there was the further assumption that untrained Type A students would demonstrate treatment-like behavior similar to that manifested by Type A therapists; similarly, Type B students would behave like Type B therapists. Actually, the students were divided into three groups of "quasi-therapists," As, ABs or middles, and Bs. All Ss were asked to respond to tape-recorded, enacted patient communications which sampled equally the responses of two patient types, one characterized by avoidance of others (schizoid) and the other, by turning against self (neurotic). More specifically, the first group of "patient" communications showed a mixture of schizoid and paranoid features, while the second group, neurotic-depressive complaints including suicidal ideation. The Ss were instructed to listen to the taped "patient" communications and to respond as they would if they were the therapist in each instance. The responses were in writing. The findings of the study provided rather impressive support for the clinically determined differential effectiveness of Type A therapists with schizophrenic patients, and Type B with neurotics. As reported greater satisfaction in responding to schizoid patients and greater ease in choosing helpful responses for them, while Bs showed the same preference for neurotic patients. These are, of course, subjective interactional impressions. The authors attempted to determine whether these impressions accorded with any systematic differences in the actual written responses. Several interesting findings emerged. The first indicated that when As responded to schizoid communications and Bs to neurotic communications, their responses were significantly longer than when they responded to the opposite types. The ABs were intermediate in length between the two extremes. Secondly, it was found that when As and Bs were matched with "compatible" types of patients, their responses took on the form of declarative formulations rather than questions much more frequently than when they were matched with "incompatible" types of patients.

A second experimental analogue study (Seidman, 1971) demonstrated the interaction effect of A and B "therapists" on schizoid (avoidance of others) and neurotic (turning against self) clients, in relation to interviewer respect and empathy, response time, and approach-avoidance behavior. Although the basic design of the study resembled the preceding one, certain important differences occurred. As in the preceding study, the three groups of Ss were student volunteers, not actual therapists, who placed at the lowest quartile (A "therapists"), the middle one-third (AB "therapists"), and top quartile (B "therapists"), of the A-B scale. This time the two enacted patient types were videotaped, rather than audiotaped. The responses of the "therapists" were not handwritten, as previously, but spoken and audiotaped. The dependent variables included some that were the same as those in the preceding study and others that were different. First, there were two therapist facilitative conditions that yielded significant interactional results. When A "interviewers" were matched with schizoid "patients" and B "interviewers" with "neurotic" patients, the interviewers' responses were rated as higher in respect (unconditional positive regard) and in accurate empathy than they were when the opposite matching occurred. Thus, the familiar interactional effect occurred again, this time in relation to variables that might mediate some of the A-B therapist results. The interaction effect may indeed occur because compatible matching generates higher facilitative conditions than incompatible matchings.

As in the preceding study, interviewer response times were longer when As interacted with schizoid patients and Bs with neurotic ones. Finally As were rated as reacting to increased stress by turning toward others and Bs by avoiding others. A complementarity of relationship model is offered by the authors to explain these diverse findings. Response time, respect, empathy and the pattern of turning toward or away from others under stress may be distributed along an approach-avoidance dimension. If long response time, high respect, high empathy, and turning toward others may be taken as indices of approach, and their opposites, avoidance, "an oversimplified description might be that the approaching A therapist works most effectively with the withdrawn schizophrenic..., while the avoidant B therapist is at his best with the verbally productive...., approaching intropunitive neurotic" (Seidman, 1971, p. 206).

The two preceding analogue studies differ in certain vital respects from actual clinical interactions. The Ss were, after all, not involved in an actual interview situation. They responded to single communications without the guidance of subsequent feedback from the patient. Nevertheless, the findings were both significant and provocative, demonstrating that there was indeed a tendency for Type A males to respond more effectively to the schizoid rather than neurotic communications, with the reverse finding characterizing the Type B males. In a third investigation in the same series (Berzins, Ross, & Cohen, 1970) there was a partial return from the therapy analogue to the actual therapy situation. Psychiatric aides, classified as Type A and Type B, were asked to interview addict patients. Each patient was given a "distrust" or a "trust" manipulation before his interview. In the "distrust" condition the patient was led to expect that his interviewer would be a shrewd, clever interrogator. It was assumed that this expectation would create a condition of guardedness and interpersonal avoidance analogous to that which would be clinically present in a schizoid patient. In the "trust" condition the patient was told that his interviewer would be direct, understanding, sincere, and warm. The authors assumed that the latter manipulation would elicit "neurotic-like" behaviors from the patients. Again, Type A aides interviewing "distrust" patients (schizoid) and Type B aides interviewing "trust" patients (neurotic) obtained better patient self-disclosure than oppositely paired dyads.

A later study (Berzins, Ross, & Friedman, 1972) represented a more complete return from the experimental analogue to the clinical situation. Its purpose was to examine the A-B interaction hypothesis in a brief psychotherapy college clinic. Three A and three B male therapists were matched with both schizoid and neurotic clients. Using a factorially derived scale for assessing the therapists' appraisal of their own effectiveness (satisfaction with therapeutic interventions, comfort, felt compatibility with the patient, and ease in generating helping responses) the predicted interaction between therapist and patient types occurred. In brief "A therapists felt more efficacious with schizoid patients than with neurotic patients.... whereas the opposite pattern characterized B therapists" (Berzins, Ross, & Friedman, 1972, p. 233).

A second factorially derived scale reflected both patient and therapist assessment of improvement in presenting problems. On this dimension, the predicted interaction effect was again evident, but not completely supported. As expected, B therapists produced more improvement in neurotic than in schizoid patients. However, A therapists were equally successful with both neurotic and schizoid patients. The efficacy of A type therapists with neurotic patients was unexpected and did not accord with the interaction hypothesis. Though the evidence supporting the interaction hypothesis in the present investigation is partial, the authors consider it adequate to justify a policy of no assignment of B therapists to schizoid patients, reserving them for neurotic patients only.

However persuasive the results of studies dealing with the A and B therapist typology appeared to be, both clinicians and researchers were uncomfortable with the frail foundation on which they rested. A brief derivative of the Strong Vocational Interest Inventory hardly provided a sufficient basis for an interactional theory of psychotherapy. The search for personality correlates of A and B therapist scores was prompted by a wish to extend the basis for the typology. If consistent psychological profiles for the A and B types could be developed, these would support the assumption that the two were stable personality categories and not transient interest patterns consequent on recent training and experience.

Evidence for personality correlates of A and B interest patterns was

sought in a research study (Berzins, Dove, & Ross, 1972) in which both professionals and nonprofessionals participated. The professionals included male
psychologists, psychiatrists, social workers, and counselors. The non-
professionals consisted of male and female undergraduate college students
and male out-patients in a student health service. A and B types in all the
population groups were compared on several dimensions of the Personality
Research Form, an inventory of personal traits. The results showed that "the
A-type S, in each sample, may be described as relatively cautious, submissive,
uninclined to seek variety or sensual pleasure for its own sake, and as
somewhat succorant. Conversely, the B-type S shows a risk-taking, dominant,
variety-seeking, and 'counter dependent' orientation to experiences" (Berzins,
Dove, & Ross, 1972, p. 391). The evidence for a personality distinction
between A and B types did indeed occur, both in the profile differences
between the two and in the consistencies in profile differences across the
various professional and nonprofessional subgroups. One additional finding of
interest was the occurrence of the same A-B profile distinctions in a female
as well as several male populations. At the time of this study, there had been
no prior evidence that the treatment relevant implications of the A-B
distinction applied to females as well as males.

Though the above findings are of interest, they provide few explanatory
clues about the particular suitability of A therapists for schizoid patients and
B therapists for neurotics. An earlier study (Segal, 1970) searched the scripts
of therapy interviews by A and B type therapists for any evidence of
differential behavior in psychotherapy. If such emerged, there was the hope
that it might help to explain the A-B interaction effect with the two patient
types. Male graduate students in a clinical psychology training program were
the therapists. Only clients with neurotic behavior and symptoms were used
in the investigation. Tape-recordings of therapist interviews were content-
analyzed using the Bales interaction process categories, a measure of
therapist directiveness, and the Lennard and Bernstein specificity scale. The
A and B therapists did not differ in amount of activity. As were more leading
and readier to express negative feeling (sarcasm) than Bs. As were also more
specific and more interpretive than Bs. It is difficult to compare these
intrainterview behavioral findings in a meaningful way with the personality
profiles drawn by Berzins, Dove, & Ross (1972). There is, however,
considerable internal consistency in the above two contrasting behavioral
patterns. Moreover, there is a suggestion of a relationship between A and B
behavioral patterns and their relative efficacy with schizoid and neurotic
patients. In the author's words:

> The A therapist might be characterized as interacting in a manner
> which provides the client with information or a frame of reference to
> which the client has to address himself. The A therapists are assuming
> responsibility for the structure and direction of the therapeutic
> process. In contrast to A therapists, B's tended to be more
> facilitative, less direct, and more encouraging to their clients."
> (Segal, 1970, p. 445)

The above behavior differences between the therapists would articulate well with the major adaptive mechanisms and deficits of the two contrasting types of patients. The schizophrenic patient, and to a lesser extent the schizoid, feels separated from the world around him/her. Relationship with others is attenuated; perceptions of the animate and inanimate environment are distorted and confused. Such a patient needs a direct, active, structured approach from the person with whom s(he) is communicating to reduce his/her own deficits and distortions. The neurotic patient, wracked with anxiety, but lacking the withdrawal and distortion of the schizophrenic or schizoid patient, is able to respond to the type of facilitation of self-exploration offered by the B-type therapist.

Additionally, it may be asked whether the two types of therapists demonstrate different styles of perception, and how these might relate to the perceptual patterns of the two kinds of patients. Basing himself on field dependence and field independence research, Silverman (1967) has found two contrasting styles of perceptual behavior for A and B therapists. He concluded that the two types of therapists perceived their physical and social worlds as well as their patients differently. A's perceptions are more like those of a schizophrenic patient than those of B. The A-type therapist does not maintain as constant and goal-directed a stance as the B therapist. S(he) responds to the environment in a less focused manner, encompassing a wider range of stimuli. These might include peripheral or incidental bits of behavior observed in others, and other forms of stiumulation that Bs might consider to be irrelevant at the moment. In brief, the A therapist is more vulnerable than the B therapist to chance inputs from a changing environment. Along with greater responsiveness to unanticipated external sources of information, there is also a greater receptiveness to such internal promptings as hunches and intuitions. The A-type therapist does not reject the distortions of the schizophrenic as irrelevant digressions, but rather accepts them as valid communications about the patient's perceptual world. B's perceptions are, by contrast, closer to those of the neurotic patient, and not at all resonant with those of the schizophrenic. B's cognitive activity is attuned to external reality, and to the logic of problem solving. S(he) does not tolerate the slippage so evident in the schizophrenic's perceptions and cognitions. In general s(he) shares with the neurotic a consensually based, sharply drawn distinction between reality and unreality, and a distinct preference for the former. These observations by Silverman (1967) suggest a greater communality of experience, and thus a readier flow of communication between As and schizophrenics, Bs and neurotics, than that which occurs when the opposite matchings are made.

A later investigation (Chartier & Weiss, 1974) further tested the conclusion by Silverman (1967) that A therapists have a highly sensitive capacity to perceive some of the essential traits of the schizophrenic patient. The Chartier and Weiss (1974) study did not develop descriptive patterns for the styles of perception of A and B therapists. Instead it compared the two on the clinical accuracy with which they perceived and selected schizophrenic and neurotic patient responses to a number of tests. The interviewer Ss were 12 male graduate students in clinical psychology whose training included an emphasis on the development of accuracy in clinical understanding and prediction. Six were A-type therapists in training and six, B-type. One neurotic patient and one schizophrenic, both female, were the other Ss in a clinical prediction exercise by the A and B therapists. The predictions were made in both a limited information condition (the auditing of an 8-10 minute excerpt of the patient in a clinical interview and the reading of a brief social history of the patient) and a more extended information condition (WAIS, Rorschach, TAT, MMPI). The task of each interviewer was to predict the responses of each of the patients to three instruments. Significant results were obtained for only one of these, the Rotter Incomplete Sentence Blank. As were superior to Bs in predicting the schizophrenic patient's responses to the sentence completion test, but only in the limited information condition. With additional information, the B therapists all but closed the gap between themselves and the As. "To the extent that accuracy of clinical understanding and prediction may mediate the course of psychotherapy, the present data clearly support the hypothesis that As are more effective than Bs with schizophrenics, while both therapist types are comparably successful with neurotics" (Chartier & Weiss, 1974, p. 312). This study, together with the preceding one by Silverman (1967) supports the theory that the differential effectiveness of A and B therapists with schizophrenic and neurotic patients is mediated by contrasting perceptual processes and accuracies in clinical perception.

In concluding this section it should be noted that studies dealing with A- and B-type interviewers or therapists are not all supportive of the hypothesized distinction. Certainly, the evidence is not impressively consistent. Moreover, one would be justified in reserving a degree of skepticism about a personality typology that is based on a frail and brief scale culled out of the Strong Vocational Interest Inventory. It is therefore not the substance of the A-B research that is persuasive, but its implication that there are systematic relations between personality types of interviewer and personality or diagnostic types of interviewee. The preceding studies, and the ones that follow, are cited not because they provide final and definitive evidence about the precise character of this relationship, but because they address themselves to the problem and provide some hope that more definitive information will be forthcoming in the future.

Many of the investigations dealing with the association between interviewer personality and his relationship behavior within the interview are based on personality inventory scores. One study yielded a rather rich harvest of significant correlations between therapist nonpossessive warmth, genuineness and empathy, and a number of EPPS personality trait measures (Truax, Silber, & Wargo, 1966). Personality inventories were administered to 16 graduate students before and after training in psychotherapy. Those students showing the highest gains in the three relationship scales were compared with those showing the least improvement. The authors addressed themselves to two questions: "What kind of trainee benefits the most from the training program?" and "What kind of personality changes occur in trainees who gain most, compared to those who gain least in therapeutic skill?" They found that the students with the greatest gains in facilitative conditions were initially lower on the EPPS Need for Order than those who showed little gain; these students also showed a significant drop on this scale posttraining. The following additional findings discriminated between the high-gain and the low-gain students in the training program: the former were significantly higher on the EPPS Change Scale both before and after training; they showed a significantly greater decline during training on the Abasement Scale; they started out significantly higher and showed larger gain in Need Autonomy; they were significantly lower at the beginning of the training program on Defensiveness. In brief, a group of personality dimensions emerged which distinguished between students who manifested high gain in therapeutic conditions during training and others who manifested low gain. The high-gain students in contrast to the low-gain manifest less rigidity, a greater readiness to change and to welcome new experiences, greater self-assertiveness, and less defensiveness.

Bergin and Jasper (1969) correlated interviewer empathy scores with a number of pathology scales on the Minnesota Multiphasic Personality Inventory. The interviewers were graduate students in psychology. It was found that interviewer Depression (D) and Anxiety (Pt) correlate negatively with Empathy rated on the basis of recorded therapy sessions. Not surprisingly, the authors conclude that personal disturbance in the therapist interferes with his/her therapeutic effectiveness.

That a high level of anxiety may decrease therapeutic competence is indicated by a second investigation in this area (Bandura, 1956). Forty-two clinical psychologists, psychiatrists, and social workers functioning as psycho-therapists in four clinics rated each other and themselves on a number of personality traits, and were also rated on therapeutic competence by their supervisors. Those who were judged more anxious by their colleagues tended also to be judged less competent as therapists by their supervisors.

Until this point, personality has been broken down into predispositional traits including pathological ones, such as high anxiety and depression, and these have been related to therapeutic competence and to such aspects of interpersonal behavior as empathy and warmth. It is now proposed to inquire into a possible relationship between an interviewer's specific conflicts and his behavior in the interview. Any interviewer or therapist who has been supervised in his work, or who has supervised others, will have an impres-sionistic awareness that an interviewer's or therapist's specific personality dynamics affect his interview work. This relationship is particularly apparent when the interviewer is still relatively inexperienced. For example, consider the interview conducted by a medical student, presented verbatim in the Gill, Newman, and Redlich (1954) book on the initial interview. It is apparent from the text of the interview that the medical student is particularly outraged by the patient's unreasonable, angry, and inconsiderate treatment of his mother. He responds with criticism and censure whenever the patient describes his immature behavior toward his mother. Less impressionistic are the findings of the following two studies, which lend support to the widely accepted belief that the individual interviewer's specific problems and conflicts do indeed affect his interview behavior.

In the first of these studies (Bandura, Lipsher, & Miller, 1960) the authors remark that a patient is not likely to be encouraged to explore areas of conflict that evoke the therapist's own anxiety. Consequently they predicted that therapists who displayed a high level of hostility anxiety would tend to respond to a patient's expressions of hostility with avoidance while therapists who had no such problem would be more likely to demonstrate approach reactions. It was further expected that whenever the therapist was avoidant of hostility as expressed by the patient, the patient would tend to decrease or inhibit his expressions of hostile feelings. The data were obtained from tape-recorded interviews of 17 parents who were engaged in psychotherapy at a parent-child clinic. There were 12 different therapists, two females and 10 males, all advanced clinical psychology students, and all, except two, themselves undergoing psychotherapy at the time of the study. Each therapist was rated independently by three staff members on three measures of hostility anxiety. These measures were then correlated with the therapist's hostility approach and avoidance responses in the interview. Approach responses included the approval of patient's expressions of hostility, exploration of such expressions, prompting the patient to speak about hostile feelings, reflecting such feelings back to the patient, and labeling them. Avoidance reactions included therapist disapproval of patient communication of hostility, change of topic whenever the patient spoke in this manner, and therapist silence, ignoring, or mislabeling of patient's hostile communication. One of the three hostility anxiety measures correlated significantly with the therapist's hostility approach-avoidance behavior. It is of interest, but hardly surprising, that therapist approach reactions to patient hostility tended to encourage the patient to continue to express such feelings, while therapist avoidance tended to prompt the patient to discontinue communication about hostile feelings. In general, it is then evident in this investigation that an interviewer's conflict and anxiety about hostility will affect his response to a patient's expression of hostility and therefore significantly affect the patient's tendency to speak about this feeling.

The second study pertaining to interviewer conflict in relation to his interview behavior (Cutler, 1958) is more general in scope than the preceding one. It investigated an anticipated association between the therapist's conflicts and his tendency to either over- or underreport the occurrence of conflict-relevant behavior in himself and in his patient. Additionally, it investigated the expectation that the therapist would deal more competently with material developed in the interview which was for him relatively conflict-free than with that which was conflict-relevant. Two therapists were studied in this investigation, one with three years of graduate training in clinical psychology and considerable experience as a therapist; the second in his second year of graduate training with very limited experience. Conflict areas were determined in the following way. Each therapist was asked to rate himself on the following 16 personality relevant adjectives: dominating, boastful, rejecting, punitive, critical, complaining, suspicious, apologetic, submissive, respectful, dependent, agreeable, affiliative, supportive, generous, advising. In addition, nine or more judges who were personally well acquainted with the therapists also rated them on the same adjectives. A 19-point scale was used by both the therapist and his raters ranging from "most characteristic" to "least characteristic." When the nine raters tended to agree with the therapist or disagree with him in a random manner, it was assumed that there was no conflict between the therapist's perception of himself and the manner in which the judges perceived him. On the other hand, when the therapist tended to systematically overrate himself or underrate himself in relation to the judges, a "plus-conflict" or a "minus-conflict" was designated for the relevant adjective. Tape-recorded interviews by the therapists were used as sources of data for this study as well as detailed accounts that they dictated immediately following therapy hours, in which they reported all that they remembered as transpiring during the session. Later, each interview was coded on the 16 adjectives referred to above so that the total number of actual manifestations by the therapist and by the patient of each of the 16 interpersonal behavior categories was determined. A similar coding was carried out on the dictated postinterview summaries. Thus, by comparing the two codings, it was possible to relate the objective behavior of the therapist and his patient during the interview series with the postinterview therapist perceptions of his own and his patient's behavior. It was expected that where a therapist tended to overestimate his possession of a trait in contrast to his evaluation by others, he would tend to overreport the occurrence of behavior in the same category, whether it be his own or his patient's. Similarly, when he tended to underestimate his possession of a trait, he would tend to underestimate the occurrence of interview behavior in the same category. While these expectations were not borne out in every instance, they were, to a significant degree, supporting in general the overall hypothesis of the study.

In addition, the investigator predicted that the therapist functioned more effectively in conflict-free rather than conflicted areas. He had each therapist's response coded by an independent judge as either "task-oriented" or "ego-oriented." He defined task-oriented behavior as that which tended to facilitate the patient's communication of therapeutically relevant material, and ego-oriented therapist behavior as that which had as its primary purpose the expression of the therapist's own needs. Ego-oriented behavior was thus defined as a sort of defensive activity on the part of the therapist. The investigator then sought an association between the occurrence in a patient's statement of material that was conflict-relevant for the therapist and the probability that the subsequent therapist remark would be ego-oriented rather than task-oriented. In fact, there was strong support for this anticipation. Patient remarks that contained material that was conflicted for the therapist rather than neutral were significantly more frequently followed by therapist ego-oriented rather than task-oriented comments. The interviewer's adequacy was significatnly greater in neutral than in conflicted areas.

Whether interviewer personality be defined in terms of type, predispositional traits, or interviewer dynamics, it is an important element in the relationship and interaction that emerge. Yet these matters cannot be understood with reference to the interviewer alone. In the next chapter the role of interviewee attributes in relationship will be considered.

APPLICATION SUMMARY

Patients and therapists often differ in their view of those aspects of the therapeutic experience that have most to do with positive therapeutic change. Therapists tend to attribute such change to the technical or procedural aspects of their work and to the theories on which they are based. Patients, instead, are inclined to emphasize the personal qualities of the therapist or the relationship that develops. If the view of the patient is a force in the unfolding of psychotherapy, the technical training and the character of the procedures used by the therapist may be less important for the effective conduct of an interview or a psychotherapeutic interaction than certain of his/her facilitating attitudes and personality attributes. Of these, interviewer warmth is given the widest recognition by both clinicians and clients as a determinant of a positive therapeutic relationship and a successful outcome of treatment.

It is difficult to think of anyone failing to have an immediate experience of recognition when one refers to a person as warm in attitude and manner. Yet definition does not come easily for this dimension of relationship. The problem is the delimitation of warmth from other positive interpersonal affects. Small wonder then that the practitioner is left with an ambiguous impression of the kind of attitude or experience that he is instructed to demonstrate if his conduct as an interviewer and a therapist is to accord with acceptable clinical values.

There is some controversy among clinicians about the teachability of warmth. (Training for high levels of relationship behavior will be considered below.) It revolves around the distinction between warmth as an attitude and warmth as an identifiable behavior pattern. Some existentially oriented psychologists take the position that a behavioral facade of warmth, which is not based on its inner experience, will be recognized as lacking in genuineness by the interviewee and will arouse distrust and other negative feelings. One may acknowledge that a cold interviewer who assumes a facade of warmth would indeed have the above effect, and yet accept the proposition that warmth does need to be communicated, and that its communication is teachable.

It is a matter of some importance to the interviewer to become sensitized to the cues used in the communication of warmth and skilled in their employment. Most of these are paralinguistic and nonverbal in character. It is possible to demonstrate a consensual recognition of a warm and cold tone of voice, and to train a person to use the former, particularly if the tone of voice is congruent with his/her inner feelings. Nonverbal cues of positive or warm feeling for the interviewee include a relaxed posture, a forward lean of the trunk toward the interviewer, and the reduction of the distance from him/her (Mehrabian, 1973), within certain normative limits. Other nonverbal signals of warmth or approval (Rosenfeld, 1973) include smiles, positive head nods, and spontaneous gesticulation by the interviewer.

However broad the intuitive consensus that warmth is a positive force in the interview, this dimension of relationship has nevertheless been the object of considerable clinical and research investigation. The findings in this area are not as consistent as one would like, but certain trends emerge with enough clarity to justify the clinician's acceptance of warmth as a positive variable in his/her work.

For example, the Principle of Reciprocal Affect (Truax & Carkhuff, 1967) has been well documented in the research literature. Warmth in the interviewer fosters positive feeling in the interviewee; and a cold attitude in the interviewer, negative feeling. Interviewees are attracted to warm rather than cold interviewers (Heller et al., 1966) and are more readily influenced by them (Greenberg, 1969). Thus, positive feeling in one member of a dyad elicits similar feeling in the other, with the ensuing resonance that is an essential part of a positive relationship.

The therapeutic influence of interviewer warmth is noted in its benign effect on the interviewee. Interviewer permissiveness (very much like warmth) reduces interviewee tension and anxiety as reflected in decreased GSR responses (Dittes, 1957) and in lower rates of speech disturbances (Pope & Siegman, 1972). The beneficial effect of warmth has been noted in the finding that therapists rated as warm have been more successful than those rated as cold in keeping unproductive patients in treatment (Hiler, 1958). Finally, warm therapists have been more successful in fostering improved adjustment in their patients than those rated as cold (Barrett-Lennard, 1962).

The effect of interviewer warmth on the course of communication in the interview has been clouded in contradictory findings. Yet there are enough results demonstrating higher interviewee verbal productivity in response to interviewer warmth rather than coldness to justify the practitioner's attentiveness to such a possible relationship as s(he) interacts with an interviewee.

In brief, warmth expressed by one member of a dyad is reciprocated by warmth from the other. Interviewer warmth has certain benign effects on the course of an interview and of a psychotherapy series: it reduces tension and anxiety; it increases the volume of verbal communication by the patient; it keeps patients in therapy; and it affects the outcome of treatment positively. It is not proposed that the interviewer learn to "fake" warmth if s(he) does not experience it. But it will be helpful to the interviewer to sensitize himself/herself to the verbal and nonverbal signals that communicate warmth and to become adept in the use of such cues.

While the concept of empathy overlaps considerably with warmth, it is by no means synonymous with it. One definition of empathy speaks of it as "the capacity of an individual to identify himself with another in terms of the way the other would act and feel. It is the essence of understanding, the why of another's attitudes and behavior" (Fenlason, 1962). In part, empathy is a cognitive process; as the above definition indicates, it is the capacity to understand another. But cognition does not capture the essence of the concept. One must add to understanding the ability to identify with another, to enter into his/her perceptual and emotional world, to resonate with him/her. In fact, any attempt to define empathy quickly impels one to use metaphoric language because expository terms are not adequate. Thus, the authors of the Accurate Empathy Scale characterize empathy as a psychological process than "involves more than just the ability of the therapist to sense the client or patient's 'private world' as if it were his own. It also involves more than just his ability to know what the patient means. Accurate Empathy involves both the therapist's sensitivity to current feelings and his verbal facilities to communicate the understanding in a language attuned to the client's current feelings" (Truax & Carkhuff, 1967, p. 46). An empathic interviewer listens, senses, perceives, and communicates empathically.

It is difficult to speak about empathy in nonexperiential terms, whether one is referring to the interviewer or the interviewee. If the empathic interviewer is understanding, the interviewee feels understood. If the empathic interviewer identifies with the interviewee's attitudes, thoughts, and feelings, the interviewee feels the reinforcing effect of the kind of interpersonal resonance that develops. But it has not been easy to partition empathy into behavioral components that might be identified and studied. Only with reference to empathic communication is one able to approach the assessment of empathy in such terms. Thus, the empathic interviewer speaks to the interviewee in a manner that is in synchrony with the latter's feelings. But here, too, there are no invariant rules. The interviewer as an empathic communicator does not always literally reflect the emotion of the interviewee. One might, for example, acknowledge and accept the depression felt by another without necessarily speaking in a depressive way oneself.

In general, however, the interviewer's style of communication is congruent with the interviewee's communication. If the interviewee is sad and restrained, the interviewer will modulate both tempo and volume in a manner that will convey to the interviewee that s(he) is aware of his/her feelings and respects them. If a paranoid interviewee speaks in cold, brittle, sarcastic tones which communicate distrust and the desire for distance, the interviewer will not crowd him/her.

But it is evident that the interviewer can achieve empathy in communication only if he is able to speak in a flexibly active and expressive manner. Indeed, research studies have demonstrated that interviewees associate interviewer empathy positively with a high level of verbal productivity and expressiveness, and negatively with interviewer silence, long reaction time, and interrupting overtalk. As in the case of warmth, the above behavioral correlates of empathy are not in themselves definitive of the condition but they do provide a context in which it occurs.

Another precondition for empathy, associated with its "understanding" aspect rather than its communication, is the interviewer's capacity to attend, to concentrate on the interviewee's communications. In their book on Micro-counseling, Ivey and Moreland (1971) analyze attending behavior into its components so that it might be taught in a condensed way to student interviewers. They include eye contact and verbal following behavior (paraphrases, neutrally toned "mm-hmm," and other attending utterances as correlates of attentiveness). They emphasize the inadequacy of simply instructing their trainees to listen. Instead, they specify the signals by which the interviewee knows that the interviewer is listening. "The counselor should look at his client to note postural movements, gestures, and facial expressions which give important indications concerning the client. Eye contact need not be constant, nor should it be fixed staring; it should be natural looking at the client.... Unless the interviewer is relaxed, he will find it difficult to focus on the client" (Ivey & Moreland, 1971, p. 41). Finally, the attentive interviewer will not utilize the above nonverbal cues as a screen for his/her own distracting boredom. S(he) will hear what the patient is saying and will acknowledge the accurate receipt of the patient's messages.

The clinician knows that the attentiveness of one person to another is a potent reinforcer that plays an important part in the establishment of a relationship. It is likely that, at least in part, the reinforcing effect of understanding and attentive listening may explain the beneficial effect of accurate empathy on the course of the interview and of psychotherapy. Two investigations (Pope et al., 1974; Staples & Sloan, 1976) found that interviewees were more productive in response to empathic than non-empathic interviewees; and one (Staples & Sloan, 1976), that interviewees responded more rapidly to empathic interviewers. Thus, interviewer empathy has a facilitating effect on interviewee communication. A number of other studies, summarized by Bergin (1967), demonstrated a positive correlation between interviewer empathic understanding and the favorable outcome of psychotherapy.

A third interviewer attribute is referred to in the Truax and Carkhuff (1967) literature as genuineness or self-congruence. A person who relates and communicates in a genuine or self-congruent manner is spontaneous, undefended, and open in manner and content. Although such openness and consistency between external style of communication and internal feeling is ordinarily appreciated in a social encounter, it is frequently lacking in the interview. Traditional schools of psychotherapy emphasize the importance of an ambiguous interviewer manner to ensure the projective character of the interview. An interviewer who may ordinarily speak quickly, with emotional color and an undefended spontaneity, may deliberately suppress his usual mode of communication when conducting an interview, becoming drab, vague, impassive, and evidently cold. S(he) may assume an impassive face, and role play the brevity, the unresponsiveness, and stereotype of a person whose speech is patently incongruent with his/her feelings and associations. The above contrast between spontaneous and incongruent styles in the same person is, to be sure, a little overdrawn. Moreover, the level of genuineness in an exchange with a friend cannot be replicated in an interview, for an interviewer is not free of some role constraints imposed by the interview situation. Therefore, one does not speak about absolute but rather relative genuineness, consistent with the requirements of the interview situation.

Research findings regarding the benign effects of interviewer genuineness on both the immediate communication of the client and on psychological improvement over a therapy sequence should help to persuade the clinician to relax the traditional taboo on open, genuine communication in the therapy interview. One auther (Bierman, 1969) has found that therapist genuineness elicits a reciprocal openness from the patient. Several have found that interviewer genuineness encourages the interviewee to engage in deep self-exploration (Truax & Carkhuff, 1965b; Van Der Veen, 1965). Finally, therapists of improved patients have been rated as significantly higher in genuineness than therapists in nonimproved cases.

The evidence for the positive effects of the three relationship conditions - warmth, empathy, and genuineness - is strengthened when interviews are selected in which all three are high in contrast to others in which the three are low. Thus, patients receiving high levels of the three conditions showed a general gain in psychological functioning, while patients who received low levels showed a loss of psychological functioning (Truax et al., 1962) over therapy. Conversely, patients receiving high levels of the three therapist conditions demonstrated a decrease in anxiety level, while those with low levels, an increase. Results such as these caused a considerable stir in the psychotherapy world. While it had never been assumed that all therapists were equally effective, it was generally believed that even the ineffective ones could do no harm. The above studies and others have shown that therapists who are not able to maintain high levels of relationship behavior may in fact increase the anxiety experienced by their patients and lead to a worsening of their psychological condition. It therefore becomes important that potential therapists be selected for their capacity to achieve high levels of relationship behavior, and indeed be trained in the exercise of such high levels.

The susceptibility of relationship behavior to training will now be examined. Much of the evidence regarding this matter has been provided by Carkhuff and his colleagues (Carkhuff, 1969; Carkhuff et al., 1969), and points to the need to teach the communication of facilitative attitudes directly, through a combination of didactic and experiential approaches. When such a course is followed, interviewers in training demonstrate significant increases in facilitative skills.

A brief summary of the essential ingredients of such a combined approach (Truax & Carkhuff, 1967) will now be given. The essence of the didactic sequence which comes first in the training program is accomplished through reading and extensive listening to taped interviews, with the task of rating taped excerpts on the three facilitative scales. The didactic sequence is followed by a graded sequence of exercises under the supervisory guidance of the instructor and feedback from student peers, ending in a closely supervised psychotherapy experience which is reviewed with peers in a quasi-group therapy situation. The success of this dual approach to the training of students in the use of empathy, warmth, and genuineness was demonstrated with advanced graduate students in clinical and counseling psychology, lay counselors (Carkhuff & Truax, 1965), and undergraduate dormitory counselors (Berenson et al., 1966).

However, one may well question whether students in training programs such as the ones referred to above develop interpersonal skills with some generality of application, or whether they simply master the content of three specific scales and learn to act out or mimic the styles of relationship and communication imbedded in the scale content. The work by Truax, Carkhuff and their colleagues does not provide the kind of evidence that would be needed to choose one of the above two alternatives.

But studies done by others (Bernstein et al., 1974) do produce some proof that students are able to transfer learned interpersonal skills beyond the operational limits of the learning procedures. Thus, understanding (or empathy) could be taught to nurses and medical students and change assessed with instruments other than those used in the training. In addition, medical students demonstrated an increase in empathy in actual interviews conducted pre- and posttraining.

Another group of investigators (Goldstein & Goedhart, 1973) was not content with demonstrating the efficacy of training in empathy and assessing its transfer to areas outside of the training situation. It set out deliberately to train the students (staff nurses, attendants, and activity therapists in a large state mental hospital) to transfer newly acquired empathic abilities from the teaching situation to actual interactions on the ward with patients. The method they used was called Structured Learning, a combined behavioral approach consisting of modeling, role playing, and social reinforcement. Both the ingroup training and its transfer to the ward were significantly successful.

In brief, the evidence, though not free of flaws, is impressive enough to persuade the interviewer in training that interpersonal attitudes and competence in their communication may be altered and improved through training that combines both experiential and didactic components.

The interviewer attributes of relationship considered above have all been components of the affective dimension in a dyadic interaction (warmth, empathy, genuineness). Orthogonal to the affective dimension is another, variously referred to as status, competence, experience, control, dominance, or power. The terms applied to it vary, but they all refer to the hierarchical aspect of relationship. One person is superior to another, above him/her, more experienced or expert, controlling rather than controlled, and more powerful. Dyadic exchanges vary in the extent to which the status dimension is salient in the relationship. At one extreme there is a conversational encounter between two persons, with no role differentiation between them and no status distinction. When two friends engage in an informal conversation there may be stylistic differences in their speech and evan a tendency for one person to assert personal dominance over another. But no status distinction is structured a priori into the encounter. Contrast this exchange, characterized by mutuality in relationship and communication, with a political or criminal interrogation in which one person is cast in the role of interrogator and the other in the role of object of the interrogation. The personal ascendancy of each participant in the interrogation is irrelevant here; certainly it is completely overshadowed by the roles assigned to each member of the dyad.

To be sure, status is not entirely determined by roles that are assigned by some agency external to the interview. There are instances in which such external assignment of status may be nullified by an assertion of power or control by one of the participants. For example, a young man in his early 20s was interviewed by a staff psychologist in an evaluation conference conducted in a large state hospital. The patient had been ordered to the hospital by the court after a rampage, ignited by alcohol and hard drugs, leading him through a succession of barroom brawls, destructive attacks on property and persons within his family, a threat to shoot a person within his home who was not exiting with sufficient speed to suit the patient, and eventually a period of intoxicated coma. However, there was nothing comatose about this young man on the day he was interviewed. Sitting in front of the group, he kept departing from the communicational channels of the interview by engaging others who were present in chatty exchanges. Very much in touch with the interviewer's inquiries, he nevertheless digressed repeatedly from the questions asked into self-enhancing anecdotal accounts of a variety of experiences. Actually, he played the role of a raconteur in a social (possibly drinking) situation. At this, he was adept, witty, and verbally facile. The 50 minutes assigned to the interview passed rapidly and pleasantly. But in the end it was evident that there had been no interview. There had not even been a dialogue. The patient had performed at a locus somewhere in between the roles of stand-up comic and sit-down raconteur. He had asserted his content and power, two aspects of status, subverting the entire interview process.

When the concept of status is applied to the interviewer, it is readily divisible into two components: one pertaining to competence or experience, the other to dominance, power, and social distance. Both clinical and research findings shed a facilitative light on the former and an inhibiting one on the latter. In clinical situations the two components of status are frequently confounded with each other. Thus, an older interviewer with considerable experience may also be perceived by the interviewee as dominant and possibly socially remote. But it has been possible to evaluate the two components separately in research studies. In general, experience in an interviewer has emerged as an attribute that inspires trust in a patient, leads to a positive relationship, and to success in therapy (Bergin, 1967; Fiedler, 1950). Additionally, an interviewee tends to be more strongly attracted to an experienced rather than an inexperienced interviewer (Greenberg, 1969).

For the most part, however, status as experience (the positive or facilitating aspect) and status as power, control, and social distance (the inhibiting aspect of status) are intermingled in research as well as in clinical situations. This confounding of positive and negative aspects has led to conflicting results. High-status interviewers in one investigation (Pope & Siegman, 1972) commanded a high level of productivity from the interviewees, interrupted however by long periods of silence expressive of caution and uncertainty. Contained within one study were both reinforcing (experience) and aversive (control) aspects of status. The exact balance between the reinforcing and aversive effects of this attribute of relationship will depend on the relative weight given to each in a clinical or research situation. When freshman students were interviewed by both sophomore students and older experienced mental health professionals (Pope et al., 1974; Pope et al., 1976), the social distance between interviewers and interviewees was much greater in the latter situation than the former. This contrast accentuated the aversive aspects of status. Thus, the student interviewees related more positively to the student rather than the professional interviewers. They viewed the student interviewers as more sympathetic, accepting, warmer, and more genuine. In addition, they communicated with the student interviewers in a more self-disclosing manner.

These results have implications both for the matching of interviewers and interviewees, and for the practice of interviewing. The goal of the clinical administrator who assigns patients to therapists should be that of minimizing the abrasive aspects of status differences between patients and therapists (differences in age, social class, education) without eliminating the benign aspects (competence and experience of therapist). In general, however, the management of this aspect of interviewee status is difficult to accomplish. In chronically understaffed clinics there is usually not enough slack in available treatment resources to make a matching program possible.

With reference to the practice of interviewing, the major consideration of the interviewer is to modulate those aspects of status behavior that have a negative effect or relationship inhibiting effect on communication. Clearly the interviewer must avoid the blatant manipulation of a patient, an authoritarian exercise of control, and the expression of excessive social distance. The gross verbal communication of status as dominance and control is relatively easy to avoid. Unfortunately, much of the expression of a superior attitude to an interviewee occurs through subtle nonverbal channels. Thus, a posture that is excessively relaxed, with an increase in distance (leaning away) signals the person to whom one is talking that one regards him/her as inferior in status (Mehrabian, 1973). The self-esteem of the interviewee is undoubtedly diminished by such a nonverbal message. The interviewer may learn much about the status attributed to him/her by the interviewee from other nonverbal cues provided by the latter. These cues all communicate an attitude of vigilance regarding the threat posed by the high-status interviewer. They include a hyperattentive sort of eye contact (Exline, 1974), a directness of posture noted in an upward tilt of the head and a direct shoulder orientation, a forward lean, and a generalized body tension. When the interviewer is sensitized to such cues, s(he) will be alerted to moments when his/her relationship behavior is excessively dominant and controlling, and will be prompted to take remedial action to reduce the status differential.

Although those who are engaged in the training enterprise tend to emphasize the susceptibility of positive interviewer relationship behavior to shaping and direction by the trainer, relationship may also be enhanced through the matching of interviewer and interviewee on the basis of personality attributes. A voluminous research effort in this area was triggered by Whitehorn and Betz (1954, 1960) when they first discovered the distinction between two types of therapists, differentially effective with hospitalized schizophrenic patients. The type that was more successful with this kind of patient came to be known as A therapists, and those less successful as B therapists. The only definitive way of distinguishing between Type A and Type B therapists, at the beginning, was through the application of a 23-item occupational interest scale derived from the Strong Vocational Interest Blank. A study that followed in 1962 (McNair et al.) completed the data base for a therapist-patient interactional scheme. These authors obtained results that appeared to contradict the earlier ones; their B therapists were the more successful with their patient sample. However, the patient sample was quite different from the earlier one, consisting of male veterans, all of whom were out-patients judged to be suitable for intensive psychotherapy. By combining the results of the first group of studies, the ingredient of the interactional theory was assembled. Type A therapists were regarded as particularly suitable for schizophrenic and schizoid patients; Type B therapists, for neurotics.

Not all the subsequent studies supported the entire interactional hypothesis, but the evidence has been sufficient to keep the theory viable. The theory appears to have been vindicated by a series of experimental analogue studies (Berzins & Seidman, 1968, 1969) and by clinical investigations (Berzins, Ross, & Friedman, 1972). The evidence includes the relative efficacy of treatment in compatible pairs (Type A therapist with schizoid or schizophrenic patient; Type B therapist with neurotic patient) rather than incompatible pairs. Investigators in this area tend to agree that certain practical measures in therapist-patient matching are indicated. Almost all studies would justify the nonassignment of B therapists to schizoid or schizophrenic patients, and the preferential assignment of A therapists to the same types of patients. There would appear not to be as much risk in the mismatching of A therapists with neurotic patients as in the mismatching of B therapists with schizophrenic patients.

While the data supporting the interaction between the above therapist and patient types accumulated, information that might flesh out an interactional theory was and remains much more sparse. The efforts that were made to develop explanatory links between the therapist and patient types were concerned chiefly with the personality traits, perceptual styles, and interactional behaviors of the therapist types. The studies based on personality traits provided few explanatory clues for the interaction (Berzins, Dove, & Ross, 1972).

Investigations dealing with the perceptual styles of the Type A and B therapists and their articulation with the perceptual styles of the two major patient groups (Silverman, 1967) came a little closer to the mark. Silverman (1967) found that the two types of therapists perceived their physical and social worlds and their patients differently. The A therapists are less disciplined in their perceptual styles, less subject to the directional control of goals, and more vulnerable to chance inputs from a changing environment than B therapists. Internally, they are more responsive to hunches and intuitions. In all these respects, there is a considerable compatibility between the perceptual style of the A therapist and that of the schizoid type of patient. B's perceptions are, by contrast, closer to those of the neurotic patient, for his/her cognitive and perceptual activity is attuned to external reality and to the logic of problem solving. Silverman (1967) concludes that As and schizoid patients, Bs and neurotics, share more perceptual and cognitive experience and hence communicate more easily with each other than would the same therapists matched with the other types of patients.

Finally, some interactional behavior contrasts between the two therapist types provide an additional rationale for the A-B interactional hypothesis. To begin with, the two therapist types seem to have more to say to their patient counterparts than to patients with whom they have been mismatched (Berzins & Seidman, 1968, 1969). This finding was later augmented by the results of another study (Seidman, 1971) in which A therapists emerged as those with greater approach behavior (more time spent talking to the patient, greater respect or positive regard for the patient, greater empathy, greater turning toward the patient rather than avoidance under conditions of stress) than B therapists. Tentatively, the author postulated that approaching A therapists are better able to cope with the withdrawal of schizophrenics, and more avoidant B therapists with verbally productive neurotics. Another author (Segal, 1970) emphasized the greater activity of A therapists, and thus their tendency to play a more leading role and to provide more structure. These are interactional patterns that are particularly helpful to schizophrenic or schizoid patients whose confusion and disorganization are accentuated by low therapist activity and ambiguity. On the other hand, B therapists, less active, less leading and structuring, may be particularly facilitative with better organized and more clearly motivated neurotic patients.

None of the above is meant to imply that the A-B therapist typology is definitively established and that therapist-patient matching may be securely based on the extant clinical and research studies. But the experience of developing the A-B typology and the associated interactional hypothesis, and the paths that have been followed in studying a matching scheme based on personality attributes, have resulted in a sense of direction and of competence in the further exploration of the enhancement of relationship through personality matching.

The discussion of interviewer attributes in relationship cannot be complete without some reference to the special problems an interviewer experiences in relating to and communicating with patients who have anxieties and conflicts that arouse the interviewer's own. Such problems are considered to be manifestations of countertransference in the psychoanalytic literature. Thus, therapists who are particularly conflicted and anxious about the experience of hostility will encounter difficulty in coping with hostility expressed by patients (Bandura et al., 1960). Their reactions tend to be avoidant of the patient's expressions of hostility with the result that such expressions are discouraged. Another study (Cutler, 1958) demonstrated the retrospective distortion of events that had occurred in an interview because of the specific areas of conflict experienced by the interviewer. In notes dictated postinterview, the interviewer would tend to underreport the occurrence of communications related to traits that s(he) avoids in himself/herself and to overreport the occurrence of communications related to traits that s(he) overestimates in himself/herself. Moreover, the therapist responded to patient communication that touched on areas of personal conflict in an ego-oriented (defensive) way rather than task-oriented (therapeutically more useful) manner. In brief, the last two studies deal not with matching but with internal therapist conflicts and how they might interfere with the conduct of the interview. These are problems with which the interviewer must learn to cope. Insight and the capacity to cope with the disrupting effects of such conflicts are acquired best by the interviewer through a personal therapy experience.

REFERENCES

Adorno, T.W., Frenkel-Brunswik, E., Levinson, D., & Sanford, R.N. The authoritarian personality. New York: Harper and Row, 1950.

Alexik, M., & Carkhuff, R.R. The effects of the manipulation of client depth of self-exploration upon high and low functioning clients. Journal of Clinical Psychology, 1967, 23, 212-215.

Allen, B.V., Wiens, A.N., Whitman, M., & Saslow, G. Effects of warm-cold set on interviewee speech. Journal of Consulting Psychology, 1965, 29, 480-482.

Baldwin, T., & Lee, J. Evaluation of programmed instruction in human relations. American Psychologist, 1965, 20, 489.

Bandura, A.   Psychotherapist's anxiety level, self-insight, and psychotherapeutic competence.   Journal of Abnormal and Social Psychology, 1956, 52,
333-337.

Bandura, A., Lipsher, D.H., & Miller, P.E.   Psychotherapists' approach-
avoidance reactions to patients' expressions of hostility.   Journal of
Consulting Psychology, 1960, 24, 1-8.

Barrett-Lennard, G.T.   Dimensions of therapist response as causal factors in
therapeutic change.   Psychological Monograph, 1962, 76 (43)(Whole
Number 562).

Berenson, B.F., Carkhuff, R.R., & Myrus, P.   The interpersonal functions and
training of college students.   Journal of Counseling Psychology, 1966, 13,
4.

Bergin, A.E.   Some implications of psychotherapy research for therapeutic
practice.   International Journal of Psychiatry, 1967, 3, 136-149.

Bergin, A.E., & Jasper, L.G.   Correlates of empathy in psychotherapy: A
replication.   Journal of Abnormal Psychology, 1969, 74, 477-481.

Bergin, A.E., & Solomon, S.   Personality and performance correlates of
empathic understanding in psychotherapy.   Paper read at American
Psychological Association, Philadelphia, 1963.

Bernstein, L., Bernstein, R.S., & Dana, R.H.   Interviewing: A guide for health
professionals.   New York: Appleton-Century-Crofts, 1974.

Berzins, J.I., Dove, J.L., & Ross, W.F.   Cross validational studies of the
personality correlates of the A-B therapist "type" distinction among
professionals and nonprofessionals.   Journal of Consulting and Clinical
Psychology, 1972, 39, 388-395.

Berzins, J.I., Ross, W.F., & Cohen, D.I.   Relation of the A-B distinction and
trust-distrust sets to addict patients' self-disclosure in brief interviews.
Journal of Consulting and Clinical Psychology, 1970, 34, 289-296.

Berzins, J.I., Ross, W.F., & Friedman, W.H.   A-B therapist distinction, patient
diagnosis, and outcome of brief psychotherapy in a college clinic.   Journal
of Consulting and Clinical Psychology, 1972, 38, 231-237.

Berzins, J.I., & Seidman, E.   Subjective reactions of A and B quasi-therapists
to schizoid and neurotic communications: A replication and extension.
Journal of Consulting and Clinical Psychology, 1968, 32, 342-347.

Berzins, J.I., & Seidman, E.   Differential therapeutic responding of A and B
quasi-therapists to schizoid and neurotic communications.   Journal of
Consulting and Clinical Psychology, 1969, 33, 279-286.

Betz, B.J.   How do personal attitudes and interests influence psychotherapeutic effectiveness?   In Proceedings of the Sixth Annual Psychiatric
Institute, 1958, 14-28, Princeton, New Jersey, Neuropsychiatric Institute.

Betz, B.J., & Whitehorn, J.C. The relationship of a therapist to the outcome of therapy in schizophrenia. Psychiatric Research Reports, 1956, 5, 89-140.

Bierman, R. Dimensions of interpersonal facilitation in psychotherapy and child development. Psychological Bulletin, 1969, 72, 338-352.

Binder, A., McConnell, D., & Sjoholm, N.A. Verbal conditioning as a function of experimental characteristics. Journal of Abnormal and Social Psychology, 1957, 55, 309-314.

Blaine, G.V., & McArthur, C.C. What happened in therapy as seen by the patient and his psychiatrist. Journal of Nervous and Mental Disease, 1958, 127, 344-350.

Bordin, E.S. Psychological counseling. New York: Appleton-Century-Crofts, 1968.

Borgatta, E.F., Cottrell, L.S., Jr., & Mann, J.M. The spectrum of individual interaction characteristics: An interdimensional analysis. Psychological Reports, 1958, 4, 279-319.

Carkhuff, R.P. Helping and human relations. Vol. I. New York: Holt, Rinehart and Winston, 1969.

Carkhuff, R.R., & Alexik, M. Effect of client depth of self-exploration upon high and low functioning counselors. Journal of Counseling Psychology, 1967, 14, 350-355.

Carkhuff, R.R., Collingwood, T., & Renz, L. The prediction of didactic training in discrimination. Journal of Clinical Psychology, 1969, 25, 460-461.

Carkhuff, R.R., Kratochvil, D., & Friel, T. The effects of professional training: The communication and discrimination of facilitative conditions. Journal of Counseling Psychology, 1968, 15, 68-74.

Carkhuff, R.R., & Truax, C.B. Training and counseling in psychotherapy: An evaluation of an integrated, didactic and experiential approach. Journal of Counseling Psychology, 1965, 29, 333-336.

Carter, L.F. Evaluating the performance of individuals as members of small groups. Personnel Psychology, 1954, 7, 477-484.

Cartwright, R.D., & Lerner, B. Empathy, need to change, and improvement in psychotherapy. Journal of Consulting Psychology, 1963, 27, 138-144.

Chartier, G.M., & Weiss, L. A-B therapists and clinical perception: Support for a "super A" hypothesis. Journal of Consulting and Clinical Psychology, 1974, 42, 312.

Cutler, R.L. Counter-transference effects of psychotherapy. Journal of Consulting Psychology, 1958, 22, 349-356.

Dittes, J.E. Galvanic skin response as a measure of patient's reaction to therapist's permissiveness. Journal of Abnormal and Social Psychology, 1957, 55, 295-303.

Exline, R.V. Visual interaction: The glances of power and preference. In S. Weitz (Ed.), Nonverbal communication. New York: Oxford University Press, 1974.

Fenlason, A.F. Essentials in interviewing. New York: Harper & Row, 1962.

Fiedler, F.E. A comparison of therapeutic relationships in psychoanalytic, non-directive and Adlerian therapy. Journal of Consulting Psychology, 1950, 14, 436-445.

Foa, U., Convergences in the analysis of the structure of interpersonal behavior. Psychological Review, 1961, 5, 341-353.

Frank, J.D. Persuasion and healing. Baltimore: The Johns Hopkins Press, 1961.

Freedman, M., Leary, T., Ossorio, A., & Coffey, H. The interpersonal dimensions of personality. Journal of Personality, 1951, 20, 143-162.

Garfield, S., & Bergin, A.E. Therapeutic conditions and outcome. Journal of Abnormal Psychology, 1971, 77, 108-114.

Gill, M., Newman, R., & Redlich, S.C. The initial interview in psychiatric practice. New York: International Universities Press, 1954.

Goldstein, A.P. Psychotherapeutic attraction. New York: Pergamon Press, 1971.

Goldstein, A.P., & Goedhart, A. The use of structured learning for empathy enhancement in paraprofessional psychotherapist training. Journal of Community Psychology, 1973, 1, 168-173.

Greenberg, R.P. Effects of pre-session information on perception of the therapist and receptivity to influence in a psychotherapy analogue. Journal of Consulting and Clinical Psychology, 1969, 33, 425-429.

Greenberg, R.P., Goldstein, A.P., & Parry, M.A. The influence of referral information upon patient perception in a psychotherapy analogue. Journal of Nervous and Mental Disease, 1970, 150, 31-36.

Hargrove, D.S. Verbal interaction analysis of empathic and nonempathic responses of therapists. Journal of Consulting and Clinical Psychology, 1974, 42, 305.

Hekmat, H., Khajavi, F., & Mehryar, A.H. Some personality correlates of empathy. Journal of Consulting and Clinical Psychology, 1975, 43, 89.

Heller, K., Davis, J.D., & Myers, R.A. The effects of interviewer's style in a standardized interview. Journal of Consulting Psychology, 1966, 30, 501-508.

Heller, K., Silver, R., Bailey, M., & Dudgeon, T. The interview reactions of patients and students to within interview changes in interviewer style. Unpublished research, 1968.

Hiler, E.W. An analysis of patient-therapist compatibility. Journal of Consulting Psychology, 1958, 22, 341-347.

Ivey, A.E., & Moreland, J.R. Microcounseling. Springfield, Ill.: Thomas, 1971.

Lorr, M., & McNair, D.M. Methods relating to therapeutic outcome. In L.A. Gottschalk & A.H. Auerbach (Eds.), Methods of research and psychotherapy. 1967. Pp. 573-594.

Maccoby, E.E., & Maccoby, M. The interview: a tool of social science. In G. Lindzey (Ed.), Handbook of social psychology. Reading, Mass.: Addison Wesley, 1954. Pp. 449-487.

Matarazzo, R.G. Research on the teaching and learning of psychotherapeutic skills. In A. Bergin & S. Garfield, Handbook of Psychotherapy and Behavior Change. New York: Wiley, 1971. Pp. 895-924.

McNair, D.M., Callahan, M., & Lorr, M. Therapist "type" and patient response to psychotherapy. Journal of Consulting Psychology, 1962, 26, 425-429.

Mehrabian, A. Nonverbal communication. Chicago: Aldine/Atherton, 1972.

Mehrabian, A. Inference of attitude from the posture, orientation and distance of a communicator. In M. Argyle (Ed.), Social encounter. Chicago: Aldine, 1973.

Melloh, R.A. Accurate empathy and counselor effectiveness. Unpublished doctoral dissertation, University of Florida, 1964.

Morris, R.J., & Suckerman, K.R. The importance of the therapeutic relationship in systematic desensitization. Journal of Consulting and Clinical Psychology, 1974, 42, 148.

Morris, R.J., & Suckerman, K.R. Therapist warmth as a factor in automated systematic desensitization. In G.R. Patterson (Ed.), Behavior change, 1974. Chicago: Aldine, 1975.

Pepitone, A., & Wallace, W. Experimental studies on the dynamics of hostility. Paper read at Pennsylvania Psychological Association meeting, 1955.

Pierce, W.D., & Mosher, D.L. Perceived empathy, interviewer behavior and interviewee anxiety. Journal of Consulting Psychology, 1967, 31, 101.

Pope, B., Nudler, S., Norden, J.S., & McGee, J.P. Changes in nonprofessional (novice) interviewers over a 3 year training period. Journal of Consulting and Clinical Psychology, 1976, 44, 819-825.

Pope, B., Nudler, S., VonKorff, M.R., & McGee, J.P. The experienced professional interviewer versus the complete novice. Journal of Consulting and Clinical Psychology, 1974, 42, 680-690.

Pope, B., & Siegman, A.W. The verbal interaction in the initial interview. Unpublished manuscript. University of Maryland, 1967.

Pope, B., & Siegman, A.W. Interviewer warmth in relation to interviewee verbal behavior. Journal of Consulting and Clinical Psychology, 1968, 32, 588-595.

Pope, B., & Siegman, A.W. Relationship and verbal behavior in the initial interview. In A.W. Siegman & B. Pope (Eds.), Studies in dyadic communication. New York: Pergamon Press, 1972.

Raush, H.L., & Bordin, E.S. Warmth in personality development and in psychotherapy. Psychiatry, 1957, 20, 351-363.

Reece, M.M., & Whitman, R.N. Expressive movements, warmth, and verbal reinforcement. Journal of Abnormal and Social Psychology, 1962, 64, 234-236.

Rogers, C.R. The characteristics of a helping relationship. In M.R. Stein (Ed.), Contemporary psychotherapies. New York: The Free Press of Glencoe, 1961.

Rogers, C.R., Gendlin, E.T., Kiesler, D.V., & Truax, C.B. The therapeutic relationship and its impact: A study of psychotherapy with schizophrenics. Madison: University of Wisconsin Press, 1967.

Rosenfeld, H.M. Non-verbal reciprocation of approval: An experimental analysis. In M. Argyle (Ed.), Social encounters. Chicago: Aldine, 1973.

Rosenthal, R. On the social psychology of the psychological experiment: The experimenter's hypothesis as unintended determinant of experimental results. American Scientist, 1963, 51, 268-282.

Sarason, I.G., & Winkel, R. Individual differences among subjects and experimenters and subjects' self descriptions. Journal of Personality and Social Psychology, 1966, 3, 448-457.

Schaefer, E.S. A circumplex model for maternal behavior. Journal of Abnormal and Social Psychology, 1959, 59, 226-235.

Segal, B. A-B distinction and therapeutic interaction. Journal of Consulting and Clinical Psychology, 1970, 34, 442-446.

Seidman, E. A and B subject-therapists' responses to videotaped schizoid and neurotic prototypes. Journal of Consulting and Clinical Psychology, 1971, 37, 201-208.

Silverman, J. Personality traits and perceptual studies of schizophrenic patients. Journal of Nervous and Mental Disorders, 1967, 145, 5-17.

Snyder, W.U. The psychotherapy relationship, New York: Macmillan, 1961.

Staples, F.R., & Sloan, R.B. Truax factors, speech characteristics, and therapeutic outcome. Journal of Nervous and Mental Disease, 1976, 163, 135-140.

Strupp, H.H. The psychotherapist's contribution to the treatment process. Behavioral Science, 1958, 3, 34-67.

Strupp, H.H. Psychotherapists in action. New York: Grune & Stratton, 1961.

Strupp, H.H., & Wallach, M.S. A further study of psychiatrists' responses in quasi-therapy situations. Behavioral Science, 1965, 10, 113-134.

Strupp, H.H., Wallach, M.S., & Wogan, M. Psychotherapy experience in retrospect: Questionnaire survey of former patients and their therapists. Psychological Monograph, 1964, 78 (XI. 588).

Truax, C.B. An approach to unraveling the patient-therapist interaction, presented at a Symposium: "The Empirical Status of Future Psychotherapy." American Psychological Association Convention, St. Louis, 1962.

Truax, C.B. Length of therapist response, accurate empathy, and patient improvement. Journal of Clinical Psychology, 1970, 26, 539-541.

Truax, C.B., & Carkhuff, R.R. The experimental manipulation of therapeutic conditions. Journal of Consulting Psychology, 1965a, 29, 119-124.

Truax, C.B., & Carkhuff, R.R. Client and therapist transparency in the psychotherapeutic encounter. Journal of Counseling Psychology, 1965b, 12, 3-9.

Truax, C.B., & Carkhuff, R.R. Toward effective counseling and psychotherapy. Chicago: Aldine, 1967.

Truax, C.B., Liccione, J., & Rosenberg, M. Psychological test evaluations of personality change in high conditions therapy, low conditions therapy and control patients. Brief Research Reports, Wisconsin Psychiatric Institute, University of Wisconsin, 1962, 10.

Truax, C.B. Silber, L.D., & Wargo, D.G. Training and change in psychotherapeutic skills. Unpublished manuscript, University of Arkansas, 1966.

Truax, C.B., Wargo, D.G., Frank, J.D., Imber, S.D., Battle, C.C., Hoehn-Sarik, R., Nash, E.H., & Stone, A.R. Therapist empathy, genuineness and warmth and patient-therapeutic outcome. Journal of Consulting Psychology, 1966, 30, 395-401.

Van Der Veen, F. Effects of the therapist and the patient on each other's therapeutic behavior. Journal of Consulting Psychology, 1965, 29, 19-26.

Van Der Veen, F. Basic elements in the process of psychotherapy: Research study. Journal of Consulting Psychology, 1967, 31, 295-303.

Welkowitz, J., & Kue, M. Interrelationships among warmth, genuineness, empathy, and temporal speech patterns in interpersonal interaction. Journal of Consulting and Clinical Psychology, 1973, 41, 472-473.

Wenegrat, A. A factor analytic study of the Truax Accurate Empathy Scale. Psychotherapy: Theory, Research and Practice, 1974, 11, 48-51.

Whitehorn, J.C., & Betz, B.J. A study of psychotherapeutic relationships between physicians and schizophrenic patients. American Journal of Psychiatry, 1954, 111, 321-331.

Whitehorn, J.C., & Betz, B.J. Further studies of the doctor as a crucial variable on the outcome of treatment with schizophrenic patients. American Journal of Psychiatry, 1960, 117, 215-223.

9 Interviewee Attributes in Relationship

The present chapter deals with the impact on the interview of certain interviewee attributes. For example, in the fictional case of Mr. A (Chapter 7), there were demographic, attitudinal, and possibly behavioral attributes that had a bearing on his response to the interview with the medical student. Coming from a lower class group, Mr. A's entire training and value system made it extremely difficult for him both to comprehend and to accept the possibility that there might be some relationship between the worries that he was experiencing and the strain in his back. So he approached the interview with a high degree of skepticism regarding the possibility of any relief coming to him from a conversation with the psychiatrist. Added to this was a sensitivity about the kind of criticism, or possibly disparagement, that might be directed toward him by members of his family and his friends for seeking psychiatric help. Under these circumstances, he found it difficult to speak freely. Moreover, there were certain topics about which he found it particularly difficult to speak at all. Unaccustomed to introspect about subjective emotional experiences, he responded to questions regarding such matters with long periods of silence interspersed with denials that he had ever been seriously depressed or anxious. He was baffled by the style of questioning used by the medical student. Thus, he was not able to reply to ambiguous questions lacking a specific focus such as, "Just tell me what comes to mind." Both with reference to topic and with reference to question format, Mr. A preferred a tangible to an ambiguous approach. If he had been asked whether there had been any troubles or worries in his recent life, he would have been able to tell the interviewer about the misfortunes of his two sons. Instead the interviewer wondered if he had been anxious. If the therapist had inquired about concrete events on the job and in his family, Mr. A would have been able to speak at length. But the interviewer had asked him to say whatever he could about these matters. One other aspect of the interview kept Mr. A from speaking freely. In all his previous contacts with doctors his role had been a passive one, responding only when the doctor asked him definite questions. In this instance the doctor (actually a medical student) assumed an ambiguous role, leaving most of the initiative to Mr. A.

393

It was up to Mr. A to choose the topics he wished to talk about. Expecting specific questions from a medical person, he received only vague invitations to talk about himself. The result was a halting, inhibited series of responses from Mr. A, with long periods of silence. He would start to speak but would bog down in uncertainty, sometimes pausing silently, and at other times filling his silences with hesitant sounds. Although Mr. A has no difficulty in communicating with his fellow workers on the job and with his relatives at home, he found that words were not flowing easily during the interview. He would start to say one thing and then hesitate in the midst of the statement, starting over again several times, before completing it. Often he would repeat a word as he became confused about what he wished to say. A similar confusion would cause him to leave certain words half spoken and sentences half completed. Occasionally, meaningless sounds would intrude into the flow of his speech. All these disruptions in his speech were associated with acute discomfort, embarrassment, and a feeling that he wished the interview were over and that he could leave.

These "clinical" notes are of course fictional, but they indicate the possible effect on interview behavior of an interviewee's expectations, values, attitudes, and habitual patterns of communication with others. To emphasize the effect of such interviewee attributes on the interview exchange it might be useful to review the contrasting picture presented by Mrs. B (Chapter 7).

Her training and life experience had made her quite adept at introspective analysis whenever some difficulty presented itself. Thus, she had become skilled at relating internal experiences to external stress and, in fact, was quite aware of the delicate balance that often obtained between the two. She had no difficulty in recognizing that she was depressed and indeed in relating her depression both to changes in her middle years within herself and to disappointing experience with her sons. Nor did her view of personality and human behavior interfere with an acceptance of the possibility that her back pain might be related to psychological stresses in her life. She had none of Mr. A's sensitivity about possible disparagement from friends and relations. She had spent her adult years in a culture that supported a person in his quest for relief and resolution of conflict in life through psychotherapy. Mr. A's reservations about turning to psychotherapy for help did not occur to her. Moreover, the psychotherapeutic milieu was a familiar one to her. As she waited in the doctor's office, she felt completely comfortable in talking to another woman, younger than herself but similarly waiting, and, as it turned out in their conversation, from the same part of the city in which Mrs. B lived.

The language the psychiatrist used was totally familiar to her. When he focused on her depression and tension, she was ready for him and communicated at great length about her recent difficulties. When he invited her to speak, however ambiguously his questions were phrased, she was not at a loss to respond because she had already introspected considerably about the matters on which he focused. Although she paused occasionally in order to collect her thoughts, she was never baffled or inhibited by the kind of inquiry that the doctor carried out. Her talk flowed smoothly without the kind of massive disruption manifested by Mr. A. To be sure, whenever a reminiscence or a reflection was painful, her speech would become a little uneven and occasionally accelerated a bit. But she was not discomfitted by any significant disruption of communication. In addition, she had none of the restrictions that Mr. A experienced when speaking with the doctor. She made a clear distinction between a medical doctor and a psychiatrist and experienced much less passivity, much more assertiveness, in the presence of the doctor than Mr. A did. It will be remembered that for her there was not the status differential with the doctor that characterized Mr. A's relationship with his. Belonging to the middle class herself, she lived in an area populated by professional people, including doctors and particularly a number of psychiatrists. Thus, at times, she felt as though she were speaking to an equal, a friend.

In the case of Mr. C the relevant factors influencing the course of the interview were not personal so much as situational. Thus, Mr. C approached the interview from a point of great social distance. The interviewer was a representative of state power in a country in which Mr. C was an alien as yet. There was also a considerable dominance-submission element in the anticipated relationship because Mr. C expected an interrogation in which he would either have to disclose information that he had previously hidden or cope with the interrogator through further guilt-inducing denials. The events that happened after he entered the interview room can only be understood within the situational context in which they unfolded. Thus, the interviewer's evident warmth and friendliness presented Mr. C with a quick reversal of his punitive interrogator expectations, throwing him off balance and prompting him to lower his defensive guards completely. It is possible, of course, that Mr. C's quick reaction to the situation, so dramatically at variance with what he expected, articulates with certain personality attributes that he may have. But this matter is not elaborated in the note. At any rate, very early in the interview there was another transient, quick reversal, when the interviewer did confront Mr. C with his previous misinformation. For a fleeting moment, the interviewer then did appear to behave in a manner that was congruent with Mr. C's anticipations of a fear-inspiring inquisitor. Then again, the confrontation subsided and the interviewer was once again friendly. Mr. C's flow of communication, both self-abasing and self-disclosing, is meaningful only if we understand the interviewer status-related anticipations with which Mr. C approached the interview.

In brief, then, the interviewee's response to the interview and his/her contribution to the relationship can be understood only if one takes account of a spectrum of interviewee attributes, including the anticipations with which s(he) approached the interview (already discussed in Chapter 7), his/her personal attributes, and a number of others that are sometimes designated as demographic, including such matters as ethnic origin and social class.

DIAGNOSTICALLY DEFINED ATTRIBUTES
OF THE INTERVIEWEES

Since the major point of reference in this book is the mental health interview, a consideration of certain clinically defined attributes of the interviewee is in order, such as patient diagnosis and personality type. In this regard, consider the contrasting interview behavior of the following two patients.

The first was a young lady, aged 20, who had been in a psychiatric hospital for two and a half years. About a year before admission, she had lost interest in school, withdrawn from family relationships and had become considerably involved in drugs and in a drug subculture. The event that precipitated hospitalization was a physical encounter with her mother after the patient had stayed out all night and was criticized by her mother when she returned home. The following excerpts are taken from an interview with a staff psychiatrist several months after admission. During the first few months in the hospital, her behavior was overtly psychotic, characterized by disrobing, masturbating openly, and behaving in other inappropriate ways. Periodically, confusion would overtake her, and at such times she was likely to become quite violent, attacking some of her fellow patients and provoking attacks on herself. Eventually, confusion lifted, psychotic misidentification of others dissipated, violence ceased, and behavior had become sufficiently well organized to prompt the staff to evaluate the patient's readiness to leave the hospital.

The excerpts that follow were taken from an interview that had as its objective an assessment of the patient's current clinical status. The interview will show that the patient still found it difficult to communicate without utilizing words that were a little hard to understand because they were condensed, with special meaning to herself, not readily shared with others. There were long periods of silence and in general the interviewer and the interviewee were not always speaking on the same wavelengths. Yet the patient was obviously struggling at this point to make herself understood and to comply with the communicational expectations of the interviewer. Parts of the interview follow:

ER: The first thing I'd like you to do is tell me a little bit about how long you've been in the hospital.

EE: Oh I've been here seven months.

ER: Seven months - does it feel like a long time?

EE: A little bit when I think about being here.

ER: Yeh.

EE: When I think of the objects around me.

ER: Ahuh

EE: The buildings and structure.

ER: And that gives you the feeling of time, huh?

EE: Ahuh, when I think about it.

ER: Yeh.

EE: And I have to think about where I'm at - then I realize how long I've been here - a long time.

ER: Ahuh and have you been on the same ward all that time?

EE: Yes.

ER: (Cough) How have you found it here?

EE: Uh (pause) complicated.

ER: Ahuh.

EE: (Pause)

ER: I guess by that you mean it's not easy to get a simple answer to that question - are there many things?

EE: Yes.

ER: Yeh well could you tell me some of them?

EE: Oh things that are unthinkable uh (pause) w- things you don't normally see in society.

ER: Ahuh. Okay,

EE: Huh (Pause)

ER: So the hospital's kind of different?

EE: Ahuh, I'd say so.

ER: Yeh could you kind of give me a few examples to illustrate that?

EE: Disagreements with other patients.

ER: Ahuh.

EE: (Pause)

ER: Disagreement with other patients have been part of your being here - you've had such disagreements huh?

EE: To a certain extent.

ER: Yeh, have they been more than you might find outside of the hospital - than you might experience outside?

EE: Yes (Pause).

ER: Well okay, you you say you've been here about seven months, huh?

EE: Seven.

ER: Yeh, do you remember when you came?

EE: November, 1968.

ER: Ahuh, you remember it quite precisely - do you remember the day you came?

EE: It was a few weeks before my birthday - right before I turned nineteen.

ER: Yeh, and why did you have to come - what problems brought you
       here?

EE: I had to be readjusted to society.

ER: You needed to be readjusted - what had, what had happened in
       your life that required this?

EE: Lot - a lot of misunderstanding and confusion and (Pause) uh
       different uh exposures to different types of people.

ER: Ahuh.

EE: And uh just being out someplace or being out in situations that I
       couldn't handle.

ER: Ahuh, you were living at home at this time, were you?

EE: Well, not really.

ER: No?

EE: No.

ER: Where were you?

EE: I was in jail.

ER: Oh, uh something happened?

EE: Just a feud.

ER: With whom - your folks?

EE: Ahuh.

ER: Parents?

EE: Parents.

ER: Ahuh, well I don't know, you know, whether uh all this comes
       through to you clearly at this time - you know, whether you
       remember it all clearly - but what was this feud all about - can
       you recall?

EE: Uh, conforming with society.

ER: Your, your parents wanted you to conform with society - is that
       it?

EE: Ahuh.

ER: And (Cough) I gather from that they didn't feel that you were
       conforming huh - they felt that you were being a nonconfor-
       mist?

EE: Well, I think it was my friends - that was about it.

ER: Ahuh, (Cough) your friends?

EE: Ahuh.

ER: Were there any other things that they took exception to?

EE: Maybe my grades in school.

ER: Oh yeh, had there been some change in these grades?

EE: Well (Pause) uh there there wasn't, there wasn't any any any motivation on my part and I was just getting confused and upset at myself and I was uh had a mental breakdown I guess.

ER: Is that what you would call it or is that what somebody else called it?

EE: Well I I'd say so for myself since I had to go through it.

ER: Yeh, do you remember what it was like - this mental breakdown?

EE: The same thing I'm going through right now in in in - well at in this hospital I've experienced the same thing as far as mental mental health goes and

ER: Ahuh

EE: I I guess I- I'm getting the right treatment - it's just disagreeing - it's like, I just, it's like disagreements are too much.

ER: Well, whom do you have the disagreements with here -

EE: It's just with other patients.

ER: Ahuh (Pause) well uh, let's go back to this idea of a mental breakdown - you know that's a term and I guess it might refer to different experiences for people - what was it for you -what did you experience when you broke down?

EE: Confusion.

ER: Ahuh, confusion - do you mean in ideas?

EE: Uh, I'd say so yes.

ER: And what else?

EE: Uh (Pause) well I just did whatever I wanted to do and having no one to talk to while I was uh feeling all these different ch-changes and ideas.

ER: Ahuh.

EE: That was going on

ER: Ahuh.

EE: With me - with myself.

ER: So it was sort of being by yourself a lot.

EE: Yeh.

ER: Being by yourself a lot with a lot of ideas going through your head huh?

EE: Ahuh.

ER: That was hard.

EE: I'd say so, yes.

ER: Was it scary?

EE: Well, I didn't think too much about anything, I was just wondering about objects and everything was like it was there but I I didn't recognize anything - it was - I didn't recognize anything.

ER: Did it seem strange to you?

EE: I felt that I'd been in this place a long time and anything that happens there is just - I I didn't - I don't react to it any more.

ER: Ahuh, you mean here?

EE: Yeh, in the hospital and

ER: Yeh so these things are familiar to you now - the objects here?

EE: Yes.

ER: But when you think of objects on the outside they seem different.

EE: Well th- that's more or less unbelievable that the outside's th- th- you know going-going into town in the city and going to the right places and

ER: Ahuh.

EE: It's just - well, what I said - I I enjoy it.

ER: You enjoy it and you called it unbelievable - and you mean pleasant.

EE: Well, I'd say -uh-well.

ER: What ahuh uh do you have periods - you use the word confusion a lot there must have been some confused periods in the hospital here too huh?

EE: Well there are times when I begin to wonder about this place.

ER: Yeh, what did you wonder?

EE: Well I I'd wonder uh what was really uh going on with other people.

ER: Yeh.

EE: I I knew it was going on with myself.

ER: Yeh.

EE: But it was just the other people - the patients really - I mean the other uh uh uh people in there on in there on category - one of the categories every-every-a lot of mass of people in one category.

ER: Ahuh.

EE: And I'd be kind of stuck there.

ER: Do you feel separate from them?

EE: Yeh like in this dormitory I was in I was just sort of - nowhere to go.

ER: Yeh.

EE: So I just sort of more or less stuck in the dormitory.

ER: Yeh, are you saying that uh you would wonder about the other patients in the dormitory?

EE: Well see, they-they- I get the notion that things w- things were going terrible there - then I'd say-were-I'd say things were going all right - well, they'd come and go like that - you know, just sort of sporadic.

ER: Ahuh yeh.

EE: Well then I I you know- I just learned to live with it and and it kept on getting out of hand till I couldn't take it.

ER: Yeh that's really not very much fun is it - when it gets out of hand.

EE: Yeh.

ER: So when it would get out of hand what would the feeling be like - would you get scared of the people around you?

EE: Scared, yeh.

ER: Would you have some feeling that they-that they-uh-uh-wanted to be harmful to you?

EE: Uh yeh.

ER: And that would come and then it would go away?

EE: Yeh, til it just, til everything just broke loose.

ER: How do you mean that - just broke loose?

EE: Well it would be (pause) it it would be like uh (pause) violence.

ER: • Yeh yeh there would be violence - would the violence be your feeling of violence - I mean would you become violent or would they become violent or was it hard to tell which was which?

EE: Both.

ER: Both huh?

EE: Well, it depended on what ward I was on.

ER: Yeh, and so there would be an outburst - things would break loose and then what would happen - would they settle down after that?

EE: Uh (Pause) yeh - well, seclusion.

ER: Yeh.

EE: Something like that - I don't know.

ER: Yeh, you would find yourself in seclusion for a while, huh?

EE: Yeh.

ER: And would that be of any help to you

EE: Well it helps a lot I guess - I - it kept me from doing it again - that's the reason that seclusion's there.

ER: Would you have some ideas at that time?

EE: Well (pause) well I I I think-uh well-what-what you know - what am I going to do?

ER: Ahuh.

EE: While - while I'm in in seclusion.

ER: Ahuh.

EE: And uh I'd just I would just uh uh (pause) I'd just wonder.

ER: You'd wonder (cough)?

EE: I'd wonder what was going on with the staff.

ER: Yeh and would you have some ideas about what might be going with the staff?

EE: Yeh I'd wonder whose side they were on.

ER: Yeh like your side or the other guy's wh- when you had this explosion.

EE: Ahuh yeh.

ER: So you would wonder and I guess that would be a pretty uncertain time huh - like you weren't awfully sure?

EE: Yeh I wouldn't know uh I wouldn't know really what was going on.

The patient in the preceding interview excerpt was diagnosed as a chronic undifferentiated schizophrenic. While she was not grossly psychotic in the interview, the highly individual, autistic cast to some of the things she said was clearly discernible. Some of her remarks were difficult to understand because the associative context necessary for grasping their meaning had not been provided by the patient. Thus, when asked whether seven months in the hospital felt like a long time, she remarked that it did when she thought of the objects around her. As it turned out she appeared to be referring to her current feeling of familiarity with the buildings and grounds of the hospital. But the interviewer needed to infer this; the patient did not state it. At other times, she appeared to be using words that were excessively abstract for the thought that she was communicating. Thus, when asked how she had found being in the hospital she spoke about experiencing things that one does not normally see in society. The answer was obscure and communicated little to the interviewer until the patient explained that she was referring to disagreements with other patients. As the interview proceeded, it became evident that she had often had explosive encounters with others. Thus, the use of the word "society" was only superficially abstract; in actuality it had a highly personal meaning for this particular patient which the interviewer could not infer without further inquiry. This very personal use of conceptual terms recurs. Instead of simply saying that she was in repeated conflict with her parents before coming into the hospital because of rebellious, nonconforming behavior, she spoke obliquely about a problem with "conforming with society." In brief, one of the characteristics of a chronic schizophrenic's mode of communicating in an interview is the highly personal, obscure character of her language. The interviewer needs to inquire persistently, and to be attuned to the interviewee's sometimes subtle and sometimes gross deviations from the normative use of language. Not surprisingly, there were moments in the interview when the interviewer and the interviewee were not with one another, but were talking at cross purposes.

An interesting example of the obscure character of some of the schizophrenic's language is provided by Beier (1966) when he quotes a patient's remark that he is "followed by a plane." On inquiry it became evident that the patient was saying that "something bothers him." Because he was insecure about letting others know about his vulnerability, he let a hint of this information escape in disguised code, simultaneously reducing direct responsibility for the remark by the obscurity of the code. Many clinicians have noted the simultaneous communication and obfuscation of that which is communicated in the language of schizophrenic interviewees. Certainly, the patient whose interview is transcribed above frequently used expressions that both expressed and disguised her feelings at the same time. What does the schizophrenic gain from this type of taxing verbal game?

The most frequently encountered view is that the schizophrenic patient's inability to communicate in a readily understandable manner, the obliqueness and indirectness of many of his/her responses are due to a lack of trust in others. Thus, while in this instance the interviewee readily agreed to the interview because of her wish to leave the hospital as soon as possible, she was not able to be open, relaxed, and self-disclosing. In addition to the autistic character of some of the language, there was also a general sort of resistiveness to communicating. There were frequent long pauses; many of her replies were extremely brief; and the ratio of interviewee to interviewer speech was remarkably low for an interactional interview of the kind recorded.

In a way it exemplifies the inverse relationship between interviewer and interviewee inputs observed by Lennard and Bernstein (1960) and Pope and Siegman (1965). Thus, when the interviewee provides relatively little information, the interviewer needs to increase his/her input in order to keep the communication system in balance. In fact, the interviewer is active both in his gross output and in his high level of specificity. The interviewer's recourse to very specific questions is noted throughout the interview. At one point he started out to ask the interviewee what her position in the family was but found that he was not likely to obtain a response unless he translated the question into more specific terms - i.e., "Are you the oldest, the youngest, the middle one?" At another point, the interviewer began to ask the interviewee what her brother did, but then realized that he would not likely get a relevant response with the ambiguous verb "did." He therefore changed his question, asking the interviewee what work her brother did. In fact, the interviewer needed to resort to a wide range of active interventions in order to keep the communication going. Thus, he would frequently reflect an unexpressed nuance of feeling to bridge some gap in the continuity of the dyadic exchange. This occurred when the interviewee spoke about her relationships with others in the hospital "getting out of hand till I couldn't take it." The interviewer reflected that it wasn't very much fun when one's feelings get out of hand. This degree of resonance of the interviewer with the interviewee seemed to be enough to keep the interviewee involved in the exchange.

The resistive character of schizophrenic communication in the interview is very much implicit in a study conducted by Kiesler (1971). Psychoneurotic patients treated in a university counseling center were compared with a group of schizophrenic patients in a state hospital on the variable of patient experiencing. Patient responses in taped excerpts from recorded psycho-therapy sessions were rated with the Experiencing Scale. Experiencing may be regarded as the antithesis of resistiveness. The scale is divided into seven stages. At the low end "the patient reveals nothing about himself and does not acknowledge his feelings". At the upper stages the patient manifests "a deep awareness of his feelings, his search for their personal meaning, and his attempt to understand them successfully and to integrate them into his experiential framework" (Kiesler, 1971, p. 371). A high level of experiencing implies an introspective opening into oneself, one's feelings, and a cognitive ability to incorporate an awareness of one's feelings with one's self-concept. Implicit in experiencing is also the capacity to communicate one's feelings and self-understanding to another person. Thus, experiencing includes elements of both self-awareness and self-disclosure. The validity of experiencing as a predictor of success in psychotherapy has been demonstrat-ed in a number of earlier studies and in the present one. In the present investigation with the first 20 therapy sessions as a base, the more successful patients, whether psychoneurotic or schizophrenic, attained higher experienc-ing scores than the less successful ones. Moreover, this difference was consistently supported across the 20 sessions. At the moment, the point of most immediate interest, however, is the comparison of the psychoneurotic and schizophrenic patients on the experiencing variable. Here, too, the results were clear cut. The author reported his findings succinctly, in the following terms: "psychoneurotics as a whole, at all points during the first 20 interviews, receive higher experiencing scores than do schizophrenics. Psychoneurotics, as expected, show a deeper level of self-exploration in their therapy interviews than do schizophrenic patients" (Kiesler, 1971, p. 376).

Although a low level of self-disclosure is quite a different kind of resistance than that expressed in autistic communication, the presence of the former in schizophrenic speech lends support to the view that, in part, the purpose of pathological communication is a self-protective one for the patient, and a resistive one in his/her relationship with the person whom s(he) is addressing.

Most of the preceding remarks evaluate the communication between the two participants in the interview. But this communication is very much a part of the relationship between the two. The interviewee was reserved at the beginning of the interview, responding only briefly and avoiding personally sensitive questions. In reviewing the above interview it is evident that most of the interviewee's responses were extremely brief and avoidant of personally disturbing material until the point at which she began to talk about the periods of confusion and violence experienced in the hospital. To be sure, the switch from a more guarded to a more trusting attitude toward the interviewer did not occur once and for all at that point in the interview. However, subsequent to this point there were some self-disclosing intervals periodically subsiding but later returning again.

Some authors go beyond the distrustful defensive tone of the schizo-phrenic's communication, emphasizing his/her actively negative attitude toward the interviewer. "The schizophrenic shows contempt for the listener in his frequent use of neologisms, whose meanings are impossible to discern from the context. Speech forms are distorted. Content is often purely idiosyncratic, and the overall effect may be one of strangeness verging on unintelligibility.... He may exhibit the ultimate in scorn by choosing to remain mute" (Vetter, 1969, p. 5). In conclusion, the interviewee's problems and her personality type appear to have a great deal to do with communication within the interview, the relationship that developed between the two participants, and the behavior of each.

To place this impression in a broader context, the preceding interview will be compared with another conducted by the same interviewer but with quite a different interviewee. In this instance the interviewee was a young man, 18 years of age, brought to a psychiatric hospital from the emergency room in a general hospital. Until four years prior to admission the patient had maintained a reasonably good adjustment. Then, with dramatic suddenness he became negativistic, antagonistic to his parents, and rebellious in school. While he had done quite well academically before the sudden change, subsequent to it school work deteriorated; he began to abuse a wide variety of drugs, and erupted belligerently with increasing frequency. Eventually he was arrested for possession of marijuana and was placed on probation by the courts on condition that he enter into psychiatric treatment. Out-patient treatment was never successful. As the patient's conflicts with his parents intensified, he made two suicidal attempts, both times by slashing his wrists. After the second attempt, he was taken to the emergency room referred to above and then admitted to a psychiatric hospital.

On admission, he was described as rather angry and depressed with a sullen, pouting expression throughout the intake interview. His dress was casual but neat. Throughout the interview, he was solemn, reticent, and uninvolved. His replies to the interviewer's questions were brief, but relevant and to the point, with no evidence of a thought disorder. When asked how he felt, he said that he was depressed but denied appreciable anxiety. He also denied his considerable involvement with drugs and firmly expressed his opposition to hospitalization. He refused to talk about his two suicide attempts.

The interview that follows was conducted about a month after his admission to the hospital. One would expect that his behavior would be quite different from that recorded by the patient in the first interview. There is no evidence of a psychosis and therefore one would not anticipate obscure or autistic communication. If problems of communication did develop, they would probably result from the patient's negativism, not from a disorder of thought and language. Because the interviewee was depressed, his tempo of speech was likely to be slow, volume low, with frequent lapses into silence. Because he was resentful at being in the hospital, there would be a lack of spontaneous self-disclosure, with considerable resistiveness. These are expectations based on interviewee attributes and the situation in which he finds himself. But it must be emphasized that any given interview has an element of unpredictability, depending on the relationship that emerges. The excerpts of this interview follow:

ER: You came here four weeks ago?

EE: Yes.

ER: What was the problem that brought you to the hospital?

EE: Well I was at another hospital. I had slashed my wrists. They thought I was still suicidal. But I don't feel suicidal anymore.

ER: I see, so coming here was not so much your idea.

EE: No.

ER: Whose was it?

EE: My doctor's at the other hospital.

ER: Did he explain to you why you needed to come?

EE: He just said I needed more help.

ER: Umhmm

EE: And I don't agree with him.

ER: Umhmm. I guess that doesn't help your frame of mind any.

EE: No.

ER: Well okay, you've been here for a month. How do you feel now?

EE: Well I had been suicidal before. But for the last two weeks you know uh here I haven't had any thoughts about harming myself come into my mind once. I'm depressed here you know because I I don't want to be here and you know that gets me depressed some... sometimes.

ER: Yea.

EE: But I haven't had the feeling of you know wanting to commit suicide at all.

ER: (Pause) You want to talk uh about what you did before you went into the hospital. What happened? (Silence)

EE: It's something I'd rather not talk about now.

ER: O.K.

Later in the interview after this inauspicious beginning, the patient was willing to open up a little about his conflicts with his parents.

EE: My parents didn't want me to go with the guys I had become friendly with in school. We stayed out late. When I would get home they would know I was smoking pot. There would always be a hassle.

ER: With both of them?

EE: No. My father usually. Even the night I was taken to the emergency room, my dad and I got in a fight. So I go- I went back to my friend's house. I bunked in his room before, But he was asleep - he went back to sleep as soon as I got there and I stayed awake. Then I decided - well - I went into the bathroom and cut my wrists. He heard me moving around - so when he found out what happened, he took me to the hospital.

ER: Well uh so the thing started out with this fight with your father. Then you left.

EE: Yeh.

ER: What did you fight about?

EE: About spending a lot of time with this friend. They don't like him. They blame him for me smoking

ER: Um Hmm.

EE: And he didn't want me to go over there again or something. And the whole thing just blew up; I don't know.

ER: And so you had a fight. What does that mean? What happened between your father and yourself? Physical fight?

EE: Just yelling and screaming. I mean I blow up - and he does - and I get afraid of him.

ER: Umhmm.

EE: But I don't hate him; I like him. He's really a pretty nice guy. I think we could get along better now. I've talked to him, you know, since then - the first day I came here umm but they don't think I should go home yet.

ER: Why do you figure they've taken that stand?

EE: They don't feel sure of me yet.

ER: Well you know we started talking about your father. I wonder if you could tell me a little bit about him? What sort of a person is he?

EE: He's a big guy (Laughs).

ER: Well, we'll start there.

EE: Umm. He's a nice guy but he's got a set rule. Everything has to be his way or - it's not right. Even if it's wrong and he says it has to be that way it's got to be that way even if it isn't right. I mean if you don't do it that way you'd better not be around.

ER: You mean he loses his temper.

EE: Yeh, quite often and easily.

ER: Umhmm.

EE: But when he doesn't he's o.k.

ER: So there must have been certain kinds of issues - that - you would sort of tangle.

EE: Yeh.

ER: What were these things that you thought he was so rigid about?

EE: Mainly - mainly just my friends. Uhm (pause) he doesn't like any of my friends because he thinks they all smoke dope and um; they all do smoke dope but all parents drink. I mean um I can't say all parents drink and um I can't say all kids smoke but I mean to me that's the same thing. Um - it's just that one is legal and one is not. It's really the same thing.

ER: Your father just couldn't stand the idea of your smoking dope huh?

EE: Yeh.

ER: Were there any incidents - I mean - did he ever catch you smoking in a way that upset him?

EE: No. I never did it in the house. I would never go that far.

ER: Umhmm.

EE: I - uh - if I did smoke dope - you know - it would be out with friends. I'd do it somewhere by myself, you know. It wouldn't be in the house.

ER: When you say dope you mean pot huh? Had you any experience with any other drugs?

EE: Yeh - but I don't want to go into that.

ER: Okay. I asked because ob- obviously your father's being upset about this is not a new thing. It's been going on for sometime.

EE: Yeh.

ER: You mention your father. Is he the chief - is he the one of your parents that you have most conflicts with?

EE: Yeh, my ma- mother just kind of stays out of it.

ER: How do you get on with your mother?

EE: Pretty good I'd say. Sometimes I wish she'd stand up for me because sometimes I feel or - I know that she thinks that I'm the one that's - um - right but if she did that then I think my dad would be pretty mad at her so; and so - she loves my dad so she sticks up for him most of the time.

ER: Still you feel kind of let down sometimes, huh?

EE: Yeh.

ER: Do you feel it would help you if you got some support from her?

EE: Yeh I do. (pause)

ER: What is she like? Can you describe her?

EE: I've always thought of her as a mouse. I don't know she's just uh - really quiet. She's not a loud person at all and uh she's eas- pretty easy to get along with and she's pretty understanding. She uh just never speaks up what she really thinks what she really feels (pause).

ER: She's never been the one to discipline you?

EE: No, just my dad. He's like (pause) the chief.

ER: Umhmm. Has it always been that way?

EE: Yeh

ER: From year one huh?

EE: Yeh

Toward the end of the interview, the interviewer asked the patient about his present depression.

EE: I'm depressed because I'm here. I don't think I should be here. That's what makes me depressed.

ER: When you're depressed do you need to be with people whom you really like to pull out of it?

EE: Yeh. Yeh, that's it.

ER: You can't sort of do it on your own?

EE: I don't think so. I don't think I could do it in this hospital. I mean, they say, you're supposed to get help, but I don't think I need any more help. I mean I've taken their help, what they've given me so far, but it's not getting me any happier. I think it's just getting worse.

ER: How do you spend your time here?

EE: Well I'm going to be starting the 12th grade um the last half of the year um on Wednesday so I'll be doing-going to school during the mornings I guess.

ER: Well what do you think of that?

EE: That's okay. It gives me something to do. I like most of the patients on my hall-yeh-they're pretty nice.

ER: Are you close to any of them?

EE: No-ever since I made these close friends in _____ I haven't really gotten close to anyone else. They're really my good friends.

ER: Are you involved in any activities here?

EE: No not really.

ER: What about your therapy. Is that helping you?

EE: Yeh I like therapy a lot. I like my doctor. I don't know, she's understanding. She knows how I feel. You know I think that's pretty good.

ER: Is there anything you want to ask me?

EE: No.

ER: How have you found the interview?

EE: It was pretty good. I didn't realize I could say all this but I have.

ER: Okay thank you.

EE: Okay.

Not all the anticipations regarding the preceding interview were actually realized. In contrast to the first, communication was remarkably rational, clear, and congruent between the two participants. There is no trace of the autism of the first interviewee, the peculiarity of expression, the very private and individual character of the interviewee's communications. This contrast was expected because of the clinical impression that had been formulated about the patient. But it was also anticipated that the patient would be sparse, limited, and hesitant in his speech. This was only partly true because, as it turned out, he was not as depressed as had been expected. Moreover, he was apparently able to relate in a positive way to the interviewer and was quite willing to tell him a lot about himself. The anticipated resistant negativism, the unwillingness to speak about his problem and about his experiences did occur, but not as massively as had been expected. In the end the interviewee remarked that he had enjoyed the experience because he had been able to disclose more about himself than he had intended.

In the above two interviews, the interviewer was the same person, but the interviewees varied. It would be reasonable to assume, then, that the difference in the character of the relationship and the communication in the interviews was a consequence of the different interactions between the single interviewer and the two different interviewees. The rest of this chapter will review some of the literature that pertains to the relationship between interviewee attributes and the interview interaction.

MacKinnon and Michels (1971) offer a rich clinical presentation of the interviewee behaviors that might be expected from patients in the major clinical syndromes. Their approach, and the kind of information that they provide, can be exemplified by a review of what they have to say about obsessive patients. To begin with, MacKinnon and Michels (1971) summarize the salient aspects of the obsessive patient's defenses. They view him/her as a person who needs to keep conflicted emotions as secret as possible from the interviewer and even from himself/herself. Hence, the authors regard the obsessive's major defense as that of emotional isolation. For the patient, life proceeds as though emotion were not real and as though one feels with one's mind. Thus, when there is an emotional conflict, it does not appear to him/her or to others with whom s(he) is communicating as a conflict of feeling at all but rather as a process of rational doubting or ruminative uncertainty. "He struggles to engage other people on the level of theories and concepts, leading to an endless discussion of details and situations in order to avoid true engagement" on the level of feelings and emotions" (p. 93). The obsessive therefore becomes quite skilled in the use of language. However, s(he) becomes particularly adept in avoiding personal communication through a complex flow of words rather than through a direct expression of feeling. The obsessive often evokes the annoyance of others by flooding them with details and thus obscuring any underlying basic theme that one might expect in his/her communication. In an interview it is difficult for the interviewer to avoid becoming bored because the patient is preoccupied with minutiae usually not relevant to the goals of the interview. If one works with an obsessive patient, one becomes aware that s(he) uses complex verbal defenses not only to avoid the expression of "such painful affects as fear and rage," but even more pointedly, such positive affects as "affection, warmth, and love" (p. 93). There is both an isolation of positive and negative feelings and a withdrawal from pleasurable and painful experiences. For life is not to be enjoyed, but rather to be stoically endured. One does not relax in the present; one works vigorously and systematically for an ever receding future release from the present strain of living.

MacKinnon and Michels (1971) emphasize the intellectual distance that the obsessive places between himself and his/her feelings. To illustrate this point they cite the example of a patient who speaks to his therapist about having been angry at him during the last session. But he does not speak directly about his anger. Instead he remarks: "After the last session, the thought of punching you in the nose came to mind." If the therapist then asks the patient whether in fact he was feeling angry at the time, the patient might add: "No, the thought just passed through my head." This pattern of transposing all experience, all feeling, into cognitive terms tends to take on a pedantic quality. Although the interviewee may be speaking about himself/herself s(he) does so as though s(he) were giving an exposition, a lecture about some objective subject or some other person.

In discussing the same type of patient, Pope and Scott (1967) described an interviewee who was identified as the daughter of an alcoholic father and the wife of an alcoholic husband. The patient was fictional and was endowed with the following obsessive characteristics:

> She would remember countless incidents in which mother and father fought, and in which she was neglected or rejected by father. At the beginning she might appear to be a very satisfactory patient because she would present a complete history. In fact she might propose plausible hypotheses about her present emotional condition, perhaps even relating it to the dissension within the family in which she grew up. Presently, however, the therapist might become frustrated by the affectless manner in which the events of her childhood would be reported. She would appear to both know what happened to her, and yet, in an emotional sense, not know. She might refer to her loneliness as a child, but loneliness would soon emerge as a verbal label, reiterated ritualistically. Another source of frustration in treating this patient would be the doubt that she would express about relationships between the events in her life. Thus, she might indeed present some convincing hypotheses about the connection between paternal rejection and her present psychological state. But soon it would be evident that the hypotheses were not believed deeply by the patient. She would think of a number of alternative explanations which might be just as credible. In fact, she would be pressing her intellectual resources into the service of an ego which needed to isolate one event in her life from another. In this sense, too, she would appear both to know and not know. To the extent that she would resist establishing connections between events and experiences she would be...screening herself from the direct experience of painful affect and anxiety... (1967, p. 161)

If the young woman with an alcoholic father and husband were to be transformed into a person with hysteric symptons and defenses, her interview behavior would contrast dramatically with that cited above.

> During her interviews she could remember few events and almost no affect about her father as she experienced him during her childhood years. She knew that he was an alcoholic, that there was constant strife between father and mother, and that father paid little attention to her when she was a child; but she could remember no disagreeable reactions to this state of affairs. In therapy it became obvious that as an adult, married to an alcoholic, she experienced boiling hostility to her husband. From time to time this hostility would blow up into an hysterical affect storm. Very early in her marriage she became aware of a painful sensitivity and feeling of injury whenever she was ignored or not overtly appreciated by her husband. For a long time, however, she rejected the therapist's repeated suggestion that her anger and

sensitivity originated during childhood years in response to her father's neglect of her. The therapist proceeded on the assumption that the amnesic void she experienced about her childhood was a result of repression that protected her from the painful blow to her self-esteem occasioned by father's neglect and from the anxiety and guilt evoked by her retaliatory rage against him. (Pope & Scott, 1967, p. 160)

Thus, two modes of coping with the same stresses in a patient's personal history, two defensive patterns, are associated with two contrasting styles of communication in the interview. The obsessive young woman relied on such cognitive processes as a vivid recall of countless details from her past life and the use of complicated networks of comparison to relate the remembered events. To be sure, that which was first associated and connected was then separated because of the doubt that permeated her perceptions, memories, and thoughts. And emotion was not noticeably present in anything that she said, however personal. In fact, it was sealed off from her cognitive processes. The hysteric young woman talked about the same themes that dominated her life. But her style of communication was completely different. Memory was blunted and the history she gave was full of amnesic voids. She would overflow with emotion as she spoke about the frustrations in her life, but was unable to relate her feelings of anger and hurt to memories of past experiences. Indeed, she had learned to avoid the use of cognitive processes as instruments for coping with the stresses in life.

The mental health interviewer learns to recognize contrasting communication styles as signals of different modes of defense against the conflicts and anxieties that might otherwise disrupt and immobilize a person. The interviewer's perceptions of interviewee communication styles provide him/her with important diagnostic information. They also alert him/her to different predispositional patterns of relationship that affect his/her interactions with different types of patients.

The preceding excerpts are clinical descriptions of the behavior of specific types of interviewees. They exemplify the impressionistic character of the information with which the clinician works. By contrast, the researcher tries, when s(he) can, to reduce the information with which s(he) deals to variables that can be manipulated experimentally. Two studies that exemplify this approach seek to establish a relationship between specified diagnostic groupings of patients and the vocal quality of their speech. In one (Markel, Meisels, & Houck, 1964) two groups of hospitalized Ss were compared, one diagnosed as schizophrenic (with delusions, hallucinations, other forms of thought pathology, mood abnormality, lack of insight, and disturbance in both speech and language), and the other, nonschizophrenic (TB patients and hospital attendants). Speech samples were recorded for the schizophrenic and nonschizophrenic Ss. To control for the possible effect of content, all Ss were asked to read the same passage into the tape. College students with no knowledge of the identity of the speakers rated the speech samples with a number of semantic differential scales. These included the following bipolar adjective pairs: kind-cruel, nice-awful, honest-dishonest, large-small, strong-weak, heavy-light, calm-agitated, relaxed-tense, and passive-active. The ratings made of the voice quality of the Ss significantly differentiated between the schizophrenic and nonschizophrenic groups. The schizophrenics were rated higher on the large-small, strong-weak, and heavy-light scales than the nonschizophrenics. In semantic differential factorial terms, schizophrenic Ss were more potent in voice quality. Other scales indicated that they were also more active in vocal tone. The authors concluded that voice quality is a channel through which some diagnostic attributes of a person may be transmitted.

A second study (Markel, 1969) dealing with the topic of the relationship between vocal tone and diagnostic attributes of the speaker, followed a reverse sequence. First, taped speech samples were categorized on the basis of certain vocal attributes. The diagnostic indentities of these vocal groupings were then determined. At the point of admission to a V.A. neuropsychiatric hospital, speech samples were collected from a group of male patients. Again, content was controlled by the procedure of asking each patient to read a standard sentence into a tape. Following prescribed instructions, six raters audited the tapes, scoring each speech sample on the vocal demensions of pitch, loudness, and tempo. Each S was assigned to one of three voice quality profile groups depending on the vocal dimension on which the highest rating was obtained. The subgroup with pitch as the highest dimension was called the Peak-Pitch group. The two others were designated the Peak-Loudness and Peak-Tempo groups. All Ss took the MMPI, and a significant interaction was obtained among the three voice quality profile groups and the MMPI scales. Clearly defined profiles emerged for the Peak-Pitch and the Peak-Loudness groups only. The MMPI profile of the former was indicative of a psychotic condition, with a poor prognosis. The Ss in this vocal group were described as keeping people at a distance and avoiding close interpersonal relationships. Those in the Peak-Loudness group were diagnosed as psychoneurotic with a good prognosis and were characterized as predominantly depressed. The two preceding studies add voice quality to the styles of verbal communication and interactional behavior emphasized earlier as correlates of the diagnostic categories to which interviewees and participants in other types of dyadic interactions belong.

Vocal tone is a paralinguistic variable. Another, that had also been related to diagnostic groupings among interviewees, is speech duration of verbal productivity. In one investigation (Matarazzo & Saslow, 1961) the authors compared the median speech duration of five groups of patients that varied widely in diagnosis. These included a hospitalized group of chronic schizophrenics, a second group of neurotic and acute psychotic in-patients and out-patients, a third group of neurotic out-patients, and two groups of normals. These groups are listed above in the sequence of decreasing severity of illness. When interviewed, Ss in these groups varied significantly in their median durations of utterances. The chronic schizophrenic patients responded with the greatest brevity; the normals with the greatest productivity. This finding accords with the observation in the first interview of the present chapter that the female schizophrenic patient gave replies of relatively short durations, prompting the interviewer to speak at greater length in order to maintain communication in the interview.

PERSONALITY ATTRIBUTES OF THE INTERVIEWEE

The above investigations, based on the study of single variables, produced results that illuminate some aspects of the interview interaction. But the control and manipulation of single variables is not always possible in interview research. The studies reviewed in this section of the chapter assume varying degrees of experimental rigor. Several are very close to the discursiveness of a clinical report. Others approximate the formality of an experimental study. The latter are usually based on experimental analogues of the interview rather than naturalistic interviews. Such analogues are actually experiments in which an interview is simulated, and a limited number of variables relevant to the interview extracted, controlled, and manipulated.

The first investigation in this section (Snyder, 1961) is based on a naturalistic psychotherapy situation in a university psychology clinic. The focus is on the interpersonal relationship between the therapist and the client, as it correlates with specified client attributes of personality.

Snyder based his study on 20 graduate students in psychology, treated psychotherapeutically. Although the entire psychotherapy sequence for each client was the source of Snyder's data, his findings regarding the interviewee's attributes affecting the therapy relationship are relevant to the dyadic interaction in the single interview. Snyder worked with his clients over considerable time periods, ranging from 12 interviews to 55 with a mean of 25.5. One would expect a client group of the kind utilized in the Snyder study to be of superior intelligence. In fact this group achieved Miller Analogy Tests Scores which ranged from 30 to 90 with a median of 73 and a mean of 72. Of the 20 clients three were women. The age range was from 22 to 42 years with a mean age of 27.4. Thirteen of the 20 were married at the time of the beginning of therapy. Students sought treatment for two basic reasons: problems related to marriage and to feeling of personal inferiority.

Both the clients and the therapist responded to questionnaires after each therapy interview, reporting their feelings toward each other and the therapy process. The clients' personal attributes were determined through the use of both the Edwards Personal Preference Schedule and the Minnesota Multiphasic Personality Inventory; those of the therapist, through the use of the EPPS only. The major statistical procedures used were correlations of various kinds and factor analyses. For the reader, this study is a rather diffuse one presenting a multitude of correlations in which patterns of interpretation are not easy to trace. The findings of present interest deal with the interviewee's contribution to the relationship and to the success of psychotherapy. To evaluate interviewee attributes within the above frame of reference, Snyder first developed a number of criteria for dividing his subjects into good and poor clients. These criteria included changes in the Edwards Personal Preference Scale between the beginning and the end of therapy, scores on the Minnesota Multiphasic Personality Inventory, ratings of the client by the therapist on rapport, and changes in the therapist's questionnaire evaluations of the clients. It should be noted that the division of clients into good and poor ones is only partly based on objective personality measurements; in part it is a matter of the subjective judgment of the therapist.

For this particular therapist, the ideal client turned out to be one who was friendly, moderately active, and at least moderately communicative. One operation carried through by Snyder consisted of intercorrelating the nine MMPI scales in the data obtained from the clients and then factor analyzing them. Four factors emerged which might briefly be designated as hypomanic, hypochondriacal, obsessive-schizoid, and depressive. The patients described by the first factor were outgoing and excitable; those by the second were preoccupied with body ailments; those described by the third were withdrawn and introverted; and those by the last were depressed. Snyder's better clients tended to be hypomanic and obsessive; the poorer clients, schizoid and depressive. Thus, Snyder appears to have been more successful with interviewees who were excitable, sociable, and introspective, and less successful with those who were withdrawn and depressed.

The preceding study is a good example of one which occurs somewhere between the level of clinical description and that of controlled experimental investigation. The design of the study provides no clues about the degree to which its findings can be generalized to other interviewers and other clients. But it does indicate, with data that is more precise and reliable than that which would be obtained from clinical impression alone, that interviewee attributes do affect the relationship with the interviewer.

The study that follows (Rayner & Hahn, 1964) probably occurs even closer to the clinical pole of the clinical-research continuum than that of Snyder. The authors set out to determine a number of patient personality traits that are related to success in psychotherapy. The investigation was carried out at Cassel Hospital in England. The patients exemplify quite a diagnostic range including both neurotic and borderline psychotic persons, but none that was overtly psychotic. Individual psychotherapy was offered once to three times a week, the duration varying from three months to a year. The instrument used to determine interviewee attributes is the Object Relations Test, a device that resembles the Thematic Apperception Test. As in the case of the Thematic Apperception Test, the subject is asked to examine a series of pictures and make up stories about them. The pictures consist of human figures whose postures, expressions, and sex are ambiguous. Each therapist at the hospital was given a list of his past patients who had taken the Object Relations Test and was asked to judge which two of these patients he considered most successful in therapy and which two, least. In this way two groups of 20 patients were assembled, one consisting of those judged by therapists to have been successful in treatment, and the other, of the unsuccessful ones. The scheme for scoring the responses given by the patients was developed specifically for the present investigation, consisting of interviewee attributes considered to be relevant to success or failure in psychotherapy. It consisted of certain traits that characterized the individuals in the stories, and it was based on the assumption that these attributes actually applied to the storyteller as well as to the characters he created and to whom he attributed them. If this assumption is tenable, it may be concluded from the data in the study that those interviewee traits that facilitate their participation in the psychotherapeutic interview include responsible initiative, introspection, persistence, and a willingness to evalute themselves.   The interfering   traits   include   nonparticipation   in social activities and passivity.

Many of the studies pertaining to interviewee attributes are based on individual dimensions of personality rather than clusters of traits such as those found in the two preceding investigations. A frequently occurring dimension is that of interviewee dependency. Andrews (1966) offered a clinical description of the dependent client in his excellent review article dealing with the psychotherapy of phobic patients. While the anxiety symptomatology of phobic patients need concern us only in passing, their dependency in relating to others is directly relevant to the present discussion.

The anxiety experienced by the phobic patient is not diffuse, but rather specific to certain situations. Thus, the altophobic patient is panicked when s(he) needs to ascend above a certain level in a public building, for example. The agoraphobic is not able to walk outdoors, particularly in wide open spaces without disorganizing certainty that s(he) will faint, die, or that some nameless terror will descend upon him/her. Similarly, there are people who are phobic about water, elevators, travel in public conveyances, and other situations.

Any attempt to help phobic persons overcome their situation-specific anxiety is likely to be a long and frustrating ordeal for the helper. Very early s(he) will encounter the phobic person's dependency as an intolerable demand on his/her time, patience, and helping efforts. With reference to the burden that the phobic person's dependency places on a relationship, Andrews has the following to say: "Individuals who have phobic problems...are often characterized by dependence and 'immaturity.' One major aspect of this pattern is that the fearfulness manifested by such individuals tends to evoke from others the care and protection which is part of such dependency relationships" (1966, p. 456). At a later point Andrews adds: "Individuals labelled phobic typically avoid activity which involves independent, self-assertive handling of difficult and fear arousing situations. This is, of course, a description of how the phobic behaves when confronted by the phobic stimulus; but frequently this lack of self assertion constitutes a broader pattern of response as well" (p. 456).

Of immediate concern is the effect on the interview process of the phobic patient, as a clinical example of a dependent type of person. MacKinnon and Michels (1971) describe the task of the interviewer in the following way:

The phobic patient relates easily during the initial portion of the interview. He comes seeking relief, and is polite and eager to talk about his problems. Silence and resistance arise later in the interview, but the opening moments are marked by an aura of good will. As the interview progresses, it becomes apparent that the patient's agreeableness continues only if the interviewer cooperates with the patient's defenses; that is, if he helps the patient avoid anxiety by not pursuing certain topics and by promising magical protection. The task of the interviewer is to direct the discussion into these forbidden areas, but at the same time to maintain the rapport necessary to sustain the relationship through the painful exploration of the patient's psychological problems. (p. 158)

Thus, the interviewer deals with a dependent interviewee through maintaining a careful balance between gratifying immediate dependency needs sufficiently to maintain the relationship, but simultaneously and in a graduated manner encouraging the interviewee to assert himself/herself enough to explore anxieties and indeed to cope with them. The clinician is concerned with how to help the client cope with dependency. The researcher has tended to be more involved with determining the correlates of interviewee dependency whether or not they are immediately relevant to the management or efficacy of the interview.

Client dependency emerged as a major interviewee variable in Snyder's two volumes (1961, 1963) dealing with the psychotherapy relationship. Regarding himself as a nurturant type of therapist (i.e., guiding, advice-giving, warm, protective), he found that those of the 20 clients in his study who expected a nurturant type of therapist were characterized as high on anxiety and high on dependency. In a comparison of the nine clients judged to be better with the 11 judged to be poorer, dependency ratings (based on MMPI and EPPS subscores and a new dependency scale developed by Snyder and his group) for the entire sequence of therapy interviews, were higher for the better rather than the poorer clients. In a content analysis of therapy interviews conducted with his two most dependent clients, Snyder found that whenever a client expressed dependency directly toward him he responded with support. This he accomplished either by talking with the client about the relationship between the interviewer (Snyder) and the interviewee (the client), or simply by reassuring the client. This particular interviewer, then, preferred dependent to nondependent clients, and when dependent clients expressed their dependency on him, he did not hesitate to provide them with the support that he felt they needed. Moreover, he found that clients, in general, rated themselves as feeling more positively about the interviewer in interviews in which he was supportive - i.e., he communicated information to the interviewee and assumed the role of an educator. "If we can draw a conclusion here, it is that the clients felt warmer to the therapist when he was using high supportive techniques" (Snyder, 1963, p. 28).

While the Snyder study utilizes measurement and statistical techniques, it must be regarded as being rather more of a clinical than an experimental investigation. Moving in the direction of the experimental pole of the clinical-experimental continuum on which the present studies are distributed, we encounter one dealing in part with the relationship between interviewee dependency and attraction to the interviewer (Heller & Goldstein, 1961). The Ss were undergraduate students undergoing psychotherapy at a university psychological clinic. They were randomly assigned to therapists who were advanced graduate students in clinical psychology. The clients met with their therapists for two 50-minute sessions per week. The following are some of the interviewee variables measured and devices used:

Client-therapist attraction. The instrument used was a projective device called the Picture Impressions Test developed by Libo (1956). Each subject was asked to respond to four pictures depicting therapy-like situations. The stories developed by the Ss were rated for interviewee-to-interviewer attraction.

Self-descriptive dependency. The Edwards Personal Preference Schedule was used because the Succorance, Deference, and Autonomy Scales were considered to be relevant to the interviewee's self-descriptive dependency. The Succorance and Deference Scales were summed and the Autonomy Scale subtracted in order to obtain a single dependency score.

Overt dependency. To determine overt or behavioral dependency, a situational test was devised involving selective role-playing tasks for the subject.

All three devices were administered to all clients immediately before their first therapy session and immediately after their last.

The results of primary interest in the present discussion pertain to the pretherapy dependency scores of the Ss and their attraction to the interviewers. Significant positive correlations were obtained between both the self-descriptive and overt dependency scores of the Ss and their attraction to the interviewer as reflected in their responses to the Picture Impressions Test. Clearly, then, those interviewees who made up stories to the Picture Impression Test that expressed an anticipated positive gratification from therapy were the ones who also described themselves as more dependent and who acted more dependently in the situation test. The authors remarked: "This finding lends support to the contention...that initial client dependence can act in ways that maintain the early stages of the psychotherapeutic relationship" (Heller & Goldstein, 1961, p. 373). It had been expected that one of the consequences of effective psychotherapy would be reduced dependency. Thus, those clients who were more positively attracted to therapy at the outset would be the ones who would reduce their dependency most during the course of psychotherapy. As it turned out, the anticipated relationship between positive attraction to therapy and client movement toward independence was evident in self-descriptive dependency scores but not in overt or behavioral dependency.

The last study pertaining to interviewee dependency is an experimental analogue of the initial interview in which the interviewers were the Ss (Heller, Myers, & Kline, 1963). The major problems for investigation was expressed in the following question: "is the behavior of the therapist in any way determined by the stimulus characteristics of the clients?" (Heller et al., 1963, p. 117). The clients were actually student actors trained to perform four standardized interviewee roles. In one role the interviewee acted out the role of a dominant-friendly client; warm, friendly, and easy to get along with, but simultaneously tending to dominate the interview by initiating conversation and choosing the topics for discussion. In a second role, as a dominant-hostile client, the interviewee was managerial, boastful, assertive, and aggressive, frequently rejecting the interviewer's statements, sometimes with sarcasm. In the dependent-friendly client role the interviewee was submissive and conforming, frequently asking the interviewer for direction and generally depending on him. He manifested a sensitive concern that the interviewer think well of him and depended on him for directing the course of the interview. Finally, as a dependent-hostile client the interviewee was suspicious, distrustful, complaining, guilty, and self-abasing. He subordinated himself to the interviewer, but with considerable resentment. Passively, he responded to the interviewer's questions but never took the lead himself.

The Ss were 34 interviewers-in-training, all graduate students in psychology ranging in age from 21 to 50. They were unaware that the interviewees were actors, believing them to be genuine clients applying for treatment. Each S interviewed the four clients (performing all four roles) for half-hour interviews, accomplishing the entire series within a 24-hour period. Each interview was observed through a one-way mirror by a judge trained to rate interviewer affect, control, and anxiety.

Only the results pertaining to the dominant-dependent variable will be considered here. Note that in this instance the interviewee's dominance-dependency was the manipulated variable. Dominant interviewee behavior was judged by the observers to evoke significantly more interviewee dependence than was the case for dependent interviewee behavior. Thus, the relationship between the two members of a dyad on this particular variable is a reciprocal one.

In a review of some of the research literature on client dependency, Bordin (1974) paid particular attention to the type of client he designated as counterdependent. He compared the overtly dependent with the counter-dependent interviewee, and explored the implications of the interpersonal behavior of each for the interview relationship. The underlying assumption was that both types of clients have high levels of dependency needs. For reasons that are embedded in the complexities of personality development, the overtly dependent person is able to display and communicate his/her anxieties in dependent behavior. Such behavior, when overt, tends to evoke either dominance or support from the interviewer. The reciprocal character of the behavior of both participants in the interview strengthens the relationship and supports the communication of the interviewee. But the needs of the counterdependent person are more paradoxical. S(he) is motivated by covert dependent feelings and probably impelled to develop expectations that the dyadic partner will be supportive. But the awareness of the need and the emergence of the expectation arouse high levels of anxiety. The referent of the anxiety is the dependency itself. Conflicted by anxiety about dependency, the counterdependent person asserts an excess of independence. S(he) refuses support; rejects any subordination of self to the interviewer; and is wary of being influenced, persuaded, or manipulated by him/her. The essence of this pattern is its excessive rigidity and the compulsive pressure with which it is acted out. Another clue about its presence is the inability of the interviewee to cope with any situation that undermines it. As a consequence, the interviewer learns to avoid any threat to the autonomy of the counterdependent person. In Bordin's terms, "when anxiety is expressed in the form of counterdependence, the therapist must be careful to offer the patient the assurance that he will be permitted to use his own resources to the fullest; the patient must build his trust in himself before he can trust the therapist" (1974, p. 199).

One investigation reviewed by Bordin (Williams, 1959) compared three patients classified as overtly dependent on the basis of initial interviews, with three others, considered to be counterdependent. Williams found that the counterdependent patients responded with more oppositional resistance than the overtly dependent ones whenever the therapist offered support. Moreover at such times the former type engaged in less self-exploration than the latter type.

The two studies that follow, both using verbal conditioning procedures, demonstrate the greater susceptibility to influence of overtly dependent rather than counterdependent Ss. In the first (Cairns & Lewis, 1962) verbal conditioning was conducted with both a high-dependency group and another composed of Ss who "tended to deny any form of dependency behavior." As expected, the high-dependency Ss conditioned positively. Beyond expectation, the counterdependent group exceeded the no-conditioning point; they actually conditioned negatively.

Somewhat later, Timmons and Noblin (1963) reported a study in which they classified their Ss, with the use of the Blacky test, into oral and anal character types. Their oral types were behaviorally similar to the high-dependency Ss of previous studies, and their anal types, to the counterdependent Ss. Using a Taffel-type of conditioning task and mild affirmative responses as reinforcers, the Es obtained opposite results for the oral and anal types. The oral (high dependency) Ss were readily extinguished. The anal (counterdependent) Ss resisted the conditioning influence to the point of negative results. They made the reinforced choice less frequently during the conditioning period than they had during the operant period.

In brief, counterdependent patients resist support, influence, and any other relationship behavior from the therapist that diminishes their independence. The task of the interviewer is particularly difficult because the patients vigilantly guard against persuasion and manipulation by him/her. In these circumstances the interviewer must guard against any display of dominance, support, control; indeed, any behavior that reduces the autonomy of the patient.

Some authors have investigated the relationship between specified personality traits of the interviewee (or other speaker) and his/her verbal content and style. The relationship between personality attributes and verbal behavior is crucially important to the mental health interviewer because much clinical assessment is based on the patient's verbal communication in an interview. In one research study (Weintraub & Aronson, 1964) the verbal communication of patients given to impulsive behavior was examined. The patients chosen as Ss were described as lacking control, unable to tolerate frustration for any period of time, and both precipitate and violent in their reactions. Impulsive behavior was noted during hospitalization "mostly in the form of temper tantrums, door-slamming, assertive behavior, and the like.... Their impulsive acts were almost always followed by attempts to undo the unfortunate consequences of the precipitate behavior" (Weintraub & Aronson, 1964, p. 76). All Ss in both the patient group and a control group were asked to talk into a tape recorder for 10 minutes about any topics that occurred to them. The transcripts of the taped monologues were then scored on certain verbal categories so that the experimental (impulsive) group might be compared with the control group.

The impulsive group exceeded the control group in a number of the verbal categories used. Impulsive patients made more direct references than the control Ss. These were remarks calculated to manipulate the E into giving them more direction and assistance than that already communicated in the instructions. This type of verbal behavior was considered to be a consequence of the very limited ability of these patients to tolerate frustration and to delay gratification. Having impulsively attempted to subvert the rules of the tasks by pressuring the E into breaking his/her silence, they then had to retract much of what they had done. This particular group of patients was in conflict about its predominantly impulse ridden behavior. Its "uncontrolled acts were immediately followed by remorseful attempts to undo the consequences of the ill-considered behavior" (Weintraub & Aronson, 1964, p. 80). Many other verbal responses of the patients were designated negators. These comments were positively correlated with retractors, and indeed the two categories were rather similar. The retractor minimizes or diminishes a statement just made ("My instructor is a very good teacher. Of course, he often wanders from the topic"). The negator totally reverses a statement already made ("I can't stand my roommate - well, he's really not bad"). Both the retractors and the negators are consequences of the conflict and anxiety that the patient experiences subsequent to the eruption of impulsive behavior. Finally, it is no surprise that the speech of impulsive patients overflows with feeling. "Just as the patients' ward behavior was characterized by temper tantrums, angry rebellion, and attempts to destroy the physical environment, so were their samples of speech frequently punctuated by 'I love,' 'I hate,' 'I'm miserable,' 'I feel terrible,' and so on" (Weintraub & Aronson, 1964, p. 81).

The applied usefulness of studies of this kind to the mental health interviewer is evident. The intake or initial interview is his/her prime instrument for assessing a patient. Linguistic research that correlates patient speech content with personality attributes, and more particularly with defensive and adaptive mechanisms, enhances the value of the interview as an assessment device.

INTERVIEWEE CAPACITY FOR SUCCESS IN RELATIONSHIP

A number of studies have investigated an interviewee attribute variously designated as capacity for relationship, relatability, attractiveness, or likability. As relatability (Isaacs & Haggard, 1966), this trait has been defined as the capacity of an individual to enter into interpersonal relationships. The higher a person's level of relatability, the more s(he) possesses those emotions and attitudes that enhance a person's ability to become attached to and interact with another. The authors were interested in correlating interviewee relatibility with success in psychotherapy.

It may be assumed that in order to participate in the psychotherapeutic process the patient must have certain capacities. In the developmental sense, the patient must have achieved a capacity for trusting others or he will not be free enough to reveal himself fully enough to his therapist to permit psychotherapy to take place. He must have sufficient empathic capacity to realize that it is possible for the therapist to recognize him as an individual. He must have sufficient objectivity about himself to be able concomitantly to experience and observe himself. (Isaacs & Haggard, 1966, p. 227)

Using the Thematic Apperception Test, judges rated each story given by a S on a relatability scale developed by the authors. In one study the investigators compared the relatability levels of seven patients designated as improved in treatment with eight designated as unimproved. The level of the improved group, determined before the beginning of therapy, was significantly higher than that of the unimproved group. Another study followed a reverse procedure. One group of patients rated high on relatability was compared on therapy outcome with another that had low relatability. The high relatability group manifested greater rate of improvement than the low group. In both investigations those interviewees with the better capacity for relationship showed more improvement in therapy than those with the poorer capacity. While it is difficult to directly translate success in therapy to behavior during the interview, it seems reasonable that capacity for relationship would be positively associated with responsiveness in the interview.

If relatability refers to a person's capacity for relationship, sociometric status refers to actual acceptance by others. In one investigation (Pope & Nudler, 1973) the sociometric status of male patients in a psychiatric hospital (i.e., the degree of their acceptance by their peers) was related to certain aspects of their interview behavior. Those who had high sociometric or acceptance scores were the ones who were liked best by their fellows; those with low scores were liked least. Without prior knowledge of the sociometric status of each patient, the senior author of the investigation interviewed each S. From the tape-recordings of the interviews, it was possible to develop certain verbal scores which were then correlated with the Ss' sociometric scores. Out of eight correlations two were significant. The first was a negative correlation between sociometric acceptance and the time that the interviewee spent in silence, indicating that the more popular Ss had fewer hesitations in interview speech and therefore greater verbal fluency. There was a second significant correlation between interviewee sociometric status and capacity to speak about psychologically meaningful rather than superficial topics. The authors had hypothesized and later concluded that popularity or acceptance by one's peers would be associated with verbal fluency (low hesitation) and self-disclosure because both may be taken as indices of interpersonal competence.

The final two studies in the present section deal with attractiveness or likability. Sociometric status is an index of actual popularity within a group, while attractiveness (like relatability) is a rating of an interpersonal trait made by a judge who has had an opportunity to observe a S. In the first of the two remaining studies (Nash, Hoehn-Saric, Battle, Stone, Imber, & Frank, 1965) interviewee attractiveness was a secondary focus of study, but is the one that will concern us at this point. The Ss were neurotic out-patients seen in individual psychotherapy by psychiatric residents. All therapy sessions were tape-recorded for the later rating of interviewee behavior. Before assignment to therapy, each patient was interviewed by a research psychiatrist (not the therapist) for a standard psychiatric screening and history. The initial interviewer rated each patient that he had screened for attractiveness, defined as "a global judgment of suitability for psychotherapy based on such factors as age, education, ability to relate to others, and the like" (Nash et al., 1965, p. 376). The attractiveness ratings, made before the beginning of therapy, were later correlated with five therapy outcome scores (based on judgments of both the patients themselves and their therapists) and three desirable interview behavior measures (based on judments by the therapists alone). The attractive patients exceeded the unattractive ones on seven of the above eight measures. In brief, those patients rated as attractive by a screening interviewer are the ones who manifest the more desirable interviewee behavior as judged by the therapists, and the more favorable therapy outcomes as judged by both the patients themselves and their therapists.

Unfortunately, the therapy outcome aspect of the findings is placed under question by a follow-up investigation that was carried out five years after the termination of treatment. In the follow-up study, based on fewer than half of the original Ss, there were no significant differences between the attractive and unattractive groups on any of the outcome measures (Liberman, Frank, Hoehn-Saric, Stone, Imber, & Pande, 1972). The five years that transpired between the investigation and its follow-up appeared to have eroded the original differences between the attractive and the unattractive groups.

In an earlier study (Stoler, 1963) interviewee likability was the term used. There is no reason to believe that there is any difference between the concept of attractiveness and that of likability. Ten raters were given 20 taped two-minute segments of therapist and client interactions drawn from 10 recorded therapy cases. One segment in each instance was drawn from an early interview in a psychotherapy sequence and one from a later interview. A number of judges were asked to listen to these segments presented to them in random order and to make a rating of the client's likability in each segment. For the judges, likability was defined as "the specific liking or disliking feeling that this client brings out in you" (Stoler, 1963, p. 176). When the five cases judged to be more successful in treatment outcome were compared with those judged to be less successful (based on both therapist and patient ratings of outcome), it was found that the more successful clients had been rated as more likable than the less successful clients.

The interviewee's behavior in the interview was rated on the Experiencing Scale (Klein, Mathieu, Gendlin, & Kiesler, 1970), a device for assessing the degree to which an interviewee is in rapport with inner experience and is able to communicate it to the interviewer. The second part of the study demonstrated that clients who obtained higher ratings on the Experiencing Scale were independently judged to have higher likability scores. It does appear that a client in good rapport with inner experience and able to communicate openly about thoughts and feelings is perceived as a more likable individual by a clinical judge, and probably by an interviewer. In conclusion, the burden of research evidence as well as that of clinical impression point to a significant association between an interviewee's capacity to enter into a relationship, his/her judged attractiveness or likability, and both effective participation in an interview and success in psychotherapy.

The first section of this chapter dealt with selected interviewee diagnostic groupings. The last will examine interviewee anxiety and depression, two reaction patterns with signficant implications for diagnosis.

INTERVIEWEE ANXIETY AND DEPRESSION

In the studies summarized in this section anxiety and depression are regarded as forms of affect which may be studied both for their relevance to therapy outcome and to interviewee communication behavior. It is a matter of general clinical impression that a psychotherapist can be more optimistic about a patient who is able to experience and communicate aroused affect rather than one who is limited or impoverished in emotional experience. Thus, one would expect patients who enter psychotherapy with significant levels of anxiety and depression to promise more favorable outcomes than those who lack these affects. In fact, many studies reported in the literature support this clinical impression. One group of authors (Luborsky, Auerbach, Chandler, Cohen, & Bachrach, 1971) summarize the findings in the literature regarding this matter as follows. "We found nine studies of psychotherapy in which initial anxiety level was assessed. In five, a significant relationship was obtained between high initial anxiety and a criterion of change" (p. 150). In four studies the results were nonsignificant. However, in one of the nonsignificant studies, there was a positive and significant relationship between anxiety and therapy outcome for women but not for men. "In sum, five and 'one-half' studies confirm that patients with high anxiety at the initial evaluation or beginning of treatment are the ones likely to benefit from psychotherapy. High initial anxiety probably indicates a readiness, or at least an openness for a change" (p. 150).

In five other studies summarized by the same authors it was found that not only anxiety but any strong affect such as depression must be regarded as a good prognostic indication for therapy. "The presence of these strong affects may indicate the patient is in pain and asking for help. The absence of affect very likely goes along with a state in which the patient is not reaching out for help, or has given up" (Luborsky et al., 1971, p. 150).

It is now proposed to take a somewhat closer look at two of the preceding five and a half studies that obtain positive results for the association between anxiety and favorable therapy outcome. The object of the first was to determine the relationship between client success in counseling and possession of anxiety and depression as personality traits (Gallagher, 1954). The Ss were students of Pennsylvania State College who came to the psychological clinic for help with their personal adjustment. Two groups of clients were selected for the study, one consisting of Ss rated as more successful in counseling outcome, and the other, of Ss rated as less successful. Three measures of anxiety were used (a short form of the MMPI, the Elizur Rorschach Anxiety Scale, and the number of problems checked on the Mooney Problem Checklist) and one of depression (The Depression Scale of the MMPI). The less successful and the more successful counseling groups were compared with each other and with a group of clients from a previous study who had left therapy following only one or two interviews. The results demonstrated a constant progression from the dropout group, through the least successful to the most successful group. On all three anxiety scales, the lowest scores were obtained by the dropout group, the median scores by the less successful group, and the highest scores by the more successful group.

However, of the nine possible differences between the three groups on the three scales, only three were significant. With reference to the Depression Scale of the MMPI, the more successful group was significantly more depressed at the beginning of therapy than the less successful group. Thus, there was a consistent but not highly significant tendency for the results of this study to support the anticipation that the more anxious and the more depressed clients at the beginning of therapy were the ones who were likely to get most out of it.

The second investigation was much too complex to be summarized in detail. It was a long term and broadly ranging investigation of factors contributing toward success in psychotherapy, conducted at the Menninger Foundation (Luborsky, 1962). The present concern is only with the relationship between patient anxiety and therapy outcome. Anxiety was measured in two ways, to determine both general anxiety level and anxiety tolerance on the part of the patient. Although it is not possible to consider in specific detail the criteria for change in therapy that were used in the investigation, it will suffice at this point to mention that an important instrument in assessing change was a Health-Sickness Rating Scale. As it turned out, there was a significant correlation between anxiety level and positive changes in the Health-Sickness ratings of the patients over the course of therapy. Once again, there was the clinically anticipated correlation between anxiety or suffering and improvement in psychotherapy. The authors took the position that a patient needs to experience an optimum level of suffering to maintain an adequate level of motivation for continuation in therapy and for a positive outcome.

Attention will now be directed to a series of experimental studies dealing with interviewee anxiety. Some of these have already been discussed in Chapter 5 but are again referred to briefly here because of their relevance to the topic of interviewee attributes of relationship. In the first of these studies (Pope & Siegman, 1965) the Ss were female nursing students, with ages ranging from 20 to 22. A standardized interview was used, divided into two content segments, including a neutral topic (past school history) and an emotional or anxiety-arousing topic (family relationships). Thus, for each S anxiety level was manipulated through the use of two contrasting topics. To ensure that past school history would indeed be a low anxiety topic for the Ss used, only students with no report of school or college maladjustment or anxiety were selected. To enhance the anxiety-arousing effect of the topic dealing with family relationships, the interviewer introduced it with a suggestive remark about the frequency with which students have problems in getting along with other members of their families. That the anxiety manipulation was in fact effective was demonstrated by the Ss themselves in their responses to a questionnaire administered after the interview. On this questionnaire, the Ss reported feeling significantly more "uncomfortable" and "tense" during the segment of the interview dealing with family relationships than with past school history.

The first result was the greater productivity of the interviewees during the anxiety-arousing topic than the neutral topic. Up to a certain point, anxiety functions as an activator of interviewee speech. In terms of the present study the interviewees were more productive during the anxiety-arousing rather than the neutral segment of the interview. This may appear to contradict the popular notion that fright is likely to bring on paralysis of speech rather than a liberation of it. The answer to the apparent contradiction between the popular notion and the results of the investigation may be provided by the concept of an optimum level of anxiety. Thus, there may be something in the nature of an inverted U curve operating. Up to a point, an increase in anxiety will prompt an increase in verbal productivity; beyond the level speech is inhibited and eventually eliminated. This would accord with drive theory (Duffy, 1962) that postulates an inverted U-relationship between the effect of drive on behavior, increasing it up to an optimum level and decreasing it beyond that level. Other results included a shorter reaction time, a faster rate of speech, fewer expressions of hesitation, and a higher level of speech disturbance during the anxious rather than the neutral segments of the interview. Thus, the interviewee who speaks more when anxiously aroused also takes a shorter time in beginning to respond, speaks more rapidly, with fewer hesitations but with more verbal flustering than s(he) would manifest when anxiety is not present. It will be recalled that speech disturbances, as measured by Kasl and Mahl (1958) include sentence changes, word incompletions, stuttering, stammering, and intruding incoherent sounds. Thus, while the interviewee is more verbally productive when anxious, his/her speech is more disrupted. One may therefore speak about a concurrent facilitating and disruptive effect of anxiety on the speech of the interviewee (Siegman & Pope, 1965).

Although the results seemed clear-cut, their interpretation was left in doubt because of the experimental procedure used. Was the greater productivity of the interviewee during the family relationship rather than the school history segment of the interview a consequence of the greater anxiety aroused by the former, or simply a result of the patient having more to say about the family than about school? "One could not rule out the possibility that the higher productivity, faster articulation rate, and fewer hesitations in the interview segment dealing with family relationships, rather than school history, were simply indications that the students had more to talk about in the area of family relationships, and therefore spoke more productively with less hesitation" (Pope, Siegman, & Blass, 1970).

To cope with the ambiguity of the first anxiety study, a second one was devised in which topical content remained constant across the high- and low-anxiety conditions. Two groups of junior and senior nursing students were used, one a control group in which there was no manipulation of anxiety, and the other, an experimental group in which anxiety was varied. All Ss took part in two interviews, with a week intervening between the first and the second. Before the first, the Ss were given a short form of the Taylor Manifest Anxiety Scale (MAS). They were then told that the interview to follow would deal with both family relations and school adjustment. At the end of the first interview, all Ss were asked to return for a second session during which they were to respond to some additional questionnaires. When they arrived, however, they were told that the tape of the first interview was flawed and not usable. They were asked to repeat the interview with the same interviewer who would cover the same topical areas as those in the first interview. In this way the topical content of the first interview could be plausibly repeated in the second. Up to this point the procedure for Ss in the control and the experimental groups was precisely the same. At this point, however, the procedures diverged. Low anxiety was fostered in the control group with the following remark: "We had a chance to evaluate the personality test you took before the first interview. You might be interested in knowing that your results on it were within the normal range expected for a student group." For the Ss in the experimental group a high level of anxiety was induced with a different comment: "We had a chance to evaluate the personality test you took before the first interview. I think it is only fair to tell you that there is clear evidence that you have some serious psychological problem with your family."

The control group showed no significant change in productivity between its first and second interviews. However, the experimental group showed a highly significant increase in productivity, confirming the finding of the first study that anxiety increases interviewee verbal productivity. The control group manifested a decrease in the occurrence of speech disturbances (a lower Non-Ah Ratio) while the anxiety group showed no decrease on this variable. Again there is a confirmation of the previous finding that with anxiety comes an increase in speech disturbance, although the confirmation is a little more indirect than in the case of productivity. One might assume that when a S is interviewed by the same interviewer for the second time s(he) feels more comfortable than the first and is likely to experience less anxiety and consequently manifest less speech disturbance. This in fact happened with the control group. Its failure to happen with the experimental group is probably an indication that the increased anxiety due to the experimental manipulation nullified the expected drop in speech disturbance. In two basic respects the second study did confirm the first, while eliminating the earlier ambiguity. When an interviewee experiences an increase in anxiety s(he) is indeed more productive although his/her speech is simultaneously more disrupted and flustered.

It may now be asked what happens to an interviewee's verbal communication when s(he) becomes depressed, and how this might differ from the changes that are brought on by anxiety. Clinical impression would lead one to expect that the depressed interviewee would tend to speak less, more slowly, with reduced volume, and that his/her speech would be interspersed with long periods of silence. These expectations have in general been confirmed in a study dealing with "Anxiety and Depression in Speech" (Pope, Blass, Siegman, & Raher, 1970). The investigators anticipated "that anxiety may...be characterized as a high-activation affect and depression as a low-activation affect" (p. 129). The activation effect of anxiety has of course been noted in the tendency of the interviewee, during anxious moments, to speak more productively, more rapidly, and to have shorter reaction times. In the Pope, Blass, et al. (1970) investigation the effects of both anxiety and depression on speech were studied. Although the investigation is relevant to the behavior of the interviewee, it does not actually use interview data. The subjects were six psychosomatic patients on a research ward of a psychiatric hospital, four females and two males, ranging in age from 17 to 39. The naturalistic fluctuations of anxiety and depression in these patients were monitored by two nurses with research training using an appropriate rating scale. These six patients taped daily 10-minute free speech monologues during tthe entire duration of their hospitalization. For the present study speech samples of each patient were selected over a three-month period to represent eight high and eight low anxiety and depression days. The following questions were posed by the investigators:

1. How does the patient's speech on high-anxious days compare with speech on low-anxious days?

2. How does the patient's speech on high-depression days compare with speech on low-depression days?

3. How do high-anxiety days compare with high-depression days?

With reference to the first question, there were the following findings. On high-anxious rather than low-anxious days the patients spoke at a faster rate, with fewer silent pauses, but with more disruption of speech. Thus, the activation effect of anxiety was noted in the higher speech rate and the lesser silence and, as in previous studies, the activation effect was associated with more flustering of speech. With reference to the second question, dealing with high- and low-depression days, the results were the reverse of those for anxiety. Thus, on high-depression days, the patients spoke at a lower rate, with longer and more frequent periods of silence, and with fewer expressions of hesitations such as Ah. The first two findings clearly reflect the anticipated tendency of depression to have a low activation effect. When depressed, the $\underline{S}$ was likely to speak at a slower rate and to manifest more silence. The apparent inconsistency in the lower Ah Ratio was a consequence of the depressed patient's preference for periods of silence over filled pauses (Ah and other expressions of hesitation). The contrasting effects of anxiety and depression were noted when one directly compared the high anxiety with high depression days for the same patients. Each patient spoke at a faster rate, spending less time in silence when s(he) was anxious than when depressed.

The previous findings regarding the effect of anxiety on verbal behavior had been obtained in studies in which the $\underline{S}$ was his/her own control. Anxiety level was varied between segments of the same interview or between interviews. In the remaining studies in this chapter the focus is on the verbal behavior correlates of differences in anxiety, defined as a predispositional personality trait. Do $\underline{S}$s who score high on anxiety scales manifest higher verbal productivity, less hesitation, and more flustering of speech than those who score low? Stated otherwise, will the interindividual differences in verbal behavior for $\underline{S}$s with high- and low-anxiety scores be the same as those obtained above for the same interviewees as they fluctuate between high- and low-anxiety periods? In an early study (Kasl & Mahl, 1958) no consistent relationship was found between interviewee scores on the Taylor Manifest Anxiety Scale and the frequency of speech disturbances (Non-Ah Ratio). A later investigation (Siegman & Pope, 1965) did produce a significant positive correlation between interviewee scores on a short form of the Manifest Anxiety Scale and verbal productivity; a significant negative correlation with hesitation expressions.

Perhaps the most sophisticated study on the effect of anxiety level as a personality trait on a $\underline{S}$'s verbal behavior was carried out by Kaplan (1966). Two groups of female undergraduate $\underline{S}$s were selected, one consisting of individuals who scored at low-anxiety levels on two anxiety questionnaires, and the other, of individuals who scored at high-anxiety levels. The method used was an experimental analogue rather than a naturalistic interview. Each S was seated in a chair directly facing a large one-way mirror. She was told that a psychologist in the adjoining room could see and hear her, and was asked to speak to him for 20 minutes through the mirror. A tape recorder, located in another room recorded the S's speech. High-anxiety Ss uttered more words (i.e., were more productive) than low-anxiety Ss.

But Kaplan (1966) was skeptical about the use of an anxiety score on a test as a valid index of anxiety. She had a hunch that Ss who report anxiety on a questionnaire may not necessarily be more anxious than those who do not, but simply more willing to disclose the anxiety that they experience. To test this out, she asked the Ss to respond to a Defensiveness Scale derived from the MMPI, a measure of the extent to which a person uses repression and denial when asked to speak about personal matters. She assumed that a significant negative correlation between defensiveness and anxiety would indicate that a high anxiety score on a questionnaire would be indicative of a lack of defensiveness (i.e., a willingness to disclose one's anxiety). In fact, the anticipated negative correlation between anxiety scores and defensiveness occurred. The author's hunch was again tested out by correlating the Ss' anxiety scores with their resistiveness as measured by a scale that assessed freedom to talk spontaneously about self, particularly about such feelings as anxiety and hostility. Again the results showed that high anxiety scoring Ss had lower resistiveness scores than low anxiety scoring Ss.

In summary, interviewees who are initially anxious are likely to do better in psychotherapy than those who are not. A moderate level of anxiety is associated with greater interviewee responsiveness - i.e., greater productivity, more expression of affect, less hesitation - and less resistiveness, associated however with increased flustering of speech. However, extreme anxiety is likely to reverse the facilitating effect of moderate levels causing the interviewee to defend against the experience of painful feeling by various degrees of withdrawal such as speaking about superficial rather than psychological content, falling into silence, or ultimately leaving the interview situation. If anxiety may be regarded as an activating motion, depression is clearly a retarding affect.

APPLICATION SUMMARY

Chapter 8 dealt with selected attributes of interviewers. In Chapter 9 the focus shifted to interviewees, their style of communication, and relationship behavior.

The diagnostic identity of the patient is an important datum to the mental health interviewer because it pertains to the major conceptual scheme used by the clinician for classifying those with whom s(he) works. Parenthetically, it does need to be noted that all diagnostic systems in the behavior disorders fall short of taxonomic criteria that would be acceptable in the physical sciences. Moreover, they have all been disappointing as explanatory frameworks for the etiology of various forms of mental illness and as guides to their treatment. Yet they are the products of a continuing effort to classify and systematize a broad range of psychological abnormality and cannot be ignored. Moreover, the different diagnostic categories are associated, to a degree, with certain patterns of communication and relationship. It is the last point, in particular, which justifies the inclusion of interviewee interactional attributes, classified according to diagnosis in the present chapter.

In a practical, applied sense, there is some value to the interviewer in becoming acquainted with the major communication and relationship patterns of interviewees in different diagnostic groups. There are two ways, one reciprocal to the other, in which the mental health interviewer may use this information. A frequent purpose of the initial interview is that of assessment or, quite simply, diagnosis. Style as reflected in the linguistic and paralinguistic aspects of speech and in nonverbal communication provides information that is relevant to the diagnostic decision that the interviewer must make. Reciprocally, as the interaction proceeds, the interviewer develops diagnostic hypotheses that lead him/her to anticipate certain forms of interviewee behavior. Such anticipation is useful to the interviewer in facilitating communication and positive relationship, the main channels through which the interview flows.

Much of the material in the section of the chapter dealing with the diagnostic classification of interviewee attributes is clinical in nature, supplemented by selected research studies. The present purpose is not to provide an encyclopedic coverage of the topic of interviewee diagnosis but to illustrate how the practitioner might use the clinical and research findings that pertain to it.

Two excerpts compare the interview behavior of a young female schizophrenic patient and a young male with late adolescent adjustment problems with associated depression. The communication of the schizophrenic patient was not grossly psychotic, but discernibly deviant nevertheless. Some remarks could not be understood because the associative context necessary for grasping the patient's meaning was not given. Other remarks were excessively abstract for the thought being communicated. But these abstractions were autistic, in the sense that they did not actually refer to the concepts that the terms would ordinarily imply but, instead, related to very private, very specific, and paradoxically, concrete meanings held by the patient. Often an exchange with a schizophrenic is obstructed by the interviewee's use of a private semantic system not shared by the interviewer.

The obscurity of the schizophrenic patient's use of language is in part a consequence of a failure to attain or a regressive loss of the capacity to remain in touch with others. Clinicians who have worked with schizophrenics also note a resistive function in schizophrenic communication. If the schizophrenic patient feels vulnerable to potential criticism, disparagement, and attack from others, s(he) retires behind an impermeable wall of speech that is not readily understandable. Mutism is, of course, a more complete defense. But silence is stressful in an interpersonal situation. In obscure speech the patient does respond, but communicates little. However, whether the patient responds with total silence or obscure speech, the task of the interviewer is a delicate one. The distrust, suspicion, and hostility of the patient cannot be overcome by frontal attack. Instead, it may yield over time to the persistent interest and commitment of the therapist.

The interview with the male patient diagnosed as an adjustment reaction was quite different. By contrast with the schizophrenic, communication was clear, lacking the autistic obscurity so prevalent in the first interview. Although the low activation quality of depressive speech (slow tempo, silent pauses, hesitation, low volume) was expected, it did not occur to a marked degree because the patient was not as depressed as had been anticipated. Certain relationship obstacles to the interview interaction had also been expected but occurred only minimally. Thus, the young man's rebelliousness led the interviewer to expect him to be resistive, negative, and unwilling to speak about his problems. Negativism did occur in relation to certain topical areas, but much more moderately than had been anticipated.

In the above two interviews the interviewer was the same person, but the interviewees varied. It would therefore be reasonable to assume that the difference in the character of the relationship and communication in the interviews was a result of the interaction between the single interviewer and the two interviewees.

A second comparison between the interview behavior of two fictional patients, one obsessive and the other hysteric, further illustrated two defensive patterns and their association with two contrasting styles of communication and relationship. The task of the interviewer is quite different with the two types. The obsessive may seem like a very gratifying patient at the beginning. S(he) produces a wealth of information, sometimes overwhelming the interviewer with memories and interpretations. But the interviewer is basically treated like a student who is being informed, often with some pedantry, about an interesting body of subject matter. Frustration with the obsessive patient grows as it becomes evident that s(he) remembers too much and knows too little. Much of the personal relevance of the information produced is attenuated by doubt and uncertainty about its meaning. The interviewer must guard against being drawn into speculative exchanges in which each participant is contending for a position of intellectual preeminence. Once drawn into an intellectual match, the interviewer becomes an accomplice of the interviewee in banning any expression of personal feeling. The goal of the obsessive interviewee is to avoid self-disclosure, that is, the expression of personal meaning and emotion. The objective of the interviewer is the introduction of personal communication where it has been eliminated by a complex cognitive filter.

The task of the interviewer with the hysteric patient is the opposite of that with the obsessive. Cognition is underutilized by the hysteric. Memory for past events is weak, impressionistic, and confused. There is little tendency to relate events in his/her life to each other and to draw inferences from such introspective analysis. By contrast, emotion erupts readily. Anxiety, hurt, depression, anger, flow easily in the interview, but attempts by the interviewer to relate them to current and past relationships and personal events are rejected. The dramatic experience of the moment is predominant, and it is into this type of immediate exchange that the patient seeks to draw the interviewer. A failure of the interviewer to resist will again make him/her an accomplice in the patient's major strategy of defense. In this instance it is the prevention of insight and understanding by repeated affect storms. In brief, if the interviewer must seek to heat up the personal response, the self-disclosing communication of the obsessive, s(he) must try to cool it with the hysteric, and assist the patient in developing cognitive channels through which emotions that have tended to flood and to retard personal growth might flow in a more regulated way.

Interacting with, but not at all identical with, diagnosis is the description of personality. There is much evidence that personality attributes or traits have a considerable bearing on interpersonal behavior in general and more specifically, on relationship and communication within the interview. An example of a widely investigated single dimension of personality is that of interviewee dependency. Much of the clinical lore in this area derives from psychotherapy with phobic patients who are both anxious and highly dependent (Andrews, 1966). Although modalities of treating phobic patients vary, there is a widely shared consensus about how the relationship should be managed. The guiding principle is that of a delicate balance between enough dependency gratification and support to the patient to maintain the relationship, and enough graduated direction of the patient into the phobically prescribed areas to insure progress in coping with the symptomatic anxiety.

Some experimental studies have emphasized the predispositional tendency of dependent patients to feel strongly attracted to potential helpers (Heller & Goldstein, 1961). Such attraction undoubtedly functions as a relationship maintaining drive. Many therapists appear to know this and therefore tend to prefer dependent to nondependent clients (Snyder, 1963).

Certainly most clinicians who have worked with both dependent and counterdependent clients (Bordin, 1974) have found the former easier to relate to than the latter. Counterdependent clients are assumed to be motivated by covert dependency needs, but their anxiety about the underlying needs is such as to make them feel helplessly vulnerable to anyone who diminishes their independence. An interviewer may arouse their dependency anxiety either by dominant or supportive behavior, because both would threaten their autonomy. Several investigators have explored the implications for relationship and communication within the interview of interviewee counterdependency. Thus, Williams (1959) found that counterdependent patients rather than overtly dependent ones responded with more oppositional resistance and with reduced levels of self-exploration when the therapist offered them support. Several verbal conditioning studies (Cairns & Lewis, 1962; Timmons & Noblin, 1963) demonstrated the reduced susceptibility to conditioning of such patients, and thus to persuasion and influence by the $\underline{E}$. Indeed, counterdependent patients were so oppositional to what they must have perceived as manipulation as to show a negative conditioning effect; that is, they performed more poorly during conditioning than during operant periods.

While the therapist may find that long-term objectives in treatment are balked by client dependency that is not alleviated over time, counterdependent resistance asserts itself more readily. The task of the interviewer is particularly difficult because patients with this problem vigilantly resist persuasion and what they perceive as manipulation. The interviewer must therefore guard against any display of dominance, overt support, and control;

indeed, against any behavior that reduces the autonomy of the patient.

Other studies correlate selected personality traits of the interviewee with his/her verbal communication. In one (Weintraub & Aronson, 1964) a diagnostically varied group of patients had one personality attribute in common - that of impulsive outbursts followed by guilty periods of self-reproach. Taped monologues of these patients, compared with those of a control group, were characterized by remarks calculated to manipulate the $\underline{E}$ into giving them more direction and assistance than that already communicated in the instructions. Having impulsively attempted to subvert the rules of their assigned tasks these patients then remorsefully retracted and negated many of the things they had said. Constantly battered by impulse, they emitted speech that overflowed with feeling.

Findings such as those cited above are useful to the interviewer in two basic ways:

1. They provide him/her with communication and relationship clues useful in diagnosis, and in personality assessment more broadly conceived.

2. They give him/her some guidance for the fostering of a positive relationship in the interview, and the encouragement of interviewee self-disclosure.

A number of studies have investigated an aspect of interviewee personality that is particularly relevant to the success of the interview. Variously designated, the attribute pertains to the interviewee's capacity for relationship. In one investigation the interviewee personality trait under discussion was called relatability (Isaacs & Haggard, 1966) and was demonstrated to be positively associated with a client's improvement in psychotherapy. Clients with higher capacities for relationship were the ones that showed more improvement in therapy. In another investigation (Pope & Nudler, 1973) in a psychiatric hospital male patients with high sociometric acceptance scores (i.e., those who were liked best by their fellows) manifested high verbal fluency in an interview (low silent hesitation) and high levels of self-disclosure. Finally two studies referred to interviewee capacity for relationship as attractiveness and likability (Nash et al., 1965; Stoler, 1963). In the first of these investigations this trait was rated in a group of neurotic out-patients, and found to correlate positively with measures of desirable interview behavior and with positive therapy outcome. In the second, patients rated as more likable were found to be the more effective participants in psychotherapy interviews (higher Experiencing scores) and the more successful in treatment. It will come as no surprise to the interviewer that those patients with a greater capacity to enter into a relationship are likely to be more self-disclosing in a mental health interview and more successful in psychotherapy.

An interviewer may acquire an enhanced capacity to perceive an interviewee's aptness for relationship. The interviewee trait under consideration is not associated with introversion-extroversion, for an introverted bent is not necessarily inconsistent with the capacity to relate. Thus, there is a critical difference between a normal, introverted person who may be capable of long hours of thoughtful, intimate conversation with another, and a schizoid individual who feels exposed and vulnerable unless s(he) is able to withdraw behind a protective wall of self-imposed isolation. The character of the relationship that the interviewer seeks to develop and the tempo and style of communication will vary with the interviewee's capacity for relationship. Compare, for example, the task of interviewing a schizoid patient, such as the one described in the first section of Chapter 6 with that of communicating with Mrs. B (Chapter 7). The schizoid patient is negative, secretive, uncommunicative, and protectively closed. With the patient's rudimentary capacity for relationship the interviewer must: guard against excessive intrusion, respect the distance assumed by the patient, adapt to the chilly flatness of the interviewee's emotional tone, and must be satisfied with a meager flow of self-disclosing communication. With Mrs. B, the interviewer could be spontaneous, expressive, and tuned up to a high level of interviewee self-disclosing speech.

Finally, the affective expressiveness of the patient is an attribute to which the clinical interviewer becomes sensitized. There is a widely shared belief among clinicians, supported by research findings, that patients who are able to experience and communicate affect freely are likely to experience more success in psychotherapy than those who are limited and impoverished in emotional experience and expression. The two emotions that are referred to most frequently in the literature are anxiety and depression. High anxiety and depression in the initial interview or early in treatment are prognostic of a favorable outcome (Luborsky et al., 1971). The presence of such strong, unpleasant emotions early in therapy indicates that the patient is in pain and is asking for help. The therapist conducting an initial interview is therefore alert to the presence of anxiety and/or depression as cues of an adequate level of motivation for treatment.

Other investigators have demonstrated the effects on interviewee communication of the above two dysphoric emotions. In several studies (Pope & Siegman, 1965; Siegman & Pope, 1965) anxiety functioned both as an activator and a disruptor of speech. The former was noted in an increase in productivity, shorter reaction time, a faster rate of speech, and fewer hesitations; the latter in an increase in speech disturbance. Depression as a low-activating emotion has quite the opposite effect on speech (Pope, Blass, Siegman & Raher, 1970). When depressed, the verbal rate of a patient decreases, and silent hesitation increases.

The interviewer tends to search an interviewee's face and posture for expressions of mood and affect. The above studies on verbal behavior indicate that the interviewer would also do well to listen to the paralinguistic attributes of the interviewee's speech.

REFERENCES

Andrews, J.D.W. Psychotherapy of phobias. Psychological Bulletin, 1966, 66, 455-480.

Beier, E.G. The silent language of psychotherapy. Chicago: Aldine, 1966.

Bordin, E.S. Research strategies in psychotherapy. New York: Wiley, 1974.

Cairns, R.B., & Lewis, D.M. Dependency and the reinforcement value of a verbal stimulus. Journal of Consulting and Clinical Psychology, 1962 26, 1-8.

Duffy, E. Activation and behavior. New York: Wiley, 1962.

Foa, U. Convergences in the analysis of the structure of interpersonal behavior. Psychological Review, 1961, 5, 341-353.

Gallagher, J.J. Test indicators for therapy prognosis. Journal of Consulting Psychology, 1954, 18, 409-413.

Heller, K., & Goldstein, A.P. Client dependency and therapist expectancy as relationship maintaining variables in psychotherapy. Journal of Consulting Psychology, 1961, 25, 371-375.

Heller, K., Myers, R.A., & Kline, L.V. Interviewer behavior as a function of standardized client roles. Journal of Consulting Psychology, 1963, 27, 117-122.

Isaacs, K.S., & Haggard, E. Some methods used in the study of affect in psychotherapy. In L.A. Gottschalk & A.H. Auerbach (Eds.), Methods of research in psychotherapy. New York: Appleton-Century-Crofts, 1966.

Kaplan, F. Effects of anxiety and defenses in a therapy-like situation. Journal of Abnormal Psychology, 1966, 71, 449-458.

Kasl, S.V., & Mahl, G.F. Experimentally induced anxiety and speech disturbance. Paper read at annual meeting of the American Psychological Association, Washington, D.C., September 1958.

Kiesler, D.J. Patient experiencing and successful outcome in individual psychotherapy of schizophrenics and psychoneurotics. Journal of Consulting and Clinical Psychology, 1971, 37, 370-385.

Klein, M.H., Mathieu, P.L., Gendlin, E.T., & Kiesler, D.J. The Experiencing Scale: A research and training manual. Madison: Wisconsin Psychiatric Institute, Bureau of Audio-Visual Instruction, 1970. Two volumes.

Lennard, H.L., & Bernstein, A. The anatomy of psychotherapy. New York: Columbia University Press, 1960.

Libo, L. Picture impressions: A projective technique for investigating the patient-therapist relationship. (Department of Psychiatry Publication Series) Baltimore: University of Maryland Medical School, 1956.

Liberman, B.L., Frank, J.D., Hoehn-Saric, R., Stone, A.R., Imber, S.D., & Pande, S.K. Patterns of change in treated psychoneurotic patients: A five-year follow-up in the investigation of the systematic preparation of patients for psychotherapy. Journal of Consulting and Clinical Psychology, 1972, 38, 36-41.

Luborsky, L. The patient's personality and psychotherapeutic change. In H.H. Strupp & L. Luborsky (Eds.), Research in psychotherapy. Washington, D.C.: American Psychological Association, 1962.

Luborsky, L., Auerbach, A.H., Chandler, M., Cohen, J., & Bachrach, H.M. Factors influencing the outcome of psychotherapy: A review of quantitative research. Psychological Bulletin, 1971, 75, 145-185.

MacKinnon, R.A., & Michels, R. The psychiatric interview in clinical practice. Philadelphia: Saunders, 1971.

Markel, N.N. Relationship between voice-quality profiles and MMPI profiles in psychiatric patients. Journal of Abnormal Psychology, 1969, 74, 61-66.

Markel, N.N., Meisels, M., & Houck, J.E. Judging personality from voice quality. Journal of Abnormal and Social Psychology, 1964, 69, 458-463.

Maslow, A.H., & Mittelmann, B. Principles of abnormal psychology. New York: Harper, 1941.

Matarazzo, J.D., & Saslow, G. Differences in interview interaction behavior among normal and deviant groups. In I.A. Berg & B.M. Bass (Eds.), Conformity and deviation. New York: Harper, 1961.

Nash, E.H., Hoehn-Saric, R., Battle, C.C., Stone, A.R., Imber, S.D., & Frank, J.D. Systematic preparation of patients for short-term psychotherapy. II: Relation to characteristics of patient, therapist and the psychotherapeutic process. The Journal of Nervous and Mental Disease, 1965, 140, 374-383.

Pope, B., Blass, T., Siegman, A.W., & Raher, J. Anxiety and depression in speech. Journal of Consulting and Clinical Psychology, 1970, 35, 128-133.

Pope, B., & Nudler, S. Some clinical and sociometric correlates of interviewee verbal behavior. Proceedings of the 81st Annual Convention of the American Psychological Association, 1973, 8, 561-562.

Pope, B., & Scott, W.H. Psychological diagnosis in clinical practice. New York: Oxford University Press, 1967.

Pope, B., & Siegman, A.W. Interviewer specificity and topical focus in relation to interviewee productivity. Journal of Verbal Learning and Verbal Behavior, 4, 1965, 188-192.

Pope, B., Siegman, A.W., & Blass, T. Anxiety and speech in the initial interview. Journal of Consulting and Clinical Psychology, 1970, 35, 233-238.

Rayner, E.H., & Hahn, H. Assessment of psychotherapy. British Journal of Medical Psychology, 1964, 37, 331-342.

Siegman, A.W., & Pope, B. Effects of question specificity and anxiety-arousing messages on verbal fluency in the initial interview. Journal of Personality and Social Psychology, 1965, 4, 188-192.

Snyder, W.U. The psychotherapy relationship. New York: MacMillan, 1961.

Snyder, W.U. Dependency in psychotherapy, A casebook. New York: MacMillan, 1963.

Stoler, N. Client likeability: A variable in the study of psychotherapy. Journal of Consulting Psychology, 1963, 27, 175-178.

Timmons, E.D., & Noblin, C.D.   The differential performance of orals and anals in a verbal conditioning paradigm.   Journal of Consulting Psychology, 1963, 27, 383-386.

Vetter, H.J.   Language behavior and psychopathology: Chicago: Rand McNally, 1969.

Waldfogel, S., Coolidge, J., & Hahn, P.   The development, meaning and management of school phobia.   American Journal of Orthopsychiatry, 1957, 27, 754-780.

Weintraub, W., & Aronson, H.   The application of verbal behavior analysis to the study of psychological defense mechanisms.   II: Speech patterns associated with impulsive behavior.   The Journal of Nervous and Mental Disease, 1964, 139, 75-82.

Williams, J.V.   The influence of therapist commitment on progress in psychotherapy.   Unpublished doctoral thesis, University of Michigan, 1959.

IV

Demographic Variables for Interviewers and Interviewees

10 Sex, Race and Social Class in the Interview

The preceding chapter has dealt with interviewee attributes defined both as personality traits and as psychological conditions. The present chapter will review investigations concerned with the effects of interviewer and interviewee sex, race, and social class on the interview interaction.

SEX

There are certain types of communication situations in which sex differences, for example, might be studied without regard to possible listeners or dyadic partners. Thus, a sample of male $\underline{S}$s and another of female $\underline{S}$s might be asked to provide taped monologues about a specific topic. Such monologues could be analyzed for sex differences in verbal behavior. Unlike a monologue, the interview is an encounter between two people. The differences that emerge between male and female interviewees may well be determined, in part, by the sexual identity of the interviewers with whom they interact. The studies that follow will therefore specify and often control the sex of both interviewer and interviewee.

Self-Reported Style

One investigation (Rice, Gurman, & Razin, 1974) explored the perceptions that male and female therapists have of their own styles of communication in therapy interviews. Using a self-report style questionnaire, male and female therapists were asked to rate themselves on such items as "talkative, supportive, reassuring; guided by theory; critical, disapproving; focusing on relationship" (Rice et al., 1974, p. 415) and others. Female therapists described themselves as more variable in their therapy behavior and less

441

"anonymous" than male therapists. Somewhat paradoxically, they also viewed themselves as more judgmental than male therapists. The authors present some evidence to show an appreciable positive correlation between the self-perceptions of the therapists and the perceptions that cotherapists had of them. Beyond this finding, there are no data to indicate how the therapists' self-reported behavior might correlate with their actual behavior. The remaining studies in this section deal with actual verbal and nonverbal behavior of male and female Ss.

Verbal Aspects

The male "chauvinist" world has always assumed that women are more verbally facile and prolific than men. The findings presented below are limited and largely applicable to the interview. They will therefore do little either to reinforce or undermine the above tenet of masculine bias. However, they do address themselves to some questions pertaining to sex differences in verbal and nonverbal communication as they may relate to the interview.

One index of verbal facility or fluency is the Mahl Non-Ah Ratio (Mahl, 1959), a measure of disturbed or flustered speech. If women are indeed more verbally facile than men, they should speak with fewer speech disturbances. Actually, two interview studies failed to demonstrate such a difference. Mahl (1959) himself found no significant difference in Non-Ah Ratio between male and female interviewees. Later, a more extensive investigation (Feldstein, Brenner, & Jaffe, 1963) again failed to find a sex difference in the rate of interviewee speech disturbance. The Ss were male and female clinic outpatients, interviewed for 20 minutes by either a male or female interviewer. Although many variables were manipulated experimentally, the ones of immediate concern are the sex of the interviewer, the sex of the interviewee, and the interaction between the two. All of these variables failed to affect significantly the level of interviewee speech disturbance. Thus, male and female interviewees did not differ from each other in level of speech disturbance whether interviewed by like-sexed or cross-sexed interviewers.

One study (Feldstein, 1964), however, did report a sex difference in level of speech disturbance. But this investigation was not based on the interview. Its primary goal was the investigation of such vocal attributes as changes in the rate and volume of speech, pitch, patterns of breathing, and speech disturbances in the expression of specific emotions. The Ss were actors and actresses asked to use the reading of a standard passage to express anger, depression, fear, hate, nervousness, and other emotions. The one finding of present interest pertains to the difference between actors and actresses in Non-Ah speech disturbances. The actor's speech was less fluent, more disrupted than that of the actresses, particularly when both were simulating nervousness.

If the preceding three studies leave some doubt about the alleged lower level of speech disturbance in female than male interviewees, one of these investigations (Feldstein et al., 1963) is quite clear-cut about another aspect of verbal fluency - i.e., hesitations in the form of such verbal expressions as

Ah. In this interview study, it was evident that men were significantly more hesitant than women. Moreover, the filled pauses (i.e., hesitation expressions such as Ah) of men took on different patterns than those of women. Men paused more frequently when talking about problems rather than neutral topics; women showed no such distinction. Both men and women were more hesitant in interactive segments of the interview than in the periods during which the interviewer instructed the interviewees to speak while he left the room.

Perhaps the male "chauvinists" have been right all along because the evidence does suggest, however faintly, that women do speak with greater facility than men. But do they speak more? Are they more productive? In two interview experiments males were actually more verbally productive than females (Heller, 1972; Siegman, 1972). In the second of these studies there was a further investigation of sex differences in interviewee productivity in the same-sexed versus cross-sexed dyads. The form of the study was prompted by a previous investigation (Pope & Siegman, 1968) which demonstrated that a friendly, warm, supportive interviewer elicits more speech from an interviewee than an unfriendly, cold, unsupportive interviewer. Siegman (1972) noticed, however, that both the interviewers and interviewees in the warm-cold study were female. Would the findings remain unaltered if interviewer warmth and coldness were studied in both same-sexed and cross-sexed interview situations? In the Siegman (1972) investigation there were two groups of interviewees, one male and the other female. The same male interviewer conducted all the interviews. By experimental design, he altered his behavior so that he was warm in one-half of the interviews, and cold in the other half. When both male and female Ss were considered together, there was no difference in interviewee productivity between the warm and cold interviews conducted by the same male interviewer. A further analysis showed that male and female interviewees were actually responding differently to the male interviewer. Males were more productive with the interviewer when they were led to expect him to be warm and he behaved warmly; and less productive when both their expectations of him and his behavior were cold. There was also a significant difference in female interviewee productivity between the two interviewer conditions; but, alas, the difference was opposite to that which had been expected. Female interviewees were more productive in the cold than in the warm condition. Siegman (1972) speculated that "perhaps warmth and friendliness on the part of the interviewer, especially somewhat exaggerated as in the present study, had seductive and threatening overtones for female interviewees, and hence its inhibiting effect on their productivity" (Siegman, 1972, p. 13). Thus, the same interviewer, conducting an interview in the same manner may be differently perceived by male and female interviewees with different consequences for the interview.

It was inevitable that the sequence of studies on self-disclosure reported by Jourard (1971a; 1971b) would, at some point, become engaged with the problem of sex differences. The following questions posed by Jourard are all of interest to the interviewer: (1) Are females, in general, more self-disclosing than males? (2) If they are, does their difference with males vary with the person who is the target of their self-disclosure? (3) Is self-disclosing behavior among females prompted more by affection for the person to whom disclosure is made than it is among males? In brief, Jourard's (1971a; 1971b) research leads to an affirmative answer to each of these questions.

The answer to the first was obtained in a study based on four small groups of undergraduate students selected from three Alabama college populations, two white liberal arts colleges, a black liberal arts college, and a school of nursing located at a medical school. The four groups in the study were composed of white males, white females, black males, and black females, all unmarried. Self-disclosure items were directed toward the following target persons: mother, father, male friend, and female friend. In general, across all target persons, females reported higher levels of self-disclosure than males.

Another study directed its attention to the question dealing with the interaction between higher female self-disclosure and the specific target person to whom self-disclosure was directed. The $\underline{S}$s were again unmarried male and female undergraduate students. The data were again elicited by a self-disclosure questionnaire similar in most respects to the one used in the first study. Once more the females were generally more disclosing than the males. With reference to specific target persons, the difference between the sexes was significant for mother, same-sex friend, and opposite-sex friend. Evidently the higher level of female self-disclosure did not apply to father.

The findings regarding the third question - that is, the difference between the sexes regarding the degree to which self-disclosure to a person was prompted by affection for him/her, were based on a comparison of two separate studies, one based on a small group of male graduate students, and the other, on a small group of female members of the faculty of a college of nursing (Jourard, 1971b). In this regard, the author summarizes his findings in the following terms: "The relatively minor role played by liking in men's disclosure contrasts sharply with the major role it played in the disclosure patterns of the female sample studied earlier....The strong association between liking and disclosure was peculiar to the females" (Jourard, 1971b, p. 25).

While the sex differences in self-disclosure outlined above have recurred in a number of studies, investigators have by no means been unanimous in obtaining these findings. Two studies conducted in the northeast of the United States (Rickers-Ovsiankina & Kusmin, 1958; Zief, 1962) and one in the middlewest (Certner, 1973) have failed to support the Jourard results. The regional locations of the studies are given because it is assumed that there may be subcultural differences based on region that affect interpersonal value differences of the two sexes. Jourard himself hinted at such an explanation in the following jocular comment: "It is tempting to suggest that in the southeast, where I collected the bulk of my data, the men are men and the women are women; whereas Harvard males and Radcliffe females, whom Zief tested, for example, may not be so different from one another" (Jourard, 1971a, p. 237).

Despite the preceding negative findings, there is enough consistency in the results of various studies to alert the interviewer to the occurrence of sex differences in self-disclosing behavior. Guided by such an explanation, the interviewer may be able to avoid the stress that occurs in an interview when expectations are incongruent with actual interview behavior.

Nonverbal Aspects

The relative dearth of sex differences in verbal dimensions of communication was more than compensated for by their frequent occurrence in nonverbal channels. A clinical study (Mahl, 1968) rich in observational data provides a striking introduction to this area of investigation. The data for the study were collected by an experienced psychiatric social worker, who tape-recorded a series of intake interviews in a university-community hospital. Since videotaping equipment was not yet readily available at the time of this investigation, an ingeniously cumbersome procedure was utilized. The interviews were recorded on audiotape while the author watched them through a one-way mirror, without hearing the spoken words. As he observed, he dictated a running account of the patient's gestural behavior onto a second tape. The two tapes were later brought into synchrony with each other. The transcriptions of both tapes were used as the basis for subsequent clinical judgments about the communication implicit in the recorded gestures. The following sex differences were noted:

1. Most women kept their legs crossed at their knees throughout the interviews. Men were more varied in their leg-crossing gestures. Although a minority of men also kept their legs crossed at their knees, others manifested an "open-leg cross" (the lower leg or ankle on the knee of the other leg), and a posture in which both feet were placed flat on the floor. These differences were partly occasioned by the clothes worn by both sexes. But Mahl emphasized the rarity with which women deviated from the "high closed cross."

2. Sex differences were most frequent in the category of communicative gestures ("those actions judged to be substitutions for verbal utterances" (Mahl, 1968, p. 301). "The men pointed more frequently than women. On the other hand, the women shrugged their shoulders, shook their heads, and turned their palms-up-and-out more frequently than did the men" (Mahl, 1968, p. 303).

3. Sex differences were relatively infrequent in autistic gestures ("those actions judged not to be common substitutions for verbal utterances" (Mahl, 1968, p. 301). In one difference that did occur women patted their hair more frequently than men.

As a clinical study, Mahl's work, largely descriptive, presents some interesting contrasts in gestural communication between male and female interviewees. The difficulty with a study of this kind is its lack of information regarding the generality with which the results might be applied. Female interviewers used communication gestures more frequently than men. Is this a sex difference that one would encounter in a variety of situations? Or is it a consequence of the interaction of the female interviewees observed with their female interviewer?

Most of the investigations that follow are experimental in nature. Many provide some information about the range of applicability of the results. Note, however, as the studies are reviewed, that they usually do not deal directly with the interview, although their relevance to it is evident.

Since several of them occur in the area of proxemics, a few comments about the interactional variables included in this specialty are in order. This matter has been dealt with once before in the chapter concerned with nonverbal communication. Mehrabian and Friar (1969) defined the areas of proxemics in the following terms:

> Some proxemic variables are distance between a communicator and his addressee, degree of directness of orientation of a communicator toward his addressee (i.e., degree to which a communicator's body is turned in the direction of his addressee vs. away from the direction of his addressee), and the presence or absence of touching, or eye contact, between communicator and addressee. Thus, the concept of proxemics subsumes variations in postural and distance variables which relate to the degree of directness or immediacy of interaction between a communicator and his addressee... In addition to eye contact and directness of body orientation, Machotka also denotes accessibility of a communicator's body to the addressee e.g., openness of arms, as a relevant aspect of attitude communicating variables. (p. 330)

Eye contact between the interviewer and the interviewee is receiving considerable research attention at the present time. Some of the findings regarding eye contact will be examined below. But first, there will be a brief consideration of a closely related topic - that of interviewee visibility to the interviewer and the interviewee's visual perception of the interviewer. Do sex differences occur under conditions that vary in degree of interviewee visibility to and visual perception of the interviewer?

One investigation (Argyle, Lalljee, & Cook, 1968) dealt directly with both of the preceding questions. The experimental procedure provided for both participants in a dyadic exchange to present themselves to each other under varying conditions of normal and reduced visibility. In general, all subjects rated themselves as feeling less comfortable under conditions of reduced visibility of the other, and of their own reduced visibility than under normal conditions. This finding would, of course, be generally anticipated. But what of sex differences?

In a follow-up study carried out by the authors at Oxford University, the Ss were students. The exchange between the experimenter and the subject in each instance was not that of an interviewer with an interviewee, but that of two equal participants in a conversation. The S and the experimenter were in adjacent rooms, with a one-way viewing mirror and an intercom between them. Each presented himself to the other at the following decreasing levels of visibility: normally, wearing dark glasses, wearing a mask, and with a mask and dark glasses. The limiting condition was that of no visibility at all, implemented by eliminating all illumination on one side of the one-way vision screen. Thus, the S or the experimenter seated on the dark side of the screen could not be seen by the other, although he himself could see the other. In this limiting condition both participants could speak with each other, but one could see the other while not being seen himself. All subjects were asked to record their attitudes toward various levels of visibility for themselves and the other by responding to a number of scales dealing with the clarity with which they could perceive the other person, the comfort that they experienced in each situation, the ease with which they could communicate their ideas and feelings, and the ease of conversation.

In general, females were uneasy if they could not see the other person, even when invisible themselves; males did not show the same discomfort. In one comparison males spoke to females with the lights alternated so that the males were on the dark side of the one-way vision mirror for one-half of the time and the females for the other half. The visible male addressing the invisible female said significantly more than the visible female addressing the invisible male. Females appeared to need vision more than males do. They wanted to see even when not seen themselves.

It has been noted that females feel more observed than males (Argyle & Williams, 1969) in dyadic situations, particularly when communicating with opposite sex partners. Thus, in a visual interaction context females are the performers and males the observers.

> People who feel observed are expected to have the perceptual goal of watching for visual feedback in order to adjust their social performances. If females feel more observed than males, they might rely on visual feedback; without such feedback they may feel unable to adjust their social performances in response to their audiences. In general these studies indicate that in a neutral or positive interaction at a given level of intimacy, females.... possibly depend more on visual feedback than do males.   (Argyle & Williams, 1969, p. 396)

In sum, one may assume that female interviewees are more sensitive to their own visibility and to that of the interviewer than are males. Moreover, they are relatively less communicative than the male interviewee when they cannot see the interviewer.

The visibility of the interviewer and interviewee is one consideration; the visual interaction between the two is another. By visual interaction is meant "The act of one person's looking into the eyes of another" (Duncan, 1969, p. 129). The term most frequently used to designate visual interaction is that of eye contact.

That eye contact is a significant factor in maintaining communication between two people is widely accepted. "In general a continued exchange of glances would seem to signal a willingness or a desire to become involved with one another, or to maintain an ongoing interaction. Avoidance, on the other hand, would seem to indicate a disinterest in initiating a relationship, or in the case of an ongoing interaction, would indicate that one or both parties wished to break away" (Exline, Gray, & Schuette, 1965).

In one investigation (Exline, 1971) U.S. and British students were asked to rate their degree of comfort on a scale with a fictional dyadic partner who, when speaking, listening, or sharing mutual silence, would be looking at the $\underline{S}$ 100% of the time, 50% of the time, and 0%. In a rather complicated design the fictional partner was older, younger, or the same age as the $\underline{S}$. And finally, in one-half of the dyadic conditions referred to above a S's partner was of the same sex, and in the other half, of the opposite sex. In general, all Ss expected to be least comfortable in the condition in which they were speaking and their partner avoided glancing at them. Similar discomfort was anticipated by Ss when they visualized their partners glancing at them constantly during periods of silence on both sides. Both men and women were less uncomforable in the latter condition when the silent partner was a younger person than a peer or older person. Similarly, both men and women preferred the 100% visual attention of a peer of the opposite sex than one of the same sex. But in this preference the male Ss were considerably more pronounced than the women. And the lowest anticipated comfort was experienced by American college women when asked to visualize themselves as the objects of complete attention of an older male (i.e., a male of their father's generation).

Exline and his colleagues have used the procedure that follows in a series of studies dealing with eye contact. The interviewer was instructed to look steadily at the interviewee throughout the entire interview exchange. Mutual glances would therefore only occur when the interviewee reciprocated the interviewer's gaze. A chronological record of the frequency and duration of the interviewee's glances was made by an observer who sat behind a one-way vision mirror facing the interviewee but a little to the side of the interviewer. One study in this series (Exline et al., 1965) investigated the problem of sex differences in frequency of mutual visual interaction. Earlier Exline (1963) had found that women communicating with women engaged in mutual glances more frequently than men communicating with men. In the study presently considered the greater tendency of women than men to engage in eye contact was investigated in both like-sex and opposite-sex pairs. Both male and female students were randomly drawn from physical education classes. One-half of the interviewees of each sex was interviewed by a male, and the other half by a female. In this study, as in the previous one, women engaged in more mutual glances than men. This time, the difference was noted not only in like-sex pairs, but also in opposite-sex pairs (Exline et al., 1965). The authors had recourse to an additional result as a possible explanation of the sex difference. They had asked the Ss to fill out a questionnaire that assessed general attitudes toward interacting with others (Schutz, 1958). The questionnaire assesses interpersonal attitudes along three dimensions known as inclusion, affection, and control. The female Ss manifested a greater need than the males did for inclusion (i.e., for satisfactory interaction and association with others) and for affection. This led the authors to infer that the greater willingness of women to enter into eye contact is due to their greater orientation toward inclusive and affectionate relationships.

Another study by Exline and his colleagues (Exline & Winters, 1965) replicated the finding that female Ss spent a significantly larger percentage of their time in eye contact with their addressees than male Ss did. The procedure called for each S to be seated at a table, facing at equal distances two addressees seated on the other side of the table. The Ss were given a verbal story task and told that the two persons on the other side of the table were evaluators of their performances. At a midpoint in the experiment, each S was escorted to an adjacent room and asked to state a preference for one of the two people. During the second half of the investigation the S was returned to the experimental room and again seated at the table, facing the same two people. At this time, after each S had already stated a preference for one of the two addressees, women markedly increased their eye contact with the preferred ones and decreased their eye contact with the nonpreferred. Men did not respond in the same way. Instead of increasing their eye contact with their preferred addressees, they reduced eye contact with the nonpreferred. "Women...seem to seek out the eyes of those they like, or to whom they are momentarily attracted, whereas men do not attempt to increase their contact with the preferred so much as to avoid contact with the less preferred" (Exline & Winters, 1965, p. 347).

As indicated in the definition of proxemics quoted earlier (Mehrabian & Friar, 1969), eye contact is only one of several variables pertaining to the distance or the directness of contact between two persons speaking to each other. Others include the actual distance one person takes from the other, and the orientation or tilt of the body toward the other.

In a study previously considered for the visibility of the two participants in a dyadic exchange (Argyle et al., 1968) all Ss were asked to converse at two distances from each other (i.e., four feet and 10 feet). It was found that opposite-sex pairs experienced the greater of the two distances as the more comfortable, and same-sex pairs, the lesser of the two distances. Another study (Mehrabian & Friar, 1969) found that for both male and female Ss the mean distance taken from a female addressee was less than from a male.

Since eye contact and the physical distance that two members of a dyad assume from each other both contribute to the sense of proximity that one feels to the other, some authors (Argyle & Dean, 1973) became interested in how these two variables interact with each other, and how such an interaction might relate to sex differences. The method used by Argyle and Dean (1973) was the same as a procedure earlier used by Exline. Two people took part in a conversation, one of these the Ss, and the other a confederate of the researcher. The confederate gazed continually at the Ss. Thus, the frequency and duration of eye contact was determined by the S. Whenever s(he) gazed at the confederate there was eye contact; when s(he) looked away eye contact was broken. The Ss were all graduate students in fields other than psychology. Each pair held three conversations at distances of two feet, six feet, and 10 feet. The authors anticipated that as physical proximity increased, eye contact would decrease; as distance increased, so would eye contact. The assumption was that a sort of proxemic equilibrium was operative. Such was actually the case, for length of glance by the S increased significantly as the distance between the S and the confederate increased. An additional finding of considerable interest was an interaction between sex of confederate and sex of Ss. There was significantly less eye contact between mixed-sex rather than same-sex pairs, and this difference was greatest when the physical proximity between the members of the opposite-sex pair was greatest. The authors hastened to place their findings within a situational context. Where intimacy has already developed, particularly under conditions of sexual attraction, the above reduction in eye contact when the two members of the dyad are physically close to each other might not occur. But in the experimental situation, analogous to an initial clinical interview, reduction in eye contact was evidently the only way open to the S to keep psychological proximity within bounds.

The directness of orientation to each other of conversational partners contributed to their sense of proximity. Mehrabian and Friar (1969) noted that the average orientation of male Ss away from female addressees was greater than that from male addressees. Female Ss showed an analogous pattern with reference to male addressees. In brief, Ss of both sexes turned away more from unlike-sex rather than like-sex conversational partners.

In one investigation (Buck, Savin, Miller, & Caul, 1974) male and female "observers" were compared for accuracy in "reading" the affect communicated by the facial expressions of Ss who functioned as "senders." The observers and senders did not face each other in the same room. Instead, they were in two rooms remote from each other, with the facial expression of the sender transmitted to the observer through closed circuit television. The facial expressions of the senders were elicited by color slides with sexual, scenic, maternal, disgusting, and unusual or ambiguous content. The sender was asked to speak about his/her emotional reaction to each slide and then to rate it on a strong-weak and a pleasant-unpleasant scale. The observer was asked to observe each facial expression as it appeared on a television screen and rate it on the same two scales. In addition the observer was given the five content categories and asked to identify the content category to which the sender was responding in each instance.

Significantly more observers in female pairs of Ss correctly identified the content of each slide from the facial expression of the sender than those in male pairs. As a group, the female observers correctly identified the content categories of the slides at greater than chance levels. The male observers, as a group, fell short of significance. A larger number of female observer-sender pairs had significant correlations between the ratings made by each on the strength of feeling and pleasantness scales, than of male observer-sender pairs. In brief, female observers more accurately read the emotions communicated facially by their partners than did male observers.

Finally, a group of researchers (Rosenthal, Archer, DiMatteo, Koivumaki, & Rogers, 1974) developed a body of information regarding the relative sensitivity of men and women to nonverbal communication. The receiver of messages who is open to the wordless communication of body and tone of voice is certain to "hear" more over a broader range of modalities than one who is closed to such nonverbal channels. Rosenthal et al. (1974) developed a test called the Profile of Nonverbal Sensitivity (PONS) to assess a person's capacity to understand tones of voice and movements of the face and body as two forms of wordless communication. The test is administered by playing a 45-minute film consisting of a series of scenes. The scenes are communicated through three pure body language channels (i.e., face only, body only - neck to knees - and face plus body). There are additionally two tone of voice channels, both based on techniques which preserve the tone of voice but make the verbal message incomprehensible. Six other nonverbal channels consisted of various combinations of the above five pure channels. The person taking the test selects one of two offered labels as his response to a given scene. Only one of the two labels is considered to be correct. "For example, the movie may show a woman's face for two seconds; she looks upset; she's saying something that sounds important, but the words aren't clear" (Rosenthal et al., 1974, p. 65).

"The PONS has corroborated the popular opinion (and some previous experimental evidence) that females are better than males at detecting nonverbal cues. Females of all ages, from third grade through adult showed a small but reliable advantage over males" (Rosenthal et al., 1974, p. 66). This would appear to provide females with an a priori advantage over males in all interpersonal encounters, and particularly in clinical roles such as interviewers or group leaders. This "sexist inequity" is reduced somewhat by the further finding that the observed sex difference is narrowed and sometimes even reversed among men training for or working in occupational fields that require nurturant, expressive, or artistic behavior. Thus, males in the mental health occupations and in the arts tend to score "like women." Such mitigating findings notwithstanding, the evidence shows that a female interviewer or interviewee is likely to be more perceptive than her male counterpart in responding to nonverbal channels of communication.

In conclusion, it is evident from the research data available to date that the sex of the interviewee and the same sex versus opposite sex character of the interview dyad are significantly related to both verbal and nonverbal communication. Sex differences in verbal communication have not turned out to be as reliable or as replicable as sex differences in nonverbal communication. Nevertheless, the differences that do occur appear to be important in dyadic communication situations. Several years ago, an often-quoted member of the French Chamber of Deputies noted that there was a difference between men and women. Another member endorsed this difference with the Gallic outcry: "Vive la Difference!" "La difference" may complicate the life of the interviewer, but it also makes his task more variable and interesting.

RACE

Does race of interviewer and interviewee make any difference in the conduct of an interview?

Consider the following sequence of events on the admission service of a large state psychiatric hospital. A tall black male, age 48, was brought to the hospital one afternoon by two white policemen on a warrant sworn out by his wife. He was tense, belligerent, and garrulous as he was escorted by the police into the hospital. Soon after he entered, he was interviewed by a black psychiatrist. After an initial few minutes of glaring silence, he began to tell the psychiatrist about the events that preceded his hospitalization, as he perceived them. He was convinced that several relatives whom he described as male cousins were projecting their voices through his house, keeping out of sight themselves while they did so. To accomplish this they used an electronic device which the patient designated a "monster." He would not repeat the content of their projected messages except to allude obscurely to some event that occurred about 23 years earlier, involving himself and his wife. Apparently this event had something to do with the birth of his

daughter, whom he described as much darker than himself; in fact much
closer in color to his wife than to himself. Having disclosed this much he
refused to say anything more about the event. With reference to the
immediate past, he admitted that he had been violent in the house, in
response to the voices, directing his anger primarily against his wife. The
patient was willing to tell the black interviewer that his difficulties began a
year ago when he sustained a back injury on his job in a steel mill. He was
never able to return to work because his back injury never healed, even
though "the doctors wrote lying reports" to the company asserting that the
medical condition had cleared up.

The black psychiatrist thus elicited a description from the patient of what
appeared to be a paranoid schizophrenic condition of increasing scope starting
about a year prior to his arrival at the hospital. The precipitating event was
a back injury, with subsequent loss of job, but there were roots in his
relationships with his wife and daughter. Though suspicious, the patient was
willing to be reasonably informative.

He was not nearly so cooperative with a white male psychiatrist, who
interviewed him two days later. For about 10 minutes he refused steadfastly
to say anything. Then he denied that there were any problems in his home at
all. The warrant that brought the police to his home was a total fabrication
of the white police who had been having some difficulty in the neighborhood
and simply picked him as a scapegoat. There had been some thefts from a
nearby food market in the neighborhood and, having failed to catch the
offenders, they had arbitrarily decided to pick on him. As for his
belligerence, who would not be angry when treated as abusively as he had
been?

The hospital staff was undecided about the second story. Was it genuinely
delusional as the information given to the black psychiatrist appeared to be,
or did the patient consciously fabricate it to put off the white psychiatrist?
One couldn't be sure. But there was no doubt that, delusional or malingered,
it was a response to the white identity of the second interviewer. The patient
trusted him less than the first; he was less informative with him, and
certainly less willing to risk making himself vulnerable by sharing recently
disturbing experiences with him. Had there been only one interview, the
second one with the white psychiatrist, the patient's delusions would have
appeared stereotyped and unconvincing, reflecting widely shared experiences
of black people with white authority. In fact, the depth of the patient's
illness would have been obscured by the plausibility of his report. As it
happened, the sequence of two interviews made it possible to trace the
interaction of the patient's pathology, with his perceptions of white agents of
authority and his use of the latter perceptions to obscure the pathology.
Clinical events of the kind described here emphasize the significance of the
racial variable in the conduct of the interview, and should prompt its
investigation.

It would be difficult to find a clinician who would deny the intrusion of the
effect of race into a dyadic encounter. But some, confident in the strength
of the procedures and attitudes that they advocate (Carkhuff, 1972), express
a sort of optimism about the ease with which racial obstacles may be
overcome in the mental health interview. Others are less sanguine about the

problems posed by racial differences between the interviewer and inter-viewee. Since the most salient racial difference in America occurs between the black and white segments of the population, the present discussion will focus on this distinction.

After many years of slavery, black Americans experienced a brief interlude of relative freedom. Then, following their liberation from servitude, a system of legally sanctioned segregation was imposed on them. In sum, over two centuries of subjugation, buttressed by violence and the threat of violence, stifled the physical well being and personal growth of black Americans. And now, with the legal basis for segregation eroded, the legacy of centuries of inhibited personal development places the black section of the population at a serious competitive disadvantage in the economic marketplace. When lack of skill and education are not the barriers to jobs, a lingering caste discrimination is. Need anyone be surprised at the rage, distrust, and sometimes self-demeaning servility that characterize the attitudes of blacks when dealing with higher status whites? Should there be any doubt that attitudes so pervasive in our society would also emerge in an interview situation?

Distrust leads to concealment, a theme that occurs in Negro literature and music depicting the black person's dealings with whites. Consider, for example, the following verse (Ames, 1950) taken out of a Negro folksong:

> Got one mind for white folk to see,
> 'Nother for what I know is me;
> He don't know, he don't know my mind
> When he sees me laughing
> Laughing just to keep from crying.

There is no reason to believe that the type of distrust and concealment expressed so poignantly in the song would not serve as obstacles to open communication, even in a professionally managed mental health interview. When a white interviewer and a black interviewee interact, one would expect the usual type of interviewee resistance to the communication of psychologi-cally sensitive material to be augmented by the lack of trust, the type of self-protective concealment expressed eloquently in the above verse.

The self-demeaning servility that characterizes the behavior of some blacks toward whites would tend to conceal much of what the black interviewee feels and thinks from the white interviewer. In referring to the comments of others regarding this matter Sattler (1970) remarks that

> Negroes...do not like to talk to whites for fear that anything they say will be twisted around so as to disparage them; suspiciousness exists even when there are no grounds. ...Genuine feelings are replaced by a facade of submissiveness, pleasure, impassivity, or humility. The fear of disparagement, however, may be subsidiary to the fear of actual bodily harm, even death, which lay and to some degree still lies at the root of all Negro-white relations in the South. Second in importance only to the fear for life itself is the fear of economic reprisal. The newer generations are rapidly losing their fear in the larger cities but it is still present in the smaller cities and rural communities. (p. 148)

As fear recedes, the rage that underlies the distrust and servility becomes more manifest. Thus, James Baldwin has remarked: "To be a Negro in this country and to be relatively conscious is to be in a rage almost all the time" (Silberman, 1964, p. 36). Rage is a difficult emotion to cope with in an interview; any attempts to do so must certainly inhibit the flow of interviewee communication.

With the above experience so pervasively characteristic of black-white interactions, small wonder that authors tend to agree that white interviewers and black interviewees, or the converse, encounter more than the usual number of communication problems in mental health interviews. Rapport tends to be difficult. In summarizing interview studies pertaining to the variable of race Carkhuff (1972) speaks of "the conditioned defensiveness of the black in a relationship with whites. Due to years of destructive experiences with whites, it is hypothesized, the black enters the situation with a set of attitudes and behaviors which, if not attended, have a deleterious effect upon both process and outcome" (p. 18).

This deleterious effect was demonstrated with simple clarity in one investigation (Baratz, 1967) which dealt with the psychological testing situation rather than the interview. The Ss were black undergraduates at Howard University, both male and female. The experimenters included one white and one black male graduate student. The task of the experimenters was simply to administer a test anxiety questionnaire to the Ss. As it turned out, level of anxiety for the black students was higher when tested by the white than the black examiner.

Other types of deleterious effects are also likely to result. For example, a white interviewer is likely to make errors in clinical judgment because he may be unduly influenced by stereotypes about lower class blacks. If a black laborer comes to a psychiatrist's or psychologist's office shabbily dressed, and speaking in an unsophisticated southern patois, his intellectual level may be seriously underestimated. The interviewer may respond more to the stereotypes associated with his concept of "lower class Negro laborer," than to the actual behavior of the interviewee (Grier & Cobbs, 1969).

But the interviewer's mistaken judgment may not always diminish the clinical status of the interviewee; in some circumstances it could enhance it. A white interviewer who regards himself as devoid of bias, might tend to overlook clinical symptoms because of his readiness to perceive social deprivation. Consider the following example:

A pair of six year old twins was seen in a Child Guidance Clinic because of suspected severe mental disorder. They showed evidence of gross neglect, and attention naturally turned to the mother. She was a poorly groomed black woman of 32. She had five other children and never been married. A worker who visited the home described it as chaotic. Mother seemed ignorant of the most fundamental ideas of childrearing. She seemed dull and uncomprehending of the investigation that had begun. After a case conference on the problem, the white clinicians concluded that this woman, who had a wretched childhood in the rural South, and little schooling, was culturally retarded because of her early life. They thought that a program of home aides and instruction in home management would move her toward more effective mothering.   (Grier & Cobbs, 1969, p. 130)

But the clinicians were wrong in their initial judgment.   On further investigation, it turned out that the woman was psychotic. Apparently the white worker who initially interviewed the woman was so impressed by the deprived conditions under which the woman and her children lived that she overlooked her very evident pathology.

The clinical and research studies that follow dealing with the effects of race on the interview interaction and its outcome will be grouped according to various black and white interviewer and interviewee combinations.

White Interviewers and Black Interviewees

A number of clinicians have found that black interviewees tend to respond to white interviewers with suspiciousness, associated either with covert or overt hostility.   Such reactions were found by Phillips (1960) when he noted that black students counseled by both white and black counselors manifested submissiveness, suspiciousness, and hostility with the former but not with the latter.   Under completely different circumstances and much earlier, Frank (1947) noted that black patients showed far more submissiveness, suspiciousness, and initial fear than white patients, when interviewed by white psychiatrists. Frank worked with World War II soldiers and veterans. As to the reason for this excessive submissiveness, another author (St. Clair, 1951) remarked that "the Negro fears the threat of retaliation by the white man and wishes to protect himself by disguising his fear and hate behind a placating submissiveness.   The white physician is still a white man and a figure of authority to the Negro patient" (p. 114). Others (Heine, 1950) stress the role of white expectation. In the presence of a white interviewer a black interviewee is likely to sense the same expectations of him that he would perceive in other white authorities. A stereotyped black response to such perceived expectations is passivity, politeness, and noncommunicativeness.

Indeed, the study of soldiers and veterans (Frank, 1947) referred to above emphasized the very limited and superficial communication of black interviewees. All personally significant topics were avoided. Thus, problems relating to the status of black Americans were seldom brought up. When they did intrude into the interview, they were discussed in general sociological but not in personal terms. Despite their awareness of the psychiatric nature of the interviews, black interviewees said remarkably little of a personal nature to their white interviewers.

The black-white interview tends to be troublesome, not only to the black interviewee, but to the white middle-class interviewer as well. The recent assertion of a positive black identity expressed, for example, in the black power movement, has given prominence to the issue of blackness and to attitudes toward this trait. Thomas (1971) speaks of steps blacks go through in affirming their blackness. In the first step, all whites are maligned; all are regarded as racist. At this stage, no distinctions are made between individual white persons. But for the black a first move is made away from self-disparagement. In the last step (the fifth) the black person is able to make realistic judgments about individual whites, particularly with reference to their attitudes toward blacks as a group, and to himself as an individual. "The person at this stage is comfortable about being black and is non prejudicial of others. It represents optimum adjustment. The further along the person is on the continuum just described, the better adjusted he will be and race will be less important as an issue in treatment" (Jackson, 1973, p. 274).

In sharp contrast to the interviewee who asserts his blackness is the one who denies it. He is not comfortable with his black identity, rejects black values, and perceives himself as separate and distinct from black culture. Self-hatred, apathy, and depression often occur, since denial of his black identity is a form of self-degradation (Jackson, 1973). Both attitudes, if extreme, lead to different problems in relationship and communication between the white interviewer and black interviewee. If the latter is a denier of his black identity, he may bring into the interview feelings of apathy, depression, and powerlessness. The white interviewer may respond in a paternalistic way, infantilizing the interviewee and accentuating the feelings of apathy and powerlessness. In this type of emotional climate the interviewer is likely to avoid painful areas, out of a wish to overprotect the interviewee. Some interviewers may respond in a contrary way, through becoming extremely authoritarian and directive. In either case the interviewer's underlying assumption is that the interviewee is dependent and helpless. With the black activist, the white interviewer may have a different set of problems. The black militant may express his rage at whites quite openly, making the white interviewer fearful of attack. Under these circumstances, the interviewer may anxiously avoid certain areas of inquiry. He may also be inhibited by his own experience of guilt, since he will recognize the validity of many of the activist's accusations against white society.

It is not inevitable that the white interviewer react in the manners described above; neither is it inevitable that each black interviewee assume one or both of the two extreme, stereotyped roles. But the problems of relationship and communication considered above do intrude to varying degrees into interviews consisting of white interviewers and black interviewees.

In a brief summary of research investigations pertaining to interracial opinion polling interviews (white interviewer-black interviewee) Sattler (1970) noted that "most studies indicate that white interviewers elicited more docile and subservient replies from Negro respondents than did the Negro interviewers. This effect occurred both in the north and in the south" (Sattler, 1970, p. 151). The general trend was that white interviewers obtained distorted opinions from black adults, who tended to provide them with "public" responses, and the black interviewers with the private responses which were desired.

The strain placed on interviewee-interviewer relationship in interracial interviews may be inferred from a series of psychotherapy studies. One of these (Yamamoto, James, Bloombaum, & Hattem, 1967) was carried out in the Psychiatric Outpatient Clinic of Los Angeles County General Hospital.

The procedure was to determine the duration of treatment and the rate of dropout of the following ethnic groups in the patient population: black, Caucasian, and Mexican-American men and women.   The findings were consistent with those of other studies.   Caucasian women were seen for the longest periods of time in psychotherapy, followed in decreasing order by Caucasian men, Mexican-American men, Mexican-American women, and black women, and black men.   When the ethnic groups were ranked on the basis of percentages remaining in treatment for more than 10 visits, Caucasian patients were first, followed by Mexican-Americans, and blacks. Clearly, a clinic that admits both white and black patients, with a staff that is largely white, retains white patients in treatment for significantly longer periods of time than blacks.   Yamamato et al.   (1967) concluded that there was a better fit or better rapport between the white therapists and white patients than between the white therapists and black patients.

Other investigations similar to the one carried out by Yamamoto et al. (1967) have found that white clinicians select fewer black than white patients for psychotherapy and retain them in treatment for shorter periods of time. However, most studies of this kind do not illuminate the differences that exist among white therapists in their capacity for and willingness to work with black patients.   The Yamamoto et al. (1967) investigation did include a component which addressed itself to this problem.   The Bogardus Social Distance Scale was used as a measure of white interviewer prejudice against specified minority groups.   In responding to this scale the $\underline{S}$ is asked to place a specified ethnic group into one of seven categories, arranged in the order of increasing social distance: (1) Would marry into the group; (2) Would have as close friend; (3) Would have as next door neighbors; (4) Would work in the same office; (5) Would have as a speaking acquaintance; (6) Would have as visitors to my nation; (7) Would have as members of another nation.   The lower an interviewer's score for a particular ethnic group, the less is the social distance between himself and the group (i.e., the less is his bias against the group).

In the analysis it was found that the interviewers with the lower social distance scores for blacks were the more likely to select black patients for treatment.   Thus, the less a white therapist's general bias against blacks, the more likely he was to select black patients for treatment.

A survey of the research literature dealing with the effect of race on the clinical interaction prompts agreement with the conclusion that "controlled investigation of interracial psychotherapy dyads is only in its beginning phase" (Sattler, 1970, p. 155).   The evidence available indicates that white therapists are more likely to select white than black psychotherapy patients, and to retain them in treatment for longer periods of time.   Reciprocally, the higher dropout rate of black patients may, in part, express the black patient's rejection of the white therapist.

Black Interviewer and White Interviewees

Although the social distance and distrust that characterizes an interracial interview is fairly general across a variety of dyadic situations, each specific cross-racial combination has its own problems. Some of those associated with the white interviewer-black interviewee dyad have been discussed in the preceding section. The reverse interview situation (i.e., black interviewer and white interviewee) will now be considered. A review of the relevant literature indicates few clinical and research studies dealing with the above-designated interview combination. This finding is not surprising since there are relatively few black professionals to play the role of interviewer. It is therefore still an infrequent occurrence for a black person to interview a white.

That the problems associated with this type of dyad cut deeply is indicated in the following social casework summary dealing with a black social worker and a white client (Curry, 1954).

> Miss K was an unmarried 33 year old white woman who had been diagnosed as suffering from a 'schizophrenic reaction, chronic undifferentiated type.' She was on convalescent leave from a psychiatric hospital, having been released as greatly improved. Altogether she had been hospitalized four times as a mental patient. On meeting the Negro worker in the initial post hospital interview, she explicitly stated that she did not like his race, his looks or his office. She said she would not return and that the worker would have to drag her into the few evaluation interviews required by the State. The worker acknowledged his concern and sympathy for her feelings. He wondered if there might be some subject that they could talk about, and he made some general comment about appreciating her frankness and honesty. His efforts failed to engage her at that point, but about three weeks later she telephoned and asked to see him. She said she was 'feeling funny again' and was thinking about suicide.
>
> She came to the interview promptly, and immediately said that she had been feeling very bad ever since she had said 'those nasty things' to the worker. The worker pointed out that he did not recall her saying anything more than that she did not like Negroes, and he had appreciated her honesty. He reminded her that the function of the agency was to help her and that he had been appointed to see her for that purpose. Miss K, appearing to relax, said that she must have been thinking some 'funny things'; perhaps she had not said them after all; anyway, perhaps she should talk with the Negro worker, since she was always having 'dark thoughts.' The worker said that he did not know what the 'dark thoughts' were but that, if she wanted to help him understand, they could arrange to see each other regularly. Miss K accepted, commenting that maybe she would have something to look for then.   (Curry, 1964, p. 132)

The social bias against blacks, so widespread in American white society, prevented the white patient from responding to the black caseworker in the first interview. The reason for the patient's later change of heart is not clear in the above summary. However, two motives are suggested: guilt and remorse over her abrasive reaction to the caseworker during the initial interview, and the resurgence of suicidal and possibly other psychotic thoughts which undoubtedly aroused anxiety in the patient and prompted her to accept the help that had been offered.

What is interesting in this case is the pervasiveness of the bias against intimacy with or closeness with the black in our society. Thus, in her first encounter with the caseworker, this patient, chronically schizophrenic and therefore alienated from others in many ways, with four previous hospitalizations, still responded to her inner promptings to reject the relationship proffered by the black caseworker. It would appear that this rejection was not, in itself, a "sick" act, but one in which the patient was being governed by social norms shared with others from her own culture.

The interview situation, and the interviewer-interviewee relationship in which a black interviewer attempts to work with a white interviewee are certain to be shaped and controlled by the relevant attitudinal cross currents in the society in which the interview occurs. Thus, one will need to consider the attitudinal climate of the country at the time the interview occurs. Has it taken place before or after the upsurge of the black power movement? If before, the black interviewer may have more difficulty in asserting the status inherent in his/her role as interviewer than after. Moreover, one needs to be specific about where the interview occurs. For example, a white interviewee in Vermont is likely to have less difficulty in accepting the authority of the black interviewer than one from Georgia. By contrast, the white interviewee from Georgia may be able to accept the black interviewer as a provider of services, while rejecting him/her as a person with some authority.

Unfortunately, there are very few research studies dealing with the particular form of interracial dyad under consideration. In fact, only two have been found; and of these two, one does not deal with the interview as such but with the operant conditioning of verbal responses.

In a verbal conditioning study (Smith & Dixon, 1968) two black and two white male experimenters carried out a classically designed verbal reinforcement study. The Ss were white female college students, subdivided into high- and low-prejudice groups, each of which was further subdivided into an experimental group and a control group. Reinforcement ("right") was given each time a first-person pronoun was used to begin a sentence in the experimental group. The effect of reinforcement was assessed by comparing the frequency of the first-person pronouns in the speech of experimental and control group Ss. Conditioning did occur in the high-prejudice group with the white experimenters, but not with the black. The findings were somewhat marred by the failure of the low-prejudice Ss to condition with both white and black experimenters. Although the latter results could not be explained, the former did prompt the conclusion that high-prejudiced white Ss tend to depreciate the positive reinforcement coming from black experimenters, but not from white.

If the verbal reinforcement paradigm may be taken as one model of the interviewer's direction and control of verbal content expressed by the interviewee, one would expect that an interview effect similar to the above laboratory result could be demonstrated. Unfortunately, the author has not been able to find a controlled study that would test out this expectation. A distantly related study (Womack & Wagner, 1967) produced negative results. The investigation was carried out on the psychiatric service of King's County

Hospital, Seattle. "This study examined the degree of distortion involved in the collection of confidential material by Negro interviewers in a psychiatric situation involving a white patient population in a predominantly white setting" (Womack & Wagner, 1967, p. 685). There were four groups of patients, two interviewed by black interviewers (one a psychiatric resident and the other a graduate student in an unrelated area) and two by white interviewers (both psychiatric residents). In order to control the content of the interview, specified questions were provided the interviewers. The authors had expected that white interviewers rather than black would elicit greater frankness and more information from the white interviewees. In fact, there were no significant findings that could be accounted for by the race of the S and of the interviewer. The authors concluded "that a Negro psychiatrist in Seattle is responded to primarily as a psychiatrist and that his race is not an important consideration during the early stages of the psychiatric contact" (Womack & Wagner, 1967, p. 690).

It may be that professional experience and role tend to reduce the distortion and inhibition that one expects in cross-racial interviews. But the single study summarized above is an insufficient basis for such a conclusion. Adequate evidence has not yet been generated regarding relationship and communication in a black interviewer-white interviewee dyad.

Same-Race and Cross-Race Interviews

A number of investigations deal with the comparison of same-race and cross-race interview situations. The emphasis in the studies included in this section is not on the racial identity of the interviewer and interviewee, but on their racial similarity or dissimilarity. In one (Banks, 1972) race, social class, and interviewer empathy were all investigated. Only the results pertaining to race will concern us here. Equal numbers of black and white counselors carried out initial interviews with black and white clients, eleventh and twelfth grade males in a border state city. The study tested the hypothesis that interviewer-interviewee racial similarity has an effect on communication and relationship in an initial interview; the hypothesis was supported. Clients interacting with racially similar counselors were rated significantly higher on self-exploration in their interview communications than were clients interacting with racially dissimilar counselors. Additionally, the rapport of clients with counselors of the same race was judged to be significantly higher than that of clients with racially dissimilar counselors.

Another investigation (Carkhuff & Pierce, 1967) also found that the interviewee is able to engage in deeper self-exploration when she is interviewed by a person of similar rather than dissimilar race. Equal numbers of black and white lay counselors, all female, interviewed hospitalized female patients diagnosed as schizophrenic, and similarly divided into white and black subgroups. Deeper levels of self-exploration occurred in interviews in which white interviewers saw white interviewees and black interviewers black interviewees, in contrast to those in which one member of the dyad was white and the other black.

The major obstacles to interview communication between blacks and whites have been found in such qualities of relationship as distrust and resentment. But there are differences in verbal and nonverbal communication style that may also interfere. Some of these are noted in a Psychology Today summary of the work of Boston University psychologists, Marianne La France and Clara Mayo (La France & Mayo, 1974). The psychologists filmed conversational exchanges between two black men and between a white man and a black man, with a focus on eye contact and direction of gaze. They found that a white speaker tended to avert his gaze from the listener when speaking, and to direct his gaze back to the other person when listening to him. A black speaker behaved in a contrary way; he looked at his listener but then averted his gaze when the listener began to speak. Such differences in style of nonverbal communication could disrupt a conversation. For example, consider the case of a black speaker communicating with a white listener. If the black speaker should pause and look at the white listener, the latter, responding in his customary way, is likely to start speaking. The white person has been trained to take a direct gaze rather than an averted one as a cue that the other has finished speaking and is ready to listen. In fact, the other, trained to look while speaking, continues to speak. Such crossed-up cues may prompt both to speak at the same time or to be simultaneously silent. Such incongruent nonverbal communication codes may disrupt a conversation for "the white may feel he is not being listened to, while the black may feel he is being unduly scrutinized" (Psychology Today, May 1974, p. 101).

In the same issue of Psychology Today (May 1974) there is a brief reference to a study by Patrick Connoly, a graduate student at the University of Iowa, dealing with the distances between speakers preferred by black and white Ss. "Whites consistently preferred more space between speakers than did blacks. Whites were most comfortable when they were 26 to 28 inches apart; blacks preferred 21 to 24 inches" (Psychology Today, May 1974, p. 101). Moreover, conversations tended to terminate at different distances for blacks and whites. Black persons tended to stop a conversation if the distance between the two participants exceeded 36 inches; whites could tolerate 44 inches. Since blacks and whites judged each other by the same standards as they judged themselves, there were tendencies toward misunderstanding between them caused by their preferences for spacing themselves.

In brief, both relationship and communication factors interfere with or impede the dyadic exchange in an interview in which the interviewer and the interviewee are of different races. To be sure, there are mitigating elements. Positive interracial attitudes, training, skill, and the possession of certain facilitating interviewer attributes may tend to reduce obstacles to positive relationship and communication that tend to intrude because the interviewer and interviewee are of different races.

SOCIAL CLASS

Social class is a demographic variable that has a highly significant effect on interview process. In two interviews reported verbatim by Gill, Newman, and Redlich (1954) the socioeconomic contrast between the interviewees is only moderate. Yet the style and content of the communication of one is quite distinct from that of the other. The first interviewee is a 30-year-old married woman who telephoned a medical school clinic for an appointment because she was irritable, depressed, and enmeshed in a destructive relationship with an alcoholic husband. She was a registered nurse. The second interviewee's age was not given but we may assume that he was in his late 20s. He complained of headaches and nervousness related to situations in which he was tense and emotionally charged. He was a manual laborer with an unstable work history.

In the first interview, the nurse spoke about her husband's alcoholism, his work as a trucker, and her disturbed marriage, attributing much of her psychological difficulty to her husband's drinking and callous indifference. The interviewer pressed the patient for some expression of awareness that her present difficulty was at least, in part, a consequence of her own psychological problems. At first, the interviewee resisted such an admission. Later she acknowledged briefly that her trouble was partly a result of her own immaturity. The interviewer persisted in his inquiry and after considerable resistance and discomfort the patient acknowledged that she was pregnant at the time she first met her husband. He offered to marry her but she. felt she could not, under the circumstances, but did, later, after a miscarriage aborted her pregnancy.

The second patient began with an account of headaches from which he had been suffering for several years, which he described as "beats" that he experienced in the back of his head. Later, the therapist inquired into the patient's constant tension and excitability. The patient explained that "everything" seemed to irritate him. For example, if the door of the house was locked when he came home he would "holler" at his mother. If his girlfriend were to observe that a television actor was handsome, he would erupt in an angry manner. Considerably later, the interviewee expressed some concern about the possible effect on his present symptoms of a sexual affair he had with a married woman about three years earlier.

An extensive analysis and comparison of the content, language, and style of communication of the two interviewees would encompass many of the issues and much of the information pertaining to the effect of social class on interview behavior. For the moment, the comparison of the preceding two interviews will be brief and impressionistic, serving as an introduction to the topic of social class in the interview.

An evident contrast between the two interviews is noted in their topical emphases. The nurse spoke in psychological terms, demonstrating a capacity for self-analysis and for integrating introspective information into a coherent psychological description of her growth, development, and current condition. Thus, she remembered a distaste for growing up sexually when she was an adolescent. This led to an account of dating and remorse for her extramarital pregnancy. There was nothing to match this psychological self-evaluation in the second interview. To be sure, the patient was critical of some of his behavior. Thus, before dropping off to sleep he had thoughts in which he berated himself for impulsively angry behavior. But his self-criticism was couched in terms of externals, of social behavior that was visible to others, not in introspective terms.   This patient's tendency not to speak in psychological terms was also evident in his major emphasis on somatic symptomatology. He began the interview with a description of his headaches ("It continually beats and I can't stop it") and returned repeatedly to this symptom as though it were the focal center of his troubles.

Particularly salient was the contrasting understanding of the goals of the interview and subsequent therapy expressed by both interviewees. The nurse indicated an awareness of treatment goals which were undoubtedly very close to the views of the interviewer himself. She remarked that she needed to talk to someone with whom her family had no emotional involvement. Later she referred to her hope that treatment would provide her with more understanding of her disturbed relationship with her husband and, consequently, with more effective means of coping with it. There was no similar expression of understanding of the goals of psychotherapy, of help that might result from an interview interaction, in the responses of the second patient.

The introspective content of the nurse's responses was associated with a style of communication that facilitated the description of inner states and feelings. Consider, for example, her account of early adolescent resentment at growing up sexually: "I hated to grow up. ....Well, I had...my breasts had started to grow then. And I remember how I resented it. And I resented the fact that I wasn't a boy" (Gill et al., 1954, p. 188). The style here is attuned to the description of feelings, memories, and thoughts. Occasionally, the nurse would go so far as to make diagnostic statements - e.g., "I think he's a chronic alcoholic."   In this, her speech reflected a special interest in psychology.   The likelihood of such an interest developing in the second interviewee, whose education may not have extended into secondary school, is very remote. In general, his speech was action oriented; his style, impulsively abrupt. His focus was an external one. His symptoms were phenomena that happened to him, often acted on him. Thus, he spoke about his headaches as outside events that intruded upon him. Even his errors in terminology were in the direction of physical metaphor, rather than psychological expression. "I know I'm nervous because I was told by a psychiatrist in the army, very high tension nerves" (Gill et al., 1954, p. 224). It need hardly be added that such superficialities as lower class dialect are absent in the nurse's speech, but abundantly present in the laborer's.

Granted that differences such as the ones outlined above occur, do they have any effect on relationship and communication within the interview? The greater social distance between the laborer and his interviewer than between the nurse and hers may be noted in the frequent occurrence of such terms of subordination as "sir," in the speech of the former but not the latter. One would expect that with social distance would come a weakening of relationship.

It is evident that the somatic and external emphasis of the second interviewee's communications would be less congruent with the focus of the mental health interviewer than the psychological and introspective emphases of the first interviewee. The nurse appears to be better attuned to the goals of treatment, the expectations of the interviewer, and the type of communication that the interviewer attempts to foster. Whether the lower class dialect of the laborer might be jarring to a middle-class interviewer may be an individual matter. But in general, one would expect that interview communication would flow more readily when the two participants speak the same language and share the same linguistic style than when they differ in these respects. In brief, membership in the lower class rather than the middle or upper class would tend to burden communication in a mental health interview conducted by a professional, generally of middle-class origin.

The pessimistic summary that follows refers to the effects of social class on psychotherapy, but is relevant as well to the single mental health interview:

> The implications of a patient's social class for his psychotherapeutic treatment destiny are numerous, pervasive, and enduring. If the patient is lower class, all such implications are decidedly and uniformly negative. In comparison with patients at higher social class levels, the lower-class patient or patient-candidate seeking psycho-therapeutic assistance in an outpatient setting is significantly more likely to: (1) be found unacceptable for treatment, (2) spend considerable time on the clinic's waiting list, (3) dropout (or be dropped out) after initial screening, (4) receive a socially less desirable formal diagnosis, (5) be assigned to the least experienced staff members, (6) hold prognostic and role expectations incongruent with those held by his therapist, (7) form a poor-quality relationship with his psycho-therapist, (8) terminate or be terminated earlier, and (9) improve significantly less from either his own or his therapist's perspective.
>
> (Goldstein, 1973, p. 3)

The remainder of the section on social class will review the clinical and research literature as it relates to the consequence of socioeconomic differences between interviewer and interviewee. Finally, there will be a summary of some studies investigating procedures designed to breach social-class barriers in the interview.

Social Class and Acceptance into Psychotherapy

Social class is an old concept, but its frequent use in social and psychological research is relatively recent. To make such research possible, the concept required definition and quantification. The most widely applied index of socioeconomic status is that developed by Hollingshead and Redlich (1958) for use in the New Haven Community in the 1950s. Although one would expect that a social-class index would require periodic revision to correct for ongoing social change, the Hollingshead-Redlich Index continues to have wide application in its original form. The basic criteria of social-class status used in the index are area of residence, occupation, and educational level attained. Five social classes are defined by the index in the following descending order:

Class I - Salaried positions at the policy-making executive level. This class is composed of the community's business and professional leaders residing in the "best" areas of the city. In the 1950s the male heads of Class I families were college graduates from private institutions and with wives who had completed from one to four years of college. Income is high, with many families affluent, often with inherited wealth.

Class II - Salaried positions in business and professions, including minor professionals. Members of this class are status conscious because they tend to be upwardly mobile persons who have moved away from the values of and connections with lower class people, aspiring toward increased contact with Class I people. Members of Class II tend to be executive and professional employees moving from job to job in order to continue their upward mobility. Thus, they tend to feel isolated from their communities. The families are reasonably well-to-do.

Class III - The white-collar group considered to be essentially middle class. Some own small business but most fill administrative, technical, clerical, and semi-professional positions. The majority are high school graduates.

Class IV - Skilled and semi-skilled manual occupations in unionized trades and industries, and minor clerical positions. This group is designated as working-class or blue-collar workers, often subdivided into ethnic groups (e.g., Italian, Irish). Education usually is limited to part of high school.

Class V - Semi-skilled and unskilled manual occupations, nonunionized, with irregular employment. These are the poor, at the bottom level of the social-class structure of our society. They are the unemployed, the welfare recipients. In the 1950s they lived in the tenements and cold-water flats of New Haven and in semi-rural slums. Ethnically they tended to consist of immigrants from Southern and Eastern Europe and, of course, much of the American black population. Constantly preoccupied with the struggle to survive, they develop much resentment about treatment received from employers, clergymen, teachers, police, doctors, and other representatives of established society. Some have completed elementary school, but many have not.

The great range in the vertical structure of American society may come as a surprise to some. However, there is a much greater awareness of it today than there was before the serious economic crisis of the 1930s. Prior to that catastrophic period, many newspapers and journals took the official position that there was one essentially American point of view about domestic and international affairs, deriving from a basically unified society. Since the Depression and subsequent events, such a stand has been untenable. The range of socioeconomic groupings, the divisions and conflicts between them, has become an integral part of our national awareness. It is easy to trace social-class differences in many of the economic and political conflicts that occur in our society. But what is the relevance of social-class division to issues in mental health? More specifically, does social class, in fact, make a difference in psychotherapy and the mental health interview?

In the case histories that follow, two teenagers manifest the same kind of disturbed behavior. The one who came from a Class I family was protected against the punitive response of society which one might have anticipated and was eventually accepted into psychotherapy; the second, from a Class V family, was neither protected from punitive treatment nor accepted into treatment.

The case histories of two compulsively promiscuous adolescent females
will be drawn upon to illustrate the differential impact of class status
on the way in which lay persons and psychiatrists perceive and appraise
similar behavior. Both girls came to the attention of the police at
about the same time but under very different circumstances. One
came from a core group Class I family, the other from a Class V
family.... The Class I girl, after one of her frequent drinking and
sexual escapades on a week-end away from an exclusive boarding
school became involved in an automobile accident while drunk. Her
family immediately arranged for bail through the influence of the
member of an outstanding law firm; a powerful friend telephoned a
newspaper contact and the report of the accident was not published.
Within twenty-four hours the girl was returned to school. In a few
weeks the school authorities realized that the girl was pregnant and
notified her parents. A psychiatrist was called in for consultation by
the parents with the expectation, expressed frankly, that he recommend a therapeutic interruption of the pregnancy. He did not see fit
to do this and, instead, recommended hospitalization in a psychiatric
institution to initiate psychotherapy. The parents, though disappointed
that the girl would not have a 'therapeutic' abortion, finally consented
to hospitalization. In due course, the girl delivered a healthy baby who
was placed for adoption. Throughout her stay in the hospital, she
received intensive psychotherapy and after being discharged continued
the treatment with a highly regarded psychoanalyst.

The Class V girl was arrested by the police after she was observed
having intercourse with four or five sailors from a nearby Naval base.
At the end of a brief and perfunctory trial, the girl was sentenced to
reform school. After two years there, she was paroled as an unpaid
domestic. While on parole, she became involved in promiscuous
activity, was caught by the police, and was sentenced to the state
reformatory for women. She accepted her sentence as deserved
'punishment' but created enough disturbance in the reformatory to
attract the attention of a guidance officer. This official recommended
that a psychiatrist be consulted. The psychiatrist who saw her was
impressed by her crudeness and inability to communicate with him....
He was alienated by the fact that she thought masturbation was 'bad,'
whereas intercourse with many men whom she hardly knew was 'o.k.'
The psychiatrist's recommendation was to return the girl to her regular
routine because she was not able to profit from psychotherapy!
                                        (Hollingshead & Redlich, 1958, p. 176)

Two girls with behavioral problems similar in some respects were seen by
two psychiatrists in consultation, with totally contrasting outcomes. The
upper class girl was accepted into treatment; the lower class girl was
rejected, ostensibly because her manner offended the psychiatrist, and her
sexual values were quite discrepant from his own. To be sure, there may have
been many other factors that entered into the rejection of the lower class
girl, not evident in the brief case summary. But it is significant that a series
of statistical studies in diverse clinics seem to tell the same story as the

preceding case summaries.

In an investigation carried out at the Henry Phipps Psychiatric Clinic of the Johns Hopkins School of Medicine in Baltimore (Rosenthal & Frank, 1958), the authors noted that "at the Phipps Clinic as elsewhere... psychiatrists tend to refer for psychotherapy persons who are most like themselves. Thus they referred significantly more white than Negro patients, the better educated and those in the upper rather than the lower income range" (p. 332). Since education and income are definitive of social class, the authors are clearly saying that more upper than lower class patients were referred for psychotherapy at the Phipps Clinic.

The consistency of the above finding across a variety of clinics is impressive. In the Adult Outpatient Division of the Department of Psychiatry at the University of Utah Medical School, social-class bias in acceptance of patients into psychotherapy was not marked as in other facilities; yet it was significant. Patients from Classes I-IV inclusive had a fairly equal chance of acceptance into therapy with rates varying between 51% and 44%, but only 31% of poor applicants from Class V were accepted (Coles, Branch, & Allison, 1962). At Tulane University Clinic (Lief, Lief, Warren, & Heath, 1961) less than half of the applicants (largely lower social class) were accepted for psychotherapy, and at the Neuropsychiatric Institute of the University of California at Los Angeles (Brill & Storrow, 1963), the rate of acceptance was 43%. The socioeconomic bias in acceptance for psychotherapy was more extreme in another clinic study (Schaffer & Myers, 1954) in which 64% of Class II applicants, 55% of Class III, 34% of Class IV, and 3% of Class V applicants were accepted for treatment.

The facts are consistent and clear. It has been asserted that the poor and uneducated are simply not good candidates for psychotherapy. This position places the onus on the patient for his rejection by psychotherapists. Later there will be some evidence presented to indicate that in certain respects the poor patient may actually not be a suitable candidate for conventional psychotherapy, and indeed may find it difficult to respond to the low active, ambiguous mental health interviewer. But the burden of adapting the interview and the psychotherapy process to the low social-class patient must rest with the mental health practitioner. Thus, many workers in the area of mental health believe "that selection factors related to socioeconomic status more often meet therapist needs than treatment requirements" (Lorion, 1973, p. 268).

Certainly lower class patients are less attractive to most therapists than middle- and upper-class patients. At the Phipps Clinic (Nash, Hoehn-Saric, Battle, Stone, Imber, & Frank, 1965), patients first seen by research psychiatrists who rated their attractiveness were later treated by psychiatric residents. The patients judged to be attractive on intake were significantly younger, more intelligent, better educated, and had higher level occupations than those rated unattractive. It is clear that intake psychiatrists found the patients from higher socioeconomic backgrounds to be more attractive to them than those from lower backgrounds.

The Rejection of Psychotherapy
by Lower Class Patients

While the studies in the preceding section have demonstrated that lower class patients are less likely than upper class to be accepted for psychotherapy, other investigations indicate that lower class patients, even when accepted, are less likely than upper class patients to participate in psychotherapy. In one study conducted in the Adult Psychiatry Clinic of the University of California Medical Center in San Francisco (Albrouda, Dean, & Starkweather, 1964) it was noted that most of the clinic patients in Classes III and IV and nearly all in Class V resisted referral to psychotherapy. That the relative failure of lower class patients to enter into psychotherapy is a consequence of the mutual rejection of each other by both patients and therapists is asserted by the following summary statement from an investigation carried out at Phipps Psychiatric Clinic: "Social class factors also made a difference with regard to acceptance of therapy. Patients of lowest educational and income levels were most likely to refuse psychotherapy when it became available. The finding complements the finding of the Yale group that psychiatrists tend to reject patients of the lower classes for psychotherapy... The rejection appears to be mutual" (Rosenthal & Frank, 1958, p. 335).

The results pertaining to duration of stay in psychotherapy are also impressively consistent. In a review of the literature (Garfield, 1971), reference is made to a study in which "about 12% of the two lower social class groups, classified according to the Hollingshead classification, remain for over 30 interviews compared with 42% for those on the highest two social class groups" (p. 277). Many other investigations have obtained similar results regarding longevity of treatment (Coles et al., 1962; Hollingshead & Redlich, 1958).

An early investigation also conducted at Phipps Clinic (Imber, Nash, & Stone, 1955) set out to control certain variables that tended to confound that of social class in previous studies. Thus, the authors discussed the practice of clinics to assign lower class patients to the least experienced therapists. They asked whether the shorter stay in therapy found in several investigations might not, under these circumstances, be a consequence of the lesser experience of the therapists assigned to them rather than social-class bias. To control for therapist experience, three senior psychiatric residents were used as therapists. As a further control, senior staff members supervising the residents encouraged them to keep patients in therapy for at least six months unless it was clear that they could not benefit at all. Patients were similarly encouraged by the therapist and research staff to continue in therapy for the six-month period. These measures increase the probability that a social-class disparity in duration of stay in treatment would be a consequence of incompatability between interviewer and interviewee, or some bias in one or both of the participants. As it turned out, the social-class disparity remained. Forty-three percent of lower class patients had no more than four psychotherapy interviews. In contrast, only 11% of the middle-class patients had similarly brief courses in psychotherapy. In addition, 56% of middle class patients remained in treatment beyond the 20th interview, while only 29% of the lower class patients stayed equally long.

In brief, low socioeconomic "applicants are significantly less likely to be assigned to individual treatment, and if assigned, are more likely to terminate prematurely. These relations have been observed across a variety of settings in different parts of the county" (Lorion, 1973, p. 266).

Social Distance Between Interviewer and Interviewee

Some evidence has been presented indicating that lower class patients are less attractive to mental health professionals than those from the middle or upper classes. Moreover, lower, rather than upper class therapists are more likely to work with lower class patients, and upper class therapists with upper class patients. Evidence for this type of social-class matching of therapist and patient is found in a study by Mitchell and Namenek (1970) that compares the social-class identity of a large sample of therapists and patients. The major hypothesis of the study was expressed in the following terms: "the social class of therapists and clients would be related in such a way that the typical client of upper class therapists would more likely also be upper class, while the typical client of lower class therapists would more likely be lower class" (p. 226). In a nationwide sample of experienced clinical psychologists and psychiatrists, each $\underline{S}$ was asked to respond to a questionnaire which requested information about parental social-class background, and the present social class of the client most typical of his/her caseload. Social class was defined in Hollingshead and Redlich terms. "There was a significant overall relationship between a therapist's socioeconomic background and the social class of his typical client. More specifically, lower class therapists reported as typical significantly fewer upper class clients than did middle and upper class therapists" (Mitchell & Namenek, 1970, p. 227).

The lack of interest in lower social-class patients by middle-class therapists may be a consequence of the social distance between the two. People who are socially remote are likely to share few experiences; their values are likely to be dissimilar and the forms of behavior for which they are rewarded, quite different. One may therefore assume that social distance will tend to weaken the relationship between an interviewer and interviewee, while social proximity will tend to strengthen it.

In this regard, there will be a second look at a study summarized in Chapter 8 (Pope, Nudler, VonKorff, & McGee, 1974). Although the social distance variable in this investigation does not pertain directly to social class, its findings are nevertheless relevant. Two sets of interviewers were involved: a group of sophomore students majoring in psychology, admitted into an undergraduate program for training baccalaureate level mental health workers, but not yet having begun their training, and a second group of experienced staff psychiatrists and third-year psychiatric residents in a private psychiatric hospital. The interviewees were female freshman students. While the professional interviewers were clearly more experienced, they were also socially more distant from the interviewees than the student interviewers. The interviews were single encounters between the two participants. They were semistructured in that the interviewers were asked to limit themselves to two specified topical areas, but to proceed naturally in other respects. Some of the results of this investigation, outlined in Chapter 8, will be repeated briefly here because they illuminate the effect of social distance in a dyadic interaction.

On postinterview rating scales, the interviewees rated student interviewers as more sympathetic, more accepting, and more sensitive than the professionals. Thus, it would appear that social proximity rather than distance between interviewer and interviewee is associated with a more benign perception of the interviewer by the interviewee. Additionally, the interviewees experienced more anxiety (i.e., they emitted higher rates of speech disturbance) when interviewed by the professionals rather than the novices. One might have expected that the more skilled and experienced interviewers would know how to modulate the anxiety of the interviewees. Actually, however, their greater distance from the interviewees, the less benign manner in which they were perceived, instigated higher levels of anxiety in the interviewees. Finally, it was evident that different patterns of communication developed when students were interviewed by students (the socially proximate dyads) than by professionals (the socially distant dyads). In the former instance the synchrony model prevailed. Very much in the manner of a conversation between equals, there was a positive association between interviewer and interviewee productivity. When the interviewer spoke at length, the interviewee did likewise; when the interviewer was brief, he was matched by a parallel brevity of the interviewee. As in the case of a conversation between equals, both participants were voluble when communication went well; both were relatively silent when it went poorly. Moreover, when the interview proceeded productively, the interviewer manifested an emotional warmth which was absent when the exchange between the two participants was skimpy. The preceding findings were based on two sets of data: an initial study and its replication. One may therefore venture to conclude that social proximity rather than distance in the interview is associated with a benign interpersonal relationship, low interviewee anxiety, and the spontaneity of an egalitarian encounter.

The synchrony model did not apply to the interviews conducted by professionals. In the first study, the inverse model prevailed. When the interviewee was highly productive, the interviewer said little. Only when the interviewee had little to say did the interviewer become more productive. This model is consistent with a general view of how the mental health professional goes about conducting an interview. Unfortunately, it was not replicated. Both in the original study and its replication there was no relationship between professional interviewer warmth and interviewee productivity. In this respect the professionals differ sharply from the novices. It would seem that a conversation or an interview between two people who are socially close, who share values and experiences, is likely to be a warmer, and a more mutual interaction than one between socially distant persons. This finding does not necessarily nullify the advantages of skill and experience for the interviewer, but implies that experience needs to be placed in balance with social distance when considering the probable course of an interview.

It is assumed that social distance due to social-class difference is likely to affect an interview in a manner that is similar to that noted in the preceding study. In the area of mental health, social proximity is a particularly salient consideration in work with low-status clients. Thus, a number of investigations have demonstrated the greater efficacy of nonprofessional indigenous mental health workers rather than professionals in helping poor clients (Guerney, 1969; Rappaport, Chinsky, & Cowen, 1971; Rioch, 1966).

In one additional study dealing with the effect of social class determined distance on the interaction between dyadic pairs (Byrne, Clore, & Worchel, 1966) each S was asked to evaluate a fictional other person, described as either similar or dissimilar to himself in economic status. The Ss rated the fictional others who were similar rather than dissimilar to themselves as more attractive. Particularly significant was the rejection by high economic status Ss of fictional others below them in status. In another study (Keith-Spiegel & Spiegel, 1967) there was an inquiry into the views of hospitalized patients, at the time of discharge, about the relative helpfulness of the different staff groups. Patients were classified in terms of years of education. Hospital personnel was grouped in the following order, of more to less complex style of communication with patients: (a) psychologists and psychiatrists, (b) nurses, (c) nursing assistants, (d) other patients. Patient's years of schooling correlated significantly with the above ordering of helping personnel. The more educated the patient, the greater the tendency to choose psychiatrists and psychologists as the most helpful; the lower the educational level, the greater the tendency to see the aides as the most helpful. One patient with limited schooling was quoted as saying: "My doctor was a nice enough guy but I never knew what the hell he was talking about. He didn't make no sense at all. Only time I felt better was when me and the boys would knock around our problems while playing pool" (Keith-Spiegel & Spiegel, 1967, p. 62).

Two people who are socially remote may find it difficult to talk to each other for several reasons. One of these may be the contrasting value and belief systems that activate and direct their social behavior. The next group of studies will deal with socioeconomic differences in social behavior values, particularly as these might relate to the interview interaction.

Social-Class Value Contrasts

The mental health interview is an interpersonal encounter with the promotion of self-disclosing communication as a major goal. It is therefore not surprising that the personal values of both participants affect the course of the exchange. In this regard, the authors of a book dealing with interviewing remark: "The clinician's behavior, like the patient's, is shaped by the shared values, beliefs, and attitudes that characterize the subculture in which he lives and has lived. Some aspects of his behavior, such as his interest in patient's families, reflect as much of his cultural origins as his professional training" (Enelow & Swisher, 1972, p. 198).

The two studies that follow deal with the values shared by young adolescents in contrasting socioeconomic subcultures. The methods and the findings of the two are quite different. However, both demonstrate the roots of social-class value differences in peer relationships during childhood and adolescence. The implications of value differences appearing as early as age 12 for a person's later participation in the clinical interview and the process of psychotherapy will be considered.

The first investigation was carried out over two decades ago (Pope, 1953a). The setting was the Oakland, California public school system and the Ss were children in sixth-grade classes selected from schools that occurred at upper and lower socioeconomic extremes. Schools with appreciable black populations were not used to avoid confounding socioeconomic with ethnic variables. The goal of the investigation was the study of contrasting behavior values among upper and lower class children that made for either status acceptance or rejection within their peer groups. If socioeconomic differences could be demonstrated, then it might be inferred that children in low and high socioeconomic groups grow up in contrasting social atmospheres, subject to different group pressures and rewards.

The instrument used was a form of the "Guess-Who" test, which consisted of descriptions of 25 social behavior traits, presented in bipolar pairs. For example, one item described aggressive behavior in the following way: "Here is someone who enjoys a fight." The opposite pole of the same trait was included in a companion item which read: "Here is someone who never fights but lets the other person have his (or her) way." Each item was followed by spaces in which a S could write the names of classmates to whom the trait applied. A S's score on a given item was the percentage of the remaining members of his class who chose him. For each of the four subgroups (high socioeconomic - male; high socioeconomic - female; low socioeconomic - male; low socioeconomic - female) item scores were intercorrelated and cluster analyzed.* The inferences about prestige values were based on the four cluster analyses and their comparisons. While the results were derived from individual expressions of choice and preference of Ss for their peers, the inferences about group values were actually descriptive abstractions for the four subgroups.

Most of the results are not directly applicable to a consideration of social class similarities and differences between mental health clinicians and clients. But some findings are provocative in their apparent relevance. Thus, Pope (1953b) found "a definite pattern of classroom-conforming, adult-conforming, good student behavior" (p. 384) in many upper class students, but not among those from the lower class. To be sure, the studious, classroom "intellectual" was not the most popular boy among his upper socioeconomic 12-year-old peers. But neither was he rejected. In fact, he was not without some respect. On the other hand, low socioeconomic 12-year-old boys did not always distinguish between effeminacy, studiousness, and conformity in the classroom. These traits were equated with acceptance of adult authority and brought about rejection by the group. The above social-class contrast was

---

* Those readers who are interested in a detailed exposition of method used may find the information in a previous publication (Pope, 1953a).

not quite as marked among the girls, but it did occur. Adolescents who are less likely to be rejected by their peers for relating positively to teachers and for good student behavior in other respects are more likely to develop the kinds of verbal communication skills that would facilitate their later participation in a clinical interview.

Another difference between upper and lower class 12-year-olds was the greater acceptability of aggressive and domineering behavior in the latter rather than the former. Other investigations (Milner, 1949) have found the ready acting out of affect and impulse in the low socioeconomic individual rather than the high to be associated with a lesser capacity to speak introspectively about thoughts and feelings. Again, the low socioeconomic pattern would be an impediment to the type of communication that the mental health clinician characteristically fosters.

In a later study (Barker, 1955) working and lower class versus middle-class boys in an Indiana junior high school were asked a series of questions designed to confront them with dilemmas that could be resolved only by resort to either working class or middle-class values. These questions are paraphrased below, and followed by the author's anticipated results and the actual results obtained.

1. Do you enjoy doing things by yourself?

It was assumed that working class boys would be more dependent on the society of their peers, and that middle-class boys would be able to enjoy some personal withdrawal into independent activity. Seventy-six percent of the middle-class boys and 43% of the working-class boys answered "yes" to this question.

2. Are there any things that you enjoy doing as hobbies?

The author assumed that middle-class approval of the cultivation of hobbies would be part of its emphasis on the constructive use of leisure. The middle-class tends to regard time as a commodity that should not be squandered in play or random activity. Seventy-six percent of the middle-class boys, and 37% of the working class boys answered "yes."

3. If you and some friends went to a movie, and you loaned one of the boys some money because he didn't have any, what would you and your friends expect this boy to do?

(a) Pay you the money back when he gets it?
(b) Do you a favor at a later time?

The answer expected was that middle-class boys would be more likely to enter into a contractual relationship with those to whom they lend money and therefore choose answer (a), while working class-boys would regard mutual aid as a reciprocal series of acts, and would therefore select (b). Forty-five percent of the middle class boys and 76% of the working-class boys chose the second answer.

4. When you and your friends were planning the movie trip nearly all the members of your group wanted to go very much. But one boy, studying to be an electrician, said he could not afford the trip because he had to save his money to buy books and tools. The other boys thought that all the members of the group ought to go together. What do you think the boy should have done?

(a) Should he have gone with the rest of the group?
(b) Should he have stayed home and saved his money?

There are two social-class-linked dilemmas here. It was expected that a middle-class boy would give greater emphasis to the long run rather than the short run, and the preparation for his own future security rather than a more immediate sense of solidarity with the group. Thirty-four percent of the middle-class boys and 51% of the working-class boys chose to go with the rest of the group.

5. What do you think you should do in the following situation? You are enjoying a baseball game with friends, but you know that the time has come when you are expected home for a meal.

(a) Should you leave the game because you are expected home for a meal?

(b) Should you go home when the game is finished, or when you get hungry?

The author expected that the middle-class boy would tend to pick the first answer because of his time consciousness, emphasis on punctuality, and self-disciplined sense of temporal obligation to others. By contrast, he expected that the working-class boy would be more responsive to the immediate pleasures and rewards of the situation. Eighty-seven percent of the middle-class boys and 69% of the working-class boys gave the first answer (Barker, 1955, p. 105-109).

The values investigated in this study are different from those studied by Pope (1953b) and the methodologies of the two studies are also quite different. Yet the Barker findings are also relevant in some ways to adult social-class differences in responsiveness to interviewing and psychotherapy. Certainly, the emphasis in psychotherapy tends not to be on immediate relief; instead its perspective is long-term change. The attainment of personality goals is not achieved instantly, but through a process of communication over time. Already in early adolescence middle-class boys demonstrate a more positive evaluation of future goals of personal attainment than working-class boys do. One would therefore expect the middle-class boys to be better prepared for the orientation of psychotherapy toward long-term goals. Although mental health professionals like to speak about the requirements of the interview and the process of therapy in socially neutral terms, it would appear that social-class values intrude rather more strongly than many of them are aware into the dyadic exchange. Many of the attitudes favored by middle-class boys in the Barker (1955) study will readily be recognized as values that are likely to be accepted by the mental health clinician. Self-reliance, the constructive use of leisure, the delay of immediate gratification in favor of future attainment and pleasure, and particularly the responsible budgeting of time are so widely accepted as desirable traits in middle-class society that they are likely to be taken as criteria of mental health by the clinician. But the working-class patient's experience may have been such as to negate or diminish the adaptive worth of some of these values for himself.

Thus, self-reliance may be less important to a member of the working class than close group solidarity with his trade union peers, for example. There may be little gain in delaying gratification if the worker's income is such as to make any attempt at saving an experience in frustration. The clinician may feel that he is formulating goals for a patient that meet mental health criteria, when in fact he is using a mental health code to communicate values that are rewarding to his middle-class patients but not to those from the working class. The latter, frustrated by a sensed incongruence between their own values and those of the therapist or interviewer, may be uncommunicative and inclined not to return.

Seward's (1972) concise statement of attitudes and values rooted in the culture of poverty is summarized below. The bracketed sections are interpretive introjections by the present author to relate Seward's summary to the mental health interview.

1. "Since the child of poverty is not required to delay his need gratification to the same extent as his middle-class age peers, he grows to adulthood behaving in ways that are often more impulsive than core culture mores condone. Holding one's own in a fight with siblings or playmates is reinforced by the family...and on the parent's part corporal punishment is the accepted way of chastising the child" (Seward, 1972, p. 46). (Most middle class psychotherapists would demur at the kind of overtly aggressive behavior referred to above. They would almost certainly regard its elimination as one of the goals of treatment, without an adequate awareness of the social stress such a change might create for the lower class patient within his peer group. More basically, a person who emphasizes action and impulse is not likely simultaneously to place a premium on introspective verbal communication, so essential to the conventional mental health interview.)

2. Self-reliance and a capacity for introspection are not expected to develop in a situation in which both personal stresses and supports are lodged externally in the immediate environment. Seward speaks of the character of stress in the life of a poor person, when she remarks: "The realistic anxiety, directed against the outer world, contrasts with the middle-class neurotic anxiety directed toward the inner self" (p. 47). This remark does not imply that there is necessarily an absence of neurosis among the poor. Rather it indicates that innerly directed, neurotic anxieties are likely to take second place to the pressing need to do whatever one needs to in order to survive in an environment of poverty. If the most urgent stresses among the poor are environmental ones, so are the immediate sources of support. The peer group (the gang) has always been the modality through which the inner-city youth has learned to achieve a measure of self-assertion. When in critical distress, a poor man may need to negotiate with society's agencies for dispensing welfare or help in some other form. In general, rewards to him came largely from externalizing rather than internalizing his efforts. (Clearly, the rewards to the interviewee in the mental health interview are for the most part a consequence of an internal orientation. A persistent focus on externals is likely to lead the interviewer to characterize the patient as superficial or resistive, with ensuing strain in the interview.)

With the type of culture conflict implied above between middle-class interviewer and lower class interviewee there is likely to be misunderstanding, disappointment, and a lack of rapport between the two.

Socioeconomic Contrasts in Patient Attitudes and Expectations

In a book entitled, Why People Go to Psychiatrists written by a sociologist (Kadushin, 1969) various social networks through which individuals approach psychiatric help are examined. The author presents two cases in which physical symptoms are prominent in the problems presented. However, the social backgrounds and training of the two persons seeking psychiatric help are quite different, leading to radically different attitudes toward the physical symptoms and related problems.

The first patient was a 24-year-old single woman, working as a social worker. She was living with her lower-middle-class, Jewish family. Her previous contact with psychiatry included considerable reading and some psychotherapy. On the present occasion she was referred for treatment by her social work supervisor and applied to a psychoanalytic clinic.

She gave the following information about her current difficulties in response to a questionnaire. As her basic problems she designated a lack of confidence in herself, free-floating anxiety, and the somatic complaint of "stomach pains." When asked to give some historical information on the development of the current problem, at first she denied any awareness of its beginning. Then she added: "I do know that as a child I was terribly frightened and afraid to leave my mother's side. I used to be afraid of going to school and would vomit every morning before leaving the house."

Clearly, the young woman had considerable knowledge about psychodynamics. Her approach to psychiatric treatment was prompted and supported by friends and associates at work. She mentioned somatic problems, but placed them in a subordinate position, and appeared to be quite accepting of a psychological explanation of the stomach pains.

If the above patient may be considered to be middle class in her present status, the next one belongs to the skilled working class (i.e., the "blue-collar" group). Consider the difference in his attitudes toward his problems and toward treatment. He was a 63-year-old airplane mechanic, born in Cuba, with about 10 years of education obtained in South America. There were three daughters, all registered nurses, living at home. He applied to a psychiatric clinic in a general hospital on the referral of a doctor in the medical clinic of the same hospital. In the psychiatric clinic his condition was diagnosed as that of reactive depression. Yet when asked what prompted him to come to the medical clinic he replied that he wanted a "physical check-up." On further inquiry into his main problems, he replied that his work was too heavy, and that he was going to try to get an easier job. In fact, he had had a siege of bronchitis recently and had lost some time at work. Not until much later in the interview did he admit to some personal difficulties such as fighting with his sisters, an inability to complete intercourse with his wife, and, more generally, feelings of disgust and unhappiness. But when asked to select the most important problems, he returned to externals (i.e., his need for a job on which he would not work as hard as he does now) and his wish to settle his social security status. Finally, when instructed to select a statement that described how he felt about the cause of his problem, from a checklist of alternatives he chose: "If I could only change my surroundings or the situation I find myself in everything would be alright."

The second patient placed a much greater emphasis on somatic symptoms than the first, and was much less inclined to describe his condition in psychological terms or to attribute a role to psychological causation. The social worker related her stomach pain to anxiety, while the airplane mechanic related his problems to fatigue due to heavy manual labor on the job. In brief, the social worker thought in internal, psychological terms; the mechanic, in external and somatic terms.

The difference in initial attitudes to their health problems would suggest a markedly different response to the initial psychiatric interview. Certainly, both applicants for psychotherapy would wish to focus on different content in the initial interview. It is readily apparent that the intake interviewer would likely find the social worker's content preferences rather than the mechanic's more congruent with his/her own. The interviewer would also note that both applicants would use different terms, would be conversant with different concepts. Thus the girl, aware that she did not have a "real" stomach disorder, would speak about her "psychosomatic symptoms." The man might suspect that there were, in fact, underlying psychological difficulties that caused or sustained his somatic problems, but he would have neither the language nor the conceptual framework with which to speak about the emotional nature of his difficulties. Instead he would use terms that have references to possible alterations in the external conditions under which he lives. Again, the interviewer would find the social worker's language and terminology more congruent with his semantic framework and would therefore find it easier to communicate with her.

It is possible that the two interviewees would have quite difficult expectations regarding the behavior of the interviewer. The social worker would expect the interviewer to listen to her self-disclosures and possibly to ask occasional questions and make some clarifying remarks. The mechanic would more likely anticipate advice on active direction from the interviewer regarding the alleviation of external stresses. Thus, he might visualize the interviewer as taking note of his complaints and advising him with reference to a possible job change. There is no doubt that the social worker's expectations rather than those of the mechanic would more closely accord with the interviewer's actual behavior. For all of the preceding reasons, the airplane mechanic would be certain to engage in the initial interview with a more defensive, a less communicative frame of mind than the social worker; analogously, the interviewer would likely be more attracted to and receptive to the social worker than the airplane mechanic.

Conflict in expectation has been considered above when it occurs between the two participants in an interview. Conflict may also occur between a patient's expectations about psychotherapy before arriving for the first interview and what s(he) perceives to occur in the initial interview. One investigation (Overall & Aronson, 1963) dealt with the association between the latter type of expectation conflict and a clinic patient's failure to return after the initial interview. The patient population in the clinic consisted almost entirely of individuals from low-socioeconomic backgrounds. The failure of applicants to return for a second interview was a high 57%. It seemed not unreasonable to assume that these patients were so discouraged by the first interview as to prompt them to discontinue clinic contact. The authors hypothesized that there would be a positive correlation between degree of discrepancy between patient expectation and actual perception of first interview and failure to return for treatment. Stated otherwise, those patients who experienced the initial interview as markedly different from what they expected would be less likely to return than those who found that it accorded well with what they expected.

The clinic was located in the general out-patient department of a university hospital, but was totally administered by the department of psychiatry. The therapists were fourth-year medical students, during their psychiatric clerkship, who were having an early experience in psychotherapy and were closely supervised by staff psychiatrists. While inexperienced, one would expect them to attempt to emulate both the attitudes and the interview behavior of their psychiatric mentors. The Ss were patients attending the clinic for the first time, each seen by a different student therapist. All Ss were classified as belonging to Social Class IV and V on the basis of income and education.

Each S was asked to indicate agreement or disagreement with 35 statements describing different therapist behaviors in the initial interview. Five aspects of possible therapist behavior were sampled:

1. Active - The therapist actively instructs or directs the patient, for example, 'Do you think the doctor will tell you what is causing your trouble?'

2. Medical - The therapist focuses on the organic or physical problems of the patient, for example, 'Do you think the doctor will be interested in your digestion?'

3. Supportive - The therapist avoids charged material in an attempt to bolster or comfort the patient, for example, 'Do you think the doctor will try to get your mind off your troubles?'

4. Passive - The therapist leaves the direction of the discussion to the patient, encouraging all patient communications, for example, 'Do you think the doctor will expect you to do most of the talking?'

5. Psychiatric - The therapist focuses on emotional or dynamic material, for example, 'Do you think the doctor will want to know how you get along with people?'   (Overall & Aronson, 1963, pp. 423-424).

The Ss were given the questionnaire orally just before their first interviews with the student-therapists assigned to work with them. Their responses at this point expressed their expectations regarding their therapy which had not yet begun. Later the questionnaire was readministered to all Ss after their initial interviews to obtain their perceptions of the interviews that had actually occurred. The differences between their two sets of responses were considered to be indices of the magnitude of the discrepancy between their expectations of therapy and their perceptions of it in the first interview.

Unlike the low-socioeconomic Ss in the Hollingshead and Redlich (1958) study, those in the present one did significantly expect the therapist to be interested in emotional and interpersonal issues. In other respects the findings of previous studies regarding therapy expectations of low social-class patients were borne out. Thus, the patients perceived the student therapists to have focused less on organic and physical problems than they had expected and to have offered less support and comfort.

The major finding pertained to the relationship between discrepancy scores (i.e., the number of items in which preinterview responses differed from postinterview responses of the patients) and their failure to return for a second interview. The result was as anticipated; there were significantly higher discrepancy scores for those patients who did not return for a second interview than for those who did. This investigation demonstrated that within Social Class IV and V patients, those who experienced considerable conflict between their expectation that their therapists would take an active, supportive role and their perceptions of the therapist's actual behavior were less likely to return for a second interview than those whose conflict was minimal. The data and, indeed, the design of the study did not permit the specific conclusion that middle- and upper class patients would experience less expectation conflict and would therefore be more likely to return for further interviews. But a comparison with the findings of previous studies is strongly supportive of such an inference.

Three years later, the same authors (Aronson & Overall, 1966) explored the possible differences between Class IV and V clinic applicants (the social-class groups represented in their 1963 study, ranging from skilled and unskilled manual occupations, the blue-collar group, down to the poor and welfare recipients) and those from Class III (the white-collar group, including the proprietors of small businesses, technical, clerical, and semi-professional workers) in attitudes and expectancies regarding psychotherapy. There was no difference between the two social-class groups in expectancies regarding the therapist's interest in emotional and interpersonal issues. (It will be recalled that in the 1963 study by Overall and Aronson, the Class IV and V Ss had recorded expectations that the therapists would be interested in emotional and interpersonal matters. It may be assumed that Class III Ss in the 1966 study also anticipated this type of focus by the interviewer.) However, the Class IV and V clinic applicants had significantly stronger expectancies for an active, supportive, therapist than did Class III Ss. Class III Ss seemed closer to the mainstream of middle-class expectations regarding the mental health interviewer than did the lower class Ss.

The Aronson and Overall (1966) findings suggest that the striking contrast between the negative attitudes toward therapy by lower class patients and the positive attitudes of middle-class patients noted earlier (Hollingshead & Redlich, 1958) might have been reduced to some extent over the eight-year period that separated the first study from the second. Certainly, such a reduction would not be inconsistent with the rather wide public dissemination of mental health information during the period referred to.

The change of attitudes over time is further suggested by a later investigation (Lorion, 1974) in which Classes III, IV, and V all reported highly similar positive attitudes toward and expectations about mental health treatment. In this investigation the Ss were divided into six subgroups of Class III, IV, and V males and females. The Ss were all applicants for treatment in the psychiatric out-patient clinic of a larger medical center. During a 30-minute screening interview prior to the beginning of the intake interview, they were asked to respond to two survey instruments, one called the Mental Health Attitude Survey which measured "pro-con" attitudes toward seeking professional help, and the other, the Treatment Expectation Survey, an inventory of expectations regarding the behavior of the mental health interviewer. The help-seeking attitudes expressed were independent of social-class level. Indeed they were uniformly positive across the three social classes. The author concluded that working-class and poor clinic applicants did not, in 1974, necessarily have the more negative attitudes than middle-class patients that Hollingshead and Redlich had found in 1958. The applicants in the present study expressed confidence in the effectiveness of treatment, acknowledged their need for professional help, did not feel stigmatized by treatment, and were quite prepared to discuss personal problems openly. Moreover, fewer than half expected the therapist to actively provide solutions for them. They knew that they would do most of the talking, and that their self-disclosing communication would include emotional topics and disturbing personal relationships and events. Thus, they did not expect a highly active, supportive, problem-solving therapist.

The possible changes in attitudes and expectations regarding mental health treatment entertained by the poor, during a period of the active extension of such treatment into low-socioeconomic segments of the community, is one possible explanation of the changes noted over a 16-year time span. But the author of the last investigation points to some methodological aspects of the study that might have accentuated the positive character of the responses given. The Ss in the study were applying for treatment. It is likely that inventories taken of their attitudes and expectations, as they were being assessed for treatment, would elicit more positive replies than those that might have been obtained at another time. Moreover, the referral process to the out-patient clinic in the Lorion study was benign in contrast to the one frequently followed by low social-class applicants. Patients came to the clinic either through self- or physician referral. In this sense, they were clearly an exceptional group of low social-class applicants for mental health treatment. In earlier studies (Hollingshead & Redlich, 1958) low-income patients were frequently sent to clinics by the courts or police, or sought them out after highly traumatic experiences.

It is hopeful that attitudes and expectations do change with time and experience. But it seems unlikely that the attitudinal obstacles to mental health treatment for the poor so voluminously reported in the literature, have been as completely eradicated as the results in the Lorion (1974) investigation would imply.

The Psychiatric Patient - An Interviewer Viewpoint

The preceding discussion has emphasized social-class differences in interviewee values as these relate to their capacity to participate in the mental health interview. The studies summarized below focus on the social-class value-based preferences of interviewers.

That mental health professionals show a social-class bias in their diagnostic decisions about patients was neatly demonstrated in a study conducted by Lee and Temerlin (1970). Psychiatric residents were divided into four groups, with 10 in each group. All observed the same filmed "interview" in which the role of interviewee was taken by an actor who was trained to present himself as an essentially healthy person with no psychiatric symptomatology. However, the four groups of residents had received different inductions before observing the interview. One group was told that the patient was of upper class origin; another that he came from the middle class; and a third, from the lower class. A control group of residents received no induction whatever. When all Ss were asked to rate the "interviewee's" mental health and prognosis, some interesting differences emerged. Those residents who received the lower class induction rated the interviewee as more disturbed and considered him to be a poorer prospect for treatment than the residents in the three other groups. It is evident that the 40 psychiatric residents in the study were not social-class neutral in their diagnostic judgments.

Nor were 60 graduate students in clinical psychology who made essentially the same kinds of diagnostic judgments as the above residents in a later investigation (DiNardo, 1975). Again the Ss responded to a filmed "interview," that was in some ways an improvement over the one used in the previous study. Social-class cues that had occurred, unwittingly, in the first interview, were eliminated from the second. In addition, the normal content of the script was assured through its prerating with a Q-sort device for normal and psychotic content. These ratings indicated that the film conveyed a normal impression. Although there were several experimental manipulations only the "middle-class" and "lower class" inductions will concern us here. One half the Ss were given a middle-class history as background of the interviewee; the other half, a lower class history. Every S rated the interview with a Q-sort scale from which a psychotic score was derived. Once again, higher pathology scores were given to the lower class rather than the middle-class interviewee.

The issue of social-class bias in diagnosis was raised pointedly in another publication. The author wondered whether

the class differences in diagnostic frequencies are directly reflective of differences in basic symptomatology or may not be reflective of differences in the 'diagnostic habits' of the clinician. One of the most ubiquitous of such habits is his more ready identification with and acceptance of the individual of his own class, the less understanding and more ready rejection of the person from a lower class matrix.
Schofield, 1964, p. 61).

The neurotic is more acceptable as a candidate for psychotherapy than the psychotic. Thus, "when confronted by a prospective patient from the upper social classes, the potential psychotherapist is subtly constrained to see the patient's illness as neurotic rather than psychotic, even if this requires forcing the diagnosis into an ambiguous category of 'character' neurosis'" (Schofield, 1964, p. 62).

In another investigation (Redlich, Hollingshead, & Bellis, 1955) the authors studied the effect of social class on the therapists' preferences for patients. Fifty patients drawn largely from clinics, state and V.A. hospitals, belonged either to Social Class III or V. The findings regarding the attitudes of therapists to their patients were based on both direct interviews with the therapists (psychiatrists in private practice, psychiatric residents, medical students, and psychologists) by research psychiatrists, and on examination of psychotherapy records. The therapists clearly preferred Social Class III to Class V patients. Many of the therapists disliked Class V patients because they judged them to be "bad cases." In their view, extreme poverty and conditions of community and family disorganization made therapeutic gain extremely unlikely.

"In many cases, the value systems pertaining to therapeutic interaction were far apart. In a number of class V patients the therapists disapproved of their sexual and aggressive behavior, their lack of discipline and responsibility. While...therapists often enough rejected class III values they at least understood them; in contrast to this, they were at a loss to understand values of class V patients" (Redlich et al., 1955, p. 67).

In a study dealing with the relationship between certain client attributes judged to be favorable for psychotherapy and social class (Lerner & Fiske, 1973), 14 therapists (experienced and inexperienced, male and female, white, social workers and psychologists) conducted psychotherapy with 30 outpatients, including a high percentage who were severely impaired and from lower socioeconomic backgrounds. Each client was rated on 11 attributes by his therapist at the beginning of treatment. These ratings were then judged by the researchers to be either high or low in prognosis for therapy. The eleven attributes considered to be favorable for therapy follow: low somatic complaints, low externalization of blame, low guardedness and suspicion, low tendency to act out, high introspectiveness, high ego strength, high therapeutic sophistication, high verbal fluency, high motivation for change, high estimated intelligence, moderate experienced anxiety. When the sums of favorable attributes for the high (Classes I, II, & III) and low (Classes IV & V) social class were compared, the number was significantly greater for the high.

One consequence of interviewer social-class bias is the attrition of communication within the interview. But problems in communication may be due to difficulties in areas other than differential interviewer preference for high and low social-class interviewees. In fact, there is evidence for the presence of a social-class-linked linguistic discrepancy between high- and low-socioeconomic groups impeding communication between them.

Language and Communication Across the Socioeconomic Barrier

In a study already referred to (Redlich, et al., 1955) neurotic patients in psychotherapy in a number of clinics and hospitals were interviewed by research psychiatrists during the course of their treatment. The interviewers rated the patients on a number of variables, including that of communication, using the categories "good," "intermediate," and "poor." These categories were "based on whether or not therapists and patients were relating meaningfully to each other on the verbal level and whether or not the patient understood the principal intent of the therapist" (Redlich et al., 1955, p. 65). When Social Class III and V patients were compared, it was found that Class III patients were rated as communicating at a significantly higher level than Class V patients. In fact all 12 Class V patients were rated as "poor," while seven out of 13 Class III patients were rated as "intermediate" or "good." The results were particularly disappointing to the therapists because many attitudes and concepts that they attempted to communicate simply did not get through to the Class V patients. The latter group was largely unable to understand or accept the concept that psychological conflict may be associated with somatic symptons. One particularly frustrating example is cited by the authors. After six months of insight therapy with a Social Class V patient, a therapist felt certain that his patient no longer accepted the notion that his emotional troubles were caused by his bad teeth, but rather by his anxieties and frustrations. Yet when this patient was interviewed by a research psychiatrist, he reiterated the belief, never abandoned, that his system had been poisoned by his teeth, rendering him weak and emotionally disturbed.

In the above study, there is no doubt that the interviewer's messages were not registering with the lower class patients. But the investigation was not devised to distinguish linguistic factors from others in the breakdown in communication. The studies that follow do focus separately on language as a distinct component in the attenuation of communication between social classes.

It is widely held that lower class persons are linguistically less skilled, less developed than those from the middle and upper classes. A study from England lends support to this notion (Bernstein, 1960). A working-class group with an age range of 15-18 years, consisting of messenger boys, none of whom had completed grammar school, was compared with an upper class group, matched for age and sex with the first. All members of the latter group were students in "public schools" (i.e., English private schools). Both groups were given the Raven's Progressive Matrices Test, 1939 (a nonverbal measure of intelligence) and the Mill-Hill Vocabulary Scale. "The mean raw score for the school it is 51.4. However, the mean raw vocabulary score for the working class group is 41.90; for the public school group it is 60.20" (Bernstein, 1960, p. 275).

While no significance data is quoted, it appears that the difference between the two groups on vocabulary is much greater than it is on the nonverbal test. On the latter, the social-class difference is small, but on the language scale the upper class clearly has the advantage.

That the linguistically skilled patients are likely to be more appealing to interviewers than the unskilled has been asserted by Schofield (1964) in his discussion of the Yavis type of patients. (Note previous reference to Yavis patient in the section of Chapter 7 dealing with interviewee expectations.) Most social workers, psychologists, and psychiatrists tend to be attracted "to clients who present the 'YAVIS' syndrome-clients who are youthful, attractive, verbal, intelligent, and successful" (Schofield, 1964, p. 135). Out of the entire syndrome, the verbal attribute is selected at the moment, for further consideration. Because the central component of the therapeutic interview is the verbal exchange, it is not surprising that the therapist would be discouraged by patients whose capacity for abstract thought and introspective verbal communication are limited.

However, the problem goes beyond a quantitative comparison of verbal skill level between upper and lower class interviewees. It is suggested that in many respects the middle and lower classes actually live in different cultures (Goldstein, 1973), with different language codes. When responding to a lower class interviewee, the middle-class interviewer is therefore hampered by a vocabulary and language different from his own in many ways. To be sure, both may be speaking English, but the semantic contexts for words that both share may be quite different.

To be very concrete, we would propose that when using terms such as the following, the middle-class therapist and the lower-class patient may often not mean the same thing, may often not be seeking to communicate the same meanings, and at times may in fact be conceptualizing very different phenomena or experiences: security, frustration, satisfaction, dependency, fear, manliness, responsibility, sex, marriage, fun, crazy, motherhood, discipline, psychotherapy, doctor, boss, feelings, happiness, etc.   (Goldstein, 1973, p. 51)

Perhaps the most subtle and complex aspect of linguistic incompatibility between the middle- or upper class interviewer and the lower class interviewee is found, not in general level of verbal skill, or in the semantics of words used, but in what the British Sociologist, Bernstein (1960; 1964; 1970) refers to as language code. In one of his articles, Bernstein (1970) quotes two stories constructed by another author (Hawkins, 1969) out of his analyses of the speech of middle-class (Story A) and working-class (Story B) five-year-old children in England. The children were asked to tell a story about a series of four pictures, presented in temporal sequence. In the first picture boys are playing football near a house; in the second the ball breaks a window; then there is a man making a threatening gesture; and, finally, the children move away while being watched by a woman looking out of the window. The author developed two composites of the responses that he obtained from middle-class and working-class children. Although the Ss were only five, certain clear distinctions in their codes of speech were evident.

1. The middle-class response was meaningful to the reader even if s(he) had not seen the picture. Thus, the narrative included explicit descriptive references to separate pictures. The reader of the working-class response would have been at a loss, had s(he) not been able to refer to the pictures. The middle-class story achieved a sort of verbal autonomy from the pictorial context; the working-class story did not.

2. Middle-class children made no assumptions about the listeners sharing common experiences with them (i.e., viewing the pictures). Their stories had a clear expository quality, as though they were talking to others who did not see what they saw, and therefore needed to be told about it in descriptive and objective terms. Thus, the persons in their stories were all designated with modified nouns - e.g., "three boys," "a man," "that lady." In each instance where a noun was used in the middle-class responses, a personal pronoun with no previous verbal referent was used in the working-class responses. Instead

of "three boys" in the middle-class child's narrative the working class child used "they"; instead of "a man," "he"; and instead of "that lady," "she." Clearly middle-class children had learned how to use language to bridge the gap between themselves and their addressees, with an awareness that the latter were not present when the events about which the Ss spoke took place. The working-class children seemed not have learned to construct purely verbal spans to others. Their language was more rudimentary and based on the narrator's assumption that there was a shared experience with the listener.

3. The predicates in the middle-class stories were more clearly explicated than those in the working class stories. Thus, "one boy kicks the ball" in the former stories was matched by "he kicks it" in the latter; "the ball goes through the window," by "goes through there," and "broken the window," with "broken it."

Bernstein (1970) designates the language code of the working class as restricted and that of the middle class as extended. There is no implication that the person who uses a restricted code is necessarily less intelligent than the one who uses an extended code. It will be recalled that a previously mentioned investigation (Bernstein, 1960) showed only a trivial difference between a working-class and upper class group of children in a nonverbal measure of intelligence, but a very marked superiority indeed for the upper class children in verbal ability. The point at issue is therefore the relative emphasis given by different socioeconomic groups to verbal skills, and more particularly their contrasting verbal codes.

The restricted code is the modal verbal style of the working-class person. The following are some of its attributes:

1. In general, it may be referred to as verbally simple, lacking in fine discrimination of meaning (Bernstein, 1964). Sentences are short, basic, without qualifiers. Speech is direct, often impulsive, skimpy in grammatical or syntactical structure and, as a result, not a very adequate vehicle in itself for the communication of meaning. Therefore, the words of a speaker who uses a restricted code must be accompanied by considerable nonverbal communication. The listener tends not to rely on the explicit structure of a verbalized message alone for decoding its meaning. S(he) listens also for tone of voice, observes gesture, posture, and other signals, all of which the speaker shares with the members of his/her own subculture. But a listener from a different socioeconomic background is likely to miss much of the meaning communicated because s(he) does not share the verbal-nonverbal code of the speaker and the life experiences in which it is imbedded.

Consider the following example of a remark made in restricted code: "It's all according like well those youths and that if they get with the gangs and that they most have a bit of a lark around and say it goes wrong and that they probably knock someone off. I think they do it just to be a bit big you know" (Bernstein, 1964, p. 58).

The above speech would be baffling to an interviewer, for example, who does not share the life experiences and the code of the speaker. Even if one did, the naked transcript of the speech might still be confusing because much of the message is nonverbal. One must be in the presence of the speaker, to both see and hear him/her in order to receive the whole message. Of course, the confusion of an interviewer would be greater if s(he) were American rather than British, because the speech is given in the restricted code of a

British working-class person. At any rate, one may readily anticipate the feeling of alienation, of social distance that a middle-class interviewer might experience in attempting to communicate with a patient who speaks in a tongue so different from his/her own.

2. The restricted code tends to be externally rather than internally oriented. Its language and simple structure lend themselves better to a focus on external objects and events rather than internal thoughts, feelings, associations, and fantasies. This attribute of the lower class restricted code was illustrated in the interview with a laborer (Gill et al., 1954) quoted at the beginning of the present section on social class and the interview. The patient could speak about his headaches, his irritable behavior with his mother and girlfriend, his arguments and conflicts with others on the job. But there was almost a complete lack of words that described emotions and other inner experiences.

By contrast, consider the range of adjectives available to persons with more extended codes for describing their inner states. The following are sampled from an adjective checklist used to describe a person's mood or feeling: "affectionate," "afraid," "aggressive," "amiable," "cautious," "fearful," "jealous," "mad," "mean," "tormented," and "worrying" (Zuckerman & Lubin, 1965). The description of shades of feeling would require the command of multiple adjectives such as those quoted above, and facility in placing them at the service of introspection.

3. The restricted code is not simply a style of speaking that is superficially acquired. It is deeply rooted in the lower class subculture. For reasons that are sociologically too complex to consider further here, lower class persons are less likely than middle- or upper class persons to resort to individual self-assertion as a means of furthering their interests, and more likely to depend on solidarity or close identity with their group. For them, security, even survival, is dependent on collective decisions and actions with neighbors and others. This pattern for them is not a superficial one; it is not an option that they pick up or drop with the shifting requirements of the moment. It is instead a value orientation acquired from the beginning. It is therefore not surprising that the collective, the group orientation is reflected in the linguistic style or code of the low socioeconomic person.

The restricted code is an outgrowth of lower class social relationships in which the intent of others is taken for granted (Bernstein, 1964). This sharing of a common intent renders the speech of lower class communicants relatively simple and predictable, for it derives from an assumed similarity of personal experience. The restricted code lends itself more readily to the expression of a social rather than a personal identity. It is therefore not as useful as the extended code for personal self-exploration.

It is well known that people who live closely with each other do not need to spell out all communication in specific verbal terms. For them, a single word may contain a surplus of shared personal experience. Often a neutral word may be given a very precise meaning if accompanied by a gesture, a posture, a facial expression that others understand. Similarly, people who show a strong group identity may not require a complete well-structured verbal explication of a communication. For them, the restricted code is a system of condensed signals that is readily understood.

For the middle-class and upper class adult, the elaborated code is the modal verbal style. It possesses linguistic attributes that are the opposites of the ones designated above for the restricted code. Thus, the elaborated code tends to be complex, capable of expressing subtle nuances of meaning. Sentences are long, enriched with qualifiers, both in the form of adjectives and adverbs and in modifying phrases and clauses. The code contains enough syntactical structure to render a transcript of a message understandable, without the nonverbal cues present in its direct communication.

While most of the studies pertaining to the two social-class-linked codes were carried out in England, analogous investigations have been conducted in the United States with similar findings. One of these was done by Heider (1971) using 10-year-old children, divided into middle-class and lower class groups. The Ss were asked to carry out both encoding (i.e., formulating and speaking certain messages) and decoding (i.e., listening and receiving the messages) tasks. The encoding part of the study required the Ss to describe both abstract figures and sketched faces so that other Ss could recognize them and select them out of groups of similar figures (i.e., the decoding part of the study). The descriptions of all Ss when functioning as encoders were tape-recorded and transcribed for scoring. The following differences occurred between the two social classes.

1. Middle-class Ss were longer and more varied in their descriptions than the lower class Ss.

2. The most frequent type of statement made by lower class Ss was ambiguous, in that it related loosely to the whole stimulus rather than more specifically to a part of it. Moreover, it was less descriptive and more inferential than the statements made by middle-class Ss, e.g., "That boy is crying."

3. Middle-class messages were more flexibly coded than lower class messages, containing both inferential and descriptive passages.

4. The greater complexity of the middle-class code was noted in both the greater length of the statements and the more frequent use of modifiers.

When the Ss functioned as decoders by selecting the abstract figures or faces in response to the tape-recorded descriptions of other Ss, the middle-class encodings were better understood by all Ss (i.e., both lower and middle-class Ss). Middle class superiority in clarity of verbal communication was due to both the greater length of its statements, and more particularly to its use of both inferential and descriptive statements (i.e., to its greater verbal flexibility).

Findings such as these have implications for communication within the interview. In general, one would expect the interviewer to understand the middle-class interviewee more readily than the working-class interviewee. In the mental health interview the aptness of the elaborated code for introspective communication is evident, for it is abundantly endowed with adjectival modifiers so necessary for the expression of thoughts, associations, fantasies, and feelings. It need hardly be added that the working-class restricted code does not lend itself well to self-disclosing communication. The interviewer may invite the interviewee to speak about thoughts, feelings, conflicts, and relationships with others. What s(he) is likely to hear from the interviewee is an account of somatic distress and stress originating in external pressures. S(he) listens for shades of feeling, but hears an emphasis on action, on conflict relative to other people. The problem is not only one of value discrepancy between the two. In addition, the interviewee lacks the language resources and the code to speak in a manner that would be congruent with the interviewer's expectations. Under these circumstances, Goldstein (1973) concludes that if it is true that "the contemporary, American, middle-class psychotherapist communicates (speaks and, in a sense listens) via an elaborate verbal code, and the typical lower-class patient utilizes a restricted code to both send and receive his verbal messages, their psychotherapeutic interaction would appear to be almost destined to fail" (p. 48).

Breaching the Communication Barrier
Between Social Classes

An attempted solution to the difficulties posed by cross social-class communication in the mental health interview has been a search for interviewer attributes and behavior that might breach the communication barrier between the middle-class interviewer and lower class interviewee. One study (Baum, Felzer, D'Zmura, & Shumaker, 1963) inquired into the characteristics of therapists who were relatively successful in retaining low-socioeconomic patients in treatment. The therapists were psychiatric residents in a clinic associated with a large medical center, working with Social Class IV and V individuals. Patients were designated as dropouts if they terminated before attending six sessions. As it turned out, the more clinically experienced residents (i.e., the residents with experience in other fields of medicine before entering the residency program) were more successful than the less experienced ones in keeping down the number of dropouts from treatment. These residents were older, more mature, more accepting and more flexible in their modes of relating to and communicating with their patients. The findings were based on the impressions of psychotherapy supervisors working individually with the residents.

Another study (Gould, 1967) is based on clinical case material collected in a program developed by a psychoanalytic institute in contract with a union to offer psychotherapy to any union member wishing help. During the first year of operation, 23 patients were seen. Although not committed to a specific set of modifications of conventional insight therapy, it was assumed "that new or modified psychotherapeutic techniques, adapted to suit the life style and value system of the blue-collar worker, might be necessary for therapy to succeed" (Gould, 1967, p. 79). A further assumption was stated in the following terms: "Since the means of working with the patient are primarily those of verbal communication, a primary aim was to bridge the gap in the styles of communication between middle-class therapist and lower-class patient" (p. 80). Basing himself on his own experience with one patient and the shared experiences of other colleagues participating in the project, the author made the following proposals for the improvement of rapport and communication with the blue-collar worker.

1. Because patients are likely to come to treatment with expectations of receiving shocks, hypnosis, or pills, it is necessary to explain to them at great length how talking can be helpful. This initial orientation period is reminiscent of the role induction interview preliminary to treatment that will be discussed below.

2. Interviewers need to shed their preference for ambiguity in their own style of conducting interview. They must not hesitate to be direct, specific, and concrete in the questions they ask. In fact, the use of concrete language tends to reduce the social distance between the interviewer and the blue-collar worker, facilitating the latter's responsiveness.

3. Low-socioeconomic interviewees often sense a linguistic difference between themselves and the interviewers, whether this be in terminology used, or in language code. Interviewers eager to reduce the social distance between themselves and the interviewees experience a dilemma. If they try to speak the interviewee's language and it is not their own, they may be perceived by the interviewees as patronizing in manner. The dictate of genuineness compels them to follow another course - that of adapting their own language so that it is understandable and nonintimidating to the interviewee.

4. Because blue-collar workers tend to be physical, and motor-oriented, therapists may permit themselves much greater activity than is their usual wont. Gould remarks: "I found myself moving about to illustrate a point, going for a book to find a passage to read to him" (1967, p. 82).

A second solution for the blunted communication between interviewer and interviewee across social-class lines, suggested by Goldstein (1973), calls for the use of paraprofessionals of lower class origin as mental health workers. One study (Pope et al., 1974) dealing with the effectiveness of the paraprofessional as an interviewer with a minimum of social distance from the interviewee has already been reviewed earlier in this chapter. Another (Carkhuff & Pierce, 1967), also referred to earlier, was concerned with the differential effect of both race and social class of interviewer on interviewee depth of self-exploration. Four lay counselors who had completed a mental health training program were used, one an upper class white, the second an upper class black, the third a lower class white, and the fourth a lower class black. Each interviewer met with four interviewees, from the four different ethnic and social class groups represented by the interviewers. The results indicated that race and social class of both interviewer and interviewee, and the interaction between the two, all affected interviewee depth of self-exploration. More specifically, interviews in which the two participants were similar in both social class and race rather than dissimilar elicited the higher levels of interviewee self-exploration. The finding that is most immediately relevant is that the interviewee is better able to engage in introspective communication if he speaks to an interviewer of his own social class, rather than one of another, either higher or lower.

The third type of solution (Goldstein, 1973) for the attenuation of communication between middle-class interviewers and lower class interviewees includes certain modifications of conventional interviewing and psychotherapy procedures. One of these modifications takes on the form of preinterview or pretherapy training of interviewees for the kind of communication that will be expected of them (or similar training early in therapy); and another, certain embellishments of or additions to the interview interaction, such as modeling procedures.

The preinterview and pretherapy (or early in therapy) training approach is based on the acceptance of the conventional mental health interview as appropriate for the lower class interviewee. The latter is prepared to participate in traditional psychotherapy, through a process of instruction with the goal of adjusting his expectations to make them accord with those of the interviewer.

Reference has been made above to the initial orientation period in a psychotherapy experience with a blue-collar worker (Gould, 1967). The patient had arrived for treatment with the expectation that he would be given shock, pills, or hypnosis. The therapist remarked: "I then explained in some detail how talking could be helpful and gave a number of examples. We discussed this again the second and third sessions until I was sure that we were on the same wave length" (Gould, 1967, p. 80).

Lennard and Bernstein (1960) refer to the same process of initial patient orientation when they speak about primary system reference in the psychotherapy interview. The term designates the comments made both by interviewer and interviewee about "reciprocal therapist patient role relations. They revolve around the obligations and activities of therapist and patient vis-a-vis each other. These references frequently consist of discussions of the purpose of therapy" (Lennard & Bernstein, 1960, p. 92). A reference to the primary interview system by a patient is generally a question soliciting information about his/her role in treatment. An analogous reference from the therapist is likely to be a statement containing instruction for the patient about his/her role in therapy. "Primary system references therefore reduce strain and disequilibrium by clarifying role expectations and reducing the lack of complimentarity between the patient's and the therapist's conceptions of therapy" (Lennard & Bernstein, 1960, p. 119). In their investigation of the communication system in the psychotherapeutic interview, Lennard and Bernstein found that the number of primary system propositions made by four therapists varied considerably. In general, however, the rate of decline for each was most rapid early in therapy, and continued at a decreasing rate subsequently. This decline is understandable since the need for role instruction is greatest early in therapy. Once both members of the dyad have congruent expectations of each other's communication roles, the initial barriers to the kind of communication required by the therapist are eliminated. The authors found that the interview dyads showing least strain were the ones in which there were most early primary system references. In their opinion, high dropout rates in mental health clinics for low-socioeconomic patients "may be related to failure to sufficiently socialize patients to their role so that they could function within the definitions provided by the therapists" (Lennard & Bernstein, 1960, p. 70).

A number of clinical investigators have used a more formal kind of initial preparation for patients considered to be ill-suited for insight therapy. This procedure is sometimes referred to as a role induction interview (Hoehn-Saric, Frank, Imber, Nash, Stone, & Battle, 1964) and at others, as an anticipatory socialization interview (Orne & Wender, 1968).

A major study of the efficacy of the role induction interview was carried out at Phipps Psychiatric Clinic in Baltimore (Hoehn-Saric et al., 1964). Forty low-socioeconomic neurotic out-patients were seen in individual psychotherapy for four months by four psychiatric residents. Each therapist was assigned 10 patients and was asked to record all sessions on tape. He was required to interview each patient at least once a week for one hour. Half of each therapist's patients received a role induction interview. All the patients in the study were of low-socioeconomic origin and were considered to have expectations about therapy that were different from those of the therapists. The role induction interviews, conducted by research psychiatrists (not the therapists), sought to alter the expectations that the patients had about the therapy process in order to make them accord with those held by the therapists.

It was found that the patients given the preparation interview, in contrast to the ones who were not, were more regular in their attendance at the weekly therapy sessions, exhibited more acceptable in-therapy behavior as judged by the therapists, and were perceived by their therapists as relating more positively to them. Both therapist and patient ratings indicated that those patients who had received the role inducation interview were more improved in treatment than those who did not. The pretherapy preparation of patients appears to have brought their in-therapy communication into line with that expected of them by the therapist, thus facilitating the psycho-therapy process.

In the next two studies the anticipatory socialization interview (another term for the role induction interview) prepared the patients for group therapy rather than individual therapeutic interviews. Hence, many of the patient variables affected by the socialization interview are not directly relevant to the dyadic interaction. Only the aspects of the studies that relate to the interview interaction will be considered.

The first of these studies "was designed to explore differences in the adequate formation of a working alliance in group psychotherapy between lower-class unsophisticated patients prepared for this process via the anticipatory socialization interview and those who were given no particular advance preparation" (Heitler, 1973, p. 252). The Ss in the study were male patients on an open psychiatric ward of a Veterans Administration Hospital. There were two distinct age groups, one consisting of young men in their 20s (Vietnam veterans) and one of middle-aged men in their 40s (Korean War veterans). Chiefly white, they were classified as Social Class IV and V persons, holding marginal jobs and semi-skilled or unskilled workers, with many of them unemployed. Those given the anticipatory socialization interview were designated experimental Ss and those not given the interview, control Ss. The experimental Ss showed a greater readiness to initiate communication than the control Ss (i.e., a shorter reaction time), a higher level of productivity (i.e., a greater number of communications), and more time spent in communication. Clearly, the experimental Ss were more responsive in the group. The prepared patients engaged in more therapeutic self-exploration than those not prepared. The therapists rated the prepared patient as participating more actively in a collaborative working alliance "on the task of trying to explore, understand and find solutions to his own personal difficulties" (p. 258). The strength of these findings is mitigated somewhat by their limitation to the first two weeks of group psychotherapy. By the 10th session, most of the significant results had dissipated.

The second study (Strupp & Bloxom, 1973) evaluated the usefulness of a role induction film as a means of preparing low-socioeconomic patients for group psychotherapy. The patients were all lower income clients selected from community agencies. Four therapists (three male clinical psychologists and one female nurse) conducted 12 groups, distributed equally among the following treatment conditions:

1. Role induction film group. The Ss in this condition were told that they were to see a motion picture before beginning their treatment. The film, prepared for the study, deals with the case of a truck driver with a volatile temper and an addiction to alcohol. Loss of several jobs, followed by loss of his family renders him suicidal. Through a friend, he finds his way into a therapy group. The process of group psychotherapy, and how it leads him to some understanding of the part that his own behavior has played in the punishing events that have overtaken him, are portrayed in the film. In the end, the truck driver regains his job and reestablishes his relationship with his wife.

2. The Ss in the second group all received individual role induction interviews that followed the pattern set by Orne and Wender (1968) and by Hoehn-Saric et al. (1964).

3. The control group viewed a neutral film dealing with early marriage.

All groups then met 12 times.

The immediate effect of role induction was assessed through a comparison of certain ratings and measurements made immediately before and after the induction sessions and the neutral film. Thus motivation of the patient to begin treatment and, indeed, understanding of the therapy process and the patient's role in it increased pre- to postinduction for both the film induction and role induction interview groups in contrast to either a decrease or no change in the neutral group. Other ratings made of themselves by patients, favoring the two role induction groups over the control group, included satisfaction with therapy sessions both early in treatment and at termination, satisfaction with progress in therapy and judgment of improvement. Some therapist ratings that demonstrated differences in favor of the two role induction groups over the neutral group included in-therapy appropriateness of patient behavior and patient attractiveness. In brief, role induction whether by individual interview or by film improved patient motivation for and knowledge of group therapy, appropriateness of in-therapy behavior, and the relationship between therapist and patients. As to the relative efficacy of the two methods of role induction, film, or interview, the authors have the following to say: "The interview seemed to be superior in conveying a detailed knowledge of the process of group therapy, whereas the film was superior over a wider range of measures" (Strupp & Bloxom, 1973, p. 381).

Role induction or anticipatory socialization is similar in many ways to modeling, especially when carried out with the use of films.

With reference to the use of modeling in facilitating low social-class interviewee responses, a review of some of the work done recently by Goldstein (1973) and his students will now be undertaken. Goldstein (1973) developed a new approach to psychotherapy for the poor, which he calls Structured Learning Therapy. This includes elements of modeling, role playing, and reinforcement procedures. In the present discussion there will be reference only to those of the many studies carried out by Goldstein and his students that investigate the role of modeling in facilitating the interview process with low-socioeconomic clients. The three investigations that follow are arranged in a sequence of increasing power of the modeling operation.

In the first (Liberman, 1970) male alcoholic in-patients were the Ss. These were divided into six subgroups for treatment under six different experimental conditions. The purpose of the study was to investigate the efficacy of modeling procedures for enhancing both self-disclosure and attraction of interviewee to interviewer. The modeling procedure consisted of a taped interview that the patient listened to before participating in an individual intake interview. In the instructions given the S prior to his listening to the taped interview the patient on the tape was identified as a person in his mid to late 30s, in a serious personal and family crisis. His hospital treatment was described as a distinct success, with improvement in every problematic sphere (i.e., vocational, family, and control of drinking). The introduction endeavored to strengthen the modeling operation by describing an interviewee with whom the patient could identify, and holding out the prospect of reinforcement to the patient by reporting the success experienced by the taped interviewee.

Four variants of the taped interview were developed by altering the interviewee's responses somewhat. The interviewer's questions remained constant across the four taped interview variants.

1. High attraction - high disclosure interview.

In this version of the taped interview the interviewee expressed positive feelings toward the interviewer and was highly self-disclosing in the information he communicated.

2. High attraction - low disclosure.

The interviewee's expression of ·positive feelings toward interviewer occurred at a high level, but his disclosure of his problems was limited. There was much denial.

3. Low attraction - high disclosure.

In the third variant of the interview the interviewee expressed negative feelings about the interviewer, but was nevertheless highly self-disclosing in his communications.

4. Low attraction - low disclosure.

In the final variant both attraction to interviewer and self-disclosure were low.

Four of the subgroups were assigned to the above four modeling conditions. The fifth and sixth subgroups were controls, one listening to a tape that recorded a conversation between two people about psychotherapy, but no actual interview; and the other not listening to any tape but proceeding directly with the intake interview. For all Ss, the intake interview (after the taped procedures in the first five subgroups) was standard in that the interviewer asked each S the same questions used by the taped interviewer. The intake interview with each S was taped and later content analyzed for self-disclosure. Interviewee attraction to interviewer was measured with a questionnaire given to each $\underline{S}$ after the completion of the intake interview.

There was support for greater self-disclosure in the initial interviews of $\underline{S}s$ exposed to the high-disclosure rather than low-disclosure model. Additionally, the $\underline{S}s$ in both groups exposed to high-disclosure tapes were more self-disclosing than the $\underline{S}s$ in the no-tape group. Clearly, exposure to a modeled interview in which the interviewee was highly self-disclosing did prompt high interviewee self-disclosure in a subsequent initial interview. However, there were no analogous results for attraction of interviewee to interviewer.

In the second investigation (Friedenberg, 1971) attraction modeling was enhanced through the addition of nonverbal cues. The $\underline{S}s$ were 60 male psychiatric in-patients, and the modeling device was a videotaped interview. Four variants of the videotaped interview were developed reflecting four experimental conditions, based on two levels of modelled attraction of interviewee to interviewer (high and low), and two modalities of display (verbal and nonverbal). Thus, the following four types of videotapes were used:

1. high attraction verbal - high attraction nonverbal;
2. high attraction verbal - low attraction nonverbal;
3. low attraction verbal - high attraction nonverbal;
4. low attraction verbal - low attraction nonverbal.

The videotaped interviews were standard across the four conditions, based on the same five interviewee questions. In those that expressed high interviewee to interviewer attraction verbally there were interviewee expressions of positive feeling toward the interviewer; in those that expressed low attraction there were interviewee expressions of negative feeling toward the interviewer. Nonverbal expressions of high and low attraction were based on findings regarding the expression of interpersonal attitude through the modality of posture (Mehrabian, 1969). High attraction rather than low was associated with the interviewee taking a position close to the interviewer, leaning toward him/her and maintaining a high level of eye contact. The attraction of $\underline{S}s$ in the present study was assessed in two ways:

1. Each $\underline{S}$ provided an index of attraction to the modeled interviewer immediately after viewing the videotape by responding to a questionnaire; and

2. Each $\underline{S}s$ was then asked to participate in an interview with the same interviewer seen on the videotape. The interview was tape recorded and observed by two raters who made an assessment of nonverbal expression of attraction using such dimensions as forward lean and eye contact. A verbal expression of interviewee attraction to the interviewer was obtained by asking each $\underline{S}$ to respond again to the questionnaire used previously immediately after the modeled interview.

The results offered partial support for the induction of interviewee attraction to interviewer through videotaped modeling interviews. Only the comparison of the first and fourth groups yielded significant results. When the group viewing the high-attraction verbal and nonverbal videotape was compared with the group viewing the low-attraction verbal and nonverbal, the former showed greater attraction immediately after viewing the videotape.

The former group also manifested less silence in the interview conducted after the videotape viewing than the latter group. The first result is actually an expression of attraction to a videotaped interviewer. It is disappointing that a similar attraction differential between experimental groups did not occur when the Ss later participated in an actual interview. However, the lesser silence of the first group in contrast to the fourth implies its greater willingness to communicate.

In a third investigation (Walsch, 1971) modeling of attraction was carried out with an audiotaped interview, amplified this time through the experimental manipulation of conforming pressures. The procedure was too complex to be discussed in detail here. Briefly, half of the Ss listened to modeled high-attraction interviews, and half to low-attraction interviews. Attraction to the modeled interviewer was again measured by Ss' responses to a questionnaire, given after auditing the modeled interview. Half of both groups of Ss were asked to listen to taped answers to the attraction questionnaire by high-status persons before giving their own replies. The taped answers providing the conformity pressure were in the direction of high attraction. As in the previous study, modeling and, in this instance, conformity pressure, too, resulted in higher attraction scores immediately after exposure to the taped modeling interview, but not after the actual interviews in which the Ss participated.

Goldstein (1973) concluded that patient change in actual interpersonal behavior rather than in an immediate postmodeling attitudinal sense would require behavioral training through role playing in addition to the modeling procedure. His investigations that followed were concerned with behavior change over psychotherapeutic time periods rather than in single interviews. Moreover, criteria of patient change applied to a range of social interaction situations rather than the interview situation alone. Since the present book is concerned with the dyadic interaction in the interview and not social behavior in a more extended sense, we must part company with Goldstein at this point.

The three investigations conducted by Goldstein (1973) and his students are moderately encouraging with reference to the use of modeling to span the social-class gap between interviewer and interviewee.

It was possible through the means of modeling to augment interviewee self-disclosing communication. Attraction of interviewee to interviewer was more difficult to judge. Studies dealing with the role induction interview used with low-socioeconomic patients indicate that this method leads to improvement in motivation to participate in an initial interview, improved communication within the interview, and improved relationship between the two participants. Other solutions for the attenuation of communication and relationship in cross social-class interviews include the use of paraprofessional interviewers as a means of reducing or eliminating the social-class differential within the dyad and an appeal to the kind of flexible clinical responsiveness that a middle-class interviewer might display with a lower class patient if he is motivated to work with him.

There is no doubt that a social-class gap between interviewer and interviewee imposes a strain on the interview. The clinical and research evidence summarized impresses one with the depth of the problem and its unyielding character since complex, culturally based values, expectations, and linguistic styles are involved. Social distance between interviewer and interviewee is not a fiction; it is a potent variable. Yet the effective expansion of mental health services into impoverished sections of the community will depend not only on the commitment and zeal of mental health professionals but even more on the development of modifications in traditional procedures that will enhance clinically relevant communication between the helper and the helpee.

APPLICATION SUMMARY

Certain demographic variables are relevant to both interviewers and interviewees, whether the two participants are viewed independently or in interaction with each other. The sex of the two members of the dyad is one of these. In some ways it does make a difference whether the interviewees are male or female and whether they are interviewed by like-sexed or cross-sexed interviewers. It has long been a tenet of masculine bias that women are verbally more facile than males; that is, that they speak with greater fluency and productivity. If this were the case, it should be of considerable interest to the interviewer, because it would affect the communication that might be expected in the interview. Actually the research results about this matter have been quite mixed. Findings regarding sex differences in speech disturbances are largely negative (Feldstein et al., 1963; Mahl, 1959) but men appear to be more hesitant in speech (Ah Ratio) than women (Feldstein et al., 1963), although they are simultaneously more verbose (Heller, 1972; Siegman, 1972). Of greater interest than interviewee sex differences in general terms is the possibility that some significant differences might occur between same-sexed and cross-sexed interview situations. Indeed, interviewer warmth does appear to function differently in such contrasting interviews. Females who were interviewed by a male who behaved in a warm manner were less productive than others interviewed by the same male when he conducted a cold interview (Siegman, 1972). With male interviewees, the same interviewer obtained opposite effects. They were less productive during his cold interviews and more productive when he was warm. It hardly needs to be added that a male interviewer may expect that personal warmth in his interview behavior is likely to be perceived quite differently by female and male interviewees. In fact the female interviewee is likely to regard his warmth as seductive with inhibiting consequences for her verbal responsiveness.

The desired communication in a mental health interview is not neutral in content, and subject only to a quantitative evaluation. The goal of the interviewer is to elicit self-disclosing communication from the interviewee. Can s(he) expect more self-disclosure from one sex rather than the other? Most of the research evidence (Jourard, 1971a, 1971b) finds the female interviewee to be more self-disclosing than the male.

The relative infrequency of sex differences in verbal dimensions of communication is more than compensated by their frequent occurrence in nonverbal channels. Many of these differences occur in channels that are constituents of the study of proxemics, including the visibility of one person to another, eye contact between them, the actual distance assumed by one from another, and body orientation.

In general, females are uneasy if they cannot see the other person, even when invisible themselves; males do not show the same discomfort (Argyle, et al., 1968). Thus, the visible male addressing an invisible female spoke significantly more than the visible female addressing an invisible male. The authors inferred that females feel more observed than males, and thus rely more on visual feedback. At issue here seems to be a set of conditions that operate in the maintenance of communication between two people. A screen placed between them, or some other method of rendering one or the other nonvisible, removes a basic condition needed to maintain their communication. If nonvisibility of the addressee has a generally inhibiting effect on the speaker, this effect is particularly pronounced when the speaker is female.

The greater dependence of female than male communicants on visual feedback is noted also in their use of eye contact. Women conversing with women engage in mutual glances more frequently than men conversing with men (Exline, 1963). Moreover, women seek eye contact with those they are addressing more than men do, in both like-sex and cross-sex dyadic communication situations (Exline et al., 1965). If the need for visual feedback is one explanation of the dependence of women on the visibility of their conversational partners and eye contact with them, their greater need for inclusion and affectionate relationship is another. Certainly, female Ss associate eye contact with affectionate feeling to a greater extent than male Ss do.

Eye contact is one dimension in the experience of psychological proximity. The actual physical distance between two people is another. In dyadic situations in which participants who are strangers to each other are asked to converse, same sex pairs are able to tolerate greater closeness than opposite sex pairs (Argyle et al., 1968). Moreover, for both male and female Ss the distance taken from a female addressee is less than from a male.

Finally, several studies support the popular notion that women are more sensitive than men to nonverbal communication. Female observers are able to "read" the emotion communicated through facial expression (Buck et al., 1974), messages sent through tone of voice, and movements of the face and body (Rosenthal et al., 1974) more accurately than male observers.

The above disparities between male and female responses to the dyadic communication situation are potential sources of tension in cross-sex interviews. If a female interviewee, for example, requires more visual feedback and eye contact than a male interviewer is able to provide, she may lack the kind of interpersonal support she needs to maintain an adequate level of self-disclosing communication. If a male interviewee feels crowded by the excessive proximity of a female interviewer whose eye contact and gaze are felt to be too searching, he may seek to increase distance and regain equilibrium by averting his gaze and reducing communication. The interviewer's training should include his/her sensitization to problems of this type in cross-sex interviews.

Equally fraught with culturally prompted tensions and barriers is the interracial interview. In the U.S. the most frequent form of the interracial interview is one in which the interviewer is white and the interviewee black. In this situation one would expect the usual type of interviewee resistance to self-disclosing communication to be augmented by the lack of trust and the self-protective concealment that are associated with undercurrents of rage that flow when a high-status white interrogates a low-status black. The discomfort of the interviewee is matched by the sense of incompetence often felt by the white clinician who is particularly prone to errors in clinical judgment when conducting an assessment interview with a black client. These may be a consequence of the clinicians's inability to cope with the biasing effect of his/her stereotyped judgments about black clients. Thus, the intellectual level of such a person may be significantly underrated if the black is poor, shabbily dressed, and speaks with the dialect of the rural South. Errors in clinical judgment may also result from the understandable unwillingness of the black client to speak in an open trusting manner to the white interviewer. Frequently, the black client, inhibited by the stressfulness of the situation, presents a picture of apathy, depression, and powerlessness, which the interviewer reinforces through a paternalistic sort of supportiveness. In this atmosphere, the clinician may avoid probing areas that arouse discomfort, thus missing pathology that may be present. This type of avoidance by the interviewer may also occur when s(he) is working with an assertive black client whose openly expressed rage is experienced as an imminent threat.

The obstacles to interview communication between blacks and whites are not limited to such qualities of relationship as distrust and resentment. There are also differences in communication style. In one study (La France & Mayo, 1974) certain differences in the deployment of gaze by black and white conversationalists were noted. Black conversationalists looked at their listeners while they spoke, but looked away when their partners began to speak. White conversationalists behaved in a converse manner. As a result, communication between the two members of a black and white dyad could be disrupted by crossed up cues, causing them both to speak at the same time, or both simultaneously to fall into silence.

In brief, there are both relationship and communication obstacles to the dyadic exchange in an interview when the two participants are of different races. But these obstacles are not inevitable. Positive interracial attitudes and focused training of the interviewer for the development of facilitating skills may mitigate the obstacles to a positive interaction.

The last, and in many ways the most pervasive demographic variable that intrudes into the interview is that of social class. Social-class differences in interview behavior can be quite striking. Such differences are demonstrated in the two interviews excerpted from the Gill et al. (1954) book on the initial psychiatric interview. The nurse (middle-class) spoke in psychological terms, demonstrating a capacity for introspection. The laborer (lower class) lacked this introspective capacity, speaking in terms of externals, of social behavior that was visible to others. Rather than communicating with psychological concepts, he preferred to couch his problems in somatic terminology. Moreover, the vocabulary commanded by the nurse and her linguistic style were attuned to the description of feelings, memories, and thoughts. These attributes of speech were largely lacking in the laborer, who somaticized his feelings ("high tension nerves") and externalized his experiences. The effect on the two relationships by the differences in communication was evident. The social distance between the laborer and his interviewer was considerably greater than that between the nurse and hers. Communication flowed more easily in the latter interview than in the former. The social-class proposition that is supported by much of reported clinical impression and research can be stated succinctly in the following way: membership in the lower class rather than the middle- or upper class tends to burden communication in a mental health interview conducted by a professional, who is generally of the middle class.

There is now a considerable body of research evidence that demonstrates that low-socioeconomic applicants for treatment in mental health clinics are less likely to be assigned to individual psychotherapy than middle- or upper socioeconomic applicants. Moreover, those who are assigned are more likely to terminate prematurely. The lack of fit between the interviewer and interviewee of different social classes, along several dimensions to be considered below, strains the dyadic system in psychotherapy often leading to its dissolution.

In part, this strain is a consequence of a lack of value congruence between lower class clients and middle- and upper class therapists. Since the mental health interview is an interpersonal encounter with the encouragement of self-disclosing communication as a major goal, conflicting values held by its two participants are certain to impede the processes that lead to the attainment of the goal. Moreover, social class value systems do not yield readily to persuasion, since they are rooted in family and peer relationships during childhood and adolescence (Barker, 1955; Pope, 1953a). In a mental health interview conducted by a middle-class clinician with a lower class client, intrapsychically determined resistances are augmented by others that stem from a culture conflict between the two participants. Some of the value elements in this culture conflict, abstracted from several studies (Barker, 1955; Seward, 1972) are listed in tabular form below:

Middle-Class Values	Lower Class Values
(a) Self-reliance, because of the opportunity for progress through individual attainment.	Group solidarity, because progress through individual attainment is not feasible.
(b) The delay of immediate gratification in favor of future attainment and pleasure. Saving and investment are the methods of attaining future security.	The rejection of gratification delay because income is too low to permit saving for future security.
(c) The responsible budgeting of time, as part of the delay of immediate gratification.	The view of time budgeting and saving for future security as equally pointless.

(d) The inhibition and control of immediate aggressive impulse. Such control is congruent with a value system that stresses delay of gratification and a future time orientation.

The indulgence of aggressive impulse, as a means of asserting immediate social control, particularly during adolescence. This impulsiveness is congruent with the rejection of gratification delay and a present time rather than a future time orientation.

(e) The emphasis, rather early in life, on verbal communication as a means of settling differences with others. This is consistent with the value placed on the control of agressive impulse.

The positive evaluation of action and impulse rather than a primary emphasis on communication.

(f) The choice of introspection as the major means of coping with problems that are perceived as basically internal.

A primary emphasis on coping with the environment, because external pressures are relatively more demanding than internal conflicts.

It is evident that the values of the middle class are the values of the therapist. It must also be clear that a lack of sensitivity of therapists to their value differences with lower-class clients is likely to make the latter feel misunderstood and, indeed, pressured in a direction that conflicts with their survival needs. Moreover, a lack of awareness of the value context from which lower class patients come is likely to cause the clinician to confuse mental health with normative social-class values. The clinician may feel that he is formulating goals for a patient that meet mental health criteria, when in fact he is using mental health code to reinforce values that are rewarding to middle-class patients but not to those from the working class. Frustrated by the incongruence that they feel between their own values and those of the therapist or interviewer, clients may become "resistive," uncommunicative, and, indeed, may not return. For the mitigation of this type of culture conflict there is no easy solution. Some specific procedures that may be used will be discussed below. But there is no substitute available to the clinician for an in-depth immersion into the subculture from which his/her clients come. The dynamic intrapsychic model is not, in itself, enough. In fact, more needs to be done to determine its generality and its culturally determined applicability. Meanwhile, it would appear that the social-class value context that governs the lives of clients is just as relevant a body of information for therapists as general intraphysic principles that have directed their work for several decades.

The step between interpersonal values and expectations is a very small one. In the two cases described by Kadushin (1969) the social worker exemplifies a middle-class orientation toward treatment, and the airplane mechanic, an orientation from the skilled (blue-collar) working class. The contrasting values of these two applicants for treatment led them both to have different anticipations regarding the behavior of the interviewer. The social worker expected the interviewer to listen to her self-disclosures, to ask occasional questions, and to make some clarifying remarks. The mechanic anticipated advice or active direction from the interviewer regarding the alleviation of external stresses. Clearly, the social worker's expectations accorded more closely with the interviewer's actual behavior than those of the mechanic. Not surprisingly, then, the mechanic was more defensive and less communicative in the initial interview than the social worker, and the interviewer was more attracted to and receptive to the social worker. The strain that a conflict of expectation places on the mental health interview is noted, also, in the studies that demonstrate a significant discrepancy between a priori expectation of lower class clients and actual observed behavior in the interview, with a subsequent high rate of failure of the client to return for treatment (Overall & Aronson, 1963). Moreover, there is a significant positive correlation between degree of discrepancy between patient expectation and actual perception of first interview and failure to return for treatment.

For the interviewer, the considerations regarding social-class differences in expectation are similar to those that hold for value differences. In fact, the two are closely related. Some work has been done on the development of methods for the adjustment of expectation discrepancies. These will be considered later.

Misperception and inaccurate expectation are not all on the side of lower class interviewees. In two separate investigations both psychiatric residents (Lee & Temerlin, 1970) and graduate students in clinical psychology (DiNardo, 1975) demonstrated a penchant to give higher pathology scores to lower class rather than middle-class interviewees when in fact there were no differences. Small wonder, then, that psychotherapists of all disciplines prefer middle-class to lower class patients (Redlich et al., 1955). This preference is in part related to the therapists' view of middle-class patients as better prospects for psychotherapy because they do not consider them to be as ill as lower-class patients. It is also related to the tendency of therapists to impart certain attributes regarded as prognostically favorable in therapy to middle-class rather than lower class interviewees (Lerner & Fiske, 1973), such as low somatic complaints, low externalization of blame, low guardedness and suspicion, high introspectiveness, high verbal fluency, and high estimated intelligence. Finally, there is the judgment by mental health clinicians (Redlich et al., 1955) that lower class patients communicate at a significantly lower level than middle-class patients - that is, the verbal interaction with them is not as satisfying and they seem not to understand the therapist as well.

However biased the perceptions of the other might be, the communication barrier between middle-class interviewers and lower class interviewees is tangible and authentic. The evidence is quite consistent that middle-class Ss and lower class Ss of equal intelligence may differ significantly in verbal skills with the former at a higher level than the latter (Bernstein, 1960). The linguistically skilled patients are certain to be more appealing to the therapists. But the communication barrier between the social classes is not only a consequence of the differential in verbal skill. In many respects the middle- and lower classes actually live in different cultures (Goldstein, 1973) and speak in different language codes. Bernstein (1960; 1964; 1970) has spelled out the extended language code of the middle and upper classes, and the restricted code of the lower classes. The restricted code lacks fine discrimination in meaning. It is direct, often impulsive, and embedded in gestures and other nonverbal signals that are subtle, and extensively shared with others in one's subculture. The restricted code is understood only with difficulty by a person who does not belong to the socioeconomic group of the speaker. Moreover, it is not a code that transmits messages clearly with verbal signals alone. The language lacks the gradation of meaning needed for this type of verbal autonomy. The listener is more likely to understand the speaker if s(he) is in the speaker's presence, and can both see and hear him/her. In a sense, the lower class speaker using a restricted code, is both transmitting a verbal message and sending out a signal that binds him/her to surrounding friends and associates. The speaker using an extended code is pursuing a more individual course in communication. The restricted code emphasizes external referents; the extended code has the capacity for making internal nuances of experience, feeling, and introspective thought explicit. The restricted code signals a strong group identity; the extended code is the vehicle par excellence for individual self-disclosure. It is not surprising, therefore, that middle-class therapists recognize the language of middle-class clients as their own, and readily feel related to them. Just as understandable is their sense of alienation from the language, and consequently from the persons of the lower class. However, even if one grants the above social-class barrier to communication in the interview, there is evidence to indicate that the barrier is permeable. There are things that the interviewer can do to breach it.

Perhaps the most conservative course to follow is that of modifying the interviewer's content and style of communication in a manner that facilitates interaction and reduces social distance between the two participants without altering the basic character of the interview. In fact, there is evidence that such modifications often occur with experience and professional maturity, even when there is no specific focus on the designated changes. For example, one group of investigators (Baum et al., 1963) found that psychiatric residents with previous work in other medical specialties were more successful than their less experienced colleagues in reducing dropout from treatment. The authors found these residents to be older, more mature, and more flexible in their modes of relating to and communicating with Social Class IV and V patients.

How might this flexibility be attained? What specific instructions or advice might be given to a clinician working with low-socioeconomic clients in a conventional therapy situation?

1. Very early in the interview, it is important that the interviewer take time to explain to the client how talking may be helpful to him/her in learning how to cope with problems that have prompted recourse to psychotherapy (Gould, 1967). Many low social-class clients come to a mental health clinic with the anticipation that some procedures (shock, pills,

hypnosis) will be applied to them.   They need to be persuaded that an exchange between two people may have a healing effect.

2. The interviewer should be sensitized to the language and the style of speech that are most appropriate when working with clients from low-socioeconomic backgrounds. As a person with an extended linguistic code, the middle-class interviewer is expected to command greater flexibility in speech than one with a restricted code (Baum, et al., 1963). When a speaker with an elaborated code seeks to shift in the direction of one with a more restricted code, s(he) must avoid mimicking the vocabulary of the latter. Such mimicry would undoubtedly be heard as patronizing.   It should be possible for interviewers to use language that is genuinely their own, but to adapt their styles of communication to their dyadic partners.

3. It is crucial that the interviewer shed the traditional ambiguity of the dynamic interview, and speak directly, specifically, concretely, and actively. These are, of course, attributes of the restricted code. In fact, the totally sedentary character of the interview may be modified; the interviewer may feel free to move about the room from time to time, if such locomotion is congruent with the communication in progress.

Another approach to penetrating the social-class barrier is, in fact, accomplished through its removal. (Goldstein, 1973; Pope et al., 1974). The use of paraprofessionals has been particularly effective with low-status interviewees.   When the social distance between the interviewer and interviewee is not readily modifiable through an ameliorating procedure, one often has recourse to its direct reduction. It has been demonstrated that there is greater interviewee self-disclosure and introspective communication when both interviewer and interviewee are from the same rather than different social classes (Carkhuff & Pierce, 1967).

Finally, certain modifications in conventional interview and psychotherapy procedures have been attempted as ways of facilitating communication between middle-class interviewers and lower class interviewees. Through the use of preinterview or pretherapy training, interviewees may be prepared to participate in the kind of communication that they will later encounter. Sometimes such preinterviews are additional procedures, inserted as separate interviews, before the beginning of a psychotherapy sequence of an initial interview (Goldstein, 1973).   At other times, the work of the preinterview may occur in the early stages of the initial or the psychotherapy interview itself (Lennard & Bernstein, 1960).   Whatever its form, the essence of the preinterview training approach is its character, as a capsule form of instruction to the interviewee about the interview process. For the most part, it is kept separate from the interview interaction as such. Those who have tested out this procedure in its varied forms have found that it reduces strain in the interview (Lennard & Bernstein, 1960), increases regularity of attendance in psychotherapy (Hoehn-Saric et al. 1964), leads to more acceptable in-therapy behavior, a better relationship with the therapist, and more improvement at the point of termination of therapy.

An additional modification in the interview process has been the introduction of modeling as a means of facilitating low social-class interviewee response (Goldstein, 1973). The procedure usually followed is that of exposing the interviewee to a taped interview, which is similar to that in which the interviewee will presently participate. Through experimental variation of the taped interview and of the instructions used to introduce the tape, several attributes of the model have been studied. It has been demonstrated that exposure to a modeled interview in which the interviewee was highly self-disclosing prompted high interviewee self-disclosure in the actual initial interview that followed (Liberman, 1970). The induction of interviewee attraction to the interviewer was not as easy to accomplish through modeling, but was attained in a limited way under certain experimental conditions (Friedenberg, 1971).

The flexibility in communication and the modification in its style needed to improve the interaction in a cross social-class interview have been presented as skills that tend to occur with interviewer maturity and experience. But the development of these skills is not inevitable. The capacity of interviewers to work with lower social-class clients should therefore be part of their basic clinical training and subsequent continuing education. They should be sensitized to problems in this area and become adept in coping with them. The modifications in basic interview process, such as preinterview and modeling, present clinicians with a somewhat different kind of challenge. There are instruments that have been developed as separate entities, through experimental investigation. Clinicians should become acquainted with their specific utilities and become skilled in their introduction into the interview whenever indicated.

REFERENCES

Albrouda, H.F., Dean, R.L., & Starkweather, J.A. Social class and psychotherapy. Archives of General Psychology, 1964, 10, 276-283.

Ames, R. Protest and irony in Negro folksong. Science and Society, 1950, 14, 193-214.

Argyle, M., & Dean, J. Eye contact, distance and affiliation. In M. Argyle (Ed.), Social encounters. Chicago: Aldine, 1973.

Argyle, M., Lalljee, M., & Cook, M. The effect of visibility on interaction in a dyad. Human Relations, 1969, 21, 3-17.

Argyle, M., & Williams, M. Observer or observed? A reversible perception in person perception. Sociometry, 1969, 32, 396-412.

Aronson, H. & Overall, B. Treatment expectations of patients in two social classes. Social Work, 1966, 11, 35-41.

Banks, W.M. The differential effects of race and social class in helping. Journal of Clinical Psychology, 1972, 28, 90-92.

Baratz, S. Effect of race of experimenter, interactions and comparison population upon level of reported anxiety in Negro subjects. Journal of Personality and Social Psychology, 1967, 7, 194-196.

Barker, L.K. Delinquent boys. Glenco, Ill.: Free Press, 1955.

Baum, O.E., Felzer, S.D., D'Zmura, T.L., & Shumaker, E. Psychotherapy dropouts, and lower socioeconomic patients. American Journal of Orthopsychiatry, 1963, 36, 629-635.

Bernstein, B. Language and social class. British Journal of Sociology, 1960, 11, 271-276.

Bernstein, B. Social class, speech systems and psychotherapy. British Journal of Sociology, 1964, 15, 54-64.

Bernstein, B. A sociolinguistic approach to socialization: With some reference to educability. In F. Williams (Ed.), Language and poverty, perspectives on a theme. Chicago: Markham, 1970.

Brill, N.Q., & Storrow, H.A. Prognostic factors in psychotherapy. Journal of the American Medical Association, 1963, 183, 913-916.

Buck, R.W., Savin, V.J., Miller, R.E., & Caul, W.F. Communication of affect through facial expression in humans. In S. Weitz (Ed.), Nonverbal communication. New York: Oxford University Press, 1974.

Byrne, D., Clore, G., & Worchel, P. Effect of economic similarity-dissimilarity on interpersonal attraction. Journal of Personality and Social Psychology, 1966, 4, 220-224.

Carkhuff, R.R. Black and white in helping. Professional Psychology, 1972, 3, 18-22.

Carkhuff, R.R., & Pierce, R. Differential effects of therapist race and social class upon patient depth of self-exploration in the initial clinical interview. Journal of Consulting Psychology, 1967, 31, 632-634.

Certner, B.C. Exchange of self-disclosures in same-sexed groups of strangers. Journal of Consulting and Clinical Psychology, 1973, 40, 292-297.

Coles, N.J., Branch, C.H., & Allison, R.B. Some relationships between social class and the practice of dynamic psychotherapy. American Journal of Psychiatry, 1962, 117, 1004-1011.

Connolly, P. Newsline, Psychology Today, May 1974, pp. 30, 101-102.

Curry, A.E. The Negro worker and the white client: A commentary on the treatment relationship. Social Casework, 1954, 45, 131-136.

DiNardo, P.A. Social class and diagnostic suggestion as variables in clinical judgment. Journal of Consulting and Clinical Psychology, 1975, 43, 363-368.

Duncan, S., Jr. Non-verbal communication. Psychological Bulletin, 1969, 72, 118-137.

Enelow, A.J., & Swisher, S.N. Interviewing and patient care. New York: Oxford University Press, 1972.

Exline, R.V. Explorations in the process of person perception. Visual interaction and relation to competition, sex, and need for affiliation. Journal of Personality, 1963, 31, 120.

Exline, R.V. Visual interaction: The glances of power and preference. In J.K. Cole (Ed.), Nebraska Symposium of motivation. Lincoln, Nebraska: University of Nebraska Press, 1971.

Exline, R.V., Gray D., & Schuette, D. Visual behavior in a dyad as affected by interview content and sex of respondent. Journal of Personality and Social Psychology, 1965, 1, 201-209.

Exline, R.V., & Winters, L.C. Affective relations and mutual glances in dyads. In S.S. Tompkins & C.E. Izard (Eds.), Affect, cognition and personality. New York: Springer, 1965.

Feldstein, S. Vocal patterning of emotional expression. In J.H. Masserman (Ed.), Science and psychoanalysis. Vol. VIII. New York: Grune & Stratton, 1964.

Feldstein, S., Brenner, M.S., & Jaffe, J. The effect of subject sex, verbal interaction and topical focus on speech disruption. Language and Speech, 1963, 6, 229-239.

Frank, J.D. Adjustment problems of selected Negro soldiers. Journal of Nervous and Mental Diseases, 1947, 105, 647-660.

Friedenberg, W.P. Verbal and non verbal attraction modeling in an initial therapy interview analogue. Unpublished masters thesis, Syracuse University, 1971.

Garfield, S. Research on client variable in psychotherapy. In A.E. Bergin & S. Garfield (Eds.), Handbook of psychotherapy and behavior change. New York: Wiley, 1971.

Gill, M.G., Newman, R., & Redlich, F.C. The initial interview in psychiatric practice. New York: International Universities Press, 1954.

Goldstein, A.P. Structured learning therapy. New York: Academic Press, 1973.

Gould, R.E. Dr. Strangeclass: Or how I stopped worrying about theory and began treating the blue-collar worker. American Journal of Orthopsychiatry, 1967, 37, 78-86.

Grier, W.H., & Cobbs, P.M. Black rage. New York: Bantam Books, 1969.

Guerney, B.G. (Ed.) Psychotherapeutic agents: New roles for nonprofessional patients, and teachers. New York: Holt, Rinehart and Winston, 1969.

Hawkins, P.R. Social class, the nominal group and reference. Language and Speech, 1969, 12, 125-135.

Heider, E.R. The style and accuracy of verbal communications within and between social classes. Journal of Personality and Social Psychology, 1971, 18, 33-47.

Heine, R.W. The Negro patient in psychotherapy. Journal of Clinical Psychology, 1950, 16, 373-376.

Heitler, J.B.   Preparation of lower class patients for expressive group psychotherapy. Journal of Consulting and Clinical Psychology, 1973, 41, 251-260.

Heller, K. Interview structure and interviewee style in initial interviews. In A.W. Siegman & B. Pope (Eds.), Studies in dyadic communication. New York: Pergamon Press, 1972.

Hoehn-Saric, R., Frank, J.D., Imber, S.D., Nash, E.H., Stone, A.R., & Battle, C.C. Systematic preparation of patients for psychotherapy. I. Effects on therapy behavior and outcome. Journal of Psychiatric Research, 1964, 2, 267-281.

Hollingshead, A.B., & Redlich, F.C.   Social class and mental illness.   New York: Wiley, 1958.

Imber, S.D., Nash, E.H., & Stone, A.R.   Social class and duration of psychotherapy. Journal of Clinical Psychology, 1955, 11, 281-284.

Jackson, A.M. Psychotherapy: Factors associated with the race of the therapist. Psychotherapy: Theory, Research and Practice, 1973, 10, 273-277.

Jourard, S.M. The transparent self. New York: Van Nostrand, 1971a.

Jourard, S.M. Self-disclosure. New York: Wiley-Interscience, 1971b.

Kadushin, C. Why people go to psychiatrists. New York: Atherton Press, 1969.

Keith-Spiegel, P., & Spiegel, D. Perceived helpfulness of others as a function of compatible intelligence levels. Journal of Counseling Psychology, 1967, 14, 61-62.

La France, M., & Mayo, C. Newsline. Psychology Today, May, 1974, pp. 30, 101-102.

Lee, S.D., & Temerlin, M.K.   Social class, diagnosis, and prognosis for psychotherapy. Psychotherapy: Theory, Research and Practice, 1970, 7, 181-185.

Lennard, H.L., & Bernstein, A. The anatomy of psychotherapy. New York: Columbia University Press, 1960.

Lerner, B., & Fiske, D.W. Client attributes and the eye of the beholder. Journal of Consulting Psychology, 1973, 40, 272-277.

Liberman, B. The effect of modeling procedures on attraction and disclosure in a psychotherapy analogue. Unpublished doctoral dissertation, Syracuse University, 1970.

Lief, H.T., Lief, V.F., Warren, C.O., & Heath, R.G. Low drop out rate in a psychiatric clinic. Archives of General Psychiatry, 1961, 5, 200-211.

Lorion, R.P. Socioeconomic status and traditional treatment approaches reconsidered. Psychological Bulletin, 1973, 79, 263-270.

Lorion, R.P. Social class, treatment attitudes, and expectations. Journal of Consulting and Clinical Psychology, 1974, 42, 920.

Machotka, P. Body movement as communication. Dialogues: Behavioral Science Research, 1965, 2, 33-66.

Mahl, G.F. Exploring emotional states by content analysis. In I. Pool (Ed.), Trends in content analysis. Urbana: University of Illinois Press, 1959. Pp. 83-110.

Mahl, G.F. Gestures and body movements in interviews. In J.M. Shlien (Ed.), Research in psychotherapy. Washington, D.C.: American Psychological Association, 1968.

Mandler, G., & Sarason, S.B. A study of anxiety and learning. Journal of Abnormal and Social Psychology, 1952, 47, 166-173.

Mehrabian, A. Some references and measures of nonverbal behavior. Behavior Research Methods and Instrumentation, 1969, 1, 203-207.

Mehrabian, A., & Friar, J.T. Encoding of attitude by seated communicator via posture and posture cues. Journal of Consulting and Clinical Psychology, 1969, 33, 330-336.

Milner, E. Effects of sex role and social status on the early adolescent personality. Genetic Psychology Monographs, 1949, 40.

Mitchell, K.M., & Namenek, T.M. A comparison of therapist and client social class. Professional Psychology, 1970, 1, 225-230.

Nash, E.H., Hoehn-Saric, R., Battle, C.G., Stone, A.R., Imber, S.D., & Frank, J.D. Systematic preparation of patients for short-term psychotherapy. II: Relation to characteristics of patient, therapist, and psychotherapeutic process. The Journal of Nervous and Mental Disease, 1965, 140, 374-383.

Orne, M.T., & Wender, P.H. Anticipatory socialization for psychotherapy: Method and rationale. The American Journal of Psychiatry, 1968, 124, 1202-1212.

Overall, B., & Aronson, H. Expectations of psychotherapy in patients of lower socioeconomic class. American Journal of Orthopsychiatry, 1963, 33, 421-430.

Phillips, W.B. Counseling Negro pupils: An educational dilemma. Journal of Negro Education, 1960, 29, 504-507.

Pope, B. Socio-economic contrasts in children's peer culture prestige values. Genetic Psychology Monographs, 1953a, 48, 157-220.

Pope, B. Prestige values in contrasting socio-economic groups of children. Psychiatry, 1953b, 16, 381-385.

Pope, B., Nudler, S., VonKorff, M., & McGee, J.P. The experienced professional interviewer vs. the complete novice. Journal of Consulting and Clinical Psychology, 1974, 42, 680-690.

Pope, B., & Siegman, A.W. Interviewer warmth in relation to interviewee verbal behavior. Journal of Consulting Psychology, 1968, 31, 588-595.

Rappaport, J., Chinsky, J.M., & Cowen, E.L. Innovations in helping chronic patients (college students in a mental institution). New York: Academic Press, 1971.

Redlich, F.C., Hollingshead, A.B., & Bellis, E. Social class differences in attitudes towards psychiatry. American Journal of Orthopsychiatry, 1955, 25, 65-70.

Rice, D.G., Gurman, A.S., & Razin, A.M. Therapist sex, "style", and theoretical orientation. Journal of Nervous and Mental Disease, 1974, 159, 413-421.

Rickers-Ovsiankina, M., & Kusmin, A.A. Individual differences in social accessibility. Psychological Reports, 1958, 4, 391-406.

Rioch, M.J. Changing concepts in the training of the therapist. Journal of Consulting Psychology, 1966, 30, 290-292.

Rosenthal, D., & Frank, J.D. The fate of psychiatric clinic outpatient assigned to psychotherapy. Journal of Nervous and Mental Disease, 1958, 127, 330-343.

Rosenthal, R., Archer, D., DiMatteo, M.R., Koivumaki, J.H., & Rogers, P.L. Body language and tone of voice: The language without words. Psychology Today, September 1974, 8, 64-68.

Sattler, J.M. Racial "experimenter effects" in experimentation, testing, interviewing and psychotherapy. Psychological Bulletin, 1970, 73, 137-160.

Sattler, J.M. Racial experimenter effects. In K.S. Miller & R.M. Dreger (Eds.), Comparative studies of blacks and whites in the United States. New York: Seminar Press, 1973.

Schaffer, L., & Myers, J.K. Psychotherapy and social stratification. Psychiatry, 1954, 17, 83-93.

Schofield, W. Psychotherapy, the purchase of friendship. Englewood Cliffs, N. J.: Prentice-Hall, 1964.

Schutz, W.C. Firo: A three dimensional theory of interpersonal behavior. New York: Rinehart, 1958.

Seward, G.H. Psychotherapy and culture conflict. New York: The Ronald Press, 1972.

Siegman, A.W. What makes interviewees talk or how effective are social reinforcers in facilitating the interviewee productivity? University of Maryland in Baltimore County: Colloquium Paper, 1972.

Silberman, C.E. Crisis in black and white. New York: Random House, 1964.

Smith, E.W., & Dixon, T.R. Verbal conditioning as a function of race of the experimenter and prejudice of the subject. Journal of Experimental Social Psychology, 1968, 4, 285-301.

Spiegel, J.P., & Machotka, P. Messages of the body. New York: The Free Press, 1974.

St. Clair, H.R. Psychiatric interview experiences with Negroes. American Journal of Psychiatry, 1951, 108, 113-119.

Strupp, H.H., & Bloxom, A.L. Preparing lower class patients for group psychotherapy: Development and evaluation of a role-induction film. Journal of Consulting and Clinical Psychology, 1973, 41, 373-384.

Thomas, C.W. Something borrowed, something black. In Boys no more: A black psychologist's view of community. Beverly Hills: Glencoe Press, 1971.

Walsch, W.G. The effects of conforming pressure and modeling on the attraction of hospitalized patients toward an interviewer. Unpublished doctoral dissertation, Syracuse University, 1971.

Womack, W.M., & Wagner, N.N. Negro interviewers and white patients. Archives of General Psychiatry, 1967, 16, 685-692.

Yamamoto, J. James, Q.C., Bloombaum, M., & Hattem, J. Racial factors in patient selection. The American Journal of Psychiatry, 1967, 124, 630-636.

Zief, R.M. Values and self disclosure. Unpublished Honors Thesis, Harvard University, 1962.

Zuckerman, M., & Lubin, B. Multiple Affect Adjective Check List. San Diego, Calif.: Educational & Industrial Testing Service, 1965.

V

The Interview—
A Temporal Perspective

11 Sequence Effects in the Interview

One may learn a good deal about the interview by dividing it somewhat arbitrarily into such gross components as communication and relationship; or, further, into the many more narrowly defined variables that are the warp and the woof of the larger components. In the end, however, the segments into which the interview have been dissected must be brought together again. In a naturalistic sense the interview is an indivisible interaction between two people, occurring at a given place, and over a definitive time span. This book will end, as it began, with a look at the interview as an unfragmented process. In Chapter 1, the focus was on certain types or schools of interviewing. In this, the last chapter, the interview is seen in a more generic sense, as a continuous process with certain patterns or trends over time. It has a beginning which differs in systematic ways from its middle, and both, in some ways from the end. Certain questions arise. If such trends do occur, how general are they? Are they rooted in the specific training of the interviewer, or do they occur across a range of types of interviews?

Each one of the three temporal segments will be evaluated on the basis of clinical impression and relevant research-generated data. In general, the clinicians will be given their say first, because they pose the various issues in an applied way. For the most part, the data produced in relevant research studies will be considered in the context of the problems raised by the clinicians. Finally, there will be an attempt to develop applied inferences from the research investigations. Thus, the progression will be from the clinic to the laboratory and back to the clinic. The focus will be on sequential stages in the development of the interview – that is, its beginning, middle, and end.

THE BEGINNING

There is a moment of magic and of some apprehension as two people cross the threshold between an oblivious lack of awareness of each other and the beginning of an acquaintanceship. Sullivan (1954) places considerable emphasis on the events that occur when the interviewer and interviewee see each other for the first time but have not yet begun to converse. His attitude is one of "respectful seriousness." This implies an avoidance of any forced or excessive hospitality. Even if the patient is strained and anxious, a display of feeling that is not genuine will be of little help. "Thus while I don't try to show a great welcome to the patient, I do try to act as if he were expected - that is, I try to know the name of a person who makes an appointment to see me for the first time, and to greet him with it, relieving him of any morbid anxiety as to whether he came on the wrong day, and so on" (Sullivan, 1954, p. 60).

The next steps are spelled out with great precision. With one exception they are conventional gestures that are associated with inviting a person into one's home or one's office. To many, such precision may seem an under-scoring of the obvious. But Sullivan appears to feel that many interviewers engage in gestures and speeches that he characterizes as "social hokum." He therefore recommends that the interviewer simply ask the patient into the office and point to his/her seat. He doesn't feel constrained to make a projective device out of the patient's choice of a seat. It must be evident by now that none of the actions of the therapist in greeting the patient is technical or essentially different from those which any person might use in greeting a stranger.

If the therapist has some information about the patient from a referring source, he may share it with him/her, avoiding the communication of any data that may be unduly disturbing. In this way, the patient is encouraged to correct or supplement what the therapist already knows. In fact, this is the beginning of the interview and the end of the initial encounter.

While the initial encounter and the greeting to the patient may not last more than a few minutes, these are very poignant minutes, for it is during this time that initial impressions take form. The interviewer may accept Sullivan's injunction not to stare at the patient, but s(he) need not blunt his/her perceptiveness. In their book, The Initial Psychiatric Interview in Clinical Practice, MacKinnon and Michels (1971) comment on the formation of first impressions: "Important clues to the conduct of the interview can often be obtained during these few moments of introduction. The patient's spontaneity and warmth may be revealed in his handshake or greeting. ...Suspicious patients might carefully glance around the office searching for 'clues' about the physician" (MacKinnon & Michels, 1971, p. 52).

If the interviewer's perceptions of the interviewee are important during the period of inception, his/her perceptions of self and how they may affect the interviewee are equally important. The capacity to monitor oneself, to be aware of one's usual patterns of behavior when getting to know a new person, and how others react to these patterns are not acquired easily. Sullivan makes the point that "the psychiatrist certainly, and any interviewer in some measure, should 'know how he acts' - that is, he should have learned from experience the usual impression obtained of him in the particular circumstances of encouraging the sort of stranger that the interviewee at first glance seems to be" (1954, p. 67). The interviewer should be aware of how his/her behavior affects the new interviewee, of how it may encourage or inhibit this person who has come for help.

These considerations and others pertain to the initial attainment of rapport. Another task of the beginning segment of the interview is the mutual adjustment of role expectations that each participant has of the other. If such expectations are not in synchrony with each other, it is not possible to move ahead to the second or main segment of the interview. Unless these expectations complement each other, the dyad lacks stability, and communication remains inhibited.

In Chapter 10, several formal procedures for establishing congruence between the role expectations of the patient and those of the therapist have been reviewed (Hoehn-Saric, Frank, Imber, Nash, Stone, & Battle, 1964; Nash, Hoehn-Saric, Battle, Stone, Imber, & Frank, 1965; Orne & Wender, 1968). In all of these there is a separate role induction interview conducted before the beginning of therapy by a person other than the therapist. The purpose of the interview is to inform clients about, and in some instances rehearse them in, the behavior expected of them. They also learn about the role behavior they may expect from the interviewer. Others (Lennard & Bernstein, 1960) accomplish the same objectives through the use of primary system references, largely during the beginning segment of a regular clinical interview. Such references "center around role discussion. The more primary system references on the part of the patient, the more information the patient is soliciting about his role in treatment. The more primary system references on the part of the therapist, the more the therapist is teaching the patient his proper role in therapy" (Lennard & Bernstein, 1960, p. 119). The roles of both participants have been defined in the following terms: "Who shall speak, how much, about what, and when?" (Lennard & Bernstein, 1960, p. 154).

It may be anticipated that primary system references will be more crucial at an early point in an interview rather than later because they are designed to reduce strain and increase equilibrium between the two members of a dyad by rendering the role expectations of both complementary to each other. Indeed, Lennard and Bernstein (1960) have demonstrated that psychotherapy dyads in which therapists make the most frequent primary system references are the ones in which strain tends to be least. Moreover, as indicated above, the crucial time for such remarks is at the beginning of an interview. Thus, when they divided their tape-recorded psychotherapy interviews into three equal segments, primary system references decreased by more than one-half between the first and second segments, and down to one-eighth, between the first and third segments. In another investigation (Karl & Abeles, 1969) based on typed psychotherapy sessions divided into five 10-minute segments, therapist primary role statements decreased steadily through the fourth 10-minute segment.

The evidence points to a significant drop in the type of structuring or role induction remark, designated as a primary system reference, between the beginning and middle segment of an interview. Evidently, these remarks help to establish rapport through reducing incongruent expectations.

THE MIDDLE

With the preparatory work of the initial segment accomplished, the participants then turn to the main business of the interview. In the initial mental health interview this usually includes presentations by the interviewees of the problems for which they are seeking help and any additional personal self-disclosures about which the interviewer may ask and/or which the interviewees are prompted to communicate. The precise content varies widely from one therapy dyad to the other, but there is fairly wide consensus about broad categories of information that are considered to be relevant to an initial assessment interview. Thus, interviews are likely to increase their focus between the beginning and middle segments on such topics as current problems, mood, predominant feelings, intrafamily relationships, relationships outside of the family, work, educational history, family of origin, significant events in childhood, and many others.

Just as interviewers vary in their topical emphases, they may differ also in their style of inquiry. Some may be more directive than others, more active, more specific, more reflective; indeed they will vary on all stylistic dimensions.   But one finding that occurs across interviewers of widely divergent schools is a drop in the specificity of the interviewer (i.e., an increase in ambiguity) after the interview has run a specified temporal course. Studies vary in conclusions regarding the precise point at which this drop occurs. Lennard and Bernstein (1960) have located it at the end of the second of three equal segments in the interview. This seems late. A study to be summarized in some detail below found the drop in interviewer specificity to occur in the transition between the beginning and the middle segments. When it occurs it signals a decrease in informational input by the interviewer (High interviewer specificity is defined in Chapter 4 as high informational input; low specificity or high ambiguity, as low informational input) and an increase in the informational input by the interviewee. A new equilibrium is established, in which the interviewer becomes more ambiguous and the interviewee more productive. One may expect this to happen after rapport has developed, the two members of the dyad have adjusted any differences between them regarding their respective roles, and communication has begun to flow in a relatively stable manner. Ordinarily, these changes should mark the transition between the beginning and the middle of the interview.

The increase in interviewee productivity has been documented in several research studies.   It emerged strikingly in an investigation reported by Matarazzo and Wiens (1972) in which the initial goal did not at all pertain to sequence effects.   The eventual finding that interviewees were more productive (i.e., they gave responses of longer durations) in the second rather than the first half of a 30-minute interview presented itself as an explanation of the failure of the study to produce a significant result in its major objective. Yet the finding is well supported, occurring as an interactional effect in an experimental group, and as main effects in two control groups. This study, and others, demonstrate that as the interview develops over time, the gross productivity of the interviewee increases. In the terminology of the present chapter, the quantity of verbal communication uttered by the interviewee should increase as the beginning segment of the interview gives way to its middle.

But the business of the mental health interview is not accomplished by interviewee verbosity alone. Clinicians are well aware that speech may conceal rather than disclose, and verbosity may serve the goal of avoidance rather than that of self-disclosure. It is important, therefore, to trace the changes in personal openness over the duration of the interview, as well as those in productivity. For example, one may ask whether the second segment of the interview, when it stabilizes as a communication system, is the time when the interviewee begins to speak more openly about personal matters. Is this when s(he) became more self-disclosing?

Some bits of evidence that the interviewee tends to move in the direction of less avoidance, and more self-disclosing communication have indeed accumulated. Lennard and Bernstein (1960) found that as primary system references decreased in the transition from the first to the second third of the psychotherapy interview there was a tendency for communication about affect to increase. In the study by Karl and Abeles (1969), referred to above, the frequency of comments about interpersonal interactions between clients and therapists increased steadily over the first four 10-minute segments of the psychotherapy interviews they investigated. Finally, there is evidence for a steady increase over interview time in the Experiencing (EXP) level (Gendlin, 1962) of the interviewee's verbalizations (Kiesler, Klein, & Mathieu, 1965). In this investigation 40-minute psychotherapy interviews were subdivided into five eight-minute segments. The Experiencing (EXP) level of the patient was traced sequentially over the five interview segments. Kiesler and his colleagues (1965) found "a consistent positive level trend of process... in which each consecutive 8-minute segment receives a slightly higher EXP rating" (p. 340).

In brief, the above findings suggest that the interviewee's passage from the beginning to the middle segment is marked by an enhanced psychological focus, reduced avoidance, and greater personal openness.

Two other paralinguistic dimensions in the interviewee's speech have been investigated in studies that deal with sequence effects in the interview. One is that of hesitation, in the form of filled pauses (Ah and allied expressions) and slow speech rate. (When a speaker becomes more uncertain, one may expect such expressions of hesitation as "Ah" to increase, and rate of speech to decrease.) The other is that of speech disturbance as measured by the Non-Ah Ratio (Kasl & Mahl, 1965), assumed to be an index of anxiety. In one investigation, the authors (Lalljee & Cook, 1973) divided the beginning of an experimental interview into nine sequential one-minute intervals to investigate changes over time with topic kept constant. They found that the Ah Ratio (filled pauses) decreased over the first three minutes and then leveled off, while speech rate increased according to the same pattern. Both of these changes are indicative of decreased uncertainty (Siegman & Pope, 1965). Non-Ah speech disturbances increased first and then subsided. Lalljee and Cook (1973) concluded that uncertainty decreases as the interaction progresses due to the cumulative feedback that the interviewee receives from the interviewer. Because of their ambiguous findings with reference to anxiety (Non-Ah), they rejected it as a variable relevant to temporal sequence in the interview.

The finding about uncertainty is readily acceptable on a commonsense basis. One may expect the information imparted to the interviewee through primary system references in the beginning segment to reduce his/her uncertainty about the interview. The middle segment should therefore be characterized by less interviewee hesitation (lower Ah) and a faster rate of interviewee speech than the beginning segment. What one might expect with reference to anxiety as reflected in disturbed speech is not quite as clear from the Lalljee and Cook (1973) study. On a clinical basis, one could anticipate that initial interpersonal anxiety would decrease as the interview proceeds. Partly due to this decline and, additionally, because of the focus of the interviewer's inquiry, after the end of the initial induction period one would look for an increase in the psychological content of the interviewee's communications, with a consequent rise in message anxiety. The passage from the beginning to the middle segment of the interview should therefore be characterized by a decrease in uncertainty and an increase in message anxiety.

THE END

The function of the last segment is, of course, the closing of the interview. When clinicians discuss this phase, they frequently emphasize the content of the exchange between the two participants and the interactional strategies that the interviewer might use. For example, many mental health interviewers signal the approach of the end by giving interviewees an opportunity to ask any questions that may be troubling them (MacKinnon & Michels, 1971). If no questions are asked, they may encourage interviewees to speak about any matters that seem important to them which had not yet been discussed. Under these circumstances, the most frequent response of the interviewee is a request for some feedback about his/her illness and the contemplated treatment. In fact, the provision of feedback by the interviewer is a way of ending the initial diagnostic interview that is frequently emphasized in the clinical literature.

Regarding the content of the feedback, there is a widely shared consensus that the onus is on the interviewer to determine where the boundary occurs between the client's right to know and the clinician's judgment about the client's ability to use a given bit of information without undue disturbance. The following advice is characteristic of that which occurs in the clinical literature on this topic: "The physician should avoid giving the patient a formal diagnostic label. Such terms have little use for the patient, and may be quite harmful, since the interviewer may be unaware of the meaning that the patient or his family attaches to them. The patient often provides clues to the proper terms to use in giving the formulation" (MacKinnon & Michels, 1971). Thus, one patient may speak about "psychological problems"; another may refer to "something emotional"; and a third may speak about his/her immaturity. The attentive clinician may be guided by the client's terminology in formulating his/her summary.

It would appear from the research literature that there is no great consensus in actual practice about the closing phase of the interview. Thus, the frequency in communications about affect that increases between the first and second segment of the interview recedes again in the last (Lennard & Bernstein, 1960). Primary system references, on the decrease between the first and second thirds, continue in a downward direction into the last third. And interviewer specificity drops between the middle and final thirds of the interview. In brief, the work of the interview appears to fade out. As an interaction between two persons, the interview appears to die, not with a bang but with a whimper. What of the feedback that the therapist is advised to provide at the end of the initial interview? If indeed his/her informational input increases as s(he) provides this feedback, should not one expect interviewer specificity to increase?

Clearly, there needs to be much more work done in tracking the mental health interview into its closing phase. And in doing so, a clear distinction should be made between the initial interview and a later one in a psychotherapy sequence. The end of a first encounter probably has more differentiated goals and attributes than the casual fade out that is more likely to occur at the end of a psychotherapy interview after the working relationship between therapist and patient has been stabilized.

Much of the rest of this chapter will be taken up with an account of a study (Pope, Nudler, Norden, & McGee, 1977) that investigates the vicissitudes in many of the interviewer and interviewee variables considered above, through a sequence of three interview segments. The interviewees were female freshman college student volunteers; and the interviewers were both male and female staff psychiatrists and third-year psychiatric residents, all experienced clinicians. There was an initial study and two replications. All findings were therefore based separately on three groups, and additionally on the three groups combined. The interviews were semi-structured. Each interviewer was asked to take no less than 15 minutes and no more than 45, in exploring two topical areas; educational history and adjustment, and primary family relationships. For the sequential analyses the typed protocol of each interview was excerpted in the following manner: a verbatim transcript of the first four pages as a sample of the opening phase, the median four pages as a sample of the body of the interview, and the last four pages for the closing phase. In the statistical analysis of sequential changes, it became evident that topic would require some form of control, since the two topics varied significantly between the three segments. To avoid the confounding of topic with sequence, an analysis of covariance for repeated measures was done, separately for each variable. Thus, any given comparison was based on eight subordinate comparisons for two topics and four groups.

The predictive hypotheses were derived from research already reviewed in preceding sections of the present chapter. All refer only to the changes anticipated between the beginning and middle segments. Because there were few guidelines in earlier research for changes in the closing segment it was left for exploratory investigation.

In the section that follows each predictive hypothesis is stated and followed immediately by the results that pertain to it. In general, the data provided suprisingly strong support for the hypotheses.

Hypothesis 1

It was expected that there would be a significantly higher frequency of primary system references in the beginning than the middle segment of the interview, since the beginning is the period in which the interviewee is inducted into the dyadic communication system.

This prediction was impressively demonstrated in all the comparisons that were made. In addition, there were significant drops between the first and third segments.

Hypothesis 2

After the interviewer's relatively high informational input in the opening segment, largely through primary system references, it was anticipated that there would be a drop in his/her specificity level between the first and second segments. Once s(he) had initiated the communication system, the interviewer could pursue a more ambiguous course, maintaining a balance with the interviewee's increased input.

The data showed that interviewer specificity did indeed drop significantly between the first and second segments. (All eight differences were in the predicted direction; six were significant.) Moreover, interviewer specificity tended to remain lower in the third than the first segment. (All differences were in the designated direction, with three at a significant level.)

Hypothesis 3

The previous hypothesis includes the assumption that interviewee productivity would increase between the opening and middle segments, both as a separate variable (interviewee words per response) and relative to interviewer productivity (interviewee words/interviewer words).

On both indices, interviewee productivity did register significant increases between the first and second segments. (For interviewee words per response, all differences were in the predicted direction; four out of the eight were significant. For interviewee words/interviewer words, all differences were as anticipated, with three at a significant level.) However, none of the differences between the first and third segments was significant. It would appear that interviewee productivity, having risen between the beginning and middle of the interview, tapered off as the two participants approached the close.

Hypothesis 4

It was assumed that the role induction of the interviewee during the opening segment would include instruction to maintain a high level of verbal

Barron Ego Strength Scale, 190, 368
Blocking, 76-77, 82, 88, 91, 152, 166, 194, 206, 242, 263
Body language, 25, 81, 83-87, 91-92, 114, 118, 124, 134, 166-167, 171, 187-188, 193-194, 202, 207, 211, 213-214, 221-222, 224, 240, 322, 335, 364-365, 377, 384, 450, 497
Bogardus Social Distance Scale, 457

Client centered, 55-56, 62, 117, 134, 137, 139, 141-142, 146-148, 150, 152, 171-172, 174, 188, 191, 221, 261, 281, 334, 350
Communication
ability, 352-353
channels, 20-23, 37, 79, 83, 87-88, 129-130, 134, 206-207, 220, 240, 276
multidimensional character of, 40
nonverbal, 25-28, 79-88, 98, 167, 171, 184-185, 187-188, 192-194, 202-204, 206-210, 213-214, 220, 337, 340, 364, 377, 384, 445, 450, 461, 485, 497, 502
styles, 345-346, 379, 381
system, 20, 155-156, 159, 162, 167-168, 176, 522-524
Conditioning
operant, 107-109
verbal, 101-102, 107-114, 116-118, 122-124, 149-150, 173, 217, 252, 272, 361, 420-421, 433, 459
Content, verbal, 41-47, 49-51, 62, 69, 75, 79-81, 88-90, 97, 102, 108, 110, 114-115, 117-120, 123-125, 129, 155, 165, 186-187, 191, 195-196, 205-206, 210-212, 221, 223, 240, 459

Dependency, interviewee, 417-421, 433
Depression
in speech, 199, 204-205, 221-222
interviewee, 424-426, 428-430, 435

Desensitization
automated, 144, 337-338
systematic, 144, 163, 337
Directive therapy, 131-132, 141-146, 172
Directiveness, 141-147, 153, 171-172, 174
Double bind, 199-201

Emotion, See Affect
Empathy, 243, 277, 339-344, 346, 348, 350-351, 353, 356-357, 378-380, 461
scale, 342-343, 349, 353, 358, 378
EPPS, 373-374, 415, 418-419
Expectations
interviewee, 289-290, 293-294, 297-302, 307-308, 308-309, 311-312, 315, 317, 323-324, 326, 394-395, 501
interviewer, 289, 293, 303-306, 308, 315-316, 324-326, 413, 431
role, 155-156, 306-307, 309-312, 316-317, 324, 515, 522
set, 313, 315-317, 323, 325
socioeconomic contrasts, 475-480, 501
Experience of therapists
experienced, 132-133, 139-140, 186, 188, 262-265, 280, 304-305, 309, 339-340, 359-361, 363, 365, 383, 469-470
inexperienced, 132-133, 139-140, 172, 175, 262-265, 280, 304-305, 309, 339, 359-361, 363, 374, 383, 469-470
Experiencing, 404
level (EXP) in interviewee verbalization, 517
Expression
facial, 28-29, 79, 82-88, 91-92, 171, 186-188, 193, 203, 207-210, 214, 221-224, 240, 322, 377, 450, 497
Expressiveness
client, 189-192, 220-222
communication of, 184-185, 188, 198, 205, 207, 209, 220-221
in movement, 130

therapist, 188-192, 215, 220-
224, 334
Eye contact, 26, 87, 108, 114, 118,
124, 188, 209, 214, 223-224, 240,
322-323, 328, 364-365, 379, 384,
446-450, 461, 494, 497

FIRO-B, 255-256, 271-272, 282

Genuineness
interviewer (self congruence),
345-351, 356, 361, 373, 380
Gestures, 28, 41, 79-82, 88, 134,
168, 171, 188, 206-207, 222,
240, 377, 445, 502
autistic, 168, 445

Hostility, verbal expression of,
111-112, 124, 374-375, 386

Immediacy, 87-88, 210-212, 214,
223, 449, 461, 497
Indiana matching project, 269-270,
281, 282
Interaction, dyadic, 20-21, 37, 42,
46, 71, 76, 119, 123, 130, 135,
157, 159, 168, 242, 252, 273, 382
Interpersonal perception
attributes of, 320-321
expectation and, 313-317, 327
in interviewee, 289, 317-319,
470
interviewer, 289, 315-317, 326-
328, 413
relationship and, 288-289, 302,
311, 313-314, 316-320, 323, 326
visual and visibility, 322-323,
328
Interpretation, 146-152, 171-173
depth of, 150-152, 173
plausibility, 150-151, 173
Interview
anticipatory socialization, 490-
492
beginning of, 513-515, 523
behavioral, 6-8, 11, 41, 108, 281
definition of, 513
end of, 518-519, 524
goals of, 3, 125, 168-170, 173-
174, 463, 471, 499

middle of, 516-518, 523
psychoanalytic, 9-13, 41-42, 71-72
124, 130, 132, 276
Rogerian, 17-19, 130-131
role induction, 103, 123, 489-492,
495, 515, 520
Sullivanian, 13-17, 19, 42, 103, 130
Interviewee instructions, 98-99, 101-
104, 106-109, 118-123, 125, 153,
177, 186
visual perception and visibility,
446-449
Intonation, 22, 24, 81, 197

Kinesics, 29, 322, 340

Libo Pictures Impressions Test,
248-250, 253, 418-419
Likeability, 423-424, 434

Mahl, See Speech Disturbance Ratio
Matching
interviewer and interviewee,
265-271, 273-274, 281-282, 369-
370, 383-386
Mill-Hill Vocabulary Scale, 483
Minnesota Multiphasic Personality
Inventory, 373-374, 414-416, 425-
426, 430
Modeling, 68-69, 99, 101, 103-109,
115, 118-123, 125, 252, 358, 382,
492, 495, 503-504
Mooney Problem Checklist, 425

Nondirective therapy, 131-132, 141-
146, 172

Object Relations Test, 416

Pause, 23, 152, 161, 164-168, 170, 177,
195, 250, 430, 435, 442, 517-518,
521
Filled Pause Ratio (Ah), 24, 164-
167, 177, 189, 197, 250, 429, 443,
496, 517-518, 521-523
frequency of hesitation, 23, 48,
164-165, 423
switching, 349
Perception, See Interpersonal
perception

Personality, interviewee and inter-
   viewer,
   See attributes
Phenomenological, 139-140
Placebo effect, 296-298
Pre-interview training, of inter-
   viewee, 489-492, 502-504
Primary system references, 99, 102,
   156, 311, 325-326, 490, 515, 517-
   521, 523
Productivity, See Activity level
Proxemics, 27, 446, 449, 497
Psycholinguistics, 129, 164

Q-sort, 243-244, 307, 339, 481

Race, 451-454, 456, 460-461, 498
   black interviewer and white
      interviewees, 457-460
   cross-race interviews, 456-461
   effects on the interview inter-
      action, 455, 457, 459-461, 489,
      498
   same race interviews, 460-461
   white interviewers and black
      interviewees, 455-456, 498
Rapport, 234, 237, 243, 275, 326,
   454, 460, 514-516
   client, 243, 415
   counselor, 243
Rate of speech, 23-24, 48-50, 81,
   89, 129-130, 164, 166-167, 171,
   197-199, 517-518, 521
Reciprocal affect, See Affect
Reciprocity, informational, 162,
   176
Reflection, 19-20, 114, 117, 124,
   134, 147-148
Reinforcers
   gestural, 114
   mechanical, 114
   symbolic, 114
   verbal, 101, 104, 107-119, 122-
      125, 149-150
Relatability, 422-423, 424, 434
Relationship
   dimensions of, 253-257, 260-265,
      270-273, 278-281, 321, 332-333,
      346, 350, 376-278

reciprocity in, 246-248, 253, 277,
   279, 325-326, 420, 431, 490
Repression, 73-74, 76
Resistance, 72-84, 86, 88, 91-92, 101,
   105, 107, 123, 148, 150-152, 161,
   173, 188, 253, 312, 420, 433, 453,
   498
   as deception, 82-87, 92
   multi-channel expression of, 79,
      91
   scale, 73-74
   stable and unstable, 78, 91
Resistiveness, 76-78, 151, 250, 263,
   265, 299, 322, 404, 430, 521, 523
Role
   interviewee, 307, 309, 419-421,
      490, 515, 521
   interviewer (therapist), 137-138,
      144, 146, 148, 172-173, 217-218,
      262, 281, 293-294, 307-308, 346,
      380, 393-394, 515

Self congruence, See Genuineness
Self disclosure, 54-56, 61-72, 76-78,
   90-91, 97-98, 102-106, 108, 115,
   120-124, 217-219, 224-225, 265-
   267, 302-303, 335, 435, 443-444,
   487, 493-496, 499, 517, 521-522
   dyadic effect, 64-65, 67-69, 90
   high, 493
   Jourard's questionnaire (J.S.D.Q.),
      54-55, 302-303, 444
   low, 493
   rating scale, 121
Self exploration, client, 55-56, 60-62,
   72, 117, 143, 148, 172, 269, 347,
   349, 351, 355, 380, 433, 460, 489
Sensitivity
   nonverbal profile (PONS), 450-451
Sex
   differences in nonverbal communi-
      cation, 445-451, 496-497
   differences in verbal communica-
      tion, 442-444, 451, 496
Social classes
   acceptance into psychotherapy,
      465-468, 499
   communication barriers between,
      482-490, 501-504

extended code, 485-487, 502-503
Hollingshead-Redlich Index, 464-
465, 468
interviewer bias, 480-482, 501
rejection of psychotherapy by
lower class patients, 468-469,
499
restricted code, 485-487, 502-
503
value contrasts, 471-475, 480,
499-501
Social distance, between interviewer
and interviewee, 469-471, 489,
495-496, 499
Sociometric status, 423
Speech
lexical aspects, 129, 155, 164,
167, 171
non lexical aspects, 129, 171,
340
Speech disturbance, 24-25, 38-39,
47-48, 77, 81, 89, 129, 161, 163-
164, 166, 171, 177, 197-199, 201-
202, 204, 221-222, 264, 378, 427-
429, 435, 442, 470, 517-518, 522
ratio of, 161, 163-164, 197-198,
200, 442
"Non Ah" ratio, 24, 164, 166,
177, 189, 197-199, 217, 335,
337, 428-429, 435, 442, 517,
522, 524
Status, 253-257, 260-265, 278-281,
358-365, 382-384, 395, 459
communication of, 364-365

Strong Vocational Interest Inventory,
(Blank), 311-312, 367-368, 370,
373, 384
Structured learning therapy, 357-
358, 382, 493
Style
interviewer, 129-133, 135-143,
147-149, 153-155, 166, 168-172,
175, 189-190, 192, 218-221, 223-
224, 243, 250, 274, 279, 282-
283, 313, 334, 341-342, 347,
350-351, 418, 420-421, 432,
435, 443, 478, 498
multi-dimensional analysis of, 131-
140, 143, 150, 162, 171-173, 175,
201-202, 516
Superficiality, 76-78, 81, 88, 91, 521,
523
Synchrony model, 158-160, 174, 185,
264, 470

Taylor Manifest Anxiety Scale, 190,
311, 368, 427, 429
Therapist Orientation Questionnaire,
136
Transference, 237, 240, 275

"Yavis" patients, 294, 324-326, 483

Vocal tone, 186-195, 197, 202, 208-
211, 214, 220-221, 223, 335, 413-
414, 450, 497

Warmth, 214-219, 224-225, 250, 277-
278, 317-318, 335-338, 344, 346,
348-351, 355-357, 373, 377-378,
380, 395, 443, 470, 496

About the Author

BENJAMIN POPE (Ph.D., University of California at Berkeley) is Director of Psychology Services at The Sheppard and Enoch Pratt Hospital in Towson, Maryland, and Director of the Sheppard-Pratt School of Mental Health Studies. He was previously Professor of Medical Psychology, Chief of the Psychology Service, and Director of the pre-doctoral Clinical Psychology Internship Program at the Psychiatric Institute of the University of Maryland School of Medicine. He has also taught at the University of British Columbia, the University of Maryland School of Medicine, and part-time at Towson State University and the University of Maryland in Baltimore County.

PERGAMON GENERAL PSYCHOLOGY SERIES

Editors: Arnold P. Goldstein, *Syracuse University*
Leonard Krasner, *SUNY, Stony Brook*

TITLES IN THE PERGAMON GENERAL PSYCHOLOGY SERIES
(Added Titles in Back of Volume)

Vol. 1. J. WOLPE—*The Practice of Behavior Therapy, Second Edition*
Vol. 2. T. MAGOON *et al.*—*Mental Health Counselors at Work*
Vol. 3. J. McDANIEL—*Physical Disability and Human Behavior, Second Edition*
Vol. 4. M.L. KAPLAN *et al.*—*The Structural Approach in Psychological Testing*
Vol. 5. H.M. LaFAUCI & P.E. RICHTER—*Team Teaching at the College Level*
Vol. 6. H.B. PEPINSKY *et al.*—*People and Information*
Vol. 7. A.W. SIEGMAN & B. POPE—*Studies in Dyadic Communication*
Vol. 8. R.E. JOHNSON—*Existential Man: The Challenge of Psychotherapy*
Vol. 9. C.W. TAYLOR—*Climate for Creativity*
Vol. 10. H.C. RICKARD—*Behavioral Intervention in Human Problems*
Vol. 11. P. EKMAN, W.V. FRIESEN & P. ELLSWORTH—*Emotion in the Human Face: Guidelines for Research and an Integration of Findings*
Vol. 12. B. MAUSNER & E.S. PLATT—*Smoking: A Behavioral Analysis*
Vol. 14. A GOLDSTEIN—*Psychotherapeutic Attraction*
Vol. 15. F. HALPERN—*Survival: Black/White*
Vol. 16. K. SALZINGER & R.S. FELDMAN—*Studies in Verbal Behavior: An Empirical Approach*
Vol. 17. H.E. ADAMS & W.K. BOARDMAN—*Advances in Experimental Clinical Psychology*
Vol. 18. R.C. ZILLER—*The Social Self*
Vol. 19. R.P. LIBERMAN—*A Guide to Behavioral Analysis & Therapy*
Vol. 22. H.B. PEPINSKY & M.J. PATTON—*The Psychological Experiment: A Practical Accomplishment*
Vol. 23. T.R. YOUNG—*New Sources of Self*
Vol. 24. L.S. WATSON, JR.—*Child Behavior Modification: A Manual for Teachers, Nurses, and Parents*
Vol. 25. H.L. NEWBOLD—*The Psychiatric Programming of People: Neo-Behavioral Orthomolecular Psychiatry*
Vol. 26. E.L. ROSSI—*Dreams and the Growth of Personality: Expanding Awareness in Psychotherapy*
Vol. 27. K.D. O'LEARY & S.G. O'LEARY—*Classroom Management: The Successful Use of Behavior Modification, Second Edition*
Vol. 28. K.A. FELDMAN—*College and Student: Selected Readings in the Social Psychology of Higher Education*
Vol. 29. B.A. ASHEM & E.G. POSER—*Adaptive Learning: Behavior Modification with Children*
Vol. 30. H.D. BURCK *et al.*—*Counseling and Accountability: Methods and Critique*
Vol. 31. N. FREDERIKSEN *et al.*—*Prediction of Organizational Behavior*
Vol. 32. R.B. CATTELL—*A New Morality from Science: Beyondism*
Vol. 33. M.L. WEINER—*Personality: The Human Potential*
Vol. 34. R.M. LIEBERT, J.M. NEALE & E.S. DAVIDSON—*The Early Window: Effects of Television on Children and Youth*
Vol. 35. R. COHEN *et al.*—*Psych City: A Simulated Community*
Vol. 36. A.M. GRAZIANO—*Child Without Tomorrow*
Vol. 37. R.J. MORRIS—*Perspectives in Abnormal Behavior*

The terms of our inspection copy service apply to all the above books. A complete catalogue of all books in the Pergamon International Library is available on request.

The Publisher will be pleased to receive suggestions for revised editions and new titles.

TITLES IN THE PERGAMON GENERAL PSYCHOLOGY SERIES (Continued)

Vol. 38.   W.R. BALLER–*Bed Wetting: Origins and Treatment*

Vol. 40.   T.C. KAHN, J.T. CAMERON, & M.B. GIFFEN–*Psychological Methods in Evaluation and Counseling*

Vol. 41.   M.H. SEGALL–*Human Behavior and Public Policy: A Political Psychology*

Vol. 42.   G.W. FAIRWEATHER *et al.*–*Creating Change in Mental Health Organizations*

Vol. 43.   R.C. KATZ & S. ZLUTNICK–*Behavior Therapy and Health Care: Principles and Applications*

Vol. 44.   D.A. EVANS & W.L. CLAIBORN–*Mental Health Issues and the Urban Poor*

Vol. 45.   K.P. HILLNER–*The Psychology of Learning*

Vol. 46.   T.X. BARBER, N.P. SPANOS & J.F. CHAVES–*Hypnosis, Imagination and Human Potentialities*

Vol. 47.   B. POPE–*Interviewing*

Vol. 48.   L. PELTON–*The Psychology of Nonviolence*

Vol. 49.   K.M. COLBY–*Artificial Paranoia–A Computer Simulation of Paranoid Processes*

Vol. 50.   D.M. GELFAND & D.P. HARTMANN–*Child Behavior Analysis and Therapy*

Vol. 51.   J. WOLPE–*Theme and Variations: A Behavior Therapy Casebook*

Vol. 52.   F.H. KANFER & A.P. GOLDSTEIN–*Helping People Change: A Textbook of Methods*

Vol. 53.   K. DANZIGER–*Interpersonal Communication*

Vol. 54.   P.A. KATZ–*Towards the Elimination of Racism*

Vol. 55.   A.P. GOLDSTEIN & N. STEIN–*Prescriptive Psychotherapies*

Vol. 56.   M. HERSEN & D.H. BARLOW–*Single-Case Experimental Designs: Strategies for Studying Behavior Changes*

Vol. 57.   J. MONAHAN–*Community Mental Health and the Criminal Justice System*

Vol. 58.   R.G. WAHLER, A.E. HOUSE & E.E. STAMBAUGH III–*Ecological Assessment of Child Behavior: A Clinical Package for Home, School, and Institutional Settings*

Vol. 59.   P.A. MAGARO–*The Construction of Madness – Emerging Conceptions and Interventions into the Psychotic Process*

Vol. 60.   P.M. MILLER–*The Behavioral Treatment of Alcoholism*

Vol. 61.   J.P. FOREYT–*Behavioral Treatment of Obesity*

Vol. 62.   A. WANDERSMAN, P. POPPEN & D.F. RICKS–*Humanism and Behaviorism: Dialogue and Growth*

Vol. 63.   M. NIETZEL, R. WINETT, M. MACDONALD & W. DAVIDSON–*Behavioral Approaches to Community Psychology*

Vol. 64.   J. FISCHER & H. GOCHROS–*Handbook of Behavior Therapy with Sexual Problems*
Vol. I: *General Procedures*
Vol. II: *Approaches to Specific Problems*

Vol. 65.   M. HERSEN & A. BELLACK–*Behavioral Assessment: A Practical Handbook*

Vol. 66.   M.M. LEFKOWITZ, L.D. ERON, L.O. WALDER & L.R. HUESMANN–*Growing Up To Be Violent: A Longitudinal Study of the Development of Aggression*

Vol. 67.   T.X. BARBER–*Pitfalls in Human Research: Ten Pivotal Points*

Vol. 68.   I. SILVERMAN–*The Human Subject in the Psychological Laboratory*

Vol. 69.   G.W. FAIRWEATHER & L.G. TORNATZKY–*Experimental Methods for Social Policy Research*

Vol. 70   A.S. GURMAN & A.M. RAZIN–*Effective Psychotherapy*

Vol. 71.   J.L. MOSES & W.C. BYHAM–*Applying the Assessment Center Method*

Vol. 72.   A.P. GOLDSTEIN–*Prescriptions for Child Mental Health and Education*

Vol. 73.   DONALD B. KEAT II–*Multimodal Therapy with Children*

Vol. 74.   M. SHERMAN–*Personality: Inquiry & Application*

Vol. 75.   R.J. GATCHEL & K.P. PRICE–*Clinical Applications of Biofeedback: Appraisal and Status*

Vol. 76.   R. CATALANO–*Health, Behavior and the Community: An Ecological Perspective*

Vol. 77.   M.T. NIETZEL–*Crime and Its Modification: A Social Learning Perpective*

Vol. 78.   A.P. GOLDSTEIN, W.J. HOYER & P.J. MONTI–*Police and the Elderly*

Vol. 79.   M.S. MIRON & A.P. GOLDSTEIN–*Hostage*

Vol. 80.   A. P. GOLDSTEIN *et al.*–*Police Crisis Intervention*

Vol. 81.   D. UPPER & J.R. CAUTELA–*Covert Conditioning*